Consumer Behavior

Buying, Having, and Being

Michael R. Solomon

Auburn University

Upper Saddle River, New Jersey 07458

Library of Congress Cataloging-in-Publication Data
Solomon, Michael R.
    Consumer behavior: buying, having, and being/Michael R. Solomon.—6th ed.
Includes bibliographical references and index.
ISBN 0-13-140406-7
1. Consumer behavior. I. Title.

JF 5415.32.s6   2004
658.8'342—dc21

Senior Editor: Wendy Craven
Assistant Editor: Melissa Pellerano
Editorial Assistant: Danielle Serra
Media Project Manager: Anthony Palmiotto
Marketing Manager: Michelle O'Brien
Marketing Assistant: Amanda Fischer
Senior Managing Editor (Production): Judy Leale
Production Editor: Cindy Durand
Production Assistant: Joseph DeProspero
Permissions Supervisor: Suzanne Grappi
Manufacturing Buyer: Arnold Vila
Design Manager: Maria Lange
Art Dirctor: Janet Slowik
Interior Design: Karen Quigley
Cover Design: Karen Quigley
Cover Illustration/Photo: Charlie Hill
Illustrator (Interior): ElectraGraphics
Photo Researcher: Kathy Ringrose
Image Permission Coordinator: Charles Morris
Manager, Print Production: Christy Mahon
Composition/Full-Service Project Management: Lynn Steines, Carlisle Communications
Printer/Binder: Von Hoffman

Credits and acknowledgments borrowed from other sources and reproduced, with permission, in this textbook appear on page 603–4.

Pearson Education LTD.   Pearson Education Australia PTY, Limited
Pearson Education Singapore, Pte. Ltd   Pearson Education North Asia Ltd
Pearson Education, Canada, Ltd   Pearson Educación de Mexico, S.A. de C.V.
Pearson Education–Japan   Pearson Education Malaysia, Pte. Ltd

10 9 8 7 6 5 4 3 2 1
ISBN 0-13-140406-7

Brief Contents

Contents

About the Author

Michael R. Solomon, Ph.D., is Human Sciences Professor of Consumer Behavior in the Department of Consumer Affairs, College of Human Sciences, at Auburn University. Prior to joining Auburn in 1995, he was Chairman of the Department of Marketing in the School of Business at Rutgers University, New Brunswick, New Jersey. He earned B.A. degrees in Psychology and Sociology magna cum laude at Brandeis University in 1977, and a Ph.D. in Social Psychology at the University of North Carolina at Chapel Hill in 1981. He received the Cutty Sark Men's Fashion Award for his research on the psychological aspects of clothing. In 1996 he was awarded the Fulbright/FLAD Chair in Market Globalization by the U.S. Fulbright Commission and the Government of Portugal.

Professor Solomon's primary research interests include consumer behavior and lifestyle issues, online research methodologies, the symbolic aspects of products, the psychology of fashion, decoration, and image, and services marketing. He has published numerous articles on these and related topics in academic journals, and he has delivered invited lectures on these subjects in the United Kingdom, Scandinavia, Australia, and Latin America. His research has been funded by the American Academy of Advertising, the American Marketing Association, the International Council of Shopping Centers, the U.S. Department of Agriculture, and the U.S. Department of Commerce. He currently sits on the Editorial Boards of the Journal of Consumer Behaviour and the Journal of Retailing, and he was elected to the Board of Governors of the Academy of Marketing Science. Professor Solomon was ranked as one of the fifteen most widely cited scholars in the academic behavioral sciences/fashion literature, and as one of the ten most productive researchers in the field of advertising and marketing communications.

In addition to his academic activities, Professor Solomon is a frequent contributor to mass media. He is the author of *Conquering Consumerspace: Marketing Strategies for a Branded World*, which was published in 2003. His feature articles have appeared in such magazines as *Psychology Today, Gentleman's Quarterly*, and *Savvy*. He has been quoted in numerous national magazines and newspapers, including *Allure, Elle, Glamour, Mademoiselle, Mirabella, Newsweek, New York Times, Self, USA Today*, and *Wall Street Journal*. He has been interviewed numerous times on radio and television, including appearances on *Today, Good Morning America*, CNBC, Channel One, *Inside Edition, Newsweek on the Air*, the *Wall Street Journal Radio Network*, and *National Public Radio*. Professor Solomon advises numerous companies on issues related to consumer behavior, services marketing, retailing, and advertising and he is a Director of Mind/Share, Inc., a consulting firm specializing in online consumer research. He frequently addresses business groups on strategic issues related to consumer behavior. Professor Solomon currently lives in Auburn, Alabama, with his wife, Gail, their three children, Amanda, Zachary, and Alexandra—and Chloe, their golden retriever.

Preface

I love to people-watch, don't you? People shopping, people flirting, people consuming. . . Consumer behavior is the study of people and the products that help to shape their identities. Because I'm a consumer myself, I have a selfish interest in learning more about how this process works—and so do you.

In many courses, students are merely passive observers, learning about topics that affect them indirectly if at all. Not everyone is a plasma physicist, a medieval French scholar, or a marketing professional. But we are all consumers. Many of the topics in this book have both professional and personal relevance to the reader, whether he or she is a student, professor, or businessperson. Nearly everyone can relate to the trials and tribulations associated with last-minute shopping, primping for a big night out, agonizing over an expensive purchase decision, fantasizing about a week in the Caribbean, celebrating a holiday, or commemorating a landmark event, such as a graduation, getting a driver's license, or (dreaming about) winning the lottery.

In this edition I have tried to introduce you to the latest and best thinking by some very bright scientists who develop models and studies of consumer behavior. But, that's not enough. Consumer behavior is an applied science, so we must never lose sight of the role of "horse sense" when we try to apply our findings to life in the real world. That's why you'll find a lot of practical examples to back up these fancy theories.

■ WHAT MAKES THIS BOOK DIFFERENT: BUYING, HAVING, AND BEING

As this book's subtitle suggests, my vision of consumer behavior goes well beyond studying the act of buying—having and being are just as important, if not more so. Consumer behavior is more than buying things; it also embraces the study of how having (or not having) things affects our lives and how our possessions influence the way we feel about ourselves and about each other—our state of being. I developed the Wheel of Consumer Behavior that appears at the beginning of text sections to underscore the complex—and often inseparable—interrelationships between the individual consumer and his or her social realities.

In addition to understanding why people buy things, we also try to appreciate how products, services, and consumption activities contribute to the broader social world we experience. Whether shopping, cooking, cleaning, playing basketball, hanging out at the beach, or even looking at ourselves in the mirror, our lives are touched by the marketing system. As if these experiences were not complex enough, the task of understanding the consumer multiplies geometrically when we take a multicultural perspective.

All of these ideas are supported by intriguing and current examples, showing consumer behavior as it relates to current events.
Throughout the sixth edition you'll discover up-to-the-minute topics including bio-terrorism, Internet piracy, consumer behavior
post 9/11, identity theft, hype versus buzz, purchase momentum, new religions (Raelians), advergaming, flow states, food
cultures, blogging, Web avatars, silent commerce, brandfests,
tribal marketing, even Botox parties.

◼ GOING GLOBAL

The American experience is important, but it's far from the whole
story. This book also considers the many other consumers around
the world whose diverse experiences with buying, having, and being
are equally vital to understand. That's why you'll find numerous
examples of marketing and consumer practices relating to consumers and companies outside the United States throughout the
book. You'll find a list of those examples on the end pages of this
book. If we didn't know it before the tragic events of September 11,
2001, we certainly know it now: Americans also are global citizens,
and it's vital that we all appreciate the perspectives of others—and
how others around the world regard us. That's why I'm excited about
a feature called The Global Looking Glass that's new to this edition.
When you come across these boxes you'll see some fascinating
examples of how consumers in other countries view Americans and
their products. Some of these views are positive, some aren't. But all
of them provide a valuable perspective on the United States
and the huge influences—both good and bad—our country
exerts on businesses and people around the world.

◼ DIGITAL CONSUMER BEHAVIOR: A VIRTUAL COMMUNITY

As more of us go online everyday, there's no doubt the world is
changing—and consumer behavior is evolving faster than you can
say "World Wide Web." This sixth edition highlights and celebrates the brave new
world of digital consumer behavior. Consumers and producers are brought
together electronically in ways we have never before experienced. Rapid transmission of information is altering the speed at which new trends develop and the direction in which they travel—especially since the virtual world lets consumers participate in the creation and dissemination of new products.

One of the most exciting aspects of the new digital world is that consumers can
interact directly with other people who live around the block or around the world.
As a result, the meaning of community is being radically redefined. It's no longer
enough to acknowledge that consumers like to talk to each other about products.
Now we share opinions and get the buzz about new movies, CDs, cars, clothes—you
name it—in electronic communities that may include a housewife in Alabama, a
disabled senior citizen in Alaska, or a teen loaded with body piercings in
Amsterdam.

We have just begun to explore the ramifications for consumer behavior when a
Web surfer can project her own picture onto a Web site to get a virtual makeover, or
a corporate purchasing agent can solicit bids for a new piece of equipment from
vendors around the world in minutes. These new ways of interacting in the marketplace create bountiful opportunities for businesspeople and consumers alike. You

will find illustrations of the changing digital world sprinkled liberally throughout this edition. In addition, each chapter features boxes called Net Profit that point to specific examples of the Net's potential to improve the way business is conducted.

But, is the digital world always a rosy place? Unfortunately just as in the "real world," the answer is no. The potential to exploit consumers, whether by invading their privacy, preying on the curiosity of children, or just providing false product information, is always there. That's why you'll also find boxes called The Tangled Web that point out some of the abuses of this fascinating new medium. Still, I can't imagine a world without the Web, and I hope you'll enjoy the ways it's changing our field. When it comes to the new virtual world of consumer behavior, you're either on the train or under it.

■ CONSUMER RESEARCH IS A BIG TENT: THE IMPORTANCE OF A BALANCED PERSPECTIVE

Like most of the readers of this book, the field of consumer behavior is young, dynamic, and in flux. It is constantly being cross-fertilized by perspectives from many different disciplines—the field is a big tent that invites many diverse views to enter. I have tried to express the field's staggering diversity in these pages. Consumer researchers represent virtually every social science discipline, plus a few from the physical sciences and the arts for good measure. From this melting pot has come a healthy "stew" of research perspectives, viewpoints regarding appropriate research methods, and even deeply held beliefs about what are and what are not appropriate issues for consumer researchers to study in the first place.

The book also emphasizes the importance of understanding consumers in formulating marketing strategy. Many (if not most) of the fundamental concepts in marketing are based on a manager's ability to know people. After all, if we don't understand why people behave as they do, how can we identify their needs? If we can't identify their needs, how can we satisfy their needs? If we can't satisfy people's needs, we don't have a marketing concept, so we might as well fold our tents and go home! To illustrate the potential of consumer research to inform marketing strategy, the text contains numerous examples of specific applications of consumer behavior concepts by marketing practitioners as well as examples of windows of opportunity in which such concepts could be used (perhaps by alert strategists after taking this course!). The Marketing Opportunity boxes you'll find in each chapter highlight the fascinating ways that marketing practitioners are (or should be) translating wisdom gleaned from consumer research into actual business activities.

■ THE GOOD, THE BAD, AND THE UGLY

A strategic focus is great, but this book does not assume that everything marketers do is in the best interests of consumers or of their environment. Likewise, as consumers we do many things that are not so positive either. People are plagued by addictions, status envy, ethnocentrism, racism, sexism, and many other isms. Regrettably, there are times when marketing activities—deliberately or not—encourage or exploit these human flaws. This book deals with the totality of consumer behavior: warts and all. Marketing mistakes or ethically suspect activities are also highlighted in special features labeled Marketing Pitfalls.

On the other hand, marketers have helped to create many wonderful (or at least unusual) things, such as holidays, comic books, techno music, Pokémon, and the many stylistic options available to us in the domains of clothing, home design, the arts, and cuisine. I have also taken pains to acknowledge the sizable impact of marketing on popular culture. Indeed, the final section of this book reflects very recent work in the field that scrutinizes, criticizes, and sometimes

Marketing Opportunity

Purple ketchup? Wildly colored products are hot, as marketers search for new ways to stand out on the shelves. First, Heinz gave us Blastin' Green ketchup in a squeeze bottle and then hit us with Funky Purple. Heinz's share of the ketchup market jumped from 50 percent to 56 percent in the 12 months after it launched its green version. ConAgra Foods caught on to the idea that kids (of all ages?) want mealtime to be fun time. Now, we can buy squeeze bottles of Parkay margarine in hot pink and bright blue, both perfect for painting pictures on corn on the cob. And for dessert, how about a pile of Nabisco's Milk Changer Blue and Orange Oreos?[9] These colorful versions of tried-and-true products still taste the same (at least with your eyes closed). For those who are a bit more darin
Africa try N
blue and t

Marketing Pitfall

Not all sales interactions are positive, but some *really* stand out. Here are a few incidents that make the rest of them easier to swallow:

- A woman sued a car dealer in Iowa, claiming that a salesperson persuaded her to climb into the trunk of a Chrysler Concorde to check out its spaciousness. He then slammed the trunk shut and bounced the car several times, apparently to the delight of his co-workers. This bizarre act apparently came about because the manager offered a prize of $100 to the salesperson who could get a customer to climb in.[87]
- A Detroit couple filed a $100 million lawsuit against McDonald's, alleging three McDonald's employees beat them after they tried to return a watery milkshake.
- In Alabama a McDonald's employee was arrested on second degree assault charges after stabbing a customer in the forehead with a ballpoint pen. The victim's attorney observed, "There was a great deal of profanity coming out of the employee prior to the stabbing."[88]

celebrates consumers in their everyday worlds. I hope you will enjoy reading about such wonderful things as much as I enjoyed writing about them. Welcome to the fascinating world of consumer behavior!

■ CRITICAL THINKING IN CONSUMER BEHAVIOR: CASES AND ASSIGNMENTS

Learning by doing is an integral part of the classroom experience. This unique casebook (authored by Judy Graham) applies consumer behavior theory to practice via 21 innovative cases and activities. Simple and complex case exercises give students the chance to critically analyze the fundamental principles of consumer behavior while providing models for the application of consumer behavior in the real world. Contact your Prentice Hall sales representative for details.

■ SUPPLEMENTS

- Instructor's Resource CD-ROM—Includes all of the print supplements, PowerPoint slides, images from the text, and test generating software.
- Instructor's Manual.
- Test Item File.
- PH TestGen EQ test generating software.
- PowerPoint presentation software.
- *NEW* Videos—This unprecedented video package, filmed by consumer researchers, faculty, and students—originally screened at the Association for Consumer Research conference—presents in-depth studies of consumer behavior in specific cultural contexts. Through interviews with consumers, faculty, and the general public, the videos explore patterns of buyer motivation and the roles that certain products play in people's lives.
- www.prenhall.com/solomon—Access free study aids and password-protected teaching resources.

Acknowledgments

I am grateful for the many helpful comments on how to improve the sixth edition that were provided by my peer reviewers. Special thanks go to the following people: Justin Peart, St. Thomas University; Ed Petkus Jr., University of Tampa; Christine L. Hansvick, Pacific Lutheran University; Avreham Horowitz, Florida Atlantic University; John Ballard, College of Mount St. Joseph; Natalie Wood, San Diego State University; and Mary Ann McGrath, Loyola University.

Many other colleagues and friends made significant contributions to this edition. I would like to thank, in particular, the following people who made constructive suggestions or who provided me with a sneak peek at their research materials and manuscripts now in press or under review:

Jennifer Aaker, Stanford University
Søren Askegaard, Odense University (Denmark)
Gary Bamossy, University of Utah
Russell Belk, University of Utah
Raymond Burke, Indiana University
Jennifer Chang Coupland, Pennsylvania State University
Janeen Costa, University of Utah
Jeff Durgee, Rensselaer Polytechnic Institute
Basil Englis, Berry College
Susan Fournier, Harvard University
Güliz Ger, Bilkent University (Turkey)
Donna Hoffman, Vanderbilt University
Robert Kozinets, Northwestern University
Tina Lowery, University of Texas at San Antonio
John Lynch, Duke University
David Mick, University of Virginia
Cele Otnes, University of Illinois
Connie Pechmann, University of California at Irvine
Greg Rose, University of Mississippi
Jonathan Schroeder, Royal Institute of Technology (Sweden)
John Sherry, Northwestern University
L. J. Shrum, University of Texas at San Antonio
Itamar Simonson, Stanford University
Barbara Stern, Rutgers University
Jerry Zaltman, Harvard University

Extra special thanks are due to the preparers of the ancillary materials: Andrew T. Norman, Drake University, for preparation of the Instructor's Manual; John R. Brooks, Houston Baptist University, for the preparation of the Test Item File; Ronald A. Clark, Florida State University, for preparation of the PowerPoint lecture slides; Gulnur Tumbat for assisting with the videographies; Gary Bamossy for his help on the Global

Looking Glass boxes; and Judy Graham for preparing the selection of cases that accompany the text.

I would also like to thank the good people at Prentice Hall who as always have done yeoman service on this edition. In particular I am indebted to my tenacious editor, Wendy Craven, for helping me to navigate the sometimes treacherous waters of publishing. Thanks also to Cindy Durand, Richard Allan, Suzanne Grappi, Tom Nixon, Michelle O'Brien, Anthony Palmiotto, Judy Leale, and Jeff Shelstad for their support and great work.

With the tolerance of my friends and colleagues, I would never have been able to sustain the illusion that I was still an active researcher while I worked on this edition. I am grateful to my department chair, Carol Warfield, and to Dean June Henton for their continuing support. Special thanks go to one of my courageous doctoral students, Gokcen Coskuner, for her help with this edition. Also, I am grateful to my undergraduate students, who have been a prime source of inspiration, examples, and feedback. The satisfaction I have garnered from teaching them about consumer behavior motivated me to write a book I felt they would like to read.

Last but not least, I would like to thank my family and friends for sticking by me during this revision. They know who they are, since their names pop up in chapter vignettes throughout the book. My apologies for "distorting" their characters in the name of poetic license! My gratitude and love go out to my parents, Jackie and Henry, and my in-laws, Marilyn and Phil. My super children, Amanda, Zachary, and Alexandra, always made the sun shine on gray days. Finally, thanks above all to the love of my life—Gail, my wonderful wife, best friend, and occasional research assistant: I still do it all for you.

M.R.S.
Auburn, Alabama
March 2003

Consumer Behavior

Buying, Having, and Being

Suddenly you'll understand   the meaning of desire.

...AND FEEL THINGS LIKE NEVER BEFORE.

...TECHNOLOGY AND

...TOGETHER SO BEAUTIFULLY

...24" ULTRATHIN HDTV READY LCD MONITOR

...RY TYPE MP3 PLAYER

...CE TECHNOLOGY

Consumers in the Marketplace

This introductory section provides an overview of the field of consumer behavior. Chapter 1 looks at how the field of marketing is influenced by the actions of consumers and also at how we as consumers are influenced by marketers. It describes the discipline of consumer behavior and some of the different approaches to understanding what makes consumers tick. It also highlights the importance of the study of consumer behavior to such public policy issues as addiction and environmentalism.

■ CHAPTERS AHEAD

CHAPTER 1
Consumers Rule

Consumers Rule

gail is killing time before her accounting class by surfing the Web in her room. Between studying for her accounting and marketing exams, she realizes she hasn't looked at any interesting sites in weeks. Enough of the serious stuff, she decides. It's time for some *really* educational surfing.

So, where to go first? Gail figures she'll start at one of the popular women's portals and see what happens. She goes to *iVillage.com*, where she checks her horoscope (cool! a good day to start a new relationship), scans a few beauty tips, and takes a Great Date quiz (uh-oh, this new guy Bruce she's been seeing may need to be replaced). Similar stuff is going on at *Oxygen.com*. Then she checks out the new Web site for her sorority at *gammaphibeta.org*, which reminds her, "the object of this organization shall be to develop the highest type of womanhood through education, social life, and service to country and humanity."[1] Very nice, but she learned all that at Rush. Maybe it's time for something a bit more interesting.

After an hour of surfing some fascinating e-commerce sites—and vowing to return to some of them to reward herself with a present after exams—Gail decides to check out what "real people" are doing on the Web. First she checks in on the clubs she belongs to at *collegeclub.com*—wow, more than 30 people from her campus are logged on right now! Looks like other students are studying as hard as she is! Then she clicks over to *http://navisite.collegeclub.com/webcams*, to decide which live webcam she'd like to peek in on today. The site has tons of them; cameras trained on real guys and women just doing their thing at work or at home. Most of these are pretty boring. There's even a "DissCam" site featuring a balding graduate student who can be observed writing his dissertation! Yawn. Gail checks out the "Campus Views" section where she can select live feeds from many schools ranging from Penn State to Humboldt State. She finally settles on a live feed from a room with four residents just doing what students do. For a few minutes, she watches the riveting spectacle of one of the guys brushing his teeth and getting ready to go to class. Hey, it's not exactly an Eminem concert, but it sure beats studying for accounting.

■ CONSUMER BEHAVIOR: PEOPLE IN THE MARKETPLACE

This book is about people like Gail. It concerns the products and services they buy and use, and the ways these fit into their lives. This introductory chapter describes some important aspects of the field of consumer behavior and some reasons why it's essential to understand how people interact with the marketing system.

For now, though, let's return to one "typical" consumer: Gail, the business major. The preceding vignette allows us to highlight some aspects of consumer behavior that will be covered in the rest of the book.

As a consumer, Gail can be described and compared to other individuals in a number of ways. For some purposes, marketers might find it useful to categorize her in terms of her age, gender, income, or occupation. These are some examples of descriptive characteristics of a population, or **demographics**. In other cases, marketers would rather know something about Gail's interests in clothing or music, or the way she spends her leisure time. This sort of information comes under the category of **psychographics**, which refers to aspects of a person's lifestyle and personality. Knowledge of consumer characteristics plays an extremely important role in many marketing applications, such as defining the market for a product or deciding on the appropriate techniques to employ when targeting a certain group of consumers.

Gail's purchase decisions are heavily influenced by the opinions and behaviors of her sorority sisters. A lot of product information, as well as recommendations to use or avoid particular brands, is transmitted by conversations among real people, rather than by way of television commercials, magazines, billboards, or even bizarre Web sites. The growth of the Web has created thousands of online **consumption communities** where members share views and product recommendations about anything from Barbie dolls to Palm Pilots. Gail forms bonds with fellow group members because they use the same products. There is also pressure on each group member to buy things that will meet with the group's approval. A consumer often pays a price in the form of group rejection or embarrassment when she does not conform to others' conceptions of what is good or bad, "in" or "out."

As members of a large society, such as the United States, people share certain cultural values or strongly held beliefs about the way the world should be structured. Other values are shared by members of subcultures or smaller groups within the culture, such as Hispanics, teens, Midwesterners, or even "riot grrls"[2] and "Hell's Angels."

While examining Web sites, Gail was exposed to many competing "brands." Numerous sites did not capture her attention at all, whereas others were noticed and rejected because they did not fit the image with which she identified or to which she aspired. The use of **market segmentation strategies** means targeting a brand only to specific groups of consumers rather than to everybody—even if it means that other consumers who don't belong to this target market aren't attracted to that product.

Brands often have clearly defined images or "personalities" created by product advertising, packaging, branding, and other marketing strategies. The choice of a favorite Web site is very much a lifestyle statement: It says a lot about what a person is interested in, as well as something about the type of person she would like to be. People often choose a product because they like its image, or because they feel its "personality" somehow corresponds to their own. Moreover, a consumer may believe that by buying and using the product or service, its desirable qualities will magically rub off onto him or her.

When a product, idea, or Web site succeeds in satisfying a consumer's specific needs or desires, it may be rewarded with many years of brand loyalty, a bond between product and consumer that is very difficult for competitors to break. Often a change in one's life situation or self-concept is required to weaken this bond.

Consumers' evaluations of products are affected by the appearance, taste, texture, or smell of the item. A good Web site helps people to feel, taste, and smell with their eyes. We may be swayed by the shape and color of a package, as well as by more subtle factors such as the symbolism used in a brand name, in an advertisement, or even in the choice of a cover model for a magazine. These judgments are affected by—and often reflect—how a society feels that people should define themselves at that point in time. If asked, Gail might not even be able to say exactly why she considered some Web sites and rejected others. Many product meanings are hidden below the surface of the packaging and advertising; this book will discuss some of the methods used by marketers and social scientists to discover or apply these meanings.

As we learned with Gail, our opinions and desires increasingly are shaped by input from around the world, which is becoming a much smaller place due to rapid advancements in communications and transportation systems. In today's global culture, consumers often prize products and services that "transport" them to different places and allow them to experience the diversity of other cultures—even if only to watch others brush their teeth.

What Is Consumer Behavior?

The field of **consumer behavior** covers a lot of ground: It is the study of the processes involved when individuals or groups select, purchase, use, or dispose of products, services, ideas, or experiences to satisfy needs and desires.[3] Consumers take many forms, ranging from an eight-year-old child begging her mother for Pokémon cards to an executive in a large corporation deciding on a multimillion-dollar computer system. The items that are consumed can include anything from canned peas to a massage, democracy, hip-hop music, or a celebrity like Eminem. Needs and desires to be satisfied range from hunger and thirst to love, status, or even spiritual fulfillment. Our attachment to everyday products is exemplified by our love affair with colas. The World of Coca-Cola in Las Vegas draws a million visitors a year. Exhibits ask, "What does Coca-Cola mean to you?" and many of the responses tell of strong emotional connections to the brand.[4]

Consumers Are Actors on the Marketplace Stage

The perspective of **role theory** takes the view that much of consumer behavior resembles actions in a play.[5] As in a play, each consumer has lines, props, and costumes necessary to put on a good performance. Because people act out many different roles, they sometimes alter their consumption decisions depending on the particular "play" they are in at the time. The criteria they use to evaluate products and services in one of their roles may be quite different from those used in another role.

Consumer Behavior Is a Process

In its early stages of development, the field was often referred to as buyer behavior, reflecting an emphasis on the interaction between consumers and producers at the time of purchase. Most marketers now recognize that consumer behavior is an ongoing process, not merely what happens at the moment a consumer hands over money or a credit card and in turn receives some good or service.

The **exchange**, a transaction in which two or more organizations or people give and receive something of value, is an integral part of marketing.[6] Although exchange remains an important part of consumer behavior, the expanded view emphasizes the entire consumption process, which includes the issues that influence the consumer before, during, and after a purchase. Figure 1.1 illustrates some of the issues that are addressed during each stage of the consumption process.

Consumer Behavior Involves Many Different Actors

We generally think of a **consumer** as a person who identifies a need or desire, makes a purchase, and then disposes of the product during the three stages in the consumption process. In many cases, however, different people may be involved in this sequence of events. The purchaser and user of a product might not be the same person, as when a parent picks out clothes for a teenager (and makes selections that can result in "fashion suicide" in the view of the teen). In other cases, another person may act as an influencer, providing recommendations for or against certain products without actually buying or using them. A friend's grimace when you try on that new pair of pants may be more influential than anything your mother or father might say.

Finally, consumers may take the form of organizations or groups. One or several persons may make the decisions involved in purchasing products that will be used by many, as when a purchasing agent orders the company's office supplies. In other organizational situations, purchase decisions may be made by a large group of people—for example, company accountants, designers, engineers, sales personnel, and others—all of whom will have a say in the various stages of the consumption process. As we'll see in Chapter 12, one important type of organization is the family, where different family members play pivotal roles in making decisions regarding products and services used by all.

■ **FIGURE 1.1**   SOME ISSUES THAT ARISE DURING STAGES IN THE CONSUMPTION PROCESS

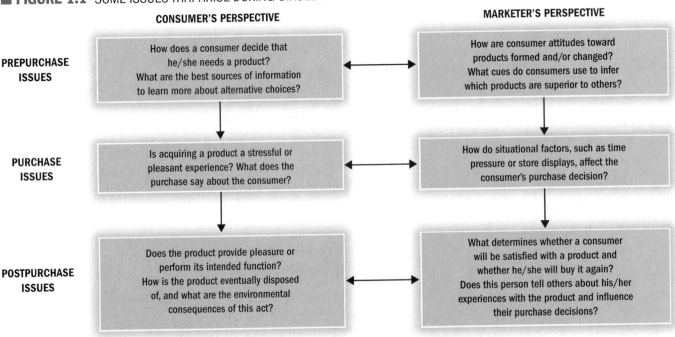

	CONSUMER'S PERSPECTIVE	**MARKETER'S PERSPECTIVE**
PREPURCHASE ISSUES	How does a consumer decide that he/she needs a product? What are the best sources of information to learn more about alternative choices?	How are consumer attitudes toward products formed and/or changed? What cues do consumers use to infer which products are superior to others?
PURCHASE ISSUES	Is acquiring a product a stressful or pleasant experience? What does the purchase say about the consumer?	How do situational factors, such as time pressure or store displays, affect the consumer's purchase decision?
POSTPURCHASE ISSUES	Does the product provide pleasure or perform its intended function? How is the product eventually disposed of, and what are the environmental consequences of this act?	What determines whether a consumer will be satisfied with a product and whether he/she will buy it again? Does this person tell others about his/her experiences with the product and influence their purchase decisions?

■ CONSUMERS' IMPACT ON MARKETING STRATEGY

Surfing cool Web sites is a lot of fun. But, on the more serious side, why should managers, advertisers, and other marketing professionals bother to learn about consumer behavior?

Very simply, understanding consumer behavior is good business. A basic marketing concept holds that firms exist to satisfy consumers' needs. These needs can only be satisfied to the extent that marketers understand the people or organizations who will use the products and services they are trying to sell, and that they do so better than their competitors.

Consumer response is the ultimate test of whether a marketing strategy will succeed. Thus, knowledge about consumers should be incorporated into every facet of a successful marketing plan. Data about consumers help organizations define the market and identify threats and opportunities to a brand. And, in the wild and wacky world of marketing, nothing is forever: This knowledge also helps to ensure that the product continues to appeal to its core market.

The Sony Walkman is a good example of a successful product that needed to update its image. Although Sony revolutionized the mobile music experience and sold almost 300 million Walkmans in the process, recent research found that today's teens see portable cassette players as dinosaurs. The company's advertising agency followed 125 teens to see how they use products in their day-to-day lives. Now Sony has relaunched the product with a removable "Memory Stick" instead of a cassette player so it can work with MP3 files. The Walkman also needed a fresh message, so Sony's advertising agency decided to use an alien named Plato to appeal to teens. They chose this character to appeal to today's ethnically diverse marketplace. As the account director explained, "An alien is no one, so an alien is everyone."[7]

Segmenting Consumers

The process of **market segmentation** identifies groups of consumers who are similar to one another in one or more ways, and then devises marketing strategies that appeal to one or more groups. *Amazon.com* tries to reach multiple segments at the same time, whereas *toysrus.com* focuses on gifts for kids.[8] If a company does its homework, it identifies a segment with unique needs and then develops products or services to meet those needs. For example, the U.S. incarceration rate has tripled since 1980. This isn't good news for those in prison, but some companies smell an opportunity to break into "The Big House" by offering products that must be modified to meet security requirements. Sony sells a line of inmate headphones, while other firms like Union Supply make clear versions of hot pots, trashcans, and shavers to prevent prisoners from hiding contraband or weapons.[9]

As we'll see later, building loyalty to a brand is a very smart marketing strategy, so sometimes companies define market segments by identifying their most faithful customers or **heavy users**. For example, in the fast-food industry the heavy user (no pun intended) accounts for only one of five customers, but for about 60 percent of all visits to fast-food restaurants. Taco Bell developed the Chalupa, a deep-fried and higher-calorie version of its Gordita stuffed taco, to appeal to its heavy users. The Checkers burger chain describes *its* core customer as a single male under age 30 who has a working-class job, loves loud music, doesn't read much, and hangs out with friends.[10] Fries with that?

Aside from heavy usage of a product, there are many dimensions that can be used to slice up a larger market. **Demographics** are statistics that measure observable aspects of a population, such as birthrate, age distribution, and income. The U.S. Census Bureau is a major source of demographic data on families, but many private firms gather additional data on specific population groups as well. The changes and trends revealed in demographic studies are of great interest to marketers, because the data can be used to locate and predict the size of markets for

Marketing Opportunity

Disabled consumers are beginning to be viewed as a profitable marketing segment rather than as charity cases. That's not surprising; they comprise a market of 52 million people with almost $800 billion in spending power. This new spirit of "handicapitalism" is being fueled by the convergence of three trends: (1) The 1990 Americans with Disabilities Act created greater awareness of this population; (2) New technology such as battery-powered bicycles and speech-recognition software is making it easier for these consumers to interact with others and with the marketplace (for example, Nokia makes cell phones that flash or vibrate for the hard of hearing); and (3) An aging population ensures continued growth in the number of disabled people. Of course, it helps to be sensitive to how disabled people are portrayed in advertising: Recently, Nike was forced to pull a print-magazine advertising campaign for a new running shoe after disabilities-rights groups claimed the ads were offensive. Small wonder; the ads for the ACG Air Dri-Goat referred to people with disabilities as "drooling and misshapen." Nike said the ad was intended to show how the right equipment could prevent injuries, but the damage had already been done.[11]

People with disabilities are beginning to be a more common focus of advertising messages, as exemplified by this South African ad for Nike.

many products, ranging from home mortgages to brooms and can openers. Imagine trying to sell baby food to a single male, or an around-the-world cruise to a couple making $15,000 a year!

In this book we explore many of the important demographic variables that make consumers the same or different from others. We also consider other important characteristics that are a bit more subtle, such as differences in consumers' personalities and tastes that can't be objectively measured, yet may be tremendously important in influencing product choices. For now, let's summarize a few of the most important demographic dimensions, each of which will be developed in more detail in later chapters.

Age

Consumers of different age groups obviously have very different needs and wants. Although people who belong to the same age group differ in many other ways, they do tend to share a set of values and common cultural experiences that they carry

throughout life.[12] For example, as we all know, teens are a hot market for many trendy products that leave their parents scratching their heads (that's part of the idea). Among others, phone manufacturers are scrambling to provide what kids want—the cell phone as fashion accessory. Wildseed designs phones specifically for teenagers that feature "smart skins"—replaceable taco shell–shaped faceplates with computer chips that allow teenagers to change functions as well as the phone's appearance. There are graffiti-splattered faceplates for skateboarders, for example, that come with edgy urban ringer tones and gritty icons. Similarly, market leader Nokia has a line of what it calls "expression" phones, which have spawned secondary products like customized faceplates, add-on lights, and downloadable ringer tones.[13]

Gender

Differentiating by gender starts at a very early age—even diapers are sold in pink versions for girls and blue for boys. Many products, from fragrances to footwear, are targeted to either men or women. In 2002, an all-female marketing team at Procter & Gamble, who jokingly call themselves "chicks in charge," introduced Crest Rejuvenating Effects, the first mass-market toothpaste positioned just for women. P&G communicates that this product is feminine by packaging the stuff in a teal tube nestled inside a glimmering "pearlescent" box. The toothpaste is sparkly and also teal-toned and tastes like vanilla and cinnamon.[14]

Family Structure

A person's family and marital status is yet another important demographic variable, because this has such a big effect on consumers' spending priorities. Not surprisingly, young bachelors and newlyweds are the most likely to exercise; go to bars, concerts, and movies; and consume alcohol (enjoy it while you can!). Families with young children are big purchasers of health foods and fruit juices, while single-parent households and those with older children buy more junk food. Home maintenance services are most likely to be used by older couples and bachelors.[15]

Social Class and Income

Social class indicates people who are approximately equal in terms of their incomes and social standing in the community. They work in roughly similar occupations, and they tend to have similar tastes in music, clothing, leisure activities, and art. They also tend to socialize with one another, and they share many ideas and values regarding the way one's life should be lived.[16] The distribution of wealth is of great interest to marketers because it determines which groups have the greatest buying power and market potential.

Race and Ethnicity

African Americans, Hispanic Americans, and Asian Americans are the three fastest-growing ethnic groups in the United States. As our society becomes increasingly multicultural, new opportunities develop to deliver specialized products to racial and ethnic groups and to introduce other groups to these offerings.

For example, many mainstream products now use hip-hop artists to push their products both in inner cities and elsewhere. The rapper J-Ro is endorsing extreme sports and promoting Mountain Dew at the same time. This brand has also enlisted the help of other "Dew Dudes" like urban music icons Run DMC and Ja Rule to promote the drink.[17]

Lifestyle

Consumers also have very different lifestyles, even if they share other characteristics such as gender or age. The way we feel about ourselves, the things we value, the things we like to do in our spare time—all of these factors help to determine which products will push our buttons. That's why SoBe Beverages, the fast-growing producer of "New Age drinks," labels its herb concoctions with names like Lizard Fuel that stress attributes such as energy rather than taste. Using an offbeat marketing campaign featuring a "Lizard Love Bus" that shows up at events such as mountain bike races, the company's lifestyle marketing campaign stresses individuality with its tagline: SoBe Yourself.[18]

Geography

Many national marketers tailor their offerings to appeal to consumers who live in different parts of the country. For example, some Southerners are fond of a "good ol' boy" image that leaves others scratching their heads. Although many Northerners regard the name "Bubba" as a negative term, businesses in Dixie proudly flaunt the name. Bubba Co. is a Charleston-based firm that licenses products such as Bubba-Q-Sauce. In Florida, restaurants, sports bars, nightclubs, and a limousine firm all proudly bear the name Bubba.[19]

Relationship Marketing: Building Bonds with Consumers

Marketers are carefully defining customer segments and listening to people in their markets as never before. Many of them have realized that a key to success is building relationships between brands and customers that will last a lifetime. Marketers who believe in this philosophy, called **relationship marketing**, interact with customers on a regular basis and give them reasons to maintain a bond with the company over time.

Another revolution in relationship building is being brought to us courtesy of the computer. **Database marketing** involves tracking consumers' buying habits very closely and crafting products and messages tailored precisely to people's wants and needs based on this information. The Ritz-Carlton hotel chain trains associates to enter detailed information into its database so that, if a guest orders decaf coffee from room service, she will also receive decaf on the next visit.[20] Sophisticated companies like American Express, General Motors, and Kraft are combining and constantly updating information from public records and marketing research surveys—with data volunteered by consumers themselves when they return warranty cards, enter sweepstakes, or purchase from catalogs—to build a complex database that fine-tunes their knowledge of what people are buying and how often.[21]

■ MARKETING'S IMPACT ON CONSUMERS

For better or for worse, we all live in a world that is significantly influenced by the actions of marketers. We are surrounded by marketing stimuli in the form of advertisements, stores, and products competing for our attention and our dollars. Marketers filter much of what we learn about the world, whether through the affluence depicted in glamorous magazines or the roles played by actors in commercials. Ads show us how we should act with regard to recycling, alcohol consumption, the types of houses and cars we might wish to own—and even how to evaluate others based on the products they buy or don't buy. In many ways we are also "at the mercy" of marketers because we rely on them to sell us products that are safe and perform as promised, to tell us the truth about what they are selling, and to price and distribute these products fairly.

Popular culture, consisting of the music, movies, sports, books, celebrities, and other forms of entertainment consumed by the mass market, is both a product of and an inspiration for marketers. Our lives are also affected in more far-reaching ways, ranging from how we acknowledge cultural events such as marriage, death, or holidays to how we view social issues such as air pollution, gambling, and addictions. Whether it's the Super Bowl, Christmas shopping, presidential elections, newspaper recycling, body piercing, cigarette smoking, in-line skating, or online video games, marketers play a significant role in our view of the world and how we live in it.

This cultural impact is hard to overlook, although many people do not seem to realize how much their views—their movie and musical heroes, the latest fashions in clothing, food and decorating choices, and even the physical features that they find attractive or ugly in men and women—are influenced by marketers. For example, consider the product icons that companies use to create an identity for their products. Many imaginary creatures and personalities, from the Pillsbury Doughboy to the Jolly Green Giant, at one time or another have been central figures in popular culture. In fact, it is likely that more consumers could recognize such

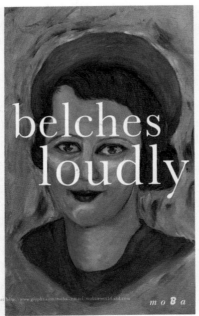

Some art speaks to you. Some just **belches loudly** in your face.

Visit the permanent collection at 580 High Street, Dedham, Massachusetts · 617.325.8224 · Or on the Web at http://www.glyphs.com/moba-em-art/mobaworld.std.com   *mo B a   m u s e u m   o f   b a d   a r t*

We are surrounded by elements of popular culture—the good, the bad, and the ugly. This ad for the Museum of Bad Art reminds us of that.

characters than could identify past presidents, business leaders, or artists. Although these figures never really existed, many of us feel as if we "know" them, and they certainly are effective spokescharacters for the products they represent. If you don't believe it, visit *www.toymuseum.com.*

The Meaning of Consumption

One of the fundamental premises of the modern field of consumer behavior is that people often buy products not for what they do, but for what they mean. This principle does not imply that a product's basic function is unimportant, but rather that the roles products play in our lives extend well beyond the tasks they perform. The deeper meanings of a product may help it to stand out from other, similar goods and services—all things being equal, people will choose the brand that has an image (or even a personality!) consistent with their underlying needs.

For example, although most people probably couldn't run faster or jump higher if they were wearing Nikes instead of Reeboks, many die-hard loyalists swear by their favorite brand. These archrivals are largely marketed in terms of their images—meanings that have been carefully crafted with the help of legions of rock stars, athletes, slickly produced commercials, and many millions of dollars. So, when you buy a Nike "swoosh" you may be doing more than choosing shoes to wear to the mall—you may also be making a lifestyle statement about the type of person you are or wish you were. For a relatively simple item made of leather and laces, that's quite a feat!

Our allegiances to sneakers, musicians, or even soft drinks help us define our place in modern society, and these choices also help each of us to form bonds with others who share similar preferences. This comment by a participant in a focus group captures the curious bonding that can be caused by consumption choices: "I was at a Super Bowl party, and I picked up an obscure drink. Somebody else across the room went 'yo!' because he had the same thing. People feel a connection when you're drinking the same thing."[22]

As we have already seen, one trademark of marketing strategies today is an emphasis on building relationships with customers. The nature of these relationships can vary, and these bonds help us to understand some of the possible mean-

 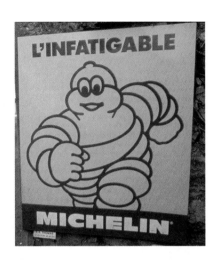 

Companies often create product icons to develop an identity for their products. Many made-up creatures and personalities, such as Mr. Clean; Bibendum, the Michelin tire man; and the Pillsbury Doughboy, are widely recognized (and often beloved) figures in popular culture. Bibendum, one of the oldest icons, dates back to the 1890s. He was born at a time when the "machine age" was dawning, so a man constructed of auto parts truly caught the spirit of the times.

ings products have to us. Here are some of the types of relationships a person might have with a product:

- *Self-concept attachment:* The product helps to establish the user's identity.
- *Nostalgic attachment:* The product serves as a link with a past self.
- *Interdependence:* The product is a part of the user's daily routine.
- *Love:* The product elicits emotional bonds of warmth, passion, or other strong emotion.[23]

One consumer researcher developed a classification scheme in an attempt to explore the different ways that products and experiences can provide meaning to people. This consumption typology was derived from a two-year analysis of spectators at Wrigley Field who were attending Chicago Cubs baseball games (of course, studying the hapless Cubbies is bound to produce some unique and frustrating experiences!).[24]

This perspective views consumption as an activity where people use products and services in a variety of ways. Focusing on an event like a ball game also is a useful reminder that when we refer to consumption, we are talking about intangible experiences, ideas, and services (the thrill of a home run hit out of the park or the antics of a team mascot) in addition to tangible objects (the hot dogs eaten at the ball park). The analysis identified four distinct types of consumption activities:

- *Consuming as experience:* An emotional or aesthetic reaction to consumption of objects. This would include reactions such as the pleasure derived from learning how to mark a scorecard or appreciating the athletic ability of a favorite player.
- *Consuming as integration:* Learning and manipulating consumption objects to express aspects of the self or society. For example, some fans wear Cubs jerseys to express their solidarity with the team. Attending ball games in person rather than watching them on TV allows the fan to more completely integrate his or her experience with that of the team.
- *Consuming as classification:* The activities that consumers engage in to communicate their association with objects, both to self and to others. For example, spectators might buy souvenirs to demonstrate to others that they are die-hard fans, or the more hard-core fans might throw the opposition team's home run ball back onto the field as a gesture of contempt.
- *Consuming as play:* Consumers use objects to participate in a mutual experience and merge their identities with that of a group. For example, happy fans might scream in unison and engage in an orgy of "high fives" when one of their

This ad for electronics products by Samsung focuses on pure desire—consuming as experience.

team's players hits a home run. This is a different dimension of shared experience than just watching the game at home by oneself.

The Global Consumer

By 2006, the majority of people on Earth will live in urban centers—the number of megacities, defined as urban centers of 10 million or more, is projected to grow to 26 in 2015.[25] One by-product of sophisticated marketing strategies is the movement toward a **global consumer culture**, one in which people around the world are united by their common devotion to brand name consumer goods, movie stars, celebrities, and leisure activities.[26] Young people in particular are in many ways the same everywhere. Indeed, those who have the time and money to do so can travel the world in one nonstop party, as some savvy tour companies develop "Adventure Travel Party Scene" packages for worldly ravers. The motto of one such company,

BringItOn! Travel, sums up this approach to life: "On the beach 'til 7 pm. In the clubs 'til 9 am."[27] Not bad work if you can get it.

The rise of global marketing means that even smaller companies are looking to expand overseas—and this increases the pressure to understand how customers in other countries are the same or different than in one's own country. In the restaurant industry, for example, Shakey's pizza restaurants are mushrooming in the Philippines, and food from the International House of Pancakes is selling like hotcakes in Tokyo. But menu changes are sometimes called for to please local palates: Schlotzky's in Malaysia offers Smokey Mountain Chicken Crunch with "half-virgin" chicken, and diners at Bob's Big Boy in Thailand snap up Tropical Shrimp, deep fried with "exotic breading."[28] This book will pay special attention to the good and bad aspects of this cultural homogenization.

Net Profit

As new technologies develop, our old model of having to be seated in front of a PC to surf the Web may vanish like the horse-and-buggy. **U-commerce** is the use of ubiquitous networks that will slowly but surely become a part of us, whether in the form of wearable computers or customized advertisements beamed to us on our cell phones ("Hey, you're walking by McDonald's. Come on in for today's burger special.").[29]

In the near future many products will carry a plastic tag containing a computer chip and a tiny antenna that lets the chip communicate with a network. Grocery items will tell the store what needs to be restocked and which items are past their expiration dates, and your house will know when you're pulling in the driveway as it turns on the lights and starts your favorite tunes spinning before you walk in the door. Already, IBM has introduced "smart" washers and dryers in some college dorms that let students keep tabs on their laundry from anywhere they can access the Internet—their dorm rooms, the library, or even a cell phone. Students can log onto a Web page to see if there are free machines and receive e-mail or a page when their load is finished.[30]

This ad from Singapore reminds us that consumers around the world increasingly are modifying their lifestyles as they gain access to modern products.

Dale color a tu vida con Levi's 517 COLLECTION BOOT CUT

American products like Levi's jeans are in demand around the world.

Virtual Consumption

There's little doubt that the Digital Revolution is one of the most significant influences on consumer behavior, and the impact of the Web will continue to expand as more and more people around the world log in. In 2001, 58 percent of Americans had access to the Internet and this proportion was even higher in some European countries like The Netherlands (61 percent) and Switzerland (60 percent).[31] Many of us are avid Web surfers, and it's hard to imagine a time when e-mail, MP3 files, or Palm Pilots weren't an accepted part of daily life. Forrester Research predicts that by 2004, U.S. consumers alone will spend $184 billion (7 percent of all retail sales) online, or nearly $4,000 per household.[32] That's a lot of CDs and sweaters.

Electronic marketing has increased convenience by breaking down many of the barriers caused by time and location. You can shop 24/7 without leaving home, you can read today's newspaper without getting drenched picking up a hard copy in a rainstorm, and you don't have to wait for the 6:00 P.M. news to find out what the weather will be like tomorrow—at home or around the globe. And, with the increasing use of handheld devices and wireless communications, you can get that same information—from stock quotes to the weather—even when you're away from your computer.[33]

And, it's not all about businesses selling to consumers (**B2C e-commerce**). The cyberspace explosion has created a revolution in consumer-to-consumer activity (**C2C e-commerce**). Welcome to the new world of virtual brand communities. Just as e-consumers are not limited to local retail outlets in their shopping, they are not limited to their local communities when looking for friends.

Picture a small group of local collectors who meet once a month at a local diner to discuss their shared interests over coffee. Now multiply that group by thousands, and include people from all over the world who are united by a shared passion for sports memorabilia, Barbie dolls, Harley-Davidson motorcycles, refrigerator magnets, or building simulated neighborhoods on *The Sims Online* (and giving your characters real products including a computer with a Pentium 4 chip or McDonald's fries). The Web also provides an easy way for consumers around the world to exchange information about their experiences with products, services, music, restaurants, and movies. The Hollywood Stock Exchange (*hsx.com*) offers a simulated entertainment stock market where traders predict the four-week box office take for each film. *Amazon.com* encourages shoppers to write reviews of

THE GLOBAL LOOKING GLASS

Mr. Zamzamy, a young Indonesian advertising executive in a pink shirt, is sitting in a Western-style café in Jakarta, his cell phone at the ready, and his fried chicken is growing cold as he explains how he tries to be a good Muslim by right action, not fighting. That, he feels, is the best way of countering what he sees as the corrupting influence of American culture and morals on traditional Indonesian ways of life in the largest Muslim country in the world.

Two years ago, in line with his growing religious beliefs, he quit the advertising agency he worked for and set up his own company along Islamic lines: He won't take banks or alcoholic-beverage producers as clients, and he doesn't conduct business on Friday, the Muslim holy day. But he is relaxed about those who don't share his beliefs: He does not insist that his wife wear a headscarf, for example, and he is not uncomfortable sitting alongside the rich young Jakartans in the café who are flirting and drinking. "They must make their own choices," he says.

And though he does not like the sexual overtones of American pop culture, he knows that "you can't hide from American culture." By living his life according to Islamic precepts, he says, "I am fighting America in my own way. But I don't agree with violence."

All over the Muslim world, young people like Zamzamy are juggling their sense of Islamic identity with the trappings of a globalized, secular society. In a classroom of Al Khair University, set in a concrete office park in Islamabad, business student Nabil Ahmed and his classmates are well-dressed, middle-class boys who represent neither the old-money security of Pakistan's elite nor dirt-poor peasants who make up the bulk of Pakistan's angry conservative masses. They are the silent majority of Pakistan, with their feet firmly planted in both the East and the West. On weekdays, they listen to Whitney Houston and Michael Bolton, wear Dockers pants and Van Heusen shirts. On weekends, many switch to traditional salwar kameez outfits and go with their fathers to the mosque to pray. They have much to gain from a Western style of life, and most have plans to move to the United States for a few years to make some money before returning home to Pakistan. Yet despite their attraction to the West, they are wary of it too. "Most of us here like it both ways, we like American fashion, American music, American movies, but in the end, we are Muslims," says Ahmed.

Source: Excerpted from Peter Ford, "Why Do They Hate Us?" *The Christian Science Monitor,* *www.csmonitor.com/2001/0927/p1s1-wogi,* September 27, 2001.

books, and you can even rate your professors from A+ to F on *virtualratings.com* (don't tell your prof about this one; it'll be our secret).

The popularity of chat rooms where consumers can go to discuss various topics with like-minded "Netizens" around the world grows every day. News reports tell us of the sometimes wonderful and sometimes horrific romances that have begun on the Internet as people check out potential mates on sites like *match.com* or Lava Life (in a recent month, 26 million people visited online dating sites!).[34] A Swiss company called *skim.com* even lets you log in to pursue someone you see in RL (real life): Registered users are issued a six-digit number worn on jackets and backpacks sold by the company. When you see someone on the street or in a club that you'd like to get to know better, you go to *skim.com*, type in the person's number, and send him or her a message. And if you're lucky enough (?) to receive one of these messages, you can decide whether to respond.[35]

Will the Web bring people closer together or drive us each into our own private virtual worlds? Wired Americans are spending less time with friends and family, less time shopping in stores, and more time working at home after hours. More than one-third of respondents who have access to the Internet reported that they were online at least five hours a week. Also, 60 percent of Internet users said they had reduced their television viewing and one-third said they spent less time reading newspapers.

On the other hand, a study by the Pew Internet and American Life Project reported that more than half of users surveyed feel that e-mail actual strengthens family ties. Users reported far more offline social contact than nonusers.[36] These results argue that people are spending more time than ever with others. It's just that they are forming strong relationships over the Internet instead of in person. But the author of the first survey disagrees. As he observes, "If I go home at 6:30 in the evening and spend the whole night sending e-mail and wake up the next morning, I still haven't talked to my wife or kids or friends. When you spend your time on the Internet, you don't hear a human voice and you never get a hug."[37]

A follow-up study found that it works both ways—extroverts tend to make even more friends on the Web, while introverts feel even more cut off from the rest of the world. This has been termed the "rich get richer" model of Internet use.[38] So, it seems that just as in the offline world, our new digital reality is both good and bad. Throughout this book, we'll look at some examples of both the pros and cons of virtual consumer behavior in boxes called "Net Profit" and "The Tangled Web."

Blurred Boundaries: Marketing and Reality

Marketers and consumers coexist in a complicated, two-way relationship. It's often hard to tell where marketing efforts leave off and "the real world" begins. One result of these blurred boundaries is that we are no longer sure (and perhaps we don't care) where the line separating this fabricated world from reality begins and ends. Sometimes, we gleefully join in the illusion. A story line in a recent *Wonder Woman*

Marketing messages often borrow imagery from other forms of popular culture to connect with an audience. This line of syrups adapts the "look" of a pulp detective novel.

comic book features the usual out-of-this-world exploits of a vivacious superhero. But, it also includes the real-world marriage proposal of Todd McDevitt, the owner of a chain of comic book stores who persuaded DC Comics to let him woo his beloved in the issue.[39] One shudders to think what he has in mind for the honeymoon!

To what degree is the world of popular culture—and even consumers' perceptions of reality—shaped by the efforts of marketers? More than many of us believe, and this influence is increasing dramatically as companies experiment with new ways to command our attention. NBC's *The Other Half* talk show has had representatives from advertisers like Clorox, Hyundai Motor America, and even Tan Towel, a "self-tanning towelette," appear on the show as part of the regular programming. During the Clorox-sponsored segment, the hosts faced off against members of the studio audience in a make-believe game show about housekeeping.[40] Going a step farther, the CBS reality-adventure program *Survivor* stranded people on an island and let them compete for products such as a new pair of sneakers or a cold Budweiser—all provided courtesy of the show's sponsors.[41] And how about sleeping with corporations? A Holiday Inn resort in Florida offers rooms decorated in corporate themes, including the Orange Minute Maid suite and the Edy's Ice Cream suite. A Coca-Cola executive (there is a polar-bear motif in the Coca-Cola suite) comments that families "feel like they can actually interact with our brands within a room."[42] Now there's a happening vacation for you!

■ MARKETING ETHICS AND PUBLIC POLICY

In business, conflicts often arise between the goal to succeed in the marketplace and the desire to maximize the well-being of consumers by providing them with safe and effective products and services. On the other hand, consumers may expect too much from companies and try to exploit these obligations. Perhaps that explains the woman who sued Celebrity Cruise Line for more than $2 million in damages because she got hit in the head with a Coco Loco drink that was dropped by a passenger on a deck above her. She claims the line should have known that passengers would try to balance their drinks on the ship's railings![43]

Business Ethics

Business ethics are rules of conduct that guide actions in the marketplace—the standards against which most people in a culture judge what is right and what is wrong, good or bad. These universal values include honesty, trustworthiness, fairness, respect, justice, integrity, concern for others, accountability, and loyalty. Ethical business is good business. A Conference Board survey of U.S. consumers found the most important criterion when forming opinions about corporations is social responsibility in such areas as labor practices, business ethics, and environmental issues.[44] Consumers think better of products made by firms they feel are behaving ethically.[45]

But just what is ethical behavior? Sometimes it's not so easy to tell. For example, when you download songs from KaZaa, Morpheus, or other file-sharing programs, are you stealing? The film and recording industry thinks you are! It's appealing to universities nationwide to help crack down on Internet-based piracy, which advocates for tighter controls on file sharing referred to as "electronic shoplifting."[46]

Notions of right and wrong differ among people, organizations, and cultures. Some businesses believe it is all right for salespeople to pull out all the stops to persuade customers to buy, even if it means giving them false information; other firms feel that anything less than total honesty with customers is terribly wrong. Because each culture has its own set of values, beliefs, and customs, ethical business behaviors are defined quite differently around the world. For example, one recent study found that due to differences in values (more on this in Chapter 4), Mexican firms

The Tangled Web

To what extent should a consumer's personal information be available online? This is one of the most controversial ethical questions today. Scott McNealy, CEO of Sun Microsystems, once commented, "You already have zero privacy—get over it." Apparently many consumers don't agree; they are not happy at the prospect of leaving an electronic trail behind. A poll conducted by the National Consumers League found that consumers are more worried about personal privacy than health care, education, crime, and taxes. People are particularly concerned that businesses or individuals will target their children.[50] Nearly 70 percent of consumers worry about keeping their information private, but according to a Jupiter Media Metrix survey only 40 percent read privacy policies posted on business Web sites. This may be because these statements are laden in legalese; and, only 30 percent of consumers who do take the time to read them say they are understandable.[51]

How can these thorny ethical issues be solved? Some analysts predict that a market for privacy will emerge; we can ensure some degree of privacy, but it will cost us. Already, it's possible to buy products from "anonymizers" that provide the capability to surf the Web and send e-mail anonymously. Zero-Knowledge Systems of Montreal sells a software package called Freedom that includes five digital pseudonyms to assign to different identities.[52]

Others believe that instead of paying to be left alone, we can actually make money by selling our personal data. As one online executive observed, "Slowly but surely consumers are going to realize that their profile is valuable. For loaning out their identity, they're going to expect something in return."[53] **Infomediaries** act as information brokers by representing consumers who want to sell their profiles (including information such as their age, sex, family status, sexual orientation, income level, assets, and current shopping interests) to interested companies.[54]

are less likely to have formal codes of ethics and they are more likely to bribe public officials than are American or Canadian companies. On the other hand, due to different attitudes about work and interpersonal relationships these companies also are more likely to treat lower-level employees better than their NAFTA partners to the north.[47]

These cultural differences certainly influence whether business practices like bribery are acceptable. In Japan, it's called *kuroi kiri* (black mist), in Germany, it's *schmiergeld* (grease money), whereas Mexicans refer to *la mordida* (the bite), the French say *pot-de-vin* (jug of wine), and Italians speak of the *bustarella* (little envelope). They're all talking about *baksheesh*, the Middle Eastern term for a "tip" to grease the wheels of a transaction. Giving "gifts" in exchange for getting business from suppliers or customers is common and acceptable in many countries, even though this may be frowned upon elsewhere. Bribing foreigners to gain business has been against the law in the United States since 1977 under the Foreign Corrupt Practices Act. The Organization for Economic Cooperation and Development (OECD), to which most industrialized countries belong, also outlaws bribery. Recently, more than 800 business experts were asked to identify the countries where this practice is most flagrant. Russian and Chinese companies emerged at the top of the list, and Tarwan and South Korea were close behind. The "cleanest" countries were Australia, Sweden, Switzerland, Austria, and Canada.[48]

Whether intentionally or not, some marketers do violate their bond of trust with consumers. In some cases, these actions are actually illegal, as when a manufacturer deliberately mislabels the contents of a package. Or a retailer may adopt a "bait-and-switch" selling strategy that lures consumers into the store by offering inexpensive products with the sole intent of getting them to switch to higher-priced goods.

In other cases, marketing practices have detrimental effects on society even though they are not explicitly illegal. Some companies erect billboards for alcohol and tobacco products in low-income neighborhoods; others sponsor commercials depicting groups of people in an unfavorable light to get the attention of a target market. Civil rights groups, for example, charge that the marketing of menthol cigarettes by R.J. Reynolds to African Americans is illegal because menthol cigarettes are less safe than regular brands. A company spokeswoman responds, "This links to the bigger issue that minorities require some special protection. We find that offensive, paternalistic, and condescending."[49] Who is right? Throughout this book, ethical issues related to the practice of marketing are highlighted. Special boxes called "Marketing Pitfalls" feature questionable practices by marketers or the possible adverse effects of certain marketing strategies on consumers.

Needs and Wants: Do Marketers Manipulate Consumers?

One of the most common and stinging criticisms of marketing is that companies convince consumers they "need" many material things and that they will be unhappy and inferior people if they do not have these "necessities." The issue is a complex one, and is certainly worth considering: Do marketers give people what they want, or do they tell people what they should want?

Welcome to Consumerspace

Who controls the market—companies or consumers? This question is even more complicated as new ways of buying, having, and being are invented everyday. It seems that the "good old days" of *marketerspace*, a time when companies called the shots and decided what they wanted their customers to know and do, are dead and gone. As we saw with Gail's surfing decisions, many people now feel empowered to choose how, when, or if they will interact with corporations as they construct their own *consumerspace*. In turn, companies need to develop and leverage brand equity in bold new ways to attract the loyalty of these consumer "nomads."

The desire by many consumers to shield their personal data is creating a new market for companies selling online privacy solutions.

People still "need" companies—but in new ways and on their own terms. As we'll see throughout this book, profound changes in consumer behavior are influencing how people search for product information and evaluate alternative brands. In the brave new world of consumerspace, we have the potential to shape our own marketing destinies.[55]

Do Marketers Create Artificial Needs?

The marketing system has come under fire from both ends of the political spectrum. On the one hand, some members of the Religious Right believe that marketers contribute to the moral breakdown of society by presenting images of hedonistic pleasure and encouraging the pursuit of secular humanism at the expense of spirituality and the environment. Recently, a coalition of religious groups called the National Religious Partnership for the Environment claimed that gas-guzzling SUVs are contrary to Christian moral teachings about protecting people and the earth (more on this in Chapter 5).[56] On the other hand, some leftists argue that the same deceitful promises of material pleasure function to buy off people who would otherwise be revolutionaries working to change the system.[57] According to this argument, the marketing system creates demand—demand that only its products can satisfy.

A Response. A need is a basic biological motive; a want represents one way that society has taught us that the need can be satisfied. For example, thirst is biologically based; we are taught to want Coca-Cola to satisfy that thirst rather than, say, goat's milk. Thus, the need is already there; marketers simply recommend ways to satisfy it. A basic objective of marketing is to create awareness that needs exist, not to create needs.

Are Advertising and Marketing Necessary?

The social critic Vance Packard wrote more than 40 years ago, "Large-scale efforts are being made, often with impressive success, to channel our unthinking habits,

This ad was created by the American Association of Advertising Agencies to counter charges that ads create artificial needs.

DESPITE WHAT SOME PEOPLE THINK, ADVERTISING CAN'T MAKE YOU BUY SOMETHING YOU DON'T NEED.

Some people would have you believe that you are putty in the hands of every advertiser in the country.

They think that when advertising is put under your nose, your mind turns to oatmeal.

It's mass hypnosis. Subliminal seduction. Brain washing. Mind control. It's advertising.

And you are a pushover for it.

It explains why your kitchen cupboard is full of food you never eat.

Why your garage is full of cars you never drive.

Why your house is full of books you don't read, TV's you don't watch, beds you don't use, and clothes you don't wear.

You don't have a choice. You are forced to buy.

That's why this message is a cleverly disguised advertisement to get you to buy land in the tropics.

Got you again, didn't we? Send in your money.

ADVERTISING

ANOTHER WORD FOR FREEDOM OF CHOICE.

American Association of Advertising Agencies

our purchasing decisions, and our thought processes by the use of insights gleaned from psychiatry and the social sciences."[58] The economist John Kenneth Galbraith charged that radio and television are important tools to accomplish this manipulation of the masses. Because virtually no literacy is required to use these media, they allow repetitive and compelling communications to reach almost everyone. This criticism may even be more relevant to online communications, where a simple click delivers a world of information to us.

Many feel that marketers arbitrarily link products to desirable social attributes, fostering a materialistic society in which we are measured by what we own. One influential critic even argued that the problem is that we are not materialistic enough—that is, we do not sufficiently value goods for the utilitarian functions they deliver but instead focus on the irrational value of goods for what they symbolize. According to this view, for example, "Beer would be enough for us, without the additional promise that in drinking it we show ourselves to be manly, young at heart, or neighborly. A washing machine would be a useful machine to wash clothes, rather than an indication that we are forward-looking or an object of envy to our neighbors."[59]

A Response. Products are designed to meet existing needs, and advertising only helps to communicate their availability.[60] According to the **economics of information** perspective, advertising is an important source of consumer information.[61] This view emphasizes the economic cost of the time spent searching for products. Accordingly, advertising is a service for which consumers are willing to pay, because the information it provides reduces search time.

Do Marketers Promise Miracles?

Consumers are led to believe through advertising that products have magical properties; products will do special and mysterious things for consumers in a way that will transform their lives. Consumers will be beautiful, have power over others' feelings, be successful, and be relieved of all ills. In this respect, advertising functions as mythology does in primitive societies: It provides simple, anxiety-reducing answers to complex problems.

A Response. Advertisers simply do not know enough about people to manipulate them. Consider that the failure rate for new products ranges from 40 to 80 percent. Although people think that advertisers have an endless source of magical tricks and scientific techniques to manipulate them, in reality the industry is successful when it tries to sell good products and unsuccessful when selling poor ones.[62]

Public Policy and Consumerism

Concern for the welfare of consumers has been an issue since at least the beginning of the twentieth century, both in the United States and elsewhere. British secondary schools are now required to teach students how to be "responsible consumers." The curriculum encourages students to take a closer look at companies' activities, from advertising to how they manufacture goods. It also asks them to examine their own roles as consumers, to think about the reasons for their purchases and the impact of their consumption.[63]

Partly as a result of consumers' efforts in the United States, many federal agencies have been established to oversee consumer-related activities. These include the Department of Agriculture, the Federal Trade Commission, the Food and Drug Administration, the Securities and Exchange Commission, and the Environmental Protection Agency. After Upton Sinclair's 1906 book *The Jungle* exposed the awful conditions in the Chicago meatpacking industry, Congress was prompted to pass important pieces of legislation—the Pure Food and Drug Act in 1906 and the Federal Meat Inspection Act a year later—to protect consumers. A summary of some important consumer legislation enacted since that time appears in Table 1.1. Other information about consumer-related issues can be found at *consumerreports.org* and *cpsc.gov* (The Consumer Product Safety Commission).

Consumer Activism: America™?

"Absolut Impotence." So reads a parody ad created by Adbusters, a nonprofit organization that advocates for "the new social activist movement of the information age." The editor of the group's magazine argues that America is no longer a country, but rather a multitrillion-dollar brand subverted by corporate agendas. He claims that America™ is no different from McDonald's, Marlboro, or General Motors.[64]

Adbusters sponsors numerous initiatives, including Buy Nothing Day and TV Turnoff Week, intended to discourage rampant commercialism. These efforts, along with biting ads and commercials that lampoon advertising messages, are part and parcel of a strategy called **culture jamming** that aims to disrupt efforts by the corporate world to dominate our cultural landscape. The movement believes "culture jamming . . . will change the way information flows, the way institutions wield

TABLE 1.1
SAMPLER OF FEDERAL LEGISLATION INTENDED TO ENHANCE CONSUMERS' WELFARE

Year	Act	Purpose
1951	Fur Products Labeling Act	Regulates the branding, advertising, and shipment of fur products.
1953	Flammable Fabrics Act	Prohibits the transportation of flammable fabrics across state lines.
1958	National Traffic and Safety Act	Creates safety standards for cars and tires.
1958	Automobile Information Disclosure Act	Requires automobile manufacturers to post suggested retail prices on new cars.
1966	Fair Packaging and Labeling Act	Regulates packaging and labeling of consumer products. (Manufacturers must provide information about package contents and origin.)
1966	Child Protection Act	Prohibits sale of dangerous toys and other items.
1967	Federal Cigarette Labeling and Advertising Act	Requires cigarette packages to carry a warning label from the Surgeon General.
1968	Truth-in-Lending Act	Requires lenders to divulge the true costs of a credit transaction.
1969	National Environmental Policy Act	Established a national environmental policy and created the Council on Environmental Quality to monitor the effects of products on the environment.
1972	Consumer Products Safety Act	Established the Consumer Product Safety Commission to identify unsafe products, establish safety standards, recall defective products, and ban dangerous products.
1975	Consumer Goods Pricing Act	Bans the use of price maintenance agreements among manufacturers and resellers.
1975	Magnuson-Moss Warranty-Improvement Act	Creates disclosure standards for consumer product warranties and allows the Federal Trade Commission to set policy regarding unfair or deceptive practices.
1990	The Nutrition Labeling and Education Act	Reaffirms the legal basis for the Food and Drug Administration's new rules on food labeling and establishes a timetable for the implementation of those rules. Regulations covering health claims became effective May 8, 1993. Those pertaining to nutrition labeling and nutrient content claims went into effect May 8, 1994.
1998	Internet Tax Freedom Act	Established a three-year moratorium on special taxation of the Internet, including taxation of access fees paid to America Online and other Internet Service Providers. An extension of the moratorium is being considered.

power, the way TV stations are run, the way the food, fashion, automobile, sports, music and culture industries set their agendas. Above all, it will change the way meaning is produced in our society."[65] The *Culture Jammers Manifesto* proclaims opposition to the "mind-polluters": "On the rubble of the old culture, we will build a new one with non-commercial heart and soul."[66]

While some in corporate America may dismiss these extreme sentiments as the ravings of a lunatic fringe, they deserve to be taken seriously. The recent scandals involving such corporate icons as Enron, Arthur Andersen, WorldCom, and Merrill Lynch have fueled a growing bonfire of mistrust and skepticism among the consuming public. Time will tell if these backlashes against companies will die down or continue to grow as new scandals continue to come to light. Clearly, dramatic steps are needed to restore public confidence as the business page of the newspaper starts to read like the crime blotter.

A few examples of coordinated consumer protest movements include:

● The Truth (sponsored by the American Legacy Foundation) was established in 1998 with significant funding from tobacco companies' settlements in lawsuits filed by numerous attorneys-general around the country. The Truth's mission

Adbusters Quarterly is a Canadian magazine devoted to culture jamming. This mock ad skewers Benetton.

"is to alert everyone to the lies and hidden practices of the cigarette companies, while giving people the tools to have a voice in changing that." This project develops marketing communications directed to adolescents and other at-risk populations to disseminate information about nicotine addiction, how tobacco products are advertised, and what these products do to the body.[67]

- Save the Redwoods/Boycott the GAP (SRBG) is an organization that specifically targets the GAP chain of stores. The group protests such policies as the alleged use of sweatshop labor on the island of Saipan, which produces some of the store's clothing.[68] In one highly visible demonstration staged in several cities, called "We'd Rather Wear Nothing Than Wear GAP!", activists stripped naked to underscore their message. Another organization called ***BehindTheLabel.org*** pushes the cause against the GAP by using a listserv to recruit protestors.[69]

- The Pittsburgh Coalition Against Pornography (PCAP) claims that the clothing company Abercrombie and Fitch produces pornographic advertising targeted to 13- to 17-year-olds. Many of the cited advertisements depict barely dressed youthful models promoting the latest adolescent styles. The organization encourages a boycott of Abercrombie products; its Web site proclaims, "Take Action: Five Steps You Can Take to Ditch Fitch!"[70]

Consumerism and Consumer Research

President John F. Kennedy ushered in the modern era of consumerism with his "Declaration of Consumer Rights" in 1962. These include the right to safety, the right to be informed, the right to redress, and the right to choice. The 1960s and 1970s were a time of consumer activism as consumers began to organize to demand better-quality products (and to boycott companies that did not provide them). These movements were prompted by the publication of books such as Rachel Carson's *Silent Spring* in 1962, which attacked the irresponsible use of pesticides; and Ralph Nader's *Unsafe at Any Speed* in 1965, which exposed safety defects in General Motors' Corvair automobile. Many consumers have a vigorous interest in consumer-related issues, ranging from environmental concerns such as pollution caused by oil spills, toxic waste, and so on, to excessive violence and sex on television or in the lyrics of popular rock and rap songs.

The field of consumer behavior can play an important role in improving our lives as consumers.[71] Many researchers play a role in formulating or evaluating public policies such as ensuring that products are labeled accurately, that people can comprehend important information presented in advertising, or that children are not exploited by program-length toy commercials masquerading as television shows.

Many firms choose to protect or enhance the natural environment as they go about their business activities, a practice known as **green marketing.** Some firms have focused their efforts on reducing wasteful packaging, as when Procter & Gamble introduced refillable containers for Downy fabric softener.[72] In other cases, successful marketers are promising donations to charity as purchase incentives or are even donating their own money to good causes.[73] For example, Pierre Omidyar, the creator of eBay who is worth more than $6 billion, is aggressively giving seed money to charities that follow solid business plans. He plans to turn over all but one percent of his astounding wealth during the next 20 years.[74]

Social marketing uses marketing techniques normally employed to sell beer or detergent to encourage positive behaviors such as increased literacy and to discourage negative activities such as drunk driving.[75] A Swedish project aimed at curbing adolescent drinking illustrates social marketing at work. The Swedish Brewer's Association invested 10 million Skr (about $7.5 million dollars) in a coop-

This German ad for Unicef makes a statement about the problem of child labor.
Source: www.unicef.de against child labor.

erative effort with the Swedish Non-Violence Project to change teens' attitudes about alcohol consumption. Consumer researchers working on the project discovered that Swedish adolescents freely admit that they "drink in order to get drunk" and enjoy the feeling of being intoxicated, so persuading them to give up alcohol is a formidable task. However, the teens reported they also are afraid of losing control over their own behavior, especially if there is a risk for them to be exposed to violence. And, while worries about the long-term health effects of drinking don't concern this group (after all, at this age many believe they will live forever), female adolescents reported a fear of becoming less attractive as a result of prolonged alcohol consumption.

Based on these findings, the group commissioned to execute this project decided to stress a more realistic message of "drink if you want to, but within a safe limit. Don't lose control, because if you do, you might get yourself into violent situations." They made up the motto "Alco-hole in your head" to stress the importance

Colguemos las armas...

...NO a la violencia

Ayudemos a las víctimas de la violencia y el terrorismo.

Cruz Roja

CREACION SAATCHI&SAATCHI GUATEMALA / GUILLERMO MARTINEZ / ALFREDO SANCHEZ

Following 9/11, ads addressed people's fears in various ways. This Guatemalan ad was created as part of the Advertising Community Together initiative.
Source: Anti-weapon ad by **CREACION NAZCA SAATCHI & SAATCHI**, Guatemala. Creatives: Guillermo Rene Martinez and Alfredo Sanchez.

of knowing one's limits. This message appeared on billboards, in video spots that depict situations involving young drinkers getting out of control, and in school presentations given by young people.[76]

■ THE DARK SIDE OF CONSUMER BEHAVIOR

Despite the best efforts of researchers, government regulators, and concerned industry people, sometimes consumers' worst enemies are themselves. Individuals are often depicted as rational decision makers, calmly doing their best to obtain products and services that will maximize the health and well-being of themselves, their families, and their society. In reality, however, consumers' desires, choices, and actions often result in negative consequences to individuals and the society in which they live.

Some of these actions are relatively harmless, but others have more onerous consequences. Some harmful consumer behaviors such as excessive drinking or cigarette smoking stem from social pressures, and the cultural value placed on money encourages activities such as shoplifting or insurance fraud. Exposure to unattainable ideals of beauty and success can create dissatisfaction with the self. Many of these issues will be touched upon later in the book, but for now, let's review some dimensions of "the dark side" of consumer behavior.

Consumer Terrorism

The terrorist attacks of 2001 were a wake-up call to the free-enterprise system. They revealed the vulnerability of nonmilitary targets and reminded us that disruptions of our financial, electronic, and supply networks can potentially be more damaging to our way of life than the fallout from a conventional battlefield. These incursions may be deliberate or not—economic shockwaves of "mad cow" disease in Europe (and now spreading to Japan and elsewhere) are still reverberating in the beef industry.[77] Assessments by the Rand Corporation and other analysts point to the susceptibility of the nation's food supply as a potential target of **bioterrorism.**[78]

Even prior to the anthrax scares of 2001, toxic substances placed in products threatened to hold the marketplace hostage. This tactic first drew public attention in the United States in 1982, when seven people died after taking Tylenol pills laced with cyanide. A decade later Pepsi weathered its own crisis when more than 50 reports of syringes found in Diet Pepsi cans surfaced in 23 states. In that case Pepsi pulled off a PR *coup de grace* by convincing the public that the syringes could not have been introduced during the manufacturing process. The company even showed an in-store surveillance video that caught a customer slipping a syringe into a Diet Pepsi can while the cashier's head was turned.[79] Pepsi's aggressive actions underscore the importance of responding to such a crisis head-on and quickly.

Addictive Consumption

Consumer addiction is a physiological or psychological dependency on products or services. These problems of course include alcoholism, drug addiction, and cigarettes—and many companies profit from addictive products or by selling solutions. For example, bottled water mixed with nicotine, called Nico Water, is the latest in a string of tobacco products that has included candy-flavored cigarettes and nicotine lollipops. The product's Web site touts it as a "safe nicotine drink for smokers trying to quit and smokers prohibited from smoking" in restaurants, offices, and airplanes. The company's CEO, responding to criticism about the potential of this product to hook kids, replied, "No one ever died of secondhand water."[80]

Although most people equate addiction with drugs, virtually any product or service can be seen as relieving some problem or satisfying some need to the point that reliance on it becomes extreme. There is even a Chap Stick Addicts support group with approximately 250 active members![81] Some psychologists are even raising concerns about "Internet addiction," a condition in which people (particularly college students!) become obsessed by online chat rooms to the point that their "virtual" lives take priority over their real ones.[82]

Compulsive Consumption

For some consumers, the expression "born to shop" is taken quite literally. They shop because they are compelled to do so, rather than because shopping is a pleasurable or functional task. **Compulsive consumption** refers to repetitive shopping, often excessive, as an antidote to tension, anxiety, depression, or boredom. "Shopaholics" turn to shopping much the way addicted people turn to drugs or alcohol.[83]

Compulsive consumption is distinctly different from impulse buying, which will be discussed in Chapter 10. The impulse to buy a specific item is temporary, and it centers on a specific product at a particular moment. In contrast, compulsive buying is an enduring behavior that centers on the process of buying, not the purchases themselves. As one woman who spent $20,000 per year on clothing confessed, "I was possessed when I went into a store. I bought clothes that didn't fit, that I didn't like, and that I certainly didn't need."[84]

In some cases, it is fairly safe to say that the consumer, not unlike a drug addict, has little to no control over consumption. Whether alcohol, cigarettes, chocolate, diet colas, or even Chap Stick, the products control the consumer. Even the act of shopping itself is an addicting experience for some consumers. Much negative or destructive consumer behavior can be characterized by three common elements:[85]

1 The behavior is not done by choice.
2 The gratification derived from the behavior is short-lived.
3 The person experiences strong feelings of regret or guilt afterwards.

Gambling is an example of a consumption addiction that touches every segment of consumer society. Whether it takes the form of casino gambling, playing the "slots," betting on sports events with friends or through a bookie, or even buying lottery tickets, excessive gambling can be quite destructive. Taken to extremes, gambling can result in lowered self-esteem, debt, divorce, and neglected children. According to one psychologist, gamblers exhibit a classic addictive cycle: They experience a "high" while in action and depression when they stop gambling, which leads them back to the thrill of the action. Unlike drug addicts, however, money is the substance that hard-core gamblers abuse.

Consumed Consumers

Consumed consumers are people who are used or exploited, willingly or not, for commercial gain in the marketplace. The situations in which consumers themselves become commodities can range from traveling road shows that feature dwarfs and midgets to the selling of body parts and babies. Some examples of consumed consumers:

- *Prostitutes:* Expenditures on prostitution in the United States alone are estimated at $20 billion annually. These revenues are equivalent to those in the domestic shoe industry.[86]
- *Organ, blood, and hair donors:* In the United States, millions of people sell their blood. A lively market also exists for organs (e.g., kidneys), and some women sell their hair to be made into wigs. Bidding for a human kidney on eBay went to more than $5.7 million before the company ended the auction (it's illegal to sell human organs online—at least so far). The seller wrote, "You can choose either

The Tangled Web

Internet addiction is becoming a big problem in South Korea, which has the largest high-speed Internet market penetration in the world. More than half of all Korean households have high-speed Internet connections (compared with fewer than 10 percent in the United States) and the exploding Web culture has "hooked" a huge number of young people on online gaming (80 percent of South Koreans under 25 play these games). Many of the gamers hang out in "PC bangs" which are coffeehouses and lounges featuring rows and rows of computers. Critics say the gaming industry is creating millions of zombified addicts who are dropping out of school and (offline) group activities, becoming uncommunicative and even violent because of the electronic games they play. South Korea is a group-oriented society where socializing in bunches is the preferred form of interaction. Critics also claim that the PC bangs are turning into pickup joints, where teenagers swap pictures electronically and decide whether or not to meet. Reversing the usual pattern in a male-dominated society, the girls tend to be in charge—they send aggressive messages to boys and provide clues to help them figure out in which bang they are playing and where they are sitting.[87]

kidney. . . . Of course only one for sale, as I need the other one to live. Serious bids only."[88]

- *Babies for sale:* Several thousand surrogate mothers have been paid to be medically impregnated and carry babies to term for infertile couples. Commercial sperm banks have become big business, and the market is international in scope as many countries rely on imports. The head of one of the largest companies boasts, "We think we can be the McDonald's of sperm." This company markets three grades of sperm including an "extra" grade, which contains twice as many sperm as the average grade. The company can deliver to almost any customer in the world within 72 hours with its special freezing techniques in which the sperm travel in liquid nitrogen tanks.[89]

Illegal Activities

A survey conducted by the McCann-Erickson advertising agency revealed the following tidbits:[90]

- Ninety-one percent of people say they lie regularly. One in three fibs about their weight, one in four about their income, and 21 percent lie about their age. Nine percent even lie about their natural hair color.
- Four out of ten Americans have tried to pad an insurance bill to cover the deductible.
- Nineteen percent say they've snuck into a theater to avoid paying admission.
- More than three out of five people say they've taken credit for making something from scratch when they have done no such thing. According to Pillsbury's CEO, this "behavior is so prevalent that we've named a category after it—speed scratch."

Many consumer behaviors are not only self-destructive or socially damaging, they are illegal as well. The cost of crimes committed by consumers against business has been estimated at more than $40 billion per year.

Consumer Theft

A retail theft is committed every five seconds. **Shrinkage** is the industry term for inventory and cash losses from shoplifting and employee theft. This is a massive problem for businesses that is passed on to consumers in the form of higher prices (about 40 percent of the losses can be attributed to employees rather than shoppers). Shopping malls spend $6 million annually on security, and a family of four spends about $300 extra per year because of markups to cover shrinkage.[91] Indeed, shoplifting is America's fastest-growing crime. A comprehensive retail study found that shoplifting is a year-round problem that costs U.S. retailers $9 billion dollars annually. The most frequently stolen products are tobacco products, athletic shoes, logo and brand name apparel, designer jeans, and undergarments. The average theft amount per incident is $58.43, up from $20.36 in a 1995 survey.[92] The problem is equally worrisome in Europe; in 2001 alone retailers apprehended 1.23 million shoplifters. Shrinkage is expected to cost European retailers more than $30 billion in 2002. The United Kingdom has the highest rate of shrinkage (as a percent of annual sales), followed by Norway, Greece, and France. Switzerland and Austria have the lowest rates.[93]

The large majority of shoplifting is not done by professional thieves or by people who genuinely need the stolen items.[94] About two million Americans are charged with shoplifting each year, but it's estimated that for every arrest, 18 unreported incidents occur.[95] About three-quarters of those caught are middle- or high-income people who shoplift for the thrill of it or as a substitute for affection. Shoplifting is also common among adolescents. Research evidence indicates that teen shoplifting is influenced by factors such as having friends who also shoplift. It is also more likely to occur if the adolescent does not believe that this behavior is morally wrong.[96]

Anticonsumption

Some types of destructive consumer behavior can be thought of as **anticonsumption**, events in which products and services are deliberately defaced or mutilated. Some of these actions are relatively harmless, as when a person goes online at *dogdoo.com* to send a bag of dog manure to a lucky recipient. This site even lets customers calibrate the size of the "gift" by choosing among three "Poo Poo Packages": Econo-Poop (20 lb. dog), Poo Poo Special (50 lb. dog), and the ultimate in payback, the Poo Poo Grande (110 lb. dog). The moral: Smell your packages before opening.

Individuals can perform acts of anticonsumption online, sometimes causing great damage to companies.

In a world where it's a different kind of threat every day, you need a different kind of security.

New threats can blow right through any firewall or anti-virus software. That's where we come in. Our dynamic protection helps you conduct business safely in the face of ever-changing threats and increased risk. From proactive research and award-winning software to 24/7 protection and response services, our solutions detect, prevent and respond to online attacks and misuse. No matter who you're up against. To learn more, call 800-776-2362. Or visit www.iss.net/ad/fortune.

INTERNET SECURITY SYSTEMS™

Anticonsumption can range from relatively mild acts like spray-painting graffiti on buildings and subways to serious incidences of product tampering or even the release of computer viruses that can bring large corporations to their knees. Anticonsumption can also take the form of political protest in which activists alter or destroy billboards and other advertisements that promote what they feel to be unhealthy or unethical acts. For example, some members of the clergy in areas heavily populated by minorities have organized rallies to protest the proliferation of cigarette and alcohol advertising in their neighborhoods; these protests sometimes include the defacement of billboards promoting alcohol or cigarettes.

■ CONSUMER BEHAVIOR AS A FIELD OF STUDY

By now it should be clear that the field of consumer behavior encompasses many things, from the simple purchase of a carton of milk to the selection of a complex networked computer system, from the decision to donate money to a charity to devious plans to rip off a company.

There's an awful lot to understand, and many ways to go about it. Although people have certainly been consumers for a long time, it is only recently that consumption per se has been the object of formal study. In fact, although many business schools now require that marketing majors take a consumer behavior course, most colleges did not even offer such a course until the 1970s.

Interdisciplinary Influences on the Study of Consumer Behavior

Many different perspectives shape the young field of consumer behavior. Indeed, it is hard to think of a field that is more interdisciplinary. People with training in a very wide range of disciplines—from psychophysiology to literature—can now be found doing consumer research. Universities, manufacturers, museums, advertising agencies, and governments employ consumer researchers. Several professional groups, such as the Association for Consumer Research and the Society for Consumer Psychology, have been formed since the mid-1970s.

To gain an idea of the diversity of interests of people who do consumer research, consider the list of professional associations that sponsor the field's major journal, the *Journal of Consumer Research:* American Association of Family and Consumer Sciences, the American Statistical Association, the Association for Consumer Research, the Society for Consumer Psychology, the International Communication Association, the American Sociological Association, the Institute of Management Sciences, the American Anthropological Association, the American Marketing Association, the Society for Personality and Social Psychology, the American Association for Public Opinion Research, and the American Economic Association. That's a pretty mixed bag.

So, with all of these researchers from diverse backgrounds interested in consumer behavior, which is the "correct" discipline to look into these issues? You might remember a children's story about the blind men and the elephant. The gist of the story is that each man touched a different part of the animal and, as a result, the descriptions each gave of the elephant were quite different. This analogy applies to consumer research as well. A given consumer phenomenon can be studied in different ways and at different levels depending on the training and interests of the researchers studying it. Table 1.2 illustrates how a "simple" topic like magazine usage can be approached in many different ways.

TABLE 1.2 INTERDISCIPLINARY RESEARCH ISSUES IN CONSUMER BEHAVIOR	
Disciplinary Focus	**Magazine Usage Sample Research Issues**
Experimental Psychology: product role in perception, learning, and memory processes	How specific aspects of magazines, such as their design or layout, are recognized and interpreted; which parts of a magazine are most likely to be read
Clinical Psychology: product role in psychological adjustment	How magazines affect readers' body images (e.g., do thin models make the average woman feel overweight?)
Microeconomics/Human Ecology: product role in allocation of individual or family resources	Factors influencing the amount of money spent on magazines in a household
Social Psychology: product role in the behavior of individuals as members of social groups	Ways that ads in a magazine affect readers' attitudes toward the products depicted; how peer pressure influences a person's readership decisions
Sociology: product role in social institutions and group relationships	Pattern by which magazine preferences spread through a social group (e.g., a sorority)
Macroeconomics: product role in consumers' relations with the marketplace	Effects of the price of fashion magazines and expense of items advertised during periods of high unemployment
Semiotics/Literary Criticism: product role in the verbal and visual communication of meaning	Ways in which underlying messages communicated by models and ads in a magazine are interpreted
Demography: product role in the measurable characteristics of a population	Effects of age, income, and marital status of a magazine's readers
History: product role in societal changes over time	Ways in which our culture's depictions of "femininity" in magazines have changed over time
Cultural Anthropology: product role in a society's beliefs and practices	Ways in which fashions and models in a magazine affect readers' definitions of masculine versus feminine behavior (e.g., the role of working women, sexual taboos)

Figure 1.2 provides a glimpse of some of the disciplines working in the field and the level at which each approaches research issues. These diverse disciplines can be roughly characterized in terms of their focus on micro versus macro consumer behavior topics. The fields closer to the top of the pyramid concentrate on the individual consumer (micro issues), and those toward the base are more interested in the aggregate activities that occur among larger groups of people, such as consumption patterns shared by members of a culture or subculture (macro issues).

The Issue of Strategic Focus

Many regard the field of consumer behavior as an applied social science. Accordingly, the value of the knowledge generated should be judged in terms of its ability to improve the effectiveness of marketing practice. However, some researchers have argued that consumer behavior should not have a strategic focus at all; the field

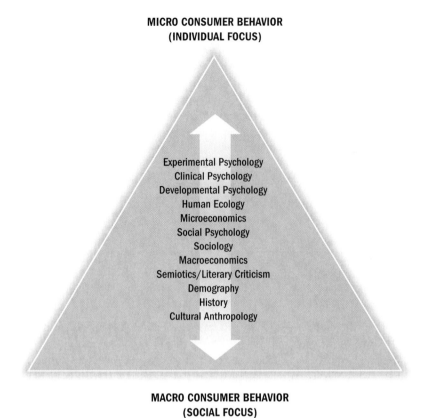

should not be a "handmaiden to business." It should instead focus on the understanding of consumption for its own sake, and not because marketers can apply this knowledge to make a profit.[97] Most consumer researchers do not hold this rather extreme view, but it has encouraged many to expand the scope of their work beyond the field's traditional focus on the purchase of consumer goods such as food, appliances, and cars to embrace social problems such as homelessness or preserving the environment. Certainly, it has led to some fiery debates among people working in the field!

The Issue of Two Perspectives on Consumer Research

One general way to classify consumer research is in terms of the fundamental assumptions the researchers make about what they are studying and how to study it. This set of beliefs is known as a **paradigm**. As in other fields of study, consumer behavior is dominated by a paradigm, but some believe it is in the middle of a paradigm shift, which occurs when a competing paradigm challenges the dominant set of assumptions.

The basic set of assumptions underlying the dominant paradigm at this point in time is called **positivism** (or sometimes *modernism*). This perspective has significantly influenced Western art and science since the late sixteenth century. It emphasizes that human reason is supreme, and that there is a single, objective truth that can be discovered by science. Positivism encourages us to stress the function of objects, to celebrate technology, and to regard the world as a rational, ordered place with a clearly defined past, present, and future.

The emerging paradigm of **interpretivism** (or *postmodernism*) questions these assumptions. Proponents of this perspective argue that there is too much emphasis on science and technology in our society, and that this ordered, rational view of behavior denies the complex social and cultural world in which we live. Others feel that positivism puts too much emphasis on material well-being, and that its logical outlook is directed by an ideology that stresses the homogenous views of a culture

TABLE 1.3
POSITIVIST VERSUS INTERPRETIVIST APPROACHES TO CONSUMER BEHAVIOR

Assumptions	Positivist Approach	Interpretivist Approach
Nature of reality	Objective, tangible Single	Socially constructed Multiple
Goal	Prediction	Understanding
Knowledge generated	Time free Context independent	Time bound Context dependent
View of causality	Existence of real causes	Multiple, simultaneous shaping events
Research relationship	Separation between researcher and subject	Interactive, cooperative with researcher being part of phenomenon under study

Source: Adapted from Laurel A. Hudson and Julie L. Ozanne, "Alternative Ways of Seeking Knowledge in Consumer Research," *Journal of Consumer Research* 14 (March 1988): 508–21. Reprinted with the permission of the University of Chicago Press.

dominated by (dead) white males. Interpretivists instead stress the importance of symbolic, subjective experience, and the idea that meaning is in the mind of the person—that is, we each construct our own meanings based on our unique and shared cultural experiences, so there are no right or wrong answers. In this view, the world in which we live is composed of a **pastiche** or mixture of images.[98] The value placed on products because they help us to create order in our lives is replaced by an appreciation of consumption as offering a set of diverse experiences. The major differences between these two perspectives on consumer research are summarized in Table 1.3.

An interpretative framework to understand marketing communications can be illustrated by an analysis of one of the best-known and longest-running (1959–1978) advertising campaigns of all time: The work done by the advertising agency Doyle Dane Bernbach for the Volkswagen Beetle. This campaign, widely noted for its self-mocking wit, found many ways to turn the Beetle's homeliness, smallness, and lack of power into positive attributes at a time when most car ads were emphasizing just the opposite. An interpretative analysis of these messages used concepts from literature, psychology, and anthropology to ground the appeal of this approach within a broader cultural context. The image created for the humble car was connected to other examples of what scholars of comedy call the "Little Man" pattern. This is a type of comedic character that is related to a clown or a trickster, a social outcast who is able to poke holes in the stuffiness and rigidity of bureaucracy and conformity. Other examples of the "Little Man" character include Hawkeye in the TV sitcom *M.A.S.H.,* the comedian Woody Allen, and Charlie Chaplin. When one looks at the cultural meaning of marketing messages this way, it is perhaps no coincidence that IBM chose the Charlie Chaplin character some years later to help it "soften" its stuffy, intimidating image as it tried to convince consumers that its new personal computer products were user-friendly.

■ TAKING IT FROM HERE: THE PLAN OF THE BOOK

This book covers many facets of consumer behavior, and many of the research perspectives briefly described in this chapter will be highlighted in later chapters. The plan of the book is simple: It goes from micro to macro. Think of it as a sort of photograph album of consumer behavior: Each chapter provides a "snapshot" of consumers, but the lens used to take each picture gets successively wider. The book begins with issues related to the individual consumer and expands its focus

An interpretative framework to understand marketing communications can be illustrated by the work done by advertising agency Doyle Dane Bernback for the Volkswagen Beetle.

Heard any Volkswagen jokes lately?

Remember the one about the lady who looked under her front hood and thought somebody stole her engine?

Or the one about the guy at the gas station who didn't know where the gas went? Or the water?

Today, the gas station attendants know enough to put the gas in front. And they don't

bother checking your water or trying to sell you some anti-freeze.

(After all, they've seen enough VWs to know that our engine's in the rear; and that it's cooled by air, not water.)

The point is this: People used to make fun of our car, now they have fun with it.

Which helps explain why our joke file's

been getting a bit low. So, if you've heard any good VW quips or sayings or jokes, why not send them on?

Just write to John Stanley, Volkswagen of America, Englewood Cliffs, N. J.

He'll start them on their rounds.

After all, nobody enjoys a good VW joke better than we do.

until it eventually considers the behaviors of large groups of people in their social settings. The topics to be covered correspond to the wheel of consumer behavior presented in Figure 1.3.

Section II, "Consumers as Individuals," considers the consumer at his or her most micro level. It examines how the individual receives information from his or her immediate environment and how this material is learned, stored in memory, and used to form and modify individual attitudes—both about products and about oneself. Section III, "Consumers as Decision Makers," explores the ways in which consumers use the information they have acquired to make decisions about consumption activities, both as individuals and as group members. Section IV, "Consumers and Subcultures," further expands the focus by considering how the consumer functions as part of a larger social structure. This structure includes the influence of different social groups with which the consumer belongs and identifies, including social class, ethnic groups, and age groups. Finally, Section V, "Consumers and Culture," completes the picture as it examines marketing's impact on mass culture. These effects include the relationship of marketing to the expression of cultural values and lifestyles, how products and services are related to rituals and cultural myths, and the interface between marketing efforts and the creation of art, music, and other forms of popular culture that are so much a part of our daily lives.

■ **FIGURE 1.3** THE WHEEL OF CONSUMER BEHAVIOR

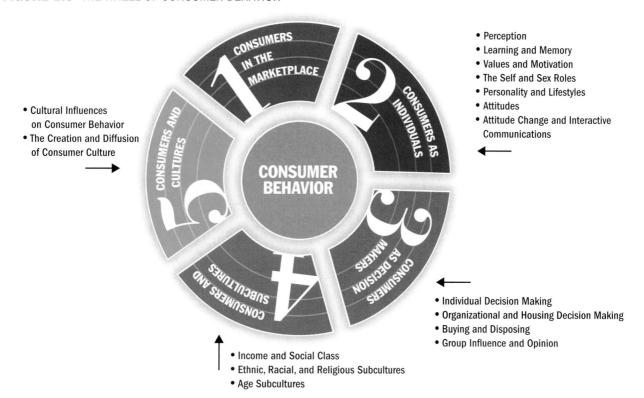

• Cultural Influences
  on Consumer Behavior
• The Creation and Diffusion
  of Consumer Culture

• Perception
• Learning and Memory
• Values and Motivation
• The Self and Sex Roles
• Personality and Lifestyles
• Attitudes
• Attitude Change and Interactive
  Communications

• Individual Decision Making
• Organizational and Housing Decision Making
• Buying and Disposing
• Group Influence and Opinion

• Income and Social Class
• Ethnic, Racial, and Religious Subcultures
• Age Subcultures

CHAPTER SUMMARY

● Consumer behavior is the study of the processes involved when individuals or groups select, purchase, use, or dispose of products, services, ideas, or experiences to satisfy needs and desires.

● A consumer may purchase, use, and dispose of a product, but different people may perform these functions. In addition, consumers may be thought of as role players who need different products to help them play their various parts.

● Market segmentation is an important aspect of consumer behavior. Consumers can be segmented according to many dimensions, including product usage, demographics (the objective aspects of a population, such as age and sex), and psychographics (psychological and lifestyle characteristics). Emerging developments, such as the new emphasis on relationship marketing and the practice of database marketing, mean that marketers are much more attuned to the wants and needs of different consumer groups. This is especially important as people are empowered to construct their own consumerspace—accessing product information where and when they want it and initiating contact with companies on the Internet instead of passively receiving marketing communications.

● The Web is transforming the way consumers interact with companies and with each other. Online commerce allows us to locate obscure products from around the world, and consumption communities provide forums for people to share opinions and product recommendations. The benefits are accompanied by potential problems, including the loss of privacy and the deterioration of traditional social interactions as people log more time online.

● Marketing activities exert an enormous impact on individuals. Consumer behavior is relevant to our understanding of both public policy issues (e.g., ethical marketing practices) and the dynamics of popular culture.

- Although textbooks often paint a picture of the consumer as a rational, informed decision maker, in reality many consumer activities are harmful to individuals or to society. The "dark side" of consumer behavior includes terrorism, addiction, the use of people as products (consumed consumers), and theft or vandalism (anticonsumption).
- The field of consumer behavior is interdisciplinary; it is composed of researchers from many different fields who share an interest in how people interact with the marketplace. These disciplines can be categorized by the degree to which their focus is micro (the individual consumer) or macro (the consumer as a member of groups or of the larger society).
- There are many perspectives on consumer behavior, but research orientations can roughly be divided into two approaches: The positivist perspective emphasizes the objectivity of science and the consumer as a rational decision maker. The interpretivist perspective, in contrast, stresses the subjective meaning of the consumer's individual experience and the idea that any behavior is subject to multiple interpretations rather than to one single explanation.

KEY TERMS

Anticonsumption   33
B2C e-commerce   18
Bioterrorism   30
Business ethics   21
C2C e-commerce   18
Compulsive consumption   31
Consumed consumers   31
Consumer   8
Consumer addiction   30
Consumer behavior   7
Consumption communities   6

Culture jamming   25
Database marketing   13
Demographics   6, 9
Economics of information   25
Exchange   8
Global consumer culture   16
Green marketing   28
Heavy users   9
Infomediaries   22
Interpretivism   36
Market segmentation   9

Market segmentation strategies   6
Paradigm   36
Pastiche   37
Popular culture   13
Positivism   36
Psychographics   6
Relationship marketing   13
Role theory   7
Shrinkage   32
Social marketing   28
U-commerce   17

CONSUMER BEHAVIOR CHALLENGE

1 This chapter states that people play different roles and that their consumption behaviors may differ depending on the particular role they are playing. State whether you agree or disagree with this perspective, giving examples from your personal life. Try to construct a "stage set" for a role you play—specify the props, costumes, and script that you use to play a role (e.g., job interviewee, conscientious student, party animal).

2 Some researchers believe that the field of consumer behavior should be a pure rather than an applied science. That is, research issues should be framed in terms of their scientific interest rather than their applicability to immediate marketing problems. Give your views on this issue.

3 Name some products or services that are widely used by your social group. State whether you agree or disagree with the notion that these products help to form group bonds, supporting your argument with examples from your list of products used by the group.

4 Although demographic information on large numbers of consumers is used in many marketing contexts, some people believe that the sale of data on customers' incomes, buying habits, and so on constitutes an invasion of privacy and should be stopped. Is Big Brother watching? Comment on this issue from both a consumer's and a marketer's point of view.

5 List the three stages in the consumption process. Describe the issues that you considered in each of these stages when you made a recent important purchase.

6 State the differences between the positivist and interpretivist approaches to consumer research. For each type of inquiry, give examples of product dimensions that would be more usefully explored using that type of research over the other.

7 What aspects of consumer behavior are likely to be of interest to a financial planner? To a university administrator? To a graphic arts designer? To a social worker in a government agency? To a nursing instructor?

8 Critics of targeted marketing strategies argue that this practice is discriminatory and unfair, especially if such a strategy encourages a group of people to buy a product that may be injurious to them or that they cannot afford. For example, community leaders in largely minority neighborhoods have staged protests against billboards promoting beer or cigarettes in these areas. On the other hand, the Association of National Advertisers argues that banning targeted marketing constitutes censorship, and thus is a violation of the First Amendment. What are your views regarding this issue?

9 Do marketers have the ability to control our desires or the power to create needs? Is this situation changing as the Internet creates new ways to interact with companies? If so, how?

10 An entrepreneur made international news when he set up a Web site to auction the eggcells of fashion models to the highest bidder (minimum bid: $15,000). He wrote, "Just watch television and you will see that we are only interested in looking at beautiful people. This site simply mirrors our current society, in that beauty usually goes to the highest bidder. . . . Any gift such as beauty, intelligence, or social skills will help your children in their quest for happiness and success. If you could increase the chance of reproducing beautiful children, and thus giving them an advantage in society, would you?"[99] Is the buying and selling of humans just another example of consumer behavior at work? Do you agree that this service is simply a more efficient way to maximize the chance of having happy, successful children? Should this kind of marketing activity be allowed? Would you sell your eggs or sperm on a Web site?

11 Many college students "share" music by downloading clips from the Internet. Is this stealing?

NOTES

1. www.gammaphibeta.org, accessed February 3, 2003.
2. www.riotsrrl.com/whatwethink.html, accessed June 2, 2000.
3. This definition is similar to the definition of marketing offered by the American Marketing Association: "Marketing is the process of planning and executing the conception, pricing, promotion, and distribution of ideas, goods, and services to create exchanges that satisfy individual and organizational goals" (www.ama.org/about/ama/markdef.asp, accessed May 27, 2000). The focus of study in the consumer behavior discipline is more on the consumer's experience or satisfaction with the product than with the organizational processes involved in creating or delivering the product. However, these issues obviously are also of great import for many consumer researchers, particularly those with an applied interest. The divergence between academic and applied perspectives will be considered later in this chapter.
4. Jill Rosenfeld, "Experience the Real Thing," *Fast Company* (January–February 2000): 184.
5. Erving Goffman, *The Presentation of Self in Everyday Life* (Garden City, NY: Doubleday, 1959); George H. Mead, *Mind, Self, and Society* (Chicago: University of Chicago Press, 1934); Michael R. Solomon, "The Role of Products as Social Stimuli: A Symbolic Interactionism Perspective," *Journal of Consumer Research* 10 (December 1983): 319–29.
6. Michael R. Solomon and Elnora W. Stuart, *Marketing: Real People, Real Choices*, 2nd ed. (Upper Saddle River, NJ: Prentice Hall, 2000): 5–6.
7. Quoted in Evan Ramstad, "Walkman's Plan for Reeling in the Ears of Wired Youths," *Wall Street Journal Interactive Edition* (May 18, 2000).
8. George Anders, "Web Giants Amazon, eToys Bet on Opposing Market Strategies," *Wall Street Journal Interactive Edition* (November 2, 1999).
9. Pamela Licalzi O'Connell, "New Economy: Behind Bars, a Market for Goods," *New York Times on the Web* (May 14, 2001).
10. Jennifer Ordonez, "Cash Cows: Burger Joints Call Them 'Heavy Users'—But Not to Their Faces," *Wall Street Journal Interactive Edition* (January 12, 2000).
11. Ann Grimes, "Nike Rescinds Advertisement, Apologizes to Disabled People," *Wall Street Journal* (October 26, 2000).
12. Natalie Perkins, "Zeroing in on Consumer Values," *Advertising Age* (March 22, 1993): 23.
13. Jennifer Lee, "Tailoring Cellphones for Teenagers," *New York Times on the Web* (May 30, 2002).
14. Jack Neff, "Crest Spinoff Targets Women," *Advertising Age* (June 3, 2002): 1.
15. Charles M. Schaninger and William D. Danko, "A Conceptual and Empirical Comparison of Alternative Household Life Cycle Models," *Journal of Consumer Research* 19 (March 1993): 580–94; Robert E. Wilkes, "Household Life-Cycle Stages, Transitions, and Product Expenditures," *Journal of Consumer Research* 22 (June 1995): 27–42.
16. Richard P. Coleman, "The Continuing Significance of Social Class to Marketing," *Journal of Consumer Research* 10 (December 1983): 265–80.
17. Maureen Tkacik, "The Worlds of Extreme Sports, Hip-Hop Are Starting to Merge," *Wall Street Journal Interactive Edition* (August 9, 2001).
18. Betsy McKay, "SoBe Hopes Edgy Ads Can Induce the Masses to Try Its 'Lizard Fuel,'" *Wall Street Journal Interactive Edition* (April 28, 2000).
19. Motoko Rich, "Region's Marketers Hop on the Bubba Bandwagon," *Wall Street Journal Interactive Edition* (May 19, 1999).
20. Alice Z. Cuneo, "Tailor-Made Not Merely 1 of a Kind," *Advertising Age* (November 7, 1994): 22.
21. Robert C. Blattberg and John Deighton, "Interactive Marketing: Exploiting the Age of Addressability," *Sloan Management Review* 331(Fall 1991): 5–14.
22. Quoted in "Bringing Meaning to Brands," *American Demographics* (June 1997): 34.
23. Susan Fournier, "Consumers and Their Brands. Developing Relationship Theory in Consumer Research," *Journal of Consumer Research* 24 (March 1998): 343–73.
24. Douglas B. Holt, "How Consumers Consume: A Taxonomy of Consumption Practices," *Journal of Consumer Research* 22 (June 1995): 1–16; Douglas B. Holt, personal communication, August 27, 1997.
25. Brad Edmondson, "The Dawn of the Megacity," *Marketing Tools* (March 1999): 64.
26. For a recent discussion of this trend, see Russell W. Belk, "Hyperreality and Globalization: Culture in the Age of Ronald McDonald," *Journal of International Consumer Marketing* 8 (1995): 23–38.
27. Lorraine Ali, "The Road to Rave," *Newsweek* (August 6, 2001): 54–56.
28. Robert Frank, "When Small Chains Go Abroad, Culture Clashes Require Ingenuity," *Wall Street Journal Interactive Edition* (April 12, 2000).
29. Richard T. Watson, Leyland F. Pitt, Pierre Berthon, and George M. Zinkhan, "U-Commerce: Expanding the Universe of Marketing," *Journal of the Academy of Marketing Science* 30 (2002): 333–47.
30. I.B.M. Unveils 'Smart' Laundry," *New York Times on the Web* (August 30, 2002).
31. Erin White, "Advertisers Aren't Following Flood of Europeans Online," *Wall Street Journal Interactive Edition* (July 26, 2002).

32. Seema Williams, David M. Cooperstein, David E. Weisman, and Thalika Oum, "Post-Web Retail," *The Forrester Report*, Forrester Research, Inc. (September 1999).

33. Some material in this section was adapted from Michael R. Solomon and Elnora W. Stuart, *Welcome to Marketing.Com: The Brave New World of E-Commerce* (Upper Saddle River, NJ: Prentice Hall, 2000).

34. Patricia Winters Lauro, "Marketing Battle for Online Dating," *New York Times on the Web* (January 27, 2003).

35. Tiffany Lee Brown, "Got Skim?" *Wired* (March 2000): 262.

36. Rebecca Fairley Raney, "Study Finds Internet of Social Benefit to Users," *New York Times on the Web* (May 11, 2000).

37. John Markoff, "Portrait of a Newer, Lonelier Crowd Is Captured in an Internet Survey," *New York Times on the Web* (February 16, 2000).

38. Lisa Guernsey, "Professor Who Once Found Isolation Online Has a Change of Heart," *New York Times on the Web* (July 26, 2001).

39. Charles Sheehan, "Upcoming Comic Features Real-Life Marriage Proposal," *Montgomery Advertiser* (February 24, 2002).

40. Stuart Elliott, "Hiding a Television Commercial in Plain View," *New York Times on the Web* (May 24, 2002).

41. Marc Gunther, "Now Starring in Party of Five—Dr. Pepper," *Fortune* (April 17, 2000): 88.

42. Rafer Guzman, "Hotel Offers Kids a Room with a Logo," *Wall Street Journal Interactive Edition* (October 6, 1999).

43. Frances A. McMorris, "Loaded Coconut Falls off Deck, Landing Cruise Line in Court," *Wall Street Journal Interactive Edition* (September 13, 1999).

44. Jennifer Lach, *American Demographics* (December 1999): 18.

45. Valerie S. Folkes and Michael A. Kamins, "Effects of Information about Firms' Ethical and Unethical Actions on Consumers' Attitudes," *Journal of Consumer Psychology* 8 (1999): 243–59.

46. Media Want Colleges to Fight Piracy," *New York Times on the Web* (October 11, 2002).

47. Jacqueline N. Hood, and Jeanne M. Logsdon, "Business Ethics in the NAFTA Countries: A Cross-Cultural Comparison," *Journal of Business Research* 55 (2002): 883–90.

48. Barbara Crossette, "Russia and China Called Top Business Bribers," *New York Times on the Web* (May 17, 2002). For more details about the survey see www.transparency.org.

49. Quoted in Ira Teinowitz, "Lawsuit: Menthol Smokes Illegally Targeted to Blacks," *Advertising Age* (November 2, 1998): 16.

50. Pamela Paul, "Mixed Signals," *American Demographics* (July 2001): 44.

51. R. Harris, "Most Customers Using Internet Fail to Read Retailers' Privacy Policies," *Ventura County Star* (June 6, 2002).

52. Jeffrey Rosen, "The Eroded Self," *New York Times Magazine* (April 29, 2000).

53. Quoted in Jennifer Lach, "The New Gatekeepers," *American Demographics* (June 1999): 41–42.

54. John Hagel III and Jeffrey F. Rayport, "The Coming Battle for Customer Information," *Harvard Business Review* (January–February 1997): 53; Toby Lester, "The Reinvention of Privacy," *The Atlantic Monthly* (March 2001): 27; Roland T. Rust, P. K. Kannan, and Na Peng, "The Customer Economics of Internet Privacy," *Journal of the Academy of Marketing Science* 30 (2002): 455–64.

55. Michael R. Solomon, *Conquering Consumerspace: Marketing Strategies for a Branded World* (New York: AMACOM, 2003).

56. Jeffrey Ball, "Religious Leaders to Discuss SUVs with GM, Ford Officials," *Wall Street Journal Interactive Edition* (November 19, 2002).

57. William Leiss, Stephen Kline, and Sut Jhally, *Social Communication in Advertising: Persons, Products, and Images of Well-Being* (Toronto: Methuen, 1986); Jerry Mander, *Four Arguments for the Elimination of Television* (New York: William Morrow, 1977).

58. Packard (1957); quoted in Leiss et al., *Social Communication*, 11.

59. Raymond Williams, *Problems in Materialism and Culture: Selected Essays* (London: Verso, 1980).

60. Leiss et al., *Social Communication*.

61. George Stigler, "The Economics of Information," *Journal of Political Economy* (1961): 69.

62. Quoted in Leiss et al., *Social Communication*, 11.

63. Erin White, "English Schoolchildren Get Lessons on Savvy Marketing," *Wall Street Journal Interactive Edition* (November 27, 2002).

64. Adbusters Media Foundation, "Adbusters" [Web site] (Vancouver, British Columbia) [cited 27 June 2002]; available from http://secure.adbusters.org/orders/culturejam.

65. Adbusters Media Foundation, "Adbusters" [Web site] (Vancouver, British Columbia) [cited 27 June 2002]; available from http://adbusters.org/information/network.

66. www.nikesweatshop.net [Web site], accessed June 29, 2002.

67. The Truth.com, "About Truth" [Web site] [cited 15 March 2002]; available from www.thetruth.com.

68. Co-op America's Boycott Action News, "Boycott updates" [Web site] [cited 15 January 2002]; available from www.coopamerica.org/boycotts/boycott_grid.htm; Greenwood Watershed Association, "We'd Rather Wear Nothing Than Wear GAP!" [Web site] (17 January 2000) [cited 11 February 2002]; available from www.elksoft.com/gwa/history/wearnothing.

69. Behind the Label, "Global Campaign News" [Web site] (31 January 2002) [cited 11 February 2002]; available from www.behindthelabel.org/infocus.

70. The Pittsburgh Coalition Against Pornography. "Take Action: Five Steps You Can Take to Ditch Fitch!" [Web site] [cited 25 February 2002]; available from www.pittsburghcoalition.com/abercrombie.html.

71. For consumer research and discussions related to public policy issues, see Paul N. Bloom and Stephen A. Greyser, "The Maturing of Consumerism," *Harvard Business Review* (November–December 1981): 130–39; George S. Day, Assessing the Effect of Information Disclosure Requirements," *Journal of Marketing* (April 1976): 42–52; Dennis E. Garrett, "The Effectiveness of Marketing Policy Boycotts: Environmental Opposition to Marketing," *Journal of Marketing* 51 (January 1987): 44–53; Michael Houston and Michael Rothschild, "Policy-Related Experiments on Information Provision: A Normative Model and Explication," *Journal of Marketing Research* 17 (November 1980): 432–49; Jacob Jacoby, Wayne D. Hoyer, and David A. Sheluga, *Misperception of Televised Communications* (New York: American Association of Advertising Agencies, 1980); Gene R. Laczniak and Patrick E. Murphy, *Marketing Ethics: Guidelines for Managers* (Lexington, MA: Lexington Books, 1985), 117–23; Lynn Phillips and Bobby Calder, "Evaluating Consumer Protection Laws: Promising Methods," *Journal of Consumer Affairs* 14 (Summer 1980): 9–36; Donald P. Robin and Eric Reidenbach, "Social Responsibility, Ethics, and Marketing Strategy: Closing the Gap Between Concept and Application," *Journal of Marketing* 51 (January 1987): 44–58; Howard Schutz and Marianne Casey, "Consumer Perceptions of Advertising as Misleading," *Journal of Consumer Affairs* 15 (Winter 1981): 340–57; Darlene Brannigan Smith and Paul N. Bloom, "Is Consumerism Dead or Alive? Some New Evidence," in Thomas C. Kinnear, ed., *Advances in Consumer Research* 11 (1984): 369–73.

72. "Concerned Consumers Push for Environmentally Friendly Packaging," *Boxboard Containers* (April 1993): 4.

73. Michal Strahilevitz and John G. Myers, "Donations to Charity as Purchase Incentives: How Well They Work May Depend on What You Are Trying to Sell," *Journal of Consumer Research* 24 (March 1998): 434–46.

74. Quentin Hardy, "The Radical Philanthropist," *Forbes* (May 1, 2000): 114.

75. Cf. Philip Kotler and Alan R. Andreasen, *Strategic Marketing for Nonprofit Organizations*, 4th ed. (Englewood Cliffs, NJ: Prentice Hall, 1991); Jeff B. Murray and Julie L. Ozanne, "The Critical Imagination: Emancipatory Interests in Consumer Research," *Journal of Consumer Research* 18 (September 1991): 192–244; William D. Wells, "Discovery-Oriented Consumer Research," *Journal of Consumer Research* 19 (March 1993): 489–504.

76. Bertil Swartz, " 'Keep Control': The Swedish Brewers Association Campaign to Foster Responsible Alcohol Consumption Among Adolescents" (paper presented at the ACR Europe Conference, Stockholm, June 1997); Anna Oloffson, Ordpolen Informations AB, Sweden, personal communication, August 1997.

77. "Japan Calls for Tighter Food Security Against Mad Cow Disease," *Xinhua News Agency* (May 20, 2002) [cited 29 June 2002]; available from www.xinhuanet.com/english.

78. Kenneth E. Nusbaum, James C. Wright, and Michael R. Solomon, "Attitudes of Food Animal Veterinarians to Continuing Education in Agriterrorism" (paper presented at the 53rd Annual Meeting of the Animal Disease Research Workers in Southern States, University of Florida, February 2001).

79. Betty Mohr, "The Pepsi Challenge: Managing a Crisis," *Prepared Foods* (March 1994): 13.

80. Wendy Koch, "Nicotine Water for Smokers Could Hook Kids," *USA Today Online* (May 23, 2002).

81. Laurie J. Flynn, "Web Site for Chap Stick Addicts," *New York Times on the Web* (November 1, 1999).

82. "Psychologist Warns of Internet Addiction," *Montgomery Advertiser* (August 18, 1997): D2.

83. Thomas C. O'Guinn and Ronald J. Faber, "Compulsive Buying: A Phenomenological Explanation," *Journal of Consumer Research* 16 (September 1989): 154.

84. Quoted in Anastasia Toufexis, "365 Shopping Days Till Christmas," *Time* (December 26, 1988): 82; see also Ronald J. Faber and Thomas

C. O'Guinn, "Compulsive Consumption and Credit Abuse," *Journal of Consumer Policy* 11 (1988): 109–21; Mary S. Butler, "Compulsive Buying—It's No Joke," *Consumer's Digest* (September 1986): 55; Derek N. Hassay and Malcolm C. Smith, "Compulsive Buying: An Examination of the Consumption Motive," *Psychology & Marketing* 13 (December 1996): 741–52.

85. Georgia Witkin, "The Shopping Fix," *Health* (May 1988): 73; see also Arch G. Woodside and Randolph J. Trappey III, "Compulsive Consumption of a Consumer Service: An Exploratory Study of Chronic Horse Race Track Gambling Behavior" (working paper #90-MKTG-04, A. B. Freeman School of Business, Tulane University, 1990); Rajan Nataraajan and Brent G. Goff, "Manifestations of Compulsiveness in the Consumer-Marketplace Domain," *Psychology & Marketing* 9 (January 1992): 31–44; Joann Ellison Rodgers, "Addiction: A Whole New View," *Psychology Today* (September–October 1994): 32.

86. Helen Reynolds, *The Economics of Prostitution* (Springfield, IL: Thomas, 1986).

87. Howard W. French, "South Korea's Real Rage for Virtual Games," *New York Times on the Web* (October 9, 2002).

88. Amy Harmon, "Illegal Kidney Auction Pops Up on ebay's Site," *New York Times on the Web* (September 3, 1999).

89. G. Paschal Zachary, "A Most Unlikely Industry Finds It Can't Resist Globalization's Call," *Wall Street Journal Interactive Edition* (January 6, 2000).

90. "Advertisers Face up to the New Morality: Making the Pitch," *Bloomberg* (July 8, 1997).

91. "Shoplifting: Bess Myerson's Arrest Highlights a Multibillion-Dollar Problem that Many Stores Won't Talk About," *Life* (August 1988): 32.

92. "New Survey Shows Shoplifting Is a Year-Round Problem," *Business Wire* (April 12, 1998).

93. "Customer Not King, but Thief," *Marketing News* (December 9, 2002): 4.

94. Catherine A. Cole, "Deterrence and Consumer Fraud," *Journal of Retailing* 65 (Spring 1989): 107–20; Stephen J. Grove, Scott J. Vitell, and David Strutton, "Non-Normative Consumer Behavior and the Techniques of Neutralization," in Terry Childers et al., eds., *Marketing Theory and Practice*, 1989 AMA Winter Educators' Conference (Chicago: American Marketing Association, 1989), 131–35.

95. Mark Curnutte, "The Scope of the Shoplifting Problems," *Gannett News Service* (November 29, 1997).

96. Anthony D. Cox, Dena Cox, Ronald D. Anderson, and George P. Moschis, "Social Influences on Adolescent Shoplifting—Theory, Evidence, and Implications for the Retail Industry," *Journal of Retailing* 69 (Summer 1993): 234–46.

97. Morris B. Holbrook, "The Consumer Researcher Visits Radio City: Dancing in the Dark," in Elizabeth C. Hirschman and Morris B. Holbrook, eds., *Advances in Consumer Research* 12 (Provo, UT: Association for Consumer Research, 1985): 28–31.

98. Alladi Venkatesh, "Postmodernism, Poststructuralism and Marketing" (paper presented at the American Marketing Association Winter Theory Conference, San Antonio, February 1992); see also Stella Proctor, Ioanna Papasolomou-Doukakis, and Tony Proctor, "What Are Television Advertisements Really Trying to Tell Us? A Postmodern Perspective," *Journal of Consumer Behavior* 1 (February 2002): 246–55; A. Fuat Firat and Alladi Venkatesh, "The Making of Postmodern Consumption," in Russell W. Belk and Nikhilesh Dholakia, eds., *Consumption and Marketing: Macro Dimensions* (Boston: PWS-Kent, 1993).

99. www.ronsangels.com/index2.html, accessed 4/3/2000.

boeri®

it's your head

Consumers as Individuals

In this section, we focus on the internal dynamics of consumers. While "no man is an island," each of us is to some degree a self-contained receptor of information about the outside world. We are constantly confronted with advertising messages, products, other people persuading us to buy something, and even reflections of ourselves that make us happy or sad. Each chapter in this section will consider a different aspect of the individual that is "invisible" to others—but of vital importance to ourselves.

Chapter 2 describes the process of perception, in which information from the outside world about products and other people is absorbed and interpreted. Chapter 3 focuses on the way this information is mentally stored and how it adds to our existing knowledge about the world during the learning process. Chapter 4 discusses our reasons of motivations for absorbing this information and how it is influenced by the values to which we subscribe as members of a particular culture.

Chapter 5 explores how our views about ourselves—particularly our sexuality and our physical appearance—affect what we do, want, and buy. Chapter 6 goes on to consider how people's individual personalities influence these decisions, and how the choices we make in terms of products, leisure activities, and so on help to define our lifestyles.

Chapters 7 and 8 discuss how our attitudes—our evaluations of all these products, messages, and so on—are formed and (sometimes) changed by marketers, and how we as individual consumers engage in our ongoing dialogue with these businesspeople by virtue of our responses to these messages.

■ CHAPTERS AHEAD

Perception

t he European vacation has been wonderful, and this stop in Lisbon is no exception. Still, after two weeks of eating his way through some of the Continent's finest pastry shops and restaurants, Gary's getting a bit of a craving for his family's favorite snack—a good old American box of Oreos and an ice-cold carton of milk. Unbeknownst to his wife, Janeen, he had stashed away some cookies "just in case"—this was the time to break them out.

Now, all he needs is the milk. On an impulse, Gary decides to surprise Janeen with a midafternoon treat. He sneaks out of the hotel room while she's napping and finds the nearest *grosa*. When he heads to the small refrigerated section, though, he's puzzled—no milk here. Undaunted, Gary asks the clerk, *"Leite, por favor?"* The clerk quickly smiles and points to a rack in the middle of the store piled with little white square boxes. No, that can't be right—Gary resolves to work on his Portuguese. He repeats the question, and again he gets the same answer.

Finally, he investigates and sure enough he sees the boxes, labeled with the brand name Parmalat, containing something called ultra heat treated (UHT) milk. Nasty! Who in the world would drink milk out of a little box that's been sitting on a warm shelf for who knows how long? Gary dejectedly returns to the hotel, his snack time fantasies crumbling like so many stale cookies. . . .

■ INTRODUCTION

Gary would be surprised to learn that many people in the world drink milk out of a box every day. UHT is Grade A pasteurized milk that has been heated until the bacteria causing spoilage are destroyed, and it can last for five to six months without refrigeration if its aseptic container is unopened. Its main manufacturer, the Parmalat Group, is one of the largest dairy companies in the world.

Shelf-stable milk is particularly popular in Europe, where refrigerator space in homes and stores tends to be more limited than in the United States. Seven out of ten Europeans drink it routinely. The company is trying to crack the American market as well, though analysts are dubious about its prospects. To begin with, milk consumption in the United States is declining steadily as teenagers choose soft drinks instead. Indeed, the Milk Industry Foundation pumped $44 million into an advertising campaign to promote milk drinking ("Got Milk?").

But enticing Americans to drink milk out of a box is even harder. In focus groups, American consumers say they have trouble believing the milk is not spoiled or unsafe. They consider the square, quart-sized boxes more suitable for dry food, and some even feel the name Parmalat sounds too much like baby formulas such as Enfamil or Similac. Parmalat USA is trying to combat this resistance by introducing new containers featuring an image of an old-fashioned milk bottle.

Parmalat is mounting an extensive distribution and marketing campaign in the United States. It has purchased numerous U.S. dairies and is constructing a new distribution base on the West Coast. Jumping on the new craze for organic products, in 2002 it introduced Organic Whole Milk to the U.S. market. A lot of Parmalat USA's sales are to schools and fast-food chains that appreciate its long shelf life.[1] Still, although Americans may not think twice about drinking a McFlurry from McDonald's made with Parmalat, it's going to be a long, uphill battle to change their perceptions about the proper accompaniment to a bagful of Oreos.

Whether it's the taste of Oreos, the sight of an Obsession perfume ad, or the sound of the music group Offspring, we live in a world overflowing with sensations. Wherever we turn, we are bombarded by a symphony of colors, sounds, and odors. Some of the "notes" in this symphony occur naturally, such as the loud barking of a dog, the shades of the evening sky, or the heady smell of a rose bush. Others come from people: The person sitting next to you in class might sport tinted blonde hair, bright pink pants, and enough nasty perfume to make your eyes water.

Marketers certainly contribute to this commotion. Consumers are never far from advertisements, product packages, radio and television commercials, and billboards—all clamoring for our attention. Sometimes consumers go out of their way to experience "unusual" sensations, whether it be bungee jumping or playing virtual reality games. Reality shows like *Fear Factor* attract people who want to test their sensations. On a very popular Peruvian TV show called *Laura en America*, contestants show just what people are capable of experiencing (with the right incentive): For $20, two women stripped to their underwear and had buckets of slime covered with toads poured over their bodies. For the same amount, three men raced to gobble down bowls of large tree grubs from the Amazon jungle. For $30, a woman licked the armpits of a sweaty body builder who had not bathed for two days.[2] And you thought college fraternities were out there?

Whether we are game-show contestants or not, each of us copes with the bombardment of sensations by paying attention to some stimuli and tuning out others. The messages to which we do choose to pay attention often wind up differing from what the sponsors intended, as we each put our "spin" on things by adopting meanings consistent with our own unique experiences, biases, and desires. This chapter focuses on the process of perception, in which sensations are absorbed by the consumer and then are used to interpret the surrounding world.

■ FIGURE 2.1 AN OVERVIEW OF THE PERCEPTUAL PROCESS

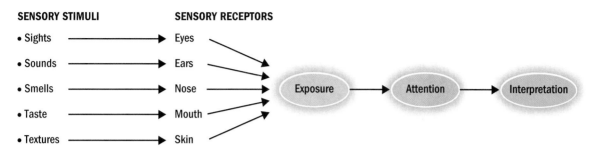

Sensation refers to the immediate response of our sensory receptors (eyes, ears, nose, mouth, fingers) to basic stimuli such as light, color, sound, odor, and texture. **Perception** is the process by which these sensations are selected, organized, and interpreted. The study of perception, then, focuses on what we add to these raw sensations in order to give them meaning.

Gary's encounter with milk in a box illustrates the perceptual process. He has learned to equate the cold temperature of refrigerated milk with freshness, so he experienced a negative physical reaction when confronted with a product that contradicted his expectations. Gary's evaluation of Parmalat was affected by factors such as the design of the package, the brand name, and even by the section in the grocery store in which the milk was displayed. These expectations are largely affected by a consumer's cultural background. Europeans do not necessarily have the same perceptions of milk, and as a result their reactions to the product are quite different.

Like computers, people undergo stages of information processing in which stimuli are input and stored. Unlike computers, though, we do not passively process whatever information happens to be present. In the first place, only a very small number of the stimuli in our environment are ever noticed. Of these, we attend to an even smaller number. The stimuli that do enter consciousness might not be processed objectively. The individual, who is influenced by his or her unique biases, needs, and experiences, interprets the meaning of a stimulus. As shown in Figure 2.1, these three stages of exposure, attention, and interpretation make up the process of perception. Before considering each of these stages, let's step back and look at the sensory systems that provide sensations to us in the first place.

Sensory Systems

External stimuli, or sensory inputs, can be received on a number of channels. We may see a billboard, hear a jingle, feel the softness of a cashmere sweater, taste a new flavor of ice cream, or smell a leather jacket. The inputs picked up by our five senses are the raw data that begin the perceptual process. For example, sensory data emanating from the external environment (e.g., hearing a tune on the radio) can generate internal sensory experiences when the song triggers a young man's memory of his first dance and brings to mind the smell of his date's perfume or the feel of her hair on his cheek. These responses are an important part of **hedonic consumption**, the multisensory, fantasy, and emotional aspects of consumers' interactions with products.[3]

The unique sensory quality of a product can play an important role in helping it to stand out from the competition, especially if the brand creates a unique association with the sensation. The Owens-Corning Fiberglass Corporation was the first company to trademark a color when it used bright pink for its insulation material and

adopted the Pink Panther cartoon character as its spokescharacter. Harley-Davidson actually tried to trademark the distinctive sound made by a "hog" revving up.[4]

Vision

Marketers rely heavily on visual elements in advertising, store design, and packaging. Meanings are communicated on the visual channel through a product's color, size, and styling. Philips is trying to give its electronics a younger feel by making them thinner and more colorful. Its audio products used to be all silver, but now each component comes in four colors, including an electric green.[5]

Colors may even influence our emotions more directly. Evidence suggests that some colors (particularly red) create feelings of arousal and stimulate appetite, and others (such as blue) are more relaxing. Products presented against a backdrop of blue in advertisements are better liked than when a red background is used, and cross-cultural research indicates a consistent preference for blue whether people live in Canada or Hong Kong.[6] American Express chose to name its new card Blue after research showed the color evokes positive feelings about the future. Its advertising agency named blue the color of the new millennium because people associate it with sky and water, "providing a sense of limitlessness and peace."[7]

Some reactions to color come from learned associations. In Western countries, black is the color of mourning, whereas in some Eastern countries, notably Japan, white plays this role. In addition, the color black is associated with power. Teams in both the National Football League and the National Hockey League who wear black uniforms are among the most aggressive; they consistently rank near the top of their leagues in penalties during the season.[8]

Other reactions are due to biological and cultural differences. Women tend to be drawn toward brighter tones and are more sensitive to subtle shadings and patterns. Some scientists attribute this to biology, since females see color better than males do, and men are 16 times more likely to be color blind. Age also influences our responsiveness to color. As we get older, our eyes mature and our vision takes on a yellow cast. Colors look duller to older people, so they prefer white and other bright tones. This helps to explain why mature consumers are much more likely to choose a white car—Lexus, which sells heavily in this market, makes 60 percent of its vehicles in white.

Marketing Opportunity

Purple ketchup? Wildly colored products are hot, as marketers search for new ways to stand out on the shelves. First, Heinz gave us Blastin' Green ketchup in a squeeze bottle and then hit us with Funky Purple. Heinz's share of the ketchup market jumped from 50 percent to 56 percent in the 12 months after it launched its green version. ConAgra Foods caught on to the idea that kids (of all ages?) want mealtime to be fun time. Now, we can buy squeeze bottles of Parkay margarine in hot pink and bright blue, both perfect for painting pictures on corn on the cob. And for dessert, how about a pile of Nabisco's Milk Changer Blue and Orange Oreos?[9] These colorful versions of tried-and-true products still taste the same (at least with your eyes closed). For those who are a bit more daring, the next time you're in South Africa try Nestlé's Gloob mayonnaise—it's blue and tastes like bubble gum.

Come to your senses.
Feel Helsinki.

2000.hel.fi
Helsinki
European City of Culture

Helsinki is a strange place. Wonderfully strange. Given the status of European City of Culture it stages such happenings as the Sauna of the Month, Forces of Light, Livingroom, the Baltic Herring Market, the Snow Church and Art goes Kapakka. And 19,994 other events. Some a bit on the odd side. Others highly cultural. So keep off the beaten track and come on over. Feel different. Feel good. Feel Helsinki.

Helsinki, Finland is the European City of Culture in the year 2000. Fly there with the official airline, Finnair. It makes sense.

This Finnish ad emphasizes the sensual reasons to visit the city of Helsinki.

Teeth are very sensitive. They hate violence.

Change from that abrasive dental cream to Phillips. The only dental cream with Phillips Milk of Magnesia.

Phillips
Phillips 2

The whitest and healthiest choice.

This Brazilian toothpaste ad uses vivid perceptual imagery to communicate a product benefit.

The trend toward brighter and more complex colors also reflects the increasingly multicultural makeup of the United States. For example, Hispanics tend to prefer brighter colors as a reflection of the intense lighting conditions in Latin America, since strong colors keep their character in strong sunlight.[10] That's why Procter & Gamble uses brighter colors in makeup it sells in Latin countries.[11]

Color plays a dominant role in Web page design. It directs a viewer's eye across the page, ties together design ideas, separates visual areas, organizes contextual relationships, creates mood, and captures attention. Saturated colors such as green, yellow, cyan, and orange are considered the best hues to capture attention, but don't overdo it: Extensive use of these hues can overwhelm people and cause visual fatigue.[12] And, of course, color is a key issue in package design. These choices used to be made casually. For example, the familiar Campbell's Soup can was produced in red and white because a company executive liked the football uniforms at Cornell University. Today, however, color is a serious business, and many companies realize that their color choices can exert a big influence on consumers' assumptions about what is inside the package.

These decisions help to "color" our expectations of what's inside the package. When introducing a white cheese as a "sister product" to an existing blue "Castello" cheese, a Danish company launched it in a red package under the name of Castello Bianco. The red package was chosen to provide maximum visibility on store shelves. Although taste tests were very positive, sales were disappointing. A subsequent analysis of consumer interpretations showed that the red packaging and the

In Western culture the color black often is associated with sophistication while white connotes innocence.

name gave the consumers wrong associations with the product type and its degree of sweetness. Danish consumers had trouble associating the color red with the white cheese. Also the name "Bianco" connoted a sweetness that was incompatible with the actual taste of the product. It was relaunched in a white package and given the name "White Castello." Almost immediately, sales more than doubled.[13]

Some color combinations come to be so strongly associated with a corporation that they become known as the company's **trade dress**, and the company may even be granted exclusive use of these colors. For example, Eastman Kodak has successfully protected its trade dress of yellow, black, and red in court. As a rule, however, trade dress protection is granted only when consumers might be confused about what they are buying because of similar coloration of a competitor's packages.[14]

As this Dutch detergent ad illustrates (Flowery orange fades without Dreft), vivid colors are often an attractive product feature.

DANKZIJ DE UNIEKE VEZELBESCHERMER IS DREFT NOG VEILIGER VOOR GEKLEURDE KATOEN. JE FAVORIETE MODEKLEUREN KOMEN DUS STRALEND FRIS UIT DE MACHINE. IEDERE KEER WEER. OOK DEZE FEL ORANJE OUTFIT. DREFT, NIETS IS VEILIGER.

Smell

Odors can stir emotions or create a calming feeling. They can invoke memories or relieve stress. One study found that consumers who viewed ads for either flowers or chocolate and who also were exposed to flowery or chocolaty odors spent more time processing the product information and were more likely to try different alternatives within each product category.[15]

Some of our responses to scents result from early associations that call up good or bad feelings, and that explains why businesses are exploring connections among smell, memory, and mood.[16] Researchers for Folger's found that for many people the smell of coffee summons up childhood memories of their mothers cooking breakfast, so the aroma reminds them of home. The company turned this insight into a commercial in which a young man in an army uniform arrives home early one morning. He goes to the kitchen, opens a Folger's package, and the aroma wafts upstairs. His mother opens her eyes, smiles, and exclaims, "He's home!"[17]

This ad pokes fun at the proliferation of scented ads. Ah, the scent of sweat.

Fragrance is processed by the limbic system, the most primitive part of the brain and the place where immediate emotions are experienced. One study even found that the scent of fresh cinnamon buns induced sexual arousal in a sample of male students![18] In another study, women sniffed T-shirts that men had worn for two days (wonder how much they paid them to do that?) and reported which ones they preferred. They tended to prefer the odor of men who are genetically similar to them, though not *too* similar. The researchers claimed the findings were evidence that we are "wired" to select compatible mates, but not those that are so similar as to cause inbreeding problems.[19]

As scientists continue to discover the powerful effects of smell on behavior, marketers are falling in line with ingenious ways to exploit these connections.

Scented marketing, now a $90 million business, is taking interesting turns. Here are a few recent developments:

- *Scented clothes:* The textile industry is developing new age fabrics with "scentual" properties by embedding fragrances in microcapsules that are sewn into clothing. A French lingerie company is selling lingerie that emits scents when touched. Korean men are even buying lavender-scented suits to cover up liquor and cigarette odors.[20]
- *Scented stores:* The Thomas Pink shirt company pumps the smell of freshly laundered clothing into its stores to stimulate its customers. Woolworth's scents its locations with its own Christmas aroma hoping that the blend of pumpkin, mulled wine, and thyme will produce not only warm, fuzzy feelings but also increased profits.
- *Scented cars and planes:* British Airways dispenses an outdoorsy scent into its first class cabins and business lounges. When the owner of a Rolls-Royce brings a car in to be repaired, it's doused with the aroma of a 1965 Silver Cloud Rolls model (this mixture of old leather and subtle wood tones is missing from newer models that now are crafted from man-made materials). Ford is trying to standardize that coveted new-car smell by replacing its staff of human sniffers with a $75,000 machine called the E-Nose 4000 that uses polymer "sponges" to detect scents.[21]
- *Scented household products:* Manufacturers are jumping on the aromatherapy bandwagon as they introduce scents with names like Ocean Breeze, Spring Blossom, and Calming Mist. Taking its cue from the recent success of more strongly scented Mexican-produced cleaning products imported to the United States, Colgate strengthened the fragrance in its Palmolive Spring Sensations. Procter & Gamble pumped up the fragrance in its Tide and Gain detergent formulas. This trend in heavy scents is a reversal from the perfume-free, lightly scented 1990s. Manufacturers cite a variety of factors for the change, such as a decrease in scent sensitivity in the aging buying public, the preference among Hispanic and Asian consumers for heavier scents, and the impact of the increased integration of fragrances into everyday bath and body products, which may leave consumers anesthetized to lighter-fragranced household products.[22]
- *Scented advertisements:* In the United Kingdom Procter & Gamble created smell-emitting ads at bus shelters as part of a campaign for its new Head & Shoulders Citrus Fresh shampoo. A poster showed a happy young woman with the wind in her hair and a button at the bottom that dispensed a mist when pressed.[23] In a more "interesting" use of fragrance, YTV (Canada's answer to Nickelodeon) teamed up with Kraft Canada to create an unusual scratch-and-sniff contest that turned viewers' televisions into "Smellvision." When kids watched YTV's weekend morning programming, an animated nose sniffed across the screen and scratched the box next to the matching Kraft product on their game cards. The 100th caller to a toll-free number to correctly identify the smell won a $500 gift certificate from Roots. The actual smells on the game cards included dill pickles, orange peels, "swamp gas"; and "grandma's toenails."[24] TV dinner anyone?

Sound

Consumers buy millions of dollars' worth of sound recordings each year—advertising jingles maintain brand awareness, and background music creates desired moods.[25] A new technology, the Hyper-Sonic Sound System (HSS), can even create a vending machine that can beckon you—and only you—with the fizz of a soft drink from 100 yards away. The process takes an audio signal from virtually any source such as a stereo or computer and converts it to an ultrasonic frequency that can be directed like a beam of light toward a target.[26]

Many aspects of sound affect people's feelings and behaviors. The Muzak Corporation estimates that 80 million people hear its recordings every day. This so-called "functional music" is played in stores, shopping malls, and offices to either relax or stimulate consumers. Research shows that workers tend to slow down during midmorning and midafternoon, so Muzak uses a system it calls "stimulus progression" that increases the tempo during those slack times. Muzak has been linked to reductions in absenteeism among factory workers, and even the milk and egg output of cows and chickens is claimed to increase under its influence.[27] Think what it might do for your term papers!

Touch

Although relatively little research has been done on the effects of tactile stimulation on consumer behavior, common observation tells us that this sensory channel is important. Moods are stimulated or relaxed on the basis of sensations reaching the skin, whether from a luxurious massage or the bite of a winter wind. Touch has even been shown to be a factor in sales interactions. In one study diners who were touched by waitpeople gave bigger tips, and food demonstrators in a supermarket who lightly touched customers had better luck in getting shoppers to try a new snack product and to redeem coupons for the brand.[28] Britain's Asda grocery chain removed the wrapping from several brands of toilet tissue in its stores so that shoppers could feel and compare textures. The result, the retailer says, was soaring sales for its own in-store brand, resulting in a 50 percent increase in shelf space for the line.[29]

The Japanese take this idea a step farther when they practice what they call **Kansei engineering**, a philosophy that translates customers' feelings into design elements. In one application of this practice, the designers of the Mazda Miata focused on young drivers who saw the car as an extension of their body; a sensation they call "horse and rider as one." After extensive research they discovered that making the stick shift exactly 9.5 cm long conveys the optimal feeling of sportiness and control.[30]

People associate the textures of fabrics and other surfaces with product qualities, and some marketers are exploring how touch can be used in packaging to arouse consumer interest. Some new plastic containers for household beauty items are incorporating "soft touch" resins that provide a soft, friction-like resistance when held. Focus group members who tested one such package for Clairol's new Daily Defense shampoo described the sensations as "almost sexy" and were actually reluctant to let go of the containers.[31]

The perceived richness or quality of the material in clothing, bedding, or upholstery is linked to its "feel," whether rough or smooth, flexible or inflexible. A smooth fabric such as silk is equated with luxury; denim is practical and durable. Some of these tactile-quality associations are summarized in Table 2.1. Fabrics that are composed of scarce materials or that require a high degree of processing to

Marketing Opportunity

Sound engineering is the latest frontier for top-end automakers that are trying to find ways to distinguish models that look and perform alike. Auto acoustics used to mean stuffing as much insulation as possible into a door panel and making the interior quiet. Now, noise is a statement about a car's quality; if it sounds well made, it probably is. Mercedes-Benz engineers record the sounds of those electric servomotors used to raise the windows and adjust the seats, then compare them with sounds made by a BMW and other competitors. A change in the motor's tone could be embarrassing if it suggested the device was having trouble moving the seat of a heavy passenger. BMW convenes groups of consumers to help designers choose which sounds should be used to signal technical problems. For example, drivers helped choose the right noise for a warning buzzer, which indicates when a door is open or the engine is having a problem.

The pursuit of the ultimate driving environment forces engineers to leave no stone unturned: In its pursuit of the perfectly silent wiper blade, BMW deadened the whine of the wiper motor with sound-absorbing padding but still found the rubber blades make a slight slap at the top or bottom of their arc. After months of testing, engineers discovered they could eliminate much of that sound if the rubber on the blade could be kept pliable—a difficult job when the blades sit still for days on end, slowly hardening and molding to the shape of the window. The solution: Every few days, wiper motors on the new 7-series flip the resting position of the blades so the rubber edges sometimes point up and sometimes down—keeping the rubber soft and silent.[32] These guys *are* driven.

TABLE 2.1
TACTILE OPPOSITIONS IN FABRICS

Perception	Male	Female	
High class	Wool	Silk	Fine
Low class	Denim	Cotton	↕
	Heavy ←→ Light		Coarse

achieve their smoothness or fineness tend to be more expensive and thus are seen as being higher class. Similarly, lighter, more delicate textures are assumed to be feminine. Roughness is often positively valued for men, and women seek out smoothness.

Taste

Our taste receptors obviously contribute to our experience of many products. For example, the new Rejuvenating Effects women's toothpaste mentioned in the last chapter is designed to produce a slight tingling sensation that P&G hopes will provide a "sensory signal" of gum health and fresh breath.[33]

Specialized companies called "flavor houses" keep busy developing new concoctions to please the changing palates of consumers. Scientists are right behind them, developing new devices to test these flavors. A company called Alpha M.O.S. sells a sophisticated electronic tongue for tasting and is working on what its executives call an electronic mouth, complete with artificial saliva, to chew food and to dissect its flavor. Coca-Cola and PepsiCo use the tongue to test the quality of corn syrups while Bristol-Myers Squibb and Roche use the device to devise medicines that don't taste bitter.[34]

Changes in our culture also determine the tastes we find desirable. For example, consumers' greater appreciation of different ethnic dishes has contributed to increased desires for spicy foods, so the quest for the ultimate pepper sauce is a hot

This Spanish ad for a hot chili-flavored chip uses a novel visual image to communicate the ferocity of the product's flavor.

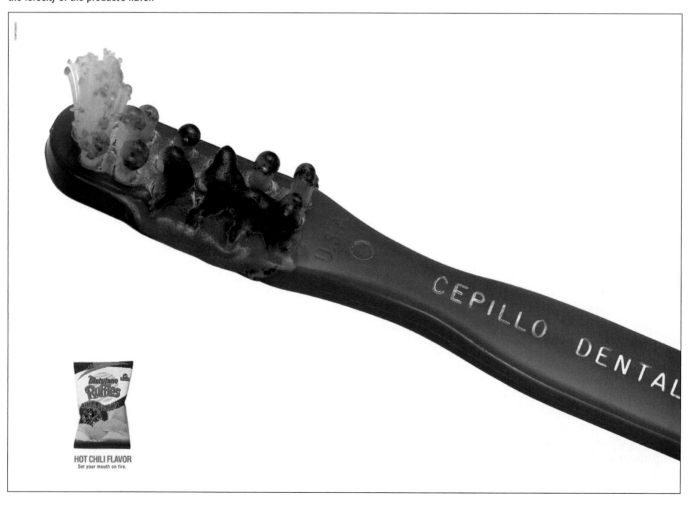

HOT CHILI FLAVOR
Set your mouth on fire.

taste trend. More than 50 stores in the United States now specialize in supplying fiery concoctions with names such as Sting and Linger, Hell in a Jar, and Religious Experience (comes in Original, Hot, and Wrath).[35] Some of these sauces are so hot that stores ask customers to sign waivers of legal liability before they will sell them. The "heat" of peppers is measured in units called Scovilles. In 1912, Wilbur Scoville asked a five-person panel to see how much sugar water it would take to eliminate the hotness of a pepper. How's this for a hot tip: It takes 1,981 gallons of sweetened water to neutralize a teaspoon of Da' Bomb, which is advertised as the hottest sauce ever made.[36]

At the other extreme of sensation, Japanese beverage companies are catching on to a new fad among younger Japanese consumers who are becoming more health conscious and who want to avoid harmful additives: bland, watery drinks. Beverage manufacturers there are working hard to make fruit drinks that you can see through. Coca-Cola introduced a new cold tea with an actor who stares at a bottle and wonders: Is it tea or is it water? Stores are stacked with cartons of "near waters," mineral waters with just a touch of flavor. Sapporo sells a watered-down iced coffee, and Asahi Breweries makes a beer that is as clear as water with a name that sums up this new trend: Beer Water.[37] Not too appealing to Americans, but perhaps good for washing down some hot sauce?

■ EXPOSURE

Exposure occurs when a stimulus comes within the range of someone's sensory receptors. Consumers concentrate on some stimuli, are unaware of others, and even go out of their way to ignore some messages. An experiment by a Minneapolis bank illustrates consumers' tendencies to miss or ignore information in which they are not interested. After a state law was passed that required banks to explain details about money transfer in electronic banking, the Northwestern National Bank distributed a pamphlet to 120,000 of its customers at considerable cost to provide the required information, which was hardly exciting bedtime reading. In 100 of the mailings, a section in the middle of the pamphlet offered the reader $10 just for finding that paragraph. Not a single person claimed the reward.[38] Before we consider what else people may choose not to perceive, let's consider what they are *capable* of perceiving.

Sensory Thresholds

If you have ever blown a dog whistle and watched pets respond to a sound you cannot hear, you won't be surprised to learn that there are some stimuli that people simply are not capable of perceiving. Some people are better able to pick up sensory information than those whose sensory channels may be impaired by disabilities or age. The science that focuses on how the physical environment is integrated into our personal, subjective world is known as **psychophysics**.

The Absolute Threshold

When we define the lowest intensity of a stimulus that can be registered on a sensory channel, we speak of a *threshold* for that receptor. It sounds like a great name for a rock band, but the **absolute threshold** refers to the minimum amount of stimulation that can be detected on a given sensory channel. The sound emitted by a dog whistle is too high to be detected by human ears, so this stimulus is beyond our auditory absolute threshold. The absolute threshold is an important consideration in designing marketing stimuli. A highway billboard might have the most entertaining copy ever written, but this genius is wasted if the print is too small for passing motorists to see it.

The Differential Threshold

The **differential threshold** refers to the ability of a sensory system to detect changes or differences between two stimuli. The minimum difference that can be detected between two stimuli is known as the **j.n.d.** (just noticeable difference).

The issue of when and if a difference between two stimuli will be noticed by consumers is relevant to many marketing situations. Sometimes a marketer may want to ensure that a change is observed, as when merchandise is offered at a discount. In other situations, the fact that a change has been made may be downplayed, as in the case of price increases or when a product is downsized.

A consumer's ability to detect a difference between two stimuli is relative. A whispered conversation that might be unintelligible on a noisy street can suddenly become public and embarrassingly loud in a quiet library. It is the *relative* difference between

Campbell's Soup has been gradually modifying its label for the last 125 years. Consumers are rushing to hoard classic Campbell's Soup cans because in 1999 the company decided to retire the label. The new cans feature photos of actual soup in the bowl but the design retains the distinctive red-and-white colors and unique script to avert a consumer backlash.

the decibel level of the conversation and its surroundings, rather than the absolute loudness of the conversation itself, that determines whether the stimulus will register.

In the nineteenth century, a psychophysicist named Ernst Weber found that the amount of change that is necessary to be noticed is systematically related to the intensity of the original stimulus. The stronger the initial stimulus, the greater a change must be for it to be noticed. This relationship is known as **Weber's Law**, and is expressed in the following equation:

$$K = \frac{\Delta i}{I}$$

where

K = a constant (this varies across the senses)
Δi = the mimimal change in intensity of the stimulus required to produce a j.n.d.
I = the intensity of the stimulus where the change occurs

For example, consider how Weber's Law might work with respect to a product that has had its price decreased for a special sale. A rule-of-thumb used by some retailers is that a markdown should be at least 20 percent for this price cut to make an impact on shoppers. If so, a pair of socks that retails for $10 should be put on sale for $8 (a $2 discount). However, a sports coat selling for $100 would not benefit from a "mere" $2 discount—it would have to be marked down to $80 to achieve the same impact.

Subliminal Perception

Most marketers are concerned with creating messages above consumers' thresholds so they will be noticed. Ironically, a good number of consumers appear to believe that many advertising messages are designed to be perceived unconsciously, or *below* the threshold of recognition. Another word for threshold is *limen*, and stimuli that fall below the limen are termed *subliminal*. **Subliminal perception** occurs when the stimulus is below the level of the consumer's awareness.

Subliminal perception is a topic that has captivated the public for more than 40 years, despite the fact that there is virtually no proof that this process has any effect on consumer behavior.[39] A survey of American consumers found that almost two-thirds believe in the existence of subliminal advertising, and more than one-half are convinced that this technique can get them to buy things they do not really want.[40]

Most examples of subliminal perception that have been "discovered" are not subliminal at all—to the contrary, these images are quite visible. Remember, if you can see it or hear it, it is not subliminal, because the stimulus is above the level of conscious awareness. Nonetheless, the continuing controversy about subliminal persuasion has been important in shaping the public's beliefs about advertisers' and marketers' ability to manipulate consumers against their will.

Subliminal Techniques

Subliminal messages supposedly can be sent on both visual and aural channels. *Embeds* are tiny figures that are inserted into magazine advertising by using high-speed photography or airbrushing. These hidden figures, usually of a sexual nature, supposedly exert strong but unconscious influences on innocent readers. Some limited evidence hints at the possibility that embeds can alter the mood of men who are exposed to sexually suggestive images presented subliminally, but the effect (if any) is very subtle—and may even work in the opposite direction by creating negative feelings among viewers.[41] To date, the only real impact of this interest in hidden messages is to sell more copies of "exposés" written by a few authors, and to make some consumers (and students of consumer behavior) look

Marketing Pitfall

The Disney Corporation is one of the companies most recently accused of using subliminal messages. The company recalled 3.4 million copies of its animated video *The Rescuers* because the film included a very brief image of a topless woman (she appeared in two frames of a 110,000-frame film, each for one-tenth of a second). This picture was embedded as a prank in the master negative way back in 1977, but "the naked truth" surfaced only recently. Disney has been combating rumors of subliminal images in its films for years, and this issue was one of the reasons given for a boycott of the company's products by the Southern Baptist Convention in 1997. In one case, CEO Michael Eisner had to rebut charges on the TV show *60 Minutes* that the clergyman in *The Little Mermaid* is shown with an erection. He argued, "Everybody knows it's his knee. It's just people spending too much time looking for things that aren't there." He's probably right in most cases, though the fact that someone pulled off *The Rescuers* prank makes it hard to mount a totally convincing argument.[42]

Critics of subliminal persuasion often focus on ambiguous shapes in drinks that supposedly spell out words like S E X as evidence for the use of this technique. This Pepsi ad, while hardly subliminal, gently borrows this message format.

NOTHING ELSE
IS A PEPSI

a bit more closely at print ads—perhaps seeing whatever their imaginations lead them to see.

The possible effects of messages hidden on sound recordings also fascinate many consumers. An attempt to capitalize on subliminal auditory perception techniques is found in the growing market for self-help cassettes. These tapes, which typically feature the sound of waves crashing or some other natural sound, supposedly contain subliminal messages to help the listener stop smoking, lose weight, gain confidence, and so on. Despite the rapid growth of this market, there is little evidence that subliminal stimuli transmitted on the auditory channel can bring about desired changes in behavior.[43]

Along with the interest in hidden self-help messages on recordings, some consumers have become concerned about rumors of satanic messages recorded backward on rock-music selections. The popular press has devoted much attention to such stories, and state legislatures have considered bills requiring warning labels about these messages. These backward messages do indeed appear on some albums, including Led Zeppelin's classic song "Stairway to Heaven," which contains the lyric "there's still time to change." When played in reverse, this phrase sounds like "so here's to my sweet Satan."

The novelty of such reversals might help to sell records, but the "evil" messages within have no effect.[44] Humans simply don't have a speech perception mechanism operating at an unconscious level that is capable of decoding a reversed signal. On the other hand, subtle acoustic messages such as "I am honest. I won't steal. Stealing is dishonest." are broadcast in more than 1,000 stores in the United States to prevent shoplifting and do appear to have some effect. Unlike subliminal perception, though, these messages are played at a (barely) audible level, using a technique known as threshold messaging.[45] Some evidence indicates, however, that these messages are effective only on individuals who are predisposed to suggestion. For example, someone who might be thinking about taking something on a dare but who feels guilty about it might be deterred, but these soft words will not sway a professional thief.[46]

Does Subliminal Perception Work? Evaluating the Evidence

Some research by clinical psychologists suggests that people can be influenced by subliminal messages under very specific conditions, though it is doubtful that these techniques would be of much use in most marketing contexts. Effective messages must be very specifically tailored to individuals, rather than the mass messages required by advertising.[47] They should also be as close to the liminal threshold as possible. Other discouraging factors include the following issues:

- There are wide individual differences in threshold levels. In order for a message to avoid conscious detection by consumers who have a low threshold, it would have to be so weak that it would not reach those who have a high threshold.
- Advertisers lack control over consumers' distance and position from a screen. In a movie theater, for example, only a small portion of the audience would be in exactly the right seats to be exposed to a subliminal message.
- The viewer must be paying absolute attention to the stimulus. People watching a television program or a movie typically shift their attention periodically and might not even be looking when the stimulus is presented.
- Even if the desired effect is induced, it operates only at a very general level. For example, a message might increase a person's thirst, but not necessarily for a specific drink. Because basic drives are affected, marketers could find that after all the bother and expense of creating a subliminal message, demand for competitors' products increases as well!

Clearly, there are better ways to get our attention—let's see how.

■ ATTENTION

As you sit in a lecture, you might find your mind wandering (yes, even you!). One minute you are concentrating on the instructor's words, and in the next, you catch yourself daydreaming about the upcoming weekend. Suddenly, you tune back in as you hear your name being spoken. Fortunately, it's a false alarm—the professor has called on another "victim" who has the same first name. But, she's got your attention now.

Nike tries to cut through the clutter by spotlighting maimed athletes instead of handsome models.

Attention refers to the extent to which processing activity is devoted to a particular stimulus. As you know from sitting through both interesting and less interesting lectures, this allocation can vary depending on both the characteristics of the stimulus (i.e., the lecture itself) and the recipient (i.e., your mental state at the time).

Although we live in an "information society," we can have too much of a good thing. Consumers often are in a state of sensory overload, exposed to far more information than they can or are willing to process. In our society, much of this bombardment comes from commercial sources, and the competition for our attention is increasing steadily. The average adult is exposed to about 3,000 pieces of advertising information every single day.[48]

Television networks are jamming a record number of commercials into their shows—an average of 16 minutes and 43 seconds per programming hour.[49] And, these mini-movies contain more information than ever before: To cope with the shortened attention spans of younger viewers, directors are cramming more shots into the same time span—more cuts to different scenes increases the pace and emotional energy of an ad. In 1978, the typical 30-second commercial contained about 8 shots, each lasting about 4 seconds. By 1991, the number of shots zoomed to 13, with each lasting only about 2 seconds.[50]

This onslaught is growing as we now are bombarded by *banner ads* when we surf the Web as well. These online ads can in fact increase brand awareness after only one exposure, but only if they motivate surfers to click through and see what information is awaiting them.[51] Indeed, some marketing analysts suggest that the Internet has transformed the way business is done—they claim we are now operating in an **attention economy**. This means that the primary goal is to attract eyeballs, not dollars, to a Web site. The idea is that the amount of information companies can provide to consumers online is infinite—but there's only so much time people can devote to accessing it. So, a goal of interactive media is to buy and sell *attention*, as when a firm is paid to divert the traffic on one Web site to another site. For example, many Web companies, including *Amazon.com*, feature affiliate programs that pay people to drive shoppers to merchants via links on their home pages. They get a cut of between 5 and 25 percent of any transaction that results from their lead.[52]

Because the brain's capacity to process information is limited, consumers are very selective about what they pay attention to. The process of **perceptual selection** means that people attend to only a small portion of the stimuli to which they are exposed. Consumers practice a form of "psychic economy," picking and choosing among stimuli to avoid being overwhelmed. How do they choose? Both personal and stimulus factors help to decide.

Personal Selection Factors

The actions of a Colorado judge illustrate how powerful our own tastes can be in determining what we want to see and hear. He requires young people convicted of violating the city's noise ordinance to listen to music they don't like—including a heavy dose of such "favorites" as Wayne Newton, Dean Martin, and bagpipe recordings.[53] What, no Nine Inch Nails? **Experience**, which is the result of acquiring and processing stimulation over time, is one factor that determines how much exposure to a particular stimulus a person accepts. *Perceptual filters* based on our past experiences influence what we decide to process.

Perceptual vigilance is one such factor. Consumers are more likely to be aware of stimuli that relate to their current needs. A consumer who rarely notices car ads will become very much aware of them when she is in the market for a new car. A newspaper ad for a fast-food restaurant that would otherwise go unnoticed becomes significant when one sneaks a glance at the paper in the middle of a five o'clock class.

The flip side of perceptual vigilance is **perceptual defense**. This means that people see what they want to see—and don't see what they don't want to see. If a stimulus is threatening to us in some way, we may not process it—or we may distort its meaning so that it's more acceptable. For example, a heavy smoker may block out images of cancer-scarred lungs because these vivid reminders hit a bit too close to home.

Still another factor is **adaptation**, the degree to which consumers continue to notice a stimulus over time. The process of adaptation occurs when consumers no longer pay attention to a stimulus because it is so familiar. A consumer can become "habituated" and require increasingly stronger "doses" of a stimulus for it to be noticed. A consumer en route to work might read a billboard message when it is first installed, but after a few days, it just becomes part of the passing scenery. Several factors can lead to adaptation:

- *Intensity:* Less-intense stimuli (e.g., soft sounds or dim colors) habituate because they have less sensory impact.
- *Duration:* Stimuli that require relatively lengthy exposure in order to be processed tend to habituate because they require a long attention span.
- *Discrimination:* Simple stimuli tend to habituate because they do not require attention to detail.

Marketing Opportunity

How can marketers attract attention in such a cluttered media environment? Many are staging elaborate public stunts to raise consumers' awareness of their products:

- Huge Altoids tins are showing up in all kinds of places. A tugboat in New York Harbor was draped to look like a big silver mint container. In Chicago a subway train received the same treatment.[54]
- VH1 promoted its annual fashion awards show by deploying a squad of models dressed as police officers to hand out fashion citations. The "fashion police" became a reality if only for a few days.
- To drum up favorable coverage for its new Web site, the Discovery Channel sent a man to magazine offices dressed as a giant mosquito to deliver baskets of cookies.
- Bigwords.com (the San Francisco–based online collegiate bookstore) hired 1,000 students to don orange jumpsuits on college campuses in order to imitate its spokesman, MTV's Tom Green. To be sure it got people's attention, the company also dropped 20,000 color-coded superballs from the tops of 50-foot cranes on some campuses.[55]
- In a promotion for Coca-Cola's Dasani water, Atlanta and Philadelphia subway riders saw an eye-catching cascading waterfall out their windows. Using a technique developed in the 1800s called the zoetrope, the images are created by a series of panels seen through narrow slits; the illusion of movement is created when the viewer is passing at the appropriate rate of speed.[56]

Despite other distractions, we tend to focus on stimuli that relate to our current needs.

- *Exposure:* Frequently encountered stimuli tend to habituate as the rate of exposure increases.
- *Relevance:* Stimuli that are irrelevant or unimportant will habituate because they fail to attract attention.

Stimulus Selection Factors

In addition to the receiver's mind-set, characteristics of the stimulus itself play an important role in determining what gets noticed and what gets ignored. These factors need to be understood by marketers, who can apply them to their messages and packages to boost their chances of cutting through the clutter and commanding attention. This idea even applies to getting animals' attention: A British ad agency did a TV commercial aimed at felines that uses fish and mouse images and sounds to attract catty consumers. In trials, 60 percent of cats showed some form of response to the ad, from twitching their ears to tapping the television screen.[57] That's a better track record than some "people commercials" have shown!

In general, stimuli that differ from others around them are more likely to be noticed (remember Weber's Law). This contrast can be created in several ways:

- *Size:* The size of the stimulus itself in contrast to the competition helps to determine if it will command attention. Readership of a magazine ad increases in proportion to the size of the ad.[58]
- *Color:* As we've seen, color is a powerful way to draw attention to a product or to give it a distinct identity. For example, Black & Decker inaugurated a new line of tools called DeWalt, targeted to the residential construction industry. The new line was colored yellow instead of black, which made them stand out against other "dull" tools.[59]

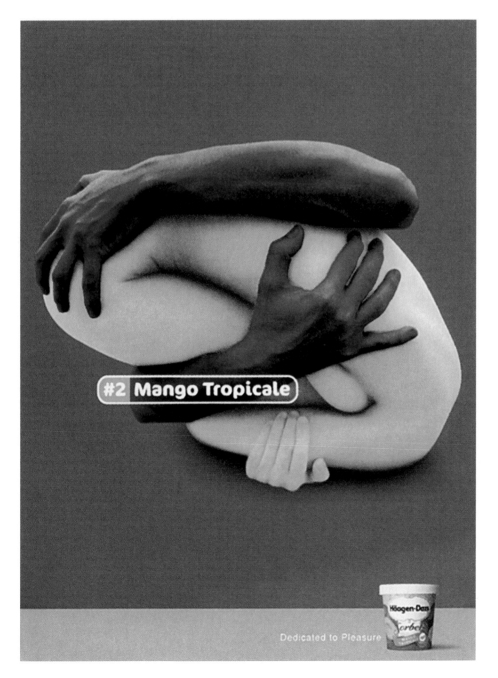

This Australian ad relies on a stark color contrast to get noticed.

● *Position:* Not surprisingly, stimuli that are in places we're more likely to look stand a better chance of being noticed. That's why the competition is so heated among suppliers to have their products displayed in stores at eye level. In magazines, ads that are placed toward the front of the issue, preferably on the right-hand side, also win out in the race for readers' attention. (Hint: The next time you read a magazine, notice which pages you're more likely to spend time looking at.)[60] A study that tracked consumers' eye movements as they scanned telephone directories also illustrates the importance of a message's position. Consumers scanned listings in alphabetical order, and they noticed 93 percent of quarter-page display ads but only 26 percent of plain listings. Their eyes were drawn to color ads first, and these were viewed longer than black-and-white ones. In addition, subjects spent 54 percent more time viewing ads for businesses they ended up choosing, which illustrates the influence of attention on subsequent product choice.[61]

● *Novelty:* Stimuli that appear in unexpected ways or places tend to grab our attention. One solution has been to put ads in unconventional places, where there will be less competition for attention. These places include the backs of shopping carts, walls of tunnels, floors of sports stadiums, and yes, even public restrooms.[62] A recent promotion to introduce Vanilla Coke in Europe illustrates how effective novelty can be. Coke put a big wooden box in shopping malls and told people to stick their head in it. The brave souls who complied were rewarded with a bottle of the stuff. This request tied into TV commercials for the new product that tell viewers to "Reward your curiosity." In one, a man walking along the street sees a hole in a wooden wall along the sidewalk. He pokes his

Advertisers know that consumers often will relate an ad to a preexisting schema in order to make sense of it (see page 69). This Singaporean ad for Toyota evokes a car schema even though the materials used in the picture are chairs and couches one might find inside a house.

Toyota Spacio

head in, which is grabbed by a mobster in a black suit as a second mobster puts a bottle of Vanilla Coke to his lips.[63]

    Interpretation refers to the meaning that we assign to sensory stimuli. Just as people differ in terms of the stimuli that they perceive, the eventual assignment of meanings to these stimuli varies as well. Two people can see or hear the same event, but their interpretation of it can be as different as night and day depending on what they had expected the stimulus to be. For example, Vernor's ginger ale did poorly in a taste test against leading ginger ales. When the research team introduced it instead as a new type of soft drink with a tangier taste, it won handily. The drink tasted good, but it didn't jibe with people's expectations of what a ginger ale should taste like.[64]

    Consumers assign meaning to stimuli based on the **schema**, or set of beliefs, to which the stimulus is assigned. That helps to explain why Gary was so revolted at the thought of warm milk. In a process known as *priming*, certain properties of a stimulus typically will evoke a schema, which leads us to evaluate the stimulus in terms of other stimuli we have encountered that are believed to be similar. Identifying and evoking the correct schema is crucial to many marketing decisions because this determines what criteria will be used to evaluate the product, package, or message. Extra Strength Maalox Whip Antacid flopped even though a spray can is a pretty effective way to deliver the product. But to consumers aerosol whips mean desert toppings, not medication.[65]

Stimulus Organization

One factor that determines how a stimulus will be interpreted is its assumed relationship with other events, sensations, or images. When RJR Nabisco introduced a version of Teddy Grahams (a children's product) for adults, restrained

A popular British retailer called French Connection relies on the priming process to evoke a response to its advertising by using an acronym that closely resembles another word.

This Swedish ad relies on gestalt perceptual principles to ensure that the perceiver organizes a lot of separate images into a familiar image.

packaging colors were used to reinforce the idea that the new product was for grown-ups. But, sales were disappointing. The box was changed to a bright yellow to convey the idea that this was a fun snack, and buyers' more positive association between a bright primary color and taste led adults to start buying the cookies.[66]

Our brains tend to relate incoming sensations to others already in memory, based on some fundamental organizational principles. These principles are based on Gestalt psychology, a school of thought that maintains that people derive meaning from the totality of a set of stimuli, rather than from any individual stimulus. The German word **Gestalt** roughly means whole, pattern, or configuration, and this perspective is best summarized by the saying "the whole is greater than the sum of its parts." A piecemeal perspective that analyzes each component of the stimulus separately will be unable to capture the total effect. The Gestalt perspective provides several principles relating to the way stimuli are organized.

- The **closure principle** states that people tend to perceive an incomplete picture as complete. That is, we tend to fill in the blanks based on our prior experience. This principle explains why most of us have no trouble reading a neon sign even if several of its letters are burned out. The principle of closure is also at work when we hear only part of a jingle or theme. Utilization of the principle of closure in marketing strategies encourages audience participation, which increases the chance that people will attend to the message.

This Land Rover ad illustrates use of the principle of closure, in which people participate in the ad by mentally filling in the gaps in the sentence.

- The **principle of similarity** tells us that consumers tend to group together objects that share similar physical characteristics. Green Giant relied on this principle when the company redesigned the packaging for its line of frozen vegetables. It created a "sea of green" look to unify all of its different offerings.

- The **figure-ground principle** states that one part of a stimulus will dominate (the figure), and other parts recede into the background (the ground). This concept is easy to understand if one thinks literally of a photograph with a clear and sharply focused object (the figure) in the center. The figure is dominant, and the eye goes straight to it. The parts of the configuration that will be perceived as figure or ground can vary depending on the individual consumer as well as other factors. Similarly, in marketing messages that use the figure-ground principle, a stimulus can be made the focal point of the message or merely the context that surrounds the focus.

The Eye of the Beholder: Interpretational Biases

The stimuli we perceive are often ambiguous. It's up to us to determine the meaning based on our past experiences, expectations, and needs. The process of "seeing what you want to see" was demonstrated in a classic experiment in which students at Princeton and Dartmouth viewed a movie of a particularly rough football game between the two schools. Although everyone was exposed to the same stimulus, the degree to which students saw infractions and the blame they assigned

This billboard for Wrangler jeans makes creative use of the figure-ground principle.

WRANGLER CAMOUFLAGE JEANS.

for those they did see was quite different depending on which college they attended.[67] As this experiment demonstrates, consumers tend to project their own desires or assumptions onto products and advertisements. This interpretation process can backfire for marketers, as occurred in these cases:

- A Detroit woman mistakenly packed a can of Anheuser-Busch's Bud Ice beer in her grandson's lunch, confusing it with a package of Hawaiian Punch. A Seattle mother thought the brew was a holiday-style can of Pepsi. Her daughter was on the losing end; she got hit with a five-day suspension for bringing beer to school.[68]
- A company called Back to Basics sells a Microbrew line of hair-care products laced with barley, yeast, and hops. They come in names like Honey Wheat Pilsner and Black Cherry Stout, packaged in brown bottles with twist-off caps. Cause for confusion? A company spokesman claims, "People should know enough to put them in the shower, not the fridge."[69]
- Planters Lifesavers Company introduced a vacuum-packed peanuts package called Planters Fresh Roast. The idea was to capitalize on consumers' growing love affair with fresh-roast coffee by emphasizing the freshness of the nuts in the same way. A great idea—until irate supermarket managers began calling to ask who was going to pay to clean the peanut gook out of their stores' coffee-grinding machines.[70]

Semiotics: The Symbols Around Us

When we try to "make sense" of a marketing stimulus, whether a distinctive package, an elaborately staged television commercial, or perhaps a model on the cover of a magazine, we do so by interpreting its meaning in light of associations we have with these images. For this reason, much of the meaning we take away is influenced by what we

Whatever you do, don't get them mixed up.

The bunny on the right is one of 12 Dung Buddies – lovable miniatures made with Zoo Doo fertilizer that dissolves in soil over time. But remember, they go in your garden, not in your mouth. **DUNG BUDDY**

make of the symbolism we perceive. After all, on the surface many marketing images have virtually no literal connection to actual products. What does a cowboy have to do with a bit of tobacco rolled into a paper tube? How can a celebrity such as basketball star Michael Jordan enhance the image of a soft drink or a fast-food restaurant?

For assistance in understanding how consumers interpret the meanings of symbols, some marketers are turning to a field of study known as **semiotics**, which examines the correspondence between signs and symbols and their role in the assignment of meaning.[71] Semiotics is important to the understanding of consumer behavior because consumers use products to express their social identities. Products have learned meanings, and we rely on marketers to help us figure out what those meanings are. As one set of researchers put it, "Advertising serves as a kind of culture/consumption dictionary; its entries are products, and their definitions are cultural meanings."[72]

From a semiotic perspective, every marketing message has three basic components: an object, a sign or symbol, and an interpretant. The **object** is the product that is the focus of the message (e.g., Marlboro cigarettes). The **sign** is the sensory image that represents the intended meanings of the object (e.g., the Marlboro cowboy). The **interpretant** is the meaning derived (e.g., rugged, individualistic, American). This relationship is diagrammed in Figure 2.2.

According to semiotician Charles Sanders Peirce, signs are related to objects in one of three ways: They can resemble objects, be connected to them, or be conventionally tied to them.[73] An **icon** is a sign that resembles the product in some way (e.g., Bell Telephone uses an image of a bell to represent itself). An **index** is a sign that is connected to a product because they share some property (e.g., the pine tree on some of Procter & Gamble's Spic and Span cleanser products conveys the shared property of fresh scent). A **symbol** is a sign that is related to a product through either conventional or agreed-upon associations (e.g., the lion in Dreyfus Fund ads provides the conventional association with fearlessness and strength that is carried over to the company's approach to investments).

People often use characteristics of a package to infer its contents. This ad for a fertilizer product reminds us, ". . . they go in your garden, not in your mouth."

■ **FIGURE 2.2**
SEMIOTIC RELATIONSHIPS

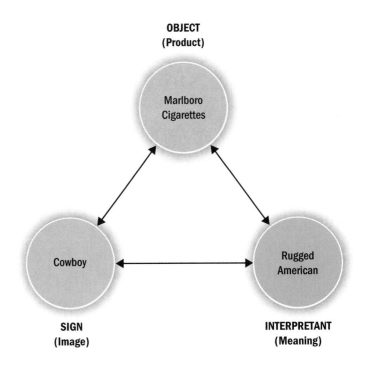

A lot of time, thought, and money goes into creating brand names and logos that will clearly communicate a product's image (even when a name like Exxon is generated by a computer!). The Nissan Xterra combines the word "terrain" with the letter *X*, which is associated with extreme sports by many young people, to give the brand name a cutting-edge, off-road feel. The choice of a logo is even more difficult when the brand has to travel across cultures. For example, as Chinese business becomes more global, companies are refashioning ancient Chinese pictograms into new corporate logos that resonate with both the East and the West. Chinese pictograms really are icons, because the ancient symbols were once graphic depictions of the words they signify. For example, China Telecom's logo features two interlocking letter Cs that together form the Chinese character for China but also represent the concept of "customer" and "competition," the firm's new focus. In addition, though, the symbol also resembles the horns of an ox, a hard-working animal. The software company Oracle recently redesigned its logo for the Chinese market by adding three Chinese characters that signify the literal translation of the word *oracle:* "writing on a tortoise shell." The expression dates back to ancient China, when prophecies were scrawled on bones. The California firm was enthusiastic about the translation because it conveyed Oracle's core competency, data storage.[74]

Hyperreality

One of the hallmarks of modern advertising is that it creates a condition known as **hyperreality**. Hyperreality refers to the process of making real what is initially simulation or "hype." Advertisers create new relationships between objects and interpretants by inventing new connections between products and benefits, such as equating Marlboro cigarettes with the American frontier spirit.[75]

In a hyperreal environment, over time the true relationship between the symbol and reality is no longer possible to discern. The "artificial" associations between product symbols and the real world may take on lives of their own. Consider for example the region of Switzerland that has been renamed "Heidiland" by tourism marketers in honor of the supposed "birthplace" of the imaginary Swiss girl. In the town of Maienfeld, new Heidi attractions are flourishing. A Heidi trail leads to a Heidi refreshment stand and then to a man there who poses full time as Heidi's grandfather. Initially, officials refused to permit "Welcome to Heidiland" highway signs because Swiss law allows only real place names. The volume of tourists making a pilgrimage to the "home" of this mythical character apparently changed their minds.[76] In our hyperreal world, Heidi lives.

Perceptual Positioning

As we've seen, a product stimulus often is interpreted in light of what we already know about a product category and the characteristics of existing brands. Perceptions of a brand comprise both its functional attributes (e.g., its features, its price, and so on) and its symbolic attributes (its image, and what we think it says about us when we use it). We'll look more closely at issues such as brand image in later chapters, but for now it's important to keep in mind that our evaluation of a product typically is the result of what it means rather than what it does. This meaning—as perceived by consumers—constitutes the product's market position, and it may have more to do with our expectations of product performance as communicated by its color, packaging, or styling than with the product itself.

How does a marketer determine where a product actually stands in the minds of consumers? One technique is to ask them what attributes are important to them, and how they feel competitors rate on these attributes. This information can be used to construct a **perceptual map**, which is a vivid way to paint a picture of where products or brands are "located" in consumers' minds. GRW Advertising created the perceptual map shown in Figure 2.3 for HMV music stores, a British company. The agency wanted to know more about how its target market, frequent buyers of CDs, perceived the different stores they might patronize. GRW plotted perceptions of such attributes of competitors as selection, price, service, and hipness on an imaginary street map. Based on this research, the firm determined that HMV's strengths were service, selection, and the stores' abilities to cater to local tastes because store managers can order their own stock. This map was used in the strategic decision to specialize in music products as opposed to competing by offering other items sold by the competition, such as video games, fragrances, and computer CD-ROMs.[77]

A **positioning strategy** is a fundamental part of a company's marketing efforts as it uses elements of the marketing mix (i.e., product design, price, distribution, and marketing communications) to influence the consumer's interpretation of its meaning. For example, although consumers' preferences for the taste of one product over another are important, this functional attribute is only one component of product evaluation. Coca-Cola found this out the hard way when it committed its famous New Coke marketing blunder in the 1980s. New Coke was preferred to Pepsi in blind taste tests (in which the products were not identified) by an average of 55 percent to 45 percent in 17 markets, yet New Coke ran into problems when it replaced the older version. Consumers' impassioned protests and letter-writing campaigns eventually forced the company to bring back "Classic Coke." People do not buy a cola for taste alone; they are buying intangibles such as brand image as well.[78] Coca-Cola's unique position as part of an American, fun-loving lifestyle is based on years of marketing efforts that involve a lot more than taste alone. In 2000, Pepsi revived its Pepsi Challenge; the original promotion was widely believed to have been a driving force behind Coke's disastrous introduction of its sweeter New Coke.[79]

There are many dimensions that can be used to establish a brand's position in the marketplace. These include:[80]

- *Lifestyle:* Grey Poupon mustard is a "higher-class" condiment.
- *Price leadership:* L'Oréal's Noisôme brand face cream is sold in upscale beauty shops, whereas its Plenitude brand is available for one-sixth the price in discount stores—even though both are based on the same chemical formula.[82]
- *Attributes:* Bounty paper towels are "the quicker picker upper."
- *Product class:* The Mazda Miata is a sporty convertible.
- *Competitors:* Northwestern Insurance is "the quiet company."

■ **FIGURE 2.3**
HMV PERCEPTUAL MAP

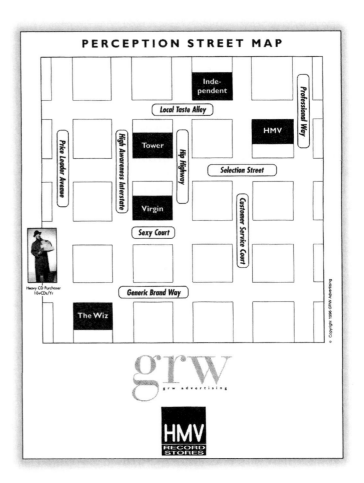

- *Occasions:* Wrigley's gum is an alternative at times when smoking is not permitted.
- *Users:* Levi's Dockers are targeted primarily to men in their twenties to forties.
- *Quality:* At Ford, "Quality is job 1."

CHAPTER SUMMARY

Perception is the process by which physical sensations such as sights, sounds, and smells are selected, organized, and interpreted. The eventual interpretation of a stimulus allows it to be assigned meaning. A perceptual map is a widely used marketing tool that evaluates the relative standing of competing brands along relevant dimensions.

Marketing stimuli have important sensory qualities. We rely on colors, odors, sounds, tastes, and even the "feel" of products when forming evaluations of them.

Not all sensations successfully make their way through the perceptual process. Many stimuli compete for our attention, and the majority are not noticed or accurately comprehended.

People have different thresholds of perception. A stimulus must be presented at a certain level of intensity before it can be detected by sensory receptors. In addition, a consumer's ability to detect whether two stimuli are different (the differential threshold) is an important issue in many marketing contexts, such as changing a package design, altering the size of a product, or reducing its price.

A lot of controversy has been sparked by so-called subliminal persuasion and related techniques, by which people are exposed to visual and aural messages below the threshold. Although evidence that subliminal persuasion is effective is virtually nonexistent, many consumers continue to believe that advertisers use this technique.

Some of the factors that determine which stimuli (above the threshold level) do get perceived are the amount of exposure to the stimulus, how much attention it generates, and how it is interpreted. In an increasingly crowded stimulus environment, advertising clutter occurs when too many marketing-related messages compete for attention.

A stimulus that is attended to is not perceived in isolation. It is classified and organized according to principles of perceptual organization. These principles are guided by a Gestalt, or overall pattern. Specific grouping principles include closure, similarity, and figure-ground relationships.

The final step in the process of perception is interpretation. Symbols help us make sense of the world by providing us with an interpretation of a stimulus that is often shared by others. The degree to which the symbolism is consistent with our previous experience affects the meaning we assign to related objects.

Marketers try to communicate with consumers by creating relationships between their products or services and desired attributes. A semiotic analysis involves the correspondence between stimuli and the meaning of signs. The intended meaning may be literal (e.g., an icon such as a street sign with a picture of children playing). The meaning may be indexical; it relies on shared characteristics (e.g., the red in a stop sign means danger). Finally, meaning can be conveyed by a symbol, in which an image is given meaning by convention or by agreement of members of a society (e.g., stop signs are octagonal, whereas yield signs are triangular). Marketer-created associations often take on a life of their own as hype is assumed to be real. This condition is known as hyperreality.

KEY TERMS

Absolute threshold   59
Adaptation   65
Attention   64
Attention economy   65
Closure principle   70
Differential threshold   60
Experience   65
Exposure   59
Figure-ground principle   71
Gestalt   70
Hedonic consumption   49
Hyperreality   74

Icon   73
Index   73
Interpretant   73
Interpretation   69
j.n.d.   60
Kansei engineering   57
Object   73
Perception   49
Perceptual defense   65
Perceptual map   75
Perceptual selection   65
Perceptual vigilance   65

Positioning strategy   75
Principle of similarity   71
Psychophysics   59
Schema   69
Semiotics   73
Sensation   49
Sign   73
Subliminal perception   61
Symbol   73
Trade dress   53
Weber's Law   61

CONSUMER BEHAVIOR CHALLENGE

1 Many studies have shown that our sensory detection abilities decline as we grow older. Discuss the implications of the absolute threshold for marketers attempting to appeal to the elderly.

2 Interview three to five male and three to five female friends about their perceptions of both men's and women's fragrances. Construct a perceptual map for each set of products. Based on your map of perfumes, do you see any areas that are not adequately served by current offerings? What (if any) gender differences did

you obtain regarding both the relevant dimensions used by raters and the placement of specific brands along these dimensions?

3 Assuming that some forms of subliminal persuasion may have the desired effect of influencing consumers, do you think the use of these techniques is ethical? Explain your answer.

4 Assume that you are a consultant for a marketer who wants to design a package for a new premium chocolate bar targeted to an affluent market. What

recommendations would you provide in terms of such package elements as color, symbolism, and graphic design? Give the reasons for your suggestions.

5 Do you believe that marketers have the right to use any or all public spaces to deliver product messages? Where would you draw the line in terms of places and products that should be restricted?

6 Using magazines archived in the library, track the packaging of a specific brand over time. Find an example of gradual changes in package design that may have been below the j.n.d.

7 Visit a set of Web sites for one type of product (e.g., personal computers, perfumes, laundry detergents, or athletic shoes) and analyze the colors and other design principles employed. Which sites work and which don't? Why?

8 Look through a current magazine and select one ad that captures your attention over the others. Give the reasons.

9 Find ads that utilize the techniques of contrast and novelty. Give your opinion of the effectiveness of each ad and whether the technique is likely to be appropriate for the consumers targeted by the ad.

10 The slogan for the movie *Godzilla* was "Size does matter." Should this be the slogan for America as well? Many marketers seem to believe so. The average serving size for a fountain drink has gone from 12 ounces to 20 ounces. An industry consultant explains that the 32-ounce Big Gulp is so popular because "people like something large in their hands. The larger the better." Hardee's Monster Burger, complete with two beef patties and five pieces of bacon, weighs in at 63 grams of fat and more than 900 calories. Clothes have ballooned as well: Kickwear makes women's jeans with 40-inch-diameter legs. The standard for TV sets used to be 19 inches; now it's 32 inches. Hulking SUVs have replaced tiny sports cars as the status vehicle of the new millennium. One consumer psychologist theorizes that consuming big things is reassuring: "Large things compensate for our vulnerability," she says. "It gives us insulation, the feeling that we're less likely to die."[83] What's up with our fascination with bigness? Is this a uniquely American preference? Do you believe that "bigger is better"? Is this a sound marketing strategy?

NOTES

1. "Going Organic," *Prepared Foods* (August 2002): 18; Cathy Sivak, "Purposeful Parmalat: Part 1 of 2," *Dairy Field* 182, no. 9 (September 1999): 1; "North Brunswick, NJ-Based Food Company Signs Deal with Online Grocer," *Home News Tribune* (March 21, 2000).
2. Rick Vecchio, "'Reality TV' Peru Style: Trashy Shows Entertain, Distract During Election Year," *Opelika-Auburn News* (March 15, 2000): 15A.
3. Elizabeth C. Hirschman and Morris B. Holbrook, "Hedonic Consumption: Emerging Concepts, Methods, and Propositions," *Journal of Marketing* 46 (Summer 1982): 92–101.
4. Glenn Collins, "Owens-Corning's Blurred Identity" *New York Times* (August 19, 1994): D4.
5. Gabriel Kahn, "Philips Blitzes Asian Market as It Strives to Become Hip," *Wall Street Journal Interactive Edition* (August 1, 2002).
6. Amitava Chattopadhyay, Gerald J. Gorn, and Peter R. Darke, "Roses are Red and Violets are Blue—Everywhere? Cultural Universals and Differences in Color Preference Among Consumers and Marketing Managers" (unpublished manuscript, University of British Columbia, Fall 1999); Joseph Bellizzi and Robert E. Hite, "Environmental Color, Consumer Feelings, and Purchase Likelihood," *Psychology & Marketing* 9 (1992): 347–63; Ayn E. Crowley, "The Two-Dimensional Impact of Color on Shopping," *Marketing Letters* 4 (January 1993); Gerald J. Gorn, Amitava Chattopadhyay, and Tracey Yi, "Effects of Color as an Executional Cue in an Ad: It's in the Shade," (unpublished manuscript, University of British Columbia, 1994).
7. Adam Bryant, "Plastic Surgery at AmEx," *Newsweek* (October 4, 1999): 55.
8. Mark G. Frank and Thomas Gilovich, "The Dark Side of Self and Social Perception: Black Uniforms and Aggression in Professional Sports," *Journal of Personality and Social Psychology* 54 (1988): 74–85.
9. Dianna Marder, "Food Coloring, Companies Market a Rainbow of Condiments to Kids," *Montgomery Advertiser* (January 16, 2002): C1.
10. Pamela Paul, "Color by Numbers," *American Demographics* (February 2002): 31–36.
11. Paulette Thomas, "Cosmetics Makers Offer World's Women an All-American Look with Local Twists," *Wall Street Journal* (May 8, 1995): B1.
12. Mike Golding and Julie White, *Pantone Color Resource Kit* (New York: Hayden Publishing, 1997); Caroline Lego, *Effective Web Site Design: A Marketing Strategy for Small Liberal Arts Colleges* (unpublished honors thesis, Coe College, 1998); T. Long, "Human Factors Principles for the Design of Computer Colour Graphics Display," *British Telecom Technology Journal* 2 (1994): 5–14; Morton Walker, *The Power of Color* (Garden City, NY: Avery Publishing Group, 1991).
13. "Ny Emballage og Nyt Navn Fordoblede Salget," *Markedsforing* 12 (1992): 24. Adapted from Michael R. Solomon, Gary Bamossy, and Soren Askegaard, *Consumer Behavior: A European Perspective*, 2nd ed. (London: Pearson Education, 2001).
14. Meg Rosen and Frank Alpert, "Protecting Your Business Image: The Supreme Court Rules on Trade Dress," *Journal of Consumer Marketing* 11 (1994): 50–55.
15. Deborah J. Mitchell, Barbara E. Kahn, and Susan C. Knasko, "There's Something in the Air: Effects of Congruent or Incongruent Ambient Odor on Consumer Decision-making," *Journal of Consumer Research* 22 (September 1995): 229–38; for a review of olfactory cues in store environments, see also Eric R. Spangenberg, Ayn E. Crowley, and Pamela W. Henderson, "Improving the Store Environment: Do Olfactory Cues Affect Evaluations and Behaviors?" *Journal of Marketing* 60 (April 1996): 67–80.
16. Pam Scholder Ellen and Paula Fitzgerald Bone, "Does It Matter if It Smells? Olfactory Stimuli as Advertising Executional Cues," *Journal of Advertising* 27 (Winter 1998): 29–40.
17. Jack Hitt, "Does the Smell of Coffee Brewing Remind You of Your Mother?" *New York Times Magazine* (May 7, 2000).
18. Maxine Wilkie, "Scent of a Market," *American Demographics* (August 1995): 40–49.
19. Nicholas Wade, "Scent of a Man is Linked to a Woman's Selection," *New York Times on the Web* (January 22, 2002).
20. Hae Won Choi, "Korean Men Seek Fashion Scents and Lavender Suits Them Just Fine," *Wall Street Journal Interactive Edition* (February 15, 1999); Susan Oh, "Scent Wear," *Maclean's* 113 (January 10, 2000): 12.
21. "A Smell That's Right on the Nose," *Newsweek* (May 31, 1999): 6.
22. Jack Neff, "Product Scents Hide Absence Of True Innovation," *Advertising Age* (February 21, 2000): 22.
23. Erin White, "The Latest Idea from Britain: Outdoor Ads That Make Scents," *Wall Street Journal Interactive Edition* (October 9, 2002).
24. Andruss Lyon Paula, " Paula Lyon Andruss 'Smell Vision' Wafts Fresh Air into Canadian Kids' Network," *Marketing News* (April 9, 2001): 4.

25. Gail Tom, "Marketing with Music," *Journal of Consumer Marketing* 7 (Spring 1990): 49–53; J. Vail, "Music as a Marketing Tool," *Advertising Age* (November 4, 1985): 24.

26. Jamie Reno and N'Gai, Croal "Hearing is Believing," *Newsweek* (August 5, 2002): 44–46.

27. Otto Friedrich, "Trapped in a Musical Elevator," *Time* (December 10, 1984): 3.

28. Jacob Hornik, "Tactile Stimulation and Consumer Response," *Journal of Consumer Research* 19 (December 1992): 449–58.

29. Sarah Ellison and Erin White, "'Sensory' Marketers Say the Way to Reach Shoppers Is the Nose," *Advertising* (November 24, 2000): 1–3.

30. Material adapted from a presentation by Glenn H. Mazur, QFD Institute, 2002.

31. "Touch Looms Large as a Sense That Drives Sales," *BrandPackaging* (May–June 1999): 39–40.

32. Miller Scott, "Acoustics Are the New Frontier in Designing Luxury Automobiles," *Marketplace* (January 24, 2002): 1–2.

33. Jack Neff, "Crest Spinoff Targets Women," *Advertising Age* (June 3, 2002): 1.

34. John Tagliabue, "Sniffing and Tasting with Metal and Wire," *New York Times Online* (February 17, 2002).

35. Becky Gaylord, "Bland Food Isn't So Bad—It Hurts Just to Think About This Stuff," *Wall Street Journal* (April 21, 1995): B1.

36. Dan Morse, "From Tabasco to Insane: When You're Hot, It May Not Be Enough," *Wall Street Journal Interactive Edition* (May 15, 2000).

37. Yumiko Ono, "Flat, Watery Drinks Are All the Rage as Japan Embraces New Taste Sensation," *Wall Street Journal Interactive Edition* (August 13, 1999).

38. "$10 Sure Thing," *Time* (August 4, 1980): 51.

39. For a recent study that did find some evidence that unconscious processing of subliminal embeds affected both upbeat and negative feelings in response to ads, see Andrew B. Aylesworth, Ronald C. Goodstein, and Ajay Kalra, "Effect of Archetypal Embeds on Feelings: An Indirect Route to Affecting Attitudes?" *Journal of Advertising* 28 (Fall 1999): 73–81.

40. Michael Lev, "No Hidden Meaning Here: Survey Sees Subliminal Ads," *New York Times* (May 3, 1991): D7.

41. Aylesworth, Goodstein, and Kalra, "Effect of Archetypal Embeds on Feelings: An Indirect Route to Affecting Attitudes?", 73–81.

42. Bruce Orwall, "Disney Recalls *The Rescuers* Video Containing Images of Topless Woman," *Wall Street Journal Interactive Edition* (January 11, 1999).

43. Philip M. Merikle, "Subliminal Auditory Messages: An Evaluation," *Psychology & Marketing* 5, no. 4 (1988): 355–72.

44. Timothy E. Moore, "The Case Against Subliminal Manipulation," *Psychology & Marketing* 5 (Winter 1988): 297–316.

45. Sid C. Dudley, "Subliminal Advertising: What Is the Controversy About?" *Akron Business and Economic Review* 18 (Summer 1987): 6–18; "Subliminal Messages: Subtle Crime Stoppers," *Chain Store Age Executive* 2 (July 1987): 85; "Mind Benders," *Money* (September 1978): 24.

46. Moore, "The Case Against Subliminal Manipulation," 297–316.

47. Joel Saegert, "Why Marketing Should Quit Giving Subliminal Advertising the Benefit of the Doubt," *Psychology & Marketing* 4 (Summer 1987): 107–20; see also Dennis L. Rosen and Surendra N. Singh, "An Investigation of Subliminal Embed Effect on Multiple Measures of Advertising Effectiveness," *Psychology & Marketing* 9 (March–April 1992): 157–73; for a more recent review, see Kathryn T. Theus, "Subliminal Advertising and the Psychology of Processing Unconscious Stimuli: A Review of Research," *Psychology & Marketing* (May–June 1994): 271–90.

48. James B. Twitchell, *Adcult USA: The Triumph of Advertising in American Culture* (New York: Columbia University Press, 1996).

49. Joe Flint, "TV Networks Are 'Cluttering' Shows with a Record Number of Commercials," *Wall Street Journal Interactive Edition* (March 2, 2000).

50. David Lewis and Darren Bridger, *The Soul of the New Consumer: Authenticity —What We Buy and Why in the New Economy* (London: Nicholas Brealey Publishing, 2000).

51. Gene Koprowsky, "Eyeball to Eyeball," *Critical Mass* (Fall 1999): 32.

52. John Browning and Spencer Reiss, "Encyclopedia of the New Economy, Part I," *Wired* (March 1998): 105; "Raking It in on the Web," *Trend Letter* (March 2, 2000): 6.

53. "Court Orders Bagpipes for Noise Violations," *Montgomery Advertiser* (March 6, 1999): 1A.

54. Verne Gay, "Best Use of Out-of-Home: Starcom Worldwide," *Adweek* 41, No. 25 (June 19, 2000): M6–M10.

55. Erik Gruenwedel, "Street Fighters," *Adweek Midwest Edition* (August 8, 2000): 36.

56. David B. Caruso, *Marketing News* (November 5, 2001): 15

57. Lucy Howard, "Trying to Fool a Feline," *Newsweek* (February 8, 1999): 8.

58. Roger Barton, *Advertising Media* (New York: McGraw-Hill, 1964).

59. Suzanne Oliver, "New Personality," *Forbes* (August 15, 1994): 114.

60. Adam Finn, "Print Ad Recognition Readership Scores: An Information Processing Perspective," *Journal of Marketing Research* 25 (May 1988): 168–77.

61. Gerald L. Lohse, "Consumer Eye Movement Patterns on Yellow Pages Advertising," *Journal of Advertising* 26 (Spring 1997): 61–73.

62. Michael R. Solomon and Basil G. Englis "Reality Engineering: Blurring the Boundaries Between Marketing and Popular Culture," *Journal of Current Issues and Research in Advertising* 16, no. 2 (Fall 1994): 1–18; Michael McCarthy, "Ads Are Here, There, Everywhere: Agencies Seek Creative Ways to Expand Product Placement," *USA Today* (June 19, 2001): 1B.

63. Erin White and David Pringle, "New Ads for Vanilla Coke Reward Curiosity in Europe," *Wall Street Journal Interactive Edition* (October 30, 2002).

64. Tim Davis, "Taste Tests: Are the Blind Leading the Blind?" *Beverage World* (April 1987): 44.

65. Robert M. McMath, "Image Counts," *American Demographics* (May 1998): 64.

66. Anthony Ramirez, "Lessons in the Cracker Market: Nabisco Saved New Graham Snack," *New York Times* (July 5, 1990): D1.

67. Albert H. Hastorf and Hadley Cantril, "They Saw a Game: A Case Study," *Journal of Abnormal and Social Psychology* 49 (1954): 129–34; see also Roberto Friedmann and Mary R. Zimmer, "The Role of Psychological Meaning in Advertising," *Journal of Advertising* 17 (1988): 31–40.

68. Gannett News Service, "Grandmother Packs Lunch with 'Punch'," *Montgomery Advertiser* (March 28, 1996): 2A.

69. "Brew Ha Ha," *Newsweek* (May 25, 1998): 8.

70. Robert M. McMath, "Chock Full of (Pea)nuts," *American Demographics* (April 1997): 60.

71. See David Mick, "Consumer Research and Semiotics: Exploring the Morphology of Signs, Symbols, and Significance," *Journal of Consumer Research* 13 (September 1986): 196–213.

72. Teresa J. Domzal and Jerome B. Kernan, "Reading Advertising: The What and How of Product Meaning," *Journal of Consumer Marketing* 9 (Summer 1992): 48–64.

73. Arthur Asa Berger, *Signs in Contemporary Culture: An Introduction to Semiotics* (New York: Longman, 1984); David Mick, "Consumer Research and Semiotics: Exploring the Morphology of Signs, Symbols, and Significance," 196–213; Charles Sanders Peirce, in Charles Hartshorne, Paul Weiss, and Arthur W. Burks, eds., *Collected Papers* (Cambridge, MA: Harvard University Press, 1931–58).

74. Gabriel Kahn, "Chinese Characters Are Gaining New Meaning as Corporate Logos," *Wall Street Journal Interactive Edition* (July 18, 2002).

75. Jean Baudrillard, *Simulations* (New York: Semiotext(e), 1983); A. Fuat Firat and Alladi Venkatesh, "The Making of Postmodern Consumption," in Russell Belk and Nikhilesh Dholakia, eds., *Consumption and Marketing: Macro Dimensions* (Boston: PWS-Kent, 1993); A. Fuat Firat, "The Consumer in Postmodernity," in Rebecca H. Holman and Michael R. Solomon, eds., *Advances in Consumer Research* 18 (Provo, UT: Association for Consumer Research, 1991): 70–76.

76. Ernest Beck, "A Minefield in Maienfeld: 'Heidiland' Is Taking Over," *Wall Street Journal Interactive Edition* (October 2, 1997).

77. Stuart Elliott, "Advertising: A Music Retailer Whistles a New Marketing Tune to Get Heard Above the Cacophony of Competitors," *New York Times* (July 2, 1996): D7; Personal communication, GRW Advertising, April 1997.

78. See Tim Davis, "Taste Tests: Are the Blind Leading the Blind?", 43–44.

79. Betsy McKay, "Pepsi to Revive a Cola-War Barb: The Decades-Old Blind Taste Test," *Wall Street Journal Interactive Edition* (March 21, 2000).

80. Adapted from Michael R. Solomon and Elnora W. Stuart, *Marketing: Real People, Real Choices*, 2nd ed. (Upper Saddle River, NJ: Prentice Hall, 2000).

81. Geoffrey A. Fowler, "Cult Film, 1999's *Office Space*, Transforms Swingline Stapler," *Wall Street Journal Interactive Edition* (July 2, 2002).

82. William Echikson, "Aiming at High and Low Markets," *Fortune* (March 22, 1993): 89.

83. Quoted in *Atlanta Journal-Constitution*, accessed via SS Newslink, May 2, 1998.

Learning and Memory

ah, Sunday morning! The sun is shining, the birds are singing, and Joe is feeling groovy! He puts on his vintage Levi's 501 jeans (circa 1968) and his Woodstock T-shirt (the "real" Woodstock, not that fake abomination they put on back in the 1990s, thank you) and saunters down to the kitchen. Joe smiles in anticipation of his morning plans. First, he's going to treat himself to a precious bowl of Quisp. Rare boxes of the cereal that was first created in 1965 sell for $10 at his grocery store in Buffalo, but after discovering that he can buy it online at netgrocer.com for $3.49 he's a happy camper. What a beautiful day to "commune" with Quisp, the propeller-headed alien character he's loved over the years. Then, perhaps a little online browsing at hippy.com, where he can check out some famous hippy quotes, visit the hippy chat room, and locate the next festival in the area on the site's Hip Planet Event Guide. Joe's got a "tune in, turn on, and drop out" vacation in mind as he eagerly awaits his trip to the Hemp World Resort in Hawaii, where according to the Web site (HempWorldResorts.com/pstindex.html), guests can "sleep, bathe, and clothe in hemp. Have a hemp oil massage, then a hemp dish with hemp beer or hemp wine and hemp ice-cream or hemp cheesecake for dessert."[1] Joe cranks up the Lava Lamp, throws a Jefferson Airplane record on the turntable (ah, the sublime joys of vinyl), sits back on his Barcalounger, and lets the memories rush in.

■ THE LEARNING PROCESS

It's the twenty-first century, but Joe's never really left the 1960s. Of course, now he's got the money to surround himself with vintage stuff from that era. Joe's a stickler for authenticity, and he is even willing to pay a premium for everyday items like cereal. Again, he's not alone. Quaker's quirky Quisp corn cereal (say that ten times fast) was on its last legs and selling only about 92,000 boxes a year, but everything changed when the manufacturer created a link between Quisp's Web site at Quisp.com and netgrocer.com. Almost overnight, the brand became the number-one seller on the site, even beating out favorites such as Cheerios and Frosted Flakes. The Quaker brand manager who saved the cereal explained, "It's the cereal I

Our tastes are formed as a result of a learning process, sometimes with painful results.

BLACK SOCKS WITH

BERMUDA SHORTS

IS AN ACQUIRED TASTE.

please, teach accessorizing skills early.

gold bug

ate when I was a kid and people around here want to keep it going."[2] Quisp memorabilia have joined the other vintage products that are hot at auction sites where Quisp decoder rings can go for more than $600. The craze for vintage American products is even stronger in Japan, where "previously worn" pairs of Adidas, Nike, and Converse sneakers sell for as much as $1,000.[3]

Many marketers realize that long-standing, learned connections between products and memories are a potent way to build and keep brand loyalty. Some companies are bringing their old trademark characters out of retirement, including the Campbell's Soup Kids, the Pillsbury Doughboy, Betty Crocker, and Planters' Mr. Peanut.[4] Several familiar faces returned in major advertising campaigns recently, including the Jolly Green Giant (born in 1925), Charlie the Tuna (who first appeared in 1961), and even Charmin's Mr. Whipple, who was brought out of retirement in 1999.[5] In this chapter, we'll explore how learned associations among feelings, events, and products—and the memories they evoke—are an important aspect of consumer behavior.

Learning is a relatively permanent change in behavior caused by experience. The learner need not have the experience directly; we can also learn by observing events that affect others.[6] We learn even when we are not trying: Consumers recognize many brand names and can hum many product jingles, for example, even for products they themselves do not use. This casual, unintentional acquisition of knowledge is known as *incidental learning*.

Learning is an ongoing process. Our knowledge about the world is being revised constantly as we are exposed to new stimuli and receive ongoing feedback that allows us to modify our behavior when we find ourselves in similar situations at a later time. The concept of learning covers a lot of ground, ranging from a consumer's simple association between a stimulus such as a product logo (e.g., Coca-Cola) and a response (e.g., "refreshing soft drink") to a complex series of cognitive activities (e.g., writing an essay on learning for a consumer behavior exam). Psychologists who study learning have advanced several theories to explain the learning process. These theories range from those focusing on simple stimulus–response connections (behavioral theories) to perspectives that regard consumers as complex-problem solvers who learn abstract rules and concepts by observing others (cognitive theories). Understanding these theories is important to marketers as well, because basic learning principles are at the heart of many consumer purchase decisions.

■ BEHAVIORAL LEARNING THEORIES

Behavioral learning theories assume that learning takes place as the result of responses to external events. Psychologists who subscribe to this viewpoint do not focus on internal thought processes. Instead, they approach the mind as a "black box" and emphasize the observable aspects of behavior, as depicted in Figure 3.1. The observable aspects consist of things that go into the box (the stimuli, or events perceived from the outside world) and things that come out of the box (the responses, or reactions to these stimuli).

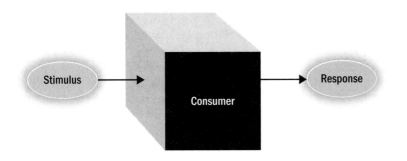

■ FIGURE 3.1

THE CONSUMER AS A "BLACK BOX": A BEHAVIORIST PERSPECTIVE ON LEARNING

The Tangled Web

Learning to love cybersex: About one-third of all visits to Web sites are to sexually oriented pages. This easy availability of formerly forbidden material has spawned a new disorder: cybersex addiction. According to one physician, "Sex on the Net is like heroin. It grabs them and takes over their lives." For some sex surfers, though, the problem is even worse. Therapists report patients who develop a conditioned response to the computer and become aroused even before turning it on.[9]

This view is represented by two major approaches to learning: classical conditioning and instrumental conditioning. According to this perspective, people's experiences are shaped by the feedback they receive as they go through life. Similarly, consumers respond to brand names, scents, jingles, and other marketing stimuli based on the learned connections they have formed over time. People also learn that actions they take result in rewards and punishments, and this feedback influences the way they will respond in similar situations in the future. Consumers who receive compliments on a product choice will be more likely to buy that brand again, but those who get food poisoning at a new restaurant will not be likely to patronize it in the future.

Classical Conditioning

Classical conditioning occurs when a stimulus that elicits a response is paired with another stimulus that initially does not elicit a response on its own. Over time, this second stimulus causes a similar response because it is associated with the first stimulus. Ivan Pavlov, a Russian physiologist doing research on digestion in animals, first demonstrated this phenomenon in dogs.

Pavlov induced classically conditioned learning by pairing a neutral stimulus (a bell) with a stimulus known to cause a salivation response in dogs (he squirted dried meat powder into their mouths). The powder was an **unconditioned stimulus (UCS)** because it was naturally capable of causing the response. Over time, the bell became a **conditioned stimulus (CS)**; it did not initially cause salivation, but the dogs learned to associate the bell with the meat powder and began to salivate at the sound of the bell only. The drooling of these canine consumers because of a sound, now linked to feeding time, was a conditioned response (CR).

This basic form of classical conditioning demonstrated by Pavlov primarily applies to responses controlled by the autonomic (e.g., salivation) and nervous (e.g., eye blink) systems. That is, it focuses on visual and olfactory cues that induce hunger, thirst, sexual arousal, and other basic drives. When these cues are consistently paired with conditioned stimuli such as brand names, consumers may learn to feel hungry, thirsty, or aroused when later exposed to the brand cues.

Classical conditioning can have similar effects for more complex reactions, too. Even a credit card becomes a conditioned cue that triggers greater spending, especially because it is a stimulus present only in situations in which consumers are spending money. People learn they can make larger purchases with credit cards, and they also have been found to leave larger tips than when paying by cash.[7] Small wonder that American Express reminds us, "Don't leave home without it."

Repetition

Conditioning effects are more likely to occur after the conditioned (CS) and unconditioned (UCS) stimuli have been paired a number of times.[8] Repeated exposures increase the strength of stimulus–response associations and prevent the decay of these associations in memory.

Many classic advertising campaigns consist of product slogans that have been repeated so many times that they are etched in consumers' minds. Conditioning will not occur or will take longer if the CS is only occasionally paired with the UCS. One result of this lack of association may be extinction, which occurs when the effects of prior conditioning are reduced and finally disappear. This can occur, for example, when a product is overexposed in the marketplace so that its original allure is lost. The Izod Lacoste polo shirt, with its distinctive crocodile crest, is a good example of this effect—when the once-exclusive crocodile started to appear on baby clothes and many other items, it lost its cachet and was successfully challenged as a symbol of casual elegance by other contenders, such as the Ralph Lauren polo player.

American Airlines uses an obvious reference to classical conditioning effects.

Stimulus Generalization

Stimulus generalization refers to the tendency of stimuli similar to a CS to evoke similar, conditioned responses. For example, Pavlov noticed in subsequent studies that his dogs would sometimes salivate when they heard noises that only resembled a bell, such as keys jangling.

People also react to other, similar stimuli in much the same way they responded to the original stimulus. A drugstore's bottle of private brand mouthwash deliberately packaged to resemble Listerine mouthwash may evoke a similar response among consumers, who assume that this "me-too" product shares other characteristics of the original. Indeed, consumers in one study on shampoo brands tended to rate those with similar packages as similar in quality and performance as well.[10] This "piggybacking" strategy can cut both ways: When the quality of the me-too product turns out to be lower than that of the original brand, consumers may exhibit even more positive feelings toward the original. However, if the quality of the two competitors is perceived to be about equal, consumers may conclude the price premium they are paying for the original is not worth it.[11]

Many classic advertising campaigns consist of product slogans that have been repeated so many times that they are etched in consumers' minds. The ad shown here brags about the high awareness of the Chiquita banana jingle ("I'm Chiquita banana, and I'm here to say . . .").

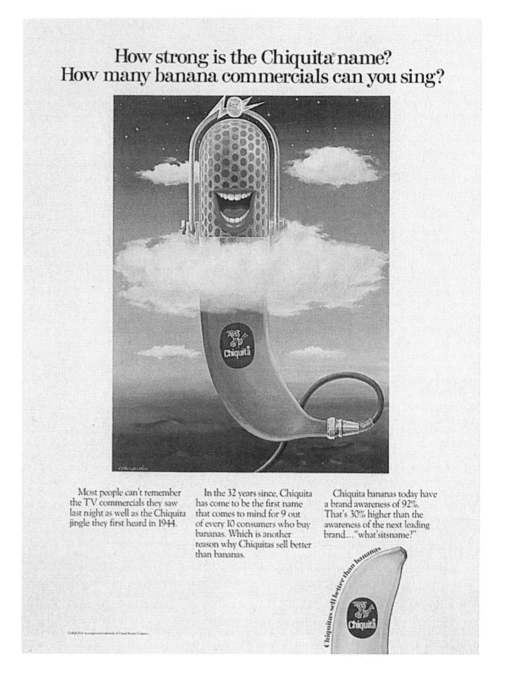

In a recent twist on this principle, some companies are using a strategy called **masked branding**, which deliberately hides a product's true origin. For example, giant corporation General Motors distanced itself from its Saturn brand and positioned the carmaker as a small-town business run by ordinary people, and Levi Strauss markets its Red Tab line to appeal to young consumers who don't want to be associated with an "old" brand. Blue Moon beers are positioned as sophisticated and the label lists the manufacturer as the Blue Moon Brewing Co., although in reality the beer is made by Coors; while Miller Brewing Co. created a dummy company called Plank Road Brewery when it launched its Icehouse and Red Dog beers.[12]

Stimulus Discrimination

Stimulus discrimination occurs when a UCS does not follow a stimulus similar to a CS. When this happens, reactions are weakened and will soon disappear. Part of the learning process involves making a response to some stimuli but not to other, similar stimuli. Manufacturers of well-established brands commonly urge consumers not to buy "cheap imitations" because the results will not be what they expect.

Marketing Applications of Behavioral Learning Principles

Many marketing strategies focus on the establishment of associations between stimuli and responses. Behavioral learning principles apply to many consumer phenomena, ranging from the creation of a distinctive brand image to the perceived linkage between a product and an underlying need.

The transfer of meaning from an unconditioned stimulus to a conditioned stimulus explains why "made-up" brand names like Marlboro, Coca-Cola, or IBM can exert such powerful effects on consumers. The association between the Marlboro Man and the cigarette is so strong that in some cases the company no

Rewarding consumers with frequent flyer miles is an effective way to reinforce them and build brand loyalty.

It's natural to want to be rewarded.

Loyalty should be rewarded. So if you're a frequent flyer member of one of our airlines, you can earn and redeem miles on the other seven. After all, **one**world™ revolves around you.

Marketing Opportunity

Marketing Opportunity

The choice of a great brand name is so important that companies often hire specialists called naming consultants to come up with a winning selection. These experts often try to find *semantic associations* that click because they evoke some desirable connection. That strategy brought us names like Qualcomm ("quality" and "communications"), Verizon ("horizon," as in forward-looking), and Intel ("intelligent" and "electronics"). The name "Viagra" rhymes with the famous waterfall Niagara. People associate water with both sexuality and life and Niagara Falls is a honeymoon Mecca. Philip Morris Companies is renaming itself Altria Group, Inc., to convey its expansion beyond cigarettes into packaged foods and brewing. This word means high which is a controversial choice; one brand consultant comments that "I'm not sure 'high' is right for a company with many mood-altering products in its brand portfolio."[21]

These combinations are getting harder to find, so some consultants are trying to appeal to consumers' more basic instincts by focusing on linkages between the raw sounds of vowels and consonants (called *phonemes*) and emotional responses. Studies on sound symbolism show that respondents who speak different languages associate the same sounds with such emotion-laden qualities as sad and insecure, alive and daring. To get at these associations, researchers usually give subjects pairs of nonsense names that differ in only a single phoneme, such as Paressa and Taressa, and ask which sounds faster, more daring, nicer, and so on. They've found that sounds that come to a full stop (p, b, t, d) connote slowness, while f, v, s, and z are fast. Prozac and Amazon convey a sense of speed (of recovery or of delivery). When naming consultants were asked to label a new handheld PDA, they first thought of Strawberry because the little keyboard buttons resembled seeds. They liked the "berry" part of the name because they knew that people associated the letter "b" with reliability and a berry communicated smallness compared to other PDAs. But, a linguist pointed out that "straw" is a slow syllable and the product needed to have a fast connotation. Voila! The Blackberry PDA was born.[22]

longer even bothers to include the brand name in its ads. When nonsense syllables (meaningless sets of letters) are paired with such evaluative words as beauty or success, the meaning is transferred to the fake words. This change in the symbolic significance of initially meaningless words shows that fairly simple associations can condition even complex meanings.[13] This study found that attitudes formed through classical conditioning are enduring.[14] These associations are crucial to many marketing strategies that rely on the creation and perpetuation of **brand equity**, in which a brand has strong positive associations in a consumer's memory and commands a lot of loyalty as a result.[15]

Applications of Repetition

One advertising researcher argued that anything more than three exposures to a marketing communication is wasted. The first exposure creates awareness of the product, the second demonstrates its relevance to the consumer, and the third serves as a reminder of the product's benefits.[16] However, even this bare-bones approach implies that repetition is needed to ensure that the consumer is actually exposed to (and processes) the message at least three times. As we saw in Chapter 2, this exposure is by no means guaranteed because people tend to tune out or distort many marketing communications. Marketers attempting to condition an association must ensure that the consumers they have targeted will be exposed to the stimulus a sufficient number of times to make it "stick."

On the other hand, it is possible to have too much of a good thing. Consumers can become so used to hearing or seeing a marketing stimulus that they no longer pay attention to it. Varying the way in which the basic message is presented can alleviate this problem, known as advertising wearout. For example, the tax preparation firm of H&R Block is famous for its long-standing "Another of the seventeen reasons to use H&R Block" campaign.

Applications of Conditioned Product Associations

Advertisements often pair a product with a positive stimulus to create a desirable association. Various aspects of a marketing message, such as music, humor, or imagery, can affect conditioning. In one study, for example, subjects who viewed a slide of pens paired with either pleasant or unpleasant music were more likely to later select the pen that appeared with pleasant music.[17]

The order in which the conditioned stimulus and the unconditioned stimulus are presented can affect the likelihood that learning will occur. Generally speaking, the conditioned stimulus should be presented prior to the unconditioned stimulus. The technique of backward conditioning, such as playing a jingle (the UCS) and then showing a soft drink (the CS) generally is not effective.[18] Because sequential presentation is desirable for conditioning to occur, classical conditioning is not as effective in static situations, such as in magazine ads, in which (in contrast to TV or radio) the marketer cannot control the order in which the CS and the UCS are perceived.

Just as product associations can be formed, they can be extinguished. Because of the danger of extinction, a classical conditioning strategy may not be as effective for products that are frequently encountered, as there is no guarantee the CS will accompany them. A bottle of Pepsi paired with the refreshing sound of a carbonated beverage being poured over ice may seem like a good application of conditioning. Unfortunately, the product would also be seen in many other contexts in which this sound was absent, reducing the effectiveness of a conditioning strategy.

By the same reasoning, a novel tune should be chosen over a popular one to pair with a product, as the popular song might also be heard in many situations in which the product is not present.[19] Music videos in particular may serve as effective UCSs because they often have an emotional impact on viewers, and this effect may transfer to ads accompanying the video.[20]

Applications of Stimulus Generalization

The process of stimulus generalization is often central to branding and packaging decisions that attempt to capitalize on consumers' positive associations with an existing brand or company name. The marketing value of an admired stimulus is clearly demonstrated at universities with winning sports teams, where loyal fans snap up merchandise, from clothing to bathroom accessories, emblazoned with the school's name. This business did not even exist 20 years ago when schools were reluctant to commercialize their images. Texas A&M was one of the first schools that even bothered to file for trademark protection, and that was only after someone put the Aggie logo on a line of handguns. Today, it's a different story. Many college administrators crave the revenue they receive from sweatshirts, drink coasters, and even toilet seats emblazoned with school logos. Strategies based on stimulus generalization include the following:

- *Family branding:* A variety of products capitalize on the reputation of a company name. Companies such as Campbell's, Heinz, and General Electric rely on their positive corporate images to sell different product lines.
- *Product line extensions:* Related products are added to an established brand. Dole, which is associated with fruit, introduced refrigerated juices and juice bars, whereas Sun Maid went from raisins to raisin bread. Other extensions include Woolite rug cleaner, Cracker Jack gourmet popping corn, and Ivory shampoo. However, there is a down side: An extension has the potential to weaken the parent brand, as the Carnation Company discovered. The company cancelled plans for "Lady Friskies," a contraceptive dog food, after tests indicated it would reduce sales of regular Friskies.[23]
- *Licensing:* Well-known names are "rented" by others. This strategy is increasing in popularity as marketers try to link their products and services with well-established figures. Even New York City firefighters and police are getting into the act. Following the tragedy of September 11, 2001, demand peaked for police and fire fighter merchandise, and unauthorized dealers cashed in. Not anymore. Now, the New York Fire Department Fire Safety Education Fund is benefiting from such licensed products as Billy Blazes Firefighter dolls by Fisher-Price, bottled water, and fire department computer software games by Activision. Not to be outdone, the New York City Police Foundation has licensed toys, stuffed animals, caps and T-shirts, and collectibles like Code 3 miniature helicopters.[24]
- *Look-alike packaging:* Distinctive packaging designs create strong associations with a particular brand. As noted earlier, makers of generic or private label brands who wish to communicate a quality image by putting their products in very similar packages often exploit this linkage.[25] Imitating the look of an existing successful brand is common in today's crowded marketplace. One study found that a negative experience with an imitator brand increased evaluations of the original brand. A positive experience with the imitator had the opposite effect of decreasing evaluations of the original brand.[26]

Applications of Stimulus Discrimination

An emphasis on communicating a product's distinctive attributes vis-à-vis its competitors is an important aspect of positioning, where consumers learn to differentiate a brand from its competitors (see Chapter 2). This is not always an easy task, especially in product categories in which the brand names of many of the alternatives look and sound alike.

Companies with a well-established brand image try to encourage stimulus discrimination by promoting the unique attributes of their brand—hence the constant reminders for American Express Traveler's Checks: "Ask for them by name." On the other hand, a brand name that is used so widely that it is no longer distinctive

Marketing Pitfall

Beware of the "curse" of paying to name a sports venue for a corporate sponsor:

- The National Car Rental Center (Sunrise, FL): Parent company ANC Rental Corp. filed for bankruptcy.
- Enron Field (Houston): After the Enron scandal it was renamed Minute Maid Park.
- Adelphia Coliseum (Nashville): The company's founder was accused of financial improprieties.
- MCI Center (Washington): MCI's parent WorldCom filed for bankruptcy and top executives were arrested.[27]

Net Profit

Marketing researchers frequently face the problem of consumers' reluctance to disclose personal information in surveys. Can online techniques help to overcome this barrier? Perhaps, if automated questioning can be made to resemble human interactions. One study found that when a computer appears to possess characteristics normally associated with human behavior, such as using everyday language and turn-taking in conversations, consumers respond favorably and form a relationship with the machine. In other words, they use rules they have learned in human interaction to tell them how to have a dialogue with a machine. The research found that consumers are more likely to divulge personal information when the computer divulges information first, and the degree of intimate disclosure gradually escalates. For example, the computer may disclose the fact that there are times when it crashes for no apparent reason and then ask the consumer to reciprocate by disclosing something about the respondent herself. And, those consumers who had engaged in self-disclosure and reciprocity with a computer were likely to evaluate products described online more favorably than those that had not engaged in this interaction. So, go give your computer a nice big hug.[31]

becomes part of the public domain and can be used by competitors, as has been the case for such products as aspirin, cellophane, the yo-yo, and the escalator.

A related problem is when fake products masquerade as the real thing. The International Anti-Counterfeiting Coalition, an industry group established to combat piracy, estimates that trademark counterfeiting robs the United States of $200 billion annually.[28] "Knockoffs" of well-known products are a problem around the world. For example, Converse's Chuck Taylor All Stars are a favorite among Brazilian kids, and only the United States and Japan post higher sales of the athletic shoes. One small problem: Though most wearers don't know it, all of the All Stars sold in Brazil are fakes. The sneakers look genuine, down to the circle with the five-pointed blue star on the high-top model. A local company registered the All Star trademark as its own back in 1979 and has been selling about one million pairs each year since for about one-third of the U.S. price.[29]

Instrumental Conditioning

Instrumental conditioning, also known as operant conditioning, occurs as the individual learns to perform behaviors that produce positive outcomes and to avoid those that yield negative outcomes. This learning process is most closely associated with the psychologist B. F. Skinner, who demonstrated the effects of instrumental conditioning by teaching pigeons and other animals to dance, play Ping-Pong, and perform other activities by systematically rewarding them for desired behaviors.[30]

Whereas responses in classical conditioning are involuntary and fairly simple, those in instrumental conditioning are made deliberately to obtain a goal and may be more complex. The desired behavior may be learned over a period of time, as intermediate actions are rewarded in a process called **shaping**. For example, the owner of a new store may award prizes to shoppers just for coming in, hoping that over time they will continue to drop in and eventually even buy something.

Also, whereas classical conditioning involves the close pairing of two stimuli, instrumental learning occurs as a result of a reward received following the desired behavior. Learning takes place over a period of time, during which other behaviors are attempted and abandoned because they are not reinforced. A good way to remember the difference is to keep in mind that in instrumental learning, the response is performed because it is *instrumental* to gaining a reward or avoiding a punishment. Over time consumers come to associate with people who reward them and to choose products that make them feel good or satisfy some need.

Instrumental conditioning occurs in one of three ways. When the environment provides **positive reinforcement** in the form of a reward, the response is strengthened and appropriate behavior is learned. For example, a woman who gets compliments after wearing Obsession perfume will learn that using this product has the desired effect, and she will be more likely to keep buying the product. **Negative reinforcement** also strengthens responses so that appropriate behavior is learned. A perfume company might run an ad showing a woman sitting home alone on a Saturday night because she did not use its fragrance. The message to be conveyed is that she could have avoided this negative outcome if only she had used the perfume. In contrast to situations in which we learn to do certain things in order to avoid unpleasantness, **punishment** occurs when a response is followed by unpleasant events (such as being ridiculed by friends for wearing an offensive-smelling perfume)—we learn the hard way not to repeat these behaviors.

To help in understanding the differences among these mechanisms, keep in mind that reactions from a person's environment to behavior can be either positive or negative, and that these outcomes or anticipated outcomes can be applied or removed. That is, under conditions of both positive reinforcement and punishment the person receives a reaction after doing something. In contrast, negative reinforcement occurs when a negative outcome is avoided—the removal of something negative is pleasurable and hence is rewarding.

The power of positive reinforcement.

Finally, when a positive outcome is no longer received, **extinction** is likely to occur, and the learned stimulus–response connection will not be maintained (as when a woman no longer receives compliments on her perfume). Thus positive and negative reinforcement strengthen the future linkage between a response and an outcome because of the pleasant experience. This tie is weakened under conditions of both punishment and extinction because of the unpleasant experience. The relationships among these four conditions are easier to understand by referring to Figure 3.2.

An important factor in operant conditioning is the set of rules by which appropriate reinforcements are given for a behavior. The issue of what is the most effective reinforcement schedule to use is important to marketers, because it relates to the amount of effort and resources they must devote to rewarding consumers to condition desired behaviors. Several schedules are possible:

- *Fixed-interval reinforcement:* After a specified time period has passed, the first response that is made brings the reward. Under such conditions, people tend to respond slowly right after being reinforced, but their responses speed up as the time for the next reinforcement looms. For example, consumers may crowd into a store for the last day of its seasonal sale and not reappear until the next one.
- *Variable-interval reinforcement:* The time that must pass before reinforcement is delivered varies around some average. Because the person does not know exactly when to expect the reinforcement, responses must be performed at a consistent rate. This logic is behind retailers' use of so-called secret shoppers, people who periodically test for service quality by posing as a customer at unannounced times. Because store employees never know exactly when to expect a visit, high quality must be maintained constantly "just in case."
- *Fixed-ratio reinforcement:* Reinforcement occurs only after a fixed number of responses. This schedule motivates people to continue performing the same behavior over and over. For example, a consumer might keep buying groceries at the same store in order to earn a prize after collecting 50 register receipts.
- *Variable-ratio reinforcement:* The person is reinforced after a certain number of responses, but he or she does not know how many responses are required. People in such situations tend to respond at very high and steady rates, and this type of behavior is very difficult to extinguish. This reinforcement schedule is responsible for consumers' attraction to slot machines. They learn that if they keep throwing money into the machine, they will eventually win something (if they don't go broke first).

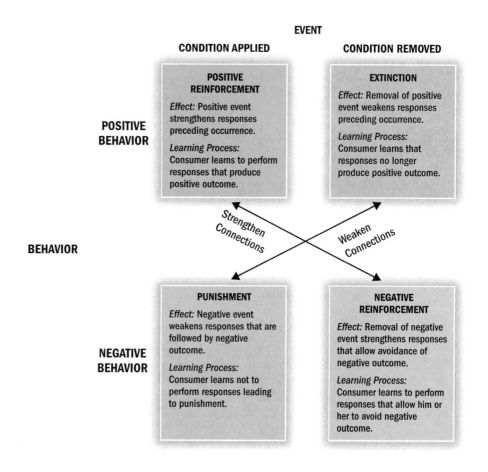

■ **FIGURE 3.2**
TYPES OF REINFORCEMENT

Applications of Instrumental Conditioning Principles

Principles of instrumental conditioning are at work when a consumer is rewarded or punished for a purchase decision. Business people shape behavior by gradually reinforcing consumers for taking appropriate actions. For example, a car dealer might encourage a reluctant buyer to just sit in a floor model, and then suggest a test drive, and then try to close the deal.

Reinforcement of Consumption

Marketers have many ways to reinforce consumers, ranging from a simple thank you after a purchase to substantial rebates and follow-up phone calls. For example, a life insurance company obtained a much higher rate of policy renewal among a group of new customers who received a thank you letter after each payment, compared to a control group that did not receive any reinforcement.[32]

Frequency Marketing

A popular technique known as **frequency marketing** reinforces regular purchasers by giving them prizes with values that increase along with the amount purchased. This instrumental learning strategy was pioneered by the airline industry, which introduced "frequent flyer" programs in the early 1980s to reward loyal customers. The practice has spread to other businesses as well, ranging from video stores to fast-food places. Perhaps the most enthusiastic fan of frequency marketing is David Phillips. He became known as the Pudding Guy because he earned a lifetime of free plane rides after noticing a frequent flyer offer on a chocolate pudding package. Phillips bought enough pudding to win 1.25 million frequent flyer miles from

American Airlines. He donated the pudding to local food banks; in exchange for free pudding, workers agreed to peel off the labels as they dished out the stuff. The final tally: 12,150 cups of pudding.[33] Whipped cream with that?

■ COGNITIVE LEARNING THEORY

In contrast to behavioral theories of learning, **cognitive learning theory** approaches stress the importance of internal mental processes. This perspective views people as problem solvers who actively use information from the world around them to master their environment. Supporters of this view also stress the role of creativity and insight during the learning process.

Is Learning Conscious or Not?

A lot of controversy surrounds the issue of whether or when people are aware of their learning processes. Whereas behavioral learning theorists emphasize the routine, automatic nature of conditioning, proponents of cognitive learning argue that even these simple effects are based on cognitive factors: Expectations are created that a stimulus will be followed by a response (the formation of expectations requires mental activity). According to this school of thought, conditioning occurs because subjects develop conscious hypotheses and then act on them.

On the one hand, there is some evidence supporting the existence of nonconscious procedural knowledge. People apparently do process at least some information in an automatic, passive way, which is a condition that has been termed "mindlessness."[34] When we meet someone new or encounter a new product, for example, we have a tendency to respond to the stimulus in terms of existing categories we have learned, rather than taking the trouble to formulate new ones. In these cases a *trigger feature*, some stimulus that cues us toward a particular pattern, activates a reaction. For example, men in one study rated a car in an ad as superior on a variety of characteristics if a seductive woman (the trigger feature) was present, despite the fact that the men did not believe the woman's presence actually had an influence on their evaluations.[35]

Nonetheless, many modern theorists are beginning to regard some instances of automatic conditioning as cognitive processes, especially where expectations are formed about the linkages between stimuli and responses. Indeed, studies using masking effects, which make it difficult for subjects to learn CS/UCS associations, show substantial reductions in conditioning.[36] An adolescent girl may observe that women on television and in real life seem to be rewarded with compliments and attention when they smell nice and wear alluring clothing. She figures out that the probability of these rewards occurring is greater when she wears perfume, and so she deliberately wears a popular scent to obtain the reward of social acceptance.

Observational Learning

Observational learning occurs when people watch the actions of others and note the reinforcements they receive for their behaviors—learning occurs as a result of vicarious rather than direct experience. This type of learning is a complex process; people store these observations in memory as they accumulate knowledge, perhaps using this information at a later point to guide their own behavior. This process of imitating the behavior of others is called **modeling**. For example, a woman shopping for a new kind of perfume may remember the reactions her friend received on wearing a certain brand several months earlier, and she will base her behavior on her friend's actions. The modeling process is a powerful form of learning, and people's tendencies to imitate others' behaviors can have negative effects.

Of particular concern is the potential of television shows and movies to teach violence to children. Children may be exposed to new methods of aggression by models (e.g., cartoon heroes) in the shows they watch. At some later point, when the child becomes angry, these behaviors will be imitated.

A classic study demonstrates the effect of modeling on children's actions. Kids who watched an adult stomp on, knock down, and otherwise torture a large inflated "Bobo doll" repeated these behaviors when later left alone in a room with the doll; children who did not witness these acts did not.[37] Unfortunately, the relevance of this study to violent TV shows seems quite clear.

Figure 3.3 shows that in order for observational learning in the form of modeling to occur, four conditions must be met:[38]

1 The consumer's attention must be directed to the appropriate model, who for reasons of attractiveness, competence, status, or similarity it is desirable to emulate.
2 The consumer must remember what is said or done by the model.
3 The consumer must convert this information into actions.
4 The consumer must be motivated to perform these actions.

Applications of Cognitive Learning Principles

Consumers' ability to learn vicariously by observing how the behavior of others is reinforced makes the lives of marketers much easier. Because people do not have to be directly reinforced for their actions, marketers do not necessarily have to actually reward or punish them for purchase behaviors (think how expensive or even ethically questionable that might be!). Instead, they can show what happens to desirable models who use or do not use their products, knowing that consumers will often be motivated to imitate these actions at a later time. For example, a perfume commercial might depict a woman surrounded by a throng of admirers who are providing her with positive reinforcement for using the product. Needless to say, this learning process is more practical than providing the same attention to each woman who actually buys the perfume!

Consumers' evaluations of models go beyond simple stimulus–response connections. For example, a celebrity's image elicits more than a simple reflexive response of good or bad.[39] It is a complex combination of many attributes. In general, the degree to which a model will be emulated depends on his or her social attractiveness. Attractiveness can be based on several components, including physical appearance, expertise, or similarity to the evaluator.

■ **FIGURE 3.3** COMPONENTS OF OBSERVATIONAL LEARNING

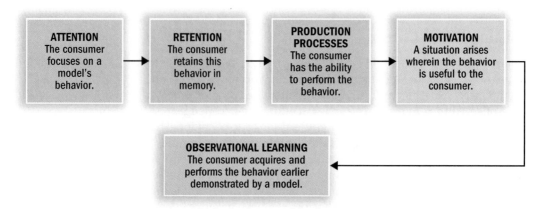

■ THE ROLE OF MEMORY IN LEARNING

Memory involves a process of acquiring information and storing it over time so that it will be available when needed. Contemporary approaches to the study of memory employ an information-processing approach. They assume that the mind is in some ways like a computer: Data are input, processed, and output for later use in revised form. In the **encoding** stage, information is entered in a way the system will recognize. In the **storage** stage, this knowledge is integrated with what is already in memory and "warehoused" until needed. During **retrieval**, the person accesses the desired information.[40] The memory process is summarized in Figure 3.4.

Many of our experiences are locked inside our heads, and they may surface years later if prompted by the right cues. Marketers rely on consumers to retain information they have obtained about products and services, trusting that it will later be applied in situations in which purchase decisions must be made. During the consumer decision-making process, this internal memory is combined with external memory, which includes all of the product details on packages and other marketing stimuli that permit brand alternatives to be identified and evaluated.[41]

The grocery shopping list is a good example of a powerful external memory aid. When consumers use shopping lists, they buy approximately 80 percent of the items on the list. And, the likelihood of a particular list item being purchased is higher if the person who wrote the list also participates in the shopping trip. Researchers also found that the likelihood of purchasing a list item increased with household size and is marginally greater during holiday periods. This means that if marketers can induce a consumer to plan an item in advance of shopping, there is a high probability that item will be purchased. One way to encourage this would be to provide peel-off stickers on packages so that when the consumer notices the supply is low, the label can be peeled off and placed directly onto a shopping list.[42]

Research supports the idea that marketers can distort a consumer's recall of a product experience. What we think we "know" about products can be influenced by advertising messages to which we are exposed after using them. This *postexperience advertising* is more likely to alter actual memories when it is very similar or activates memories about the actual experience. For example, advertising can make a remembered product experience more favorable than it actually was.[43]

Encoding Information for Later Retrieval

The way information is encoded, or mentally programmed, helps to determine how it will be represented in memory. In general, incoming data that are associated with other information already in memory stand a better chance of being retained. For example, brand names that are linked to physical characteristics of a product category (e.g., Coffee-Mate creamer or Sani-Flush toilet bowl cleaner) or that are easy to

Net Profit

Here's a new way to remember your loved ones. FinalThoughts.com offers a place to store e-mail messages online so they can be sent to family and friends after you die. The creator of the site came up with the idea during a turbulent airplane ride. As the plane shook, he realized he hadn't properly said goodbye to people who mattered to him. The site is set up to encourage advanced planning. Each user chooses a "guardian angel" who will notify the site when the time comes so that the appropriate messages can be sent out. The site also includes resource centers with links to articles on coping with loss and forms that can be used to notify survivors of the deceased's final wishes. More than 10,000 customers have signed up; most hope they won't be using the service anytime soon.[44]

■ FIGURE 3.4 THE MEMORY PROCESS

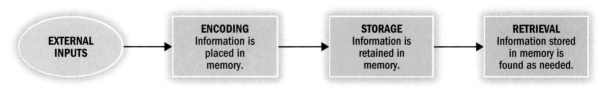

| EXTERNAL INPUTS | → | ENCODING Information is placed in memory. | → | STORAGE Information is retained in memory. | → | RETRIEVAL Information stored in memory is found as needed. |

Rocky Road, a classic candy product, uses a brief narrative to remind consumers of its long-lasting value.

This Brazilian ad illustrates that external memory aids like Post-its can help us to remember many of the details of modern life.

visualize (e.g., Tide detergent or Mercury Cougar cars) tend to be more easily retained in memory than more abstract brand names.[45]

Types of Meaning

A consumer may process a stimulus simply in terms of its **sensory meaning**, such as its color or shape. When this occurs, the meaning may be activated when the person sees a picture of the stimulus. We may experience a sense of familiarity on seeing an ad for a new snack food we have recently tasted, for example. In many cases, though, meanings are encoded at a more abstract level. **Semantic meaning** refers to symbolic associations, such as the idea that rich people drink champagne or that fashionable women have navel piercings.

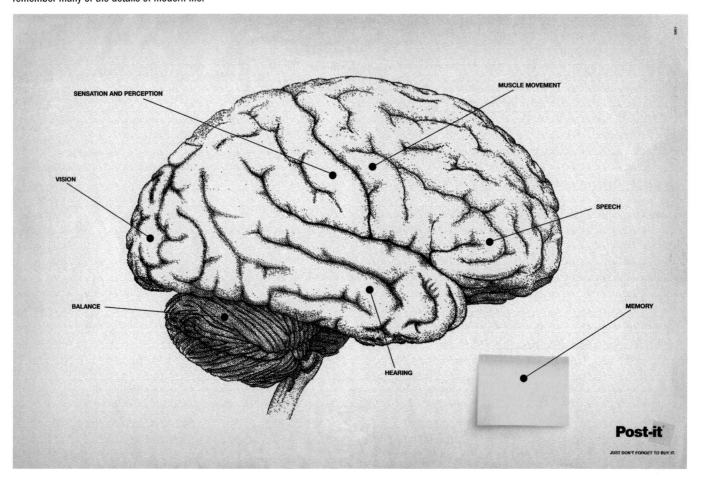

Personal Relevance

Episodic memories are those that relate to events that are personally relevant.[46] As a result, a person's motivation to retain these memories will likely be strong. Couples often have "their song" that reminds them of their first date or wedding. Some especially vivid associations are called *flashbulb memories*. And, recall of the past may have an effect on future behavior. For example, a college fund-raising campaign can get higher donations by evoking pleasant college memories.

One method of conveying product information is through a *narrative* or a story. Much of the social information that an individual acquires is represented in memory this way. Therefore, utilizing this method in product advertising can be an effective marketing technique. Narratives persuade people to construct a mental representation of the information that they are viewing. Pictures aid in this construction and allow for a more developed and detailed mental representation.[47]

Memory Systems

According to the information-processing perspective, there are three distinct memory systems: sensory memory, short-term memory (STM), and long-term memory (LTM). Each plays a role in processing brand-related information. The interrelationships of these memory systems are summarized in Figure 3.5.

Sensory Memory

Sensory memory permits storage of the information we receive from our senses. This storage is very temporary; it lasts a couple of seconds at most. For example, a person might be walking past a donut shop and get a quick, enticing whiff of something baking inside. Although this sensation would last only for a few seconds, it would be sufficient to allow the person to determine if he or she should investigate further. If the information is retained for further processing, it passes through an **attentional gate** and is transferred to short-term memory.

Short-Term Memory

Short-term memory (STM) also stores information for a limited period of time, and its capacity is limited. Similar to a computer, this system can be regarded as working memory; it holds the information we are currently processing. Verbal input may be stored acoustically (in terms of how it sounds) or semantically (in terms of what it means).

■ **FIGURE 3.5** RELATIONSHIPS AMONG MEMORY SYSTEMS

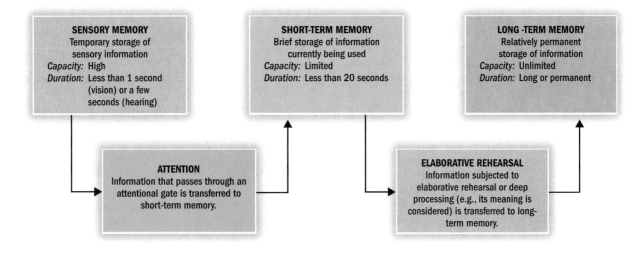

The information is stored by combining small pieces into larger ones in a process known as **chunking**. A chunk is a configuration that is familiar to the person and can be manipulated as a unit. For example, a brand name can be a chunk that summarizes a great deal of detailed information about the brand.

Initially, it was believed that STM was capable of processing between five and nine chunks of information at a time, and for this reason phone numbers were designed to have seven digits.[48] It now appears that three to four chunks is the optimal size for efficient retrieval (seven-digit phone numbers can be remembered because the individual digits are chunked, so we may remember a three-digit exchange as one piece of information).[49]

Long-Term Memory

Long-term memory (LTM) is the system that allows us to retain information for a long period of time. In order for information to enter into long-term memory from short-term memory, elaborative rehearsal is required. This process involves thinking about the meaning of a stimulus and relating it to other information already in memory. Marketers sometimes assist in the process by devising catchy slogans or jingles that consumers repeat on their own.

Storing Information in Memory

Relationships among the types of memory are a source of some controversy. The traditional perspective, known as multiple-store, assumes that STM and LTM are separate systems. More recent research has moved away from the distinction between the two types of memory, instead emphasizing the interdependence of the systems. This work argues that depending on the nature of the processing task, different levels of processing occur that activate some aspects of memory rather than others. These approaches are called **activation models of memory**.[50] The more effort it takes to process information (so-called "deep processing"), the more likely it is that information will be placed in long-term memory.

Associative Networks

Activation models propose that an incoming piece of information is stored in an associative network containing many bits of related information organized according to some set of relationships. The consumer has organized systems of concepts relating to brands, manufacturers, and stores.

These storage units, known as **knowledge structures**, can be thought of as complex spider webs filled with pieces of data. This information is placed into **nodes**, which are connected by associative links within these structures. Pieces of information that are seen as similar in some way are chunked together under some more abstract category. New, incoming information is interpreted to be consistent with the structure already in place.[51]

According to the *hierarchical processing model*, a message is processed in a bottom-up fashion: Processing begins at a very basic level and is subject to increasingly complex processing operations that require greater cognitive capacity. If processing at one level fails to evoke the next level, processing of the ad is terminated and capacity is allocated to other tasks.[52]

An associative network is developed as links form between nodes. For example, a consumer might have a network for "perfumes." Each node represents a concept related to the category. This node can be an attribute, a specific brand, a celebrity identified with a perfume, or even a related product. A network for perfumes might include concepts like the names Chanel, Obsession, and Charlie, as well as attributes such as sexy and elegant.

When asked to list perfumes, the consumer would recall only those brands contained in the appropriate category. This group constitutes that person's **evoked set**. The task of a new entrant that wants to position itself as a category member

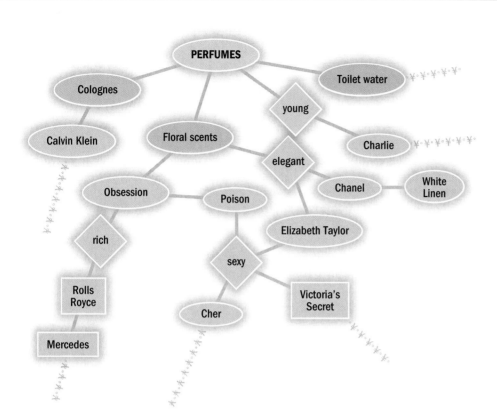

(e.g., a new luxury perfume) is to provide cues that facilitate its placement in the appropriate category. A sample network for perfumes is shown in Figure 3.6.

Spreading Activation

A meaning can be activated indirectly; energy spreads across nodes of varying levels of abstraction. As one node is activated, other nodes associated with it also begin to be triggered. Meaning thus spreads across the network, bringing up concepts including competing brands and relevant attributes that are used to form attitudes toward the brand.

This process of **spreading activation** allows consumers to shift back and forth between levels of meaning. The way a piece of information is stored in memory depends on the type of meaning assigned to it. This meaning type will in turn determine how and when the meaning is activated. For example, the memory trace for an ad could be stored in one or more of the following ways:

- *Brand-specific:* in terms of claims made for the brand.
- *Ad-specific:* in terms of the medium or content of the ad itself.
- *Brand identification:* in terms of the brand name.
- *Product category:* in terms of how the product works or where it should be used.
- *Evaluative reactions:* positive or negative emotions, such as "that looks like fun."[53]

Levels of Knowledge

Knowledge is coded at different levels of abstraction and complexity. Meaning concepts are individual nodes (e.g., elegant). These may be combined into a larger unit, called a *proposition* (also known as a *belief*). A proposition links two nodes together to form a more complex meaning, which can serve as a single chunk of information. For example, a proposition might be that "Chanel is a perfume for elegant women."

Propositions are in turn integrated to produce a complex unit known as a schema which, as we have already seen, is a cognitive framework that is developed through experience. Information that is consistent with an existing schema is encoded more readily.[54] The ability to move up and down among levels of abstraction greatly increases processing flexibility and efficiency. For this reason, young children, who do not yet have well-developed schemas, are not able to make as efficient use of purchase information as are older children.[55]

One type of schema that is relevant to consumer behavior is a script, a sequence of events that is expected by an individual. For example, consumers learn **service scripts** that guide their behavior in commercial settings. Consumers learn to expect a certain sequence of events, and they may become uncomfortable if the service departs from the script. A service script for a visit to the dentist might include such events as (1) drive to the dentist, (2) read old magazines in the waiting room, (3) hear name called and sit in dentist's chair, (4) dentist puts funny substance on teeth, (5) dentist cleans teeth, and so on. This desire to follow a script helps to explain why such service innovations as automatic bank machines, self-service gas stations, or "scan-your-own" grocery checkouts have met with resistance by some consumers, who have trouble adapting to a new sequence of events.[56]

Retrieving Information for Purchase Decisions

Retrieval is the process whereby information is recovered from long-term memory. As evidenced by the popularity of the TV show *Who Wants to Be a Millionaire?* and the board game *Trivial Pursuit,* people have a vast quantity of information stored in their heads that is not necessarily available on demand. Although most of the information entered in long-term memory does not go away, it may be difficult or impossible to retrieve unless the appropriate cues are present.

Factors Influencing Retrieval

Some differences in retrieval ability are affected by physiological factors. Older adults consistently display inferior recall ability for current items such as prescription drug instructions, though events that happened to them when they were younger may be recalled with great clarity.[57]

Other factors are situational, relating to the environment in which the message is delivered. Not surprisingly, recall is enhanced when the consumer pays more attention to the message in the first place. Some evidence indicates that information about a *pioneering brand* (the first brand to enter a market) is more easily retrieved from memory than follower brands because the first product's introduction is likely to be distinctive and, for the time being, no competitors divert the consumer's attention.[58] In addition, descriptive brand names are more likely to be recalled than are those that do not provide adequate cues as to what the product is.[59]

The viewing environment of a marketing message also can affect recall. For example, commercials shown during baseball games yield the lowest recall scores among sports programs because the activity is stop-and-go rather than continuous. Unlike football or basketball, the pacing of baseball gives many opportunities for attention to wander even during play. Similarly, General Electric found that its commercials fared better in television shows with continuous activity, such as stories or dramas, compared to variety shows or talk shows that are punctuated by a series of acts.[60] Finally, a large-scale analysis of TV commercials found that commercials shown first in a series of ads are recalled better than those shown last.[61]

Recent research on *postexperience advertising effects* underscores how powerful marketing communications can be in shaping our daily experiences. Language and imagery from ads we have seen recently can become confused with our own experiential memories so that we may come to believe that what we saw in advertising actually was our own experience with products. This study showed that when consumers were exposed to advertising after they had directly experienced a product, the ad altered their recollections of the experience.[62]

State-Dependent Retrieval

In a process called *state-dependent retrieval,* people are better able to access information if their internal state is the same at the time of recall as when the information was learned. This phenomenon, called the *mood congruence effect,* underscores the desirability of matching a consumer's mood at the time of purchase when planning exposure to marketing communications. A consumer is more likely to recall an ad, for example, if his or her mood or level of arousal at the time of exposure is similar to that in the purchase environment. Recreating the cues that were present when the information was first presented can enhance recall. For example, Life cereal uses a picture of "Mikey" from its commercial on the cereal box, which facilitates recall of brand claims and favorable brand evaluations.[63]

A few marketing researchers are using *hypnosis* to dredge up past memories of experiences with products.[64] Shell Oil was having trouble finding out why there was a decade-long sales slump at the company. After trying many different research methods, managers decided to try focus groups conducted under hypnosis. People were able to go back in their lives to talk about their first experience in a gas station when they were very young. Shell discovered that current preferences for gasoline were related to these very early memories. As a result, the firm is working on ways to make a positive impression on people at a very early age rather than waiting for them to be old enough to get a driver's license.[65]

Familiarity and Recall

As a general rule, prior familiarity with an item enhances its recall. Indeed, this is one of the basic goals of marketers who are trying to create and maintain awareness of their products. The more experience a consumer has with a product, the better use he or she is able to make of product information.[66] However, there is a possible fly in the ointment: As noted earlier in the chapter, some evidence indicates that extreme familiarity can result in inferior learning and recall. When consumers are highly familiar with a brand or an advertisement, they may attend to fewer attributes because they do not believe that any additional effort will yield a gain in knowledge.[67] For example, when consumers are exposed to a radio replay in which the audio track from a television ad is replayed on the radio, they do very little critical, evaluative processing and instead mentally replay the video portion of the ad.[68]

Salience and Recall

The **salience** of a brand refers to its prominence or level of activation in memory. As noted in Chapter 2, stimuli that stand out in contrast to their environment are more likely to command attention which, in turn, increases the likelihood they will be recalled. Almost any technique that increases the novelty of a stimulus also improves recall (a result known as the *von Restorff Effect*).[69] This effect explains why unusual advertising or distinctive packaging tends to facilitate brand recall.[70]

Introducing a surprise element in an ad can be particularly effective in aiding recall even if it is not relevant to the factual information being presented.[71] In addition, **mystery ads**, in which the brand is not identified until the end of the ad, are more effective at building associations in memory between the product category and that brand—especially in the case of relatively unknown brands.[72]

Pictorial Versus Verbal Cues: Is a Picture Worth a Thousand Words?

There is some evidence for the superiority of visual memory over verbal memory, but this advantage is unclear because it is more difficult to measure recall of pictures.[73] However, the available data indicate that information presented in picture form is more likely to be recognized later.[74] Certainly, visual aspects of an ad are more likely to grab a consumer's attention. In fact, eye-movement studies indicate that about 90 percent of viewers look at the dominant picture in an ad before they bother to view the copy.[75]

Although pictorial ads may enhance recall, they do not necessarily improve comprehension. One study found that television news items presented with illustrations (still pictures) as a backdrop result in improved recall for details of the news story, even though understanding of the story's content does not improve.[76]

Factors Influencing Forgetting

Marketers obviously hope that consumers will not forget about their products. However, in a poll of more than 13,000 adults, more than half were unable to remember any specific ad they had seen, heard, or read in the last 30 days.[77] Clearly, forgetting by consumers is a big headache for marketers (not to mention a problem for students when studying for exams!).

Early memory theorists assumed that memories simply fade with the passage of time. In a process of **decay**, the structural changes in the brain produced by learning simply go away. Forgetting also occurs due to interference; as additional information is learned, it displaces the earlier information.

Stimulus–response associations will be forgotten if the consumers subsequently learn new responses to the same or similar stimuli in a process known as *retroactive interference*. Or, prior learning can interfere with new learning, a process termed *proactive interference*. Because pieces of information are stored in memory as nodes that are connected to one another by links, a meaning concept that is connected by a larger number of links is more likely to be retrieved. But, as new responses are learned, a stimulus loses its effectiveness in retrieving the old response.[78]

These interference effects help to explain problems in remembering brand information. Consumers tend to organize attribute information by brand.[79] Additional attribute information regarding a brand or similar brands may limit the person's ability to recall old brand information. Recall may also be inhibited if the brand name is composed of frequently used words. These words cue competing associations and result in less retention of brand information.[80]

In one study, brand evaluations deteriorated more rapidly when ads for the brand appeared with messages for 12 other brands in the same category than when the ad was shown with ads for 12 dissimilar products.[81] By increasing the salience of a brand, the recall of other brands can be impaired.[82] On the other hand, calling a competitor by name can result in poorer recall for one's own brand.[83]

Finally, a phenomenon known as the *part-list cueing effect* allows marketers to strategically utilize the interference process. When only a portion of the items in a category are presented to consumers, the omitted items are not as easily recalled. For example, comparative advertising that mentions only a subset of competitors (preferably those that the marketer is not very worried about) may inhibit recall of the unmentioned brands with which the product does not favorably compare.[84]

Products as Memory Markers

Products and ads can themselves serve as powerful retrieval cues. Indeed, the three types of possessions most valued by the majority of consumers are furniture, visual art, and photos. The most common explanation for this attachment is the ability of these things to call forth memories of the past.[85] The power of these cues helps to explain the great scrapbooking trend that is sweeping America. *Creating Keepsakes*, the leading scrapbook trade magazine, estimates that 4 million people, almost all of them women, gather for "crop-alongs" or "power layouts" every month. Scrapbookers typically meet in somebody's home, but there also are scrapbooking cruises to the Caribbean and Alaska and weekend sessions at resort hotels.[86]

Researchers are just beginning to probe the effects of *autobiographical memories* on buying behavior. These memories appear to be one way that advertisements create emotional responses; ads that succeed in getting us to think about our own past also appear to get us to like these ads more—especially if the linkage between the nostalgia experience and the brand is strong.[87]

Products are particularly important as markers when our sense of past is threatened, as when a consumer's current identity is challenged due to some change in role caused by divorce, moving, graduation, and so on.[88] Our possessions often have *mnemonic* qualities that serve as a form of external memory by prompting consumers to retrieve episodic memories. For example, family photography allows consumers to create their own retrieval cues, with the 11 billion amateur photos taken annually forming a kind of external memory bank for our culture. A sadder example is the popularity in some neighborhoods of memorial T-shirts for friends and family members who have been murdered. The shirts often feature poems and prayers along with a picture of the dead person. This practice has become so prevalent in gang areas that a common threat has become: "Keep it up—you'll end up on a shirt."[89]

The Marketing Power of Nostalgia

Nostalgia has been described as a bittersweet emotion; the past is viewed with both sadness and longing.[90] As Joe's passion for the 1960s illustrates, references to "the good old days" are increasingly common, as advertisers call up memories of youth—and hope these feelings will translate to what they're selling today. That may help to explain why reunions have become such a booming business; about 22 million Americans attend one every year.[91] A stimulus is at times able to evoke a weakened response even years after it was initially perceived, an effect known as *spontaneous recovery*, and this reestablished connection may explain consumers' powerful nostalgic reactions to songs or pictures they have not been exposed to in quite a long time.

Why are nostalgia appeals so welcomed by consumers? According to one consumer analyst, "We are creating a new culture, and we don't know what's going to happen. So we need some warm fuzzies from our past."[92] Or, this strategy may work because more than half of adults think things were better in the past than they are today, according to research by Roper Starch Worldwide.[93] In the aftermath of September 11, 2001, consumers seem to be craving the comfort of items from the past even more. Marketers like Ford, GE, S.C. Johnson, and Sears are sponsoring campaigns that celebrate their heritage. Once-popular products like Breck shampoo, Sea & Ski sun-care lotion, St. Joseph's aspirin, and the Care Bears are being revived. Other advertisers are bringing back themes and characters from old shows to sell new products, as when Old Navy transforms "The Brady Bunch" into "The Rugby Bunch" to push its shirts, Mr. T endorses a phone company, and Robin Leach of *Lifestyles of the Rich and Famous* fame appears in ads for Courtyard by Marriott hotels.[94]

Memory and Aesthetic Preferences

In addition to liking ads and products that remind us of our past, our past experiences also help to determine what we like now. Consumer researchers have created a nostalgia index that measures the critical ages during which our preferences are likely to be formed and endure over time. For example, liking for specific songs appears to be related to how old a person was when that song was popular—on average songs that were popular when he or she was 23.5 years old are the most likely to be favored, whereas preferences for fashion models peak at age 33 and for movie stars at age 26 to 27.[95]

Measuring Memory for Marketing Stimuli

Because marketers pay so much money to place their messages in front of consumers, they are naturally concerned that people will actually remember these

Lifetime TV uses a nostalgia appeal to attract female viewers.

messages at a later point. It seems that they have good reason to be concerned. In one study, fewer than 40 percent of television viewers made positive links between commercial messages and the corresponding products, only 65 percent noticed the brand name in a commercial, and only 38 percent recognized a connection to an important point.[96]

Even more sadly, only 7 percent of television viewers can recall the product or company featured in the most recent television commercial they watched. This figure represents less than half the recall rate recorded in 1965 and may be attributed to such factors as the increase of 30- and 15-second commercials, and the practice of airing television commercials in clusters rather than in single-sponsor programs.[97]

Recognition Versus Recall

One indicator of good advertising is, of course, the impression it makes on consumers. But how can this impact be defined and measured? Two basic measures of

Fossil's product designs evoke memories of earlier, classic styles.

impact are *recognition* and *recall*. In the typical recognition test, subjects are shown ads one at a time and asked if they have seen them before. In contrast, free recall tests ask consumers to independently think of what they have seen without being prompted for this information first—obviously this task requires greater effort on the part of respondents. Intermedia Advertising Group is a research firm that measures advertising effectiveness by monitoring the TV-viewing population's ability to remember an ad within 24 hours. The firm assigns a recall index to each ad to indicate the strength of the impact it had. Scores for 2002 attest to the power of a memorable character in aiding recall. Although ads with well-known celebrities like Britney Spears, Austin Powers, and Michael Jordan tend to have very high recall rates, three of the top five most remembered ads starred another (and taller) celebrity: Toys "R" Us spokesanimal Geoffrey the Giraffe! [98]

Under some conditions, these two memory measures tend to yield the same results, especially when the researchers try to keep the viewers' interest in the ads constant.[99] Generally, though, recognition scores tend to be more reliable and do not decay over time the way recall scores do.[100] Recognition scores are almost always better than recall scores because recognition is a simpler process and more retrieval cues are available to the consumer.

Both types of retrieval play important roles in purchase decisions, however. Recall tends to be more important in situations in which consumers do not have product data at their disposal, so they must rely on memory to generate this information.[101] On the other hand, recognition is more likely to be an important factor in a store, where consumers are confronted with thousands of product options and information (i.e., external memory is abundantly available) and the task may simply be to recognize a familiar package. Unfortunately, package recognition and familiarity can have a negative consequence in that warning labels may be ignored, because their message is taken for granted and not really noticed.[102]

The Starch Test

A widely used commercial measure of advertising recall for magazines is called the *Starch Test,* a syndicated service founded in 1932. This service provides scores on a number of aspects of consumers' familiarity with an ad, including such categories as "noted," "associated," and "read most." It also scores the impact of the component parts of an overall ad, giving such information as "seen" for major illustrations and "read some" for a major block of copy.[103] Factors such as the size of the ad, whether it appears toward the front or the back of the magazine, if it is on the right or left page, and the size of illustrations play an important role in affecting the amount of attention given to an ad, as determined by Starch scores.

Problems with Memory Measures

Although the measurement of an ad's memorability is important, the ability of existing measures to accurately assess these dimensions has been criticized for several reasons, which we explore now.

Response Biases

Results obtained from a measuring instrument are not necessarily due to what is being measured, but rather to something else about the instrument or the respondent. This form of contamination is called a **response bias**. For example, people tend to give "yes" responses to questions, regardless of what is asked. In addition, consumers often have an eagerness to be "good subjects" by pleasing the experimenter. They will try to give the responses they think he or she is looking for. In some studies, the claimed recognition of bogus ads (ads that have not been seen before) is almost as high as the recognition rate of real ads.[104]

Memory Lapses

People are also prone to unintentionally forgetting information. Typical problems include *omitting* (leaving facts out), *averaging* (the tendency to "normalize" memories by not reporting extreme cases), and *telescoping* (inaccurate recall of time).[105] These distortions call into question the accuracy of product usage databases that rely on consumers to recall their purchase and consumption of food and household items. In one study, for example, people were asked to describe what portion of various foods—small, medium, or large—they ate in a typical meal. However, different definitions of "medium" were used. Regardless of the measurement used, about the same number of people claimed they typically ate "medium" portions.[106]

Memory for Facts Versus Feelings

Although techniques are being developed to increase the accuracy of memory scores, these improvements do not address the more fundamental issue of whether recall is necessary for advertising to have an effect. In particular, some critics argue that these measures do not adequately tap the impact of "feeling" ads in which the objective is to arouse strong emotions rather than to convey concrete product benefits. Many ad campaigns, including those for Hallmark cards, Chevrolet, and Pepsi, use this approach.[107] An effective strategy relies on a long-term buildup of feeling rather than on a one-shot attempt to convince consumers to buy the product.

Also, it is not clear that recall translates into preference. We may recall the benefits touted in an ad but not believe them. Or, the ad may be memorable because it is so obnoxious and the product becomes one we "love to hate." The bottom line:

Although recall is important, especially for creating brand awareness, it is not necessarily sufficient to alter consumer preferences. To accomplish this, more sophisticated attitude-changing strategies are needed. These issues will be discussed in Chapters 7 and 8.

CHAPTER SUMMARY

- Learning is a change in behavior that is caused by experience. Learning can occur through simple associations between a stimulus and a response, or via a complex series of cognitive activities.
- Behavioral learning theories assume that learning occurs as a result of responses to external events. Classical conditioning occurs when a stimulus that naturally elicits a response (an unconditioned stimulus) is paired with another stimulus that does not initially elicit this response. Over time, the second stimulus (the conditioned stimulus) comes to elicit the response even in the absence of the first.
- This response can also extend to other, similar stimuli in a process known as stimulus generalization. This process is the basis for such marketing strategies as licensing and family branding, where a consumer's positive associations with a product are transferred to other contexts.
- Operant or instrumental conditioning occurs as the person learns to perform behaviors that produce positive outcomes and avoid those that result in negative outcomes. Whereas classical conditioning involves the pairing of two stimuli, instrumental learning occurs when reinforcement is delivered following a response to a stimulus. Reinforcement is positive if a reward is delivered following a response. It is negative if a negative outcome is avoided by not performing a response. Punishment occurs when a response is followed by unpleasant events. Extinction of the behavior will occur if reinforcement is no longer received.
- Cognitive learning occurs as the result of mental processes. For example, observational learning takes place when the consumer performs a behavior as a result of seeing someone else performing it and being rewarded for it.
- Memory refers to the storage of learned information. The way information is encoded when it is perceived determines how it will be stored in memory. The memory systems known as sensory memory, short-term memory, and long-term memory each play a role in retaining and processing information from the outside world.
- Information is not stored in isolation; it is incorporated into knowledge structures, in which it is associated with other related data. The location of product information in associative networks, and the level of abstraction at which it is coded, help to determine when and how this information will be activated at a later time. Some factors that influence the likelihood of retrieval include the level of familiarity with an item, its salience (or prominence) in memory, and whether the information was presented in pictorial or written form.
- Products also play a role as memory markers; they are used by consumers to retrieve memories about past experiences (autobiographical memories) and are often valued for their ability to do this. This function also contributes to the use of nostalgia in marketing strategies.
- Memory for product information can be measured through either recognition or recall techniques. Consumers are more likely to recognize an advertisement if it is presented to them than they are to recall one without being given any cues. However, neither recognition nor recall automatically or reliably translate into product preferences or purchases.

KEY TERMS

Activation models of memory   98
Behavioral learning theories   83
Brand equity   88
Chunking   98
Classical conditioning   84
Cognitive learning theory   93
Conditioned stimulus (CS)   84
Decay   102
Encoding   95
Evoked set   98
Extinction   91
Frequency marketing   92
Instrumental conditioning   90
Knowledge structures   98

Learning   83
Long-term memory (LTM)   98
Masked branding   86
Memory   95
Modeling   93
Mystery ads   101
Negative reinforcement   90
Nodes   98
Nostalgia   103
Observational learning   93
Positive reinforcement   90
Punishment   90
Response bias   106

Retrieval   95
Salience   101
Semantic meaning   96
Sensory meaning   96
Sensory memory   97
Service scripts   100
Shaping   90
Short-term memory (STM)   97
Spreading activation   99
Stimulus discrimination   86
Stimulus generalization   85
Storage   95
Unconditioned stimulus (UCS)   84

CONSUMER BEHAVIOR CHALLENGE

1 Identify three patterns of reinforcement and provide an example of how each is used in a marketing context.

2 Describe the functions of short-term and long-term memory. What is the apparent relationship between the two?

3 Devise a "product jingle memory test." Compile a list of brands that are or have been associated with memorable jingles, such as Chiquita Banana or Alka-Seltzer. Read this list to friends, and see how many jingles are remembered. You may be surprised at the level of recall.

4 Identify some important characteristics of a product with a well-known brand name. Based on these attributes, generate a list of possible brand extension or licensing opportunities, as well as some others that would most likely not be accepted by consumers.

5 Collect some pictures of "classic" products that have high nostalgia value. Show these pictures to consumers, and allow them to free associate. Analyze the types of memories that are evoked, and think about how these associations might be employed in a product's promotional strategy.

6 Some die-hard fans were not pleased when the Rolling Stones sold the tune "Start Me Up" for about $4 million to Microsoft, which wanted the classic song to promote its Windows 95 launch. The Beach Boys sold "Good Vibrations" to Cadbury Schweppes for its Sunkist soft drink, Steppenwolf offered its "Born to be Wild" to plug the Mercury Cougar, and even Bob Dylan sold "The Times They Are A-Changin'" to Coopers & Lybrand (now called PriceWaterhouseCoopers).[108] Other rock legends have refused to play the commercial game, including Bruce Springsteen, the Grateful Dead, Led Zeppelin, Fleetwood Mac, R.E.M., and U2. According to U2's manager, "Rock 'n roll is the last vestige of independence. It is undignified to put that creative effort and hard work to the disposal of a soft drink or beer or car."[109] Singer Neil Young is especially adamant about not selling out; in his song "This Note's for You," he croons, "Ain't singing for Pepsi, ain't singing for Coke, I don't sing for nobody, makes me look like a joke." What's your take on this issue? How do you react when one of your favorite songs turns up in a commercial? Is this use of nostalgia an effective way to market a product? Why or why not?

NOTES

1. HempWorldResorts.com/pstindex.html, accessed February 4, 2003.
2. Jonathan Eig, "Nostalgic Fans Use Internet to Save Quirky Quisp from a Cereal Killing," *Wall Street Journal Interactive Edition* (April 24, 2000).
3. Jennifer Cody, "Here's a New Way to Rationalize Not Cleaning Out Your Closets," *New York Times* (June 14, 1994): B1.
4. Stuart Elliott, "At 75, Mr. Peanut Is Getting Expanded Role at Planters," *New York Times* (September 23, 1991): D15.
5. Todd Pruzan, "Brand Illusions," *New York Times on the Web* (September 12, 1999).
6. Robert A. Baron, *Psychology: The Essential Science* (Boston: Allyn & Bacon, 1989).
7. Richard A. Feinberg, "Credit Cards as Spending Facilitating Stimuli: A Conditioning Interpretation," *Journal of Consumer Research* 13 (December 1986): 348–56.
8. R. A. Rescorla, "Pavlovian Conditioning: It's Not What You Think It Is," *American Psychologist* 43 (1988): 151–60; Elnora W. Stuart, Terence A. Shimp, and Randall W. Engle, "Classical Conditioning of Consumer Attitudes: Four Experiments in an Advertising Context," *Journal of Consumer Research* 14 (December 1987): 334–39.

9. Jane E. Brody, "Cybersex Gives Birth to a Psychological Disorder," *New York Times on the Web* (May 16, 2000).

10. James Ward, Barbara Loken, Ivan Ross, and Tedi Hasapopoulous, "The Influence of Physical Similarity of Affect and Attribute Perceptions from National Brands to Private Label Brands," in Terence A. Shimp et al., eds, *American Marketing Educators' Conference* (Chicago: American Marketing Association, 1986), 51–56.

11. Judith Lynne Zaichkowsky and Richard Neil Simpson, "The Effect of Experience with a Brand Imitator on the Original Brand," *Marketing Letters* 7, no. 1 (1996): 31–39.

12. Janice S. Griffiths and Mary Zimmer, "Masked Brands and Consumers' Need for Uniqueness," *American Marketing Association* (Summer 1998): 145–53.

13. Chris T. Allen and Thomas J. Madden, "A Closer Look at Classical Conditioning," *Journal of Consumer Research* 12 (December 1985): 301–15; Chester A. Insko and William F. Oakes, "Awareness and the Conditioning of Attitudes," *Journal of Personality and Social Psychology* 4 (November 1966): 487–96; Carolyn K. Staats and Arthur W. Staats, "Meaning Established by Classical Conditioning," *Journal of Experimental Psychology* 54 (July 1957): 74–80.

14. Randi Priluck Grossman and Brian D. Till, "The Persistence of Classically Conditioned Brand Attitudes," *Journal of Advertising* 21, no. 1 (1998): 23–31.

15. Kevin Lane Keller, "Conceptualizing, Measuring, and Managing Customer-Based Brand Equity," *Journal of Marketing* 57 (January 1993): 1–22.

16. Herbert Krugman, "Low Recall and High Recognition of Advertising," *Journal of Advertising Research* (February–March 1986): 79–80.

17. Gerald J. Gorn, "The Effects of Music in Advertising on Choice Behavior: A Classical Conditioning Approach," *Journal of Marketing* 46 (Winter 1982): 94–101.

18. Noreen Klein, Virginia Tech, personal communication (April 2000); Calvin Bierley, Frances K. McSweeney, and Renee Vannieuwkerk, "Classical Conditioning of Preferences for Stimuli," *Journal of Consumer Research* 12 (December 1985): 316–23; James J. Kellaris and Anthony D. Cox, "The Effects of Background Music in Advertising: A Reassessment," *Journal of Consumer Research* 16 (June 1989): 113–18.

19. Frances K. McSweeney and Calvin Bierley, "Recent Developments in Classical Conditioning," *Journal of Consumer Research* 11 (September 1984): 619–31.

20. Basil G. Englis, "The Reinforcement Properties of Music Videos: 'I Want My . . . I Want My . . . I Want My . . . MTV' " (paper presented at the meetings of the Association for Consumer Research, New Orleans, 1989).

21. Stuart Elliott, "A Name Change at Philip Morris," *New York Times on the Web* (November 19, 2001).

22. Sharon Begley, "StrawBerry Is No BlackBerry: Building Brands Using Sound," *Wall Street Journal Interactive Edition* (August 26, 2002).

23. Peter H. Farquhar, "Brand Equity," *Marketing Insights* (Summer, 1989): 59.

24. Patricia Winters Lauro, "Fire and Police Try to Market Goods," *New York Times on the Web* (June 10, 2002).

25. "Look-Alikes Mimic Familiar Packages," *New York Times* (August 9, 1986): D1.

26. Zaichkowsky and Simpson, "The Effect of Experience with a Brand Imitator on the Original Brand," 31–39.

27. "Cursed?" *Advertising Age* (September 16, 2002): 19.

28. www.iacc.org/, accessed November 27, 2002.

29. Miriam Jordan, "In Wooing Brazil's Teenagers, Converse Has Big Shoes to Fill," *Wall Street Journal Interactive Edition* (July 18, 2002).

30. For a comprehensive approach to consumer behavior based on operant conditioning principles, see Gordon R. Foxall, "Behavior Analysis and Consumer Psychology," *Journal of Economic Psychology* 15 (March 1994): 5–91.

31. Youngme Moon, "Personalization and Personality: Some Effects of Customizing Message Style Based on Consumer Personality," *Journal of Consumer Psychology* 12 (4 April 2002): 313–26; Youngme Moon, "Intimate Exchanges: Using Computers to Elicit Self-Disclosure from Consumers," *Journal of Consumer Research* 26 (March 2000): 323–39.

32. Blaise J. Bergiel and Christine Trosclair, "Instrumental Learning: Its Application to Customer Satisfaction," *Journal of Consumer Marketing* 2 (Fall 1985): 23–28.

33. Jane Costello, "Do Offers of Free Mileage Sell? The Proof Is in Pudding Guy," *Wall Street Journal Interactive Edition* (January 24, 2000).

34. Ellen J. Langer, *The Psychology of Control* (Beverly Hills, CA: Sage, 1983).

35. Robert B. Cialdini, *Influence: Science and Practice*, 2nd ed. (New York: William Morrow, 1984).

36. Allen and Madden, "A Closer Look at Classical Conditioning," 301–15; see also Terence A. Shimp, Elnora W. Stuart, and Randall W. Engle, "A Program of Classical Conditioning Experiments Testing Variations in the Conditioned Stimulus and Context," *Journal of Consumer Research* 18 (June 1991): 1–12.

37. Terence A. Shimp, "Neo-Pavlovian Conditioning and Its Implications for Consumer Theory and Research," in Thomas S. Robertson and Harold H. Kassarjian, eds., *Handbook of Consumer Behavior* (Upper Saddle River, NJ: Prentice Hall, 1991).

38. Albert Bandura, *Social Foundations of Thought and Action: A Social Cognitive View* (Upper Saddle River, NJ: Prentice Hall, 1986).

39. Bandura, *Social Foundations of Thought and Action.*

40. R. C. Atkinson and I. M. Shiffrin, "Human Memory: A Proposed System and Its Control Processes," in K. W. Spence and J. T. Spence, eds., *The Psychology of Learning and Motivation: Advances in Research and Theory* 2 (New York: Academic Press, 1968): 89–195.

41. James R. Bettman, "Memory Factors in Consumer Choice: A Review," *Journal of Marketing* (Spring 1979): 37–53. For a study that explores the relative impact of internal versus external memory on brand choice, see Joseph W. Alba, Howard Marmostein, and Amitava Chattopadhyay, "Transitions in Preference over Time: The Effects of Memory on Message Persuasiveness," *Journal of Marketing Research* 29 (1992): 406–16.

42. Lauren G. Block and Vicki G. Morwitz "Shopping Lists as an External Memory Aid for Grocery Shopping: Influences on List Writing and List Fulfillment," *Journal of Consumer Psychology* 8, no. 4 (1999): 343–75.

43. Kathryn R. Braun, "Postexperience Advertising Effects on Consumer Memory," *Journal of Consumer Research* 25 (March 1999): 319–34.

44. David S. Koeppel, "Tales from the Crypt: Storing E-mail to be Sent After Your Death," *New York Times on the Web* (April 13, 2000); www.FinalThoughts.com, accessed November 27, 2002.

45. Kim Robertson, "Recall and Recognition Effects of Brand Name Imagery," *Psychology & Marketing* 4 (Spring 1987): 3–15.

46. Endel Tulving, "Remembering and Knowing the Past," *American Scientist* 77 (July–August 1989): 361.

47. Rashmi Adaval and Robert S. Wyer Jr., "The Role of Narratives in Consumer Information Processing," *Journal of Consumer Psychology* 7, no. 3 (1998): 207–46.

48. George A. Miller, "The Magical Number Seven, Plus or Minus Two: Some Limits on Our Capacity for Processing Information," *Psychological Review* 63 (1956): 81–97.

49. James N. MacGregor, "Short-Term Memory Capacity: Limitation or Optimization?" *Psychological Review* 94 (1987): 107–8.

50. See Catherine A. Cole and Michael J. Houston, "Encoding and Media Effects on Consumer Learning Deficiencies in the Elderly," *Journal of Marketing Research* 24 (February 1987): 55–64; A. M. Collins and E. F. Loftus, "A Spreading Activation Theory of Semantic Processing," *Psychological Review* 82 (1975): 407–28; Fergus I. M. Craik and Robert S. Lockhart, "Levels of Processing: A Framework for Memory Research," *Journal of Verbal Learning and Verbal Behavior* 11 (1972): 671–84.

51. Walter A. Henry, "The Effect of Information-Processing Ability on Processing Accuracy," *Journal of Consumer Research* 7 (June 1980): 42–48.

52. Anthony G. Greenwald and Clark Leavitt, "Audience Involvement in Advertising: Four Levels," *Journal of Consumer Research* 11 (June 1984): 581–92.

53. Kevin Lane Keller, "Memory Factors in Advertising: The Effect of Advertising Retrieval Cues on Brand Evaluations," *Journal of Consumer Research* 14 (December 1987): 316–33. For a discussion of processing operations that occur during brand choice, see Gabriel Biehal and Dipankar Chakravarti, "Consumers' Use of Memory and External Information in Choice: Macro and Micro Perspectives," *Journal of Consumer Research* 12 (March 1986): 382–405.

54. Susan T. Fiske and Shelley E. Taylor, *Social Cognition* (Reading, MA: Addison-Wesley, 1984).

55. Deborah Roedder John and John C. Whitney Jr., "The Development of Consumer Knowledge in Children: A Cognitive Structure Approach," *Journal of Consumer Research* 12 (March 1986): 406–17.

56. Michael R. Solomon, Carol Surprenant, John A. Czepiel, and Evelyn G. Gutman, "A Role Theory Perspective on Dyadic Interactions: The Service Encounter," *Journal of Marketing* 49 (Winter 1985): 99–111.

57. Roger W. Morrell, Denise C. Park, and Leonard W. Poon, "Quality of Instructions on Prescription Drug Labels: Effects on Memory and Comprehension in Young and Old Adults," *The Gerontologist* 29 (1989): 345–54.

58. Frank R. Kardes, Gurumurthy Kalyanaram, Murali Chandrashekaran, and Ronald J. Dornoff, "Brand Retrieval, Consideration Set Composition, Consumer Choice, and the Pioneering Advantage" (unpublished manuscript, the University of Cincinnati, Ohio, 1992).

59. Judith Lynne Zaichkowsky and Padma Vipat, "Inferences from Brand Names" (paper presented at the European meeting of the Association for Consumer Research, Amsterdam, June 1992).

60. Herbert E. Krugman, "Low Recall and High Recognition of Advertising," *Journal of Advertising Research* (February–March 1986): 79–86.

61. Rik G. M. Pieters and Tammo H. A. Bijmolt, "Consumer Memory for Television Advertising: A Field Study of Duration, Serial Position, and Competition Effects," *Journal of Consumer Research* 23 (March 1997): 362–72.

62. Braun, "Postexperience Advertising Effects on Consumer Memory," 319–34.

63. Keller, "Memory Factors in Advertising."

64. Michelle Wirth Fellman, "Mesmerizing Method Gets Real Results," *Marketing News* (July 20, 1998): 1.

65. Ruth Shalit, "The Return of the Hidden Persuaders," www.salon.com (September 27, 1999).

66. Eric J. Johnson and J. Edward Russo, "Product Familiarity and Learning New Information," *Journal of Consumer Research* 11 (June 1984): 542–50.

67. Eric J. Johnson and J. Edward Russo, "Product Familiarity and Learning New Information," in Kent Monroe, ed., *Advances in Consumer Research* 8 (Ann Arbor, MI: Association for Consumer Research, 1981): 151–55; John G. Lynch and Thomas K. Srull, "Memory and Attentional Factors in Consumer Choice: Concepts and Research Methods," *Journal of Consumer Research* 9 (June 1982): 18–37.

68. Julie A. Edell and Kevin Lane Keller, "The Information Processing of Coordinated Media Campaigns," *Journal of Marketing Research* 26 (May 1989): 149–64.

69. Lynch and Srull, "Memory and Attentional Factors in Consumer Choice."

70. Joseph W. Alba and Amitava Chattopadhyay, "Salience Effects in Brand Recall," *Journal of Marketing Research* 23 (November 1986): 363–70; Elizabeth C. Hirschman and Michael R. Solomon, "Utilitarian, Aesthetic, and Familiarity Responses to Verbal versus Visual Advertisements," in Thomas C. Kinnear, ed., *Advances in Consumer Research* 11 (Provo, UT: Association for Consumer Research, 1984): 426–31.

71. Susan E. Heckler and Terry L. Childers, "The Role of Expectancy and Relevancy in Memory for Verbal and Visual Information: What is Incongruency?" *Journal of Consumer Research* 18 (March 1992): 475–92.

72. Russell H. Fazio, Paul M. Herr, and Martha C. Powell, "On the Development and Strength of Category-Brand Associations in Memory: The Case of Mystery Ads," *Journal of Consumer Psychology* 1, no. 1 (1992): 1–13.

73. Hirschman and Solomon, "Utilitarian, Aesthetic, and Familiarity Responses to Verbal Versus Visual Advertisements."

74. Terry Childers and Michael Houston, "Conditions for a Picture-Superiority Effect on Consumer Memory," *Journal of Consumer Research* 11 (September 1984): 643–54; Terry Childers, Susan Heckler, and Michael Houston, "Memory for the Visual and Verbal Components of Print Advertisements," *Psychology & Marketing* 3 (Fall 1986): 147–50.

75. Werner Krober-Riel, "Effects of Emotional Pictorial Elements in Ads Analyzed by Means of Eye Movement Monitoring," in Thomas C. Kinnear, ed., *Advances in Consumer Research* 11 (Provo, UT: Association for Consumer Research, 1984): 591–96.

76. Hans-Bernd Brosius, "Influence of Presentation Features and News Context on Learning from Television News," *Journal of Broadcasting & Electronic Media* 33 (Winter 1989): 1–14.

77. Raymond R. Burke and Thomas K. Srull, "Competitive Interference and Consumer Memory for Advertising," *Journal of Consumer Research* 15 (June 1988): 55–68.

78. Burke and Srull, "Competitive Interference and Consumer Memory for Advertising."

79. Johnson and Russo, "Product Familiarity and Learning New Information."

80. Joan Meyers-Levy, "The Influence of Brand Name's Association Set Size and Word Frequency on Brand Memory," *Journal of Consumer Research* 16 (September 1989): 197–208.

81. Michael H. Baumgardner, Michael R. Leippe, David L. Ronis, and Anthony G. Greenwald, "In Search of Reliable Persuasion Effects: II. Associative Interference and Persistence of Persuasion in a Message-Dense Environment," *Journal of Personality and Social Psychology* 45 (September 1983): 524–37.

82. Alba and Chattopadhyay, "Salience Effects in Brand Recall."

83. Margaret Henderson Blair, Allan R. Kuse, David H. Furse, and David W. Stewart, "Advertising in a New and Competitive Environment: Persuading Consumers to Buy," *Business Horizons* 30 (November–December 1987): 20.

84. Lynch and Srull, "Memory and Attentional Factors in Consumer Choice."

85. Russell W. Belk, "Possessions and the Extended Self," *Journal of Consumer Research* 15 (September 1988): 139–68.

86. Johnson Dirk, "Beyond the Quilting Bee," *Newsweek* (October 21, 2002).

87. Hans Baumgartner, Mita Sujan, and James R. Bettman, "Autobiographical Memories, Affect and Consumer Information Processing," *Journal of Consumer Psychology* 1 (January 1992): 53–82; Mita Sujan, James R. Bettman, and Hans Baumgartner, "Autobiographical Memories and Consumer Judgments" (Working Paper No. 183, Pennsylvania State University, University Park, 1992).

88. Russell W. Belk, "The Role of Possessions in Constructing and Maintaining a Sense of Past," in Marvin E. Goldberg, Gerald Gorn, and Richard W. Pollay, eds., *Advances in Consumer Research* 16 (Provo, UT: Association for Consumer Research, 1989): 669–78.

89. Dan Morse, no headline, *Wall Street Journal Interactive Edition* (February 4, 1999).

90. Susan L. Holak and William J. Havlena, "Feelings, Fantasies, and Memories: An Examination of the Emotional Components of Nostalgia," *Journal of Business Research* 42 (1998): 217–26.

91. Paula Mergenhagen, "The Reunion Market," *American Demographics* (April 1996): 30–34.

92. Keith Naughton and Bill Vlasic, "Nostalgia Boom," *BusinessWeek* (March 23, 1998): 59–64.

93. Diane Crispell, "Which Good Old Days," *American Demographics* (April 1996): 35.

94. Stuart Elliot, "Ads from the Past with Modern Touches," *New York Times on the Web* (September 9, 2002); Julia Cosgrove, "Listen up, Sucka the 80s are back," *BusinessWeek* (August 5, 2002): 16.

95. Morris B. Holbrook and Robert M. Schindler, "Some Exploratory Findings on the Development of Musical Tastes," *Journal of Consumer Research* 16 (June 1989): 119–24; Morris B. Holbrook and Robert M. Schindler, "Market Segmentation Based on Age and Attitude Toward the Past: Concepts, Methods, and Findings Concerning Nostalgic Influences on Consumer Tastes," *Journal of Business Research* 37 (September 1996)1: 27–40.

96. "Only 38% of T.V. Audience Links Brands with Ads," *Marketing News* (January 6, 1984): 10.

97. "Terminal Television," *American Demographics* (January 1987): 15.

98. Vanessa O'Connell, "Toys 'R' Us Spokesanimal Makes Lasting Impression: Giraffe Tops List of Television Ads Viewers Found the Most Memorable," *Wall Street Journal Interactive Edition* (January 2, 2003).

99. Richard P. Bagozzi and Alvin J. Silk, "Recall, Recognition, and the Measurement of Memory for Print Advertisements," *Marketing Science* 2 (1983): 95–134.

100. Adam Finn, "Print Ad Recognition Readership Scores: An Information Processing Perspective," *Journal of Marketing Research* 25 (May 1988): 168–77.

101. James R. Bettman, "Memory Factors In Consumer Choice: A Review," *Journal of Marketing* (Spring 1979): 37–53.

102. Mark A. Deturck and Gerald M. Goldhaber, "Effectiveness of Product Warning Labels: Effects of Consumers' Information Processing Objectives," *Journal of Consumer Affairs* 23, no. 1 (1989): 111–25.

103. Adam Finn, "Print Ad Recognition Readership Scores: An Information Processing Perspective," *Journal of Marketing Research* 25 (May 1988): 168–77.

104. Surendra N. Singh and Gilbert A. Churchill Jr., "Response-Bias-Free Recognition Tests to Measure Advertising Effects," *Journal of Advertising Research* (June–July 1987): 23–36.

105. William A. Cook, "Telescoping and Memory's Other Tricks," *Journal of Advertising Research* 27 (February–March 1987): 5–8.

106. "On a Diet? Don't Trust Your Memory," *Psychology Today* (October 1989): 12.

107. Hubert A. Zielske and Walter A. Henry, "Remembering and Forgetting Television Ads," *Journal of Advertising Research* 20 (April 1980): 7–13; Cara Greenberg, "Future Worth: Before It's Hot, Grab It," *New York Times* (1992): C1; S. K. List, "More Than Fun and Games," *American Demographics* (August 1992): 44.

108. Thomas F. Jones, "Our Musical Heritage Is Being Raided," *San Francisco Examiner* (May 23, 1997).

109. Kevin Goldman, "A Few Rockers Refuse to Turn Tunes into Ads," *New York Times* (August 25, 1995): B1.

Motivation and Values

as Basil scans the menu at the trendy health food restaurant Juanita has dragged him to, he reflects on what a man will give up for love. Now that Juanita has become a die-hard vegetarian, she's slowly but surely working on him to forsake those juicy steaks and burgers for healthier fare. He can't even hide from tofu and other vegan delights at school; the dining facility in his dorm just started offering "veggie" alternatives to its usual assortment of greasy "mystery meats" and other delicacies he has come to love.

Juanita is totally into it; she claims that eating this way not only cuts out unwanted fat, but also is good for the environment. Just his luck to fall head-over-heels for a "tree-hugger." As Basil gamely tries to decide between the stuffed artichokes with red pepper vinaigrette and the grilled marinated zucchini, fantasies of a sizzling 24-ounce T-bone dance before his eyes.

■ INTRODUCTION

Paula certainly is not alone in believing that eating green is good for the body, the soul, and the planet. It is estimated that 7 percent of the general population is vegetarian, and women and younger people are even more likely to adopt a meatless diet. An additional 10 to 20 percent of consumers are interested in vegetarian options in addition to their normal fare of dead animals. In a 2003 survey of 12- to 19-year-olds, 20 percent of respondents (and close to one in three of the females) said vegetarianism is "in." Even the beef industry is taking notice and fighting back: The National Cattleman's Beef Association has gone so far as to post a Web site called "Cool-2B-Real" that encourages young girls to build self-esteem and eat a healthy diet—with various beef recipes thrown in for good measure. On the other hand, People for the Ethical Treatment of Animals (PETA) is joining the battle to promote vegetarianism with an ad showing an obese child eating a hamburger and the slogan, "Feeding Kids Meat is Child Abuse—Fight the Fat."[1] It's obvious our menu choices have deep-seated consequences.

The forces that drive people to buy and use products are generally straightforward, as when a person chooses what to have for lunch. As hard-core vegans demonstrate, however, even the consumption of basic food products may also be related to wide-ranging beliefs regarding what is appropriate or desirable. In some cases, these emotional responses create a deep commitment to the product. Sometimes people are not even fully aware of the forces that drive them toward some products and away from others. Often a person's values—his or her priorities and beliefs about the world—influence these choices.

To understand motivation is to understand why consumers do what they do. Why do some people choose to bungee jump off a bridge or stand in Times Square screaming for Carson Daly to bring them up to the studio on MTV's *Total Request Live* (*TRL*) show, whereas others spend their leisure time playing chess or gardening? Whether to quench a thirst, kill boredom, or to attain some deep spiritual experience, we do everything for a reason, even if we can't articulate what that reason is. Marketing students are taught from Day One that the goal of marketing is to satisfy consumers' needs. However, this insight is useless unless we can discover *what* those needs are and *why* they exist. A beer commercial once asked, "Why ask why?" In this chapter, we'll find out.

■ THE MOTIVATION PROCESS

Motivation refers to the processes that lead people to behave as they do. It occurs when a need is aroused that the consumer wishes to satisfy. Once a need has been activated, a state of tension exists that drives the consumer to attempt to reduce or eliminate the need. This need may be *utilitarian* (i.e., a desire to achieve some functional or practical benefit, as when a person loads up on green vegetables for nutritional reasons) or it may be *hedonic* (i.e., an experiential need, involving emotional responses or fantasies, as when Basil thinks longingly about a juicy steak). The desired end state is the consumer's **goal**. Marketers try to create products and services that will provide the desired benefits and permit the consumer to reduce this tension.

Whether the need is utilitarian or hedonic, a discrepancy exists between the consumer's present state and some ideal state. This gulf creates a state of tension. The magnitude of this tension determines the urgency the consumer feels to reduce the tension. This degree of arousal is called a **drive**. A basic need can be satisfied in any number of ways, and the specific path a person chooses is influenced both by his or her unique set of experiences and by the values instilled by the culture in which the person has been raised.

This could be your body.

Soloflex could be the way.

For a free brochure and video, call
SOLOFLEX® 1-800-356-5344

This ad for exercise equipment shows men a desired state (as dictated by contemporary Western culture), and suggests a solution (purchase of the equipment) to attain it.

These personal and cultural factors combine to create a **want**, which is one manifestation of a need. For example, hunger is a basic need that must be satisfied by all; the lack of food creates a tension state that can be reduced by the intake of such products as cheeseburgers, double fudge Oreo cookies, raw fish, or bean sprouts. The specific route to drive reduction is culturally and individually determined. Once the goal is attained, tension is reduced and the motivation recedes (for the time being). Motivation can be described in terms of its *strength*, or the pull it exerts on the consumer, and its *direction*, or the particular way the consumer attempts to reduce motivational tension.

■ MOTIVATIONAL STRENGTH

The degree to which a person is willing to expend energy to reach one goal as opposed to another reflects his or her underlying motivation to attain that goal. Many theories have been advanced to explain why people behave the way they do. Most share the basic idea that people have some finite amount of energy that must be directed toward certain goals.

Biological Versus Learned Needs

Early work on motivation ascribed behavior to *instinct*, the innate patterns of behavior that are universal in a species. This view is now largely discredited. For one thing, the existence of an instinct is difficult to prove or disprove. The instinct is inferred from the behavior it is supposed to explain (this type of circular explanation is called a *tautology*).[2] It is like saying that a consumer buys products that are status symbols because he or she is motivated to attain status, which is hardly a satisfying explanation.

Drive Theory

Drive theory focuses on biological needs that produce unpleasant states of arousal (e.g., your stomach grumbles during a morning class). We are motivated to reduce the tension caused by this arousal. Tension reduction has been proposed as a basic mechanism governing human behavior.

In a marketing context, tension refers to the unpleasant state that exists if a person's consumption needs are not fulfilled. A person may be grumpy if he hasn't eaten, or he may be dejected or angry if he cannot afford that new car he wants. This state activates goal-oriented behavior, which attempts to reduce or eliminate this unpleasant state and return to a balanced one called **homeostasis**.

Those behaviors that are successful in reducing the drive by satisfying the underlying need are strengthened and tend to be repeated. (This aspect of the learning process was discussed in Chapter 3.) Your motivation to leave class early to grab a snack would be greater if you hadn't eaten in 24 hours than if you had eaten only 2 hours earlier. If you did sneak out and got indigestion after, say, wolfing down a package of Twinkies, you would be less likely to repeat this behavior the next time you wanted a snack. One's degree of motivation, then, depends on the distance between one's present state and the goal.

Drive theory runs into difficulties when it tries to explain some facets of human behavior that run counter to its predictions. People often do things that increase a drive state rather than decrease it. For example, people may delay gratification. If you know you are going out for a lavish dinner, you might decide to forego a snack earlier in the day even though you are hungry at that time.

Expectancy Theory

Most current explanations of motivation focus on cognitive factors rather than biological ones to understand what drives behavior. **Expectancy theory** suggests that behavior is largely pulled by expectations of achieving desirable outcomes—positive incentives—rather than pushed from within. We choose one product over another because we expect this choice to have more positive consequences for us. Thus the term *drive* is used here more loosely to refer to both physical and cognitive processes.

■ MOTIVATIONAL DIRECTION

Motives have direction as well as strength. They are goal oriented in that they drive us to satisfy a specific need. Most goals can be reached by a number of routes, and the objective of a company is to convince consumers that the alternative it offers

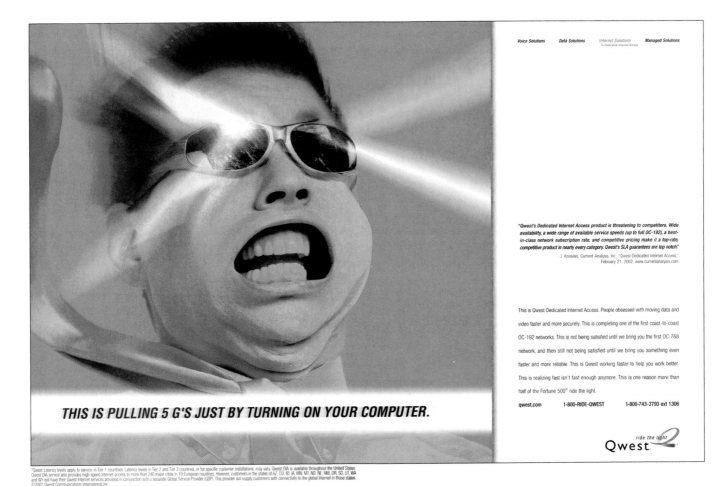

A technical product can satisfy hedonic desires.

provides the best chance to attain the goal. For example, a consumer who decides that she needs a pair of jeans to help her reach her goal of being accepted by others can choose among Levi's, Wranglers, Jnco, Diesel, Seven, and many other alternatives, each of which promises to deliver certain benefits.

Needs Versus Wants

The specific way a need is satisfied depends on the individual's unique history, learning experiences, and cultural environment. A want is the particular form of consumption used to satisfy a need. For example, two classmates may feel their stomachs rumbling during a lunchtime lecture. If neither person has eaten since the night before, the strength of their respective needs (hunger) would be about the same. However, the ways each person goes about satisfying this need might be quite different. The first person may be a vegan like Juanita who fantasizes about gulping down a big handful of trail mix, whereas the second person may be a meat hound like Basil who is aroused by the prospect of a greasy cheeseburger and fries.

Types of Needs

People are born with a need for certain elements necessary to maintain life, such as food, water, air, and shelter. These are called *biogenic needs*. People have many other needs, however, that are not innate. We acquire *psychogenic needs* as we become members of a specific culture. These include the need for status, power, affiliation, and so on. Psychogenic needs reflect the priorities of a culture, and their effect on behavior will vary from environment to environment. For example, an

American consumer may be driven to devote a good chunk of his income to products that permit him to display his individuality, whereas his Japanese counterpart may work equally hard to ensure that he does not stand out from his group.

Consumers can also be motivated to satisfy either utilitarian or hedonic needs. The satisfaction of *utilitarian needs* implies that consumers will emphasize the objective, tangible attributes of products, such as miles per gallon in a car; the amount of fat, calories, and protein in a cheeseburger; and the durability of a pair of blue jeans. *Hedonic needs* are subjective and experiential; consumers might rely on a product to meet their needs for excitement, self-confidence, or fantasy. Of course, consumers can be motivated to purchase a product because it provides *both* types of benefits. For example, a mink coat might be bought because of the luxurious image it portrays and because it also happens to keep one warm through the long, cold winter.

Motivational Conflicts

A goal has *valence*, which means that it can be positive or negative. A positively valued goal is one toward which consumers direct their behavior; they are motivated to *approach* the goal and will seek out products that will help them to reach it. However, not all behavior is motivated by the desire to approach a goal. As we saw in the previous chapter's discussion of negative reinforcement, consumers may instead be motivated to *avoid* a negative outcome. They will structure their purchases or consumption activities to reduce the chances of attaining this end result. For example, many consumers work hard to avoid rejection, a negative goal. They will stay away from products that they associate with social disapproval. Products

We expect today's technical products to satisfy our needs—instantly.

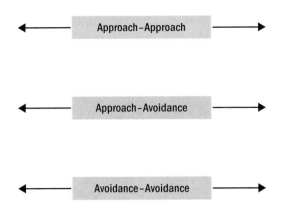

■ **FIGURE 4.1**
THREE TYPES OF MOTIVATIONAL
CONFLICTS

such as deodorants and mouthwash frequently rely on consumers' negative motivation by depicting the onerous social consequences of underarm odor or bad breath.

Because a purchase decision can involve more than one source of motivation, consumers often find themselves in situations in which different motives, both positive and negative, conflict with one another. Because marketers are attempting to satisfy consumers' needs, they can also be helpful by providing possible solutions to these dilemmas. As shown in Figure 4.1, three general types of conflicts can occur. Let's review each kind.

Approach–Approach Conflict

In an **approach–approach conflict**, a person must choose between two desirable alternatives. A student might be torn between going home for the holidays or going on a skiing trip with friends. Or, she might have to choose between two CDs at the store.

The **theory of cognitive dissonance** is based on the premise that people have a need for order and consistency in their lives and that a state of tension is created when beliefs or behaviors conflict with one another. The conflict that arises when choosing between two alternatives may be resolved through a process of *cognitive dissonance reduction*, where people are motivated to reduce this inconsistency (or dissonance) and thus eliminate unpleasant tension.[3]

A state of dissonance occurs when there is a psychological inconsistency between two or more beliefs or behaviors. It often occurs when a consumer must make a choice between two products, both of which usually possess both good and bad qualities. By choosing one product and not the other, the person gets the bad qualities of the chosen product and loses out on the good qualities of the unchosen one.

This loss creates an unpleasant, dissonant state that the person is motivated to reduce. People tend to convince themselves, after the fact, that the choice they made was the smart one by finding additional reasons to support the alternative they chose, or perhaps by "discovering" flaws with the option they did not choose. A marketer can resolve an approach–approach conflict by bundling several benefits together. For example, Miller Lite's claim that it is "less filling" and "tastes great" allows the drinker to "have his beer and drink it too."

Approach–Avoidance Conflict

Many of the products and services we desire have negative consequences attached to them as well. We may feel guilty or ostentatious when buying a status-laden product such as a fur coat, or we might feel like a glutton when contemplating a tempting package of Twinkies. An **approach–avoidance conflict** exists when we desire a goal but wish to avoid it at the same time.

Some solutions to these conflicts include the proliferation of fake furs, which eliminate guilt about harming animals to make a fashion statement, and the success

The Partnership for a Drug-Free America points out the negative consequences of drug addiction for those who are tempted to start.

of diet foods, such as those produced by Weight Watchers, that promise good food without the calories (***weight-watchers.com***). Many marketers try to overcome guilt by convincing consumers that they are deserving of luxuries (e.g., when the model for L'Oréal cosmetics exclaims, "Because I'm worth it!").

Avoidance–Avoidance Conflict

Sometimes consumers find themselves "caught between a rock and a hard place." They may face a choice with two undesirable alternatives, for instance, the option of either throwing more money into an old car or buying a new one. Marketers frequently address an **avoidance–avoidance conflict** with messages that stress the unforeseen benefits of choosing one option (e.g., by emphasizing special credit plans to ease the pain of car payments).

Classifying Consumer Needs

Much research has been done on classifying human needs. On the one hand, some psychologists have tried to define a universal inventory of needs that could be traced systematically to explain virtually all behavior. One such effort, developed by Henry Murray, delineates a set of 20 psychogenic needs that (sometimes in combination) result in specific behaviors. These needs include such dimensions as *autonomy* (being independent), *defendance* (defending the self against criticism), and even *play* (engaging in pleasurable activities).[4]

Murray's need structure serves as the basis for a number of widely used personality tests such as the Thematic Apperception Technique (TAT). In the TAT, test subjects are shown four to six ambiguous pictures and they're asked to write answers to four direct questions about the pictures. These questions are: (1) What is happening? (2) What has led up to this situation? (3) What is being thought? (4) What will happen? Each answer is then analyzed for references to certain needs and scored whenever that need is mentioned. The theory behind the test is that people will freely project their own subconscious needs onto the stimulus. By getting responses to the picture, you are really getting at the person's true needs for achievement or affiliation or whatever other need may be dominant. Murray believed that everyone has the same basic set of needs, but that individuals differ in their priority ranking of these needs.[5]

Specific Needs and Buying Behavior

Other motivational approaches have focused on specific needs and their ramifications for behavior. For example, individuals with a high *need for achievement* strongly value personal accomplishment.[6] They place a premium on products and services that signify success because these consumption items provide feedback about the realization of their goals. These consumers are good prospects for products that provide evidence of their achievement. One study of working women found that those who were high in achievement motivation were more likely to choose clothing they considered businesslike, and less likely to be interested in apparel that accentuated their femininity.[7] Some other important needs that are relevant to consumer behavior include the following:

- *Need for affiliation* (to be in the company of other people):[8] This need is relevant to products and services that are "consumed" in groups and alleviate loneliness, such as team sports, bars, and shopping malls.
- *Need for power* (to control one's environment):[9] Many products and services allow consumers to feel that they have mastery over their surroundings, ranging from "hopped-up" muscle cars and loud boom boxes (large portable radios) that impose one's musical tastes on others to luxury resorts that promise to respond to every whim of their pampered guests.
- *Need for uniqueness* (to assert one's individual identity):[10] Products can satisfy this need by pledging to accentuate a consumer's distinctive qualities. For example, Cachet perfume claims to be "as individual as you are."

Maslow's Hierarchy of Needs

The psychologist Abraham Maslow proposed one influential approach to motivation. His approach was originally developed to understand personal growth and the attainment of "peak experiences."[11] Maslow formulated a hierarchy of biogenic and psychogenic needs that specifies certain levels of motives. This *hierarchical* approach implies that the order of development is fixed—that is, a certain level must be attained before the next, higher one is activated. Marketers have embraced this perspective because it (indirectly) specifies certain types of product benefits people might be looking for, depending on the different stages in their development or their environmental conditions.[12]

Figure 4.2 summarizes this model. At each level, different priorities exist in terms of the product benefits a consumer is looking for. Ideally, an individual progresses up the hierarchy until his or her dominant motivation is a focus on "ultimate" goals, such as justice and beauty. Unfortunately, this state is difficult to achieve (at least on a regular basis); most of us have to be satisfied with occasional glimpses, or *peak experiences*.

■ **FIGURE 4.2** LEVELS OF NEEDS IN THE MASLOW HIERARCHY

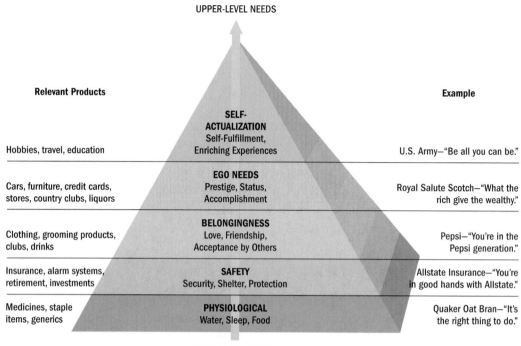

UPPER-LEVEL NEEDS

Relevant Products		Example
	SELF-ACTUALIZATION Self-Fulfillment, Enriching Experiences	
Hobbies, travel, education		U.S. Army—"Be all you can be."
	EGO NEEDS Prestige, Status, Accomplishment	
Cars, furniture, credit cards, stores, country clubs, liquors		Royal Salute Scotch—"What the rich give the wealthy."
	BELONGINGNESS Love, Friendship, Acceptance by Others	
Clothing, grooming products, clubs, drinks		Pepsi—"You're in the Pepsi generation."
	SAFETY Security, Shelter, Protection	
Insurance, alarm systems, retirement, investments		Allstate Insurance—"You're in good hands with Allstate."
	PHYSIOLOGICAL Water, Sleep, Food	
Medicines, staple items, generics		Quaker Oat Bran—"It's the right thing to do."

LOWER-LEVEL NEEDS

Source: Motivation and Personality, 2nd ed., by A. H. Maslow, 1970. Reprinted by permission of Pearson Education, Upper Saddle River, New Jersey.

The basic lesson of Maslow's hierarchy is that one must first satisfy basic needs before progressing up the ladder (i.e., a starving man is not interested in status symbols, friendship, or self-fulfillment). That implies that consumers value different product attributes depending upon what is currently available to them. For example, consumers in the former Eastern bloc are now bombarded with images of luxury goods, yet may still have trouble obtaining basic necessities. In one study Romanian students named the products they hoped to acquire. Their wish lists included not only the expected items such as sports cars and the latest model televisions, but also staples like water, soap, furniture, and food.[13]

The application of this hierarchy by marketers has been somewhat simplistic, especially as the same product or activity can satisfy a number of different needs. For example, one study found that gardening could satisfy needs at every level of the hierarchy:[14]

- *Physiological:* "I like to work in the soil."
- *Safety:* "I feel safe in the garden."
- *Social:* "I can share my produce with others."
- *Esteem:* "I can create something of beauty."
- *Self-actualization:* "My garden gives me a sense of peace."

Another problem with taking Maslow's hierarchy too literally is that it is culture-bound. The assumptions of the hierarchy may be restricted to Western culture. People in other cultures (or, for that matter, in Western culture as well) may question the order of the levels as specified. A religious person who has taken a vow of celibacy would not necessarily agree that physiological needs must be satisfied before self-fulfillment can occur.

Similarly, many Asian cultures value the welfare of the group (belongingness needs) more highly than needs of the individual (esteem needs). The point is that this hierarchy, although widely applied in marketing, is helpful to marketers because it reminds us that consumers may have different need priorities in different consumption situations and at different stages in their lives—not because it exactly specifies a consumer's progression up the ladder of needs.

Paradise: Satisfying Needs?

Presumably, a person who has had all of his or her needs satisfied lives in "paradise." Conceptualizations of paradise have implications for the marketing and consumption of any products, such as vacation travel, that try to invoke an ideal state. However, the definition of just what constitutes paradise appears to differ across cultures. A study compared American and Dutch college students' concepts of paradise to explore these variations. The students each constructed a collage of images to illustrate their overall concept of paradise, and then they wrote an essay to explain their choices. Some similarities were evident in the two societies; both Americans and Dutch emphasized the personal, experiential aspects of paradise, saying "paradise is different for everyone . . . a feeling . . . a state of being." In addition, individuals in both societies said that paradise must include family, friends, and significant others.

However, the Dutch and Americans differed in important and interesting ways. The Americans consistently emphasized hedonism, materialism, individuality, creativity, and issues of time and space consistent with a society in which time is segmented and viewed almost as a commodity (more on this in Chapter 10). Conversely, the Dutch respondents showed a concern for social and environmental responsibility, collective societal order and equality, and a balance between work and play as part of paradise. For instance, one Dutch student said that "Respect for animals, flowers, and plants . . . regenerating energy sources, such as wind, water, and sun are all important parts of paradise." Marketers should expect that, because concepts of paradise appear to vary across cultures, different images and behaviors might be evoked when consumers are confronted with marketing messages such as "Hawaii is paradise," or "You can experience paradise when you drive this car."[15]

A Dutch respondent's collage emphasizes this person's conception of paradise as a place where there is interpersonal harmony and concern for the environment.

■ CONSUMER INVOLVEMENT

Do consumers form strong relationships with products and services? If you don't believe so, consider these recent events:

● A consumer in Brighton, England loves a local restaurant called the All In One so much, he had its name and phone number tattooed on his forehead. The owner remarked, "whenever he comes in, he'll go straight to the front of the queue."[16]

● *Lucky* is a magazine devoted to shopping for shoes and other fashion accessories. The centerfold of the first issue featured rows of makeup sponges. The editor observes, "It's the same way that you might look at a golf magazine and see a spread of nine irons. *Lucky* is addressing one interest in women's lives, in a really obsessive, specific way."[17]

● After being jilted by his girlfriend, a Tennessee man tried to marry his car. His plan was thwarted, however, after he listed his fiancée's birthplace as Detroit, her father as Henry Ford, and her blood type as 10W40. Under Tennessee law, only a man and a woman can legally wed.[18] So much for that exciting honeymoon at the carwash.

These examples illustrate that people can get pretty attached to products. As we have seen, a consumer's motivation to attain a goal increases her desire to acquire the products or services she believes will satisfy that goal. However, not everyone is motivated to the same extent—one person might be convinced she can't live without the latest style or modern convenience, whereas another is not interested in this item at all.

Involvement is defined as "a person's perceived relevance of the object based on their inherent needs, values, and interests."[19] The word *object* is used in the generic sense and refers to a product (or a brand), an advertisement, or a purchase situation. Consumers can find involvement in all these *objects*. Figure 4.3 shows

■ FIGURE 4.3 CONCEPTUALIZING INVOLVEMENT

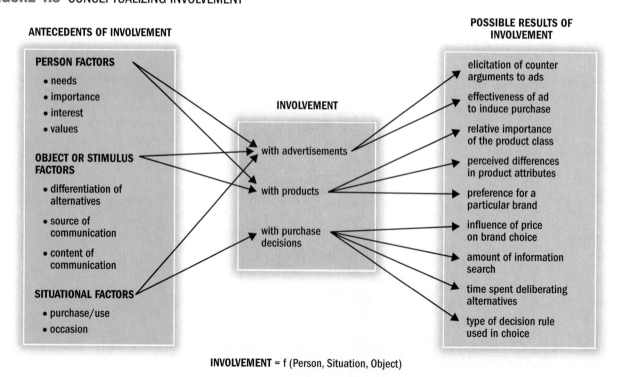

INVOLVEMENT = f (Person, Situation, Object)

The level of involvement may be influenced by one or more of these three factors. Interactions among persons, situation, and object factors are likely to occur.

that because involvement is a motivational construct, different antecedents can trigger it. These factors can be something about the person, something about the object, or something about the situation.

We can view involvement as the motivation to process information.[20] To the degree that there is a perceived linkage between a consumer's needs, goals, or values and product knowledge, the consumer will be motivated to pay attention to product information. When relevant knowledge is activated in memory, a motivational state is created that drives behavior (e.g., shopping). As involvement with a product increases, the consumer devotes more attention to ads related to the product, exerts more cognitive effort to understand these ads, and focuses more attention on the product-related information in them.[21]

Levels of Involvement: From Inertia to Passion

The type of information processing that will occur thus depends on the consumer's level of involvement. It can range from *simple processing*, in which only the basic

The Swiss Potato Board is trying to increase involvement with its product. The ad reads, "Recipes against boredom."

Rezepte gegen die Langeweile: www.kartoffel.ch

Marketing Opportunity

Anyone who can create a cult brand goes straight to marketing heaven, but this is very difficult to do from scratch. One entrepreneur is well on his way. In 1996, Peter van Stolk was barely getting shelf space for his Jones Soda brand. He started putting his colorful drinks in unconventional places like record stores, hair salons, tattoo parlors, even sex shops. After a buzz started around Jones, van Stolk stoked it by asking fans to send him their photographs, which he plastered on his labels. The company's Web site (**www.jonessoda.com**) has become a forum for Jones fans to chat about school, life, or soda.[24]

features of a message are considered, all the way to *elaboration*, in which the incoming information is linked to one's preexisting knowledge system.[22]

Inertia

We can think of a person's degree of involvement as a continuum, ranging from absolute lack of interest in a marketing stimulus at one end to obsession at the other. Consumption at the low end of involvement is characterized by **inertia**, where decisions are made out of habit because the consumer lacks the motivation to consider alternatives. At the high end of involvement, we can expect to find the type of passionate intensity reserved for people and objects that carry great meaning for the individual. For example, the passion of some consumers for famous people (those living, such as Michael Jordan, or—supposedly—dead, such as Elvis Presley) demonstrates the high end of the involvement continuum.

When consumers are truly involved with a product, an ad, or a Web site, they enter what has been called a **flow state**. This state is the Holy Grail of Web designers who want to create sites that are so entrancing the surfer loses all track of time as he becomes engrossed in the site's contents (and hopefully buys stuff in the process!). Flow is an optimal experience characterized by:

- A sense of playfulness
- A feeling of being in control
- Concentration and highly focused attention
- Mental enjoyment of the activity for its own sake
- A distorted sense of time
- A match between the challenge at hand and one's skills.[23]

Cult Products

Cult products command fierce consumer loyalty, devotion—and maybe even worship by consumers who are very highly involved with a brand. These items take many forms, from Apple computers and Harley-Davidson motorcycles to Krispy Kreme donuts and Beanie Babies. What else explains the willingness of many women to shell out up to $3,400 for a pair of shoes designed by Manolo Blahnik?

Loyal users can log in and hang out at the Jones Soda Web site.

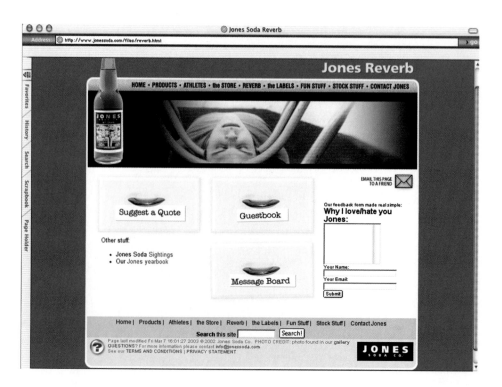

The Many Faces of Involvement

Involvement can take many forms. It can be cognitive, as when a "Webhead" is motivated to learn all she can about the latest specs of a new multimedia PC, or emotional, as when the thought of a new Armani suit gives a clotheshorse goosebumps.[25] Further, the very act of buying the Armani may be very involving for people who are passionately devoted to shopping. To complicate matters further, advertisements, such as those produced for Nike or Adidas, may themselves be involving for some reason (e.g., because they make us laugh, cry, or inspire us to work harder). It seems that involvement is a fuzzy concept, because it overlaps with other things and means different things to different people. Indeed, the consensus is that there are actually several broad types of involvement related to the product, the message, or the perceiver.[26]

Many marketing messages, such as this ad for a cosmetics company in Taiwan, focus on emotions rather than cognitions.

Product Involvement

Product involvement is related to a consumer's level of interest in a particular product. Many sales promotions are designed to increase this type of involvement. When Lifesavers announced that it was going to eliminate the pineapple flavor unless consumers went to its Web site and voted to keep it, over 400,000 consumers heard the call and saved the flavor.[27]

Message–Response Involvement

Message–response involvement (also known as *advertising involvement*) refers to the consumer's interest in processing marketing communications.[28] Television is considered a low-involvement medium because it requires a passive viewer who exerts relatively little control (remote control "zipping" notwithstanding) over content (on the other hand, the young fans of MTV's *TRL Show* certainly seem pretty involved with this experience!). In contrast, print is a high-involvement medium. The reader is actively involved in processing the information and is able to pause and reflect on what he or she has read before moving on.[29] We'll discuss the role of message characteristics in changing attitudes in Chapter 8.

Purchase Situation Involvement

Purchase situation involvement refers to differences that may occur when buying the same object for different contexts. Here the person may perceive a great deal of social risk or none at all. For example, when you want to impress someone you may try to buy a brand or a product with a certain image that you think reflects good taste. When you have to buy a gift for someone in an obligatory situation, like a wedding gift for a cousin you do not really like, you may not care what image the gift portrays. Or you may actually pick something cheap that reflects your desire to distance yourself from that cousin.

Measuring Involvement

The measurement of involvement is important for many marketing applications. For example, research evidence indicates that a viewer who is more involved with a television show will also respond more positively to commercials contained in that show, and that these spots will have a greater chance of influencing his or her purchase intentions.[30] One of the most widely used measures of the state of involvement is the scale shown in Table 4.1.

Teasing Out the Dimensions of Involvement

French researchers devised a scale to measure the antecedents of product involvement. Recognizing that consumers can be involved with a product because it is a risky purchase and its use reflects on or affects the self, they advocate the development of an *involvement profile* containing five components:[31]

1 The personal interest a consumer has in a product category, its personal meaning or importance;
2 The perceived importance of the potential negative consequences associated with a poor choice of the product (risk importance);
3 The probability of making a bad purchase;
4 The pleasure value of the product category;
5 The sign value of the product category (how closely it's related to the self).

These researchers asked a sample of homemakers to rate a set of 14 product categories on each of the facets of involvement. The results are shown in Table 4.2. These data indicate that no single component captures consumer involvement. For example, the purchase of a durable product such as a vacuum cleaner is seen as

TABLE 4.1
A SCALE TO MEASURE INVOLVEMENT

To Me [Object to be Judged] Is

1.	important	_:_:_:_:_:_:_	unimportant*
2.	boring	_:_:_:_:_:_:_	interesting
3.	relevant	_:_:_:_:_:_:_	irrelevant*
4.	exciting	_:_:_:_:_:_:_	unexciting*
5.	means nothing	_:_:_:_:_:_:_	means a lot to me
6.	appealing	_:_:_:_:_:_:_	unappealing*
7.	fascinating	_:_:_:_:_:_:_	mundane*
8.	worthless	_:_:_:_:_:_:_	valuable
9.	involving	_:_:_:_:_:_:_	uninvolving*
10.	not needed	_:_:_:_:_:_:_	needed

Note: Totaling the 10 items gives a score from a low of 10 to a high of 70.
*Indicates item is reverse scored. For example, a score of 7 for item no. 1 (important/unimportant) would actually be scored as 1.
Source: Judith Lynne Zaichkowsky, "The Personal Involvement Inventory: Reduction, Revision, and Application to Advertising," *Journal of Advertising* 23, no. 4 (December 1994): 59–70.

risky, because one is stuck with a bad choice for many years. However, the vacuum cleaner does not provide pleasure (hedonic value), nor is it high in sign value (i.e., its use is not related to the person's self-concept). In contrast, chocolate is high in pleasure value but is not seen as risky or closely related to the self. Dresses and bras, on the other hand, appear to be involving for a combination of reasons. Note also that involvement with a product class may vary across cultures. Although this sample of French consumers rated champagne high in both sign value and personal value, the ability of champagne to provide pleasure or to be central to self-definition might not transfer to other countries (e.g., Islamic cultures).

Segmenting by Involvement Levels
A measurement approach of this nature allows consumer researchers to capture the diversity of the involvement construct, and it also provides the potential to use involvement as a basis for market segmentation. For example, a yogurt manufacturer might find that even though its product is low in sign value for one group of consumers, it might be highly related to the self-concept of another market segment, such as health food enthusiasts or avid dieters. The company could adapt its strategy to account for the motivation of different segments to process information about the product. One study looked at the role of affective versus cognitive and level of involvement (high versus low) in promoting Canadian universities. The researchers found that students who were cognitively involved conducted an intense search for university information, whereas students who were affectively involved made their university choice based mainly on emotional factors.[32]

Strategies to Increase Involvement
Although consumers differ in their levels of involvement with respect to a product message, marketers do not have to just sit back and hope for the best. By being aware of some basic factors that increase or decrease attention, they can take steps

TABLE 4.2
INVOLVEMENT PROFILES FOR A SET OF FRENCH CONSUMER PRODUCTS

	Importance of Negative Consequences	Subjective Probability of Mispurchase	Pleasure Value	Sign Value
Dresses	121	112	147	181
Bras	117	115	106	130
Washing machines	118	109	106	111
TV sets	112	100	122	95
Vaccum cleaners	110	112	70	78
Irons	103	95	72	76
Champagne	109	120	125	125
Oil	89	97	65	92
Yogurt	86	83	106	78
Chocolate	80	89	123	75
Shampoo	96	103	90	81
Toothpaste	95	95	94	105
Facial soap	82	90	114	118
Detergents	79	82	56	63

Average product score = 100.
Note the first two antecedents of personal importance and importance of negative consequences are combined in these data.

Source: Gilles Laurent and Jean-Noël Kapferer, "Measuring Consumer Involvement Profiles," *Journal of Marketing Research 22* (February 1985): 45, Table 3. By permission of American Marketing Association.

to increase the likelihood that product information will get through. A marketer can boost consumers' motivations to process relevant information by using one or more of the following techniques:[33]

- *Appeal to the consumers' hedonic needs.* For example, ads using sensory appeals generate higher levels of attention.[34]
- *Use novel stimuli, such as unusual cinematography, sudden silences, or unexpected movements in commercials.* When a British firm called Egg Banking introduced a credit card to the French market in 2002, its ad agency created unusual commercials to make people question their assumptions. One ad stated "Cats always land on their paws," and then two researchers in white lab coats dropped a kitten off a rooftop—never to see it again (animal rights activists were not amused).[35]
- *Use prominent stimuli, such as loud music and fast action, to capture attention in commercials.* In print formats, larger ads increase attention. Also, viewers look longer at colored pictures as opposed to black and white.
- *Include celebrity endorsers to generate higher interest in commercials.* (We'll discuss this strategy in Chapter 8.)
- *Build a bond with consumers by maintaining an ongoing relationship with them.* Learn from the actions of tobacco companies, which have figured out how to keep smokers' loyalties (at least until they die). R.J. Reynolds Co. hosted nearly 3,700 Doral smokers at its factory for Western line dancing lessons, bowl-

ing, blackjack, and plenty of free cigarettes. Said one happy attendee, "I'd quit altogether before I'd change brands."[36] Now there's a thought.

■ VALUES

A **value** is a belief that some condition is preferable to its opposite. For example, it's safe to assume that most people place a priority on freedom, preferring it to slavery. Others avidly pursue products and services that will make them look young, believing that this is preferable to appearing old. A person's set of values plays a very important role in consumption activities. Consumers purchase many products and services because they believe these products will help to attain a value-related goal.

Two people can believe in the same behaviors (e.g., vegetarianism), but their underlying belief systems may be quite different (e.g., animal activism versus health concerns). The extent to which people share a belief system is a function of individual, social, and cultural forces. Advocates of a belief system often seek out others with similar beliefs so that social networks overlap, and as a result believers tend to be exposed to information that supports their beliefs (e.g., "tree-huggers" rarely hang out with loggers).[37]

Core Values

More than 8.2 million women in 50 countries read versions of *Cosmopolitan* in 28 different languages—even though due to local norms about modesty some of them have to hide the magazine from their husbands! Adapting the *Cosmo* credo of "Fun, Fearless Female" in all these places gets a bit tricky. Different cultures emphasize varying belief systems that define what it means to be female, feminine, or appealing—and what is considered appropriate to see in print on these matters. In India, you won't come across any *Cosmo* articles about sexual positions. Publishers of the Chinese version aren't even permitted to mention sex at all, so articles about uplifting cleavage are replaced by uplifting stories about youthful dedication. Ironically, there isn't much down and dirty material in the Swedish edition either—but for the opposite reason: The culture is so open about this topic that it doesn't grab readers' attention the way it would in the United States.[38]

Every culture has a set of values that it imparts to its members.[39] People in one culture might feel that being a unique individual is preferable to subordinating one's identity to the group, whereas another culture may emphasize the virtues of group membership. A study by Wirthlin Worldwide found that the most important values to Asian executives are hard work, respect for learning, and honesty. In contrast, North American businesspeople emphasize the values of personal freedom, self-reliance, and freedom of expression.[40]

These differences in values often explain why marketing efforts that are a big hit in one country can flop in another. For example, a hugely successful advertisement in Japan promoted breast cancer awareness by showing an attractive woman in a sundress drawing stares from men on the street as a voice-over says, "If only women paid as much attention to their breasts as men do." The same ad flopped in France because the use of humor to talk about a serious disease offended the French.[41]

In many cases, of course, values are universal. Who does not desire health, wisdom, or world peace? What sets cultures apart is the *relative importance*, or ranking, of these universal values. This set of rankings constitutes a culture's **value system**.[42] For example, one study found that North Americans have more favorable attitudes toward advertising messages that focus on self-reliance, self-improvement, and the achievement of personal goals as opposed to themes stressing family integrity, collective goals, and the feeling of harmony with others. Korean consumers exhibited the reverse pattern.[43]

Net Profit

It's human nature to be more involved with a product that's directly relevant to your individual wants and needs. One of the exciting advantages of the Internet is the ability to *personalize* content, so that a Web site offers unique information or products tailored to each Web surfer. Consider these approaches to personalization that build the different kinds of involvement we've been discussing:

● *Product involvement:* A recent survey found that 75 percent of American adults want more customized products and—more importantly—70 percent are willing to pay extra for them. This desire is even more acute among young people; 85 percent of 18- to 24-year-olds want more customized products, particularly in such domains as clothing, shoes, electronics, and travel services.[44] **Venturoma.com** lets the shopper create her own blend of massage oils, skin creams, or body washes, while **Customatix.com** lets you design your own sports and casual shoes. In Asia, Coca-Cola is testing its "Style-A-Coke" shrink-wrap system that lets consumers customize their Coke bottles with different sleeve designs.[45]

● *Message-response involvement:* An ad campaign in the Netherlands directs teens to a Web-design site where they can create their own Coca-Cola commercials. At the end of the month, about 10 to 15 finalists will appear on a Web site, where people can view them and vote for their favorite.[46] In a more powerful application of this idea, a British ad for a homeless charity lets viewers create their own message by selecting different story lines. The ad traces the story of Paul, a teenager from a troubled family. Viewers can click to make different choices for Paul as his fortunes decline, such as whether to report his bullying stepfather to the police, or whether to prostitute himself ("To have sex for money press Green now").[47] Or, how about movie posters that talk back to you? ThinkPix Smart

—continued

Displays are part of a new wave of posters that will enable a celebrity on the wall to wink at you as you pass by. And, to personalize the process, moviegoers will insert a card indicating their tastes in order to see posters that show trailers featuring stars they like.[48]

- *Purchase situation involvement:* To a denizen of the online world, a **skin** is a graphical interface that acts as both the face and the control panel of a computer program. Rather than settling for the boring skins that come with most programs, many people prefer to make and trade their own unique ones. According to the product manager for Real Player, "This kind of customization is a huge factor in driving product use. . . We're getting into a world were one size doesn't fit all, and one of the great benefits of technology is having the experience tailored to you." In addition to the more than 15 million skins that have been created for Real Player, many other games, including The Sims and the multiplayer Unreal Tournament have Web sites devoted to user-created skins. Players swap skins of the Incredible Hulk or Rambo or even playable skins of themselves. Movie companies and record labels now routinely commission artists to create promotional skins for films like "Blow" and "Frequency" and for music artists like U2, Britney Spears, and 'N Sync.[49]

Every culture is characterized by its members' endorsement of a value system. These values may not be equally endorsed by every individual, and in some cases, values may even seem to contradict one another (e.g., Americans appear to value both conformity and individuality, and seek to find some accommodation between the two). Nonetheless, it is usually possible to identify a general set of **core values** that uniquely define a culture. Core values such as freedom, youthfulness, achievement, materialism, and activity have been said to characterize American culture.

How do we figure out what a culture values? The process of learning the beliefs and behaviors endorsed by one's own culture is termed **enculturation**. In contrast, the process of learning the value system and behaviors of another culture (often a priority for those who wish to understand consumers and markets in foreign countries) is called **acculturation**. These beliefs are taught to us by *socialization agents*, including parents, friends, and teachers. Another important type of agent is the media; we learn a lot about a culture's priorities by looking at the values advertising

Cleanliness is a core value in many cultures.

communicates. For example, sales strategies differ significantly between the United States and China. American commercials are more likely to present facts about products and suggestions from credible authorities, while Chinese advertisers tend to focus more on emotional appeals without bothering too much to substantiate their claims. American ads tend to be youth-oriented, while Chinese ads are more likely to stress the wisdom of older people.[50]

Applications of Values to Consumer Behavior

Despite their importance, values have not been as widely applied to direct examinations of consumer behavior as might be expected. One reason is that broad-based concepts such as freedom, security, or inner harmony are more likely to affect general purchasing patterns than to differentiate between brands within a product category. For this reason some researchers have found it convenient to make distinctions among broad-based *cultural values* such as security or happiness, *consumption-specific values* such as convenient shopping or prompt service, and *product-specific values* such as ease of use or durability, which affect the relative importance people in different cultures place on possessions.[51]

While some aspects of brand image such as sophistication tend to be common across cultures, others are more likely to be relevant in specific places. The characteristic of peacefulness is valued to a larger extent in Japan, while the same holds true for passion in Spain and ruggedness in the United States.[52] Because values drive much of consumer behavior (at least in a very general sense), we might say that virtually all consumer research ultimately is related to the identification and measurement of values. This section will describe some specific attempts by researchers to measure cultural values and apply this knowledge to marketing strategy.

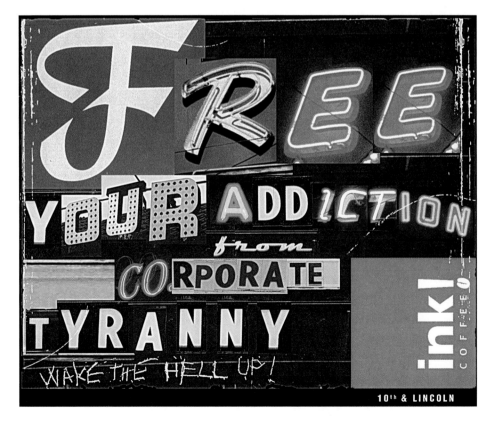

The positive value we place on the activities of large corporations is changing among some consumers who prefer to go "anti-corporate." This ad for a coffee shop in Boulder, Colorado reflects that sentiment.

Marketing Opportunity

The values treasured by a culture create opportunities for new products that might seem strange or a bit excessive to foreigners. Consider the "toilet wars" now underway in Japan, as companies vie with each other to produce the most sophisticated and luxurious bathroom fixture.

Why the commotion over commodes? As one marketing executive explains, in a Japanese house, "the only place you can be alone and sit quietly is likely to be the toilet." Take cramped living conditions, and then factor in a love of new technology. Now, add a strong cultural emphasis on cleanliness: Many Japanese wear gloves to protect themselves from strangers' germs and some ATM machines dispense cash that's been sanitized (yes, banks literally "launder" their money!). Nearly half of Japanese homes already have toilets with a water jet spray used to wash and massage the buttocks. Let the games begin:

- It all started when Matsushita unveiled a toilet seat equipped with electrodes that send a mild electric charge through the user's buttocks, yielding a digital measurement of body-fat ratio.
- Engineers from Inax counterattacked with a toilet that glows in the dark. When in use, the toilet plays any of six soundtracks, including chirping birds, rushing water, tinkling wind chimes, or the strumming of a traditional Japanese harp.
- Matsushita retaliated with a $3,000 throne that greets a user by flipping its lid, and by blasting its twin air nozzles that provide air conditioning in the summer and heat in the winter.
- Toto weighed in with the Wellyou II model that automatically measures the user's urine sugar levels by making a collection with a little spoon held by a retractable, mechanical arm.
- What's next? Matsushita is working on devices to measure weight, heartbeat, blood pressure, and other health indicators; the toilet will send results to a doctor via a built-in, Internet-capable cell phone. Also in the works are talking toilets equipped with microchips that will greet each user with a personalized message such as words of encouragement from Mom, and soon people will be able to give their toilets simple verbal commands.[56]

The Rokeach Value Survey

The psychologist Milton Rokeach identified a set of **terminal values**, or desired end states, that apply to many different cultures. The Rokeach Value Survey, a scale used to measure these values, also includes a set of **instrumental values**, which are composed of actions needed to achieve these terminal values.[53] Table 4.3 lists these two sets of values.

Some evidence indicates that differences on these global values do translate into product-specific preferences and differences in media usage. Nonetheless, marketing researchers have not widely used the Rokeach Value Survey.[54] One reason is that our society is evolving into smaller and smaller sets of *consumption microcultures* within a larger culture, each with its own set of core values. For example, in the United States a sizeable number of people are strong believers in natural health practices and alternative medicines. This focus on wellness instead of mainstream medical approaches to sickness influences many of their behaviors, from food choices to use of alternative medical practitioners as well as their opinions on political and social issues.[55] Indeed, American value structures seem to shift a bit as one moves around the country: Researchers find that people in the Mountain region, for example, are relatively more concerned with environmental mastery,

TABLE 4.3
TWO TYPES OF VALUES IN THE ROKEACH VALUE SURVEY

Instrumental Values	Terminal Values
Ambitious	A comfortable life
Broad-minded	An exciting life
Capable	A sense of accomplishment
Cheerful	A world of peace
Clean	A world of beauty
Courageous	Equality
Forgiving	Family security
Helpful	Freedom
Honest	Happiness
Imaginative	Inner harmony
Independent	Mature love
Intellectual	National security
Logical	Pleasure
Loving	Salvation
Obedient	Self-respect
Polite	Social recognition
Responsible	True friendship
Self-controlled	Wisdom

Source: Richard W. Pollay, "Measuring the Cultural Values Manifest in Advertising," *Current Issues and Research in Advertising* (1983): 71–92. Reprinted by permission of University of Michigan Division of Research.

THE GLOBAL LOOKING GLASS

It may not be unusual for an American to be booed at an environmental conference these days, but it may be noteworthy that many of the countries attending the event are friends of the United States. "I think a lot of people see a greedy bully," says Vuyo Mvoko, a journalist with SABC television in South Africa, "someone who is prepared to run roughshod over other people's interests." It was a theme that was repeated when ABCNEWS consulted journalists around the world about the way the United States is perceived at the moment.

"The people in Germany, we accept that you are, in a way, stronger," said Peter Kloeppel of RTL television in Germany. "But what we don't accept is that you just come to conclusions and make decisions without ever putting into consideration what it might mean for other names—like, for example, the Germans."

"Japanese people think the American people are a friendly people," said Hidetoshi Fujisawa of the Japanese television network NHK. "But these days, some are thinking of them as a little bit self-centered and not knowing much about what is happening outside of the United States."

In France, a poll published this week reported a rise in hostility to U.S. policies. "They are too much interested in their own personal business," said Christian Malar, a senior foreign analyst for France 3 TV. "They're concerned only by their own personal interest, not caring enough about the interest or sharing interest with their own friendly countries and their own allies." "What we have seen for the last year is a strong environmental movement," said Kloeppel, the German journalist. "We have the feeling America should really be more conscious about the global environment, and not just always say, 'It's our economy that's first.' I think what a lot of Germans say is 'Let's think about our global environment because it's something that belongs to all of us.'"

And some so-called anti-American feeling, these correspondents said, was really just acknowledgement that the fate of small nations is so inextricably bound to desires of the United States, the world's sole superpower and largest economy. "We know that when the United States sneezes we get pneumonia," said Félix de Bedout of UniNoticias television in Colombia.

*Source: Adapted from Michael Martin, "A Greedy Bully: Foreign Journalists Say Regard for the U.S. Abroad Has Dropped," **ABCNews.com**, April 28, 2003.*

while those in the West South Central region focus on personal growth and feeling cheerful and happy; the West North Central area emphasizes feeling calm, peaceful, and satisfied; and people in the East South Central area are more concerned with contributing to others' well-being.[57]

The List of Values (LOV)

The List of Values (LOV) Scale was developed to isolate values with more direct marketing applications. This instrument identifies nine consumer segments based on the values they endorse and relates each value to differences in consumption behaviors. These segments include consumers who place a priority on such values as a sense of belonging, excitement, warm relationships with others, and security. For example, people who endorse the value of sense of belonging are older and more likely to read *Reader's Digest* and *TV Guide,* drink and entertain more, and prefer group activities more than people who do not endorse this value as highly. In contrast, those who endorse the value of excitement are younger and prefer *Rolling Stone* magazine.[58]

The Means–End Chain Model

Another research approach that incorporates values is termed a means–end chain model. This approach assumes that very specific product attributes are linked at levels of increasing abstraction to terminal values. The person has valued end states, and he or she chooses among alternative means to attain these goals. Products are thus valued as the means to an end. Through a technique called **laddering**, consumers' associations between specific attributes and general consequences are uncovered. Consumers are helped to climb up the "ladder" of abstraction that connects functional product attributes with desired end states.[59] Based on consumer feedback, researchers create *hierarchical value maps* that show how specific product attributes get linked to end states.

Figure 4.4 shows three different hierarchical value maps from a study of consumers' perceptions of cooking oils in three European countries.[60] The laddering technique illustrates how different product/values links can be across cultures. For Danish people, health is the most important end state. The British also focus on health, but saving money and avoiding waste are more important than for people elsewhere. And, unlike the other two countries, French people link oil (especially olive oil) to their cultural identity.

The notion that products are consumed because they are instrumental in attaining more abstract values is central to one application of this technique, called the Means–End Conceptualization of the Components of Advertising Strategy (MECCAS). In this approach, researchers first generate a map depicting relationships between functional product or service attributes and terminal values. This information is then used to develop advertising strategy by identifying elements such as the following:[61]

- *Message elements:* The specific attributes or product features to be depicted.
- *Consumer benefit:* The positive consequences of using the product or service.
- *Executional framework:* The overall style and tone of the advertisement.
- *Leverage point:* The way the message will activate the terminal value by linking it with specific product features.
- *Driving force:* The end value on which the advertising will focus.

This technique was used to develop an advertising strategy for the Danish fish trade organization.[62] In spite of the country's huge fishing industry and ample supply of fresh fish, the Danish per capita consumption of fish was considerably lower than in several other European countries. Researchers used a means–end approach to investigate Danish consumers' attitudes about eating fish. They concluded that a big problem was that Danish housewives didn't feel they could prepare a sufficient variety of fish-based meals to please their families.

Based on these results, an advertising campaign was created. Instead of its usual emphasis on fish as a healthy food, this time message elements emphasized convenience and good taste. The consumer benefit was quick and easy preparation, which made dinner or lunch an easy task to accomplish. The executional framework was a humorous one. Two middle-aged, traditional-looking people are portrayed in various situations, where the male is skeptical about the idea of eating fish for lunch or dinner. In one of the TV spots, the wife is talking to somebody else over the telephone. Her remarks lead the TV viewers (and the husband listening in the background) to think that they are talking about the other family's sex life ("You do it TWICE a week!" "It takes FIFTEEN minutes!!!," "so HE likes that?"). In fact, a friend is telling the wife how she prepares fish for dinner. The leverage point is that these recipes allow the wife to prepare delicious meals very quickly, which in turn provides a happy family life, the driving force (terminal value). Almost immediately after the campaign, the trade organization registered an increase in the consumption of fresh fish.

Syndicated Surveys

A number of companies track changes in values through large-scale surveys. They sell the results of these studies to marketers, who often also pay a fee to receive regular updates on changes and trends. This approach originated in the mid-1960s, when Playtex was concerned about sagging girdle sales. The company commissioned the market research firm of Yankelovich, Skelly & White to see why sales had dropped. Their research determined that sales had been affected by a shift in values regarding appearance and naturalness. Playtex went on to design lighter, less restrictive garments, while Yankelovich went on to track the impact of these types of changes in a range of industries. Gradually, the firm developed the idea of one big study to track American attitudes. In 1970, it introduced the Yankelovich *Monitor*,™ which is based on two-hour interviews with 4,000 respondents.[63]

■ **FIGURE 4.4** HIERARCHICAL VALUE MAPS FOR VEGETABLE OIL IN THREE COUNTRIES

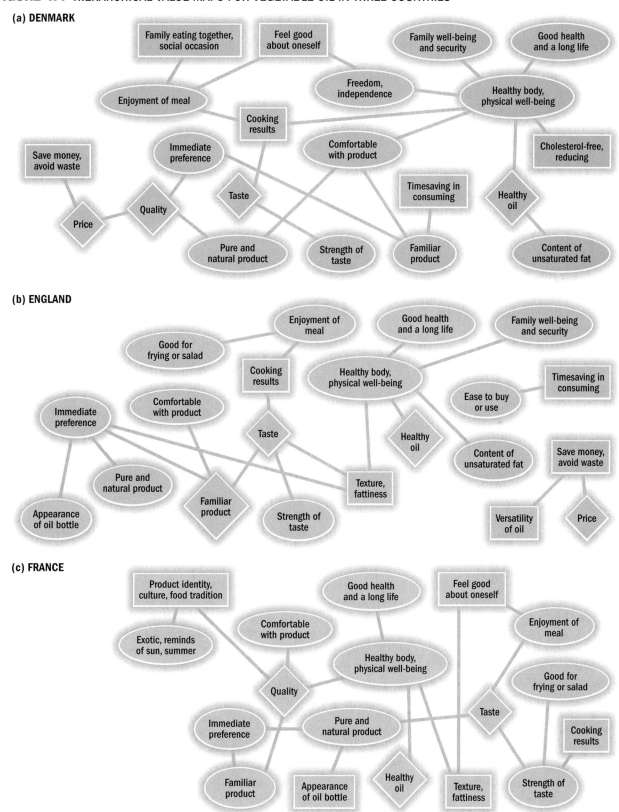

Source: N. A. Nielsen, T. Bech-Larsen, and K. G. Grunert, "Consumer Purchase Motives and Product Perceptions: A Laddering Study on Vegetable Oil in Three Countries," *Food Quality and Preference* 9(6) (1998): 455-66.

Marketing Pitfall

Strongly held values can make life very difficult for marketers who sell personal-care products. This is the case with tampons; 70 percent of American women use them, but only 100 million out of a potential market of 1.7 billion eligible women around the world do. Resistance to using this product posed a major problem for Tambrands. This company makes only one product, so it needs to sell tampons in as many countries as possible to continue growing. But, Tambrands has trouble selling its feminine hygiene products in some cultures such as Brazil, where many young women fear they will lose their virginity if they use a tampon. A commercial developed for this market included an actress who says in a reassuring voice, "Of course, you're not going to lose your virginity."

Prior to launching a new global advertising campaign for Tampax in 26 countries, the firm's advertising agency conducted research and divided the world into three clusters based on residents' resistance to using tampons. Resistance was so intense in Muslim countries that the agency didn't even try to sell there!

In Cluster One (including the United States, the United Kingdom, and Australia), women felt comfortable with the idea and offered little resistance. A teaser ad was developed to encourage more frequency of use: "Should I sleep with it, or not?"

In Cluster Two (including France, Israel, and South Africa), about 50 percent of women use the product, but some concerns about the loss of virginity remain. To counteract these objections, the marketing strategy focused on obtaining the endorsements of gynecologists within each country.

In Cluster Three (including Brazil, China, and Russia), Tambrands encountered the greatest resistance. To try to make inroads in these countries, the researchers found that the first priority is simply to explain how to use the product without making women feel squeamish—a challenge they still are trying to puzzle out. If they do—and that's a big if—Tambrands will have changed the consumer behavior of millions of women and added huge new markets to its customer base in the process.[67]

This survey attempts to pick up changes in values; for example, it reported a movement among American consumers toward simplification and away from hype as people try to streamline their hectic lives and reduce their concerns about gaining the approval of others through their purchases. **Voluntary simplifiers** believe that once basic material needs are sated, additional income does not add to happiness. Instead of adding yet another SUV to the collection in the garage, simplifiers are into community building, public service, and spiritual pursuits.[64] Voluntary simplifiers range from senior citizens who downsize their homes to young, mobile professionals who don't want to be tied down to their possessions. These sentiments snowballed after the tragedy of September 11, 2001, when many people became more reflective and less materialistic. In the months that followed, stories abounded of successful careerists who gave it all up to spend time with their families.

Today, many other syndicated surveys also track changes in values. Some of these are operated by advertising agencies to allow them to stay on top of important cultural trends and help them to shape the messages they craft on behalf of their clients. These services include VALS 2 (more on this in Chapter 6), GlobalScan (operated by the advertising agency Backer Spielvogel Bates), New Wave (the Ogilvy & Mather advertising agency), and the Lifestyles Study conducted by the DDB World Communications Group. The Angus Reid Group in Canada surveys changes in values of specific groups or industry segments.

As we'll see in later chapters, it's often useful to go beyond simple demographics like a person's age to understand the values and preferences a group of people might have in common. This philosophy applies to understanding the youth market—we'll show in Chapter 15 that as much as adults would like to lump all kids together, in fact there are important differences among them in terms of what they value—and these priorities may mean that they have more in common with a young person halfway around the globe than the guy sitting in the next seat in homeroom.

The *New World Teen Study* surveyed over 27,000 teenagers in 44 countries and identified six values segments that characterize young people from Cairo to Caracas. Companies like Coca-Cola and Royal Phillips Electronics have used the results of this massive segmentation exercise to develop ads that appeal to youth around the world. Table 4.4 on pages 140–141 summarizes some of the findings from this study.

Materialism: "He Who Dies with the Most Toys, Wins"

During World War II, members of "cargo cults" in the South Pacific literally worshiped cargo salvaged from crashed aircraft or washed ashore from ships. These people believed that their ancestors piloted the ships and planes passing near their islands so they tried to attract them to their villages. They went so far as to construct fake planes from straw in hopes of luring the real ones![65]

Although most people don't literally worship material goods in quite this way, things do play a central role in many people's lives and influence their value systems. **Materialism** refers to the importance people attach to worldly possessions. We sometimes take the bounty of products and services for granted, until we remember how recent this abundance is. For example, in 1950 two of five American homes did not have a telephone, and in 1940 half of all households still did not possess complete indoor plumbing.

Today, though, many Americans now energetically seek "the good life," which abounds in material comforts. Most young people can't imagine a life without cell phones, MP3 players, and other creature comforts. In fact, one way to think about marketing is as a system that provides a certain standard of living to consumers. To some extent, then, our lifestyles are influenced by the standard of living we have come to expect and desire. However, the priorities of materialism tend to emphasize the well-being of the individual versus the group, which may conflict with family or religious values. That conflict may help to explain why people with highly material values tend to be less happy.[66]

Americans inhabit a highly materialistic society in which people often gauge the worth of themselves and others in terms of how much they own (see Chapter 13). The popular bumper sticker, "He Who Dies with the Most Toys, Wins" is a comment on this philosophy. Of course, Americans are not alone; many people around the world crave "the good life." In Africa, the Winners Church is less than 15 years old but it already has branches in 32 countries. This sect is one of several booming Pentecostal churches whose leaders are attracting followers by preaching what they call a Prosperity Theology: Success comes to those who pray, and wealth is celebrated.[68]

Materialists are more likely to value possessions for their status and appearance-related meanings, whereas those who do not emphasize this value tend to prize products that connect them to other people or that provide them with pleasure in using them.[69] As a result, products valued by high materialists are more likely to be publicly consumed and to be more expensive. A study that compared specific items valued by both types of people found that products associated with high materialists include jewelry, china, or a vacation home, whereas those linked to low materialists included a mother's wedding gown, picture albums, a rocking chair from childhood, or a garden.[70]

Although there is still no shortage of materialistic consumers who relish the race to acquire as much as possible before they die, there are signs that a sizable number of Americans are evolving a different value system. The Brain Waves/Market Facts survey reports that about a quarter of the population is displaying a value system characterized by a rejection of tradition and conformity. Significantly, more than half of this group is under the age of 35. They are still interested in achievement, but they are trying to balance life in the fast lane with an emphasis on developing close personal relationships and having fun. Through observation and in some cases direct

Materialists value visible symbols of success such as expensive watches.

TAGHeuer
SWISS MADE SINCE 1860

SUCCESS.
IT'S A
MIND
GAME.

TABLE 4.4
NEW WORLD TEEN STUDY

Segment	Key Countries	Driving Principles	Overview	Marketing Approach
Thrills and Chills	Germany, England, Lithuania, Greece, Netherlands, South Africa, United States, Belgium, Canada, Turkey, France, Poland, Japan, Italy, Denmark, Argentina, and Norway	Fun, friends, irreverence, and sensation	Stereotype of the devil-may-care, trying-to-become-independent hedonist. For the most part, they come from affluent or middle-class parents, live mainly in developed countries, and have allowance money to spend.	Respond to sensory stimulation. Tend to get bored easily so stale advertising messages will escape their notice. They want action ads with bells and whistles, humor, novelty, color, and sound. Edgier than their peers. Constantly seek out the new. First ones to hear of the newest technology or the hippest Web site. Experimenting is second nature. Wear all sorts of body rings and wear their hair in different shades.
Resigned	Denmark, Sweden, Korea, Japan, Norway, Germany, Belgium, Netherlands, Argentina, Canada, Turkey, England, Spain, France, and Taiwan	Friends, fun, family, and low expectations	Resemble the thrills-and-chills teens, often decorating their bodies with rings and dye. However, they are alienated from society and very pessimistic about their chances for economic success. The punk rockers of the world, who sometimes take drugs and drink to excess. Respond to heavy metal and grunge music that emphasizes the negative and angry side of society.	Do not have as much discretionary income to spend as teens in other segments. Infrequent consumers save for some fast-food, low-ticket clothes items, tobacco, and alcohol. They are drawn to irony and to ads that make fun of the pompousness of society.
World Savers	Hungary, Philippines, Venezuela, Brazil, Spain, Colombia, Belgium, Argentina, Russia, Singapore, France, Poland, Ukraine, Italy, South Africa, Mexico, and England	Environment, humanism, fun, and friends	A long list of do-good global and local causes that spark their interest. The intelligentsia in most countries who do well in school. They are the class and club leaders who join many organizations. They attend the same parties as the thrills-and-chills kids. But, they are more into romance, relationships, and strong friendships. Eagerly attend concerts, operas, and plays. They exhibit a *joie de vivre* about life and enjoy dancing or drinking at bars and cafes with friends. They love the outdoors as well, including camping, hiking, and other sports activities.	Attracted by honest and sincere messages that tell the truth. Offended by any ad that puts people down or makes fun of another group. Piggyback a promotion with a worthwhile cause.
Quiet Achievers	Thailand, China, Hong Kong, Ukraine, Korea, Lithuania, Russia, and Peru	Success, anonymity, anti-individualism, and social optimism	Value anonymity and prefer to rest in the shadows. They are the least rebellious of all the groups, avoid the limelight and do not ever want to stand out in the crowd. These are the bookish and straight kids who study long hours, are fiercely ambitious and highly goal-directed. Their top priority is to make good grades in school and use higher education to further their career advancement. Most of the quiet achievers live in Asia, especially Thailand and China.	Love to purchase stuff. Part of the reward for working diligently is being able to buy products. Their parents will defer to their children's needs when it comes to computers and other technological products that will aid in homework. This group is also keen on music; they are inner directed and adept at creating their own good times. Prefer ads that address the benefits of a product. They are embarassed by ads that display rampant

Segment	Key Countries	Driving Principles	Overview	Marketing Approach
			But these somewhat stereotypical studious types also exist in the United States, where they are sometimes regarded as being techies or nerds.	sexuality. And they do not respond to the sarcastic or the irreverent.
Boot-strappers	Nigeria, Mexico, United States, India, Chile, Puerto Rico, Peru, Venezuela, Colombia, and South Africa	Achievement, individualism, optimism, determination, and power	Most dreamy and childlike of the six segments. They live sheltered and ordered lives that seem bereft of many forms of typical teen fun and wild adult-emulating teen behavior. Spend a lot of time at home, doing homework and helping around the house. Eager for power; they are the politicians in every high school who covet the class offices. They view the use of authority as a means for securing rewards, and they are constantly seeking out recognition. Geographically many of these teens come from emerging nations such as Nigeria and India. In the United States, bootstrappers represent one in every four teens. Moreover, they represent 40% of young African Americans. A major error of U.S. marketers is to misread the size and purchasing power of this ambitious African American segment.	Young yuppies in training. They want premium brands and luxury goods. Bootstrappers are also on the lookout for goods and services that will help them get ahead. They want to dress for success, have access to technology and software, and stay plugged into the world of media and culture to give them a competitive edge. They are attracted by messages that portray aspirations and possibilities for products and their users.
Upholders	Vietnam, Indonesia, Taiwan, China, Italy, Peru, Venezuela, Puerto Rico, India, Philippines, and Singapore	Family, custom, tradition, and respect for individuals	Traditions act as a rigid guideline, and these teens would be hard-pressed to rebel or confront authority. They are content to rest comfortably in the mainstream of life, remaining unnoticed. The girls seek mostly to get married and have families. The boys perceive that they are fated to have jobs similar to their fathers'. Predominate in Asian countries, such as Indonesia and Vietnam that value old traditions and extended family relationships. Teens in these countries are helpful around the home and protective of their siblings. Moreover, many upholders are in Catholic countries where the Church and tradition guide schooling, attitudes, and values.	Advertisers and marketers have had success selling to upholders using youthful, almost childlike communication and fun messages. These are teens that still watch cartoons and are avid media consumers. They are highly involved in both watching and playing sports, particularly basketball and soccer. More than any other group, they plan to live in their country of birth throughout adulthood. Essentially upholders are homebodies. They are deeply rooted in family and community and they like to make purchase decisions that are safe and conform to their parents' values. Brands that take a leadership stance will attract upholders for their risk-free quality value and reliability.

Source: Adapted from "The Six Value Segments of Global Youth," *Brandweek* 11, no. 21 (May 22, 2000), 38, based on data initially presented in *The $100 Billion Allowance: How to Get Your Share of the Global Teen Market* by Elissa Moses (New York: John Wiley & Sons, 2000).

Participants at the anti-corporate Burning Man Festival find novel ways to express their individuality.

Source: Photographs courtesy of Professor Robert Kozinets, Northwestern University.

experience, these consumers have come to believe that (unlike the "good old days") a diploma does not guarantee a job, getting a job is no guarantee of keeping a job, retirement may not happen, and marriages often fail. This lack of stability has instilled a value of self-reliance and the desire to build personal networks rather than relying on the government or corporations to take care of them, as these institutions did for their parents. Marketing communications like Saab's "Find Your Own Road" and Prudential's "Be Your Own Rock" are designed to appeal to this group.[71]

These changes are not confined to young people. In the past, there was often a sharp divide in values between young and old, but it seems these old categories no longer make sense. As one analyst recently noted, for example, even conservative small towns now often feature "new age" stores and services where people of all ages shop. Retailers that used to be considered "bohemian" now are mainstream; grocers such as Fresh Fields sell Mayan Fungus soap and vegetarian dog biscuits to a hodgepodge of consumers. Big corporations such as Apple and The Gap use countercultural figures like Gandhi and Jack Kerouac in their advertising, and Ben & Jerry's boasts of its unconventional corporate philosophy. It's become hard to separate establishment from anti-establishment as bohemian attitudes of the hippie 1960s have merged with the bourgeois attitudes of the yuppie 1980s to form a new culture that is a synthesis of the two. The people who dominate our culture (this analyst calls them "BoBos," or Bourgeois Bohemians) now are richer and worldlier than hippies, but more spiritual than yuppies.[72] As we noted earlier, even core values do change over time; stay tuned to see how our always-evolving culture continues to put a fresh spin on materialism and other values.

The disenchantment among some people with a culture dominated by big corporations shows up in events that promote uniqueness and anti-corporate statements. Probably the most prominent movement is the annual Burning Man project. This is a one-week-long annual anti-market event, where thousands of people gather at Black Rock Desert in Nevada to express themselves and proclaim their emancipation from corporate America. The highlight of the festival involves the burning of a huge figure of a man made out of wood that symbolizes the freedom from market domination. Ironically, some critics point out that even this high-profile, anti-market event is being commercialized as it becomes more popular each year![73]

Consumer Behavior in the Aftermath of 9/11

The need for balance became even more of a mantra for many after September 11, 2001. Certainly no other event in our recent history has forced such a dramatic and public reexamination of consumer values. The threats to our safety and security have had a direct impact on businesses ranging from travel and hospitality (e.g., United Airlines, the second-largest carrier in the world, was forced to declare bankruptcy at the end of 2002) to home improvement products and carry-out foods as people seek the sanctuary of their homes rather than venturing out as much as they did before.

Even television programming has been affected; conventional situation comedies and family-oriented shows have reemerged as ratings favorites after many years of decline.[74] As noted earlier, some of us are coping by redirecting our focus from

Following 9/11, ads addressed people's fears in various ways. This ad was created as part of the Advertising Community Together initiative.

Marketing Pitfall

Following the terrorist attacks, America was awash in patriotic imagery as companies wrapped themselves in the flag to proclaim the strength of traditional values. This approach has been effective, but it can backfire if consumers feel the company is merely using patriotism as a marketing tool or is inappropriately reviving fears of terrorism to make a point or move a product. In a poll taken a few months after 9/11, about half those surveyed believed companies exploit patriotism for their own profits. An equal number said using patriotism to encourage spending in order to revive the economy is wrong.[77]

A more recent controversy over an advertisement illustrates how sensitive this issue can be even after some time has elapsed. In November of 2002, People for the Ethical Treatment of Animals, the nation's largest animal rights group, released a "turkey terror" commercial that drew upon Americans' fear of terrorism to discourage them from eating birds (and other animals) during Thanksgiving. The ad depicts a terrorist takeover of a supermarket. The store manager is shown bound and gagged, with shoppers cowering, as an unseen hostage taker warns that "innocent creatures" will be beaten, scalded, and dismembered if anyone resists. In the wake of protests, most stations declined to run the ad.[78]

luxury goods to community activities and family quality time. A 2002 study found that 73 percent of Americans have postponed treats and luxuries since the incident. Still, not everyone has reacted in the same way; following the attacks many luxury goods marketers such as high-end auto dealers reported a surge in purchases, as some people seemed to be splurging in a "you can't take it with you" mentality.[75]

One of the biggest value shifts is related to consumers' willingness to sacrifice their privacy for security. Polls taken since 9/11 indicate a large majority of Americans favor wider use of facial-recognition systems, and they want closer monitoring of banking and credit card transactions. A majority even supports the creation of a national ID card, which until 2001 had been anathema to most Americans. Many high-tech surveillance tools that were deemed too intrusive before 9/11, including the FBI's "Carnivore" Internet eavesdropping system, are being unleashed. Cameras equipped with facial-recognition software can pick out known criminals in a crowd at airports, stadiums, and other public areas. Cars and cell phones equipped with location technology make it possible to track down people to within about 10 feet. Meanwhile, sophisticated x-ray machines that can see through people's clothes may be more widely deployed at airports, government buildings, and even in corporate lobbies.[76]

CHAPTER SUMMARY

Marketers try to satisfy consumer needs, but the reasons any product is purchased can vary widely. The identification of consumer motives is an important step in ensuring that a product will satisfy appropriate needs.

Traditional approaches to consumer behavior have focused on the abilities of products to satisfy rational needs (utilitarian motives), but hedonic motives (e.g., the need for exploration or for fun) also play a key role in many purchase decisions.

As demonstrated by Maslow's hierarchy of needs, the same product can satisfy different needs, depending on the consumer's state at the time. In addition to his or her objective situation (e.g., have basic physiological needs already been satisfied?), the consumer's degree of involvement with the product must be considered.

Product involvement can range from very low, where purchase decisions are made via inertia, to very high, where consumers form very strong bonds with what they buy. In addition to considering the degree to which consumers are involved with a product, marketing strategists also need to assess their extent of involvement with marketing messages and with the purchase situation.

Underlying values often drive consumer motivations. Products thus take on meaning because they are seen as being instrumental in helping the person to achieve some goal that is linked to a value, such as individuality or freedom. Each culture is characterized by a set of core values to which many of its members adhere.

Materialism refers to the importance people attach to worldly possessions. Although many Americans can be described as being materialists, there are indications of a value shift within a sizable portion of the population—especially in the aftermath of 9/11.

KEY TERMS

Acculturation   132
Approach–approach conflict   119
Approach–avoidance conflict   119
Avoidance–avoidance conflict   120
Core values   132
Cult products   126
Drive   114
Drive theory   116
Enculturation   132

Expectancy theory   116
Flow state   126
Goal   114
Homeostasis   116
Inertia   126
Instrumental values   134
Involvement   124
Laddering   135
Materialism   138

Motivation   114
Skin (graphical interface)   132
Terminal values   134
Theory of cognitive dissonance   119
Value   131
Value system   131
Voluntary simplifiers   138
Want   115

CONSUMER BEHAVIOR CHALLENGE

1 Describe three types of motivational conflicts, citing an example of each from current marketing campaigns.

2 Devise separate promotional strategies for an article of clothing, each of which stresses one of the levels of Maslow's hierarchy of needs.

3 Collect a sample of ads that appeal to consumers' values. What value is being communicated in each ad, and how is this done? Is this an effective approach to designing a marketing communication?

4 What is your conception of paradise? Construct a collage consisting of images you personally associate with paradise, and compare the results with those of your classmates. Do you detect any common themes?

5 Construct a hypothetical means–end chain model for the purchase of a bouquet of roses. How might a florist use this approach to construct a promotional strategy?

6 Describe how a man's level of involvement with his car would affect how he is influenced by different marketing stimuli. How might you design a strategy for a line of car batteries for a segment of low-involvement consumers, and how would this strategy differ from your attempts to reach a segment of men who are very involved in working on their cars?

7 Interview members of a celebrity fan club. Describe their level of involvement with the "product" and devise some marketing opportunities to reach this group.

8 "High involvement is just a fancy term for expensive." Do you agree?

9 "College students' concerns about the environment and vegetarianism are just a passing fad; a way to look 'cool.'" Do you agree?

10 Some market analysts see a shift in values among young people. They claim that this generation has not had a lot of stability in their lives. They are fed up with superficial relationships, and are yearning for a return to tradition. This change is reflected in attitudes toward marriage and family. One survey of 22- to 24-year-old women found that 82 percent thought motherhood was the most important job in the world. *Brides* magazine reports a swing toward traditional weddings—80 percent of brides today are tossing their garters. Daddy walks 78 percent of them down the aisle.[79] So, what's your take on this? Are young people indeed returning to the values of their parents (or even their grandparents)? How have these changes influenced your perspective on marriage and family?

NOTES

1. Martha Ivine, "Beef, Veggie Activists Compete for Teen Palate," *Montgomery Advertiser* (February 19, 2003): 3A.
2. Robert A. Baron, *Psychology: The Essential Science* (Needham, MA: Allyn & Bacon, 1989).
3. Leon Festinger, *A Theory of Cognitive Dissonance* (Stanford, CA: Stanford University Press, 1957).
4. See Paul T. Costa and Robert R. McCrae, "From Catalog to Classification: Murray's Needs and the Five-Factor Model," *Journal of Personality and Social Psychology* 55 (1988): 258–65; Calvin S. Hall and Gardner Lindzey, *Theories of Personality*, 2nd ed. (New York: Wiley, 1970); James U. McNeal and Stephen W. McDaniel, "An Analysis of Need-Appeals in Television Advertising," *Journal of the Academy of Marketing Science* 12 (Spring 1984): 176–90.
5. Michael R. Solomon, Judith L. Zaichkowsky, and Rosemary Polegato, *Consumer Behaviour: Buying, Having, and Being—Canadian Edition* (Scarborough, Ontario: Prentice Hall Canada, 1999).
6. See David C. McClelland, *Studies in Motivation* (New York: Appleton-Century-Crofts, 1955).
7. Mary Kay Ericksen and M. Joseph Sirgy, "Achievement Motivation and Clothing Preferences of White-Collar Working Women," in Michael R. Solomon, ed., *The Psychology of Fashion* (Lexington, MA: Lexington Books, 1985), 357–69.
8. See Stanley Schachter, *The Psychology of Affiliation* (Stanford, CA: Stanford University Press, 1959).
9. Eugene M. Fodor and Terry Smith, "The Power Motive as an Influence on Group Decision Making," *Journal of Personality and Social Psychology* 42 (1982): 178–85.
10. C. R. Snyder and Howard L. Fromkin, *Uniqueness: The Human Pursuit of Difference* (New York: Plenum, 1980).

11. Abraham H. Maslow, *Motivation and Personality*, 2nd ed. (New York: Harper & Row, 1970).

12. A more recent integrative view of consumer goal structures and goal-determination processes proposes six discrete levels of goals wherein higher-level (versus lower-level) goals are more abstract, more inclusive, and less mutable. In descending order of abstraction, these goal levels are life themes and values, life projects, current concerns, consumption intentions, benefits sought, and feature preferences. See Cynthia Huffman, S. Ratneshwar, and David Glen Mick, "Consumer Goal Structures and Goal-Determination Processes, An Integrative Framework," in S. Ratheshwar, David Glen Mick, and Cynthia Huffman, eds., *The Why of Consumption* (London: Routledge, 2000), 9–35.

13. Russell W. Belk, "Romanian Consumer Desires and Feelings of Deservingness," in Lavinia Stan, ed., *Romania in Transition* (Hanover, NH: Dartmouth Press, 1997), 191–208, quoted on p. 193.

14. Study conducted in the Horticulture Department at Kansas State University, cited in "Survey Tells Why Gardening's Good," *Vancouver Sun* (April 12, 1997): B12.

15. Gary J. Bamossy and Janeen Costa, "Consuming Paradise: A Cultural Construction" (paper presented at the Association for Consumer Research Conference, Stockholm, June 1997); Professor Janeen Costa, personal communication, August 1997.

16. "Forehead Advertisement Pays Off," *Montgomery Advertiser* (May 4, 2000): 7A.

17. Alex Kuczynski, "A New Magazine Celebrates the Rites of Shopping," *New York Times on the Web* (May 8, 2000).

18. "Man Wants to Marry His Car," *Montgomery Advertiser* (March 7, 1999): 11A.

19. Judith Lynne Zaichkowsky, "Measuring the Involvement Construct in Marketing," *Journal of Consumer Research* 12 (December 1985): 341–52

20. Andrew Mitchell, "Involvement: A Potentially Important Mediator of Consumer Behavior," in William L. Wilkie, ed., *Advances in Consumer Research* 6 (Provo, UT: Association for Consumer Research, 1979): 191–96.

21. Richard L. Celsi and Jerry C. Olson, "The Role of Involvement in Attention and Comprehension Processes," *Journal of Consumer Research* 15 (September 1988): 210–24.

22. Anthony G. Greenwald and Clark Leavitt, "Audience Involvement in Advertising: Four Levels," *Journal of Consumer Research* 11 (June 1984): 581–92.

23. Mihaly Csikszentmihalyi, *Flow: The Psychology of Optimal Experience* (New York: HarperCollins, 1991); Donna L. Hoffman and Thomas P. Novak, "Marketing in Hypermedia Computer-Mediated Environments: Conceptual Foundations," *Journal of Marketing* (July 1996): 50–68.

24. Melanie Wells, "Cult Brands," *Forbes* (April 16, 2001): 198–205.

25. Judith Lynne Zaichkowsky, "The Emotional Side of Product Involvement," in Paul Anderson and Melanie Wallendorf, eds., *Advances in Consumer Research* 14 (Provo, UT: Association for Consumer Research): 32–35.

26. For a recent discussion of interrelationships between situational and enduring involvement, see Marsha L. Richins, Peter H. Bloch, and Edward F. McQuarrie, "How Enduring and Situational Involvement Combine to Create Involvement Responses," *Journal of Consumer Psychology* 1, no. 2 (1992): 143–53. For more information on the involvement construct, see "Special Issue on Involvement," *Psychology & Marketing* 10, no. 4 (July–August 1993).

27. Rob Wherry, "Stunts for Blue Chips," *Forbes* (November 11, 1999): 232.

28. Rajeev Batra and Michael L. Ray, "Operationalizing Involvement as Depth and Quality of Cognitive Responses," in Alice Tybout and Richard Bagozzi, eds., *Advances in Consumer Research* 10 (Ann Arbor, MI: Association for Consumer Research, 1983): 309–13.

29. Herbert E. Krugman, "The Impact of Television Advertising: Learning Without Involvement," *Public Opinion Quarterly* 29 (Fall 1965): 349–56.

30. Kevin J. Clancy, "CPMs Must Bow to 'Involvement' Measurement," *Advertising Age* (January 20, 1992): 26.

31. Gilles Laurent and Jean-Noël Kapferer, "Measuring Consumer Involvement Profiles," *Journal of Marketing Research* 22 (February 1985): 41–53. This scale was validated on an American sample as well; see William C. Rodgers and Kenneth C. Schneider, "An Empirical Evaluation of the Kapferer–Laurent Consumer Involvement Profile Scale," *Psychology & Marketing* 10 (July–August 1993): 333–45. For an English translation of this scale, see Jean Noël Kapferer and Gilles Laurent, "Further Evidence on the Consumer Involvement Profile: Five Antecedents of Involvement," *Psychology & Marketing* 10 (July–August 1993): 347–56.

32. Carmen W. Cullen and Scott J. Edgett, "The Role of Involvement in Promoting Management," *Journal of Promotion Management* 1, no. 2 (1991): 57–71.

33. David W. Stewart and David H. Furse, "Analysis of the Impact of Executional Factors in Advertising Performance," *Journal of Advertising Research* 24 (1984): 23–26; Deborah J. MacInnis, Christine Moorman, and Bernard J. Jaworski, "Enhancing and Measuring Consumers' Motivation, Opportunity, and Ability to Process Brand Information from Ads," *Journal of Marketing* 55 (October 1991): 332–53.

34. Morris B. Holbrook and Elizabeth C. Hirschman, "The Experiential Aspects of Consumption: Consumer Fantasies, Feelings, and Fun," *Journal of Consumer Research* 9 (September 1982): 132–40.

35. Elaine Sciolino, "Disproving Notions, Raising a Fury," *New York Times on the Web* (January 21, 2003).

36. Gordon Fairclough, "Dancing, Music and Free Smokes in Good Ol' Tobaccoville, N.C.," *The Wall Street Journal Interactive Edition* (October 26, 1999).

37. Ajay K. Sirsi, James C. Ward, and Peter H. Reingen, "Microcultural Analysis of Variation in Sharing of Causal Reasoning About Behavior," *Journal of Consumer Research* 22 (March 1996): 345–72.

38. David Carr, "Romance, in Cosmo's World, Is Translated in Many Ways," *New York Times on the Web* (May 26, 2002).

39. Richard W. Pollay, "Measuring the Cultural Values Manifest in Advertising," *Current Issues and Research in Advertising* 6, no. 1 (1983): 71–92.

40. Paul M. Sherer, "North American and Asian Executives Have Contrasting Values, Study Finds," *Wall Street Journal* (March 8, 1996).

41. Sarah Ellison, "Sexy-Ad Reel Shows What Tickles in Tokyo Can Fade Fast in France," *Wall Street Journal Interactive Edition* (March 31, 2000).

42. Milton Rokeach, *The Nature of Human Values* (New York: Free Press, 1973).

43. Han, Sang-Pil and Sharon Shavitt, "Persuasion and Culture: Advertising Appeals in Individualistic and Collectivistic Societies," *Journal of Experimental Social Psychology* 30 (1994): 326–50.

44. Rebecca Gardyn, "Swap Meet," *American Demographics* (July 2001): 51–56.

45. Lawrence Speer and Magz Osborne, "Coke Tests Custom Bottles," *Advertising Age* (November 4, 2002): 16

46. Erin White, "Coke Moves to Let Teens Pitch Soda to Themselves," *Wall Street Journal Interactive Edition* (January 10, 2003).

47. Erin White, "Interactive Commercials Face One Big Challenge: Laziness," *Wall Street Journal Interactive Edition* (August 2, 2002).

48. Michel Marriot, "Movie Posters That Talk Back," *New York Times on the Web* (December 12, 2002).

49. David Kushner, "From the Skin Artist, Always a Free Makeover," *New York Times on the Web* (March 21, 2002).

50. Carolyn A. Lin, "Cultural Values Reflected in Chinese and American Television Advertising," *Journal of Advertising* 30 (Winter 2001): 83–94.

51. Donald E. Vinson, Jerome E. Scott, and Lawrence R. Lamont, "The Role of Personal Values in Marketing and Consumer Behavior," *Journal of Marketing* 41 (April 1977): 44–50; John Watson, Steven Lysonski, Tamara Gillan, and Leslie Raymore, "Cultural Values and Important Possessions: A Cross-Cultural Analysis," *Journal of Business Research* 55 (2002): 923–31.

52. Jennifer Aaker, Veronica Benet-Martinez, and Jordi Garolera, "Consumption Symbols as Carriers of Culture: A Study of Japanese and Spanish Brand Personality Constructs," *Journal of Personality and Social Psychology* (2001).

53. Milton Rokeach, *Understanding Human Values* (New York: Free Press, 1979); see also J. Michael Munson and Edward McQuarrie, "Shortening the Rokeach Value Survey for Use in Consumer Research," in Michael J. Houston, ed., *Advances in Consumer Research* 15 (Provo, UT: Association for Consumer Research, 1988): 381–86.

54. B. W. Becker and P. E. Conner, "Personal Values of the Heavy User of Mass Media," *Journal of Advertising Research* 21 (1981): 37–43; Vinson, Scott, and Lamont, "The Role of Personal Values in Marketing and Consumer Behavior," 44–50.

55. Craig J. Thompson and Maura Troester, "Consumer Value Systems in the Age of Postmodern Fragmentation: The Case of the Natural Health Microculture," *Journal of Consumer Research* 28 (March 2002): 550–71.

56. James Brooke, "Japanese Masters Get Closer to the Toilet Nirvana," *New York Times on the Web* (October 8, 2002).

57. Victoria C. Plaut and Hazel Rose Markus, "Place Matters: Consensual Features and Regional Variation in American Well-Being and Self," *Journal of Personality and Social Psychology* 83 (2002): 160–84.

58. Sharon E. Beatty, Lynn R. Kahle, Pamela Homer, and Shekhar Misra, "Alternative Measurement Approaches to Consumer Values: The List

of Values and the Rokeach Value Survey," *Psychology & Marketing* 2 (1985): 181–200; Lynn R. Kahle and Patricia Kennedy, "Using the List of Values (LOV) to Understand Consumers," *Journal of Consumer Marketing* 2 (Fall 1988): 49–56; Lynn Kahle, Basil Poulos, and Ajay Sukhdial, "Changes in Social Values in the United States During the Past Decade," *Journal of Advertising Research* 28 (February–March 1988): 35–41; see also Wagner A. Kamakura and Jose Alfonso Mazzon, "Value Segmentation: A Model for the Measurement of Values and Value Systems," *Journal of Consumer Research* 18 (September 1991): 28; Jagdish N. Sheth, Bruce I. Newman, and Barbara L. Gross, *Consumption Values and Market Choices: Theory and Applications* (Cincinnati: South-Western Publishing Co., 1991).

59. Thomas J. Reynolds and Jonathan Gutman, "Laddering Theory, Method, Analysis, and Interpretation," *Journal of Advertising Research* (February–March 1988): 11–34; Beth Walker, Richard Celsi, and Jerry Olson, "Exploring the Structural Characteristics of Consumers' Knowledge," in Melanie Wallendorf and Paul Anderson, eds., *Advances in Consumer Research* 14 (Provo, UT: Association for Consumer Research, 1986): 17–21.

60. This example was adapted from Michael R. Solomon, Gary Bamossy, and Søren Askegaard, *Consumer Behaviour: A European Perspective*, 2nd ed. (London: Pearson Education Limited, 2002).

61. Thomas J. Reynolds and Alyce Byrd Craddock, "The Application of the MECCAS Model to the Development and Assessment of Advertising Strategy: A Case Study," *Journal of Advertising Research* (April–May 1988): 43–54.

62. This example was adapted from Solomon, Bamossy, and Askegaard, *Consumer Behaviour: A European Perspective*.

63. "25 Years of Attitude," *Marketing Tools* (November–December 1995): 38–39.

64. Amitai Etzioni, "The Good Society: Goals Beyond Money," *The Futurist* 35, no. 4 (2001); D. Elgin, *Voluntary Simplicity: Toward a Way of Life That is Outwardly Simple, Inwardly Rich* (New York: Quill, 1993); Ascribe Higher Education News Service, "PNA Trend in Consumer Behavior Called 'Voluntary Simplicity' Poses Challenges for Marketers," (6 December 2001).

65. Russell W. Belk, "Possessions and the Extended Self," *Journal of Consumer Research* 15 (September 1988): 139–68; Melanie Wallendorf and Eric J. Arnould, "'My Favorite Things': A Cross-Cultural Inquiry into Object Attachment, Possessiveness, and Social Linkage," *Journal of Consumer Research* 14 (March 1988): 531–47.

66. James E. Burroughs and Aric Rindfleisch, "Materialism and Well-Being: A Conflicting Values Perspective," *Journal of Consumer Research* 29 (December 2002): 348–370

67. Yumiko Ono, "Tambrands Ads Try to Scale Cultural, Religious Obstacles," *Wall Street Journal Interactive Edition* (March 17, 1997).

68. Norimitsu Onishi, "Africans Fill Churches That Celebrate Wealth," *New York Times on the Web* (March 13, 2002).

69. Marsha L. Richins, "Special Possessions and the Expression of Material Values," *Journal of Consumer Research* 21 (December 1994): 522–33.

70. Richins, "Special Possessions and the Expression of Material Values."

71. Paul H. Ray, "The Emerging Culture," *American Demographics* (February 1997): 29.

72. David Brooks, "Why Bobos Rule," *Newsweek* (April 3, 2000): 62–64.

73. Robert V. Kozinets, "Can Consumers Escape the Market? Emancipatory Illuminations from Burning Man," *Journal of Consumer Research* 29 (June 2002): 20–38; see also Douglas B. Holt, "Why Do Brands Cause Trouble? A Dialectical Theory of Consumer Culture and Branding," *Journal of Consumer Research* 29 (June 2002): 70–90.

74. Bill Carter, "Mom, Dad and the Kids Reclaim TV Perch," *New York Times on the Web* (October 15, 2002).

75. J. Cosgrove, "What-The-Hell Consumption," *BusinessWeek* (2001): 12. For a study that examined value changes following a terrorist attack (the Oklahoma City bombing), see Dwight D. Frink, Gregory M. Rose, and Ann L. Canty, "The Effects of Values on Worries Associated with Acute Disaster: A Naturally Occuring Quasi-Experiment," *Journal of Applied Social Psychology* (forthcoming).

76. M. France et al., "Privacy in an Age of Terror," *BusinessWeek* (November 5, 2001): 83.

77. Lisa Sanders, "Agencies Study a New America," *Advertising Age* (November 26, 2001): 3–5.

78. "'Turkey Terror' Ad by Animal Rights Group," *New York Times Online* (November 28, 2002).

79. Helene Stapinski, "Y Not Love?" *American Demographics* (February 1999): 62–68.

The Self

Lisa is trying to concentrate on the report her client is expecting by five o'clock. She has always worked hard to maintain this important account for the firm, but today she is distracted, thinking about her date with Eric last night. Although things seemed to go okay, why couldn't she shake the feeling that Eric regarded her more as a friend than as a potential romantic partner?

Leafing through *Glamour* and *Cosmopolitan* during her lunch hour, Lisa is struck by all of the articles about ways to become more attractive by dieting, exercise, and wearing sexy clothes. She begins to feel depressed as she looks at the svelte models in the many advertisements for perfumes, apparel, and makeup. Each woman is more glamorous and beautiful than the next. She could swear that some of them must have had assorted "adjustments"— women just don't look that way in real life. Then again, it's unlikely that Eric could ever be mistaken for hunk model Fabio on the street.

In her down mood, though, Lisa actually entertains the thought that maybe she should look into cosmetic surgery. Even though she's never considered herself unattractive, who knows—maybe a new nose or removing that mole on her cheek would make her feel better about herself. On second thought, though, is Eric even worth it?

■ PERSPECTIVES ON THE SELF

Lisa is not alone in feeling that her physical appearance and possessions affect her "value" as a person. Consumers' insecurities about their appearance are rampant. We buy many products, from cars to cologne, because we want to highlight or hide some aspect of the self. In this chapter, we'll focus on how consumers' feelings about themselves shape their consumption practices, particularly as they strive to fulfill their society's expectations about how a male or female should look and act.

Does the Self Exist?

The 1980s were called the "Me Decade" because many people were so self-absorbed. More recently, *Self* magazine designated March 7 as Self Day and it encourages women to spend a minimum of one hour doing something for themselves.[1]

Although it seems natural to think about each consumer as having a self, this concept is actually a relatively new way of regarding individuals and their relationship to society. The idea that each single human life is unique, rather than a part of a group, only developed in late medieval times (between the eleventh and fifteenth centuries). The notion that the self is an object to be pampered is even more recent. Furthermore, the emphasis on the unique nature of the self is much greater in Western societies.[2] Many Eastern cultures instead stress the importance of a *collective self,* where the person's identity is derived in large measure from his or her social group.

Both Eastern and Western cultures see the self as divided into an inner, private self and an outer, public self. But where they differ is in terms of which part is seen as the "real you"—the West tends to subscribe to an independent construal of the self, which emphasizes the inherent separateness of each individual. Non-Western cultures, in contrast, tend to focus on an interdependent self in which one's identity is largely defined by the relationships one has with others.[3]

For example, a Confucian perspective stresses the importance of "face"—others' perceptions of the self and maintaining one's desired status in their eyes. One dimension of face is *mien-tzu*—reputation achieved through success and ostentation. Some Asian cultures developed explicit rules about the specific garments and even colors that certain social classes and occupations were allowed to display. These traditions live on today in Japanese style manuals that provide very detailed instructions for dressing and for addressing people of differing status.[4]

That orientation is a bit at odds with such Western conventions as "Casual Fridays," which encourage employees to express their unique selves (at least within reason). To further illustrate these cross-cultural differences, a recent Roper Starch Worldwide survey compared consumers in 30 countries to see which were the most and least vain. Women living in Venezuela were the chart-toppers; 65 percent said they thought about their appearance all the time.[5] Other high-scoring countries include Russia and Mexico. The lowest scorers lived in the Philippines and in Saudi Arabia, where only 28 percent of consumers surveyed agreed with this statement.

Self-Concept

The **self-concept** refers to the beliefs a person holds about his or her own attributes, and how he or she evaluates these qualities. Although one's overall self-concept may be positive, there certainly are parts of the self that are evaluated more positively than others. For example, Lisa feels better about her professional identity than she does about her feminine identity.

The self-concept is a very complex structure. It is composed of many attributes, and we emphasize some over others when we evaluate the overall self. We can describe attributes of self-concept along such dimensions as their *content* (e.g., facial attractiveness versus mental aptitude), *positivity* (i.e., self-esteem), *intensity*, *stability* over time, and *accuracy* (i.e., the degree to which one's self-assessment corresponds to reality).[6] As we'll see later in this chapter, consumers' self-assessments can be quite distorted, especially with regard to their physical appearance.

Self-Esteem

Self-esteem refers to the positivity of a person's self-concept. People with low self-esteem expect that they will not perform very well, and they will try to avoid embarrassment, failure, or rejection. In developing a new line of snack cakes, for example, Sara Lee found that consumers low in self-esteem preferred portion-controlled snack items because they felt they lacked self-control.[7] In contrast, people with high self-esteem expect to be successful, will take more risks, and are more willing to be the center of attention.[8] Acceptance by others often influences self-esteem. As you probably remember from your own experience, high school students who hang out in high-status "crowds" seem to have higher self-esteem than their classmates (even though this may not be deserved).[9]

Marketing communications can influence a consumer's level of self-esteem. Exposure to ads like the ones Lisa was checking out can trigger a process of *social comparison*, where the person tries to evaluate his or her self by comparing it to the people depicted in these artificial images. This form of comparison appears to be a basic human tendency, and many marketers tap into this need by supplying idealized images of happy, attractive people who just happen to be using their products.

A study that illustrates the social comparison process showed that female college students tend to compare their physical appearance with models in advertising. Furthermore, study participants who were exposed to beautiful women in advertisements afterwards expressed lowered satisfaction with their own appearance, as compared to other participants who did not view ads with attractive models.[10] Another study demonstrated that young women's perceptions of their own body shapes and sizes can be altered after being exposed to as little as 30 minutes of TV programming.[11] Similar findings have been reported for men.[12]

Self-esteem advertising attempts to change product attitudes by stimulating positive feelings about the self. One strategy is to challenge the consumer's self-esteem and then show a linkage to a product that will provide a remedy. For example, the Marine Corps uses this strategy with its theme "If you have what it takes . . .". Another strategy is outright flattery, as when Virginia Slims cigarettes proclaims, "You've come a long way, baby."

Real and Ideal Selves

In South Korean shopping malls, teenage girls line up at photo machines that provide high-tech makeovers with options including glamour lighting, a hair-blowing breeze, and virtual plastic surgery. At the Beauty Plus booth, for example, the fashion model wannabees can digitally trim jawlines, puff up lips, eliminate blemishes, and give themselves Western-style eyelids (this is the most popular option at booths in Seoul).[13]

When a consumer compares some aspect of herself to an ideal this judgment influences her self-esteem. A consumer might ask, "Am I as attractive as I would like to be?" or "Do I make as much money as I should?" The **ideal self** is a person's conception of how he or she would like to be, whereas the **actual self** refers to our more realistic appraisal of the qualities we have and don't have.

The ideal self is partly molded by elements of the consumer's culture, such as heroes or people depicted in advertising, who serve as models of achievement or appearance.[14] We might purchase products because we believe they will be instrumental in helping us achieve these goals. We choose some products because we think they are consistent with our actual self, while we buy others to help us to reach the standard set by the ideal self.

Fantasy: Bridging the Gap Between the Selves

Most people experience a discrepancy between their real and ideal selves, but for some consumers this gap is especially large. These people are especially good targets for marketing communications that employ *fantasy appeals*.[15] A **fantasy** or daydream is a self-induced shift in consciousness, which is sometimes a way of compensating for a lack of external stimulation or of escaping from problems in the real world.[16] Many products and services are successful because they appeal to consumers' fantasies. These marketing strategies allow us to extend our vision of ourselves by placing us in unfamiliar, exciting situations or by permitting us to "try on" interesting or provocative roles. And with today's technology, such as *Cosmopolitan*'s online makeover (***virtualmakeover.com***), consumers can experiment with different looks before actually taking the plunge in the real world.

Multiple Selves

In a way, each of us really is a number of different people—your mother probably would not recognize the "you" that emerges at a rave at 2:00 A.M. with a group of friends! We have as many selves as we do different social roles. Depending on the situation, we act differently, use different products and services, and even vary in terms of how much we *like* the aspect of ourselves that is on display. A person may require a different set of products to play each of her roles: She may choose a sedate, understated perfume when she is being her professional self, but splash on something more provocative on Saturday night as she becomes her *femme fatale* self.

As we saw in Chapter 1, the dramaturgical perspective on consumer behavior views people as actors who play different roles. We each play many roles, and each has its own script, props, and costumes.[17] We can think of the self as having different components, or *role identities*, and only some of these are active at any given time. Some identities (e.g., husband, boss, student) are more central to the self than others, but other identities (e.g., stamp collector, dancer, or advocate for the homeless) may be dominant in specific situations. Strategically, this means a marketer may want to take steps to ensure the appropriate role identity is active before pitching products needed to play that particular role. One obvious way to

A Japanese company called Paris Miki has developed a sophisticated system that collects information about a consumer's preferences. After the customer uploads a picture, the software selects an eyeglass frame and superimposes it on her face so she can see what it will look like.

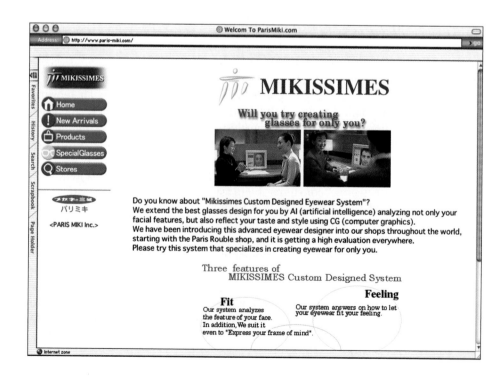

do that is to place advertising messages in contexts where people are likely to be well aware of that role identity—for example, by promoting fitness and energy products at a marathon.

Symbolic Interactionism

If each person potentially has many social selves, how does each develop and how do we decide which self to "activate" at any point in time? The sociological tradition of **symbolic interactionism** stresses that relationships with other people play a large part in forming the self.[18] This perspective maintains that people exist in a symbolic environment, and we assign meaning to any situation or object by interpreting these symbols. As members of society, we learn to agree on shared meanings. Thus, we "know" that a red light means stop, the "golden arches" means fast food, and "blondes have more fun." That's important in understanding consumer behavior, because it implies that our possessions play a key role as we evaluate ourselves and decide "who we are."[19]

Like other social objects, consensus defines the meanings of consumers themselves. The consumer interprets his or her own identity, and this assessment is continually evolving as he or she encounters new situations and people. In symbolic interactionist terms, we *negotiate* these meanings over time. Essentially, the consumer poses the question, "Who am I in this situation?" The answer to this question is greatly influenced by those around us: "Who do *other people* think I am?" We tend to pattern our behavior on the perceived expectations of others in a form of *self-fulfilling prophecy*. By acting the way we assume others expect us to act, we often wind up confirming these perceptions.

The Looking-Glass Self

This process of imagining the reactions of others toward us is known as "taking the role of the other," or the **looking-glass self**.[20] According to this view, our desire to define ourselves operates as a sort of psychological sonar: We take readings of our own identity by "bouncing" signals off others and trying to project what impression they have of us. The looking-glass image we receive will differ, depending on whose views we are considering.

Like the distorted mirrors in a funhouse, our appraisal of who we are can vary, depending on whose perspective we are taking and how accurately we are able to predict their evaluations of us. A confident career woman such as Lisa may sit morosely at a nightclub, imagining that others see her as an unattractive woman with little sex appeal (whether these perceptions are true or not). A *self-fulfilling prophecy* can operate here because these "signals" can influence Lisa's actual behavior. If she doesn't believe she's attractive, she may choose dowdy clothing that actually does make her less attractive. On the other hand, her confidence in herself in a professional setting may cause her to assume that others hold her "executive self" in even higher regard than they actually do (we've all known people like that!).

Self-Consciousness

There are times when people seem to be painfully aware of themselves. If you have ever walked into a class in the middle of a lecture and noticed that all eyes were on you, you can understand this feeling of *self-consciousness*. In contrast, consumers sometimes behave with shockingly little self-consciousness. For example, people may do things in a stadium, a riot, or at a fraternity party that they would never do if they were highly conscious of their behavior.[21]

Some people seem to be more sensitive in general to the image they communicate to others. On the other hand, we all know people who act as if they're oblivious to the impression they are making. A heightened concern about the nature of one's public "image" also results in more concern about the social appropriateness of products and consumption activities. Several techniques have been devised to

Marketing Pitfall

measure this tendency. Consumers who score high on a scale of *public self-consciousness*, for example, are also more interested in clothing and are heavier users of cosmetics.[22] A similar measure is *self-monitoring*. High self-monitors are more attuned to how they present themselves in their social environments, and their product choices are influenced by their estimates of how these items will be perceived by others.[23] Self-monitoring is assessed by consumers' extent of agreement with statements such as "I guess I put on a show to impress or entertain others," or "I would probably make a good actor."[24] High self-monitors are more likely than low self-monitors to evaluate products consumed in public in terms of the impressions they make on others.[25] Similarly, groups such as college football players and fashion models tend to score higher on vanity, which includes a fixation on physical appearance or on the achievement of personal goals.[26]

■ CONSUMPTION AND SELF-CONCEPT

A British marketing firm is paying five people to transform themselves into human billboards for a fantasy superhero. This so-called "identity marketing" technique will require each participant to legally change his or her name for one year to "Turok," the hero of a video game series about a time-traveling American Indian who slays bionically enhanced dinosaurs. A company spokesman notes, "It's not a gimmick. . . . Every form of their identity will have to change for this to work. They'll be walking, talking, living, breathing advertisements." This tactic pushes the boundaries between people and products, though this video promotion is not the first to do so: A few years ago a Kansas couple was paid $5,000 by a Web site called the Internet Underground Music Archive (IUMA) to name their baby boy Iuma.[27]

By extending the dramaturgical perspective a bit farther, it is easy to see how the consumption of products and services contributes to the definition of the self. For an actor to play a role convincingly, he or she needs the correct props, stage setting, and so on. Consumers learn that different roles are accompanied by constellations of products and activities that help to define these roles.[28] Some "props" are so important to the roles we play that they can be viewed as a part of the extended self, a concept to be discussed shortly.

Products That Shape the Self: You Are What You Consume

Recall that the reflected self helps to shape self-concept, which implies that people see themselves as they imagine others see them. Because what others see includes a person's clothing, jewelry, furniture, car, and so on, it stands to reason that these products also help to determine the perceived self. A consumer's possessions place him or her into a social role, which helps to answer the question, "Who am I now?"

People use an individual's consumption behaviors to help them make judgments about that person's social identity. In addition to considering a person's clothes and grooming habits, we make inferences about personality based on a person's choice of leisure activities (e.g., squash versus bowling), food preferences (e.g., tofu and beans versus steak and potatoes), cars, home decorating choices, and so on. People who are shown pictures of someone's living room, for example, are able to make surprisingly accurate guesses about his or her personality.[29] In the same way that a consumer's use of products influences others' perceptions, the same products can help to determine his or her own self-concept and social identity.[30]

A consumer exhibits attachment to an object to the extent that he or she uses it to maintain his or her self-concept.[31] Objects can act as a sort of security blanket by reinforcing our identities, especially in unfamiliar situations. For example, students who decorate their dorm rooms with personal items are less likely to drop out of college. This coping process may protect the self from being diluted in a strange environment.[32]

Consumers often express their self-concepts through their choice of an automobile. These British ads take the process a step farther.

Closure principle from Gestalt psychology

The use of consumption information to define the self is especially important when an identity is yet to be adequately formed, as occurs when we play a new or unfamiliar role. **Symbolic self-completion theory** suggests that people who have an incomplete self-definition tend to complete this identity by acquiring and displaying symbols associated with it.[34] Adolescent boys, for example, may use "macho" products such as cars and cigarettes to bolster their developing masculinity; these items act as a "social crutch" during a period of uncertainty about identity.

The contribution of possessions to self-identity is perhaps most apparent when these treasured objects are lost or stolen. One of the first acts performed by institutions that want to repress individuality and encourage group identity, such as prisons or the military, is to confiscate personal possessions.[35] Victims of burglaries and natural disasters commonly report feelings of alienation, depression, or of being "violated." One consumer's comment after being robbed is typical: "It's the next worse thing to being bereaved; it's like being raped."[36] Burglary victims exhibit a diminished sense of community, lowered feelings of privacy, and less pride in their houses' appearance than do their neighbors.[37]

Studying postdisaster conditions, where consumers may have lost literally everything but the clothes on their backs following a fire, hurricane, flood, or earthquake, highlights the dramatic impact of product loss. Some people are reluctant to undergo the process of recreating their identity by acquiring new possessions. Interviews with disaster victims reveal that some hesitate to invest the self in new possessions and so become more detached about what they buy. This comment from a woman in her fifties is representative of this attitude: "I had so much love tied up in my things. I can't go through that kind of loss again. What I'm buying now won't be as important to me."[38]

Self/Product Congruence

Because many consumption activities are related to self-definition, it is not surprising to learn that consumers demonstrate consistency between their values (see Chapter 4) and the things they buy.[39] **Self-image congruence models** suggest that products will be chosen when their attributes match some aspect of the self.[40] These models assume a process of cognitive matching between product attributes and the consumer's self-image.[41]

Although results are somewhat mixed, the ideal self appears to be more relevant than the actual self as a comparison standard for highly expressive social products such as perfume. In contrast, the actual self is more relevant for everyday, functional products. These standards are also likely to vary by usage situation.[42] For example, a consumer might want a functional, reliable car to commute to work every day and a flashier model with more "zing" when going out on a date in the evening.

Research tends to support the idea of congruence between product usage and self-image. One of the earliest studies to examine this process found that car owners' ratings of themselves tended to match their perceptions of their cars: Pontiac drivers saw themselves as more active and flashy than did Volkswagen drivers.[43] Congruity also has been found between consumers and their most-preferred brands of beer, soap, toothpaste, and cigarettes relative to their least-preferred brands, as well as between consumers' self-images and their favorite stores.[44] Some specific attributes useful in describing matches between consumers and products include rugged/delicate, excitable/calm, rational/emotional, and formal/informal.[45]

Although these findings make some intuitive sense, we cannot blithely assume that consumers will always buy products whose characteristics match their own. It is not clear that consumers really see aspects of themselves in down-to-earth, functional products that don't have very complex or human-like images. It is one thing to consider a brand personality for an expressive, image-oriented product such as perfume and quite another to impute human characteristics to a toaster.

Another problem is the old "chicken-and-egg" question: Do people buy products because the products are seen as similar to the self, or do people assume that these products must be similar to themselves because they have bought them? The similarity between a person's self-image and the images of products purchased does tend to increase over the time the product is owned, so this explanation cannot be ruled out.

The Extended Self

Recently, a young man named John Freyer sold all his possessions on eBay to see if our "stuff" really defines who we are. These treasures included an open box of taco shells, half a bottle of mouthwash, and his sideburns packaged in a plastic bag (yes, it seems people will buy just about anything!). Those who bought any of the artifacts he listed for sale registered them on a Web site called *allmylifeforsale.com*. Freyer then undertook a decidedly nonspiritual odyssey as he set out to "visit" all of his possessions in their new homes around the world—including a bag of PorkyO's BBQ Pork Skins that wound up in Japan.[46]

As noted earlier, many of the props and settings consumers use to define their social roles become parts of their selves. Those external objects that we consider a part of us comprise the **extended self**. In some cultures, people literally incorporate objects into the self—they lick new possessions, take the names of conquered enemies (or in some cases eat them), or bury the dead with their possessions.[47]

We don't usually go that far, but some people do cherish possessions as if they were a part of them. Many material objects, ranging from personal possessions and pets to national monuments or landmarks, help to form a consumer's iden-

This Italian ad demonstrates that our favorite products are part of the extended self.

FRANCESCO**BIASIA**
HANDBAGS

tity. Just about everyone can name a valued possession that has a lot of the self "wrapped up" in it, whether it is a beloved photograph, a trophy, an old shirt, a car, or a cat. Indeed, it is often possible to construct a pretty accurate "biography" of someone just by cataloguing the items on display in his or her bedroom or office.

Understanding the importance of the extended self helps to explain why in Japan something as seemingly inconsequential as the mishandling of a business card can be a deal killer. Japanese businesspeople view the card as an extension of their selves and they expect it to be treated respectfully. A business card should not be bent or ever serve double duty as a tooth pick. Arriving in Japan without an ample stock of business cards is akin to arriving barefoot. There is an elaborate etiquette connected to giving and receiving cards. This should be done solemnly and

She might look like you.
But she doesn't have to eat the same food.
Cesar. For special dogs.

Cesar
Beef & Cheese
Gourmet

Our pets often become part of our extended selves. This Brazilian pet food ad plays on the popular belief that over time pets and their owners start to resemble each other.

the card should be studied, not shoved in a coat pocket to file later.[50] Japanese take a failure to follow these rules as a personal insult.

In one study on the extended self, people were given a list of items that ranged from electronic equipment, facial tissues, and television programs to parents, body parts, and favorite clothes. They were asked to rate each in terms of its closeness to the self. Objects were more likely to be considered a part of the extended self if "psychic energy" was invested in the effort to obtain them, or because they were personalized and kept for a long time.[51]

We can describe four levels of the extended self, ranging from very personal objects (like Freyer's used bottle of mouthwash) to places and things that allow people to feel as though they are rooted in their larger social environments:[52]

1 *Individual level:* Consumers include many of their personal possessions in self-definition. These products can include jewelry, cars, clothing, and so on. The saying "You are what you wear" reflects the belief that one's things are a part of one's identity.
2 *Family level:* This part of the extended self includes a consumer's residence and the furnishings in it. The house can be thought of as a symbolic body for the family, and often is a central aspect of identity.
3 *Community level:* It is common for consumers to describe themselves in terms of the neighborhood or town from which they come. For farm families or other residents with close ties to a community, this sense of belonging is particularly important.

4 *Group level:* Our attachments to certain social groups also can be considered a part of the self—we'll consider some of these consumer subcultures in later chapters. A consumer also may feel that landmarks, monuments, or sports teams are a part of the extended self.

■ SEX ROLES

Sexual identity is a very important component of a consumer's self-concept. People often conform to their culture's expectations about how those of their gender should act, dress, or speak. Of course, these guidelines change over time, and they differ radically across societies. It's unclear to what extent gender differences are innate versus culturally shaped—but they're certainly evident in many consumption situations.

Consider the gender differences market researchers observe when comparing the food preferences of men to those of women. Women eat more fruit; men are more likely to eat meat. As one food writer put it, "Boy food doesn't grow. It is hunted or killed." Men are more likely to eat Frosted Flakes or Corn Pops, but women prefer multigrain cereals. Men are big root beer drinkers; women account for the bulk of sales of bottled water.[53]

The sexes also differ sharply in the quantities of food they eat: When researchers at Hershey's discovered that women eat smaller amounts of candy, the company created a white chocolate confection called Hugs, one of the most successful food introductions of all time. On the other hand, men are more likely to take their food and drink in larger servings. When Lipton advertised its iced tea during the Super Bowl, it told its (predominantly male) viewers, "This ain't no sippin' tea," and encouraged them to chug it down.

Gender Differences in Socialization

A society communicates its assumptions about the proper roles of men and women by stressing ideal behaviors for each gender. It's likely, for instance, that many women eat smaller quantities because they have been "trained" to be more delicate and dainty (which explains why many women eat before going out on a dinner date so they won't order too much).

Advertising reinforces these expectations which, as we've already seen in the last chapter, tend to mirror cultural values. Even countries that are physically close to each other may send very different messages. In a comparison between Malaysian and Singaporean commercials, for example, the researchers found that Malaysian males tend to dominate ads for technical products while females dominate the Singaporean ones, which suggests that Singaporean women are more widely accepted as partners in the business world. To support this argument, they also found that men are portrayed more often in high-level business/professional roles in Malaysia while in Singapore both genders were portrayed equally. [In addition, when women appear in commercials in Malaysia they are less likely to be shown in professional or executive roles.[54]]

In many societies, males are expected to pursue **agentic goals**, which stress self-assertion and mastery. Females, on the other hand, are taught to value **communal goals**, such as affiliation and the fostering of harmonious relations.[55] One study found that even a male voice emanating from a computer is perceived as more accurate and authoritative than when the same words are read by a female voice. And, computer-generated words of praise were valued to a greater extent when the voice was male![56] Each society creates a set of expectations regarding the behaviors appropriate for men and women and finds ways to communicate these priorities. A recent analysis of TV commercials aimed at children in the United

Marketing Opportunity

From product promotions to video games, consumers are responding to the opportunity to cement the bonds between their selves and the things they own and use. Here are a few recent examples of the extended self at work:

- NFL fans can now wear NFL Crazy Lenses, contact lenses imprinted with the logo of their favorite team. The Green Bay Packers lens, for example, is primarily yellow, with a green "Packers" and two green-and-white Packer G's printed atop the yellow, around a transparent space left for the pupil.[57]
- Drinkers of Bud Light can insert their own faces into ads for the beer that they then can e-mail to friends. Just store a digital photo at the brand's Web site and write a script. The character will appear to be live with blinking eyes and lips that move in synch with its voice. You can choose from several voices including a sportscaster and a California Valley Girl.[58]
- A patient sued her surgeon because he branded the initials of his alma mater, the University of Kentucky, on her uterus during a hysterectomy.[59]
- Enter a Q Cloning Booth and put down your $25. Three digital cameras will take your picture, transform your face into a 3-D file, and burn it onto a CD/ROM. Then you can upload your own face to selected video games so you can literally be a player.[60]

Net Profit

Game developers agree that women's interest in community, as opposed to men's drive to compete, makes them gravitate toward role-playing games that let players communicate rather than shoot each other's guts out. Males traditionally dominate online games, but all that is changing as a new genre of multiplayer games is attracting droves of women. Although the developers of the hugely popular games Ultima Online, Asheron's Call, and EverQuest did not design their products with women in mind, they have been pleasantly surprised. These games just happen to offer what women want: social interaction including chatting, buying and selling food and weapons, running businesses, or making friends. Industry insiders estimate that today at least 20 to 30 percent of the players are women. As a sign of this change in the gender makeup of its audience, the developers of Asheron's Call bowed to requests from female players and bestowed its characters with two new abilities: curtsying and wearing dresses.[63]

States and Australia found that boys continue to be depicted as more knowledgeable, active, aggressive, and instrumental.[61]

These differences in orientation show up early in our development. When Mattel decided to develop a new brand of building toy called Ello to appeal to girls, its designers began by watching the play patterns of 5- to 10-year-old girls. The new toy features interconnecting plastic squares, balls, triangles, squiggles, flowers, and sticks, in pastel colors and with rounded corners that let users snap pieces together to create houses, people, jewelry, and picture frames. As one of the developers observed, "boys enjoy stacking blocks and working towards a goal, such as finishing a building. Their play is more physically active, and they like to create conflict between characters. Girls don't like repetitive stacking. They prefer to create relationships between characters, building communities and decorative spaces."[62] Along the same lines, another study found that female characters in children's books are far more likely to take on nurturing roles such as baking and

This French shoe ad pokes fun at ads that demean women by proclaiming: "No woman's body was exploited in the making of this advertisement."

gift-giving, while the male in these stories often is cast in the role of a miraculous provider of gifts.

Gender Versus Sexual Identity

Gender role identity is a state of mind as well as body. A person's biological gender (i.e., male or female) does not totally determine whether he or she will exhibit **sex-typed traits**, characteristics that are stereotypically associated with one gender or the other. A consumer's subjective feelings about his or her sexuality are crucial as well.[64]

Unlike maleness and femaleness, masculinity and femininity are *not* biological characteristics. A behavior considered masculine in one culture might not be viewed as such in another. For example, the norm in the United States is that male friends avoid touching each other (except in "safe" situations such as on the football field). In some Latin and European cultures, however, it is common for men to hug and kiss one another. Each society determines what "real" men and women should and should not do.

Sex-Typed Products

There was a popular book entitled, *Real Men Don't Eat Quiche*. Many products (in addition to quiche) also are *sex-typed*. They take on masculine or feminine attributes, and consumers often associate them with one gender or another.[65] The sex typing of products is often created or perpetuated by marketers (e.g., Princess telephones, boys' and girls' bicycles, and Luvs color-coded diapers). A new brand of

This ad for Bijan illustrates how sex-role identities are culturally bound by contrasting the expectations of how women should appear in two different countries.

Marketing Opportunity

From the time we're swathed in pink or blue diapers in the maternity ward, our culture bombards us with sex-typed products that reinforce differences between the sexes. For example, the ever-popular Barbie doll is a product many people "love to hate" because its many variations over the years have reflected certain cultural assumptions about what it means to be female. In addition to teaching little girls what an "ideal" female body should look like (more on that later), dolls like Barbie also send messages about how girls should dress and what occupations they should aspire to. Barbie has taken on the role of doctor, astronaut, even president but she's still retained her squeaky-clean image. That's a problem for Mattel; its core user is getting younger and younger (primarily 3- to 7-year-olds) and in order to keep growing the company has to entice older girls to keep playing with their dolls.

Now, Mattel is trying to keep girls who outgrow their Barbies as customers with its new line called My Scene Barbie. Out with the ball gowns and flight attendant outfits, in with the skintight, low-rise jeans, platform boots, leather and faux-fur jackets, and cropped shirts that stop just above the belly button.[73] And in case that's not risqué enough, you can buy a "limited edition" Lingerie Barbie dressed in bustier, stiletto heels, and thigh-high stockings.[74] Even as Mattel scrambles to change with the times, it's being challenged by upstarts like Bratz dolls that also are outfitted in racy fashions such as platform shoes, hip huggers, tube tops, and fur vests. They are multiethnic and have cool names like Yasmin, Jade, and Sasha; not to mention their cool activity sets, including a bubble-making Jacuzzi. To add insult to injury, Bratz dolls are an inch shorter than Barbie, so the rivals can't share their wardrobes. A company executive explained, "At first we thought no one is going to buy a doll named Bratz. But in focus groups, girls really liked it. It meant everything that Barbie is not." Mattel is hoping the new generation of Barbie will prove him wrong.[75]

vodka introduced in 2000 called Thor's Hammer illustrates this stereotyping. The booze comes in a short, squat bottle and is described by the company's VP of marketing as being "bold and broad and solid. This is a man's kind of vodka . . . it's not your frosted . . . girly-man vodka." Thor was the Norse god of thunder, and the company claims the name has no connection to the slang phrase "getting hammered," which can happen if you drink too much of the stuff.[66]

Androgyny

Androgyny refers to the possession of both masculine and feminine traits.[67] Researchers make a distinction between *sex-typed people*, who are stereotypically masculine or feminine, and *androgynous people*, whose mixture of characteristics allows them to function well in a variety of social situations.

Differences in sex-role orientation can influence responses to marketing stimuli, at least under some circumstances.[68] For example, research indicates that females are more likely to undergo more elaborate processing of message content, so they tend to be more sensitive to specific pieces of information when forming a judgment, whereas males are more influenced by overall themes.[69] In addition, women with a relatively strong masculine component in their sex-role identity prefer ad portrayals that include nontraditional women.[70] Some research indicates that sex-typed people are more sensitive to the sex-role depictions of characters in advertising, although women appear to be more sensitive generally to gender-role relationships than men.

In one study, subjects read two versions of a beer advertisement, couched in either masculine or feminine terms. The masculine version contained phrases such as "X beer has the strong aggressive flavor that really asserts itself with good food and good company," and the feminine version made claims such as "Brewed with tender care, X beer is a full-bodied beer that goes down smooth and gentle." People who rated themselves as highly masculine or highly feminine preferred the version that was described in (respectively) very masculine or feminine terms.[71] Sex-typed people in general are more concerned with ensuring that their behavior is consistent with their culture's definition of gender appropriateness.

Female Sex Roles

In the 1949 movie *Adam's Rib*, Katherine Hepburn played a stylish and competent lawyer. This film was one of the first to show that a woman can have a successful career and still be happily married. Today, the evolution of a new managerial class of women has forced marketers to change their traditional assumptions about women as they target this growing market.

And, younger women's views of themselves are quite different from those of their mothers who fought the good fight for feminism 20 or 30 years ago. To some extent they may take for granted that they have certain rights that their mothers had to fight for. After all, they have grown up with female role models who are strong leaders; they participate to a much greater degree in organized sports; and they spend a lot of time on the Internet where factors like gender, race, and social status tend to disappear. In one study only 34 percent of girls aged 13 to 20 labeled themselves as feminists—even though they strongly endorse the principles of the feminist movement. Ninety-seven percent of the same respondents believe a woman should receive the same pay for the same work a man does; 92 percent agree that a woman's lifestyle choices should not be limited by her gender; and 89 percent say a woman can be successful without either a man or children. But, 56 percent also believe that "a man should always open the door for a woman."[72]

These changes have forced marketers to reexamine their strategies. For example, 10 years ago most sporting goods manufacturers sold products for women, but this often meant just creating an inferior version of the male product and slapping a pink label on it. Then the companies discovered that many women were buying products intended for boys because they wanted better quality, so some of them figured out that they needed to take this market segment seriously.

Burton Snowboard Company was one of the early learners. When the company started to offer high-quality clothing and gear made specifically for women, female boarders snapped them up. Burton also changed the way it promotes these products. It recently redesigned its Web site after getting feedback from female riders. Now, models in the women's section are shot from the bottom looking up, which makes them look more empowered. In contrast, the photos in the men's section feature tighter shots of the gear itself, since Burton's research showed that males were more interested in the technical details.[76]

The evolution of female sex roles is even more apparent in Asia, where until recently women were expected to be docile and subservient to men. That's changing rapidly in many Asian countries. In sharp contrast to traditional attitudes, for example, today one-quarter of urban, unmarried women say they want to marry but not have kids. A comment by one young Chinese woman in a study typifies this change in mind-set. She wrote: "I am the center of the world, I am the [focal point]. Draw a circle and you can find me. I'm quite realistic, but sometimes I daydream. I'm a little bit selfish, but I'm always there for my friends."

Some marketers have noted these changes and have responded strategically. Motivated by surveys that showed women were becoming more career-focused, Procter & Gamble pulled an ad for Rejoice shampoo that featured an airline hostess and replaced it with a spot showing a female working as a mechanical engineer for the airline.[77]

Another sign of changing attitudes is the huge popularity of HBO's hit series *Sex and the City* among single, working women in Asia. Events like a fashion show called "Shoes in the City" in Bangkok and Manila attract hordes of wannabe Sarah Jessica Parkers. Passionate devotion to a show with such sexually explicit content is unusual in most of the region, and in Muslim countries like Malaysia censors delete parts of the program. It's banned entirely in Singapore, but that hasn't stopped the show from becoming an underground hit as fans go online to order DVDs or watch when they travel abroad. As the editor of a Singapore lifestyle magazine observes, "The show has created personas for women to base themselves on. What happens in the show reflects our lives in a lot of ways, even here in Singapore. They get a lot more sex and a lot more men, but we aspire."[78]

Still, announcing the death of traditional sex-role stereotypes is premature. This is certainly true in traditional Islamic countries like Saudi Arabia, where women are required to be completely covered in public and they are not allowed to work as salespeople in stores open to the public (even if the store sells female intimate apparel).[79] Or, consider the extremely popular Singapore Girl—encased in her snug sarong, she has been the familiar symbol of Singapore Airlines since 1972. The sarongs are tailored to fit so closely that they have been known to split open during flights. Candidates for the job must be younger than 26, at least 5 feet, 2 inches tall, slim, and attractive with a good complexion. The rigorous selection process includes a swimsuit test in which the women are inspected for scars. A spokesman for the airline said, "We want to present a complete picture of femininity." The airline's slogan: "Singapore Girl, you're a great way to fly."[80]

Male Sex Roles

The traditional conception of the ideal male is as a tough, aggressive, muscular man who enjoys "manly" sports and activities. Just as for women, however, the true story is more complicated than that. Indeed, the field of study known as **masculinism** is devoted to the study of the male image and the cultural meanings of masculinity.[81] Like women, men receive mixed messages about how they are supposed to behave and feel. It's more common these days to see men holding babies or being involved in meaningful relationships with women or with male friends in advertisements.

Reinforcing gender stereotypes.

While you don't necessarily dress for men, it doesn't hurt, on occasion, to see one drool like the pathetic dog that he is.

On the other hand, it's easy to find examples of a return to "old-fashioned" male roles that celebrate leering, boyish behavior—think about the very popular "Man Show" on Comedy Central. An ad for Rheingold beer says, "for the few real men still left," and a character in a Wendy's commercial points out, "This is a burger town, pretty boy."

An ad campaign for Brut cologne, targeted to men aged 18 to 34, exemplifies this new emphasis on being "politically incorrect." The campaign features head-lines like "Actually, yes. That outfit does make you look fat." An executive involved with the campaign explains, "These ads reflect the style of how these young guys feel today. It accepts it and speaks in their language that it's good to be Neanderthal again." The campaign was developed after focus groups including men and women of all ages told researchers that crass humor is acceptable now. They were shown a preliminary version, for example, of an ad featuring a man surrounded by buxom women, with the tagline "Brut has been considered an effective treatment for erectile dysfunction." A "disclaimer" says, "Brut antiperspirant should be applied to armpits only." According to the executive, "We showed this to young women in concept form, and they thought it was funny. Certain people might take offense, but overall we were surprised by how both men and women of a wide age range seemed to have a really relaxed attitude about this now." Research findings led to the core insight that drove the campaign: "Inside every man, there's a guy."[82]

Perhaps this shift in attitudes is due to the idea that now everyone—women and men—is fair game. Regardless of your gender, your appearance (and perhaps sex appeal) is important. Indeed, just as advertisers are often criticized for so-called "cheesecake" ads depicting women as sex objects, the same accusations can be made about how males are portrayed—a practice correspondingly known as "beefcake." In a typical example, the copy for a Sansabelt trousers ad reads, "What women look for in men's pants."

In a display of "what's good for the goose is good for the gander," men are concerned as never before with their appearance. Men spend $7.7 billion on grooming products globally each year. A wave of male cleansers, moisturizers, sunscreens, depilatories, and body sprays is washing up on U.S. shores, largely from European marketers. Unilever spent $90 million to launch its Axe body spray after its research showed that a sizeable number of American men would put on a spritz or two in addition to their usual deodorant.

Men are showing a willingness to use other traditionally feminine products such as depilatories to give them that smooth-torso look (depilatory sales increased by 16 percent between 2001 and 2002).[83] Many of these same guys also are coloring their hair; men between the ages of 18 and 24 are 64 percent more likely to dye their hair than the average adult male.[84] Other vanity products introduced in recent years include Bodyslimmers underwear that sucks in the waist, and Super Shaper Briefs that round out the buttocks.

Japanese men are taking it a step farther; it's fashionable for everyone from high school students to professional baseball players to tweeze their eyebrows. Others are putting mudpacks on their cheeks and using hairpins, and market researchers are starting to see an interest among men in wearing foundation makeup. These choices illustrate the lengths to which one sex will go to please the other; the men apparently are trying to compete with the large number of boyish, clean-cut actors and singers who are the rage among young Japanese women.[85]

Gay, Lesbian, Bisexual, and Transgender (GLBT) Consumers

The proportion of the population that is gay or lesbian is difficult to determine, and efforts to measure this group have been controversial.[86] Estimates among academics and marketing experts range widely, from about 4 percent to 8 percent of the total U.S. population, or between 11 million and 23 million people. The 2000 Census reported 1.2 million same-sex "unmarried" partners in the United States, and this number excludes single gays and lesbians.[87] The respected research company Yankelovich Partners Inc., which as we saw in Chapter 4 has tracked consumer values and attitudes since 1971 in its annual *Monitor*™ survey, now includes a question about sexual identity in its survey and reports that about 6 percent of respondents identify themselves as gay/homosexual/lesbian. This study was virtually the first to use a sample that reflects the population as a whole instead of polling only smaller or biased groups (such as readers of gay publications) whose responses may not be as representative of all consumers.

One barrier to computing an accurate estimate is that some respondents are reluctant to answer questions about their sexual orientation. The anonymity of the Internet has helped a bit—Harris Interactive found that while just about 2 percent of adult respondents identify themselves as "gay or lesbian" in telephone surveys, 4 percent self-identify when online. Harris has also discovered that how the question

Billy, an openly gay doll who is anatomically correct, was created by a London-based firm. He comes with a range of macho outfits including a bell-bottomed sailor and a San Francisco leatherman.

is asked can boost response rates. When given the option to self-identify as "gay," "lesbian," "bisexual," or "transgendered" (those who have physically changed their sex) as opposed to "gay or lesbian," a full 6 percent respond affirmatively.[88]

These results help to paint a more accurate picture of the potential size and attractiveness of this segment to marketers. To put things in perspective, the GLBT market is at least as large if not larger than the Asian American population (currently at around 12 million people). The GLBT consumer market spends in the range of $250 to $350 billion a year. A Simmons study of readers of gay publications found that readers are almost 12 times more likely to hold professional jobs, twice as likely to own a vacation home, and eight times more likely to own a notebook computer compared to heterosexuals.

In the mid-1990s, IKEA, a Swedish furniture retailer with stores in several major U.S. markets, broke new ground by running a TV spot featuring a gay couple that purchased a dining room table at the store.[89] Now, many big corporations such as American Express, American Airlines, and Procter & Gamble actively court this market segment: Over 60 national advertisers now place ads in gay publications.[90] At one time Mattel even sold an Earring Magic Ken doll, complete with faux-leather vest, lavender mesh shirt, and two-tone hairdo, though the company removed the product from its line following reports that it had become a favorite of gay men.[91] A few current examples of marketing activities in this area include:

● Recognizing that gay consumers tend to be active Web surfers, the travel portal Orbitz launched a gay and lesbian version of its site with features and promotions pegged to popular gay destinations like Palm Springs, California, and Provincetown, Massachusetts, as well as advice for gay and lesbian parents traveling with children. An Orbitz executive said that about 100,000 people visited the gay section of the site each month, and those visitors booked travel at a rate 50 percent higher than visitors to the other parts of ***Orbitz.com***.[92]

● MTV Networks and Showtime (both cable divisions of Viacom) are developing a plan to create the first cable channels aimed directly at gay viewers. According to Viacom's research, gay viewers make up about 6.5 percent of television households.[93]

● The first gay central character in a comic book was unveiled in late 2002 when "Green Lantern" introduced Terry, who is the victim of a gay bashing. One of the creators commented, "Where we're bringing Terry is very similar to the Brandon Teena and Matthew Shepard moments," referring to the cross-dressing woman in Nebraska who was murdered in 1993 and the gay University of Wyoming student who was beaten, tied to a post, and left to die in 1998.[94]

This ad for Alize, a cognac drink, is geared toward lesbians.

In addition to gay men, lesbian consumers have recently been in the cultural spotlight. Perhaps the trendiness of "lesbian chic" is due in part to such high-profile cultural figures as tennis star Martina Navratilova, singers k.d. lang and Melissa Etheridge, and actresses Ellen deGeneres and Anne Heche. A readers' survey by a lesbian-oriented publication called *Girlfriends* magazine found that 54 percent hold professional/managerial jobs, 57 percent have partners, and 22 percent have children. But, lesbian women are harder to reach than gay men because they don't tend to concentrate in urban neighborhoods or in bars and don't read as many gay publications. Some marketers have chosen to focus instead on such venues as women's basketball games and women's music festivals.[95] American Express, Stolichnaya vodka, Atlantic Records, and Naya bottled water are among those corporations that run ads in lesbian publications (an ad for American Express Travelers Cheques for Two shows two women's signatures on a check). Acting on research that showed lesbians are four times as likely as the average consumer to own one of their cars, Subaru of America decided to target this market in a big way.

■ BODY IMAGE

A person's physical appearance is a large part of his or her self-concept. **Body image** refers to a consumer's subjective evaluation of his or her physical self. As was the case with the overall self-concept, this image is not necessarily accurate. A man may think of himself as being more muscular than he really is, or a woman may feel she appears fatter than is the case. It is not uncommon to find marketing strategies that exploit consumers' tendencies to distort their body images by preying on insecurities about appearance, thereby creating a gap between the real and ideal physical self and, consequently, the desire to purchase products and services to narrow that gap. Indeed, the success of the photo chain Glamour Shots, which provides dramatic makeovers to customers and then gives them a pictorial record of their pinup potential, is due to the fantasies of everyday people to be supermodels—at least for an hour or two.

Body cathexis means a person's feelings about his or her body. The word *cathexis* refers to the emotional significance of some object or idea to a person, and some parts of the body are more central to self-concept than are others. One study of young adults' feelings about their bodies found that the respondents were the most satisfied with their hair and eyes and had the least positive feelings about their waists. These feelings also were related to usage of grooming products. Consumers who were more satisfied with their bodies were more frequent users of such "preening" products as hair conditioner, blow dryers, cologne, facial bronzer, tooth polish, and pumice soap.[96]

Ideals of Beauty

A person's satisfaction with the physical image he or she presents to others is affected by how closely that image corresponds to the image valued by his or her culture.[97] An **ideal of beauty** is a particular model, or *exemplar*, of appearance. Ideals of beauty for both men and women may include physical features (e.g., big breasts or small, bulging muscles or not) as well as clothing styles, cosmetics, hairstyles, skin tone (pale versus tan), and body type (petite, athletic, voluptuous, etc).

Is Beauty Universal?

Recent research indicates that preferences for some physical features over others are "wired in" genetically, and that these reactions tend to be the same among people around the world. Specifically, people appear to favor features associated with good health and youth, attributes linked to reproductive ability and strength. These characteristics include large eyes, high cheekbones, and a narrow jaw. Another cue

Some research indicates that balanced or symmetrical facial features are a cue used by men and women to decide who is attractive. Country singer Lyle Lovett is an example of a man with asymmetrical features. The left picture is the real Lovett; the right is a computerized image that is really two left sides of his face.

that apparently is used by people across ethnic and racial groups to signal sexual desirability is whether the person's features are balanced. One study reported that men and women with greater facial symmetry started having sex three to four years earlier than people with asymmetric features.

Men also are more likely to use a woman's body shape as a sexual cue, and one explanation is because feminine curves provide evidence of reproductive potential. During puberty a typical female gains almost 35 pounds of "reproductive fat" around hips and thighs that supply the approximately 80,000 extra calories needed to support a pregnancy. Most fertile women have waist–hip ratios of 0.6 to 0.8, an hourglass shape that also happens to be the one men rank highest. Even though preferences for overall weight change over time, waist–hip ratios tend to stay in this range. Figure 5.1 illustrates how body shape changes (sometimes subtly) as

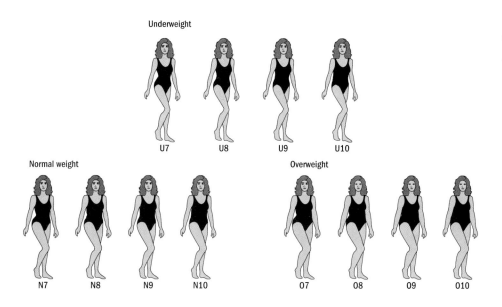

■ **FIGURE 5.1**
WAIST-HIP RATIOS
Source: Newsweek (June 3, 1996): 65 © 1996 Newsweek, Inc. All rights reserved. Reprinted by permission.

waist–hip ratios increase or decrease. Even the superthin model Twiggy (who pioneered the "waif look" decades before Kate Moss) had a ratio of 0.73.[98] Other positively valued female characteristics include a higher than average forehead, fuller lips, a shorter jaw, and a smaller chin and nose.

Women, on the other hand, favor men with a heavy lower face (an indication of high concentration of androgens that impart strength), those who are slightly above-average height, and males with a prominent brow. One study found these preferences actually fluctuate during the course of a woman's menstrual cycle: Researchers showed women in Japan and Scotland a series of computer-generated photos of male faces that were systematically altered in terms of such dimensions as the size of the jaw and the prominence of the eyebrow ridge.[99] Women in the study preferred the more heavy, masculine features when they were ovulating, but these choices shifted during other parts of their monthly cycles. If true, these results indicate a "wired-in" preference for strong men who can pass this trait on to offspring.

Of course, the way these faces are "packaged" still varies enormously, and that's where marketers come in: Advertising and other forms of mass media play a significant role in determining which forms of beauty are considered desirable at any point in time. An ideal of beauty functions as a sort of cultural yardstick. Consumers compare themselves to some standard (often advocated by the fashion media) and they are dissatisfied with their appearance to the extent that they don't match up to it. This may lower their own self-esteem or in some cases possibly diminish the effectiveness of an ad because of negative feelings aroused by a highly attractive model.[100]

These cultural ideals often are summed up in a sort of cultural shorthand. We may talk about a "bimbo," a "girl-next-door," or an "ice queen," or we may refer to specific women who have come to embody an ideal, such as J-Lo, Gwyneth Paltrow, or the late Princess Diana.[101] Similar descriptions for men include "jock," "pretty boy," and "bookworm," or a "Brad Pitt type," a "Wesley Snipes type," and so on.

The Western Ideal

Beauty is about more than aesthetics—people use cues such as skin color and eye shape to make inferences about a person's status, sophistication, and social desirability. These linkages are part of our socialization process and often are associated with political and social issues—the standards of beauty prevalent in dominant cultures tend to be adopted by people in less powerful cultures who want to identify with these groups.

An ad on Malaysian television shows an attractive college student who can't get a second glance from a boy at the next desk. "She's pretty," he says to himself, "but . . ." Then, she applies Pond's Skin Lightening Moisturizer by Unilever PLC and she reappears looking several shades paler. Now the boy wonders, "Why didn't I notice her before?" In many Asian cultures, historically light skin was equated with wealth and status. People associated dark skin with the laboring class that toils in the fields. This stereotype persists today: In a 2002 survey, 74 percent of men in Malaysia, 68 percent in Hong Kong, and 55 percent in Taiwan say they are more attracted to women with fair complexions. Accordingly, about a third of the female respondents in each country said they use skin-whitening products.[102]

As media images of glamorous American (Caucasian) celebrities proliferate around the globe, the Western ideal of beauty—big round eyes, tiny waists, large breasts, blond hair, and blue eyes—is being adopted by cultures that have to literally go under the knife to achieve these attributes:

● The proportion of African-African women who are using plastic surgery to enhance their looks has almost doubled in the last decade. A growing middle class is fueling this trend, since these people can afford the surgery and improved technology that leaves less scarring on dark skin. A columnist for *Essence* magazine recently expressed her concerns about black women wanting to exchange their African features for European ones by buying into "a culture that dictates the feminine ideal."[103]

● A few years ago, a model named Cindy Burbridge, who was the local spokeswoman for Lux soap and Omega watches, became the first blue-eyed Miss Thailand. She's one of a generation of racially mixed Thais who now dominate the local fashion and entertainment industries as the public abandons the round face, arched eyebrows, and small mouth of the classical Thai look in favor of a Western ideal. Many buy blue contact lenses to enhance their looks. In a poll conducted to name the sexiest men and the sexiest women in Thailand, seven out of the nine top scorers were of mixed blood.[104]

● Year after year, winners of the Most Beautiful Girl in Nigeria performed very poorly in the Miss World competition. Local organizers had about given up on the idea that an African woman could win a contest dominated by Western beauties. Then, Agbani Darego, the 2001 Most Beautiful Girl, went on to win the Miss World title. She was the first African winner in the contest's 51-year history. However, pride was mixed with puzzlement: The new Miss World didn't possess the voluptuous figure prized in African culture. In West and Central Africa, big women are revered and many beauty contestants weigh over 200 pounds. In Niger, women even eat livestock feed or special vitamins to bulk up. The Calabari in southeastern Nigeria send prospective brides to fattening farms, where they are fed huge amounts of food and massaged into rounder shapes. After weeks of this regimen, the bigger brides are proudly paraded in the village square.[105] As one African explained, "Plumpness means prosperity. Thin represents everything you don't want: poverty, AIDS, and other diseases, misery and hunger." In contrast, Ms. Darego is six feet tall and skinny. Older Nigerians did not find the winner especially attractive at all, and some bitingly described her as a white girl in black skin. But, younger people are a different story. For them, thin is in. In Lagos, fashionable thin girls are called *lepa* and there is even a popular song with this title. A movie called *Lepa Shandi* celebrates the new look; the title means a girl as slim as a 20-naira bill.[106]

● It's good to be a plastic surgeon in Seoul. Many Korean women are lifting their noses, shaving their jaws, and widening their eyes in pursuit of a Western image of beauty. The newest craze is a leg job to reduce the size of thick calves that are common in this country as women seek the slender legs of Western supermodels.[107]

Ideals of Beauty over Time

Although beauty may be only skin deep, throughout history women have worked very hard to attain it. They have starved themselves, painfully bound their feet, inserted plates into their lips; spent countless hours under hair dryers, in front of mirrors, and beneath tanning lights; and opted for breast reduction or enlargement operations to alter their appearance and meet their society's expectations of what a beautiful woman should look like.

In retrospect, periods of history tend to be characterized by a specific "look," or ideal of beauty. American history can be described in terms of a succession of dominant ideals. For example, in sharp contrast to today's emphasis on health and vigor, in the early 1800s, it was fashionable to appear delicate to the point of looking ill. The poet John Keats described the ideal woman of that time as "a milk white lamb that bleats for man's protection." Other looks have included the voluptuous, lusty woman as epitomized by Lillian Russell, the athletic Gibson Girl of the 1890s, and the small, boyish flapper of the 1920s as exemplified by Clara Bow.[108] One study compared measures of the public's favorite actresses with socioeconomic indicators between 1932 and 1995. When conditions were bad, people preferred actresses with mature features including small eyes, thin cheeks, and a large chin. When the economy was in good shape, however, the public embraced women with babyish features such as large eyes and full cheeks.[109]

To play *refreshed*

Drink
Coca-Cola

This 1951 bathing beauty exemplified an
ideal of American femininity at that time.

In much of the nineteenth century, the desirable waistline for American women was 18 inches, a circumference that required the use of corsets pulled so tight that they routinely caused headaches, fainting spells, and possibly even the uterine and spinal disorders common among women of the time. Although modern women are not quite as "straight laced," many still endure such indignities as high heels, body waxing, eyelifts, and liposuction. In addition to the millions spent on cosmetics, clothing, health clubs, and fashion magazines, these practices remind us that—rightly or wrongly—the desire to conform to current standards of beauty is alive and well.

The ideal body type of Western women has changed radically over time, and these changes have resulted in a realignment of *sexual dimorphic markers*—those aspects of the body that distinguish between the sexes. The first part of the 1990s saw the emergence of the controversial "waif" look in which successful models (most notably Kate Moss) were likely to have bodies resembling those of young boys. Using heights and weights from winners of the Miss America pageant, nutrition experts concluded that many beauty queens were in the undernourished range. In the 1920s, contestants had a body mass index in the range now considered normal—20–25. Since then, an increasing number of winners have had indexes under 18.5, which is the World Health Organization's standard for undernutrition.[110] Similarly, a study of almost 50 years of *Playboy* centerfolds shows that the women have become less shapely and more androgynous since Marilyn Monroe graced the first edition with a voluptuous hourglass figure of 37–23–36. However, a magazine spokesman comments, "As time has gone on and women have become more athletic, more in the business world and more inclined to put themselves through fitness regimes, their bodies have changed, and we reflect that as well. But I would think that no one with eyes to see would consider playmates to be androgynous."[111] Fair enough.

We can also distinguish among ideals of beauty for men in terms of facial features, musculature, and facial hair—who could confuse Tom Cruise with George Clooney? In fact, one national survey that asked both men and women to comment on male aspects of appearance found that the dominant standard of beauty for men is a strongly masculine, muscled body—though women tend to prefer men with less muscle mass than men themselves strive to attain.[112] Advertisers appear to have the males' ideal in mind—a study of men appearing in advertisements found that most sport the strong and muscular physique of the male stereotype.[113]

Working on the Body

Because many consumers are motivated to match some ideal of appearance, they often go to great lengths to change aspects of their physical selves. From cosmetics to plastic surgery, tanning salons to diet drinks, a multitude of products and services are directed toward altering or maintaining aspects of the physical self in order to present a desirable appearance. It is difficult to overstate the importance of the physical self-concept (and the desire by consumers to improve their appearance) to many marketing activities.

Fattism

As reflected in the expression "you can never be too thin or too rich," our society has an obsession with weight. We are continually bombarded by images of thin, happy people. Various surveys have reported that as early as nursery school children prefer drawings of peers in wheelchairs, on crutches, or with facial disfigurements to those of fat children. One survey of girls aged 12 to 19 reported that 55 percent said they see ads "all the time" that make them want to go on a diet.[114]

Although Americans' obsession with thinness is legendary worldwide, the weight-loss obsession is spreading—often with help from American media figures. In traditional Fijian culture, for example, the body ideal for females is, to put it delicately, robust. When a woman started to lose weight in Fiji, this was cause for concern and a sign of probable illness. Then, a few years ago satellite TV started showing skinny actresses in imported shows such as *Melrose Place* and *Beverly Hills 90210*. Now, the tables have turned and teenaged girls in Fiji are starting to exhibit eating disorders. A study found that teens who watched TV three or more nights per week were 50 percent more likely to feel too fat than were other girls. Participants cited characters such as Heather Locklear as an inspiration for changing their bodies.[115]

Or, consider changes now occurring in the Middle East. As in Fiji, Egyptians traditionally preferred somewhat plumper women—and the belly dancing tradition encouraged this. Now, though, weight-loss diets are fashionable. The head of Egyptian television announced that overweight female newscasters have three months to shed those extra pounds (10 to 20 pounds in most cases) or they will be fired. Egypt's first lady, Suzanne Mubarak, visits schools to promote thinness, and Egyptian advertising increasingly uses skinny, blond, light-skinned models to sell products to customers who don't look anything like them. An entrepreneur named Samia Allouba is Egypt's answer to Jane Fonda. She sells home-exercise and diet videos, and her twice-weekly exercise program is beamed to millions of potential viewers around the Middle East via satellite. Of course, Fonda never had to face the obstacles Mrs. Allouba does. In deference to Islamic sensibilities, she and female guests exercising on her shows wear only loose-fitting clothes. Though they are doing aerobic exercises, the women aren't allowed to breathe too heavily.[116]

How realistic are our appearance standards? Fashion dolls, such as the ubiquitous Barbie, reinforce an unnatural ideal of thinness. The dimensions of these dolls, when extrapolated to average female body sizes, are unnaturally long and thin.[117] If the traditional Barbie doll were a real woman, her dimensions would be 38–18–34! In 1998, Mattel conducted "plastic surgery" on Barbie to give her a less pronounced bust and slimmer hips, but she is still not exactly dumpy.[118] The company now sells an even more realistic Barbie featuring wider hips and a smaller bust (and for the first time Barbie has a belly button).[119]

One reason for Mattel's change is to meet the growing competition from other doll makers who are responding to the public's desire for more down-to-earth figures. Emme, a full-figure fashion doll based on the voluptuous supermodel is selling out. Visitors to the model's Web site can read about Emme's acceptance of her

This ad for an online weight-loss site drives home the idea that the media often communicate unrealistic expectations about body shape.

This is not normal.
(Despite what you see at the Oscars®.)

weight: "There is nothing more freeing after many years of not feeling comfortable in my own skin and going on every diet you could imagine, to learn that I wasn't crazy . . . millions of other women and men felt the same way. . . . I've learned that after many years of trying to fit into others' ideals of beauty, I had to learn that my own image of beauty was perfect just as it is, as long as I took care of myself.[120]

Lane Bryant, the specialty retailer for plus-size women, sends a similar message with an advertising campaign featuring Mr. Big, a character in the HBO series *Sex and the City.* The debonair Mr. Big (portrayed by actor Chris Noth) is shown cavorting with several plus-size models.[121] Lane Bryant has carefully groomed a hip image, featuring full-figured celebrity spokesmodels such as Camryn Manheim of *The Practice* TV show. The chain is introducing sexy lingerie with the tagline "Big girls take back the night." A Lane Bryant executive comments, "If a short-sleeve rib sweater is the hot item this fall it is our challenge to deliver that for our customer, too. But not to do it in a way that makes her look as though she's pushed into a sausage casing."[122]

Lane Bryant offers lingerie for plus-sized women with the slogan, "Big girls take back the night."

Still, many consumers focus on attaining an unrealistic ideal weight, sometimes by relying on height and weight charts compiled by the insurance industry that show what one *should* weigh. These charts are often outdated because they don't take into account today's larger body frames or such factors as muscularity, age, or activity level. And, as much as we admire razor-thin models, our behavior says otherwise: In 2002 the Centers for Disease Control reported that 60 percent of Americans are overweight, and more than one in four are obese.[123]

Body Image Distortions

Some people unfortunately exaggerate the connection between self-esteem and appearance to such an extent that they sacrifice their health to attain what they consider to be a desirable body image. Women tend to pick up messages from the media more than men that the quality of their bodies reflects their self-worth, so it

Society's emphasis on thinness makes many consumers insecure about their body image. This South American ad promises, "You'll never have to go to the beach in a T-Shirt again."

You'll never have to go to the beach in a T-shirt again.

is not surprising that most major distortions of body image occur among females. These cultural messages are everywhere—perhaps even in the supermarket if a study conducted by one grocery chain is to be believed. Managers at Tesco, Britain's largest supermarket, were perplexed that its large, 2-pound-2-ounce melons were not selling well, especially when they discovered that sales actually increased when the product was replaced with a smaller, 1-pound-3-ounce version. In research done to explore this curious finding, 7 out of 10 women cited unfavorable comparison to their breast size as the reason they avoided the larger fruit. Tesco instructed its produce suppliers to grow smaller melons.[124]

Men do not tend to differ in ratings of their current figure, their ideal figure, and the figure they think is most attractive to women. In contrast, women rate both the figure they think is most attractive to men and their ideal figure as much thinner than their actual figure.[125] In one survey, two-thirds of college women admitted resorting to unhealthy behavior to control weight. Advertising messages that convey an image of slimness help to reinforce these activities by arousing insecurities about weight.[126]

A distorted body image has been linked to eating disorders, which are particularly prevalent among young women. People with *anorexia* perceive themselves as being too fat, and they virtually starve themselves in the quest for thinness. This condition often results in *bulimia*, which involves two stages. First, binge eating occurs (usually in private), in which more than 5,000 calories may be consumed at one time. The binge is then followed by induced vomiting, abuse of laxatives, fasting, or overly strenuous exercise—a "purging" process that reasserts the woman's sense of control.

Most eating disorders are found in white, upper-middle-class teens and college-age women. Victims often have brothers or fathers who are hypercritical of their weight, and these disorders are also associated with a history of sexual abuse.[127] In addition, one's peers can encourage binge eating. Groups such as athletic teams, cheerleading squads, and sororities may develop positive norms regarding binge eating. In one study of a college sorority, members' popularity within the group increased the more they binged.[128]

Although about 90 percent of teens treated for eating disorders are female, body image disturbances in men may be more widespread than is believed. Psychiatrists report increasing cases of *body dysmorphic disorder* (an obsession with perceived flaws in appearance) among young males (the average age of onset is 15). Symptoms of this disorder include excessive checking of mirrors and attempts to camouflage imagined deformities. Male eating disorders are especially common among jockeys, boxers, and other athletes who must conform to weight requirements.[129]

As with women, perhaps men are influenced by media images and products encouraging an unrealistic physique. Consider, for example, that if the dimensions of the original GI Joe action figure were projected onto a real 5-feet-10-inch man, he would have a 32-inch waist, a 44-inch chest, and 12-inch biceps. Or how about the same exercise for the Batman action figure: If this superhero came to life he would boast a 30-inch waist, 57-inch chest, and 27-inch biceps.[130] Holy steroids, Robin!

Cosmetic Surgery

Consumers are increasingly electing to have cosmetic surgery to change a poor body image or simply to enhance appearance.[131] Virtually any body part is fair game for surgical alteration. For example, bellybutton reconstruction is a popular form of cosmetic surgery in Japan. The navel is an important part of Japanese culture, and mothers often save a baby's umbilical cord in a wooden box. In Japanese, a "bent navel" is a grouch, and a phrase meaning, "give me a break" translates as "yeah, and I brew tea in my bellybutton." A popular insult among children is "Your mother has an outie."[132]

Interest in the United States tends to center elsewhere. More than 6 percent of the U.S. adult population has had cosmetic surgery, and the number of procedures rose eightfold from 1990 to 1999.[133] And going under the knife is not just for women anymore: Men now account for as many as 20 percent of plastic surgery patients, with liposuction the most common procedure. Other popular operations for men include the implantation of silicon pectoral muscles (for the chest) and even calf implants to fill out "chicken legs."[134]

Breast Augmentation

As the female shoppers at Tesco testified, our culture tends to equate breast size with sex appeal. The impact of breast size on self-concept is demonstrated by consumer research undertaken by an underwear company. While conducting focus groups on bras, an analyst noted that small-chested women typically reacted with hostility when discussing the subject. The participants would unconsciously cover their chests with their arms as they spoke and complained that they were ignored by the fashion industry. To meet this overlooked need, the company introduced a line of A-cup bras called "A-OK" and a new market segment was born.

Some women elect to have breast augmentation procedures because they feel that larger breasts will increase their allure.[135] Although some of these procedures have generated controversy due to negative side effects, it is unclear whether potential medical problems will deter large numbers of women from choosing surgical options to enhance their (perceived) femininity. And, as Lisa discovered, many companies are promoting nonsurgical alterations by pushing pushup bras that merely create the illusion of a larger cleavage. These products offer "cleavage enhancement" that uses a combination of wires and internal pads (called "cookies" in the industry) to create the desired effect.

Body Decoration and Mutilation

The body is adorned or altered in some way in every culture. Decorating the self serves a number of purposes.[136]

Marketing Pitfall

Supersize that? One reason Americans suffer from an epidemic of obesity is staring us right in the face: The portions we eat are getting bigger and bigger. Although many of us accuse fast-food restaurants of introducing the colossal serving idea, new research shows that we've taken the lesson home. Nutritionists argue that we've gotten so used to large servings when we dine out that we've lost sight of what a normal portion is. The average size of a cheeseburger people make at home grew from 5.7 to 8.4 ounces between 1977 and 1996, while the size of a typical soft drink serving went from 13.1 to 19.9 fluid ounces and a salty snack ballooned from 1 to 1.6 ounces.[137]

- *To separate group members from nonmembers:* Chinook Indians of North America pressed the head of a newborn between two boards for a year, permanently altering its shape. In our society, teens go out of their way to adopt distinctive hair and clothing styles that will separate them from adults.
- *To place the individual in the social organization:* Many cultures engage in puberty rites, during which a boy symbolically becomes a man. Young men in Ghana paint their bodies with white stripes to resemble skeletons to symbolize the death of their child status. In Western culture, this rite may involve some form of mild self-mutilation or engaging in dangerous activities.
- *To place the person in a gender category:* The Tchikrin Indians of South America insert a string of beads in a boy's lip to enlarge it. Western women wear lipstick to enhance femininity. At the turn of the century, small lips were fashionable because they represented women's submissive role at that time.[138] Today, big, red lips are provocative and indicate an aggressive sexuality. Some women, including a number of famous actresses and models, receive collagen injections

Body piercing has practically become a mainstream fashion statement.

or lip inserts to create large, pouting lips (known in the modeling industry as "liver lips").[139]

- *To enhance sex-role identification:* The modern use of high heels, which podiatrists agree are a prime cause of knee and hip problems, backaches, and fatigue, can be compared with the traditional Asian practice of foot-binding to enhance femininity. As one doctor observed, "When [women] get home, they can't get their high-heeled shoes off fast enough. But every doctor in the world could yell from now until Doomsday, and women would still wear them."[140]

- *To indicate desired social conduct:* The Suya of South America wear ear ornaments to emphasize the importance placed on listening and obedience in their culture. In Western society some gay men may wear an earring in the left or right ear to signal what role (submissive or dominant) they prefer in a relationship.

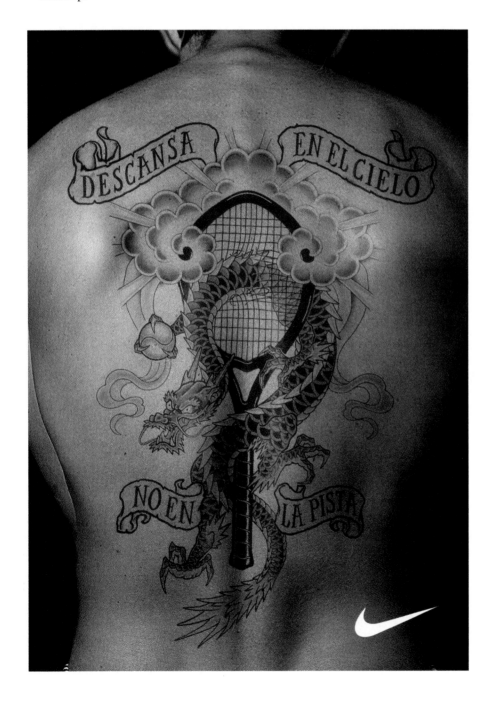

Tattooing is becoming mainstream. This Spanish ad for Nike tennis products says, "Rest in heaven, not on the court."

Body piercing has become a form of
expression for young people the world over.

- *To indicate high status or rank:* The Hidates Indians of North America wear
  feather ornaments that indicate how many people they have killed. In our society, some people wear glasses with clear lenses, even though they do not have
  eye problems, to enhance their perceived status.
- *To provide a sense of security:* Consumers often wear lucky charms, amulets,
  and rabbits' feet to protect them from the "evil eye." Some modern women wear
  a "mugger whistle" around their necks for a similar reason.

Tattoos

Tattoos—both temporary and permanent—are a popular form of body adornment.
People use this body art to make statements about the self, and these skin designs
serve some of the same functions that other kinds of body painting do in primitive
cultures. Tattoos (from the Tahitian *ta-tu*) have deep roots in folk art. Until recently,

the images were crude and were primarily death symbols (e.g., a skull), animals (especially panthers, eagles, and snakes), pinup women, or military designs. More current influences include science fiction themes, Japanese symbolism, and tribal designs. Tattoos have a long history of association with people who are social outcasts. For example, the faces and arms of criminals in sixth-century Japan were tattooed as a means of identifying them, as were Massachusetts prison inmates in the nineteenth century and concentration camp internees in the twentieth century. Marginal groups, such as bikers or Japanese *yakuze* (gang members) often use these emblems to express group identity and solidarity.

Today, a tattoo is a fairly risk-free way of expressing an adventurous side of the self. One recent trend is for middle-aged women to get one in order to commemorate a milestone like a big birthday, a divorce, or becoming an "empty nester." So, now these skin designs are more of a fashion statement than a declaration of rebellion—especially since 10 percent of Americans have one.[141] What are you waiting for?

Body Piercing

Decorating the body with various kinds of metallic inserts also has evolved from a practice associated with some fringe groups to become a popular fashion statement. The initial impetus for the mainstreaming of what had been an underground West Coast fad is credited to Aerosmith's 1993 video "Cryin'" in which Alicia Silverstone gets both a navel ring and a tattoo.[142] Piercings can range from a hoop protruding from a navel to scalp implants, where metal posts are inserted in the skull (do not try this at home!). Publications such as *Piercing Fans International Quarterly* are seeing their circulations soar, and Web sites are attracting numerous followers.

CHAPTER SUMMARY

- Consumers' self-concepts are reflections of their attitudes toward themselves. Whether these attitudes are positive or negative, they will help to guide many purchase decisions; products can be used to bolster self-esteem or to "reward" the self.
- Many product choices are dictated by the consumer's perceived similarity between his or her personality and attributes of the product. The symbolic interactionist perspective on the self implies that each of us actually has many selves, and a different set of products is required as props to play each role. Many things other than the body can also be viewed as part of the self. Valued objects, cars, homes, and even attachments to sports teams or national monuments are used to define the self, when these are incorporated into the extended self.
- A person's sex-role identity is a major component of self-definition. Conceptions about masculinity and femininity, largely shaped by society, guide the acquisition of "sex-typed" products and services.
- Advertising and other media play an important role in socializing consumers to be male and female. Although traditional women's roles have often been perpetuated in advertising depictions, this situation is changing somewhat. The media do not always portray men accurately either.
- A person's conception of his or her body also provides feedback to self-image. A culture communicates certain ideals of beauty, and consumers go to great lengths to attain these. Many consumer activities involve manipulating the body, whether through dieting, cosmetic surgery, piercing, or tattooing.
- Sometimes these activities are carried to an extreme, as people try too hard to live up to cultural ideals. One common manifestation is eating disorders, diseases in which women in particular become obsessed with thinness.

- Body decoration and/or mutilation may serve such functions as separating group members from nonmembers, marking the individual's status or rank within a social organization or within a gender category (e.g., homosexual), or even providing a sense of security or good luck.

KEY TERMS

Actual self   151
Agentic goals   159
Androgyny   162
Body cathexis   168
Body image   168
Communal goals   159

Extended self   156
Fantasy   152
Ideal of beauty   168
Ideal self   151
Identity theft   154
Looking-glass self   153

Masculinism   163
Self-concept   150
Self-image congruence models   156
Sex-typed traits   161
Symbolic interactionism   153
Symbolic self-completion theory   155

CONSUMER BEHAVIOR CHALLENGE

1 How might the creation of a self-conscious state be related to consumers who are trying on clothing in dressing rooms? Does the act of preening in front of a mirror change the dynamics by which people evaluate their product choices? Why?

2 Is it ethical for marketers to encourage infatuation with the self?

3 List three dimensions by which the self-concept can be described.

4 Compare and contrast the real versus the ideal self. List three products for which each type of self is likely to be used as a reference point when a purchase is considered.

5 Watch a set of ads featuring men and women on television. Try to imagine the characters with reversed roles (i.e., the male parts played by women and vice versa). Can you see any differences in assumptions about sex-typed behavior?

6 To date, the bulk of advertising targeted to gay consumers has been placed in exclusively gay media. If it were your decision to make, would you consider using mainstream media as well to reach gays, who constitute a significant proportion of the general population? Or, remembering that members of some targeted segments have serious objections to this practice, especially when the product (e.g., liquor, cigarettes) may be viewed as harmful in some way, should gays be singled out at all by marketers?

7 Do you agree that marketing strategies tend to have a male-oriented bias? If so, what are some possible consequences for specific marketing activities?

8 Construct a "consumption biography" of a friend or family member. Make a list of or photograph his or her most favorite possessions, and see if you or others can describe this person's personality just from the information provided by this catalogue.

9 Some consumer advocates have protested the use of superthin models in advertising, claiming that these women encourage others to starve themselves in order to attain the "waif" look. Other critics respond that the media's power to shape behavior has been overestimated, and that it is insulting to people to assume that they are unable to separate fantasy from reality. What do you think?

10 Interview victims of burglaries, or people who have lost personal property in floods, hurricanes, or other natural disasters. How do they go about reconstructing their possessions, and what effect did the loss appear to have on them?

11 Locate additional examples of self-esteem advertising. Evaluate the probable effectiveness of these appeals—is it true that "Flattery gets you everywhere?"

12 Does sex sell? There's certainly enough of it around, whether in print ads, television commercials, or on Web sites. When Victoria's Secret broadcast a provocative fashion show of skimpy lingerie live on the Web (after advertising the show on the Super Bowl), 1.5 million visitors checked out the site before it crashed due to an excessive number of hits. Of course, the retailer was taking a risk since by its own estimate 90 percent of its sales are from women. Some of them did not like this display of skin. One customer said she did not feel comfortable watching the Super Bowl ad with her boyfriend: "It's not that I'm offended by it; it just makes me feel inferior."[143] Perhaps the appropriate question is not does sex sell, but *should* sex sell? What are your feelings about the blatant use of sex to sell products? Do you think this tactic works better when selling to men than to women? Does exposure to unbelievably attractive men and women models only make the rest of us "normal" folks unhappy and insecure? Under what conditions (if any) should sex be used as a marketing strategy?

NOTES

1. Ann-Christine P. Diaz, "*Self* Declares Its Own Holiday," *Advertising Age* (January 31, 2000): 20.
2. Harry C. Triandis, "The Self and Social Behavior in Differing Cultural Contexts," *Psychological Review* 96, no. 3 (1989): 506–20; H. Markus and S. Kitayama, "Culture and the Self: Implications for Cognition, Emotion, and Motivation," *Psychological Review* 98 (1991): 224–53.
3. Markus and Kitayama, "Culture and the Self."
4. Nancy Wong and Aaron Ahuvia, "A Cross-Cultural Approach to Materialism and the Self," in Dominique Bouchet, ed., *Cultural Dimensions of International Marketing* (Denmark: Odense University, 1995), 68–89.
5. Lisa M. Keefe, "You're So Vain," *Marketing News* (February 28, 2000): 8.
6. Morris Rosenberg, *Conceiving the Self* (New York: Basic Books, 1979); M. Joseph Sirgy, "Self-Concept in Consumer Behavior: A Critical Review," *Journal of Consumer Research* 9 (December 1982): 287–300.
7. Emily Yoffe, "You Are What You Buy," *Newsweek* (June 4, 1990): 59.
8. Roy F. Baumeister, Dianne M. Tice, and Debra G. Hutton, "Self-Presentational Motivations and Personality Differences in Self-Esteem," *Journal of Personality* 57 (September 1989): 547–75; Ronald J. Faber, "Are Self-Esteem Appeals Appealing?" in Leonard N. Reid, ed., *Proceedings of the 1992 Conference of the American Academy of Advertising* (1992), 230–35.
9. B. Bradford Brown and Mary Jane Lohr, "Peer-Group Affiliation and Adolescent Self-Esteem: An Integration of Ego-Identity and Symbolic-Interaction Theories," *Journal of Personality and Social Psychology* 52, no. 1 (1987): 47–55.
10. Marsha L. Richins, "Social Comparison and the Idealized Images of Advertising," *Journal of Consumer Research* 18 (June 1991): 71–83; Mary C. Martin and Patricia F. Kennedy, "Advertising and Social Comparison: Consequences for Female Preadolescents and Adolescents," *Psychology & Marketing* 10 (November–December 1993): 513–30.
11. Philip N. Myers Jr. and Frank A. Biocca, "The Elastic Body Image: The Effect of Television Advertising and Programming on Body Image Distortions in Young Women," *Journal of Communication* 42 (Summer 1992): 108–33.
12. Charles S. Gulas and Kim McKeage, "Extending Social Comparison: An Examination of the Unintended Consequences of Idealized Advertising Imagery," *Journal of Advertising* 29 (Summer 2000): 17–28.
13. J. C. Herz, "Flash Face-Lift," *Wired* (March 2002): 45.
14. Sigmund Freud, *New Introductory Lectures in Psychoanalysis* (New York: Norton, 1965).
15. Harrison G. Gough, Mario Fioravanti, and Renato Lazzari, "Some Implications of Self versus Ideal-Self Congruence on the Revised Adjective Check List," *Journal of Personality and Social Psychology* 44, no. 6 (1983): 1214–20.
16. Steven Jay Lynn and Judith W. Rhue, "Daydream Believers," *Psychology Today* (September 1985): 14.
17. Erving Goffman, *The Presentation of Self in Everyday Life* (Garden City, NY: Doubleday, 1959); Michael R. Solomon, "The Role of Products as Social Stimuli: A Symbolic Interactionism Perspective," *Journal of Consumer Research* 10 (December 1983): 319–29.
18. George H. Mead, *Mind, Self and Society* (Chicago: University of Chicago Press, 1934).
19. Debra A. Laverie, Robert E. Kleine, and Susan Schultz Kleine, "Reexamination and Extension of Kleine, Kleine, and Kernan's Social Identity Model of Mundane Consumption: The Mediating Role of the Appraisal Process," *Journal of Consumer Research* 28 (March 2002): 659–69.
20. Charles H. Cooley, *Human Nature and the Social Order* (New York: Scribner's, 1902).
21. J. G. Hull and A. S. Levy, "The Organizational Functions of the Self: An Alternative to the Duval and Wicklund Model of Self-Awareness," *Journal of Personality and Social Psychology* 37 (1979): 756–68; Jay G. Hull, Ronald R. Van Treuren, Susan J. Ashford, Pamela Propsom, and Bruce W. Andrus, "Self-Consciousness and the Processing of Self-Relevant Information," *Journal of Personality and Social Psychology* 54, no. 3 (1988): 452–65.
22. Arnold W. Buss, *Self-Consciousness and Social Anxiety* (San Francisco: Freeman, 1980); Lynn Carol Miller and Cathryn Leigh Cox, "Public Self-Consciousness and Makeup Use," *Personality and Social Psychology Bulletin* 8, no. 4 (1982): 748–51; Michael R. Solomon and John Schopler, "Self-Consciousness and Clothing," *Personality and Social Psychology Bulletin* 8, no. 3 (1982): 508–14.
23. Morris B. Holbrook, Michael R. Solomon, and Stephen Bell, "A Re-Examination of Self-Monitoring and Judgments of Furniture Designs," *Home Economics Research Journal* 19 (September 1990): 6–16; Mark Snyder, "Self-Monitoring Processes," in Leonard Berkowitz, ed., *Advances in Experimental Social Psychology* (New York: Academic Press, 1979): 85–128.
24. Mark Snyder and Steve Gangestad, "On the Nature of Self-Monitoring: Matters of Assessment, Matters of Validity," *Journal of Personality and Social Psychology* 51 (1986): 125–39.
25. Timothy R. Graeff, "Image Congruence Effects on Product Evaluations: The Role of Self-Monitoring and Public/Private Consumption," *Psychology & Marketing* 13 (August 1996): 481–99.
26. Richard G. Netemeyer, Scot Burton, and Donald R. Lichtenstein, "Trait Aspects of Vanity: Measurement and Relevance to Consumer Behavior," *Journal of Consumer Research* 21 (March 1995): 612–26.
27. "Video Game Company Tries Human Branding," *New York Times on the Web* (August 12, 2002).
28. Michael R. Solomon and Henry Assael, "The Forest or the Trees? A Gestalt Approach to Symbolic Consumption," in Jean Umiker-Sebeok, ed., *Marketing and Semiotics: New Directions in the Study of Signs for Sale* (Berlin: Mouton de Gruyter, 1987), 189–218.
29. Jack L. Nasar, "Symbolic Meanings of House Styles," *Environment and Behavior* 21 (May 1989): 235–57; E. K. Sadalla, B. Verschure, and J. Burroughs, "Identity Symbolism in Housing," *Environment and Behavior* 19 (1987): 579–87.
30. Solomon, "The Role of Products as Social Stimuli, 319–28; Robert E. Kleine III, Susan Schultz-Kleine, and Jerome B. Kernan, "Mundane Consumption and the Self: A Social-Identity Perspective," *Journal of Consumer Psychology* 2, no. 3 (1993): 209–35; Newell D. Wright, C. B. Claiborne, and M. Joseph Sirgy, "The Effects of Product Symbolism on Consumer Self-Concept," in John F. Sherry Jr. and Brian Sternthal, eds., *Advances in Consumer Research* 19 (Provo, UT: Association for Consumer Research, 1992): 311–18; Susan Fournier, "A Person-Based Relationship Framework for Strategic Brand Management" (doctoral dissertation, University of Florida, 1994).
31. A. Dwayne Ball and Lori H. Tasaki, "The Role and Measurement of Attachment in Consumer Behavior," *Journal of Consumer Psychology* 1, no. 2 (1992): 155–72.
32. William B. Hansen and Irwin Altman, "Decorating Personal Places: A Descriptive Analysis," *Environment and Behavior* 8 (December 1976): 491–504.
33. Jennifer Lee, "Identity Theft Complaints Double in '02," *New York Times on the Web* (January 23, 2003); Susan J. Wells, "When It's Nobody's Business but Your Own," *New York Times on the Web* (February 13, 2000); Deborah Lohse, "Travelers Offers Insurance to Borrowers to Cover Expenses of Stolen Identities," *Wall Street Journal Interactive Edition* (September 29, 1999).
34. R. A. Wicklund and P. M. Gollwitzer, *Symbolic Self-Completion* (Hillsdale, NJ: Erlbaum, 1982).
35. Erving Goffman, *Asylums* (New York: Doubleday, 1961).
36. Floyd Rudmin, "Property Crime Victimization Impact on Self, on Attachment, and on Territorial Dominance," *CPA Highlights, Victims of Crime Supplement* 9, no. 2 (1987): 4–7.
37. Barbara B. Brown, "House and Block as Territory" (paper presented at the Conference of the Association for Consumer Research, San Francisco, 1982).
38. Shay Sayre and David Horne, "I Shop, Therefore I Am: The Role of Possessions for Self Definition," in Shay Sayre and David Horne, eds., *Earth, Wind, and Fire and Water: Perspectives on Natural Disaster* (Pasadena CA: Open Door Publishers, 1996), 353–70.
39. Deborah A. Prentice, "Psychological Correspondence of Possessions, Attitudes, and Values," *Journal of Personality and Social Psychology* 53, no. 6 (1987): 993–1002.
40. Jennifer L. Aaker, "The Malleable Self: The Role of Self-Expression in Persuasion," *Journal of Marketing Research* 36 (February 1999): 45–57; Sak Onkvisit and John Shaw, "Self-Concept and Image Congruence: Some Research and Managerial Implications," *Journal of Consumer Marketing* 4 (Winter 1987): 13–24. For a related treatment of congruence between advertising appeals and self-concept, see George M. Zinkhan and Jae W. Hong, "Self-Concept and Advertising Effectiveness: A Conceptual Model of Congruency, Conspicuousness, and Response Mode," in Rebecca H. Holman and Michael R. Solomon, eds., *Advances in Consumer Research* 18 (Provo, UT: Association for Consumer Research, 1991): 348–54.

41. C. B. Claiborne and M. Joseph Sirgy, "Self-Image Congruence as a Model of Consumer Attitude Formation and Behavior: A Conceptual Review and Guide for Further Research" (paper presented at the Academy of Marketing Science Conference, New Orleans, 1990).

42. Jennifer L. Aaker, "The Malleable Self: The Role of Self-Expression in Persuasion," *Journal of Marketing Research* 36 (February 1999): 45–57.

43. A. L. E. Birdwell, "A Study of Influence of Image Congruence on Consumer Choice," *Journal of Business* 41 (January 1964): 76–88; Edward L. Grubb and Gregg Hupp, "Perception of Self, Generalized Stereotypes, and Brand Selection," *Journal of Marketing Research* 5 (February 1986): 58–63.

44. Ira J. Dolich, "Congruence Relationship Between Self-Image and Product Brands," *Journal of Marketing Research* 6 (February 1969): 80–84; Danny N. Bellenger, Earle Steinberg, and Wilbur W. Stanton, "The Congruence of Store Image and Self Image as It Relates to Store Loyalty," *Journal of Retailing* 52, no. 1 (1976): 17–32; Ronald J. Dornoff and Ronald L. Tatham, "Congruence Between Personal Image and Store Image," *Journal of the Market Research Society* 14, no. 1 (1972): 45–52.

45. Naresh K. Malhotra, "A Scale to Measure Self-Concepts, Person Concepts, and Product Concepts," *Journal of Marketing Research* 18 (November 1981): 456–64.

46. Leslie Walker, "More Than the Sum of His Stuff," *Washington Post* (August 11, 2001): E1.

47. Ernest Beaglehole, *Property: A Study in Social Psychology* (New York: Macmillan, 1932).

48. Jeffrey Ball, "Religious Leaders to Discuss SUVs with GM, Ford Officials," *Wall Street Journal Interactive Edition* (September 17, 2002).

49. David R. Shoonmaker, "Book Review: High and Mighty: SUVs—The World's Most Dangerous Vehicles and How They Got That Way," *American Scientist* (January–February 2003): 69; Keith Bradsher, *High and Mighty: SUVs—The World's Most Dangerous Vehicles and How They Got That Way* (New York: Public Affairs, 2002).

50. James Brooke, "Learning to Avoid a Deal-Killing Faux Pas in Japan," *New York Times on the Web* (September 17, 2002).

51. M. Csikszentmihalyi and Eugene Rochberg-Halton, *The Meaning of Things: Domestic Symbols and the Self* (Cambridge, UK: Cambridge University Press, 1981).

52. Russell W. Belk, "Possessions and the Extended Self," *Journal of Consumer Research* 15 (September 1988): 139–68.

53. Diane Goldner, "What Men and Women Really Want . . . to Eat," *New York Times* (March 2, 1994): C1 (2).

54. Thomas Tsu Wee Tan, Lee Boon Ling, and Eleanor Phua Cheay Theng, "Gender-role Portrayals in Malaysian and Singaporean Television Commercials: An International Advertising Perspective," *Journal of Business Research* 55 (2002): 853–61.

55. Joan Meyers-Levy, "The Influence of Sex Roles on Judgment," *Journal of Consumer Research* 14 (March 1988): 522–30.

56. Anne Eisenberg, "Mars and Venus, on the Net: Gender Stereotypes Prevail," *New York Times Online* (October 12, 2000).

57. Michael Wentzel, "NFL Logos Make Eye Contact with Fans," *Montgomery Advertiser* (September 15, 2002): 1G.

58. Vanessa O'Connell, "Bud Light's Online Campaign Could Attract Underage Users," *Wall Street Journal Interactive Edition* (September 16, 2002).

59. "Branding of Uterus Defended," *Montgomery Advertiser* (January 29, 2003): 4A.

60. Fisher Adam, "The First Time Ever I Shot Your Face," *Wired* (February 2001): 76.

61. Beverly A. Browne, "Gender Stereotypes in Advertising on Children's Television in the 1990s: A Cross-National Analysis," *Journal of Advertising* 27 (Spring 1998): 83–97.

62. Lisa Bannon, "Mattel Sees Untapped Market for Blocks: Little Girls," *Wall Street Journal* (June 6, 2002): B1.

63. Hassan Fattah and Pamela Paul, "Gaming Gets Serious," *American Demographics* (May 2002): 39–43; Emily Laber, "Men Are from Quake, Women Are from Ultima," *New York Times on the Web* (January 11, 2001).

64. Eileen Fischer and Stephen J. Arnold, "Sex, Gender Identity, Gender Role Attitudes, and Consumer Behavior," *Psychology & Marketing* 11 (March–April 1994): 163–82.

65. Clifford Nass, Youngme Moon, and Nancy Green, "Are Machines Gender Neutral? Gender-Stereotypic Responses to Computers with Voices," *Journal of Applied Social Psychology* 27, no. 10 (1997): 864–76; Kathleen Debevec and Easwar Iyer, "Sex Roles and Consumer Perceptions of Promotions, Products, and Self: What Do We Know and Where Should We Be Headed," in Richard J. Lutz, ed., *Advances in Consumer Research* 13 (Provo, UT: Association for Consumer Research, 1986): 210–14; Joseph A. Bellizzi and Laura Milner, "Gender

66. Positioning of a Traditionally Male-Dominant Product," *Journal of Advertising Research* (June–July 1991): 72–79.

66. Hillary Chura, "Barton's New High-End Vodka Exudes a 'Macho Personality'," *Advertising Age* (May 1, 2000): 8.

67. Sandra L. Bem, "The Measurement of Psychological Androgyny," *Journal of Consulting and Clinical Psychology* 42 (1974): 155–62; Deborah E. S. Frable, "Sex Typing and Gender Ideology: Two Facets of the Individual's Gender Psychology That Go Together," *Journal of Personality and Social Psychology* 56, no. 1 (1989): 95–108.

68. See D. Bruce Carter and Gary D. Levy, "Cognitive Aspects of Early Sex-Role Development: The Influence of Gender Schemas on Preschoolers' Memories and Preferences for Sex-Typed Toys and Activities," *Child Development* 59 (1988): 782–92; Bernd H. Schmitt, France Le Clerc, and Laurette Dube-Rioux, "Sex Typing and Consumer Behavior: A Test of Gender Schema Theory," *Journal of Consumer Research* 15 (June 1988): 122–27.

69. Carol Gilligan, *In a Different Voice: Psychological Theory and Women's Development* (Cambridge, MA: Harvard University Press, 1982); Joan Meyers-Levy and Durairaj Maheswaran, "Exploring Differences in Males' and Females' Processing Strategies," *Journal of Consumer Research* 18 (June 1991): 63–70.

70. Lynn J. Jaffe and Paul D. Berger, "Impact on Purchase Intent of Sex-Role Identity and Product Positioning," *Psychology & Marketing* (Fall 1988): 259–71; Lynn J. Jaffe, "The Unique Predictive Ability of Sex-Role Identity in Explaining Women's Response to Advertising," *Psychology & Marketing* 11 (September–October 1994): 467–82.

71. Leila T. Worth, Jeanne Smith, and Diane M. Mackie, "Gender Schematicity and Preference for Gender-Typed Products," *Psychology & Marketing* 9 (January 1992): 17–30.

72. Rebecca Gardyn, "Granddaughters of Feminism," *American Demographics* (April 2001): 43–47.

73. Sherri Day, "As It Remakes Itself, Mattel Does Same for Barbie," *New York Times on the Web* (November 9, 2002).

74. Deborah Roffman, "A Sign Culture's Gone too Far: Lingerie Barbie," *Washington Post* (December 26, 2002): A40.

75. Lisa Bannon, "Fashion Coup? Bratz Grabs Some of Barbie's Limelight," *Wall Street Journal Interactive Edition* (November 29, 2002).

76. Ibid.

77. Cris Prystay, "Marketers to Chinese Women Offer 'More Room to Be Vain'," *Wall Street Journal Interactive Edition* (May 29, 2002).

78. Cris Prystay and Montira Narkvichien, "*Sex and the City* Singles Out Asian Women for Marketers," *Wall Street Journal Interactive Edition* (August 8, 2002).

79. Craig S. Smith, "Underneath, Saudi Women Keep Their Secrets," *New York Times on the Web* (December 3, 2002).

80. Wayne Arnold, "For the Singapore Girl, It's Her Time to Shine," *New York Times* (December 31, 1999): C4.

81. Barbara B. Stern, "Masculinism(s) and the Male Image: What Does It Mean to Be a Man?" in Tom Reichert and Jacqueline Lambiase, eds., *Advertising: Multi-disciplinary Perspectives on the Erotic Appeal* (Mahwah, NJ: Lawrence Erlbaum Associates 2002).

82. Anthony Vagnoni, "Brut Ad Reeks of Bad-Boy Attitude," *Advertising Age* (October 18, 1999): 24–25.

83. Jack Neff, "Marketers Rush into Men's Care Category," *Advertising Age* (July 29, 2002): 6.

84. Peroxide Tales," *American Demographics* (July–August 2002): 9.

85. Jim Carlton, "Hair-Dye Makers, Sensing a Shift, Step up Campaigns Aimed at Men," *Wall Street Journal Interactive Edition* (January 17, 2000).

86. Projections of the incidence of homosexuality in the general population often are influenced by assumptions of the researchers, as well as the methodology they employ (e.g., self-report, behavioral measures, fantasy measures). For a discussion of these factors, see Edward O. Laumann, John H. Gagnon, Robert T. Michael, and Stuart Michaels, *The Social Organization of Homosexuality* (Chicago: University of Chicago Press, 1994).

87. Lee Condon, "By the Numbers (Census 2000)," *The Advocate: The National Gay and Lesbian Newsmagazine* (September 25, 2001): 37.

88. R. Gardyn, "A Market Kept in the Closet," *American Demographics* (November 2001): 37–43.

89. Kate Fitzgerald, "IKEA Dares to Reveal Gays Buy Tables, Too," *Advertising Age* (March 28, 1994); Cyndee Miller, "Top Marketers Take Bolder Approach in Targeting Gays," *Marketing News* (July 4, 1994): 1; Michael Wilke, "Big Advertisers Join Move to Embrace Gay Market," *Advertising Age* (August 4, 1997): 1.

90. R. Gardyn, "A Market Kept in the Closet," 37–43; see also Lisa Peñaloza, "We're Here, We're Queer, and We're Going Shopping! A Critical Perspective on the Accommodation of Gays and Lesbians in the U.S. Marketplace," *Journal of Homosexuality* 31 (Summer 1996): 9–41.

91. Joseph Pereira, "These Particular Buyers of Dolls Don't Say, 'Don't Ask, Don't Tell'," *Wall Street Journal* (August 30, 1993): B1.

92. Bob Tedeschi, "Gays Draw Attention of Retailers," *New York Times on the Web* (August 26, 2002).

93. Bill Carter, "MTV and Showtime Plan Cable Channel for Gay Viewers," *New York Times on the Web* (January 10, 2002).

94. George Gene Gustines, "A Comic Book Gets Serious on Gay Issues," *New York Times on the Web* (August 13, 2002).

95. Ronald Alsop, "Lesbians Are Often Left Out When Firms Market to Gays," *Wall Street Journal Interactive Edition* (October 11, 1999).

96. Dennis W. Rook, "Body Cathexis and Market Segmentation," in Michael R. Solomon, ed., *The Psychology of Fashion* (Lexington, MA: Lexington Books, 1985), 233–41.

97. Carrie Goerne, "Marketing to the Disabled: New Workplace Law Stirs Interest in Largely Untapped Market," *Marketing News* 3 (September 14, 1992): 1; "Retailers Find a Market, and Models, in Disabled," *New York Times* (August 6, 1992): D4.

98. Geoffrey Cowley, "The Biology of Beauty," *Newsweek* (June 3, 1996): 61–66.

99. Corky Siemaszko, "Depends on the Day: Women's Sex Drive a Very Cyclical Thing," *New York Daily News* (June 24, 1999): 3.

100. Amanda B. Bower, "Highly Attractive Models in Advertising and the Women Who Loathe Them: The Implications of Negative Affect for Spokesperson Effectiveness," *Journal of Advertising* 30 (Fall 2001): 51–63.

101. Basil G. Englis, Michael R. Solomon, and Richard D. Ashmore, "Beauty Before the Eyes of Beholders: The Cultural Encoding of Beauty Types in Magazine Advertising and Music Television," *Journal of Advertising* 23 (June 1994): 49–64; Michael R. Solomon, Richard Ashmore, and Laura Longo, "The Beauty Match-Up Hypothesis: Congruence Between Types of Beauty and Product Images in Advertising," *Journal of Advertising* 21 (December 1992): 23–34.

102. Cris Prystay, "Critics Say Ads for Skin Whiteners Capitalize on Malaysian Prejudice," *Wall Street Journal Interactive Edition* (April 29, 2002).

103. Lewis Gregory, "Cosmetic Cover-Up: Growing Number of Minority Women Seek Plastic Surgery," *Montgomery Advertiser* (January 14, 2002): 1D.

104. Seth Mydans, "Oh Blue-Eyed Thais, Flaunt Your Western Genes!" *New York Times on the Web* (August 29, 2002).

105. Norimitsu Onishi, "Globalization of Beauty Makes Slimness Trendy," *New York Times on the Web* (October 3, 2002).

106. Ellen Knickermeyer, "Full-Figured Females Favored," *Opelika-Auburn News* (August 7, 2001).

107. Michael Schuman, "Some Korean Women Are Taking Great Strides to Show a Little Leg," *Wall Street Journal Interactive Edition* (February 21, 2001).

108. Lois W. Banner, *American Beauty* (Chicago: University of Chicago Press, 1980); for a philosophical perspective, see Barry Vacker and Wayne R. Key, "Beauty and the Beholder: The Pursuit of Beauty Through Commodities," *Psychology & Marketing* 10 (November–December 1993): 471–94.

109. Abraham Tesser and Terry Pettijohn II, reported in "And the Winner Is . . . Wall Street," *Psychology Today* (March–April 1998): 12.

110. "Report Delivers Skinny on Miss America," *Montgomery Advertiser* (March 22, 2000): 5A.

111. "Study: Playboy Models Losing Hourglass Figures," (December 20, 2002), CNN.com.

112. Jill Neimark, "The Beefcaking of America," *Psychology Today* (November–December 1994): 32.

113. Richard H. Kolbe and Paul J. Albanese, "Man to Man: A Content Analysis of Sole-Male Images in Male-Audience Magazines," *Journal of Advertising* 25 (Winter 1996): 1–20.

114. David Goetzl, "Teen Girls Pan Ad Images of Women," *Advertising Age* (September 13, 1999): 32; Carey Goldberg, "Citing Intolerance, Obese People Take Steps to Press Cause," *New York Times on the Web* (November 5, 2000).

115. "Fat-Phobia in the Fijis: TV-Thin Is In," *Newsweek* (May 31, 1999): 70.

116. Amy Dockser Marcus, "With an Etiquette of Overeating, It's Not Easy Being Lean in Egypt," *Wall Street Journal Interactive Edition* (March 4, 1998).

117. Elaine L. Pedersen and Nancy L. Markee, "Fashion Dolls: Communicators of Ideals of Beauty and Fashion" (paper presented at the International Conference on Marketing Meaning, Indianapolis, IN, 1989); Dalma Heyn, "Body Hate," *Ms.* (August 1989): 34; Mary C. Martin and James W. Gentry, "Assessing the Internalization of Physical Attractiveness Norms," *Proceedings of the American Marketing Association Summer Educators' Conference* (Summer 1994): 59–65.

118. Lisa Bannon, "Barbie Is Getting Body Work, and Mattel Says She'll Be 'Rad'," *Wall Street Journal Interactive Edition* (November 17, 1997).

119. Lisa Bannon, "Will New Clothes, Bellybutton Create 'Turn Around' Barbie," *Wall Street Journal Interactive Edition* (February 17, 2000).

120. www.emmesupermodel.com/, accessed December 17, 2002; www.tonnerdoll.com/emme.htm, accessed December 17, 2002; Jennifer Barrett, "Must Have, Plus Size," *Newsweek* (August 26, 2002): 60.

121. Kane Courtney, "Advertising: A Male Sex Symbol Enjoys the Company of Larger Women," *New York Times on the Web* (February 1, 2001).

122. Yumiko Ono, "For Once, Fashion Marketers Look to Sell to Heavy Teens," *Wall Street Journal Interactive Edition* (July 31, 1998).

123. www.cbsnews.com/stories/2002/01/31/health/main326811.shtml, accessed December 17, 2002.

124. Fruit Cups," *Details* (August 1999): 37.

125. Debra A. Zellner, Debra F. Harner, and Robbie I. Adler, "Effects of Eating Abnormalities and Gender on Perceptions of Desirable Body Shape," *Journal of Abnormal Psychology* 98 (February 1989): 93–96.

126. Robin T. Peterson, "Bulimia and Anorexia in an Advertising Context," *Journal of Business Ethics* 6 (1987): 495–504.

127. Jane E. Brody, "Personal Health," *New York Times* (February 22, 1990): B9.

128. Christian S. Crandall, "Social Contagion of Binge Eating," *Journal of Personality and Social Psychology* 55 (1988): 588–98.

129. Judy Folkenberg, "Bulimia: Not for Women Only," *Psychology Today* (March 1984): 10.

130. Stephen S. Hall, "The Bully in the Mirror," *New York Times Magazine*, (downloaded August 22, 1999); Natalie Angier, "Drugs, Sports, Body Image and G.I. Joe," *New York Times* (December 22, 1998): D1.

131. John W. Schouten, "Selves in Transition: Symbolic Consumption in Personal Rites of Passage and Identity Reconstruction," *Journal of Consumer Research* 17 (March 1991): 412–25.

132. Jane E. Brody, "Notions of Beauty Transcend Culture, New Study Suggests," *New York Times* (March 21, 1994): A14; Norihiko Shirouzu, "Reconstruction Boom in Tokyo: Perfecting Imperfect Belly-buttons," *Wall Street Journal* (October 4, 1995): B1.

133. Nancy Hass, "Nip, Tuck, Click: Plastic Surgery on the Web Is Hip," *New York Times on the Web* (September 19, 1999); Celeste McGovern, "Brave New World," *Newsmagazine* (Alberta edition) 26 (February 7, 2000): 50–52.

134. Stephen S. Hall, "The Bully in the Mirror," Emily Yoffe, "Valley of the Silicon Dolls," *Newsweek* (November 26, 1990): 72.

135. Jerry Adler, "New Bodies for Sale," *Newsweek* (May 27, 1985): 64.

136. Ruth P. Rubinstein, "Color, Circumcision, Tatoos, and Scars," in Michael R. Solomon, ed., *The Psychology of Fashion* (Lexington, MA: Lexington Books, 1985), 243–54; Peter H. Bloch and Marsha L. Richins, "You Look 'Mahvelous': The Pursuit of Beauty and Marketing Concept," *Psychology & Marketing* 9 (January 1992): 3–16. For a visual overview of these processes, visit amnh.org/exhibitions/bodyart/ to view an exhibit mounted by the American Museum of Natural History.

137. Deanna Bellandi, "U.S. Suffers 'Portion Distortion'," *Montgomery Advertiser* (January 22, 2003): 3A.

138. Sondra Farganis, "Lip Service: The Evolution of Pouting, Pursing, and Painting Lips Red," *Health* (November 1988): 48–51.

139. Michael Gross, "Those Lips, Those Eyebrows; New Face of 1989 (New Look of Fashion Models)," *New York Times Magazine* (February 13, 1989): 24.

140. High Heels: Ecstasy's Worth the Agony," *New York Post* (December 31, 1981).

141. Elizabeth Hayt, "Over-40 Rebels with a Cause: Tattoos," *New York Times* (December 22, 2002): sec. 9: 2.

142. www.pathfinder.com:80/altculture/aentries/p/piercing.html, accessed August 22, 1997.

Personality and Lifestyles

j

ackie and Hank, executives in a high-powered Los Angeles advertising agency, are exchanging ideas about how they are going to spend the big bonus everyone in the firm has been promised for landing the Gauntlet body jewelry account. They can't help but snicker at their friend Debbie in accounting, who has been avidly surfing the Internet for information about a state-of-the-art home theater system she plans to put into her condo. What a couch potato! Hank, who fancies himself a bit of a thrill seeker, plans to blow his bonus on a wild trip to Colorado, where a week of outrageous bungee jumping awaits him (assuming he lives to tell about it, but that uncertainty is half the fun). Jackie replies, "Been there, done that. . . . Believe it or not, I'm staying put right here—heading over to Santa Monica to catch some waves." Seems that the surfing bug has bitten her since she started leafing through Wahine, a magazine targeted to the growing number of women taking up the sport.

Jackie and Hank are sometimes amazed at how different they are from Debbie, who's content to spend her downtime watching sappy old movies or reading books. All three make about the same salary, and Jackie and Debbie even went to college together. How can their tastes be so different? Oh well, they figure, that's why they make chocolate and vanilla.

■ PERSONALITY

Jackie and Hank are typical of many people who search for new (and even risky) ways to spend their leisure time. This desire has meant big business for the "adventure travel" industry, which specializes in providing white-knuckle experiences. Sports such as bungee jumping, white-water rafting, sky diving, mountain biking, and other physically stimulating activities now account for about one-fifth of the U.S. leisure travel market.[1] In the old days, the California beach culture relegated women to the status of land-locked "Gidgets" who sat on shore while their boyfriends rode the big one. Now (spurred by the female surfers featured in the movie *Blue Crush*), it's women who are fueling the sport's resurgence in popularity. Quiksilver, the largest maker of surf apparel, is reaping huge profits with its female surfing gear, which includes a line of board shorts called Roxy. Quiksilver also teamed up with Nextel Communications to market a cell phone targeted at teenage girls that flips open to a pink screen emblazoned with the Roxy logo.[2]

Just what does make Jackie and Hank so different from their more sedate friend Debbie? One answer may lie in the concept of **personality**, which refers to a person's unique psychological makeup and how it consistently influences the way a person responds to her environment.

Do people have personalities (certainly we can wonder about some we meet!)? Actually, some psychologists argue that the concept of personality may not be valid. Many studies have found that people do not seem to exhibit stable personalities. Since people don't necessarily behave the same way in all situations, they argue that this is merely a convenient way to categorize people.

Intuitively, this argument is a bit hard to accept because we tend to see others in a limited range of situations, and so they *do* appear to act consistently. On the other hand, we each know that we are not all *that* consistent; we may be wild and crazy at times and serious and responsible at others. Although certainly not all psychologists have abandoned the idea of personality, many now recognize that a person's underlying characteristics are but one part of the puzzle, and situational factors often play a very large role in determining behavior.[3] Still, some aspects of personality continue to be included in marketing strategies. These dimensions are usually employed in conjunction with a person's choices of leisure activities, political outlook, aesthetic tastes, and other individual factors to segment consumers in terms of lifestyles, a process we'll focus on more fully later in this chapter.

Consumer Behavior on the Couch: Freudian Theory

Sigmund Freud developed the idea that much of one's adult personality stems from a fundamental conflict between a person's desire to gratify his or her physical needs and the necessity to function as a responsible member of society. This struggle is carried out in the mind among three systems. (Note: These systems do *not* refer to physical parts of the brain.)

Freudian Systems

The **id** is entirely oriented toward immediate gratification—it is the "party animal" of the mind. It operates according to the **pleasure principle**; behavior is guided by the primary desire to maximize pleasure and avoid pain. The id is selfish and illogical. It directs a person's psychic energy toward pleasurable acts without regard for any consequences.

The **superego** is the counterweight to the id. This system is essentially the person's conscience. It internalizes society's rules (especially as communicated by parents) and works to prevent the id from seeking selfish gratification.

Finally, the **ego** is the system that mediates between the id and the superego. It is in a way a referee in the fight between temptation and virtue. The ego tries to balance these opposing forces according to the **reality principle**, whereby it finds ways to gratify the id that will be acceptable to the outside world. These conflicts occur on an unconscious level, so the person is not necessarily aware of the underlying reasons for his behavior.

Consumer researchers have adapted some of Freud's ideas. In particular, his work highlights the potential importance of unconscious motives underlying purchases. The implication is that consumers cannot necessarily tell us their true motivation for choosing a product, even if we can devise a sensitive way to ask them directly. The Freudian perspective also hints at the possibility that the ego relies on the symbolism in products to compromise between the demands of the id and the prohibitions of the superego. The person channels his or her unacceptable desire into acceptable outlets by using products that signify these underlying desires. This is the connection between product symbolism and motivation: The product stands for, or represents, a consumer's true goal, which is socially unacceptable or unattainable. By acquiring the product, the person is able to vicariously experience the forbidden fruit.

This ad focuses on the conflict between the desire for hedonic gratification (represented by the id) versus the need to engage in rational, task-oriented activities (represented by the superego).

Sometimes a Cigar Is Just a Cigar

Most Freudian applications in marketing are related to the sexuality of products. For example, some analysts have speculated that a sports car is a substitute for sexual gratification for many men. Indeed, some men do seem inordinately attached to their cars and may spend many hours lovingly washing and polishing them. An Infiniti ad reinforces the belief that cars symbolically satisfy consumers' sexual needs in addition to their functional ones by describing one model as "what happens when you cross sheet metal and desire."

Others focus on male-oriented symbolism—so-called *phallic symbols*—that appeals to women. Although Freud himself joked that "sometimes a cigar is just a cigar," many popular applications of Freud's ideas revolve around the use of objects that resemble sex organs (e.g., cigars, trees, or swords for male sex organs; tunnels for female sex organs). This focus stems from Freud's analysis of dreams, which he interpreted as communicating repressed desires through symbols.

Motivational Research

In the 1950s, a perspective called **motivational research** attempted to use Freudian ideas to understand the deeper meanings of products and advertisements. This approach was largely based on psychoanalytic (Freudian) interpretations, with a heavy emphasis on unconscious motives. A basic assumption is that socially unacceptable needs are channeled into acceptable outlets.

This form of research relies on *depth interviews* with individual consumers. Instead of asking many consumers a few general questions about product usage and combining these responses with those of many other consumers in a representative statistical sample, this technique uses relatively few consumers but probes deeply into each person's purchase motivations. An in-depth interview might take several hours, and it's based on the assumption that the respondent cannot immediately articulate his or her *latent*, or underlying motives. These can be derived only after extensive questioning and interpretation on the part of a carefully trained interviewer.

Ernest Dichter, a psychoanalyst who was trained in Vienna in the early part of the century, pioneered this work. Dichter conducted in-depth interview studies on more than 230 different products, and many of his findings were incorporated into actual marketing campaigns.[4] For example, Esso (now Exxon) for many years reminded consumers to "Put a Tiger in Your Tank" after Dichter found that people responded well to this powerful animal symbolism containing vaguely sexual undertones. A summary of major consumption motivations identified by using this approach appears in Table 6.1.

Motivational research has been attacked for two opposing reasons. Some feel it does not work, whereas others feel it works *too* well. On the one hand, social critics reacted much the same way they had to subliminal perception studies (see Chapter 2). They attacked this school of thought for giving advertisers the power to manipulate consumers.[5] On the other hand, many consumer researchers felt the research lacked sufficient rigor and validity, as interpretations were subjective and indirect.[6] Because conclusions are based on the analyst's own judgment and are derived from discussions with a small number of people, some researchers are dubious as to the degree to which these results can be generalized to a large market. In addition, because the original motivational researchers were heavily influenced by orthodox Freudian theory, their interpretations usually involved sexual themes. This emphasis tends to overlook other plausible causes for behavior.

Still, motivational research had great appeal to at least some marketers for several reasons, including these:

● Motivational research tends to be less expensive than large-scale, quantitative survey data because interviewing and data-processing costs are relatively minimal.
● The knowledge derived from motivational research can possibly help develop marketing communications that appeal to deep-seated needs and thus provide

TABLE 6.1
MAJOR MOTIVES FOR CONSUMPTION AS IDENTIFIED BY ERNEST DICHTER

Motive	Associated Products
Power-masculinity-virility	Power: Sugary products and large breakfasts (to charge oneself up), bowling, electric trains, hot rods, power tools Masculinity-virility: Coffee, red meat, heavy shoes, toy guns, buying fur coats for women, shaving with a razor
Security	Ice cream (to feel like a loved child again), full drawer of neatly ironed shirts, real plaster walls (to feel sheltered), home baking, hospital care
Eroticism	Sweets (to lick), gloves (to be removed by woman as a form of undressing), a man lighting a woman's cigarette (to create a tension-filled moment culminating in pressure, then relaxation)
Moral purity-cleanliness	White bread, cotton fabrics (to connote chastity), harsh household cleaning chemicals (to make housewives feel moral after using), bathing (to be equated with Pontius Pilate, who washed blood from his hands), oatmeal (sacrifice, virtue)
Social acceptance	Companionship: Ice cream (to share fun), coffee
	Love and affection: Toys (to express love for children), sugar and honey (to express terms of affection)
	Acceptance: Soap, beauty products
Individuality	Gourmet foods, foreign cars, cigarette holders, vodka, perfume, fountain pens
Status	Scotch; ulcers, heart attacks, indigestion (to show one has a high-stress, important job!); carpets (to show one does not live on bare earth like peasants)
Femininity	Cakes and cookies, dolls, silk, tea, household curios
Reward	Cigarettes, candy, alcohol, ice cream, cookies
Mastery over environment	Kitchen appliances, boats, sporting goods, cigarette lighters
Disalienation (a desire to feel connectedness to things)	Home decorating, skiing, morning radio broadcasts (to feel "in touch" with the world)
Magic-mystery	Soups (having healing powers), paints (change the mood of a room), carbonated drinks (magical effervescent property), vodka (romantic history), unwrapping of gifts

Source: Adapted from Jeffrey F. Durgee, "Interpreting Dichter's Interpretations: An Analysis of Consumption Symbolism," in *The Handbook of Consumer Motivation, Marketing and Semiotics: Selected Papers from the Copenhagen Symposium,* ed. Hanne Hartvig-Larsen, David Glen Mick, and Christian Alstead (Copenhagen, 1991).

a more powerful hook to reel in consumers. Even if not necessarily valid for all consumers in a target market, these insights can be valuable when used in an exploratory way. For example, the rich imagery that may be associated with a product can be used creatively when developing advertising copy.
• Some of the findings seem intuitively plausible after the fact. For example, motivational studies concluded that coffee is associated with companionship, that people avoid prunes because they remind them of old age, and that men fondly equate the first car they owned as an adolescent with the onset of their sexual freedom.

Other interpretations were hard for some researchers to swallow, such as the observation that to a woman baking a cake symbolizes giving birth, or that men are reluctant to give blood because they feel that their vital fluids are being drained. On the other hand, a pregnant woman *is* sometimes described as "having a bun in the oven," and Pillsbury claims, "nothing says lovin' like something from the oven." Motivational research for the American Red Cross did find that men (but not women) tend to drastically overestimate the amount of blood that is taken during a donation. The Red Cross counteracted the fear of loss of virility by symbolically equating the act of giving blood with fertilization: "Give the gift of life." Despite its drawbacks, motivational research continues to be employed as a useful diagnostic tool. Its validity is enhanced, however, when used in conjunction with the other research techniques available to the consumer researcher.

Neo-Freudian Theories

Freud's work had a huge influence on subsequent theories of personality. Although Freud opened the door to the realization that explanations for behavior may lurk beneath the surface, many of his colleagues and students felt that an individual's personality was more influenced by how he or she handled relationships with others than by unresolved sexual conflicts. These theorists are often called *neo-Freudian* (meaning following from or being influenced by Freud).

Karen Horney

One of the most prominent neo-Freudians was a psychoanalyst named Karen Horney. She described people as moving toward others (*compliant*), away from others (*detached*), or against others (*aggressive*).[7] Indeed, one early study found that compliant people are more likely to gravitate toward name-brand products, detached types are more likely to be tea drinkers, and males classified as aggressive prefer brands with a strong masculine orientation (e.g., Old Spice deodorant).[8]

Other well-known neo-Freudians include Alfred Adler, who proposed that many actions are motivated by people's desire to overcome feelings of inferiority relative to others; and Harry Stack Sullivan, who focused on how personality evolves to reduce anxiety in social relationships.[9]

Carl Jung

Carl Jung was also a disciple of Freud (and was being groomed by Freud to be his successor). However, Jung was unable to accept Freud's emphasis on sexual aspects of personality, and this was a contributing factor in the eventual dissolution of their relationship. Jung went on to develop his own method of psychotherapy, which became known as *analytical psychology.*

Jung believed that people are shaped by the cumulative experiences of past generations. A central part of his perspective was an emphasis on what he called the collective unconscious, a storehouse of memories inherited from our ancestral past. For example, Jung would argue that many people are afraid of the dark because their distant ancestors had good reason to exhibit this fear. These shared memories create **archetypes**, or universally shared ideas and behavior patterns. Archetypes involve themes, such as birth, death, or the devil, that appear frequently in myths, stories, and dreams.

Jung's ideas may seem a bit far-fetched, but (at least intuitively) advertising messages often invoke archetypes to link products with underlying meanings. For example, some of the archetypes identified by Jung and his followers include the "old wise man" and the "earth mother."[10] These images appear frequently in marketing messages that use characters such as wizards, revered teachers, or even Mother Nature to convince people of the merits of products. Our culture's current infatuation with stories like *Harry Potter* and *The Lord of the Rings* speaks to the power of these images.

Trait Theory

One approach to personality is to focus on the quantitative measurement of **personality traits**, or identifiable characteristics that define a person. For example, people can be distinguished by the degree to which they are socially outgoing (the trait of *extroversion*)—Debbie might be described as an *introvert* (quiet and reserved), whereas her co-worker Jackie is an *extrovert.*

Some specific traits that are relevant to consumer behavior include: *innovativeness* (the degree to which a person likes to try new things); *materialism* (amount of emphasis placed on acquiring and owning products); *self-consciousness* (the degree to which a person deliberately monitors and controls the image of the self that is projected to others), and *need for cognition* (the degree to which a person likes to think about things and by extension expands the necessary effort to process brand information).[11] Another trait relevant to consumer behavior is *frugality*. Frugal people deny short-term purchasing whims, choosing instead to resourcefully use what they already own. For example, people who have been classified as frugal tend to do things like timing their showers and bringing leftovers from home to have for lunch at work.[12]

Are You an Innie or an Outie?

Perhaps the trait dimension most relevant to consumer behavior is the extent to which a person is motivated to consume in order to please others or to fit in versus consuming to express a unique sense of self without much concern about being accepted by a group. A sociologist named David Reisman first introduced the terms *inner-directed* and *outer-directed* to our culture.[13] This general idea has resurfaced in a variety of ways. As we'll see in Chapter 16, some cultures tend to stress individualism while others reward those who try to fit in. We'll talk more about the power of conformity (the impact of shaping one's behavior to meet the expectations of a group) in Chapter 11. Each of us is a conformist by definition to some extent because as members of society we follow certain rules. As a simple example, we each (with the exception of some New York City drivers!) "agree" to stop at a corner when the light turns red. Still, some of us are more concerned about the reactions of others to what we do, while some seem to "march to their own tune." One personality trait we can measure is the *need for uniqueness* (the degree to which a person is motivated to conform to the preferences of others versus standing apart from the crowd).[14]

Some recent research examines consumption differences between individuals who are classified as **idiocentrics** (having an individualist orientation) and those classified as **allocentrics** (having a group orientation). Some differences between these two personality types include:

- *Contentment:* Idiocentrics scored higher than allocentrics on the statement "I am very satisfied with the way things are going in my life these days." They also are more satisfied with their financial situations.
- *Health Consciousness:* Allocentrics are more likely to avoid foods that are high in cholesterol, have a high salt content, have additives in them, or have a high amount of fat.

Net Profit

As the saying goes, "Birds of a feather flock together." We tend to like people who are like us. New research reveals that the same folk wisdom may apply to our computers. People respond to the personality cues in computer-generated speech just as they would to flesh-and-blood individuals. People in a study who were classified as either extroverts or introverts listened to an identical book review read by a computer with a synthesized voice designed to sound either like an extrovert or an introvert (quieter, slower). Subjects were more likely to buy the book if the computer's voice matched their own personality.[15]

THE GLOBAL LOOKING GLASS

The author Thomas Friedman defines healthy glocalization as "... the ability of a culture, when it encounters other strong cultures, to absorb influences that naturally fit into and can enrich the culture, to resist those things that are truly alien, and to compartmentalize those things that, while different, can nevertheless be enjoyed and celebrated as different." Glocalization, then, seems to be the art of attaining a fine balance of assimilating foreign influences into a society that add to its diversity without overwhelming it.

Robinson Department Stores in Bangkok, Thailand have "glocalized" their store's fashion departments by offering "Life Code"—a computer analysis that helps consumers determine what type of clothing fashion is best for them. The Life Code system aims to build loyalty between Robinson, and its target audience of 25 to 45 year olds, by asking a set of survey like questions that correlate personality and individual preferences with dressing style. The in-store use of the computer analysis appeals to the Thai urban consumer's sense of modernity. Buddhist beliefs are also taken into account, as the Life Code will interpret fashion preferences from four basic elements: earth, water, air, and fire. A person with an earth element is believed to prefer clothes with basic and timeless design, while those born with the water element prefer bright and lively colors, and a sweet, youthful look.

Sources: Quoted in Thomas L. Friedman, *The Lexus and the Olive Tree* (New York: Farrar, Straus and Giroux, 1999) p. 236; Jarunee Taemsamran and Charoen Kittikanya, "Unlocking the 'Life Code' " *Bangkok Post*, December 31, 2002, p. 6; Annama Joy and Melanie Wallendorf, "The Development of Consumer Culture in the Third World," *Consumption and Macromarketing*, eds. R. W. Belk, N. Dholakia and A. Venkatesh (Cincinnati: Southwestern College Publishing; 1996), 104–142.

- *Food Preparation:* The kitchen is the favorite room of allocentrics, who spend more time preparing meals than do idiocentrics.
- *Workaholics:* Idiocentrics are more likely to say they work very hard most of the time, and they stay late at work more than do allocentrics.
- *Travel and Entertainment:* Idiocentrics are more interested in other cultures and traveling than are allocentrics. They also are more likely to go to movies, art galleries, and museums. Compared to idiocentrics, allocentrics visited the public library and finished reading books with a greater frequency. Allocentrics reported working on crafts projects such as needlework and model building. On the other hand, idiocentric individuals were more likely to collect stamps, rocks, work on do-it-yourself projects, and take photos. They also were more likely to play the lottery.[16]

Problems with Trait Theory in Consumer Research

Because large numbers of consumers can be categorized according to whether they exhibit various traits, these approaches potentially can be used to segment markets. If a car manufacturer, for example, could determine that drivers who fit a given trait profile are more likely to prefer a car with certain features, this match could be used to great advantage. The notion that consumers buy products that are extensions of their personalities makes intuitive sense. As we'll see shortly, many marketing managers endorse this idea as they try to create *brand personalities* that will appeal to different types of consumers.

Unfortunately, the use of standard personality trait measurements to predict product choices has met with mixed success at best. In general, marketing researchers simply have not been able to predict consumers' behaviors on the basis of measured personality traits. A number of explanations have been offered for these equivocal results.[17]

- Many of the scales are not sufficiently valid or reliable; they do not adequately measure what they are supposed to measure, and their results may not be stable over time.
- Personality tests are often developed for specific populations (e.g., mentally ill people); these tests are then "borrowed" and applied to the general population where their relevance is questionable.
- Often the tests are not administered under the appropriate conditions; people who are not properly trained may give them in a classroom or at a kitchen table.
- The researchers often make changes in the instruments to adapt them to their own situations, in the process deleting or adding items and renaming variables. These *ad hoc* changes dilute the validity of the measures and also reduce researchers' ability to compare results across consumer samples.
- Many trait scales are intended to measure gross, overall tendencies (e.g., emotional stability or introversion); these results are then used to make predictions about purchases of specific brands.
- In many cases, a number of scales are given with no advance thought about how these measures should be related to consumer behavior. The researchers then use a "shotgun approach," following up on anything that happens to look interesting.

Although the use of personality measures by marketing researchers was largely abandoned after many studies failed to yield meaningful results, some researchers have not given up on the early promise of this line of work. More recent efforts (mainly in Europe) have tried to benefit from past mistakes. Researchers are using more specific measures of personality traits that they have reason to believe are relevant to economic behavior. They are trying to increase the validity of these measures, primarily by using multiple measures of behavior rather than relying on the common practice of trying to predict purchasing responses from a single item on a personality test.

In addition, these researchers have toned down their expectations of what personality traits can tell them about consumers. They now recognize that traits are only part of the solution, and that personality data must be incorporated with information about people's social and economic conditions in order to be useful.[18] As a result, some more recent research has had better success at relating personality traits to such consumer behaviors as alcohol consumption among young men or shoppers' willingness to try new, healthier food products.[19]

Brand Personality

In 1886, a momentous event occurred in marketing history—the Quaker Oats man first appeared on boxes of hot cereal. Quakers had a reputation in nineteenth-century America for being shrewd but fair, and peddlers sometimes dressed as members of this religious group for this reason. When the cereal company decided to "borrow" this imagery for its packaging, this signaled the recognition that purchasers might make the same associations with its product.[20] A **brand personality** is the set of traits people attribute to a product as if it were a person.

These inferences are an important part of **brand equity**, which refers to the extent to which a consumer holds strong, favorable, and unique associations with a brand in memory.[21] Building strong brands is good business—if you don't believe it consider that in a study of 760 *Fortune* 1000 companies, after the stock market took a nosedive in October of 1997, the 20 strongest corporate brands (e.g., Microsoft, GE) actually gained in market value whereas the 20 weakest lost an average of $1 billion each.[22] Name recognition has become so valuable that some companies are completely outsourcing production to focus on nurturing the brand. Nike doesn't own any sneaker factories, and Sara Lee sold off many of its bakeries, meat-processing plants, and textile mills to become a "virtual" corporation. Its CEO commented, "Slaughtering hogs and running knitting machines are businesses of yesterday."[23]

So, how do people think about brands? Advertisers are keenly interested in this question, and several of them conduct extensive consumer research to help them understand how consumers connect to a brand before they roll out campaigns. DDB Worldwide does a global study called "Brand Capital" of 14,000 consumers for this purpose; Leo Burnett's "Brand Stock" project involves 28,000 interviews. WPP Group has "BrandZ" and Young & Rubicam uses its "Brand Asset Valuator." DDB's worldwide brand planning director observes, "We're not marketing just to isolated individuals. We're marketing to society. How I feel about a brand is directly related and affected by how others feel about that brand." The logic behind this bonding approach is that if a consumer feels a strong connection with a brand, he or she is less likely to succumb to peer pressure and switch brands.[24]

Some personality dimensions that can be used to compare and contrast the perceived characteristics of brands in various product categories include:[25]

- Old-fashioned, wholesome, traditional
- Surprising, lively, with it
- Serious, intelligent, efficient
- Glamorous, romantic, sexy
- Rugged, outdoorsy, tough, athletic

The following memo was written to help an advertising agency figure out how a client should be portrayed in advertising. Based on this description of the "client," can you guess who he is? "He is creative . . . unpredictable . . . an imp. . . . He not only walks and talks, but has the ability to sing, blush, wink, and work with little devices like pointers. . . . He can also play musical instruments. . . . His walking motion is characterized as a 'swagger.' . . . He is made of dough and has mass."[26] Of course, we all know today that packaging and other physical cues create a "personality" for a product (in this case, the Pillsbury Doughboy). The marketing activities

TABLE 6.2
BRAND BEHAVIORS AND POSSIBLE PERSONALITY TRAIT INFERENCES

Brand Action	Trait Inference
Brand is repositioned several times or changes its slogan repeatedly	Flighty, schizophrenic
Brand uses continuing character in its advertising	Familiar, comfortable
Brand charges a high price and uses exclusive distribution	Snobbish, sophisticated
Brand frequently available on deal	Cheap, uncultured
Brand offers many line extensions	Versatile, adaptable
Brand sponsors show on PBS or uses recycled materials	Helpful, supportive
Brand features easy-to-use packaging or speaks at consumer's level in advertising	Warm, approachable
Brand offers seasonal clearance sale	Planful, practical
Brand offers five-year warranty or free customer hot line	Reliable, dependable

Source: Adapted from Susan Fournier, "A Consumer-Brand Relationship Framework for Strategic Brand Management," unpublished doctoral dissertation. University of Florida, 1994, Table 2.2, p. 24.

undertaken on behalf of the product also can influence inferences about its "personality," and Table 6.2 shows some of these actions.

Indeed, consumers appear to have little trouble assigning personality qualities to all sorts of inanimate products, from personal care products to more mundane, functional ones—even kitchen appliances. Whirlpool's research showed that people saw its products as more feminine than competing brands. When respondents were asked to imagine the appliance as a person, many of them pictured a modern, family-oriented woman living in the suburbs—attractive but not flashy. In contrast, they envisioned the company's Kitchen Aid brand as a modern professional woman who was glamorous, wealthy, and who enjoyed classical music and the theater.[27]

The creation and communication of a distinctive brand personality is one of the primary ways marketers can make a product stand out from the competition and inspire years of loyalty. This process can be understood in terms of **animism**, the practice found in many cultures whereby inanimate objects are given qualities that make them somehow alive. Animism is in some cases a part of a religion: Sacred objects, animals, or places are believed to have magical qualities or to contain the spirits of ancestors. In our society, objects may be "worshiped" in the sense that they are believed to impart desirable qualities to the owner or they may in a sense become so important to a person that they can be viewed as a "friend."

Two types of animism can be identified to describe the extent to which human qualities are attributed to the product:[28]

- *Level 1:* People believe the object is possessed by the soul of a being—as is sometimes the case for spokespersons in advertising. This strategy allows the consumer to feel that the spirit of the celebrity is available through the brand. In other cases, a brand may be strongly associated with a loved one, alive or deceased ("My grandmother always served Knott's Berry Farm jam.").
- *Level 2:* Objects are anthropomorphized, or given human characteristics. A cartoon character or mythical creation may be treated as if it were a person, and even assumed to have human feelings. Think about familiar spokescharacters such as Charlie the Tuna, the Keebler Elves, or the Michelin Man, or even the frustration some people feel when they come to believe their computer is smarter than they are or may even be "conspiring" to make them crazy! In

research for its client Sprint Business Services, Grey Advertising found that when customers were asked to imagine long-distance carriers as animals, they envisioned AT&T as a lion, MCI as a snake, and Sprint as a puma. Grey used these results to position Sprint as a company that could "help you do more business" rather than taking the more aggressive approach of its competitors.[29]

As we saw in Chapter 2, a brand's positioning strategy is a statement about what that brand wants to be in the eyes of its customers—especially relative to the competition. Marketers are used to thinking in these terms (even if they haven't read this book) and they routinely describe their brands and the competition as if they were people. For example, here's how the marketing director for Philips Electronics in Asia sums up the problem he faces in updating his brand so that it's seen as hip and young by Chinese consumers: "To put it bluntly, we are received well by middle-aged gentlemen. . . . But a brand like Sony is seen as younger, more arrogant, with a space-age personality."[30]

In a sense, then, a brand personality is a statement about how the brand is positioned. Understanding this is crucial to marketing strategy, especially if consumers don't see the brand the way its makers intend them to and an attempt must be made to *reposition* the product (i.e., give it a personality makeover). That's the problem now being faced by Volvo, whose cars are renowned for safety but are not exactly seen as exciting or sexy. A safe and solid brand personality makes it hard to sell a racy convertible like the C70 model, so a British ad tries to change that perception with the tagline "Lust, envy, jealousy. The dangers of a Volvo."

Just as with people, however, you can only go so far to convince others that your personality has changed. Volvo has been trying to jazz up its image for years, but for the most part consumers aren't buying it. In an earlier attempt in the United

The Zaltman Metaphor Elicitation Technique (ZMET) is one tool used to assess the strategic aspects of brand personality and is based on the premise that brands are expressed in terms of metaphors; that is, a representation of one thing in terms of another. These associations often are nonverbal, so the ZMET approach is based on a nonverbal representation of brands. Participants collect a minimum of twelve images representing their thoughts and feelings about a topic, and are interviewed in depth about the images and their feelings. Eventually, digital imaging techniques are used to create a collage summarizing these thoughts and feelings, and the person tells a story about the image created. This collage was created by a young woman to express her feelings about Tide detergent. It includes such images as a sunrise to represent freshness and a teddy bear that stands for the soft and comfortable way her laundry feels when she's done. However, the facial expressions also give a clue about her 'fondness' for doing laundry!

Kingdom, the company paired action images like a Volvo pulling a helicopter off a cliff with the headline, "Safe Sex"—but market research showed people didn't believe the new image. As one brand consultant observed, "You get the sort of feeling you get when you see your grandparents trying to dance the latest dance. Slightly amused and embarrassed."[31]

■ LIFESTYLES AND PSYCHOGRAPHICS

Jackie, Hank, and Debbie strongly resemble one another demographically. They all were raised in middle-class households, have similar educational backgrounds, are about the same age, and work for the same company. However, as their leisure choices show, it would be a big mistake to assume that their consumption choices are similar as well. Each person chooses products, services, and activities that help define a unique *lifestyle*. This section first explores how marketers approach the issue of lifestyle and then how they use information about these consumption choices to tailor products and communications to individual lifestyle segments.

Lifestyle: Who We Are, What We Do

In traditional societies, class, caste, village, or family largely dictate a person's consumption options. In a modern consumer society, however, people are freer to select the set of products, services, and activities that define themselves and, in turn, create a social identity that is communicated to others. One's choice of goods and services indeed makes a statement about who one is and about the types of people with which one desires to identify—and even those whom we wish to avoid.

Lifestyle refers to a pattern of consumption reflecting a person's choices of how he or she spends time and money. In an economic sense, one's lifestyle represents the way one has elected to allocate income, both in terms of relative allocations to different products and services, and to specific alternatives within these categories.[32] Other somewhat similar distinctions describe consumers in terms of their broad patterns of consumption, such as those differentiating consumers in terms of those who devote a high proportion of total expenditures to food, advanced technology, or to such information-intensive goods as entertainment and education.[33]

A lifestyle marketing perspective recognizes that people sort themselves into groups on the basis of the things they like to do, how they like to spend their leisure time, and how they choose to spend their disposable income.[34] These choices are reflected, for example, in the growing number of niche magazines that cater to specialized interests. In one recent year, *WWF Magazine* (World Wrestling Federation) gained 913,000 readers and *4 Wheel & Off Road* gained 749,000, while mainstream *Reader's Digest* lost more than 3 million readers and *People* lost more than 2 million.[35] These finely tuned choices in turn create opportunities for market segmentation strategies that recognize the potency of a consumer's chosen lifestyle in determining both the types of products purchased and the specific brands most likely to appeal to a designated lifestyle segment.

Lifestyles As Group Identities

Economic approaches are useful to track changes in broad societal priorities, but they do not begin to embrace the symbolic nuances that separate lifestyle groups. Lifestyle is more than the allocation of discretionary income. It is a statement about who one is in society and who one is *not*. Group identities, whether of hobbyists, athletes, or drug users, gel around forms of expressive symbolism. The self-definitions of group members are derived from the common symbol system to which the group is dedicated. Such self-definitions have been described by a number of terms, including lifestyle, taste public, consumer group, symbolic community, and status culture.[36]

Many people in similar social and economic circumstances may follow the same general consumption pattern. Still, each person also provides a unique "twist" to the pattern that allows him or her to inject some individuality into a lifestyle. For example, a "typical" college student (if there is such a thing) may dress much like his friends, hang out in the same places, and like the same foods, yet still indulge a passion for marathon running, stamp collecting, or community activism that makes him unique.

And, lifestyles are not set in stone. Unlike the deep-seated values we discussed in Chapter 4, people's tastes and preferences evolve over time. In fact, consumption patterns that were viewed favorably during one life phase may be laughed at (or sneered at) a few years later. If you don't believe that, simply think back to what you and your friends were wearing five or ten years ago—where *did* you find those clothes? Because people's attitudes regarding physical fitness, social activism, sex roles for men and women, the importance of home life and family, and so on do change, it is vital for marketers to continually monitor the social landscape to try to anticipate where these changes will lead. The responses to the Lifestyle Study conducted by the DDB Worldwide advertising agency in Figure 6.1 illustrate how consumer behaviors and attitudes can change over time.

The Tangled Web

The Web's power to unite thousands or even millions of people who share attitudes or consumption preferences is a mixed blessing. Many groups spreading a gospel of hate use the Internet to reach fellow believers and to recruit new ones. These include neo-Nazi groups, skinheads, and black separatist organizations. As the man who founded the White Aryan Resistance group boasted, "[Now that we are online] our reach is much, much farther." And, because many relatively affluent, educated people frequent the Web, the targets of these messages are changing as hate groups now can reach those who used to be out of reach. As noted by a spokesman for the Southern Poverty Law Center, a human rights organization that tracks hate groups, "The movement is interested not so much in developing street thugs who beat up people in bars, but college-bound teens who live in middle-class and upper-class homes." Racism is just a click away on the Tangled Web.[37]

Escape in a 200-horsepower Camry Solera. But do it soon.
Unused vacation days cannot be carried over into your next lifetime.

TOYOTA
live a little.
every day

This ad illustrates the way that products like cars are tightly integrated into consumers' lifestyles, along with leisure activities, travel, music, and so on.

■ **FIGURE 6.1** RESPONSES TO SELECTED ITEMS IN THE DDB NEEDHAM LIFESTYLE STUDY FROM 1990–1999

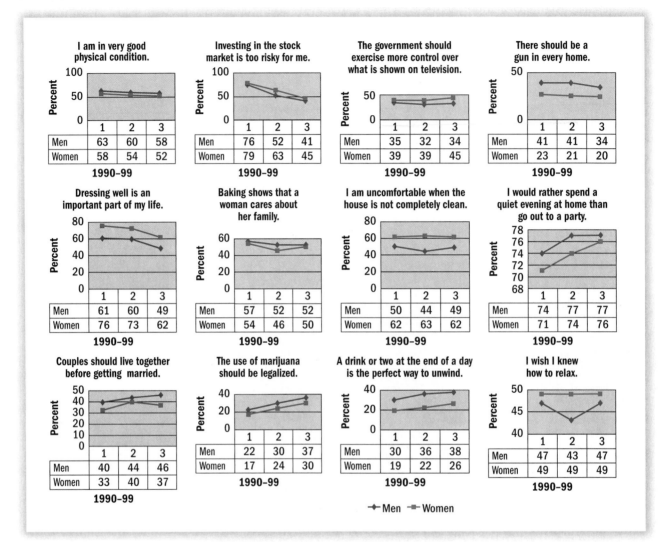

Products Are the Building Blocks of Lifestyles

We often choose a product precisely because it's associated with a certain lifestyle. For this reason, lifestyle-marketing strategies attempt to position a product by fitting it into an existing pattern of consumption. That explains why hip restaurants, bars, and hotels like the Standard Hotel in Los Angeles, the Sunset Beach hotel/restaurant in New York's Hamptons, and the Buddha Bar and Man Ray in Paris are branching out by selling CDs featuring the music playing on site. Aspiring lounge lizards can re-create the "insider" experience without leaving home.[38]

Because a goal of lifestyle marketing is to allow consumers to pursue their chosen ways to enjoy their lives and express their social identities, a key aspect of this strategy is to focus on product usage in desirable social settings. The goal of associating a product with a social situation is a long-standing one for advertisers, whether the product is included in a round of golf, a family barbecue, or a night at a glamorous club surrounded by the hip-hop elite.[39] Thus people, products, and settings are combined to express a certain consumption style, as diagrammed in Figure 6.2.

The adoption of a lifestyle marketing perspective implies that we must look at *patterns of behavior* to understand consumers. We can get a clearer picture of how people use products to define lifestyles by examining how they make choices in a

The White Aryan Resistance is one of many hate groups with an active presence on the World Wide Web.

variety of product categories. As one study noted, "All goods carry meaning, but none by itself. . . . The meaning is in the relations between all the goods, just as music is in the relations marked out by the sounds and not in any one note."[40]

Indeed, many products and services do seem to "go together," usually because they tend to be selected by the same types of people. In many cases, products do not

The recreational-vehicle ad shown here demonstrates how a market segment is defined by a particular allocation of time and money to a leisure activity. The ad's claim that the RV dealer has the product that 'says you're you!' implies that dedicated RVers derive a significant portion of their self-identities from the activities associated with this lifestyle.

■ **FIGURE 6.2**
LINKING PRODUCTS TO LIFESTYLES

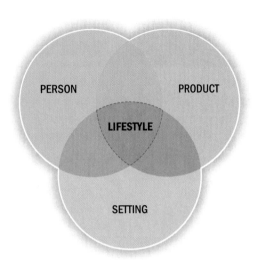

Interior designers rely on consumption constellations when choosing items to furnish a room. A decorating style involves integrating products from many different categories—such as appliances, furnishings, knick-knacks, and even artwork—into a unified whole that conveys a certain 'look.'

seem to "make sense" if they are unaccompanied by companion products (e.g., fast food and paper plates, or a suit and tie) or are incongruous in the presence of others (e.g., a Chippendale chair in a high-tech office or Lucky Strike cigarettes with a solid gold lighter). Therefore, an important part of lifestyle marketing is to identify the set of products and services that seems to be linked in consumers' minds to a specific lifestyle. And, research evidence suggests that even a relatively unattractive product becomes more appealing when evaluated with other, liked products.[41] Marketers who pursue **co-branding strategies** like these recent deals understand this:

Monogram, by GE. It solves the riddle of how to integrate the appliances into custom kitchen design.

No matter what design theme you choose, the one thing you don't have to worry about nowadays is how the appliances will look.

The Monogram line of built-in appliances now offers such an array of models that you have virtually infinite choice and options.

This year we add the first 36" built-in refrigerator that is trimless and completely cabinet friendly. The decorative door panels accept custom handles, so they co-ordinate with the pulls on your cabinets. Because there is no bottom air vent, the base of the cabinet can now extend across the bottom of the refrigerator. No other built-in refrigerator integrates so beautifully.

Monogram now offers a built-in convection wall oven that provides new technology for faster cooking and sleek flush design.

Our Component Cooktops continue to be the only ones that can be installed perpendicular or horizontal to the counter edge to form clusters in gas, electric, updraft and downdraft. And there's also a 5-burner gas cooktop.

The remarkable idea of getting everything from your dishwasher to your microwave from *one* manufacturer also simplifies the complex process of shopping and delivery. And when you buy Monogram, you buy the assurance of the appliance industry's most extensive network of factory service professionals.

Going one step further is the extraordinary GE Answer Center™ service on duty 24 hours a day *every* day of the year at 800.626.2000. We're there to help in any way. If you would like a brochure that tells you more about Monogram, and if you would like to know where you can see the line, please call.

Monogram, from GE. A synonym for the best in built-in appliances.

Monogram.™

- The German car maker Porsche is teaming up with Canada's Fairmont Hotels & Resorts chain to appeal to one another's customers. Fairmont's best-known properties are its regal hotel on San Francisco's Nob Hill and New York's Plaza Hotel, but the chain wants to spread its cachet to other, lesser-known properties. In turn, Porsche figures Fairmont's upscale clientele is the perfect market for its recently upgraded Boxster convertible and new Cayenne sport-utility vehicle.[42]
- Unilever will be handing out samples of its new Dove Body Refreshers body care product to women as they enter Bally Total Fitness gyms.[43]
- Nike and Polaroid formed a partnership to promote the I-Zone, targeted to teens. Now, buyers of the portable camera can also pick up shoes with a clear pocket that will let them display their photos as they walk.[44]
- Remember Roxy surfwear from the beginning of the chapter? They've also teamed up with Toyota to create a surf-friendly version of the Echo sedan for the young female market. It features water-resistant, neoprene-covered seats, a Yakima roof rack, and wet-gear storage bins. If this surfmobile succeeds, Toyota hopes to develop a similar male-oriented vehicle (most likely a sport wagon or pickup) linked to the Quiksilver name.[45]

Product complementarity occurs when the symbolic meanings of different products are related to each other.[46] Consumers use these sets of products, termed **consumption constellations**, to define, communicate, and perform social roles.[47] For example, the American "yuppie" of the 1980s was defined by such products as a Rolex watch, a BMW automobile, a Gucci briefcase, a squash racket, fresh pesto, white wine, and brie cheese. Somewhat similar constellations could be found for "Sloane Rangers" in the United Kingdom and "Bon Chic Bon Genres" in France. Although people today take pains to avoid being classified as yuppies, this social

Net Profit

Choosing your own lifestyle is complicated enough. Now, the Web lets you "play God" by creating your own family online. By joining The Sims™, you can design and furnish a house and put people in it who look and act as you choose. Starting at the game's Web site, ***thesims.com***, you can make up an endless variety of characters, insult your neighbors, fall in love, whatever turns you on. Your "skins" can follow a wide range of career paths (lounge singer, golf caddy, talk show host, maybe even a marketing professor?), and you can "buy" tons of goodies for your virtual family, including hot tubs and giant-screen TVs (and program in nasty stuff like roach infestations to keep Sim life interesting). What's more, you can exchange your simulated world with other players using The Sims Teleportation Device. And, in late 2002 The Sims Online was launched online as a massively multiplayer game where a flesh-and-blood player controls every Sim. So what are you waiting for? Get a life.[48]

Create your own consumers by playing the Sims.

role had a major influence on defining cultural values and consumption priorities in the 1980s.[49] What consumption constellation might characterize you and your friends today?

Psychographics

In 1998, Cadillac introduced its sport utility vehicle called the Escalade. Critics scoffed at the bizarre pairing of this old-line luxury brand with a truck, but the vehicle quickly became associated with the hip-hop lifestyle. Artists like Jennifer Lopez, Outkast, and Jay-Z referred to it in songs, and Jermaine Dupri proclaimed "gotta have me an Escalade." Three years later, Cadillac went even farther when it rolled out its 18-foot Escalade EXT pickup with a sticker price of $50,000.

The brand manager describes the target customer for luxury pickups as a slightly earthier version of the SUV buyer. She says that while the two drivers may own $2 million homes next door to each other, the typical luxury SUV driver is about 50, has an MBA from Harvard, belongs to a golf club, maintains connections with his college friends, and works hard at keeping up with the Joneses. In contrast, the luxury pickup driver is roughly five years younger. He might have inherited his father's construction business, and he's been working since he was 18 years old. He may or may not have attended college, and unlike the SUV driver he is absolutely still connected to his high school friends.[50]

As this example shows, marketers often find it useful to develop products that appeal to different lifestyle groups—just knowing a person's income doesn't predict whether he will drive a Cadillac Escalade SUV, pickup, or a Cadillac El Dorado sedan. As Jackie's, Hank's, and Debbie's choices demonstrated, consumers can share the same demographic characteristics and still be very different people. For this reason, marketers need a way to "breathe life" into demographic data to really identify, understand, and target consumer segments that will share a set of preferences for their products and services. Earlier this chapter discussed some of the differences in consumers' personalities that play a role in determining product choices. When personality variables are combined with knowledge of lifestyle preferences, marketers have a powerful lens with which to focus on consumer segments.

This tool is known as **psychographics**, which involves the "use of psychological, sociological, and anthropological factors . . . to determine how the market is segmented by the propensity of groups within the market—and their reasons—to make a particular decision about a product, person, ideology, or otherwise hold an attitude or use a medium."[51] Psychographics can help a marketer fine-tune its offerings to meet the needs of different segments. For example, the Discovery Channel surveyed those who watch at least one-half hour of its programming a week. It found that, in fact, there were eight distinct groups of watchers with different motivations and preferences—psychographic segments that were given descriptive names such as Entertain-Mes, Practicals, Scholars, and Escapists. Based on these results, Discovery was able to tailor its programming to different segments and increase its market share in the competitive cable television industry.[52]

The Roots of Psychographics

Psychographic research was first developed in the 1960s and 1970s to address the shortcomings of two other types of consumer research: *motivational research* and *quantitative survey research*. Motivational research, which involves intensive, one-to-one interviews and projective tests, yields a lot of information about a few people. As we've seen though, this information is often idiosyncratic and may not be very reliable. At the other extreme, quantitative survey research, or large-scale demographic surveys, yields only a little information about a lot of people. As some researchers observed, "The marketing manager who wanted to know why people ate the competitor's cornflakes was told '32 percent of the respondents said taste, 21 percent said flavor, 15 percent said texture, 10 percent said price, and

22 percent said don't know or no answer.'"[54] There's not a lot you can do with that kind of feedback.

We can use many psychographic variables to segment consumers, but they all share the underlying principle of going beyond surface characteristics to understand consumers' motivations for purchasing and using products. Demographics allow us to describe *who* buys, but psychographics tells us *why* they do. A classic example was a very popular Canadian advertising campaign for Molson Export beer that included commercials based on psychographic findings. Research showed that Molson's target customers tended to be like boys who never grew up, who were uncertain about the future, and who were intimidated by women's new-found freedoms. Accordingly, the ads featured a group of men, "Fred and the boys," whose get-togethers emphasize male companionship, protection against change, and the message that the beer "keeps on tasting great."[55]

Doing a Psychographic Analysis

Some early attempts at lifestyle segmentation "borrowed" standard psychological scales (often used to measure pathology or personality disturbances) and tried to relate scores on these tests to product usage. As we saw earlier in the chapter, such efforts were largely disappointing. These tests were never intended to be related to everyday consumption activities, so they didn't do much to explain people's purchases. The technique is more effective when the variables included are more closely related to actual consumer behaviors. If you want to understand purchases of household cleaning products, you are better off asking people about their attitudes toward household cleanliness than testing for personality disorders!

Psychographic studies can take several different forms:

- A *lifestyle profile* looks for items that differentiate between users and nonusers of a product.
- A *product-specific profile* identifies a target group and then profiles these consumers on product-relevant dimensions.
- A *general lifestyle segmentation* places a large sample of respondents into homogenous groups based on similarities of their overall preferences.
- A *product-specific segmentation* tailors questions to a product category. For example, in a study done specifically for a stomach medicine, the item "I worry too much" might be rephrased as "I get stomach problems if I worry too much." This allows the researcher to more finely discriminate between users of competing brands.[56]

AIOs

Most contemporary psychographic research attempts to group consumers according to some combination of three categories of variables—activities, interests, and opinions—known as **AIOs**. Using data from large samples, marketers create profiles of customers who resemble each other in terms of their activities and patterns of product usage.[57] Table 6.3 lists commonly used AIO dimensions.

To group consumers into AIO categories, respondents are given a long list of statements and are asked to indicate how much they agree with each one. Lifestyle is thus "boiled down" by discovering how people spend their time, what they find interesting and important, and how they view themselves and the world around them. By the way, the single most common use of leisure time among Americans overall is—you guessed it—watching television![58]

Typically, the first step in conducting a psychographic analysis is to determine which lifestyle segments are producing the bulk of customers for a particular product. According to a very general rule of thumb frequently used in marketing research, called the **80/20 rule**, only 20 percent of a product's users account for 80 percent of the volume of product sold. Researchers attempt to determine who

TABLE 6.3
LIFESTYLE DIMENSIONS

Activities	Interests	Opinions	Demographics
Work	Family	Themselves	Age
Hobbies	Home	Social issues	Education
Social events	Job	Politics	Income
Vacation	Community	Business	Occupation
Entertainment	Recreation	Economics	Family size
Club membership	Fashion	Education	Dwelling
Community	Food	Products	Geography
Shopping	Media	Future	City size
Sports	Achievements	Culture	Stage in life cycle

Source: William D. Wells and Douglas J. Tigert, "Activities, Interests, and Opinions." *Journal of Advertising Research* 11 (August 1971): 27–35. © 1971 by The Advertising Research Foundation.

uses the brand and try to isolate heavy, moderate, and light users. They also look for patterns of usage and attitudes toward the product. In many cases, just a few lifestyle segments account for the majority of brand users.[59] Marketers primarily target these heavy users, even though they may constitute a relatively small number of total users.

After the heavy users are identified and understood, we consider the brand's relationship to them. Heavy users may have quite different reasons for using the product; they can be further subdivided in terms of the *benefits* they derive from using the product or service. For instance, marketers at the beginning of the walking shoe craze assumed that purchasers were basically burned-out joggers. Subsequent psychographic research showed that there were actually several different groups of "walkers," ranging from those who walk to get to work to those who walk for fun. This realization resulted in shoes aimed at different segments, from Footjoy Joy-Walkers to Nike Healthwalkers.

Uses of Psychographic Segmentation

Psychographic segmentation can be used in a variety of ways:

- *To define the target market:* This information allows the marketer to go beyond simple demographic or product usage descriptions (e.g., middle-aged men or frequent users).
- *To create a new view of the market:* Sometimes marketers create their strategies with a "typical" customer in mind. This stereotype may not be correct because the actual customer may not match these assumptions. For example, marketers of a face cream for women were surprised to find their key market was composed of older, widowed women rather than the younger, sociable women to whom they were pitching their appeals.
- *To position the product:* Psychographic information can allow the marketer to emphasize features of the product that fit in with a person's lifestyle. Products targeted to people whose lifestyle profiles show a high need to be around other people might focus on the product's ability to help meet this social need.
- *To better communicate product attributes:* Psychographic information can offer very useful input to advertising creatives who must communicate something

about the product. The artist or writer obtains a much richer mental image of the target consumer than that obtained through dry statistics, and this insight improves his or her ability to "talk" to that consumer. For example, research conducted for Schlitz beer found that heavy beer drinkers tended to feel that life's pleasures were few and far between. Commercials were developed using the theme that told these drinkers, "You only go around once, so reach for all the gusto you can."[60]

- *To develop overall strategy:* Understanding how a product fits, or does not fit, into consumers' lifestyles allows the marketer to identify new product opportunities, chart media strategies, and create environments most consistent and harmonious with these consumption patterns.
- *To market social and political issues:* Psychographic segmentation can be an important tool in political campaigns and can also be employed to find commonalities among types of consumers who engage in destructive behaviors, such as drug use or excessive gambling. A psychographic study of men aged 18 to 24 who drink and drive highlights the potential for this perspective to help in the eradication of harmful behaviors. Researchers divided this segment into four groups: "good timers," "well adjusted," "nerds," and "problem kids." They found that one group in particular—"good timers"—is more likely to believe that it is fun to be drunk, that the chances of having an accident while driving drunk are low, and that drinking increases one's appeal to the opposite sex. Because the study showed that this group is also the most likely to drink at rock concerts and parties, is most likely to watch MTV, and tends to listen to album-oriented rock radio stations, reaching "good timers" with a prevention campaign was made easier because messages targeted to this segment could be placed where these drinkers are most likely to see and hear them.[61]

Psychographic Segmentation Typologies

Marketers are constantly on the prowl for new insights that will allow them to identify and reach groups of consumers that are united by a common lifestyle. To meet this need, many research companies and advertising agencies have developed their own *segmentation typologies.* Respondents answer a battery of questions that allow the researchers to cluster them into a set of distinct lifestyle groups. The questions usually include a mixture of AIOs, plus other items relating to their perceptions of specific brands, favorite celebrities, and media preferences. These systems are usually sold to companies that want to learn more about their customers and potential customers.

At least at a superficial level, many of these typologies are fairly similar to one another, in that a typical typology breaks up the population into roughly five to eight segments. Each cluster is given a descriptive name, and a profile of the "typical" member is provided to the client. Unfortunately, it is often difficult to compare or evaluate different typologies, as the methods and data used to devise these systems frequently are *proprietary;* that is, the information is developed and owned by the company, and the company feels that it would not be desirable to release this information to outsiders. Let's review a few typical approaches to classifying consumers in terms of lifestyles.

Vals 2

One well-known segmentation system is **The Values and Lifestyles (VALS™) System**, developed at SRI International in California. The original VALS™ system was based on how consumers agreed or disagreed with various social issues such as abortion rights. After about 10 years, SRI discovered that the social issues used to categorize consumers were not as predictive of consumer behavior as they once had been because greater numbers of people agreed with these ideas. SRI searched for a more powerful way to segment consumers, and the company discovered that certain lifestyle indicators such as "I like a lot of excitement in my life" were better predictors of purchase behavior than the degree to which a person agreed or disagreed with a social value.

Marketing Pitfall

When the R.J. Reynolds Company made plans to introduce a new brand of cigarettes called "Dakota" in several test markets, the tobacco company found out the hard way that a psychographic approach can be controversial. The marketing plan, submitted in the early 1990s to the company by an outside consulting firm, specifically targeted the cigarette to 18- to 24-year-old women with a high school education or less who work in entry-level factory or service jobs. This segment is one of the few remaining consumer segments in the United States that exhibits an increase in smoking rates, so from a purely financial point of view it clearly has market potential.

The brand was developed to appeal to a lifestyle segment the company called the "Virile Female." This woman had the following psychographic characteristics: Her favorite pastimes are cruising, partying, and going to hot rod shows and tractor pulls with her boyfriend, and her favorite TV shows are evening soap operas. Her chief aspirations are to get married in her early twenties and to spend time with her boyfriend, doing whatever he does. This psychographic strategy resulted in a flood of unfavorable publicity as critics charged the company was trying to persuade more young women to take up the habit.[62]

■ **FIGURE 6.3**
VALS 2 SEGMENTATION SYSTEM

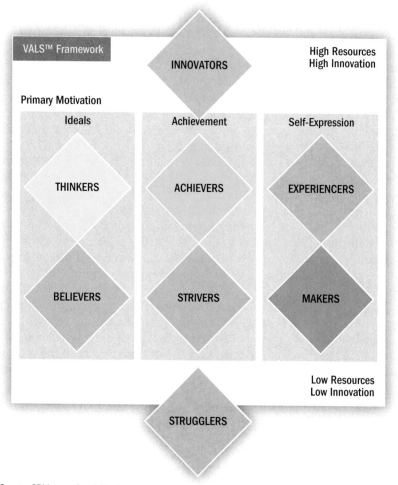

Source: SRI International, Menlo Park, CA.

The current VALS 2™ system uses a battery of 39 items (35 psychological and four demographic) to divide U.S. adults into groups, each with distinctive characteristics. As shown in Figure 6.3, groups are arranged vertically by their resources (including such factors as income, education, energy levels, and eagerness to buy), and horizontally by self-orientation.

Key to the VALS 2™ system is three self-orientations that comprise the horizontal dimension. Consumers with a *Principle* orientation make purchase decisions guided by a belief system, and they are not concerned with the views of others. People with a *Status* orientation make decisions based on the perceived opinions of their peers. *Action*, or self-oriented individuals, buy products to have an impact on the world around them.

The top VALS 2™ group is termed *Actualizers*, who are successful consumers with many resources. This group is concerned with social issues and is open to change. As one indication of this group's interest in cutting-edge technology, although only one in ten American adults is an Actualizer, half of all regular Internet users belong to this category.[63]

The next three groups also have sufficient resources but differ in their outlooks on life:[64]

- *Fulfilleds* are satisfied, reflective, and comfortable. They tend to be practical and value functionality.
- *Achievers* are career-oriented and prefer predictability to risk or self-discovery.
- *Experiencers* are impulsive, young, and enjoy offbeat or risky experiences.

The next four groups have fewer resources:

- *Believers* have strong principles and favor proven brands.
- *Strivers* are similar to Achievers, but have fewer resources. They are very concerned about the approval of others.
- *Makers* are action-oriented and tend to focus their energies on self-sufficiency. They will often be found working on their cars, canning their own vegetables, or building their own houses.
- *Strugglers* are at the bottom of the economic ladder. They are most concerned with meeting the needs of the moment, and have limited ability to acquire anything beyond the basic goods needed for survival.

The VALS 2™ system has been a useful way to understand people like Jackie and Hank. SRI estimates that 12 percent of American adults are thrill seekers, who tend to fall into the system's Experiencer category and who are likely to agree with statements like "I like a lot of excitement in my life" and "I like to try new things." Experiencers like to break the rules, and are strongly attracted to extreme sports such as sky surfing or bungee jumping.

Not too surprisingly, fully one-third of consumers aged 18 to 34 belong in this category, so it has attracted the interest of many marketers who are trying to appeal to younger people (more on this in Chapter 15). For example, VALS 2™ helped Isuzu market its Rodeo sport utility vehicle by focusing on Experiencers, many of whom believe it is fun to break rules in ways that do not endanger others. The car was positioned as a vehicle that lets a driver break the rules. Advertising was created to support this idea by showing kids jumping in mud puddles, running with scissors, and coloring out of the lines.[65] Isuzu sales increased significantly after this campaign. If you want to see what VALS type you would be classified as, go to ***www.sric-bi.com/VALS/presurvey.shtml***.

A system like VALS is useful to identify different consumer types within the United States, but of course in many cases multinational marketers need to reach customers who live in many countries. That's why VALS is developing similar systems to be used elsewhere—its Japan VALS identifies people there who are more or less receptive to change. In addition, though, increasingly sophisticated efforts are being made to develop lifestyle typologies that transcend national borders.

Global MOSAIC

Global MOSAIC was developed by a British firm called Experian. This system analyzes consumers in 19 countries including Australia, South Africa, and Peru. Experian boiled down 631 different MOSAIC types to come up with 14 common lifestyles, classifying 800 million people who produce roughly 80 percent of the world's GDP. This allows marketers to identify consumers who share similar tastes around the world. An Experian executive explained, "the yuppie on the upper East side of New York has more in common with a yuppie in Stockholm than a downscale person in Brooklyn."

These yuppies (labeled Education Cosmopolitans in MOSAIC) are the first consumers to accept new products and ideas and are influential in fueling the globalization of lifestyles. Although they are found in every country they are not present in equal proportions. MOSAIC says that they make up 10 percent of households in the United States, 7.1 percent in Japan, 5.8 percent in New Zealand, 4.2 percent in Great Britain, and only 3.7 percent in Australia. Figure 6.4 illustrates how an Irish band used this information to identify Americans most likely to want to hear their music.[66]

RISC

Since 1978, a Paris-based organization called the Research Institute on Social Change (RISC) has conducted international measurements of lifestyles and sociocultural change in more than 40 countries.[67] Its long-term measurement of the

■ **FIGURE 6.4**
GLOBAL FANS OF AN IRISH
ROCK BAND

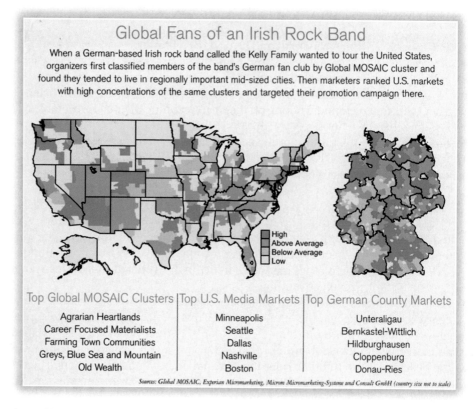

Global Fans of an Irish Rock Band

When a German-based Irish rock band called the Kelly Family wanted to tour the United States, organizers first classified members of the band's German fan club by Global MOSAIC cluster and found they tended to live in regionally important mid-sized cities. Then marketers ranked U.S. markets with high concentrations of the same clusters and targeted their promotion campaign there.

High
Above Average
Below Average
Low

Top Global MOSAIC Clusters	Top U.S. Media Markets	Top German County Markets
Agrarian Heartlands	Minneapolis	Unteraligau
Career Focused Materialists	Seattle	Bernkastel-Wittlich
Farming Town Communities	Dallas	Hildburghausen
Greys, Blue Sea and Mountain	Nashville	Cloppenburg
Old Wealth	Boston	Donau-Ries

Sources: Global MOSAIC, Experian Micromarketing, Microm Micromarketing-Systeme und Consult GmbH (country size not to scale)

Source: Michael Weiss. "Parallel Universe." *American Demographics* (October 1999): 51–63.

social climate around the world makes it possible to anticipate future change and to identify signs of change in one country before it eventually spreads to other countries. For example, concern for the environment appeared in Sweden in the early 1970s, then in Germany in the late 1970s, in France in the beginning of the 1980s, and in Spain in the early 1990s.[68]

RISC asks a battery of questions to identify people's values and attitudes about a wide range of issues. The answers are combined to measure 40 "trends" such as "spirituality" or "blurring of the sexes." Based upon statistical analysis of the respondents' score on each trend, each individual is located in a virtual space described by three axes. RISC then divides the population into 10 segments referring to their position in this virtual space. Figure 6.5 illustrates the 10 segments (G for global, L for Local (behind)) and their main life aspirations. The three axes are:

1 *Exploration/Stability:* The vertical axis separates people motivated by change, creativity, volatility, and openness from people motivated by stability, familiarity, tradition, and structure.
2 *Social/Individual:* The horizontal axis distinguishes people oriented toward collective needs from people oriented more toward satisfaction of individual needs.
3 *Global/Local:* The third axis indicates a distance between people who are comfortable with unfamiliar environments, multiple loose connections and large-scale networking from people preferring close-knit relationships and a desire for the elements of life to be connected in a predictable manner.

■ **FIGURE 6.5**
THE TEN RISC SEGMENTS

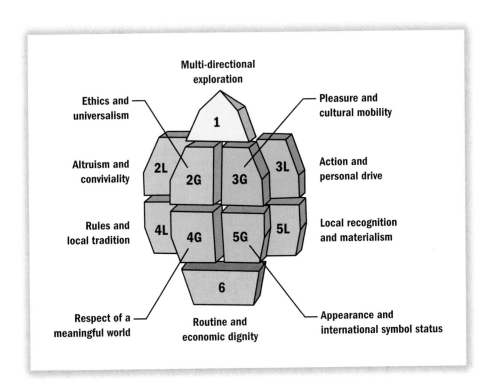

Source: "RISC Methodology" (Paris: RISC International, 1997): 14.

Each of the 40 trends can also be located in the space according to the gravity point of the people who scored highest on the particular trend. Trends that are related to exploration will thus be located near the top of the map, individualism trends to the right; local trends are smaller because they are at the back, and so on. While the position of the trends tends not to vary greatly, the percentage of various populations (countries, age groups, heavy users of a brand) supporting each trend will differ quite a bit.

The example shown in Figure 6.6 indicates how consumers in the United Kingdom compare to people in the rest of Europe. Darker colors indicate the trends that are relatively more important in Britain: cultural mobility, expanded vitality, narrow bounds, law and order, social recognition, well-being and epicurism (a quality-of-life orientation toward "the finer things" in life).

The use of RISC typically involves identifying users of a brand and understanding those users better, and it's also possible to monitor changes in the profiles of users over time. Furthermore, RISC data can be used to hone in on potential target groups and to tell marketers the types of product benefits and communications that would be likely to attract these groups. Figure 6.7 shows how the system was used in Germany to differentiate between likely buyers of two car brands. Consumers were asked if each of the two brands would be their first, second, or third choice if they were going to buy a new car. Brand B has a strong profile, individual and experimental; about 21 percent of respondents expressed interest in it. About 19 percent liked Brand M instead, which has more of a "vanilla" personality.

While overall popularity of the two cars is about the same in the German population, the key is to identify segments within the country that are much more receptive to the brand. The number in each cell is an *index value* that quickly tells

■ FIGURE 6.6
TREND MAP OF THE UK

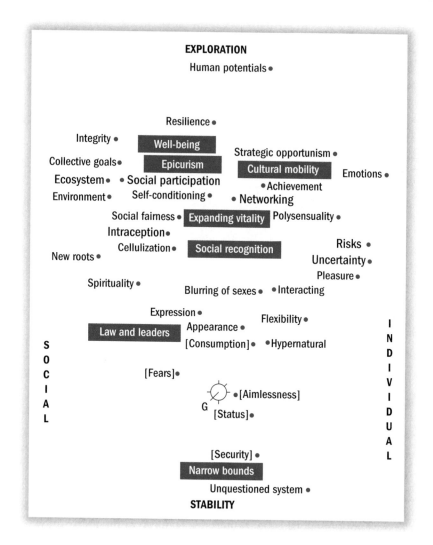

Source: RISC International, Paris, 1997.

us how people in that group stack up to the average German. IQ scores are computed the same way—if you have an IQ of 100 your intelligence level is exactly average compared to the population, while an IQ of 120 means a person is 20 percent more intelligent than average, and an IQ of 80 means a person is 20 percent less intelligent than average. So for example, the score of 152 in the top cell of Brand B (the group which is most interested in new designs, technologies, and function) means consumers in that segment are 152 percent more interested in this car than is the average German.

By comparing these index values you can get a sense of how different the two cars are: Both cars appeal to people in the multi-directional exploration segment (topmost cell), but otherwise there isn't a clear difference among cells for Brand M. In contrast, Germans who like Brand B skew heavily toward those who value appearance and status (with an index value of 131) and those who value pleasure and exploring other cultures (an index value of 151). This difference implies, for example, that marketers of Brand B might appeal to this segment in their advertising by linking the car with images of rich, worldly *bon vivants* (James Bond might be a prime endorser candidate!).

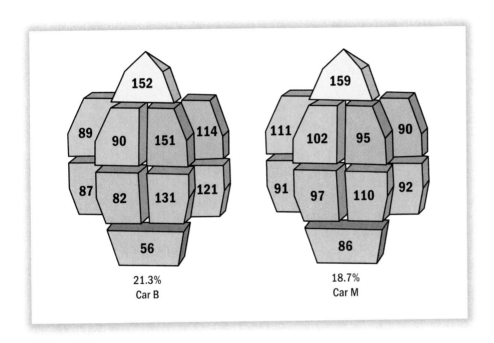

Source: RISC International, Paris, 1997.

■ **FIGURE 6.7**
CHOICE OF BRAND FOR
THE NEXT NEW CAR, GERMANY,
BRAND B/BRAND M, 1995

■ REGIONAL CONSUMPTION DIFFERENCES: YOU ARE WHAT YOU EAT!

If you have traveled to or lived in other parts of the country, you may have experienced the weird feeling of being slightly out of sync with your environment. The people may speak the same language, yet you may have difficulty understanding some things they say. Brands and store names may be confusing; some are familiar and some are not. Some familiar items may masquerade under different names. One person's "hero" is another person's "grinder" and one person's "submarine sandwich" is another person's "hoagie." These regional differences often exert a big impact on consumers' lifestyles because many of our preferences in foods, entertainment, and so on are dictated by local customs and the availability of some diversions rather than others: A resident of the Midwest would have to work hard to cultivate a "Florida beach bum" lifestyle, whereas a New Englander might be hard-pressed to find a rodeo show to attend on the weekend.

These regional differences are important for many product categories, from entertainment to favorite cars, decorating styles, or leisure activities (for example, BMW found that drivers in France prized a car for its road-handling abilities and the self-confidence it gave them, while those in Austria were more interested in its value as a status symbol).[69] One of the most telling domains in which lifestyle is influenced by where a person lives is in the area of food products. Many national marketers regionalize their offerings to appeal to different tastes, as when Campbell's Soup puts a stronger dose of jalapeño pepper in its nacho cheese soup in the Southwest.

Americans' differing preferences for "munchies" illustrates how something as simple as the act of snacking is largely defined by where you live. The average American eats 21 pounds of snack foods in a year (hopefully not all at one sitting), but people in the west central part of the country consume the most (24 pounds per person), whereas those in the Pacific and southeast regions eat "only" 19 pounds per person. Pretzels are the most popular snack in the mid-Atlantic area, pork rinds are most likely to be eaten in the South, and multigrain chips turn up as a favorite in the West. Not surprisingly, the Hispanic influence in the Southwest influences snacking preferences there—consumers eat about 50 percent more tortilla chips than do people elsewhere.[70]

Food Cultures

There's a lot of truth to the expression, "You are what you eat." Our food preferences say a lot about us, and many of our likes and dislikes are learned responses to dishes valued or not by the people who matter to us. Sheep eyeballs are considered a delicacy in Saudi Arabia, while snake is prized in China. People in Spain and Portugal consume 10 times the amount of fresh fish as those in Austria or the United Kingdom, and the consumption of pork in Denmark is about 10 times that of France. Not surprisingly, the Irish eat a lot of potatoes, but not as many as the Greeks. In contrast, Italians avoid the tuber; instead they consume approximately four times more pasta per person than the Swiss, who are the second most avid spaghetti eaters.[71]

A **food culture** is a pattern of food and beverage consumption that reflects the values of a social group. Citizens of the United States share the same national identity, yet a large country's many unique climates, cultural influences, and resources shape different food cultures. Such differences allow us to legitimately talk about "regional personalities" as well as a "national personality." That helps to explain, for example, why visitors to the southern United States may be surprised to discover some locals drinking Dr. Pepper for breakfast to wash down their Krispy Kreme donuts, or why "natural" foods like sprouts and tofu are associated with trendy restaurant menus in California.[72]

Similar differences in food cultures exist in Europe. An analysis of 138 food-related variables in 15 countries revealed the 12 distinct food cultures shown in Figure 6.8, many of which parallel national or linguistic borders. For example, the French/French-Swiss, Wallonian, and Italian cultures are characterized by, among other things, the importance of the sensory pleasure and high consumption of red wine; the Germanic cluster of countries exhibit a high degree of health consciousness; the Portuguese and Greek food cultures show relatively traditional eating patterns with a fascination for new "global" food; the Norwegian and Danish food cultures are unique in their openness to convenience products (and, for the Danes, also for the love of beer); and the British and Irish are distinguished by their extraordinary desire for sweets and tea.

Even the meaning of a dining occasion varies across countries and regions. This explains why American tourists who show up at a restaurant in Europe for their customary 6:00 P.M. dinner are perplexed to find that the place is empty, since locals don't start arriving until 9:00 P.M. The things we consume at different times during the day also vary widely, even though we may call the occasion by the same name. Thus a North American consumer may associate breakfast with eggs and bacon, a Spaniard may think of a strong cup of coffee at the local bar, and a Dane may salivate at the thought of his traditional cheese and marmalade meal.[73]

Geodemography

Geodemography refers to analytical techniques that combine data on consumer expenditures and other socioeconomic factors with geographic information about the areas in which people live, in order to identify consumers who share common consumption patterns. This approach is based on the assumption that "birds of a feather flock together"; people who have similar needs and tastes also tend to live near one another, so it should be possible to locate "pockets" of like-minded people

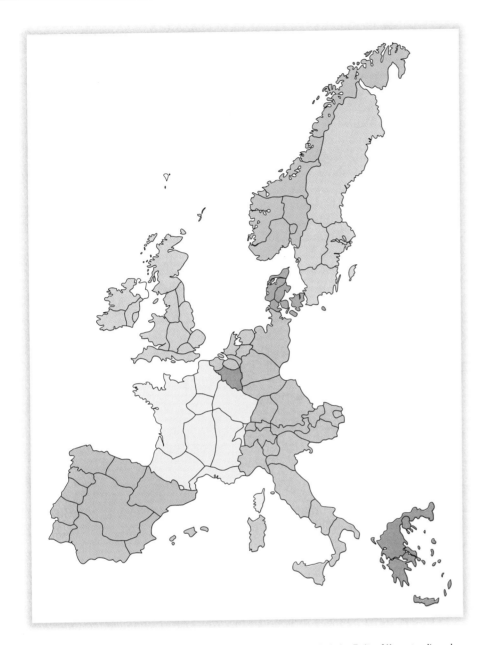

■ **FIGURE 6.8**
EUROPEAN FOOD CULTURES

Source: Søren Askegaard and Tage Koed Madsen, "The Local and the Global: Exploring Traits of Homogeneity and Heterogeneity in European Food Cultures," *International Business Review* 7(6) (1998).

who can then be reached more economically by direct mail and other methods. For example, a marketer who wants to reach white, single consumers who are college-educated and tend to be fiscally conservative may find that it is more efficient to mail catalogs to zip codes 20770 (Greenbelt, MD) and 90277 (Redondo Beach, CA) than to adjoining areas in either Maryland or California, where there are fewer consumers who exhibit these characteristics.

Single-Source Data

A statistical technique called *cluster analysis* allows marketers to identify groups of people who share important characteristics even though they may live in different parts of the country. Geographic information is increasingly being combined with other data to paint an even more complete picture of the American consumer. Several marketing research ventures now employ **single-source data**, in which information about a person's actual purchasing history is combined with geodemographic data, thus allowing marketers to learn even more about the types of marketing strategies that motivate some people—but not others—to respond.

This comprehensive strategy was first implemented in the BehaviorScan project conducted by Information Resources, Inc. The system combined grocery store UPC scanners, household consumer panels, and responses to different television commercials that were transmitted to selected parts of a market area to track purchases. This approach allows marketers to test the impact of changes in advertising, pricing, shelf placement, and promotions on consumer behavior patterns. Similar systems are now available or under development by other organizations, such as Nielsen and SAMI/ Burke.[74]

Marketers have been successful at adapting sophisticated analytical techniques originally developed for other applications, such as the military and oil and gas exploration. These techniques, which can now employ data at the neighborhood or even household level, are being used in a variety of ways:

- A bank examined its penetration of accounts by customer zip codes.
- A utility company compared demographic data with billing patterns to fine-tune energy conservation campaigns.
- A chain of ice cream stores helped franchisees develop sales promotion programs for local markets by providing them with demographic profiles of actual users and information about the sales potential of untapped customer groups.
- The Western Union Company improved the cost-effectiveness of its network of offices by analyzing the number of Western Union agents needed in an area and determining where new agents would most profitably be located.[75]

PRIZM

One popular clustering technique is the **PRIZM** system developed by Claritas, Inc. (PRIZM stands for Potential Rating Index by Zip Market). This system classifies every U.S. zip code into one of 62 categories, ranging from the most affluent "Blue-Blood Estates" to the least well-off "Public Assistance."[76] A resident of southern California might be classified as "Money & Brains" if he or she lives in Encino (zip code 91316), whereas someone living in Sherman Oaks (zip code 91423) would be a "Young Influential."[77] The system was updated from its original set of 40 clusters to reflect the growing ethnic and economic diversity of the United States; some new clusters include "American Dreams," "Kids & Cul-de-Sacs," and "Young Literati."[78]

Residents of different clusters display marked differences in their consumption of products, from annuities to zip-lock bags. These groupings also are ranked in terms of income, home value, and occupation (i.e., a rough index of social class) on a ZQ (Zip Quality) scale. Table 6.4 provides an idea of how dramatically different the consumption patterns of two clusters can be. This table compares consumption data for "Furs & Station Wagons," the third-highest-ranking cluster, with "Tobacco Roads," the third lowest.

Systems like PRIZM often are useful to maximize the effectiveness of marketing communications, especially direct-mail pieces where fine-tuning which households receive the messages makes them more cost-efficient and impactful. When Cox Communications wanted to boost the number of its cable subscribers who bought pay-per-view (PPV) service, the company launched a direct-mail campaign in 12 of its markets. The campaign targeted "nevers," those customers who had never purchased a pay-per-view movie, with enticements to try the service. Cox's Arizona cable system (the company's largest market) decided to use PRIZM cluster-

TABLE 6.4
A COMPARISON OF TWO PRIZM CLUSTERS

Furs & Station Wagons (ZQ3)		Tobacco Roads (ZQ38)	
New money, parents in 40s and 50s		Racially mixed farm towns in the South	
Newly built subdivisions with tennis courts, swimming pools, gardens		Small downtowns with thrift shops, diners, and laundromats; shanty-type homes without indoor plumbing	
Sample neighborhoods		Sample neighborhoods	
Plano, TX (75075)		Belzoni, MI (39038)	
Dunwoody, GA (30338)		Warrenton, NC (27589)	
Needham, MA (02192)		Gates, VA (27937)	

High Usage	**Low Usage**	**High Usage**	**Low Usage**
Country clubs	Motorcycles	Travel by bus	Knitting
Wine by the case	Laxatives	Asthma relief remedies	Live theater
Lawn furniture	Nonfilter cigarettes	Malt liquors	Smoke detectors
Gourmet magazine	Chewing tobacco	*Grit* magazine	*Ms.* magazine
BMW 5 Series	*Hunting* magazine	Pregnancy tests	Ferraris
Rye bread	Chevrolet Chevettes	Pontiac Bonnevilles	Whole-wheat bread
Natural cold cereal	Canned stews	Shortening	Mexican foods

Note: Usage rates as indexed to average consumption across all 40 clusters.
Source: "A Comparison of Two Prizm Clusters" from *The Clustering of America* by Michael J. Weiss. Copyright © 1988 by Michael J. Weiss. Reprinted by permission of HarperCollins, Publishers, Inc.

ing to sharpen its targeting efforts. The analysis found that in Arizona the "New Beginnings," "Towns & Gowns," and "Smalltown Downtown" clusters had higher-than-average likelihood of buying PPV service. Cox mailed a promotion to 41,000 customers in these clusters that included a list of the pay-per-view movies available during the month of the campaign and two coupons that could only be redeemed for movies purchased during the month of the campaign. The coupons were coded so that responses to the mailing could be tracked. Although the system mailed fewer pieces than other Cox cable companies, the response rate was considerably higher and 20 percent of the responders to the promotion were repeat buyers in the following month. Four months later, nearly 11 percent of those who were targeted continued to use pay-per-view. [79]

What's more, although consumers in two very different clusters may purchase a product at an equivalent rate, these similarities end when other purchases are taken into account. These differences highlight the importance of going beyond simple product-category purchase data and demographics to really understand a market (remember the earlier discussion of product complementarity). For example, people in "Urban Gold Coast," "Money & Brains," and "Blue-Blood Estates" communities buy a lot of high-quality binoculars, but so do those in the "Grain Belt," "New Homesteaders," and "Agri-Business" clusters. The difference is that the former groups use the binoculars to watch birds and other wildlife, while the latter use them to help line up the animals in their gun sights. Furthermore, whereas the bird watchers do a lot of foreign travel, listen to classical music, and host cocktail parties, the bird hunters travel by bus, like country music, and belong to veterans' clubs.

These two bowling centers, both located in a Kansas City suburb, are only six miles apart. However, they are light years apart in terms of the PRIZM clusters they draw upon as their clientele. The architectural firm that designed both centers found that the patrons at Olathe Lanes East came for relaxation and exercise, while those at the West Lanes were hard-core bowlers who came to compete. The customers at East came from three upscale clusters: Young Suburbia, Pools and Patios, and Furs and Station Wagons, and the firm selected an Art Deco motif and used soft lines to create a relaxing, upscale atmosphere. Bowlers at West came from the Blue Collar Nursery, Middle America, Blue Chip Blues, and Shotguns and Pickups clusters. The firm redid the bowling alley, using a Southwest theme with squares and energetic triangles to appeal to these groups.[80]

CHAPTER SUMMARY

The concept of *personality* refers to a person's unique psychological makeup and how it consistently influences the way a person responds to his or her environment. Marketing strategies based on personality differences have met with mixed success, partly because of the way these differences in *personality traits* have been measured and applied to consumption contexts. Some approaches have attempted to understand underlying differences in small samples of consumers by employing techniques based on Freudian psychology and variations of this perspective, whereas others have tried to assess these dimensions more objectively in large samples using sophisticated quantitative techniques.

A consumer's *lifestyle* refers to the ways he or she chooses to spend time and money and how his or her values and tastes are reflected in consumption choices. Lifestyle research is useful to track societal consumption preferences and also to position specific products and services to different segments. Marketers segment by lifestyle differences, often by grouping consumers in terms of their AIOs (activities, interests, and opinions).

Psychographic techniques attempt to classify consumers in terms of psychological, subjective variables in addition to observable characteristics (demographics). A variety of systems, such as VALS, have been developed to identify consumer "types" and to differentiate them in terms of their brand or product preferences, media usage, leisure time activities, and attitudes toward broad issues such as politics and religion.

Interrelated sets of products and activities are associated with social roles to form *consumption constellations*. People often purchase a product or service because it is associated with a constellation that, in turn, is linked to a lifestyle they find desirable.

Place of residence often is a significant determinant of lifestyle. Many marketers recognize regional differences in product preferences and develop different versions of their products for different markets that share a common *food culture*. A set of techniques called *geodemography* analyzes consumption patterns using geographical and demographic data, and identifies clusters of consumers who exhibit similar psychographic characteristics.

KEY TERMS

80/20 rule   205
AIOs   205
Allocentrics   193
Animism   196
Archetypes   192
Brand equity   195
Brand personality   195
Co-branding strategies   202
Consumption constellations   203

Ego   188
Food culture   214
Geodemography   214
Id   188
Idiocentrics   193
Lifestyle   198
Motivational research   190
Personality   188
Personality traits   192

Pleasure principle   188
PRIZM   216
Product complementarity   203
Psychographics   204
Reality principle   188
Single-source data   216
Superego   188
The Values and Lifestyles (VALS™)
   System   207

CONSUMER BEHAVIOR CHALLENGE

1 Construct a brand personality inventory for three different brands within a product category. Ask a small number of consumers to rate each brand on about 10 different personality dimensions. What differences can you locate? Do these "personalities" relate to the advertising and packaging strategies used to differentiate these products?

2 In what situations is demographic information likely to be more useful than psychographic data, and vice versa?

3 Alcohol drinkers vary sharply in terms of the number of drinks they may consume, from those who occasionally have one at a cocktail party to regular imbibers. Explain how the 80/20 principle applies to this product category.

4 Compile a set of recent ads that attempt to link consumption of a product with a specific lifestyle. How is this goal usually accomplished?

5 Psychographic analyses can be used to market politicians. Conduct research on the marketing strategies used in a recent, major election. How were voters segmented in terms of values? Can you find evidence that communications strategies were guided by this information?

6 Construct separate advertising executions for a cosmetics product targeted to the Belonger, Achiever, Experiencer, and Maker VALS types. How would the basic appeal differ for each group?

7 Using media targeted to the group, construct a consumption constellation for the social role of college students. What set of products, activities, and interests tend to appear in advertisements depicting "typical" college students? How realistic is this constellation?

8 Geodemographic techniques assume that people who live in the same neighborhood have other things in common as well. Why is this assumption made, and how accurate is it?

9 Single-source data systems give marketers access to a wide range of information about a consumer, just by knowing his or her address. Do you believe this "knowledge power" presents any ethical problems with regard to consumers' privacy? Should the government regulate access to such information? Should consumers have the right to limit access to these data?

10 Should organizations or individuals be allowed to create Web sites that advocate potentially harmful practices? Should hate groups such as the White Aryan Resistance be allowed to recruit members online? Why or why not?

11 Extreme sports. Day trading. Chat rooms. Vegetarianism. Can you predict what will be "hot" in the near future? Identify a lifestyle trend that is just surfacing in your universe. Describe this trend in detail, and justify your prediction. What specific styles and/or products are part of this trend?

NOTES

1. For an interesting ethnographic account of sky diving as a voluntary high-risk consumption activity, see Richard L. Celsi, Randall L. Rose, and Thomas W. Leigh, "An Exploration of High-Risk Leisure Consumption Through Skydiving," *Journal of Consumer Research* 20 (June 1993): 1–23. See also Jerry Adler, "Been There, Done That," *Newsweek* (July 19, 1993): 43.

2. Maureen Tkacik, "Quiksilver Keeps Marketing to a Minimum to Stay 'Cool'," *Wall Street Journal Interactive Edition* (August 28, 2002).

3. See J. Aronoff and J. P. Wilson, *Personality in the Social Process* (Hillsdale, NJ: Erlbaum, 1985); Walter Mischel, *Personality and Assessment* (New York: Wiley, 1968).

4. Ernest Dichter, *A Strategy of Desire* (Garden City, NY: Doubleday, 1960); Ernest Dichter, *The Handbook of Consumer Motivations* (New York: McGraw-Hill, 1964); Jeffrey J. Durgee, "Interpreting Dichter's Interpretations: An Analysis of Consumption Symbolism" in *The Handbook of Consumer Motivations*, unpublished manuscript

(Rensselaer Polytechnic Institute, Troy, New York, 1989); Pierre Martineau, *Motivation in Advertising* (New York: McGraw-Hill, 1957).

5. Vance Packard, *The Hidden Persuaders* (New York: D. McKay, 1957).

6. Harold Kassarjian, "Personality and Consumer Behavior: A Review," *Journal of Marketing Research* 8 (November 1971): 409–18.

7. Karen Horney, *Neurosis and Human Growth* (New York: Norton, 1950).

8. Joel B. Cohen, "An Interpersonal Orientation to the Study of Consumer Behavior," *Journal of Marketing Research* 6 (August 1967): 270–78; Pradeep K. Tyagi, "Validation of the CAD Instrument: A Replication," in Richard P. Bagozzi and Alice M. Tybout, eds., *Advances in Consumer Research* 10 (Ann Arbor, MI: Association for Consumer Research, 1983): 112–14.

9. For a comprehensive review of classic perspectives on personality theory, see Calvin S. Hall and Gardner Lindzey, *Theories of Personality*, 2nd ed. (New York: Wiley, 1970).

10. See Carl G. Jung, "The Archetypes and the Collective Unconscious," in H. Read, M. Fordham, and G. Adler, eds., *Collected Works*, vol. 9, part 1 (Princeton, NJ: Princeton University Press, 1959).

11. Linda L. Price and Nancy Ridgway, "Development of a Scale to Measure Innovativeness," in Richard P. Bagozzi and Alice M. Tybout, eds., *Advances in Consumer Research* 10 (Ann Arbor, MI: Association for Consumer Research, 1983): 679–84; Russell W. Belk, "Three Scales to Measure Constructs Related to Materialism: Reliability, Validity, and Relationships to Measures of Happiness," in Thomas C. Kinnear, ed., *Advances in Consumer Research* 11 (Ann Arbor, MI: Association for Consumer Research, 1984): 291; Mark Snyder, "Self-Monitoring Processes," in Leonard Berkowitz, ed., *Advances in Experimental Social Psychology* (New York: Academic Press, 1979), 85–128; Gordon R. Foxall and Ronald E. Goldsmith, "Personality and Consumer Research: Another Look," *Journal of the Market Research Society* 30, no. 2 (1988): 111–25; Ronald E. Goldsmith and Charles F. Hofacker, "Measuring Consumer Innovativeness," *Journal of the Academy of Marketing Science* 19, no. 3 (1991): 209–21; Curtis P. Haugtvedt, Richard E. Petty, and John T. Cacioppo, "Need for Cognition and Advertising: Understanding the Role of Personality Variables in Consumer Behavior," *Journal of Consumer Psychology* 1, no. 3 (1992): 239–60.

12. John L. Lastovicka, Lance A. Bettencourt, Renee Shaw Hughner, and Ronald J. Kuntze, "Lifestyle of the Tight and Frugal: Theory and Measurement," *Journal of Consumer Research* 26 (June 1999): 85–98.

13. David Reisman, *The Lonely Crowd: A Study of the Changing American Character* (New Haven, CT: Yale University Press, 1969).

14. Kelly Tepper Tian, William O. Bearden, and Gary L. Hunter, "Consumers' Need for Uniqueness: Scale Development and Validation," *Journal of Consumer Research* 28 (June 2001): 50–66.

15. Bennett Courtney, "Robotic Voices Designed to Manipulate," *Psychology Today* (January–February 2002): 20.

16. Mohan J. Dutta-Bergman and William D. Wells, "The Values and Lifestyles of Idiocentrics and Allocentrics in an Individualist Culture: A Descriptive Approach," *Journal of Consumer Psychology* 12 (March 2002): 231–42.

17. Jacob Jacoby, "Personality and Consumer Behavior: How Not to Find Relationships," in *Purdue Papers in Consumer Psychology*, no. 102 (Lafayette, IN: Purdue University, 1969); Harold H. Kassarjian and Mary Jane Sheffet, "Personality and Consumer Behavior: An Update," in Harold H. Kassarjian and Thomas S. Robertson, eds., *Perspectives in Consumer Behavior*, 4th ed. (Glenview, IL: Scott, Foresman, 1991): 291–353; John Lastovicka and Erich Joachimsthaler, "Improving the Detection of Personality Behavior Relationships in Consumer Research," *Journal of Consumer Research* 14 (March 1988): 583–87. For an approach that ties the notion of personality more directly to marketing issues, see Jennifer L. Aaker, "Dimensions of Brand Personality," *Journal of Marketing Research* 34 (August 1997): 347–57.

18. See Girish N. Punj and David W. Stewart, "An Interaction Framework of Consumer Decision-making," *Journal of Consumer Research* 10 (September 1983): 181–96.

19. J. F. Allsopp, "The Distribution of On-Licence Beer and Cider Consumption and Its Personality Determinants Among Young Men," *European Journal of Marketing* 20, no. 3 (1986): 44–62; Gordon R. Foxall and Ronald E. Goldsmith, "Personality and Consumer Research: Another Look," *Journal of the Market Research Society* 30, no. 2 (April 1988): 111–25.

20. Thomas Hine, "Why We Buy: The Silent Persuasion of Boxes, Bottles, Cans, and Tubes," *Worth* (May 1995): 78–83.

21. Kevin L. Keller, "Conceptualization, Measuring, and Managing Customer-Based Brand Equity," *Journal of Marketing* 57 (January 1993): 1–22.

22. Linda Keslar, "What's in a Name?" *Individual Investor* (April 1999): 101–2.

23. Rebecca Piirto Heath, "The Once and Future King," *Marketing Tools* (March 1998): 38–43.

24. Kathryn Kranhold, "Agencies Beef Up Brand Research to Identify Consumer Preferences," *Wall Street Journal Interactive Edition* (March 9, 2000).

25. Aaker, "Dimensions of Brand Personality."

26. Bradley Johnson, "They All Have Half-Baked Ideas," *Advertising Age* (May 12, 1997): 8.

27. Tim Triplett, "Brand Personality Must Be Managed or It Will Assume a Life of Its Own," *Marketing News* (May 9, 1994): 9.

28. Susan Fournier, "Consumers and Their Brands: Developing Relationship Theory in Consumer Research," *Journal of Consumer Research* 24, no. 4 (March 1998): 343–73.

29. Rebecca Piirto Heath, "The Frontiers of Psychographics," *American Demographics* (July 1996): 38–43.

30. Gabriel Kahn, "Philips Blitzes Asian Market As It Strives to Become Hip," *Wall Street Journal Online* (August 1, 2002).

31. Erin White, "Volvo Sheds Safe Image for New, Dangerous Ads," *Wall Street Journal Online* (June 14, 2002).

32. Benjamin D. Zablocki and Rosabeth Moss Kanter, "The Differentiation of Life-Styles," *Annual Review of Sociology* (1976): 269–97.

33. Mary Twe Douglas and Baron C. Isherwood, *The World of Goods* (New York: Basic Books, 1979).

34. Zablocki and Kanter, "The Differentiation of Life-Styles."

35. The Niche's the Thing, *American Demographics* (February 2000): 22.

36. Richard A. Peterson, "Revitalizing the Culture Concept," *Annual Review of Sociology* 5 (1979): 137–66.

37. Hate Group Web Sites on the Rise," CNN.com (February 23, 1999); www.resist.com/, accessed December 18, 2002.

38. Julia Cosgrove, "Campari and CD?" *BusinessWeek* (July 1, 2002): 14.

39. William Leiss, Stephen Kline, and Sut Jhally, *Social Communication in Advertising* (Toronto: Methuen, 1986).

40. Douglas and Isherwood, *The World of Goods*, quoted on pp. 72–73.

41. Christopher K. Hsee and France Leclerc, "Will Products Look More Attractive When Presented Separately or Together?" *Journal of Consumer Research* 25 (September 1998): 175–86.

42. Christina Binkley, "Fairmont and Porsche Team Up in Luxury Cross-Marketing Deal," *Wall Street Journal Online* (October 8, 2002).

43. Karen J. Banyan, "Bally, Unilever and Free Product Add Up to a Sampling Campaign," *New York Times on the Web* (April 23, 2002).

44. Cara Beardi, "Photo Op: Nike, Polaroid Pair Up for Footwear Line," *Advertising Age* (April 2, 2001): 8.

45. Mark Rechtin, "Surf's Up for Toyota's Co-Branded Roxy Echo," *Automotive News* (June 25, 2001): 17.

46. Michael R. Solomon, "The Role of Products as Social Stimuli: A Symbolic Interactionism Perspective," *Journal of Consumer Research* 10 (December 1983): 319–29.

47. Michael R. Solomon and Henry Assael, "The Forest or the Trees? A Gestalt Approach to Symbolic Consumption," in Jean Umiker-Sebeok, ed., *Marketing and Semiotics: New Directions in the Study of Signs for Sale* (Berlin: Mouton de Gruyter, 1988), 189–218; Michael R. Solomon, "Mapping Product Constellations: A Social Categorization Approach to Symbolic Consumption," *Psychology & Marketing* 5, no. 3 (1988): 233–58; see also Stephen C. Cosmas, "Life Styles and Consumption Patterns," *Journal of Consumer Research* 8, no. 4 (March 1982): 453–55.

48. Russell W. Belk, "The Retro Sims," in Stephen Brown and John Sherry, eds., *No Then There: Ecumenical Essays on the Rise of Retroscapes*, (forthcoming); www.ea.com/eagames/official/thesimsonline/home/index.jsp, accessed December 18, 2002; Michael R. Solomon, *Conquering Consumerspace: Marketing Strategies for a Branded World* (New York: AMACOM, 2003).

49. Russell W. Belk, "Yuppies as Arbiters of the Emerging Consumption Style," in Richard J. Lutz, ed., *Advances in Consumer Research* 13 (Provo, UT: Association for Consumer Research, 1986): 514–19.

50. Danny Hakim, "Cadillac, Too, Shifting Focus to Trucks," *New York Times on the Web* (December 21, 2001).

51. See Lewis Alpert and Ronald Gatty, "Product Positioning by Behavioral Life Styles," *Journal of Marketing* 33 (April 1969): 65–69; Emanuel H. Demby, "Psychographics Revisited: The Birth of a Technique," *Marketing News* (January 2, 1989): 21; William D. Wells, "Backward Segmentation," in Johan Arndt, ed., *Insights into Consumer Behavior* (Boston: Allyn & Bacon, 1968): 85–100.

52. Rebecca Piirto Heath, "Psychographics: 'Q'est-ce que c'est'?" *Marketing Tools* (November–December 1995): 73.

53. Seth Stevenson, "How to Beat Nike," *New York Times on the Web* (January 5, 2003).

54. William D. Wells and Douglas J. Tigert, "Activities, Interests, and Opinions," *Journal of Advertising Research* 11 (August 1971): 27.
55. Ian Pearson, "Social Studies: Psychographics in Advertising," *Canadian Business* (December 1985): 67.
56. Piirto Heath, "Psychographics: 'Q'est-ce que c'est'?"
57. Alfred S. Boote, "Psychographics: Mind over Matter," *American Demographics* (April 1980): 26–29; William D. Wells, "Psychographics: A Critical Review," *Journal of Marketing Research* 12 (May 1975): 196–213.
58. "At Leisure: Americans' Use of Down Time," *New York Times* (May 9, 1993): E2.
59. Joseph T. Plummer, "The Concept and Application of Life Style Segmentation," *Journal of Marketing* 38 (January 1974): 33–37.
60. Berkeley Rice, "The Selling of Lifestyles," *Psychology Today* (March 1988): 46.
61. John L. Lastovicka, John P. Murry, Erich A. Joachimsthaler, Gurav Bhalla, and Jim Scheurich, "A Lifestyle Typology to Model Young Male Drinking and Driving," *Journal of Consumer Research* 14 (September 1987): 257–63.
62. Anthony Ramirez, "New Cigarettes Raising Issue of Target Market," *New York Times* (February 18, 1990): 28.
63. Rebecca Piirto Heath, "The Frontiers of Psychographics," 38–43.
64. Martha Farnsworth Riche, "VALS 2," *American Demographics* (July 1989): 25. Additional information provided by William D. Guns, Director, Business Intelligence Center, SRI Consulting, Inc., personal communication, May 1997.
65. Rebecca Piirto Heath, "You Can Buy a Thrill: Chasing the Ultimate Rush," *American Demographics* (June 1997): 47–51.
66. Michael Weiss, "Parallel Universe," *American Demographics* (October 1999): 58–63, p. 62.
67. Some of this section is adapted from material presented in Michael R. Solomon, Gary Bamossy, and Søren Askegaard, *Consumer Behaviour: A European Perspective*, 2nd ed. (London: Prentice Hall Europe, 2002).
68. Document, RISC.
69. Horst Kern, Hans-Christian Wagner and Roswitha Harris, "European Aspects of a Global Brand: The BMW Case," *Marketing and Research Today* (February 1990): 47–57.
70. Marcia Mogelonsky, "The Geography of Junk Food," *American Demographics* (July 1994): 13–14.
71. "Euromonitor," European Marketing Data and Statistics (1997): 328–31.
72. Søren Askegaard and Tage Koed Madsen, "The Local and the Global: Patterns of Homogeneity and Heterogeneity in European Food Cultures," *International Business Review* (in press).
73. Michael R. Solomon, Suzanne C. Beckmann, and Basil G. Englis, "Exploring and Understanding of Cultural Meaning Systems: Visualizing the Underlying Meaning Structure of Brands," presented at a conference, Branding: Activating & Engaging Cultural Meaning Systems, Innsbruck Austria, May 2003.
74. Thomas W. Osborn, "Analytic Techniques for Opportunity Marketing," *Marketing Communications* (September 1987): 49–63.
75. Osborn, "Analytic Techniques for Opportunity Marketing."
76. Michael J. Weiss, *The Clustering of America* (New York: Harper & Row, 1988).
77. Bob Minzesheimer, "You Are What You Zip," *Los Angeles* (November 1984): 175.
78. Christina Del Valle, "They Know Where You Live and How You Buy," *BusinessWeek* (February 7, 1994): 89.
79. Adapted from a case study provided by Cox Communications, www.claritas.com/index.html, accessed December 18, 2002.
80. Barbra J. Eichorn, "Selling by Design: Using Lifestyle Analysis to Revamp Retail Space," *American Demographics* (October 1996): 45–48.

Attitudes

it's a lazy Tuesday night, and Jan, Terri, and Nancy are hanging out at Nancy's apartment doing some channel surfing. Jan clicks to ESPN and the three friends see that there's a women's soccer game on. Jan has been a fan for as long as she can remember—even before the World Cup that pro-pelled players like Mia Hamm and Brandi Chastain into the media spotlight. She loves the subtle intensity of the game—the traps, the moves, the way players make it look easy to move a ball around a huge field as if it were a small patch of grass. Nancy's a glutton for thrills and chills; she converted to soccer after the emotional cliffhanger of the World Cup final game in which the United States beat China on the team's fifth penalty kick after 120 scoreless minutes. Terri, on the other hand, doesn't know a banana kick from a rainbow kick. Still, you'd have to be living in a cave not to have seen the footage over and over of Brandi Chastain whipping her shirt off to reveal her sports bra when the game was won. Jan even bought one a few weeks later. Still, soccer doesn't really ring her chimes—but as long as she gets to hang out with her girlfriends she doesn't really care if they watch noncontact sports like soccer or contact sports like *The Jerry Springer Show*.

■ THE POWER OF ATTITUDES

Jan is just the kind of fan sponsoring brands like McDonald's and Coca-Cola hope will turn women's soccer into an ongoing source of sports fanaticism. Americans' attitudes toward the game have changed dramatically since the women's team lost in the 1996 semifinals in Sweden before a crowd of less than 3,000. The 1999 World Cup was won before an audience of more than 90,000 screaming fans, many of whom were soccer moms who saw the players as important role models for their young daughters. Professional women's soccer is off to a shaky start following the launch of the WUSA league in 2001, but investors including Comcast and AOL Time Warner are committed to funding the league at least through the 2006 season. The league is attracting top-notch athletes including Mia Hamm, who plays for the Washington Freedom.

On the other hand, following Chastain's exuberant show of skin, there is concern about the so-called "Babe Factor" as some critics wonder whether women's athletics will ever be taken seriously by male fans. It probably didn't help when the league risked alienating its core fans (families with young girls) by sending glamour shots of selected players to *Playboy.com* before the 2002 season, or when the magazine did an Internet poll and selected Philadelphia Charge defender Heather Mitts as the sexiest player. Time will tell if this ambitious project will score big or be red-carded and left to dwindle on the sidelines.[1] To score big in professional sports, it's all a question of attitudes.

The term *attitude* is widely used in popular culture. You might be asked, "What is your attitude toward abortion?" A parent might scold, "Young man, I don't like your attitude." Some bars even euphemistically refer to Happy Hour as "an attitude adjustment period." For our purposes, though, an **attitude** is a lasting, general evaluation of people (including oneself), objects, advertisements, or issues.[2] Anything toward which one has an attitude is called an attitude object (A_o).

An attitude is lasting because it tends to endure over time. It is general because it applies to more than a momentary event such as hearing a loud noise, though you might over time develop a negative attitude toward all loud noises. Consumers have attitudes toward a wide range of attitude objects, from very product-specific behaviors (e.g., using Crest toothpaste rather than Colgate) to more general consumption-related behaviors (e.g., how often one should brush one's teeth). Attitudes help to determine whom a person chooses to date, what music he or she listens to, whether he or she will recycle or discard aluminum cans, or whether he or she chooses to become a consumer researcher for a living. This chapter will consider the contents of an attitude, how attitudes are formed, and how they can be measured. It will also review some of the surprisingly complex relationships between attitudes and behavior. In the next chapter, we'll take a closer look at how attitudes can be changed—certainly an issue of prime importance to marketers.

The Functions of Attitudes

Psychologist Daniel Katz developed the **functional theory of attitudes** to explain how attitudes facilitate social behavior.[3] According to this pragmatic approach, attitudes exist *because* they serve some function for the person. That is, they are determined by a person's motives. Consumers who expect that they will need to deal with similar situations at a future time will be more likely to start forming attitudes in anticipation of this event.[4] Two people can each have an attitude toward some object for very different reasons. As a result it can be helpful for a marketer to know *why* an attitude is held before attempting to change it. The following are attitude functions as identified by Katz:

●   *Utilitarian function:* The utilitarian function is related to the basic principles of reward and punishment. We develop some attitudes toward products simply on the basis of whether these products provide pleasure or pain. If a person likes the taste of a cheeseburger, that person will develop a positive attitude toward cheeseburgers. Ads that stress straightforward product benefits (e.g., you should drink Diet Coke "just for the taste of it") appeal to the utilitarian function.

● *Value-expressive function:* Attitudes that perform a value-expressive function express the consumer's central values or self-concept. A person forms a product attitude not because of its objective benefits, but because of what the product says about him or her as a person (e.g., "What sort of man reads *Playboy*?"). Value-expressive attitudes are highly relevant to lifestyle analyses, which look at how consumers cultivate a cluster of activities, interests, and opinions to express a particular social identity.

● *Ego-defensive function:* Attitudes that are formed to protect the person, either from external threats or internal feelings, perform an ego-defensive function. An early marketing study indicated that housewives in the 1950s resisted the use of instant coffee because it threatened their conception of themselves as capable homemakers.[5] Products that promise to help a man project a "macho" image (e.g., Marlboro cigarettes) may be appealing to his insecurities about his masculinity. Another example is deodorant campaigns that stress the dire, embarrassing consequences of being caught with underarm odor in public.

● *Knowledge function:* Some attitudes are formed as the result of a need for order, structure, or meaning. This need is often present when a person is in an ambiguous situation or is confronted with a new product (e.g., "Bayer wants you to know about pain relievers").

This Norwegian ad addresses young people's smoking attitudes by arousing strong negative feelings. The ad reads (left panel): "Smokers are more sociable than others." (Right panel): "While it lasts."

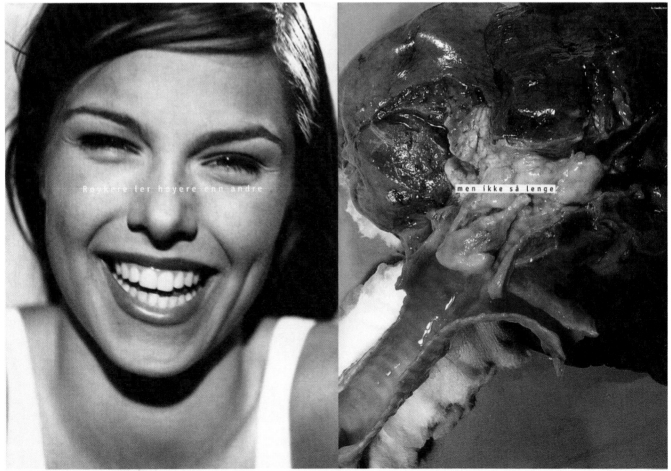

Annonsen er betalt av DET OPPLYSTE TOBAKKSKOUPANI AS Idé: La Familia Reklamebyrå. Foto: Alistair Taylor-Young. Modeller: Elite/heartbreak. Repro: Rep-Rek   DU BLIR IKKE STILIG, SOFISTIKERT ELLER SEXY AV Å RØYKE. DU BARE DØR.

An attitude can serve more than one function, but in many cases a particular one will be dominant. By identifying the dominant function a product serves for consumers—what *benefits* it provides—marketers can emphasize these benefits in their communications and packaging. Ads relevant to the function prompt more favorable thoughts about what is being marketed and can result in a heightened preference for both the ad and the product.

One study determined that for most people coffee serves more of a utilitarian function than a value-expressive function. As a consequence, subjects responded more positively to copy for a (fictitious) coffee that read, "The delicious, hearty flavor and aroma of Sterling Blend coffee comes from a blend of the freshest coffee beans" (utilitarian appeal) than to, "The coffee you drink says something about the type of person you are. It can reveal your rare, discriminating taste" (value-expressive function).[6]

As we saw in the experiences of the three women watching a soccer game, the importance of an attitude object may differ quite a bit for different people. Understanding the attitude's centrality to an individual and to others who share similar characteristics can be useful to marketers who are trying to devise strategies that will appeal to different customer segments. A study of football game attendance illustrates that varying levels of commitment result in different fan "profiles."[7] The study identified three distinct clusters of fans:[8]

- One cluster consisted of the real die-hard fans like Jan who were highly committed to their team and who displayed an enduring love of the game. To reach these fans, the researchers recommend that sports marketers should focus on providing them with greater sports knowledge and relate their attendance to their personal goals and values.
- A second cluster was like Nancy—their attitudes were based on the unique, self-expressive experience provided by the game. They enjoy the stimulation of cheering for a team and the drama of the competition itself. They are more likely to be "brand switchers" who are fair-weather fans, shifting allegiances when the home team no longer provides the thrills they need. This segment can be appealed to by publicizing aspects of the visiting teams, such as advertising the appearance of stars who are likely to give the fans a game they will remember.

Sports fans can be divided into clusters based on the type and intensity of attitudes they have toward the game and their team. In which cluster would you guess these fans belong?

● A third cluster was like Terri—they were looking for camaraderie above all. These consumers attend games primarily to take part in small-group activities such as tailgating that accompany the event. Marketers could appeal to this cluster by providing improved peripheral benefits, such as making it easier for groups to meet at the stadium, improving parking, and offering multiple-unit pricing.

The ABC Model of Attitudes

Most researchers agree that an attitude has three components: affect, behavior, and cognition. **Affect** refers to the way a consumer *feels* about an attitude object. **Behavior** involves the person's intentions to *do* something with regard to an attitude object (but, as will be discussed at a later point, an intention does not always result in an actual behavior). **Cognition** refers to the *beliefs* a consumer has about an attitude object. These three components of an attitude can be remembered as the **ABC model of attitudes**.

This model emphasizes the interrelationships among knowing, feeling, and doing. Consumers' attitudes toward a product cannot be determined by simply identifying their beliefs about it. For example, a researcher may find that shoppers "know" a particular camcorder has an 8:1 power zoom lens, auto focus, and a flying erase head, but such findings do not indicate whether they feel these attributes are good, bad, or irrelevant, or whether they would actually buy the camcorder.

All three components of an attitude are important, but their relative importance will vary depending on a consumer's level of motivation with regard to the attitude object. The differences in athletic interests among the three women in Nancy's apartment illustrate how these elements can be combined in different ways to create an attitude. Attitude researchers have developed the concept of a **hierarchy of effects** to explain the relative impact of the three components. Each hierarchy specifies that a fixed sequence of steps occurs en route to an attitude. Three different hierarchies are summarized in Figure 7.1.

The Standard Learning Hierarchy

Jan's positive attitude toward women's soccer closely resembles the process by which most attitudes are assumed to be constructed. A consumer approaches a product decision as a problem-solving process. First, he or she forms beliefs about a product by accumulating knowledge (beliefs) regarding relevant attributes. Next, the consumer evaluates these beliefs and forms a feeling about the product

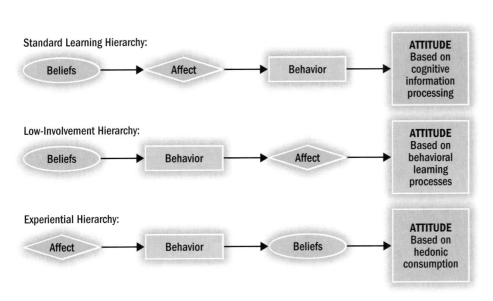

■ FIGURE 7.1
THREE HIERARCHIES OF EFFECTS

(affect).[9] Over time, Jan assembled information about the sport, began to recognize the players, and learned which teams were superior to others. Finally, based on this evaluation, the consumer engages in a relevant behavior, such as buying the product or supporting a particular team by wearing its jersey. This careful choice process often results in the type of loyalty displayed by Jan; the consumer "bonds" with the product over time and is not easily persuaded to experiment with other brands. The standard learning hierarchy assumes that a consumer is highly involved in making a purchase decision.[10] The person is motivated to seek out a lot of information, carefully weigh alternatives, and come to a thoughtful decision.

The Low-Involvement Hierarchy

In contrast to Jan, Nancy's interest in the attitude object (women's soccer) is at best lukewarm. She is not particularly knowledgeable about the sport, and she may have an emotional response to an exciting game but not to a specific team. Nancy is typical of a consumer who forms an attitude via the *low-involvement hierarchy of effects*. In this sequence, the consumer does not initially have a strong preference for one brand over another, but instead acts on the basis of limited knowledge and then forms an evaluation only after the product has been purchased or used.[11] The attitude is likely to come about through behavioral learning in which the consumer's choice is reinforced by good or bad experiences with the product after purchase. Nancy will probably be more likely to tune in to future games if they continue to come down to the wire like the World Cup game.

The possibility that consumers simply don't care enough about many decisions to carefully assemble a set of product beliefs and then evaluate them is important, because it implies that all of the concern about influencing beliefs and carefully communicating information about product attributes may be largely wasted. Consumers aren't necessarily going to pay attention anyway; they are more likely to respond to simple stimulus–response connections when making purchase decisions. For example, a consumer choosing among paper towels might remember that "Bounty is the quicker picker-upper" rather than bothering to systematically compare all of the brands on the shelf.

The notion of low involvement on the part of consumers is a bitter pill for some marketers to swallow. Who wants to admit that what they market is not very important or involving? A brand manager for, say, a brand of bubble gum or cat food may find it hard to believe that consumers don't put that much thought into purchasing her product, because she herself spends many of her waking (and perhaps sleeping) hours thinking about it.

For marketers, the ironic silver lining to this low-involvement cloud is that under these conditions, consumers are not motivated to process a lot of complex, brand-related information. Instead, they will be swayed by principles of behavioral learning, such as the simple responses caused by conditioned brand names, point-of-purchase displays, and so on. This results in what we might call the *involvement paradox:* The less important the product is to consumers, the more important are many of the marketing stimuli (e.g., packages, jingles) that must be devised to sell it.

The Experiential Hierarchy

Researchers in recent years have begun to stress the significance of emotional response as a central aspect of an attitude. According to the *experiential hierarchy of effects*, consumers act on the basis of their emotional reactions. Terri just enjoys watching the tube with her friends, regardless of what is on. For this reason Coca-Cola is starting to promote Coke in more emotional ways. Consumers told researchers they value attributes like authenticity and optimism as they move toward beverages like water, juices, and flavored teas. To combat this erosion of the cola market, ads for Coke now use phrases like "unique taste sensation" and "sparkle on your tongue." Coke's core proposition now is "Only the unique sensory experience of an ice-cold Coca-Cola brings a magical delight to the real moments of my life."[12]

The experiential perspective highlights the idea that attitudes can be strongly influenced by intangible product attributes, such as package design, and by consumers' reactions toward accompanying stimuli, such as advertising, brand names, and the nature of the setting in which the experience occurs. As discussed in Chapter 4, resulting attitudes will be affected by consumers' hedonic motivations, such as how the product makes them feel or the fun its use will provide. Even the emotions expressed by the communicator have an impact. A smile is infectious; in a process termed *emotional contagion*, messages delivered by happy people enhance our attitude toward the product.[13] Numerous studies indicate that the mood a person is in when exposed to a marketing message influences how the ad is processed, the likelihood that the information presented will be remembered, and how the person will feel about the advertised item and related products in the future.[14]

One important debate about the experiential hierarchy concerns the independence of cognition and affect. On the one hand, the *cognitive-affective* model argues that an affective judgment is but the last step in a series of cognitive processes. Earlier steps include the sensory registration of stimuli and the retrieval of meaningful information from memory to categorize these stimuli.[15]

On the other hand, the *independence hypothesis* takes the position that affect and cognition involve two separate, partially independent systems; affective responses do not always require prior cognitions.[16] A number-one song on the *Billboard* "Top 40" may possess the same attributes as many other songs (e.g., dominant bass guitar, raspy vocals, persistent downbeat), but beliefs about these attributes cannot explain why one song becomes a classic while another sharing the

Marketing Opportunity

The recognition that emotional responses play a key role in product attitudes has sparked renewed interest in developing high-tech approaches to measuring and manipulating emotional responses. Traditionally, these reactions have been measured in terms of physiological arousal, but the problem with this approach is that it is hard to interpret the results because arousal can be either positive or negative. Several companies are marketing more finely tuned alternatives that track specific responses. IBM is working on a gadget called the emotion mouse. It tracks the user's skin temperature, heart rate, and even very tiny hand movements, along with the electrical conductivity of the skin, which changes with moisture. The company is a leader in the new field of *affective computing*, where it is hoped that computers will eventually be able to determine the user's current emotional state and actually adjust its interface to reduce frustration, sense when an employee may be burning out, automatically boost computer game action, or base an automatic search for television shows on a user's personal feelings of what is funny. Right now the emotion mouse is about 75 percent successful at determining a user's emotional state. Eventually, these devices are likely to find their way into other objects, such as a car steering wheel that could sense when a driver is getting drowsy or a key chain that will tell a policeman if someone he's stopped seems unusually frightened. And, teachers offering lectures over the Internet may be able to judge the reactions of their faceless students and even replay parts of lectures where students' minds had wandered.[17]

Steak is our life. All we ask is that you make it your lunch.

Smith & Wollensky.
The quintessential New York City steakhouse.
49th St. & 3rd Ave. (212) 753-1530.

Winner of The *Wine Spectator's* 1987 Grand Award.

This ad for New York's famous Smith & Wollensky restaurant emphasizes that marketers and others associated with a product or service are often more involved with it than are their consumers.

same characteristics winds up in the bargain bin at the local record store. The independence hypothesis does not eliminate the role of cognition in experience. It simply balances this traditional, rational emphasis on calculated decision making by paying more attention to the impact of aesthetic, subjective experience. This type of holistic processing is more likely to occur when the product is perceived as primarily expressive or delivers sensory pleasure rather than utilitarian benefits.[18]

Product Attitudes Don't Tell the Whole Story

Marketers who are concerned with understanding consumers' attitudes have to contend with an even more complex issue: In decision-making situations, people form attitudes toward objects other than the product itself that can influence their ultimate selections. One additional factor to consider is attitudes toward the act of buying in general—as we'll see later in this chapter, sometimes people simply are reluctant, embarrassed, or just plain too lazy to expend the effort to actually obtain a desired product or service.

Attitude Toward the Advertisement

Consumers' reactions to a product are also influenced by their evaluations of its advertising, over and above their feelings about the product itself. Our evaluation of a product can be determined solely by our appraisal of how it's depicted in marketing communications—we don't hesitate to form attitudes toward products we've never even seen in person, much less used.

One special type of attitude object, then, is the marketing message itself. The **attitude toward the advertisement** (A_{ad}) is defined as a predisposition to respond in a favorable or unfavorable manner to a particular advertising stimulus during a particular exposure occasion. Determinants of A_{ad} include attitude toward the advertiser, evaluations of the ad execution itself, the mood evoked by the ad, and the degree to which the ad affects viewers' arousal levels.[19] A viewer's feelings about the context in which an ad appears can also influence brand attitudes. For example, atti-

In addition to a product attitude, a consumer's attitude toward an advertisement for the product (A_{ad}) can also make it more or less likely that he would buy the item.

tudes about an ad and the brand depicted will be influenced if the consumer sees the ad while watching a favorite TV program.[20] The effects demonstrated by A_{ad} emphasize the potential importance of an ad's entertainment value in the purchase process.[21] If consumers are not able to view an ad again, both belief and attitude confidence about that ad rapidly diminish. This research supports the marketer's effort to pulse or frequently repeat advertisements in the media.[22]

Ads Have Feelings Too

The feelings generated by an ad have the capacity to directly affect brand attitudes. Commercials can evoke a wide range of emotional responses, from disgust to happiness. These feelings can be influenced both by the way the ad is done (i.e., the specific advertising *execution*) and by the consumer's reactions to the advertiser's motives. For example, many advertisers who are trying to craft messages for adolescents and young adults are encountering problems because this age group, having grown up in a "marketing society," tends to be skeptical about attempts to get them to buy things.[23] These reactions can in turn influence memory for advertising content.[24]

At least three emotional dimensions have been identified in commercials: pleasure, arousal, and intimidation.[25] Specific types of feelings that can be generated by an ad include the following:[26]

- *Upbeat feelings:* amused, delighted, playful
- *Warm feelings:* affectionate, contemplative, hopeful
- *Negative feelings:* critical, defiant, offended

■ FORMING ATTITUDES

We all have lots of attitudes, and we don't usually question how we got them. Certainly, a person isn't born with the conviction that, say, Pepsi is better than Coke, or that alternative music liberates the soul. Where do these attitudes come from?

An attitude can form in several different ways, depending on the particular hierarchy of effects in operation and how the attitude is learned (see Chapter 3). It can occur because of classical conditioning, in which an attitude object such as the Pepsi name is repeatedly paired with a catchy jingle ("You're in the Pepsi Generation"). Or, it can be formed through instrumental conditioning, in which consumption of the attitude object is reinforced (e.g., Pepsi quenches one's thirst). Or the learning of an attitude can be the outcome of a very complex cognitive process. For example, a teenager may come to model the behavior of friends and media endorsers like Beyonce Knowles who drink Pepsi because they believe that this will allow them to fit in with the desirable lifestyle portrayed in Pepsi commercials.

Not All Attitudes Are Created Equal

It is thus important to distinguish among types of attitudes, because not all are formed the same way.[27] For example, a highly brand-loyal consumer like Jan, the soccer fan, has an enduring, deeply held positive attitude toward an attitude object, and this involvement will be difficult to weaken. On the other hand, another consumer like Nancy may be a more fickle consumer: She may have a mildly positive attitude toward a product but be quite willing to abandon it when something better comes along. This section will consider the differences between strongly and weakly held attitudes, and briefly review some of the major theoretical perspectives that have been developed to explain how attitudes form and relate to one another in the minds of consumers.

Levels of Commitment to an Attitude

Consumers vary in their *commitment* to an attitude; the degree of commitment is related to their level of involvement with the attitude object.[28]

Marketing Pitfall

In a study of irritating advertising, researchers examined more than 500 prime-time network commercials that had registered negative reactions by consumers. The most irritating commercials were for feminine hygiene products, hemorrhoid medication or laxatives, and women's underwear. The researchers identified the following factors as prime offenders:

- A sensitive product is shown (e.g., hemorrhoid medicine), and its use or package is emphasized.
- The situation is contrived or overdramatized.
- A person is put down in terms of appearance, knowledge, or sophistication.
- An important relationship, such as a marriage, is threatened.
- There is a graphic demonstration of physical discomfort.
- Uncomfortable tension is created by an argument or by an antagonistic character.
- An unattractive or unsympathetic character is portrayed.
- A sexually suggestive scene is included.
- The commercial suffers from poor casting or execution.[29]

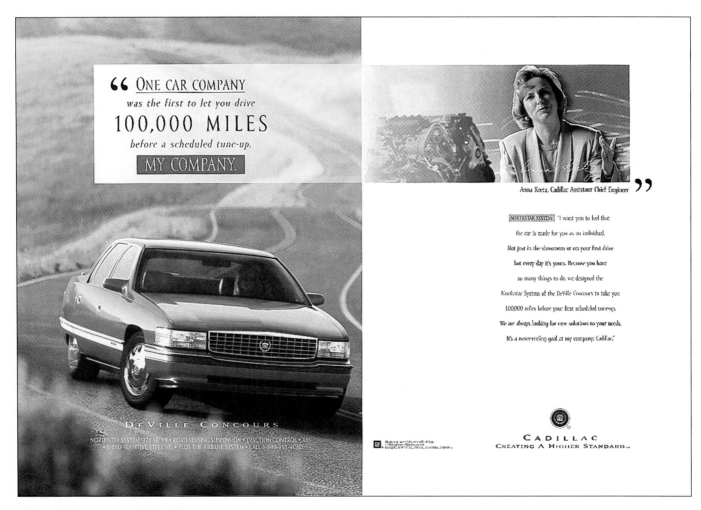

By describing Cadillac as "my company," the woman in this ad exhibits a high level of attitudinal commitment to her employer.

- *Compliance:* At the lowest level of involvement, *compliance*, an attitude is formed because it helps in gaining rewards or avoiding punishments from others. This attitude is very superficial; it is likely to change when others no longer monitor the person's behavior or when another option becomes available. A person may drink Pepsi because this brand is sold in the cafeteria, and it is too much trouble to go elsewhere for a Coca-Cola.
- *Identification:* A process of identification occurs when attitudes are formed in order to conform to another person or group. Advertising that depicts the social consequences of choosing some products over others is relying on the tendency of consumers to imitate the behavior of desirable models.
- *Internalization:* At a high level of involvement, deep-seated attitudes are internalized and become part of the person's value system. These attitudes are very difficult to change because they are so important to the individual. For example, many consumers had strong attitudes toward Coca-Cola and reacted quite negatively when the company attempted to switch to the New Coke formula. This allegiance to Coke was obviously more than a minor preference for these people; the brand had become intertwined with their social identities, taking on patriotic and nostalgic properties.

The Consistency Principle

Have you ever heard someone say, "Pepsi is my favorite soft drink. It tastes terrible," or "I love my boyfriend. He's the biggest idiot I've ever met"? Probably not, because these beliefs or evaluations are not consistent with one another. According

Woman's Day is 54 years old. Its readers aren't.

We're not the woman you think we are.

This ad for a magazine illustrates that consumers often distort information so that it fits with what they already believe or think they know.

to the **principle of cognitive consistency**, consumers value harmony among their thoughts, feelings, and behaviors, and they are motivated to maintain uniformity among these elements. This desire means that, if necessary, consumers will change their thoughts, feelings, or behaviors to make them consistent with their other experiences. That boyfriend may slip up and act like an idiot occasionally, but usually his girlfriend will (eventually) find a way to forgive him. The consistency principle is an important reminder that attitudes are not formed in a vacuum. A significant determinant of the way an attitude object will be evaluated is how it fits with other, related attitudes already held by the consumer.

Cognitive Dissonance and Harmony among Attitudes

The **theory of cognitive dissonance** states that when a person is confronted with inconsistencies among attitudes or behaviors, he or she will take some action to resolve this "dissonance," perhaps by changing an attitude or modifying a behavior. The theory has important ramifications for attitudes, because people are often confronted with situations in which there is some conflict between their attitudes and behaviors.[30]

According to the theory, people are motivated to reduce the negative feelings caused by dissonance by somehow making things fit with one another. The theory focuses on situations in which two cognitive elements are inconsistent with one another. A cognitive element can be something a person believes about himself, a behavior he performs, or an observation about his surroundings. For example, the two *cognitive elements*, "I know smoking cigarettes causes cancer" and "I smoke cigarettes" are *dissonant* with one another. This psychological inconsistency creates a feeling of discomfort that the smoker is motivated to reduce. The magnitude

Smokers often reduce cognitive dissonance by modifying or minimizing their beliefs about the negative effects of their behavior.

of dissonance depends on both the importance and number of dissonant elements.[31] In other words, the pressure to reduce dissonance is more likely to be observed in high-involvement situations in which the elements are more important to the individual.

Dissonance reduction can occur either by eliminating, adding, or changing elements. For example, the person could stop smoking (eliminating) or remember great-aunt Sophie, who smoked until the day she died at age 90 (adding). Alternatively, he might question the research that links cancer and smoking (changing), perhaps by believing industry-sponsored studies that try to refute this connection.

Dissonance theory can help to explain why evaluations of a product tend to increase *after* it has been purchased. The cognitive element, "I made a stupid decision," is dissonant with the element "I am not a stupid person," so people tend to find even more reasons to like something after it becomes theirs.

A classic study performed at a horse race demonstrated postpurchase dissonance. Bettors evaluated their chosen horse more highly and were more confident of its success *after* they had placed a bet than before. Because the bettor is financially committed to the choice, he or she reduces dissonance by increasing the attractiveness of the chosen alternative relative to the unchosen ones.[32] One implication of this phenomenon is that consumers actively seek support for their purchase decisions, so marketers should supply them with additional reinforcement to build positive brand attitudes.

Self-Perception Theory

Do attitudes necessarily change following behavior because people are motivated to feel good about their decisions? **Self-perception theory** provides an alternative explanation of dissonance effects.[33] It assumes that people use observations of their own behavior to determine what their attitudes are, just as we assume that we know the attitudes of others by watching what they do. The theory states that we maintain consistency by inferring that we must have a positive attitude toward an object if we have bought or consumed it (assuming that we freely made this choice). Thus, Jan might say to herself, "I guess I must be into sports pretty big time. I sure choose to watch it a lot."

Self-perception theory is relevant to the *low-involvement hierarchy*, because it involves situations in which behaviors are initially performed in the absence of a

In one demonstration of postpurchase dissonance, bettors tend to be more confident about their chances of winning *after* they place their bets than beforehand.

strong internal attitude. After the fact, the cognitive and affective components of attitude fall into line. Thus, buying a product out of habit may result in a positive attitude toward it after the fact—why would I buy it if I didn't like it?

Self-perception theory helps to explain the effectiveness of a sales strategy called the **foot-in-the-door technique**, which is based on the observation that a consumer is more likely to comply with a request if he or she has first agreed to comply with a smaller request.[34] The name for this technique comes from the practice of door-to-door selling in which salespeople were taught to plant their foot in a door so the prospect could not slam it on them. A good salesperson knows that he or she is more likely to get an order if the customer can be persuaded to open the door and

Door-to-door salespeople know that their chances of making a sale go up considerably if they can first persuade the potential customer to let them in the door.

talk. By agreeing to do so, the customer has established that she or he is willing to listen to the salesperson. Placing an order is consistent with this self-perception.

This technique is especially useful for inducing consumers to answer surveys or to donate money to charity. Such factors as the time lag between the first and second request, the similarity between the two requests, and whether the same person makes both requests have been found to influence its effectiveness.[35] Other variations on this strategy include the *low-ball technique*, in which a person is asked for a small favor and is informed after agreeing to it that it will be very costly; or the *door-in-the-face technique*, in which a person is first asked to do something extreme (a request that is usually refused) and then is asked to do something smaller. In each of these cases, people tend to go along with the smaller request, possibly because they feel guilty about denying the larger one.[36]

Social Judgment Theory

Social judgment theory also assumes that people assimilate new information about attitude objects in light of what they already know or feel.[37] The initial attitude acts as a frame of reference, and new information is categorized in terms of this existing standard. Just as our decision that a box is heavy depends in part on the weight of other boxes we have lifted, we develop a subjective standard when making judgments about attitude objects.

One important aspect of the theory is the notion that people differ in terms of the information they will find acceptable or unacceptable. They form **attitudes of acceptance and rejection** around an attitude standard. Ideas that fall within a latitude will be favorably received, but those falling outside of this zone will not. Because Jan already had a favorable attitude toward the concept of women playing professional soccer, she is likely to be receptive to ads such as Nike's that promote female athletic participation. If she were opposed to these activities, these messages would probably not be considered.

Messages that fall within the latitude of acceptance tend to be seen as more consistent with one's position than they actually are. This process is called an *assimilation effect*. On the other hand, messages falling in the latitude of rejection tend to be seen as even farther from one's position than they actually are, resulting in a *contrast effect*.[38]

As a person becomes more involved with an attitude object, his or her latitude of acceptance gets smaller. In other words, the consumer accepts fewer ideas that are removed from his or her own position and tends to oppose even mildly divergent positions. This tendency is evident in ads that are directed at discriminating buyers, which claim that knowledgeable people will reject anything but the very best (e.g., "choosy mothers choose Jif peanut butter"). On the other hand, relatively uninvolved consumers will consider a wider range of alternatives. They are less likely to be brand loyal and will be more likely to be brand switchers.[39]

Balance Theory

Balance theory considers relations among elements a person might perceive as belonging together.[40] This perspective involves relations (always from the perceiver's subjective point of view) among three elements, so the resulting attitude structures are called *triads*. Each triad contains: (1) a person and his or her perceptions of (2) an attitude object, and (3) some other person or object.

These perceptions can be either positive or negative. More importantly, people *alter* these perceptions in order to make relations among them consistent. The theory specifies that people desire relations among elements in a triad to be harmonious, or *balanced*. If they are not, a state of tension will result until somehow perceptions are changed and balance is restored.

Elements can be perceived as going together in one of two ways: They can have either a *unit relation*, in which one element is seen as somehow belonging to or being a part of the other (something like a belief), or a *sentiment relation*, in which the two elements are linked because one has expressed a preference (or dislike) for the other. A dating couple might be seen as having a positive sentiment relation. On getting married, they will have a positive unit relation. The process of divorce is an attempt to sever a unit relation.

To see how balance theory might work, consider the following scenario:

- Alex would like to date Larry, who is in her consumer behavior class. In balance theory terms, Alex has a positive sentiment relation with Larry.
- One day, Larry shows up in class wearing an earring. Larry has a positive unit relation with the earring. It belongs to him and is literally a part of him.
- Alex does not like men who wear earrings. She has a negative sentiment relation with men's earrings.

According to balance theory, Alex faces an unbalanced triad, and she will experience pressure to restore balance by altering some aspect of the triad, as shown in Figure 7.2. She could, for example, decide that she does not like Larry after all. Or, her liking for Larry could prompt a change in her attitude toward earrings. She might even try to negate the unit relation between Larry and the earring by deciding that he must be wearing it as part of a fraternity initiation (thus reducing the free-choice element). Finally, she could choose to "leave the field" by not thinking any more about Larry and his controversial earring.

Note that although the theory does not specify which of these routes will be taken, it does predict that one or more of Alex's perceptions will probably change in order to achieve balance. Although this example is an oversimplified representation of most attitude processes, it helps to explain a number of consumer behavior phenomena.

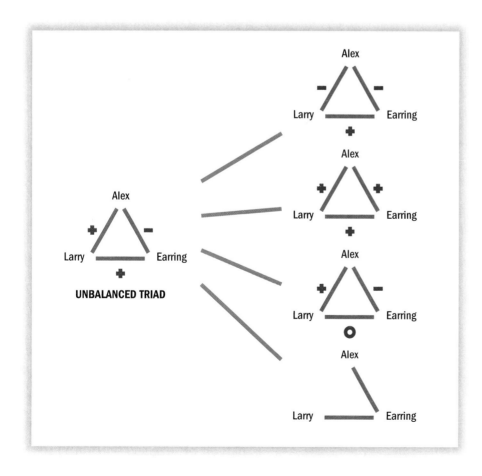

■ **FIGURE 7.2**
ALTERNATIVE ROUTES TO
RESTORING BALANCE IN A TRIAD

Marketing Applications of Balance Theory

Balance theory reminds us that when perceptions are balanced, attitudes are likely to be stable. On the other hand, when inconsistencies are observed, we are more likely to observe changes in attitudes. Balance theory also helps explain why consumers like to be associated with positively valued objects. Forming a unit relation with a popular product (e.g., buying and wearing fashionable clothing, driving a flashy car) may improve one's chances of being included as a positive sentiment relation in other people's triads.

Finally, balance theory is useful in accounting for the widespread use of celebrities to endorse products. When a triad is not fully formed (e.g., perceptions about a new product or one about which the consumer does not yet have a well-defined attitude), the marketer can create a positive sentiment relation between the consumer and the product by depicting a positive unit relation between the product and a well-known personality. In other cases, behaviors are discouraged when admired people argue against them, as is the goal when athletes appear in antidrug public service advertisements.

This "balancing act" is at the heart of celebrity endorsements, in which marketers hope that the star's popularity will transfer to the product. This strategy will be considered at length in the next chapter. For now, it pays to remember that this creation of a unit relation between product and star can backfire if the public's opinion of the celebrity endorser shifts from positive to negative, as happened when Pepsi pulled an ad featuring Madonna after she was associated with a controversial music video involving religion and sex. The strategy can also cause trouble if the star–product unit relation is questioned, as happened when singer Michael Jackson, who also did promotions for Pepsi, subsequently confessed that he does not drink soda.

College merchandise helps students and fans alike to "bask in reflected glory."

■ ATTITUDE MODELS

A consumer's overall evaluation of a product sometimes accounts for most of his attitude. When market researchers want to assess attitudes, it can be sufficient for them to simply ask a bunch of guys, "How do you feel about Budweiser?" However, as we saw earlier, attitudes can be a lot more complex than that. One problem is that a product or service may be composed of many attributes, or qualities—some of these may be more important than others to particular people. Another problem is that a person's decision to act on his or her attitude is affected by other factors, such as whether it is felt that buying a product would be met with approval by friends or family. As a result, *attitude models* try to specify the different elements that might work together to influence people's evaluations of attitude objects.

Multiattribute Attitude Models

A simple response does not always tell us everything we need to know about either *why* the consumer feels a certain way toward a product or about what marketers can do to change the consumer's attitude. Beliefs about specific brand attributes can be pivotal for a product. Warner-Lambert discovered this in research it did for its Fresh Burst Listerine mouthwash. A research firm paid 37 families to allow it to set up cameras in their bathrooms to watch their daily routines. Users of both Fresh Burst and rival Scope said they used mouthwash to make their breath smell good. But, Scope users swished the liquid and then spit it out, while Listerine users kept the product in their mouths for a long time (one user kept it in until he got in the car and finally spit it out in a sewer a block away!). These findings meant Listerine hadn't shaken its medicine-like image.[42]

Because attitudes can be complex, **multiattribute attitude models** have been extremely popular among marketing researchers. This type of model assumes that a consumer's attitude (evaluation) toward an attitude object (A_o) will depend on the beliefs he or she has about several or many attributes of the object. The use of a multiattribute model implies that identifying these specific beliefs and combining them to derive a measure of the consumer's overall attitude can predict an attitude toward a product or brand. We'll describe how these work, using the example of a consumer evaluating a complex attitude object that should be very familiar to you: a college.

Basic multiattribute models specify three elements.[43]

● *Attributes* are characteristics of the A_o. Most models assume that the relevant characteristics can be identified. That is, the researcher can include those attributes that consumers take into consideration when evaluating the A_o. For example, scholarly reputation is an attribute of a college.
● *Beliefs* are cognitions about the specific A_o (usually relative to others like it). A belief measure assesses the extent to which the consumer perceives that a brand possesses a particular attribute. For example, a student might have a belief that the University of North Carolina has a strong academic standing.
● *Importance weights* reflect the relative priority of an attribute to the consumer. Although an A_o can be considered on a number of attributes, some are likely to be more important than others (i.e., they will be given greater weight). Furthermore, these weights are likely to differ across consumers. In the case of colleges and universities, for example, one student might stress research opportunities, whereas another might assign greater weight to athletic programs.

the team's performance. If the team had won, students were more likely to show off their school affiliation (basking in reflected glory) than if the team had lost. This relationship was affected by the magnitude of the win—the bigger the point spread, the more likely were observers to note a sea of ASU insignias the following Monday.

The desire to bask in reflected glory by purchasing products associated with a valued attitude object has created numerous marketing opportunities. These include the revenues colleges reap by licensing their school's name and logo. Schools with strong athletic programs like Michigan, Penn State, and Auburn clean up by selling millions of dollars worth of merchandise (everything from T-shirts to toilet seats). Yale was a relative latecomer to this game, but the director of licensing explained the recent decision to profit from the use of the school's name and the likeness of bulldog mascot Handsome Dan: "We recognize that our name means a lot—even to people who didn't go here. Plus, this way we can crack down on the Naked Coed Lacrosse shirts out there with Yale on them."[41]

The Fishbein Model

The most influential multiattribute model is called the Fishbein model, named after its primary developer.[44] The model measures three components of attitude:

1 *Salient beliefs* people have about an A_o (i.e., those beliefs about the object that are considered during evaluation).

2 *Object-attribute linkages*, or the probability that a particular object has an important attribute.

3 *Evaluation* of each of the important attributes.

Note, however, that the model makes some assumptions that may not always be warranted. It assumes that we have been able to adequately specify all of the relevant attributes that, for example, a student will use in evaluating his or her choices about which college to attend. The model also assumes that he or she will go through the process (formally or informally) of identifying a set of relevant attributes, weighing them, and summing them. Although this particular decision is likely to be highly involving, it is still possible that his or her attitude will instead be formed by an overall affective response (a process known as *affect referral*).

By combining these three elements, a consumer's overall attitude toward an object can be computed (we'll see later how this basic equation has been modified to increase its accuracy). The basic formula is

$$A_{ijk} = \Sigma \beta_{ijk} I_{ik}$$

where

i = attribute
j = brand
k = consumer
I = the importance weight given attribute i by consumer k
β = consumer k's belief regarding the extent to which brand j possesses attribute i
A = a particular consumer's (k's) attitude score for brand j

The overall attitude score (A) is obtained by multiplying a consumer's rating of each attribute for all of the brands considered by the importance rating for that attribute.

A prospective student's attitude toward a college is influenced by the attributes she considers to be important and the extent to which she feels that school possesses those attributes.

TABLE 7.1
THE BASIC MULTIATTRIBUTE MODEL: SAUNDRA'S COLLEGE DECISION

Attribute(I)	Importance(I)	Beliefs(B)			
		Smith	Princeton	Rutgers	Northland
Academic reputation	6	8	9	6	3
All women	7	9	3	3	3
Cost	4	2	2	6	9
Proximity to home	3	2	2	6	9
Athletics	1	1	2	5	1
Party atmosphere	2	1	3	7	9
Library facilities	5	7	9	7	2
Attitude score		163	142	153	131

Source: These hypothetical ratings are scored from 1 to 10, and higher numbers indicate "better" standing on an attribute. For a negative attribute (e.g., cost), higher scores indicate that the school is believed to have "less" of that attribute (i.e., to be cheaper).

To see how this basic multiattribute model might work, let's suppose we want to predict which college a high school senior is likely to attend. After months of waiting, Saundra has been accepted to four schools. Because she must now decide among these, we would first like to know which attributes Saundra will consider in forming an attitude toward each school. We can then ask Saundra to assign a rating regarding how well each school performs on each attribute and also determine the relative importance of the attributes to her.

By summing scores on each attribute (after weighting each by its relative importance), we can compute an overall attitude score for each school. These hypothetical ratings are shown in Table 7.1. Based on this analysis, it seems that Saundra has the most favorable attitude toward Smith. She is clearly someone who would like to attend an all-woman's school with a solid academic reputation rather than a school that offers a strong athletic program or a party atmosphere.

Strategic Applications of the Multiattribute Model

Suppose you were the director of marketing for Northland College, another school Saundra was considering. How might you use the data from this analysis to improve your image?

Capitalize on Relative Advantage. If one's brand is viewed as being superior on a particular attribute, consumers like Saundra need to be convinced that this particular attribute is an important one. For example, although Saundra rates Northland's social atmosphere highly, she does not believe this attribute is a valued aspect for a college. As Northland's marketing director, you might emphasize the importance of an active social life, varied experiences, or even the development of future business contacts forged through strong college friendships.

Strengthen Perceived Product/Attribute Linkages. A marketer may discover that consumers do not equate his or her brand with a certain attribute. This problem is commonly addressed by campaigns that stress the product's qualities to consumers (e.g., "new and improved"). Saundra apparently does not think much of Northland's academic quality, athletic programs, or library facilities. You might develop an informational campaign to improve these perceptions (e.g., "little known facts about Northland").

Add a New Attribute. Product marketers frequently try to distinguish themselves from their competitors by adding a product feature. Northland College might try to emphasize some unique aspect, such as a hands-on internship program for business majors that takes advantage of ties to the local community.

Influence Competitors' Ratings. Finally, you might try to decrease the positivity of competitors. This type of action is the rationale for a strategy of comparative advertising. One tactic might be to publish an ad that lists the tuition rates of a number of area schools, as well as their attributes, with which Northland can be favorably compared as the basis for emphasizing the value obtained for the money at Northland.

■ USING ATTITUDES TO PREDICT BEHAVIOR

Consumer researchers have used multiattribute models for many years, but they are plagued by a major problem: In many cases, knowledge of a person's attitude is *not* a very good predictor of behavior. In a classic demonstration of "do as I say, not as I do," many studies have obtained a very low correlation between a person's reported attitude toward something and his or her actual behavior toward it. Some researchers have been so discouraged that they have questioned whether attitudes are of any use at all in understanding behavior. [45]

This questionable linkage between attitudes and behavior can be a big headache for advertisers: Consumers can love a commercial, yet still not buy the product. For example, one of the most popular TV commercials in recent years featured basketball player Shaquille O'Neal for Pepsi. Although the company spent $67 million on this spot and other similar ones in a single year, sales of Pepsi-Cola fell by close to two percent, even as sales of arch rival Coca-Cola increased by eight percent in the same period.[46]

The Extended Fishbein Model

The original Fishbein Model, which focused on measuring a consumer's attitude toward a product, has been extended in several ways to improve its predictive ability. The newer version is called the **theory of reasoned action**.[47] This model contains several important additions to the original, and although the model is still not perfect, its ability to predict relevant behavior has been improved.[48] Some of the modifications to this model are considered here.

Intentions Versus Behavior

Like the motivations discussed in Chapter 4, attitudes have both direction and strength. A person may like or dislike an attitude object with varying degrees of confidence or conviction. It is helpful to distinguish between firmly held attitudes and those that are more superficial, especially because an attitude held with greater conviction is more likely to be acted on.[49] One study on environmental issues and marketing activities found, for example, that people who express greater conviction in their feelings regarding environmentally responsible behaviors such as recycling show greater consistency between attitudes and behavioral intentions.[50]

However, as the old expression goes, "the road to hell is paved with good intentions." Many factors might interfere with performance of actual behavior, even if the consumer has sincere intentions. He or she might save up with the intention of buying a stereo system. In the interim, though, any number of things could happen: losing a job, getting mugged on the way to the store, or arriving at the store to find that the desired model is out of stock. It is not surprising, then, that in some instances past purchase behavior has been found to be a better predictor of future behavior than is a consumer's behavioral intention.[51] The theory of reasoned action

The likelihood of performing socially desirable behaviors like recycling may be influenced by our *subjective norms*—the belief that others would approve or disapprove of the behavior.

aims to measure behavioral intentions, recognizing that certain uncontrollable factors inhibit prediction of actual behavior.

Social Pressure

The theory acknowledges the power of other people in influencing behavior. Many of our behaviors are not determined in a vacuum. Much as we may hate to admit it, what we think others would *like* us to do may be more crucial than our own individual preferences. Some research approaches try to assess the extent to which people's "public" attitudes and purchase decisions might be different from what they would do if they were in private. For example, one firm uses a technique it calls "engineered theatre." Researchers go to the actual site where a product is being consumed, such as a bar. They arrange for the wrong product to "mistakenly" be served, and then observe the consumer's "naked response" to the brand and her reaction to consuming the brand in a social context.[52]

In the case of Saundra's college choice, note that she was very positive about going to a predominantly female school. However, if she felt that this choice would be unpopular (perhaps her friends would think she was crazy), she might ignore or downgrade this preference when coming to a decision. A new element, the subjective norm (SN), was thus added to include the effects of what we believe other people think we should do. The value of SN is arrived at by including two other factors: (1) the intensity of a *normative belief* (NB) that others believe an action should be taken or not taken, and (2) the *motivation to comply* (MC) with that belief (i.e., the degree to which the consumer takes others' anticipated reactions into account when evaluating a course of action or a purchase).

Attitude Toward Buying

The model now measures **attitude toward the act of buying** (A_{act}), rather than only the attitude toward the product itself. In other words, it focuses on the perceived consequences of a purchase. Knowing how someone feels about buying or using an object turns out to be more valid than merely knowing the consumer's evaluation of the object itself.[53]

To understand this distinction, consider a problem that might arise when measuring attitudes toward condoms. Although a group of college students might have a positive attitude toward condoms, does this necessarily predict that they will buy and use them? A better prediction would be obtained by asking the students how likely they are to *buy* condoms. A person might have a positive A_o toward condoms, but A_{act} might be negative due to the embarrassment or the hassle involved.

Obstacles to Predicting Behavior in the Theory of Reasoned Action

Despite improvements to the Fishbein Model, problems arise when it is misapplied. In many cases, the model is used in ways for which it was not intended, or where certain assumptions about human behavior may not be warranted.[54] Other obstacles to predicting behavior include the following:

- The model was developed to deal with actual behavior (e.g., taking a diet pill), not with the *outcomes* of behavior that are instead assessed in some studies (e.g., losing weight).
- Some outcomes are beyond the consumer's control, such as when the purchase requires the cooperation of other people. For instance, a woman might *want* to get a mortgage, but this intention will be worthless if she cannot find a banker to give her one.
- The basic assumption that behavior is intentional may be invalid in a variety of cases, including impulsive acts, sudden changes in one's situation, novelty seeking, or even simple repeat buying. One study found that such unexpected events as having guests, changes in the weather, or reading articles about the healthfulness of certain foods exerted a significant effect on actual behaviors.[55]
- Measures of attitude often do not really correspond to the behavior they are supposed to predict, either in terms of the A_o or when the act will occur. One common problem is a difference in the level of *abstraction* employed. For example, knowing a person's attitude toward sports cars may not predict whether he or she will purchase a BMW Z4. It is very important to match the level of specificity between the attitude and the behavioral intention.
- A similar problem relates to the *time frame* of the attitude measure. In general, the longer the time between the attitude measurement and the behavior it is supposed to assess, the weaker the relationship will be. For example, predictability would improve markedly by asking consumers the likelihood that they would buy a house in the next week as opposed to within the next five years.
- Attitudes formed by direct, personal experience with an A_o are stronger and more predictive of behavior than those formed indirectly, such as through advertising.[56] According to the *attitude accessibility perspective*, behavior is a function of the person's immediate perceptions of the A_o in the context of the situation in which it is encountered. An attitude will guide the evaluation of the object, but *only* if it is activated from memory when the object is observed. These findings underscore the importance of strategies that induce trial (e.g., by widespread product sampling to encourage the consumer to try the product at home, by taste tests, test drives, etc.) as well as those that maximize exposure to marketing communications.

In addition, the theory of reasoned action has primarily been applied in Western settings. Certain assumptions inherent in the model may not necessarily apply to consumers from other cultures. Several cultural roadblocks diminish the universality of the theory of reasoned action:

- The model was developed to predict the performance of any voluntary act. Across cultures, however, many consumer activities, ranging from taking exams and entering military service to receiving an inoculation or even choosing a marriage partner, are not necessarily voluntary.
- The relative impact of subjective norms may vary across cultures. For example, Asian cultures tend to value conformity and "face saving," so it is possible that subjective norms that involve the anticipated reactions of others to the choice will have an even greater impact on behavior for many Asian consumers. Indeed, a recent study conducted among voters in Singapore was able to predict voting for political candidates from their voting intentions, which in turn were influenced by such factors as voters' attitudes toward the candidate, attitudes toward the political party, and subjective norms—which in Singapore included an emphasis on harmonious and close ties among members of the society.
- The model measures behavioral intentions, and thus presupposes that consumers are actively thinking ahead and planning future behaviors. The intention concept assumes that consumers have a linear time sense; they think in terms of past, present, and future. As will be discussed in Chapter 10, this perspective on time is not held by all cultures.
- A consumer who forms an intention is (implicitly) claiming that he or she is in control of his or her actions. Some cultures (e.g., Muslim peoples) tend to be fatalistic and do not necessarily believe in the concept of free will. Indeed, one study comparing students from the United States, Jordan, and Thailand found evidence for cultural differences in assumptions about fatalism and control over the future. [57]

Trying to Consume

Another perspective tries to address some of these problems by focusing instead on consumers' goals and what they believe is required to attain them. The *theory of trying* states that the criterion of behavior in the reasoned action model should be replaced with *trying* to reach a goal.[58] This perspective recognizes that additional factors might intervene between intent and performance—both personal and environmental barriers might prevent the individual from attaining the goal. For example, a person who intends to lose weight may have to deal with numerous issues: He may not believe he is capable of slimming down, he may have a roommate who loves to cook and who leaves tempting goodies lying around the apartment, his friends may be jealous of his attempts to diet and will encourage him to pig out, or he may be genetically predisposed to obesity and cutting down on calories simply will not produce the desired results.

The theory of trying includes several new components that attempt to account for the complex situations in which many factors either help or hurt our chances of turning intentions into actions, as shown in Figure 7.3. These factors include the amount of control the person has over the situation, his or her expectations of success or failure in achieving the goal, social norms related to attaining the goal, and his or her attitude toward the process of trying (i.e., how the action required to attain the goal makes him or her feel, regardless of the outcome). Still other new variables are the frequency and recency of past trying of the behavior— for example, even if a person does not have specific plans to go on a diet in the next month, the frequency with which he or she has tried to do so in the recent past (and the success—however fleeting—he or she may have experienced) would be the best predictor of future attempts to shed some pounds. To predict whether someone would try to lose weight, here are a few sample issues that might be addressed:

- *Past frequency:* How many times in the past year did the person try to lose weight?
- *Recency:* Did he try to lose weight in the last week?
- *Beliefs:* Did he believe he would be healthier if he lost weight?

■ **FIGURE 7.3** THEORY OF TRYING (TT)

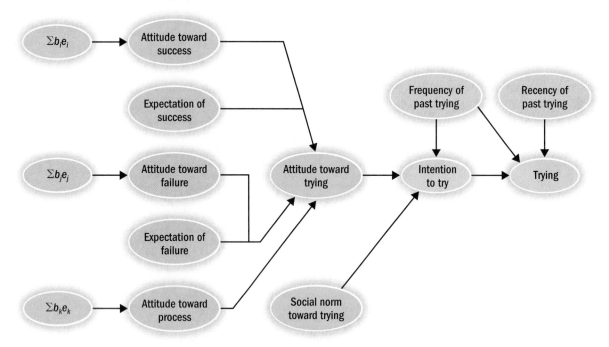

● *Evaluations of consequences:* Did he believe his girlfriend would be happier if he succeeded in losing weight? Did he believe his friends would make fun of him if he tried but failed to lose weight?
● *The process:* Would the diet make him uncomfortable or depressed?
● *Expectations of success and failure:* Did he believe it likely he would be able to lose weight if he tried?
● *Subjective norms toward trying:* Would the people who are important to him approve of his efforts to lose weight?

Tracking Attitudes over Time

An attitude survey is like a snapshot taken at a single point in time. It may tell us a lot about a brand's position at that moment, but it does not permit many inferences about progress the brand has made over time or any predictions about possible future changes in consumer attitudes. To accomplish that, it is necessary to develop an *attitude-tracking* program. This activity helps to increase the predictability of behavior by allowing researchers to analyze attitude trends during an extended period of time. It is more like a movie than a snapshot. For example, a longitudinal survey conducted by the Food Marketing Institute of consumers' attitudes toward food content during the last decade illustrates how priorities can shift in a fairly short time.[59] Concerns about fat and cholesterol content rose dramatically during this period, while a focus on nutritional issues such as interest in sugar content decreased.

Ongoing Tracking Studies

Attitude tracking involves the administration of an attitude survey at regular intervals. Preferably, the identical methodology is used each time so that results can be reliably compared. Several syndicated services, such as the Gallup Poll or the

■ **FIGURE 7.4**
PERCENTAGE OF 16- TO 24-YEAR-
OLDS WHO AGREE "WE MUST TAKE
RADICAL ACTION TO CUT DOWN ON
HOW WE USE OUR CARS."

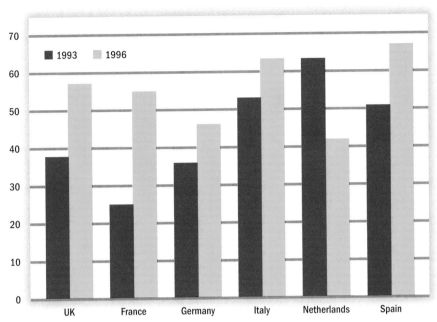

Source: The Henley Centre Frontiers: Planning for Consumer Change in Europe, 1996/97.

Yankelovich Monitor, track consumer attitudes over time (see Chapter 6). Results from a tracking study of ecological attitudes among young people in a set of European countries are shown in Figure 7.4.

This activity can be extremely valuable for many strategic decisions. For example, one firm monitored changes in consumer attitudes toward one-stop financial centers. Although a large number of consumers were warm to the idea when it was first introduced, the number of people who liked the concept did not increase over time despite the millions of dollars invested in advertising to promote the centers. This finding indicated some problems with the way the concept was being presented to consumers, and the company decided to "go back to the drawing board," eventually coming up with a new way to communicate the advantages of this service.

Changes to Look for over Time

Some of the dimensions that can be included in attitude tracking include the following:

- *Changes in different age groups:* Attitudes tend to change as people age (a life-cycle effect). In addition, cohort effects occur, whereby members of a particular generation tend to share certain outlooks (e.g., the yuppie). Also, historical effects can be observed as large groups of people are affected by profound cultural changes (such as the Great Depression, the terrorist attacks of 2001, or the crash of the Columbia space shuttle in 2003).
- *Scenarios about the future:* Consumers are frequently tracked in terms of their future plans, confidence in the economy, and so on. These measures can provide valuable data about future behavior and yield insights for public policy. For example, Americans tend to overestimate how much they will earn after retirement, which is a potentially dangerous miscalculation.
- *Identification of change agents:* Social phenomena can alter people's attitudes toward basic consumption activities over time, as when consumers' willingness

to buy fur changes. Or, consumers' likelihood of desiring a divorce may be affected by such facilitators as changes in the legal system that make this action easier, or by inhibitors, such as the prevalence of AIDS and the value of two paychecks in today's economy.[60]

CHAPTER SUMMARY

An *attitude* is a predisposition to evaluate an object or product positively or negatively.

Social marketing refers to attempts to change consumers' attitudes and behaviors in ways that are beneficial to the society as a whole.

Attitudes are made up of three components: beliefs, affect, and behavioral intentions.

Attitude researchers traditionally assumed that attitudes were learned in a fixed sequence, consisting first of the formation of beliefs (*cognitions*) regarding an attitude object, followed by some evaluation of that object (*affect*) and then some action (*behavior*). Depending on the consumer's level of involvement and the circumstances, though, attitudes can result from other hierarchies of effects as well.

A key to attitude formation is the function the attitude holds for the consumer (e.g., is it utilitarian or ego defensive?).

One organizing principle of attitude formation is the importance of consistency among attitudinal components—that is, some parts of an attitude may be altered to be in line with others. Such theoretical approaches to attitudes as *cognitive dissonance theory, self-perception theory,* and *balance theory* stress the vital role of the need for consistency.

The complexity of attitudes is underscored by multiattribute attitude models, in which a set of beliefs and evaluations is identified and combined to predict an overall attitude. Factors such as subjective norms and the specificity of attitude scales have been integrated into attitude measures to improve predictability.

KEY TERMS

CONSUMER BEHAVIOR CHALLENGE

1 Contrast the hierarchies of effects outlined in this chapter. How will strategic decisions related to the marketing mix be influenced by which hierarchy is operative among target consumers?

2 List three functions performed by attitudes, giving an example of how each function is employed in a marketing situation.

3 Think of a behavior someone does that is inconsistent with his or her attitudes (e.g., attitudes toward cholesterol, drug use, or even buying things to make him or her stand out or attain status). Ask the person to elaborate on why he or she does the behavior, and try to identify the way the person has resolved dissonant elements.

4 Devise an attitude survey for a set of competing automobiles. Identify areas of competitive advantage or disadvantage for each model you incorporate.

5 Construct a multiattribute model for a set of local restaurants. Based on your findings, suggest how restaurant managers can improve an establishment's image via the strategies described in this chapter.

6 More than 500 universities have signed up commercial companies to run campus Web sites and e-mail services. These agreements provide Web services to colleges at little or no cost. But, these actions have aroused controversy, because major companies pay to place advertising on the sites. That gives marketers entreé to influence the attitudes of thousands of students who are involuntarily exposed to product messages. One professor complained, "we're throwing our freshmen to the wolves. The University has become a shill for the corporate community." But University administrators argue that they could not provide the services by themselves—students expect to be able to fill out financial aid forms and register for classes online. Colleges that do not offer such services may lose their ability to attract students.[61] How do you feel about this situation? Do you agree that you're being "thrown to the wolves"? Should companies be able to buy access to your eyeballs from the school you pay to attend?

NOTES

1. Grant Wahl, "Foreign Aid: The Carolina Courage Tapped into the International Pipeline and Came Up Champs in WUSA's Year 2," *Sports Illustrated* (September 2, 2002): R2; Bill Saporito, "Flat-Out Fantastic," *Time* (July 19, 1999): 58; Mark Hyman, "The 'Babe Factor' in Women's Soccer," *BusinessWeek* (July 26, 1999): 118.

2. Robert A. Baron and Donn Byrne, *Social Psychology: Understanding Human Interaction*, 5th ed. (Boston: Allyn & Bacon, 1987).

3. Daniel Katz, "The Functional Approach to the Study of Attitudes," *Public Opinion Quarterly* 24 (Summer 1960): 163–204; Richard J. Lutz, "Changing Brand Attitudes through Modification of Cognitive Structure," *Journal of Consumer Research* 1 (March 1975): 49–59.

4. Russell H. Fazio, T. M. Lenn, and E. A. Effrein, "Spontaneous Attitude Formation," *Social Cognition* 2 (1984): 214–34.

5. Mason Haire, "Projective Techniques in Marketing Research," *Journal of Marketing* 14 (April 1950): 649–56.

6. Sharon Shavitt, "The Role of Attitude Objects in Attitude Functions," *Journal of Experimental Social Psychology* 26 (1990): 124–48; see also J. S. Johar and M. Joseph Sirgy, "Value-Expressive versus Utilitarian Advertising Appeals: When and Why to Use Which Appeal," *Journal of Advertising* 20 (September 1991): 23–34.

7. For the original work that focused on the issue of levels of attitudinal commitment, see H. C. Kelman, "Compliance, Identification, and Internalization: Three Processes of Attitude Change," *Journal of Conflict Resolution* 2 (1958): 51–60.

8. Lynn R. Kahle, Kenneth M. Kambara, and Gregory M. Rose, "A Functional Model of Fan Attendance Motivations for College Football," *Sports Marketing Quarterly* 5, no. 4 (1996): 51–60.

9. For a study that found evidence of simultaneous causation of beliefs and attitudes, see Gary M. Erickson, Johny K. Johansson, and Paul Chao, "Image Variables in Multi-Attribute Product Evaluations: Country-of-Origin Effects," *Journal of Consumer Research* 11 (September 1984): 694–99.

10. Michael Ray, "Marketing Communications and the Hierarchy-of-Effects," in P. Clarke, ed., *New Models for Mass Communications* (Beverly Hills, CA: Sage, 1973), 147–76.

11. Herbert Krugman, "The Impact of Television Advertising: Learning without Involvement," *Public Opinion Quarterly* 29 (Fall 1965): 349–56; Robert Lavidge and Gary Steiner, "A Model for Predictive Measurements of Advertising Effectiveness," *Journal of Marketing* 25 (October 1961): 59–62.

12. Stuart Elliott and Constance L. Hays, "Coca-Cola Will Try to Promote Its Top Brand with More Emotion," *New York Times on the Web* (October 19, 1999).

13. Daniel J. Howard and Charles Gengler, "Emotional Contagion Effects on Product Attitudes," *Journal of Consumer Research* 28 (September 2001): 189–201.

14. For some recent studies, see Andrew B. Aylesworth and Scott B. MacKenzie, "Context Is Key: The Effect of Program-Induced Mood on Thoughts about the Ad," *Journal of Advertising* 27 (Summer 1998): 17; Angela Y. Lee and Brian Sternthal, "The Effects of Positive Mood on Memory," *Journal of Consumer Research* 26 (September 1999): 115–28; Michael J. Barone, Paul W. Miniard, and Jean B. Romeo, "The Influence of Positive Mood on Brand Extension Evaluations," *Journal of Consumer Research* 26 (March 2000): 386–401. For a study that compared the effectiveness of emotional appeals across cultures, see Jennifer L. Aaker and Patti Williams, "Empathy versus Pride: The Influence of Emotional Appeals across Cultures," *Journal of Consumer Research* 25 (December 1998): 241–61. For research that relates mood (depression) to acceptance of health-related messages, see Punam Anand Keller, Isaac M. Lipkus, and Barbara K. Rimer, "Depressive Realism and Health Risk Accuracy: The Negative Consequences of Positive Mood," *Journal of Consumer Research* 29 (June 2002): 57–69.

15. Punam Anand, Morris B. Holbrook, and Debra Stephens, "The Formation of Affective Judgments: The Cognitive–Affective Model versus the Independence Hypothesis," *Journal of Consumer Research* 15 (December 1988): 386–91; Richard S. Lazarus, "Thoughts on the Relations between Emotion and Cognition," *American Psychologist* 37, no. 9 (1982): 1019–24.

16. Robert B. Zajonc, "Feeling and Thinking: Preferences Need No Inferences," *American Psychologist* 35, no. 2 (1980): 151–75.

17. Patricia Winters Lauro, "Advertisers Want to Know What People Really Think," *New York Times on the Web* (April 13, 2000); Ian Austen, "Soon: Computers That Know You Hate Them," *New York Times on the Web* (January 6, 2000).

18. Banwari Mittal, "The Role of Affective Choice Mode in the Consumer Purchase of Expressive Products," *Journal of Economic Psychology* 4, no. 9 (1988): 499–524.

19. Scot Burton and Donald R. Lichtenstein, "The Effect of Ad Claims and Ad Context on Attitude Toward the Advertisement," *Journal of Advertising* 17, no. 1 (1988): 3–11; Karen A. Machleit and R. Dale Wilson, "Emotional Feelings and Attitude toward the Advertisement: The Roles of Brand Familiarity and Repetition," *Journal of Advertising* 17, no. 3 (1988): 27–35; Scott B. Mackenzie and Richard J. Lutz, "An Empirical Examination of the Structural Antecedents of Attitude toward the Ad in an Advertising Pretesting Context," *Journal of Marketing* 53 (April 1989): 48–65; Scott B. Mackenzie, Richard J. Lutz, and George E. Belch, "The Role of Attitude toward the Ad as a Mediator of Advertising Effectiveness: A Test of Competing Explanations," *Journal of Marketing Research* 23 (May 1986): 130–43; Darrel D. Muehling and Russell N. Laczniak, "Advertising's Immediate and Delayed Influence on Brand Attitudes: Considerations Across Message-Involvement Levels," *Journal of Advertising* 17, no. 4 (1988): 23–34; Mark A. Pavelchak, Meryl P. Gardner, and V. Carter Broach, "Effect of Ad Pacing and Optimal Level of Arousal on Attitude toward the Ad," in Rebecca H. Holman and Michael R. Solomon, eds., *Advances in Consumer Research* 18 (Provo, UT: Association for Consumer Research, 1991): 94–99. Some research evidence indicates that a separate attitude is also formed regarding the brand name itself; see George M. Zinkhan and Claude R. Martin Jr., "New Brand Names and Inferential Beliefs: Some Insights on Naming New Products," *Journal of Business Research* 15 (1987): 157–72.

20. John P. Murry Jr., John L. Lastovicka, and Surendra N. Singh, "Feeling and Liking Responses to Television Programs: An Examination of Two Explanations for Media-Context Effects," *Journal of Consumer Research* 18 (March 1992): 441–51.

21. Barbara Stern and Judith Lynne Zaichkowsky, "The Impact of 'Entertaining' Advertising on Consumer Responses," *Australian Marketing Researcher* 14 (August 1991): 68–80.

22. H. Shanker Krishnan and Robert E. Smith, "The Relative Endurance of Attitudes, Confidence, and Attitude Behavior Consistency: The Role of Information Source and Delay," *Journal of Consumer Psychology* 7, no. 3 (1998): 273–98.

23. For a recent study that examined the impact of skepticism on advertising issues, see David M. Boush, Marian Friestad, and Gregory M. Rose, "Adolescent Skepticism toward TV Advertising and Knowledge of Advertiser Tactics," *Journal of Consumer Research* 21 (June 1994): 167–75.

24. Basil G. Englis, "Consumer Emotional Reactions to Television Advertising and Their Effects on Message Recall," in S. Agres, J. A. Edell, and T. M. Dubitsky, eds., *Emotion in Advertising: Theoretical and Practical Explorations* (Westport, CT: Quorum Books, 1990), 231–54.

25. Morris B. Holbrook and Rajeev Batra, "Assessing the Role of Emotions as Mediators of Consumer Responses to Advertising," *Journal of Consumer Research* 14 (December 1987): 404–20.

26. Marian Burke and Julie Edell, "Ad Reactions over Time: Capturing Changes in the Real World," *Journal of Consumer Research* 13 (June 1986): 114–18.

27. Herbert Kelman, "Compliance, Identification, and Internalization: Three Processes of Attitude Change," *Journal of Conflict Resolution* 2 (1958): 51–60.

28. See Sharon E. Beatty and Lynn R. Kahle, "Alternative Hierarchies of the Attitude–Behavior Relationship: The Impact of Brand Commitment and Habit," *Journal of the Academy of Marketing Science* 16 (Summer 1988): 1–10.

29. David A. Aaker and Donald E. Bruzzone, "Causes of Irritation in Advertising," *Journal of Marketing* 49 (Spring 1985): 47–57.

30. Leon Festinger, *A Theory of Cognitive Dissonance* (Stanford, CA: Stanford University Press, 1957).

31. Chester A. Insko and John Schopler, *Experimental Social Psychology* (New York: Academic Press, 1972).

32. Robert E. Knox and James A. Inkster, "Postdecision Dissonance at Post Time," *Journal of Personality and Social Psychology* 8, no. 4 (1968): 319–23.

33. Daryl J. Bem, "Self-Perception Theory," in Leonard Berkowitz, ed., *Advances in Experimental Social Psychology* (New York: Academic Press, 1972), 1–62.

34. Jonathan L. Freedman and Scott C. Fraser, "Compliance Without Pressure: The Foot-in-the-Door Technique," *Journal of Personality and Social Psychology* 4 (August 1966): 195–202. For further consideration

of possible explanations for this effect, see William DeJong, "An Examination of Self-Perception Mediation of the Foot-in-the-Door Effect," *Journal of Personality and Social Psychology* 37 (December 1979): 221–31; Alice M. Tybout, Brian Sternthal, and Bobby J. Calder, "Information Availability as a Determinant of Multiple-Request Effectiveness," *Journal of Marketing Research* 20 (August 1988): 280–90.

35. David H. Furse, David W. Stewart, and David L. Rados, "Effects of Foot-in-the-Door, Cash Incentives and Follow-ups on Survey Response," *Journal of Marketing Research* 18 (November 1981): 473–78; Carol A. Scott, "The Effects of Trial and Incentives on Repeat Purchase Behavior," *Journal of Marketing Research* 13 (August 1976): 263–69.

36. R. B. Cialdini, J. E. Vincent, S. K. Lewis, J. Catalan, D. Wheeler, and B. L. Darby, "Reciprocal Concessions Procedure for Inducing Compliance: The Door-in-the-Face Effect," *Journal of Personality and Social Psychology* 31 (1975): 200–215.

37. Muzafer Sherif and Carl I. Hovland, *Social Judgment: Assimilation and Contrast Effects in Communication and Attitude Change* (New Haven, CT: Yale University Press, 1961).

38. See Joan Meyers-Levy and Brian Sternthal, "A Two-Factor Explanation of Assimilation and Contrast Effects," *Journal of Marketing Research* 30 (August 1993): 359–68.

39. Mark B. Traylor, "Product Involvement and Brand Commitment," *Journal of Advertising Research* (December 1981): 51–56.

40. Fritz Heider, *The Psychology of Interpersonal Relations* (New York: Wiley, 1958).

41. R. B. Cialdini, R. J. Borden, A. Thorne, M. R. Walker, S. Freeman, and L. R. Sloan, "Basking in Reflected Glory: Three (Football) Field Studies," *Journal of Personality and Social Psychology* 34 (1976): 366–75; "Boola Boola, Moola Moola," *Sports Illustrated* (February 16, 1998): 28.

42. Leslie Kaufman, "Enough Talk," *Newsweek* (August 18, 1997): 48–49.

43. William L. Wilkie, *Consumer Behavior* (New York: Wiley, 1986).

44. M. Fishbein, "An Investigation of the Relationships between Beliefs about an Object and the Attitude toward that Object," *Human Relations* 16 (1983): 233–40.

45. Allan Wicker, "Attitudes versus Actions: The Relationship of Verbal and Overt Behavioral Responses to Attitude Objects," *Journal of Social Issues* 25 (Autumn 1969): 65.

46. Laura Bird, "Loved the Ad. May (or May Not) Buy the Product," *Wall Street Journal* (April 7, 1994): B1.

47. Icek Ajzen and Martin Fishbein, "Attitude–Behavior Relations: A Theoretical Analysis and Review of Empirical Research," *Psychological Bulletin* 84 (September 1977): 888–918.

48. Morris B. Holbrook and William J. Havlena, "Assessing the Real-to-Artificial Generalizability of Multi-Attribute Attitude Models in Tests of New Product Designs," *Journal of Marketing Research* 25 (February 1988): 25–35; Terence A. Shimp and Alican Kavas, "The Theory of Reasoned Action Applied to Coupon Usage," *Journal of Consumer Research* 11 (December 1984): 795–809.

49. R. P. Abelson, "Conviction," *American Psychologist* 43 (1988): 267–75; R. E. Petty and J. A. Krosnick, *Attitude Strength: Antecedents and Consequences* (Mahwah, NJ: Erlbaum, 1995); Ida E. Berger and Linda F. Alwitt, "Attitude Conviction: A Self-Reflective Measure of Attitude Strength," *Journal of Social Behavior and Personality* 11, no. 3 (1996): 557–72.

50. Berger and Alwitt, "Attitude Conviction: A Self-Reflective Measure of Attitude Strength."

51. Richard P. Bagozzi, Hans Baumgartner, and Youjae Yi, "Coupon Usage and the Theory of Reasoned Action," in Rebecca H. Holman and Michael R. Solomon, eds., *Advances in Consumer Research* 18 (Provo, UT: Association for Consumer Research, 1991): 24–27; Edward F. McQuarrie, "An Alternative to Purchase Intentions: The Role of Prior Behavior in Consumer Expenditure on Computers," *Journal of the Market Research Society* 30 (October 1988): 407–37; Arch G. Woodside and William O. Bearden, "Longitudinal Analysis of Consumer Attitude, Intention, and Behavior Toward Beer Brand Choice," in William D. Perrault Jr., ed., *Advances in Consumer Research* 4 (Ann Arbor, MI: Association for Consumer Research, 1977): 349–56.

52. Andy Greenfield, "The Naked Truth (Studying Consumer Behavior)," *Brandweek* (October 13, 1997): 22.

53. Michael J. Ryan and Edward H. Bonfield, "The Fishbein Extended Model and Consumer Behavior," *Journal of Consumer Research* 2 (1975): 118–36.

54. Blair H. Sheppard, Jon Hartwick, and Paul R. Warshaw, "The Theory of Reasoned Action: A Meta-Analysis of Past Research with Recommendations for Modifications and Future Research," *Journal of Consumer Research* 15 (December 1988): 325–43.

55. Joseph A. Cote, James McCullough, and Michael Reilly, "Effects of Unexpected Situations on Behavior–Intention Differences: A

Garbology Analysis," *Journal of Consumer Research* 12 (September 1985): 188–94.

56. Russell H. Fazio, Martha C. Powell, and Carol J. Williams, "The Role of Attitude Accessibility in the Attitude-to-Behavior Process," *Journal of Consumer Research* 16 (December 1989): 280–88; Robert E. Smith and William R. Swinyard, "Attitude–Behavior Consistency: The Impact of Product Trial Versus Advertising," *Journal of Marketing Research* 20 (August 1983): 257–67.

57. Kulwant Singh, Siew Meng Leong, Chin Tiong Tan, and Kwei Cheong Wong, "A Theory of Reasoned Action Perspective of Voting Behavior: Model and Empirical Test," *Psychology & Marketing* 12, no. 1 (January 1995): 37–51; Joseph A. Cote and Patriya S. Tansuhaj, "Culture Bound Assumptions in Behavior Intention Models," in Thom Srull, ed., *Advances in Consumer Research* 16 (Provo, UT: Association for Consumer Research, 1989): 105–109.

58. Richard P. Bagozzi and Paul R. Warshaw, "Trying to Consume," *Journal of Consumer Research* 17 (September 1990): 127–40.

59. Barbara Presley Noble, "After Years of Deregulation, a New Push to Inform the Public," *New York Times* (October 27, 1991): F5.

60. Matthew Greenwald and John P. Katosh, "How to Track Changes in Attitudes," *American Demographics* (August 1987): 46.

61. Lisa Guernsey, "Welcome to College. Now Meet Our Sponsor," *New York Times on the Web* (August 17, 1999).

Attitude Change and Interactive Communications

Carrie is sorting through today's mail. Bill, ad, bill, fund-raising letter from a political candidate, an offer for yet another credit card . . . aha! The new edition of *Launch!* Carrie throws down the other junk mail and pops the CD/ROM into her PC. Time to check out the latest music and movies . . . and yes, probably watch some cool commercials also. She's been looking forward to getting her monthly online magazine since she overheard Natalie down at the health club talking about the video interview with Avril Lavigne on this edition.

Carrie fires up the CD/ROM and the interface that looks like a city full of buildings and billboards soon appears. She enters "The Hang" and watches the interview, and then she clicks on the Toyota icon for Toyota and drools through a new commercial for the MR2 Spider. Something to think about. After that, she watches a public service message courtesy of a tobacco company that shows a teenager burning up all of his money to buy cigarettes ("Tobacco is whacko if you're a teen."), and then she previews a few new computer games she might buy for her spaced-out brother Ken. Carrie putters around in a few more locations; she listens to some new music by Afroman, watches a preview of that new J-Lo flick (and a Q/A session with the star), and then just for fun she clicks over to the live *Launch.com* Web site to take a survey and download some more music information. Watching commercials and participating in marketing research projects sure makes a lot more sense when she gets to pick which ones to see and when.

■ CHANGING ATTITUDES THROUGH COMMUNICATION

Consumers are constantly bombarded by messages inducing them to change their attitudes. These persuasion attempts can range from logical arguments to graphic pictures, and from intimidation by peers to exhortations by celebrity spokespeople. And, communications flow both ways—the consumer may seek out information sources in order to learn more about these options. As Carrie's actions show, the choice to access marketing messages on your own terms is changing the way we think about persuasion attempts.

This chapter will review some of the factors that help to determine the effectiveness of marketing communications. Our focus will be on some basic aspects of communication that specifically help to determine how and if attitudes will be created or modified. This objective relates to **persuasion**, which refers to an active attempt to change attitudes. Persuasion is, of course, the central goal of many marketing communications. We'll learn more about how marketers try to accomplish this throughout the chapter, but for now we can set the stage by listing some basic psychological principles that influence people to change their minds or comply with a request:[1]

- *Reciprocity:* People are more likely to give if they receive. That's why including money in a mail survey questionnaire increases the response rate by an average of 65 per cent over surveys that come in an empty envelope.
- *Scarcity:* Items become more attractive when they are less available. In one study that asked people to rate the quality of chocolate chip cookies, participants who only got two cookies liked them better than did those who got 10 of the same kind of cookie. That helps to explain why we tend to value "limited edition" items.
- *Authority:* We'll talk more about the importance of who delivers the message. We tend to believe an authoritative source much more readily. That explains why the American public's opinion shifts 2 percent when a news article is printed in The *New York Times*.
- *Consistency:* As we saw in the last chapter, people try not to contradict themselves in terms of what they say and do about an issue. In one study, students at an Israeli university who solicited donations to help the handicapped doubled the amount they normally collected in a neighborhood by first asking the residents to sign a petition supporting the handicapped two weeks before asking for donations.
- *Liking:* As we'll see later, we tend to agree with those we like or admire. In one study good-looking fund-raisers raised almost twice as much as other volunteers who were not as attractive.
- *Consensus:* We often take into account what others are doing before we decide what to do. We'll talk more about the power of conformity in Chapter 11. This desire to fit in with what others are doing influences our actions—for example, people are more likely to donate to a charity if they first see a list of the names of their neighbors who have already done so.

Decisions, Decisions: Tactical Communications Options

Suppose a car company wants to create an advertising campaign for a new ragtop targeted to young drivers. As it plans this campaign, it must develop a message that will create desire for the car by potential customers. To craft persuasive messages that might persuade someone to buy this car instead of the many others available, we must answer several questions:

- Who will be shown driving the car in an ad? A NASCAR driver? A career woman? A rock star? The source of a message helps to determine consumers' acceptance of it as well as their desire to try the product.

- How should the message be constructed? Should it emphasize the negative consequences of being left out when others are driving cool cars and you're still tooling around in your old clunker? Should it directly compare the car with others already on the market, or maybe present a fantasy in which a tough-minded female executive meets a dashing stranger while cruising down the highway with the top down?
- What media should be used to transmit the message? Should it be depicted in a print ad? On television? Sold door to door? On a Web site? If a print ad is produced, should it be run in the pages of *Jane? Good Housekeeping? Car and Driver?* Sometimes *where* something is said can be as important as *what* is said. Ideally, the attributes of the product should be matched to those of the medium. For example, magazines with high prestige are more effective at communicating messages about overall product image and quality, whereas specialized expert magazines do a better job at conveying factual information.[2]
- What characteristics of the target market might influence the ad's acceptance? If targeted users are frustrated in their daily lives, they might be more receptive to a fantasy appeal. If they're status-oriented, maybe a commercial should show bystanders swooning with admiration as the car cruises by.

The Elements of Communication

Marketers and advertisers have traditionally tried to understand how marketing messages can change consumers' attitudes by thinking in terms of the **communications model**, which specifies that a number of elements are necessary for communication to be achieved. One of these is a source; where the communication originates. Another is the message itself. There are many ways to say something, and the structure of the message has a big effect on how it is perceived. The message must be transmitted via a medium, which could be television, radio, magazines, billboards, personal contact, or even a matchbook cover. Toyota placed its message about the Spider in a sophisticated CD/ROM format that it knew would be accessed by young, cutting-edge consumers—just the ones it was trying to reach. One or more *receivers* (like Carrie) then interpret the message in light of their own experiences. Finally, *feedback* must be received by the source, which uses the reactions of receivers to modify aspects of the message. *Launch* uses the Web to collect such information from its subscribers. Figure 8.1 depicts the traditional communications process.

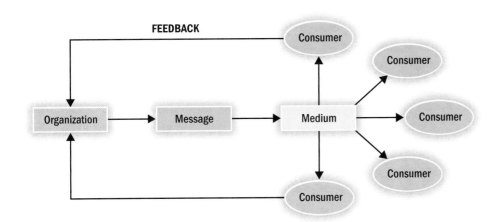

■ FIGURE 8.1
THE TRADITIONAL COMMUNICATIONS MODEL

An Updated View: Interactive Communications

Although Carrie managed to ignore most of the "junk mail" that arrived at her door, she didn't avoid marketing messages—instead she chose which ones she wanted to see. Although the traditional communications model is not entirely wrong, it also doesn't tell the whole story—especially in today's dynamic world of interactivity, in which consumers have many more choices available to them and greater control over which messages they will choose to process.[3] In fact, a popular strategy known as **permission marketing** is based on the idea that a marketer will be much more successful in persuading consumers who have agreed to let him or her try—consumers who "opt out" of listening to the message probably weren't good prospects in the first place.[4] On the other hand, those who say they are interested in learning more are likely to be receptive to marketing communications they have already chosen to see or hear. As the permission marketing concept reminds us, we don't have to just sit there and take it. We have a voice in deciding what messages we choose to see and when—and we exercise that option more and more.

The traditional model was developed to understand mass communications, in which information is transferred from a producer (source) to many consumers (receivers) at one time—typically via print, television, or radio. This perspective essentially views advertising as the process of transferring information to the buyer before a sale. A message is seen as perishable—it is repeated (perhaps frequently) for a fairly short period of time and then it "vanishes" as a new campaign eventually takes its place.

This model was strongly influenced by a group of theorists known as the Frankfurt School, which dominated mass communications research for most of the last century. In this view, the media exert direct and powerful effects on individuals, and often are used by those in power to brainwash and exploit the population. The receiver is basically a passive being—a "couch potato" who simply is the receptacle for many messages—and who is often duped or persuaded to act based on the information he or she is "fed" by the media.

Uses and Gratifications

Is this an accurate picture of the way we relate to marketing communications? Proponents of **uses and gratifications theory** argue instead that consumers are an active, goal-directed audience that draws on mass media as a resource to satisfy needs. Instead of asking what media do *for* or *to* people, they ask what people do *with* the media.[5]

The uses and gratifications approach emphasizes that media compete with other sources to satisfy needs, and that these needs include diversion and entertainment as well as information. This also means that the line between marketing information and entertainment is continuing to blur—especially as companies are being forced to design more attractive retail outlets, catalogs, and Web sites in order to attract consumers. *Launch* accomplishes this by ensuring that the commercial messages it burns into its discs are sufficiently entertaining that its subscribers will *want* to watch them.

Research with young people in Great Britain finds that they rely on advertising for many gratifications including entertainment (some report that the "adverts" are better than the programs), escapism, play (some report singing along with jingles, others make posters out of magazine ads), and self-affirmation (ads can reinforce their own values or provide role models). It's important to note that this perspective is not arguing that media play a uniformly positive role in our lives, only that recipients are making use of the information in a number of ways. For example, marketing messages have the potential to undermine self-esteem as consumers use the media to establish unrealistic standards for behavior, attitudes, or even their own appearance. A comment by one study participant illustrates this negative impact. She observes that when she's watching TV with her boyfriend, "really, it makes you

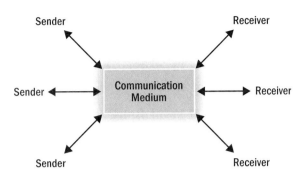

think 'oh no, what must I be like?' I mean you're sitting with your boyfriend and he's saying 'oh, look at her. What a body!' "[6]

Who's in Charge of the Remote?

Whether for good or bad, though, exciting technological and social developments certainly are forcing us to rethink the picture of the passive consumer, as people increasingly are playing a proactive role in communications. In other words, they are to a greater extent becoming partners—rather than potatoes—in the communications process. Their input is helping to shape the messages they and others like them receive, and furthermore, they may seek out these messages rather than sit home and wait to see them on TV or in the paper. Figure 8.2 illustrates this updated approach to interactive communications.

One of the early signs of this communications revolution was the humble hand-held remote control device. As VCRs began to be commonplace in homes, suddenly consumers had more input into what they wanted to watch—and when. No longer did the TV networks decide when they saw their favorite shows, and neither did they necessarily have to forsake a show because it conflicted with another's time slot.

Since that time, of course, our ability to control our media environment has mushroomed. Just ask some of the more than one million people who are now using DVRs (digital video recorders) like TiVo to watch TV shows whenever they wish—and who are skipping over the commercials.[7] Many others have access to video-on-demand or pay-per-view TV. Home-shopping networks encourage us to call in and discuss our passion for cubic zirconium jewelry live on the air. Caller ID devices and answering machines allow us to decide if we will accept a phone call during dinner, and to know if a telemarketer is lurking on the other end before we pick up the phone. A bit of Web surfing allows us to identify kindred spirits around the globe, to request information about products, and even to provide suggestions to product designers and market researchers.

Levels of Interactive Response

A key to understanding the dynamics of interactive marketing communications is to consider exactly what is meant by a response.[8] The early perspective on communications primarily regarded feedback in terms of behavior—did the recipient run out and buy the laundry detergent after being exposed to an ad for it?

However, a variety of other responses are possible as well, including building awareness of the brand, informing us about product features, reminding us to buy a new package when we've run out, and—perhaps most importantly—building a long-term relationship. Therefore, a transaction is one type of response, but forward-thinking marketers realize that customers can interact with them in other valuable ways as well. For this reason it is helpful to distinguish between two basic types of feedback.

● *First-order response:* Direct-marketing vehicles such as catalogs and television infomercials are interactive—if successful, they result in an order, which is most definitely a response! So, let's think of a product offer that directly yields a transaction as a first-order response. In addition to providing revenue, sales data are a valuable source of feedback that allows marketers to gauge the effectiveness of their communications efforts.

● *Second-order response:* However, a marketing communication does not have to immediately result in a purchase to be an important component of interactive marketing. Messages can prompt useful responses from customers, even though these recipients do not necessarily place an order immediately after being exposed to the communication. Carrie may get around to buying that Spider eventually as a result of being exposed to persuasive messages about it. Customer feedback in response to a marketing message that is not in the form of a transaction is a second-order response.

■ THE SOURCE

Regardless of whether a message is received by "snail mail" (netheads' slang for the postal service) or e-mail, common sense tells us that the same words uttered or written by different people can have very different effects. Research on *source effects* has been carried out for more than 50 years. By attributing the same message to different sources and measuring the degree of attitude change that occurs after listeners hear it, it is possible to determine which aspects of a communicator will induce attitude change.[9]

Under most conditions, the source of a message can have a big impact on the likelihood that the message will be accepted. The choice of a source to maximize attitude change can tap into several dimensions. The source can be chosen because he or she is an expert, attractive, famous, or even a "typical" consumer who is both likable and trustworthy. Two particularly important source characteristics are *credibility* and *attractiveness.*[10]

How do marketing specialists decide whether to stress credibility or attractiveness when choosing a message source? There should be a match between the needs of the recipient and the potential rewards offered by the source. When this match occurs, the recipient is more motivated to process the message. People who tend to be sensitive about social acceptance and the opinions of others, for example, are more persuaded by an attractive source, whereas those who are more internally oriented are swayed by a credible, expert source.[11]

The choice may also depend on the type of product. A positive source can help to reduce risk and increase message acceptance overall, but particular types of sources are more effective at reducing different kinds of risk. Experts are effective at changing attitudes toward utilitarian products that have high performance risk, such as vacuums (i.e., they may be complex and not work as expected). Celebrities are more effective when they focus on products such as jewelry and furniture that have high social risk; the user of such products is aware of their effect on the impression others have of him or her. Finally, "typical" consumers, who are appealing sources because of their similarity to the recipient, tend to be most effective when providing real-life endorsements for everyday products that are low risk, such as cookies.[12]

Source Credibility

Source credibility refers to a source's perceived expertise, objectivity, or trustworthiness. This dimension relates to consumers' beliefs that a communicator is competent, and he or she is willing to provide the necessary information to adequately evaluate competing products. A credible source can be particularly persuasive when the consumer has not yet learned much about a product or formed an opinion of it.[13] The decision to pay an expert or a celebrity to tout a product can be a very costly one, but researchers have concluded that on average the investment is worth it simply because the announcement of an endorsement contract is often used by market analysts to evaluate a firm's potential profitability, thereby affecting its expected return. On average, then, the impact of endorsements on stock returns appears to be so positive that it offsets the cost of hiring the spokesperson.[14]

The Sleeper Effect

Although in general more positive sources tend to increase attitude change, exceptions can occur. Sometimes a source can be obnoxious or disliked and still manage to be effective at getting the product's message across. A case in point is Mr. Whipple, the irritating but well-known television character who scolds toilet paper shoppers, "Please don't squeeze the Charmin!" In some instances the differences in attitude change between positive sources and less positive sources seem to get erased over time. After a while people appear to "forget" about the negative source and wind up changing their attitudes anyway. This process is known as the **sleeper effect**.[15]

The explanation for the sleeper effect is a subject of debate, as is the more basic question regarding whether and when it really exists. Initially, the *dissociative cue hypothesis* proposed that over time the message and the source become disassociated in the consumer's mind. The message remains on its own in memory, causing the delayed attitude change.[16]

Another explanation is the *availability-valence hypothesis*, which emphasizes the selectivity of memory owing to limited capacity.[17] If the associations linked to the negative source are less available than those linked to the message information, the residual impact of the message enhances persuasion. Consistent with this view, the sleeper effect has been obtained only when the message was encoded deeply; it had stronger associations in memory than did the source.[18]

Building Credibility

Credibility can be enhanced if the source's qualifications are perceived as somehow relevant to the product being endorsed. This linkage can overcome other objections people may have to the endorser or the product. Ronald Biggs, whose claim to fame was his 1963 role in "The Great Train Robbery" in the United Kingdom, successfully served as a spokesman in Brazil for a company that makes door locks—a topic about which he is presumably knowledgeable![19]

That's what makes Josh Sundquist a great message source for Jones Soda, even though he's not exactly someone most would think of as a glamorous celebrity. Sundquist lost a leg to cancer and he sports a funky, neon-green metal pole instead of a natural limb. The cult drink company sponsors the teenager on the motivational speaking circuit, and in return the cancer survivor wears a Jones sweatshirt and drinks a Jones Soda while he gives his speeches.[20]

It's important to note that what is credible to one consumer segment may be a turn-off to another. To the disbelief and outrage of many in the Western world, there are reports that Yeslam bin Laden, one of Osama bin Laden's 53 siblings, is going to introduce a Bin Laden clothing line in Arab markets.[21] Indeed, rebellious or even deviant celebrities may be attractive to some for just that reason. Tommy Hilfiger cultivated a rebellious, street-smart image by using rapper Snoop Doggy Dogg (who was acquitted of murder charges) to help launch his clothing line and Coolio, a former crack addict and thief, as a runway model.[22] Parents may not be thrilled by these message sources—but isn't that the point?

Source Biases

A consumer's beliefs about a product's attributes can be weakened if the source is perceived to be the victim of bias in presenting information.[23] *Knowledge bias* implies that a source's knowledge about a topic is not accurate. *Reporting bias*

Marketing Pitfall

Testimonials by authority figures are strongly valued in the medical arena, where patients often need to make costly and important (sometimes life-or-death) decisions without a whole lot of scientific knowledge to evaluate competing brands or treatments. Physicians are authority figures that we count on to give us objective advice, but occasionally this trust is violated. Recent court cases involving pharmaceutical companies show how this can happen. In some situations doctors have been paid to allow pharmaceutical sales representatives into their examining rooms to meet with patients, review medical charts, and even recommend what medicines to prescribe—without identifying them as salespeople. Drug manufacturers also may reward physicians who prescribe high volumes of their products with lavish dinners and trips, or by paying them as speakers and consultants. One major company paid doctors to write favorable articles for medical journals about one of its new drugs and even hired a marketing company to write the first drafts.[30] A recent survey of physicians found that 37 percent said they had accepted some kind of compensation from pharmaceutical companies.

Drug companies also pursue celebrity endorsements to persuade the rest of us to try their products. In most cases the firms simply pay a famous person for his or her endorsement because they use the drug, as when Lance Armstrong touts cancer drugs for Bristol-Myers Squibb or Bob Dole plugs Viagra. More recently, though, drug companies are turning to a more subtle approach by placing stars on television talk shows to promote a drug. For example, actor Rob Lowe went on the air to raise public awareness of a side effect of chemotherapy called febrile neutropenia (his father suffered from the condition at one point). He was paid to make the appearances by Amgen, a company that happens to make a treatment for the condition called Neulasta.

occurs when a source has the required knowledge, but his or her willingness to convey it accurately is compromised, as when a star tennis player is paid by a racket manufacturer to use its products exclusively. The source's credentials might be appropriate, but the fact that the expert is perceived as a "hired gun" compromises believability.

Companies appreciate the value of having experts validate their products and sometimes their efforts to pile up these testimonials can get them into trouble. For example, Microsoft was criticized when it offered to pay "travel costs" for professors if they presented papers at conferences and mentioned how Microsoft programs helped them in their work.[24]

Concerns are growing in the advertising world about the public's skepticism regarding celebrities who endorse products for money. It doesn't help matters when Britney Spears appears in lavish commercials for Pepsi-Cola but is caught on camera drinking Coca-Cola, or when Shaquille O'Neal at various times pledges his fast-food allegiance to Burger King, McDonald's, *and* Taco Bell. Tiger Woods promoted Rolex's Tudor watches for five years, but then he abruptly switched to Swiss rival TAG Heuer. Although Tiger explained the defection simply by noting that "My tastes have changed," it's possible that the estimated $2 million he's now getting for this new endorsement was a factor.[25]

What's a marketer to do? One increasingly popular solution is to involve celebrities in the actual design of the products they're pitching. Michael Jordan oversees the design of Nike's Jordan line of apparel and footwear, Star Jones of TV's *The View* is director of style for Payless shoes, and actresses like Meredith Baxter and Victoria Principal create skin-care products for home-shopping networks. Jennifer Lopez even had veto power over the design of the bottle for her new fragrance, "Glow by J-Lo."[26]

Hype Versus Buzz: The Corporate Paradox

Obviously, many marketers spend lavishly to create marketing messages that they hope will convince hordes of customers that they are the best. There's the rub—in many cases they may be trying too hard! We can think of this as the **Corporate Paradox**—the more involved a company appears to be in the dissemination of news about its products, the less credible it becomes.[27] As we'll see in Chapter 11, consumer word of mouth typically is the most convincing kind of message. As Table 8.1 shows, **buzz** is word of mouth that is viewed as authentic and generated by customers. In contrast, **hype** is dismissed as inauthentic—corporate propaganda planted by a company with an axe to grind. So, the challenge to marketers is to get the word out there without looking like they are working at it. That's why Coca-Cola decided to promote its newly redesigned can that resembles the trendy Red Bull brand by placing it in select Manhattan nightclubs and boutiques. Marketing strategists reasoned that young trendsetters would be more likely to tune in to the brand's new look if they "discovered" it in chic watering holes rather than learning about it in a bells-and-whistles ad campaign.[28]

The now-famous movie *Blair Witch Project*, which led many viewers to believe the fictional treatment was in fact a real documentary, demonstrated the power of a brand that seems as if it's not one. Some marketers are trying to borrow the veneer of buzz by mounting "stealth" campaigns that seem as if they are untouched by the corporate world. *Buzz building* has become the new mantra at many companies that recognize the power of underground word of mouth.[29] Indeed, a bit of a cottage industry has sprung up as some firms begin to specialize in the corporate shill business by planting comments on Web sites made to look as if they originated from actual consumers. Consider these recent examples:

- Building on the success of its resurrected Buddy Lee icon, Lee Apparel commissioned 15 Web sites devoted to the diminutive doll that looked "horrible, as if fans created them" according to an employee of the company that created the

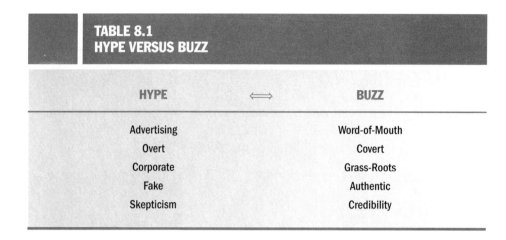

**TABLE 8.1
HYPE VERSUS BUZZ**

HYPE	⟺	BUZZ
Advertising		Word-of-Mouth
Overt		Covert
Corporate		Grass-Roots
Fake		Authentic
Skepticism		Credibility

In this case, the actor did not violate U.S. Food and Drug Administration regulations because he didn't mention the drug by name. If he had, he would be required to summarize the main side effects of the drug and to tell consumers where to find more detailed information via an 800 number or a Web site. Other movie stars including Lauren Bacall and Kathleen Turner have been paid to help promote drugs or other medical products on morning shows like *Today* and *Good Morning America*. In a segment on *The Early Show*, rock singer Ann Wilson of the band Heart promoted a silicon band that is surgically fastened around the stomach to control obesity. After learning that some celebrities who appeared on its news programs to talk about their health problems were being paid by drug companies, CNN recently announced a new policy requiring the network to tell viewers about the stars' financial ties to corporations.[31]

sites. The goal of was to make it look as if people were spontaneously turning on to the Buddy Lee phenomenon.[32]

- Dodge's Ram truck made a splash with a Web site supposedly generated by fans to organize drag races in several cities. The e-mail features amateurishly shot footage of a drag race and contains no reference to the Dodge connection, just a shot of the Ram's grille. Staged drag races were held where, of course, only Ram trucks emerged victorious. Videos of the wins were then posted to the Web site. Bogus letters were sent to editors of local newspapers protesting the rise in street racing and mentioning the Dodge Ram involvement. Supposedly, the guerrilla campaign was so hush-hush even the top brass at the car company were kept in the dark.[33]

- When RCA records wanted to create a buzz around teen pop singer Christina Aguilera, it hired a team of young people to swarm the Web and chat about her on popular teen sites like ***alloy.com***, ***bolt.com***, and ***gurl.com***. Posing as fans, they posted entries raving about her new material. Just before one of her albums debuted, RCA also hired a direct-marketing company to e-mail electronic postcards filled with song snippets and biographical information to 50,000 Web addresses.[34] The album quickly went to number one on the charts.

As powerful as these tactics are, they have the potential to poison the well in a big way. Web surfers, already skeptical about what they see and hear, may get to the point where they assume every "authentic" site they find is really a corporate front. Until then, however, buzz building online is going strong. Still, there's no beating the impact of a marketing message that really does originate with product users. For example, a homemade Web site created by two self-confessed "nerds" named Louis and Ish documented their quest for coolness—which for some bizarre reason they decided would be found at a Wendy's restaurant. Their search took on mystical qualities: "As though from the voice of God Himself, we realized our purpose: to visit every Wendy's we had knowledge of, limited only by our $5.50–$6 an hour jobs."[35] Maybe they need to get out more?

Source Attractiveness

Source attractiveness refers to the source's perceived social value. This quality can emanate from the person's physical appearance, personality, social status, or his or her similarity to the receiver (we like to listen to people who are like us). A compelling source has great value and endorsement deals are constantly in the works. Even dead sources can be attractive: The great-grandson of the artist Renoir is putting his famous ancestor's name on bottled water, and the Picasso family licensed their name to the French auto maker Citroen.[36] Former boxer George Foreman made endorsement history by becoming the first celebrity to sell his

To stimulate demand for milk, an industry trade group tapped a huge range of celebrities to show off their milk mustaches.

name in perpetuity to the company that has sold more than 10 million of George Foremans Lean Mean Fat Reducing Grilling Machines. In exchange for $137.5 million, Foreman agreed never to endorse rival cookware, though he is still free to pitch other products.[37] That's a lot of low-fat burgers.

"What Is Beautiful Is Good"

Almost everywhere we turn, beautiful people are trying to persuade us to buy or do something. Our society places a very high premium on physical attractiveness, and we tend to assume that people who are good-looking are smarter, cooler, and happier. Such an assumption is called a halo effect, which occurs when persons who rank high on one dimension are assumed to excel on others as well. We can explain this effect in terms of the consistency principle discussed in Chapter 7, which states that people are more comfortable when all of their judgments about a person go together. This notion has been termed the "what is beautiful is good" stereotype.[38]

A physically attractive source tends to facilitate attitude change. His or her degree of attractiveness exerts at least modest effects on consumers' purchase intentions or product evaluation.[39] How does this happen?

One explanation is that physical attractiveness functions as a cue that facilitates or modifies information processing by directing consumers' attention to relevant marketing stimuli. Some evidence indicates that consumers pay more attention to ads that contain attractive models, though not necessarily to the ad copy.[40] In other words, an ad with a beautiful person may stand a better chance of getting noticed but not necessarily read. We may enjoy looking at a beautiful or handsome person, but these positive feelings do not necessarily affect product attitudes or purchase intentions.[41]

Beauty can also function as a source of information. The effectiveness of highly attractive spokespeople in ads appears to be largely limited to those situations in which the advertised product is overtly related to attractiveness or sexuality.[42] The *social adaptation perspective* assumes that the perceiver will weight information seen to be instrumental in forming an attitude more heavily. As we saw in Chapter 2, we filter out irrelevant information to minimize cognitive effort.

Under the right circumstances, an endorser's level of attractiveness constitutes a source of information instrumental to the attitude change process and thus functions as a central, task-relevant cue.[43] An attractive spokesperson, for this reason, is more likely to be an effective source when the product is relevant to attractiveness. For example, attractiveness affects attitudes toward ads about perfume or cologne (where attractiveness is relevant) but not toward coffee ads (where attractiveness is not relevant).

Star Power: Celebrities as Communications Sources

Celebrity endorsers don't come cheap, but many advertisers continue to believe in their effectiveness. Tiger Woods is now the richest endorser in sports history, with an estimated income of $62 million per year (not counting the money he makes actually winning golf tournaments!).[44] Why do stars command this kind of money? One study found that famous faces capture attention and are processed more efficiently by the brain than are "ordinary" faces.[45] Celebrities increase awareness of a firm's advertising and enhance both company image and brand attitudes.[46] A celebrity endorsement strategy can be an effective way to differentiate among similar products; this is especially important when consumers do not perceive many actual differences among competitors, as often occurs when brands are in the mature stage of the product life cycle.

Star power works because celebrities embody *cultural meanings*—they symbolize important categories such as status and social class (a "working-class hero," such as Drew Carey), gender (a "ladies man," such as Leonardo diCaprio), age (the boyish Michael J. Fox), and even personality types (the eccentric Kramer on *Seinfeld*). Ideally, the advertiser decides what meanings the product should convey (that is, how it should be positioned in the marketplace), and then chooses a celebrity who has come to embody a similar meaning. The product's meaning thus moves from the manufacturer to the consumer, using the star as a vehicle.[47]

Singer/actress J-Lo or Beyonce Knowles? Quarterback Brett Favre or Michael Vick? With all those famous people out there, how does a firm decide who should be the source of its marketing messages? For celebrity campaigns to be effective, the endorser must have a clear and popular image. In addition, the celebrity's image and that of the product he or she endorses should be similar—this is known as the **match-up hypothesis**.[48] Many promotional strategies employing stars fail because the endorser has not been selected very carefully—some marketers just assume that because a person is "famous" he or she will serve as a successful spokesperson. Pretesting the images of celebrities can increase the probability of consumer acceptance.

One widely used technique is the *Q rating* (Q stands for quality) developed by a market research company. This rating considers two factors in surveys: consumers' level of familiarity with a name, and the number of respondents who indicate that a

Marketing Opportunity

Celebrities often pitch well-known brands, but sometimes they're also responsible for making the products stars in their own right. Nowhere is this star-making power more pronounced than in the world of hip-hop. For example, Busta Rhymes and P. Diddy almost single-handedly made Courvoisier the "official" drink of the hip-hop nation. In a popular video, the two music idols defeat evildoers, get the girls, and toast their triumphs with "yack," hip-hop's shorthand for cognac. Courvoisier's U.S. sales have skyrocketed and the drink's brand manager says this is largely because Busta made the drink "the hero of the song." Other luxury products that have benefited from becoming hip-hop icons include the Cadillac Escalade, Cristal champagne, Burberry, Prada, and Louis Vuitton.

Now, some hip-hop artists are recognizing their power to push a brand, so the free ride may be ending. Steve Stout, an influential executive with Interscope Records, is introducing an expensive new cigar brand called Vino Platinum. Jay-Z and his partners bought a European vodka concern called Armadale after seeing how big a boost he gave to Belvedere (another pricey vodka) by mentioning it in several of his hit songs. And, it seems the record labels have figured things out as well—the talk is they are going to try to charge brands in return for giving them a starring role in songs and videos.[49]

Omega uses tennis star Anna Kournikova as a celebrity endorser.

Anna Kournikova's Choice

Tennis star Anna Kournikova chooses the Constellation «Quadra» in steel

Ω
OMEGA
www.omegawatches.com

person, program, or character is a favorite. For example, one of the reasons Amgen chose actor Rob Lowe to spearhead the Neulasta drug campaign we mentioned previously is that his Q rating was particularly high among women age 50 and older; they are prime targets for the drug.[50]

Nonhuman Endorsers

Celebrities can be effective endorsers, but there are drawbacks to using them. As noted previously, their motives may be suspect if they plug products that don't fit their images or if they come to be seen as never having met a product they didn't like (for a fee). They may be involved in a scandal or upset customers, as when Madonna's controversial comments about the Catholic Church caused trouble for Coca-Cola. Or, they may be *prima donnas* who don't show up on time for a shoot or who are overly demanding.

For these reasons some marketers seek alternatives, including cartoon characters and mascots. After all, as the marketing director for a company that manufactures costumed characters for sports teams and businesses points out, "You don't have to worry about your mascot checking into rehab."

Some big companies are trying this approach. As we saw in Chapter 1, Sony Electronics adopted a blue alien character named Plato to sell its Walkman brand. Roots Canada Ltd., the Toronto clothing company behind the 2002 U.S. Olympic team's popular uniforms, employs a "Buddy the Beaver" mascot to promote its outlets. Roots' director of communications observed, "A lot of our stores are in shopping malls. Malls are crowded. People don't pay attention. But it's hard to ignore a seven-foot-tall beaver."[51]

Talking stuffed animals aside, a lot of the real action these days is in the use of virtual models. An **avatar** is the manifestation of a Hindu deity in superhuman or animal form. In the computing world it has come to mean a cyberspace presence represented by a character that you can move around inside a visual, graphical world. Many consumers became more aware of these cybermodels following the recent movie *Simone*, which starred Al Pacino as a washed-up director who creates a virtual actress that the public believes is real. Although a flesh-and-blood woman named Rachel Roberts played the title role, New Line Cinema kept her existence a secret for almost two years as it tried to create a buzz that Simone really was a computer concoction.[52]

Avatars like Simone originated in computer games like The Sims, but now they are starting to appear in online advertising and on e-commerce sites as a mechanism for enhancing the online experience. For example, Brown & Williamson Tobacco Corp. developed a high-tech vending machine featuring a cast of virtual characters on a video screen who "speak" to customers as they are choosing a brand. When a smoker tries to buy a pack of Marlboros made by rival Philip Morris Cos., a virtual vixen with a sultry voice and lurid red lipstick entices him or her to switch to Lucky Strikes instead: "Toasted and delicious, and I'll give you a pack for 75 cents off."[53]

Now, rock bands, soft drink makers, and other big-time marketers are using avatars. Coca-Cola Co. recently launched an avatar-populated site for the Hong Kong market where avatars mill around and chat in a Coke-sponsored world. British Telecom also is testing such products as avatar e-mail, software that makes the sender's face appear and speak the message aloud.[54]

The creation of avatars for commercial formats is evolving into a cottage industry as demand for compelling figures begins to grow. For example, the German firm No DNA GmbH (*www.nodna.com*) offers a variety of "virtualstars." These are computer-generated figures that appear as caricatures, "vuppets" (cartoon-type mascots and animals) and "replicants" that are doubles of real people. Its models receive hundreds of love letters and even a few marriage proposals.[55]

THE GLOBAL LOOKING GLASS

Like the Romans before it, the empire of the Golden Arches has finally succumbed to the indomitable spirit of Asterix the Gaul. Ronald McDonald has been retired as the icon of McDonald's France, replaced by the Gallic nationalist comic-book hero. Ironies abound, of course, since Asterix had been something of an anti-McDonald's icon, appropriated by anti-globalization protestors such as Mac-basher Jose Bove to symbolize French resistance to foreign encroachment. Resentment of the perceived "McDonaldization" of their culture runs high in France—the influential daily *Le Monde*, for example, warns that McDonald's "commercial hegemony threatens agriculture and (its) cultural hegemony insidiously ruins alimentary behavior—sacred reflections of French identity."

Protestors in France and around the world take McDonald's to symbolize all that America stands for; the company's own marketers work to identify the brand with the tastes and cultural preferences of the target population. In France, that has meant deploying "ugly American" caricatures in its ads and substituting Asterix for Ronald McDonald. The general idea is to make the famously malcontented French youth (in their Levis and Nikes) feel comfortable stopping in for a Big Mac on their way home from an anti-American demonstration.

Source: Adapted from Tony Karon, "Adieu, Ronald McDonald: McDonald's Doesn't Want to Change the World, It Simply Wants to Fit In," *Time.com*, January 24, 2002.

A German firm called NoDNA offers its own stable of cybermodels such as Tyra, who is shown here.

www.noDNA.com

The advantages of virtual avatars compared to flesh-and-blood models include the ability to change the avatar in real time to suit the needs of the target audience or individual consumer. From an advertising perspective they are likely to be more cost-effective than hiring a real person. From a personal selling and customer service perspective they have the ability to handle multiple customers at any one time, they are not geographically limited, and they are operational 24/7, thus freeing up company employees and sales personnel to perform other activities.

■ THE MESSAGE

A major study of more than 1,000 commercials identified factors that determine whether or not a commercial message will be persuasive. The single most important feature was whether the communications contained a brand-differentiating message. In other words, did the communication stress a unique attribute or benefit of the product?[56] Table 8.2 lists some other good and bad elements.

TABLE 8.2 POSITIVE AND NEGATIVE EFFECTS OF ELEMENTS IN TELEVISION COMMERCIALS	
Positive Effects	**Negative Effects**
Showing convenience of use	Extensive information on components, ingredients, or nutrition
Showing new product or improved features	Outdoor setting (message gets lost)
Costing background (i.e., people are incidental to message)	Large number of on-screen characters
Indirect comparison to other products	Graphic displays
Demonstration of the product in use	
Demonstration of tangible results (e.g., bouncy hair)	
An actor playing the role of an ordinary person	
No principal character (i.e., more time is devoted to the product)	

Source: Adapted from David W. Stewart and David H. Furse. "The Effects of Television Advertising Execution on Recall, Comprehension, and Persuasion." *Psychology of Marketing* 2 (Fall 1985): 135–60. Copyright © 1985 by John Wiley & Sons, Inc. Reprinted by permission.

Characteristics of the message itself help to determine its impact on attitudes. These variables include *how* the message is said as well as *what* is said. Some of the issues facing marketers include the following:

- Should the message be conveyed in words or pictures?
- How often should the message be repeated?
- Should a conclusion be drawn, or should this be left up to the listener?
- Should both sides of an argument be presented?
- Is it effective to explicitly compare one's product to competitors?
- Should a blatant sexual appeal be used?
- Should negative emotions, such as fear, ever be aroused?
- How concrete or vivid should the arguments and imagery be?
- Should the ad be funny?

Sending the Message

The saying "one picture is worth a thousand words" captures the idea that visual stimuli can economically deliver big impact, especially when the communicator wants to influence receivers' emotional responses. For this reason, advertisers often place great emphasis on vivid and creative illustrations or photography.[57]

On the other hand, a picture is not always as effective at communicating factual information. Different reactions are elicited from ads that contain the same information, presented in either visual or verbal form. The verbal version affects ratings on the utilitarian aspects of a product, whereas the visual version affects aesthetic evaluations. Verbal elements are more effective when reinforced by an accompanying picture, especially if the illustration is *framed* (the message in the picture is strongly related to the copy).[58]

Because it requires more effort to process, a verbal message is most appropriate for high-involvement situations, such as in print contexts in which the reader is motivated to really pay attention to the advertising. Because verbal material decays more rapidly in memory, more frequent exposures are needed to obtain the desired effect. Visual images, in contrast, allow the receiver to *chunk* information at the time of encoding (see Chapter 3). Chunking results in a stronger memory trace that aids retrieval over time.[59]

Visual elements may affect brand attitudes in one of two ways. First, the consumer may form inferences about the brand and change his or her beliefs because

■ **FIGURE 8.3** DUAL COMPONENT MODEL OF BRAND ATTITUDES

of an illustration's imagery. For example, people in a study who saw an ad for a facial tissue accompanied by a photo of a sunset were more likely to believe that the brand came in attractive colors. Second, brand attitudes may be affected more directly; for example, a strong positive or negative reaction elicited by the visual elements will influence the consumer's attitude toward the ad (A_{ad}), which will then affect brand attitudes (A_b). Figure 8.3 illustrates this dual component model of brand attitudes.[60]

Vividness

Both pictures and words can differ in *vividness*. Powerful descriptions or graphics command attention and are more strongly embedded in memory. The reason may be because they tend to activate mental imagery, whereas abstract stimuli inhibit this process.[61] Of course, this effect can cut both ways: Negative information presented in a vivid manner may result in more negative evaluations at a later time.[62]

The concrete discussion of a product attribute in ad copy also influences the importance of that attribute, because more attention is drawn to it. For example, the copy for a watch that read "According to industry sources, three out of every four watch breakdowns are due to water getting into the case" was more effective than this version: "According to industry sources, many watch breakdowns are due to water getting into the case."[63]

Repetition

Repetition can be a double-edged sword for marketers. As noted in Chapter 3, multiple exposures to a stimulus are usually required for learning (especially conditioning) to occur. Contrary to the saying "familiarity breeds contempt," people tend to like things that are more familiar to them, even if they were not that keen on them initially.[64] This is known as the *mere exposure* phenomenon. Positive effects for advertising repetition are found even in mature product categories—repeating product information has been shown to boost consumers' awareness of the brand, even though nothing new has been said.[65] On the other hand, as we saw in Chapter 2, too much repetition creates *habituation*, whereby the consumer no longer pays attention to the stimulus because of fatigue or boredom. Excessive exposure can cause advertising wear-out, which can result in negative reactions to an ad after seeing it too much.[66]

The **two-factor theory** explains the fine line between familiarity and boredom by proposing that two separate psychological processes are operating when a person is repeatedly exposed to an ad. The positive side of repetition is that it increases familiarity and thus reduces uncertainty about the product. The negative side is that over time boredom increases with each exposure. At some point the amount of boredom incurred begins to exceed the amount of uncertainty reduced, resulting in wear-out. Figure 8.4 depicts this pattern. Its effect is especially pronounced when each exposure is of a fairly long duration (such as a 60-second commercial).[67]

■ **FIGURE 8.4** TWO-FACTOR THEORY

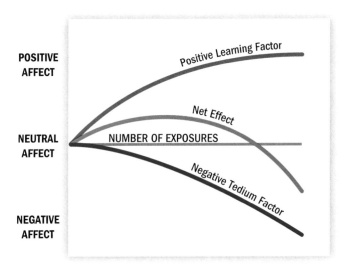

The theory implies that advertisers can overcome this problem by limiting the amount of exposure per repetition (such as using 15-second spots). They can also maintain familiarity but alleviate boredom by slightly varying the content of ads over time through campaigns that revolve around a common theme, although each spot may be different. Recipients who are exposed to varied ads about the product absorb more information about product attributes and experience more positive thoughts about the brand than do those exposed to the same information repeatedly. This additional information allows the person to resist attempts to change his or her attitude in the face of a counterattack by a competing brand.[68]

Constructing the Argument

Many marketing messages are similar to debates or trials, in which someone presents arguments and tries to convince the receiver to shift his or her opinion accordingly. The way the argument is presented may be as important as what is said.

One- Versus Two-Sided Arguments

Most messages merely present one or more positive attributes about the product or reasons to buy it. These are known as *supportive arguments*. An alternative is to use a *two-sided message*, in which both positive and negative information is presented. Research has indicated that two-sided ads can be quite effective, yet they are not widely used.[69]

Why would a marketer want to devote advertising space to publicizing a product's negative attributes? Under the right circumstances, the use of **refutational arguments**, in which a negative issue is raised and then dismissed, can be quite effective. This approach can increase source credibility by reducing reporting bias. Also, people who are skeptical about the product may be more receptive to a balanced argument instead of a "whitewash."[70]

This is not to say that the marketer should go overboard in presenting major problems with the product. The typical refutational strategy discusses relatively minor attributes that may present a problem or fall short when compared with competitors. Positive, important attributes then refute these drawbacks. For example, Avis got a lot of mileage out of claiming to be only the "No. 2" car rental company, whereas an ad for Volkswagen woefully described one of its cars as a "lemon" because there was a scratch on the glove compartment chrome strip.[71] A two-sided

As this Dutch ad illustrates, the way something is said can be as significant as what is said.

strategy appears to be the most effective when the audience is well educated (and presumably more impressed by a balanced argument).[73] It is also best to use when receivers are not already loyal to the product; "preaching to the choir" about possible drawbacks may raise doubts unnecessarily.

Drawing Conclusions

Should the argument draw conclusions, or should the points merely be presented, permitting the consumer to arrive at his or her own decision? On the one hand, consumers who make their own inferences instead of having them spoon-fed to them will form stronger, more accessible attitudes. On the other hand, leaving the conclusion ambiguous increases the chance that the desired attitude will not be formed.

The response to this issue depends on the consumers' motivation to process the ad and the complexity of the arguments. If the message is personally relevant, people will pay attention to it and spontaneously form inferences. However, if the arguments are hard to follow or consumers' motivation to follow them is lacking, it is safer for the ad to draw conclusions.[74]

Comparative Advertising

In 1971, the FTC issued guidelines that encouraged advertisers to name competing brands in their ads. This action was taken to improve the information available to consumers in ads, and indeed recent evidence indicates that at least under some conditions this type of presentation does result in more informed decision making.[75] **Comparative advertising** refers to a strategy in which a message compares two or more specifically named or recognizably presented brands and makes a comparison of them in terms of one or more specific attributes.[76] For example, Schering-Plough claimed that "New OcuClear relieves three times longer than Visine," and Bristol-Myers stated, "New Liquid Vanish really does clean tough rust stains below the water line better than Lysol."

This strategy can cut both ways, especially if the sponsor depicts the competition in a nasty or negative way. Although some comparative ads result in desired attitude change or positive A_{ad}, they have also been found to be lower in believability and may result in more source derogation (i.e., the consumer may doubt the credibility of a biased presentation).[77] Indeed, in some cultures (such as Asia) comparative advertising is rare because people find such a confrontational approach offensive.

Comparative ads do appear to be effective for new products that are trying to build a clear image by positioning themselves vis-à-vis dominant brands in the market. For example, Procter & Gamble recently introduced a new chip called Torengos by comparing them to an unnamed rival in a bag that happens to be a dead ringer for Frito Lay's Tostitos.[78] These ads work well at generating attention, awareness, favorable attitudes, and purchase intentions—but ironically consumers may not like the ad itself because of its aggressiveness.[79] When Michelob recently slammed imported beer rival Stella Artois as ordinary and overpriced, its smaller competitor's sales doubled.[80]

But, if the aim is to compare the new brand with the market leader in terms of specific product attributes, merely saying it is as good or better than the leader is not sufficient. For example, the use of the claim "Spring has the same fluoride as Crest" in a study resulted in attitude change for the fictitious product, but the more global statement "Preferred by Europeans in comparison with Crest" did not.[81] And, comparative ads are only credible if they don't reach too far by comparing a brand to a competitor that is obviously superior. Not too surprisingly, for example, a survey of new-car buyers found that TV commercials comparing a Nissan Altima to a Mercedes were not effective.[82]

Types of Message Appeals

The *way* something is said can be as significant as *what* is said. A persuasive message can tug at the heartstrings or scare you, make you laugh, make you cry, or leave you yearning to learn more. In this section, we'll review the major alternatives available to communicators who wish to *appeal* to a message recipient.

Emotional Versus Rational Appeals

The French firm L'Oréal persuades millions of women around the world to buy its personal care products by promising them Parisian chic, associating them with its sexy spokeswomen, and touting the self-assured slogan "Because I'm worth it." Now the company is feeling pressure from an unlikely rival. Procter & Gamble is applying the no-nonsense comparative advertising strategy that it has long used to sell soap and diapers to cosmetics as well. After P&G acquired Clairol in 2001, the company, better known for Tide detergent and many other household products, suddenly became the largest seller of cosmetics in supermarkets and club stores. A current P&G promotion for Pantene hair conditioner offers a "10-day challenge," promising hair that is 60 percent healthier, 85 percent shinier, 80 percent less prone to breakage, and 70 percent less frizzy. In another case, after using 60 different methods to measure the size of pores, length of wrinkles, and the color and size of age spots, P&G researchers used results from one of the tests to proclaim in national ads that Olay Total Effects Night Firming Cream worked better than leading department-store brands (including those made by L'Oréal). Now P&G is trying to penetrate the high-end market, where L'Oréal rules. The head of L'Oréal sneers at this factual approach by arguing that when it comes to selling cosmetics, "you have to both inform, convince but also seduce consumers . . . and not just ram facts down their throats."[83]

So, which is better: To appeal to the head or to the heart? The answer often depends upon the nature of the product and the type of relationship consumers have with it. This issue was at the core of a fierce debate at Polaroid, a company

These ads demonstrate rational versus emotional message appeals. At the time of the initial ad campaign for the new Infiniti automobiles, the ads for rival Lexus (top) emphasized design and engineering, while the ads for Infiniti (bottom) did not even show the car.

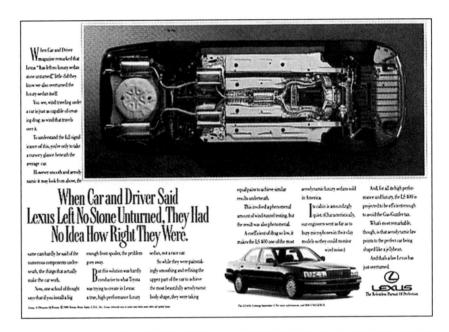

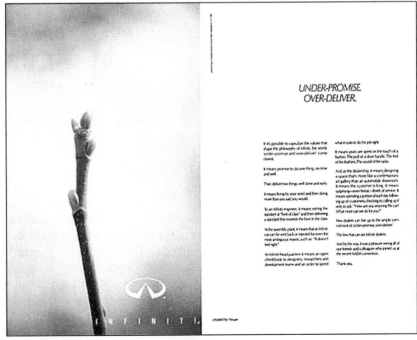

known for technological innovation rather than "warm and fuzzy" products. Marketers at the photographic products firm argued strenuously that the company needed to develop new, "fun" products to recapture younger consumers. Engineers were antagonistic about this idea; they felt a "toy" camera would cheapen Polaroid's reputation. In this case, the marketers prevailed and convinced the engineers to create a small instant camera with a cheap lens to produce fuzzy thumbnail-size photos. The I-Zone Instant Pocket camera was born. In a radical move for the company the ad campaign is based on the theme "being a little bit bad is good." One execution features a young man who sticks instant pictures on his nipples and then wiggles his chest. Half of the I-Zone's buyers are 13- to 17-year-old girls, and Polaroid reaped revenues of $270 million for the product in one year.[84]

Many companies turned to an emotional strategy after realizing that consumers do not find many differences among brands, especially those in well-established, mature categories. Ads for products ranging from cars (Lincoln Mercury) to cards (Hallmark) focus instead on emotional aspects. Mercury's capitalization on emotional attachments to old rock songs succeeded in lowering the median age of its consumers for some models by 10 years.[85]

It's hard to gauge the precise effects of rational versus emotional appeals. Although recall of ad contents tends to be better for "thinking" ads than for "feeling" ads, conventional measures of advertising effectiveness (e.g., day-after recall) may not be adequate to assess cumulative effects of emotional ads. These open-ended measures are oriented toward cognitive responses, and feeling ads may be penalized because the reactions are not as easy to articulate.[86]

Sexual Appeals

Echoing the widely held belief that "sex sells," many marketing communications for everything from perfumes to autos feature heavy doses of erotic suggestions that range from subtle hints to blatant displays of skin. Of course, the prevalence of sexual appeals varies from country to country. Even American firms run ads elsewhere that would not go over at home. For example, a recent "cheeky" ad campaign designed to boost the appeal of American-made Lee jeans among Europeans features a series of bare buttocks. The messages are based on the concept that if bottoms could choose jeans, they would opt for Lee: "Bottoms feel better in Lee Jeans."[87]

Bare flesh is so much a part of French advertising that a minor backlash is brewing as some critics complain the advertising industry is making sex boring![88] Perhaps not surprisingly, female nudity in print ads generates negative feelings and tension among female consumers, whereas men's reactions are more positive.[89] In a case of turnabout being fair play, another study found that males dislike nude males in ads, whereas females responded well to undressed males—but not totally nude ones.[90]

Does sex work? Although the use of sex does appear to draw attention to an ad, its use may actually be counterproductive to the marketer. In one recent survey, an overwhelming 61 percent of the respondents said that sexual imagery in a product's ad makes them less likely to buy it.[91] Ironically, a provocative picture can be *too* effective; it attracts so much attention that it hinders processing and recall of the ad's contents. Sexual appeals appear to be ineffective when used merely as a "trick" to grab attention. They do, however, appear to work when the product is *itself* related to sex (e.g., lingerie or condoms). Overall, though, use of a strong sexual appeal is not very well received.[92]

Humorous Appeals

A recent TV commercial for Metamucil caused a bit of a stir in the United States. The spot showed a National Park Service ranger pouring a glass of it down Old Faithful and announcing that the product keeps the famous geyser "regular." Yellowstone National Park started getting letters from offended viewers such as this one who wrote, "I suppose that in an era when people sell naming rights to sports arenas and when we hear that some even propose selling the naming rights to the Golden Gate

Marketing Pitfall

Nike is the master craftsman of "in-your-face" emotional messages about sports that barely acknowledge the shoes they are trying to sell. These appeals have played very well in the United States, but now the company has hit some bumps in the road as it tries to export this attitude overseas. As the company searches for new markets, it is trying to conquer soccer the way it did basketball. An ad in *Soccer America* magazine announced the impending invasion: "Europe, Asia, and Latin America: Barricade your stadiums. Hide your trophies. Invest in some deodorant." This message was not very well received in some soccer quarters, and similarly, a successful American TV commercial featuring Satan and his demons playing soccer against Nike endorsers was banned by some European stations on the grounds that it was too scary for children to see and offensive to boot. A British TV ad featuring a French soccer player saying how his spitting at a fan and insulting his coach won him a Nike contract resulted in a scathing editorial against Nike in the sport's international federation newsletter. Nike has a tough task ahead of it: to win over European soccer fans where rival Adidas is king—in a game that traditionally doesn't have the glitz and packaging of basketball. Now a bit chastised, Nike is modifying its "question authority" approach as it tries to win over the sports organizations in countries that don't appreciate its violent messages and antiestablishment themes.[93]

Depending upon the audience, sexual humor either can be effective or backfire.

Bridge that some in the National Park Service would see nothing wrong with selling the image of a National Park ranger for the marketing of a product promoting bowel regularity." Park officials also had their own concerns; they didn't want people to think that the geyser needed "help"—or that it's okay to throw things down into it![94]

The use of humor can be tricky, particularly because what is funny to one person may be offensive or incomprehensible to another. Specific cultures may have different senses of humor and use funny material in diverse ways. For example, commercials in the United Kingdom are more likely to use puns and satire than they are in the United States.[95]

Does humor work? Overall, humorous advertisements do get attention. One study found that recognition scores for humorous liquor ads were better than average. However, the verdict is mixed as to whether humor affects recall or product

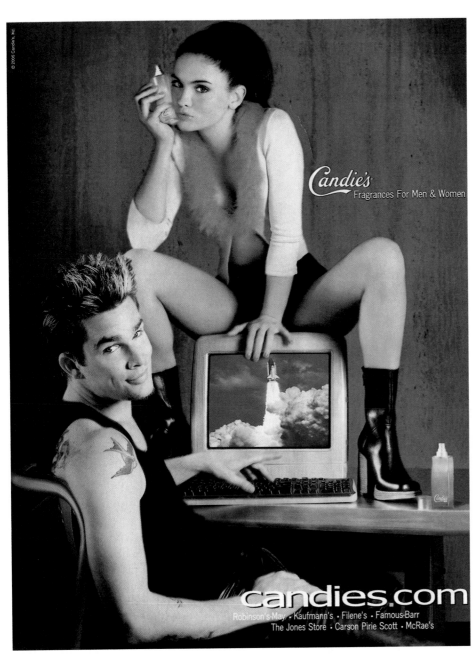

attitudes in a significant way.[96] One function it may serve is to provide a source of *distraction*. A funny ad inhibits the consumer from *counterarguing* (thinking of reasons why he doesn't agree with the message), thereby increasing the likelihood of message acceptance.[97]

Humor is more likely to be effective when the brand is clearly identified and the funny material does not "swamp" the message. This danger is similar to one we've already discussed about beautiful models diverting attention from copy points. Subtle humor is usually better, as is humor that does not make fun of the potential consumer. Finally, humor should be appropriate to the product's image. An undertaker or a bank might want to avoid humor, but other products adapt to it quite well. Sales of Sunsweet pitted prunes improved dramatically based on the claim, "Today the pits, tomorrow the wrinkles."[98]

Remember to ski and snowboard responsibly. www.boeriusa.com

boeri®
it's your head

This ad relies upon humor to communicate the message that skiers and snowboarders should wear helmets.

Fear Appeals

Fear appeals emphasize the negative consequences that can occur unless the consumer changes a behavior or an attitude. Schering-Plough placed ads that read "A government panel has determined some laxatives may cause cancer." The ads implicated Ex-Lax, a rival brand, even though the Food and Drug Administration hadn't yet made a final determination regarding this issue (Ex-Lax eventually did withdraw the product to reformulate it after the FDA decided to ban its active ingredient).[99] A fear appeal strategy is widely used in marketing communications, though more commonly in social marketing contexts in which organizations are encouraging people to convert to a healthier lifestyle by quitting smoking, using contraception, relying on a designated driver, and so on.

Does fear work? Most research on this topic indicates that these negative appeals are usually most effective when only a moderate threat is used, and when a solution to the problem is presented. Otherwise, consumers will tune out the ad because they can do nothing to solve the problem.[100] This approach also works better when source credibility is high.[101]

When a weak threat is ineffective, this may be because there is insufficient elaboration of the harmful consequences of engaging in the behavior. When a strong threat doesn't work, it may be because *too much* elaboration interferes with the processing of the recommended change in behavior—the receiver is too busy thinking of reasons why the message doesn't apply to him or her to pay attention to the offered solution.[102]

A study that manipulated subjects' degree of anxiety about AIDS, for example, found that condom ads were evaluated most positively when a moderate threat was

Humorous ads like this one from Budapest, grab our attention.

used. In this context, copy that promoted the use of the condom because "Sex is a risky business" (moderate threat) resulted in more attitude change than either a weaker threat that instead emphasized the product's sensitivity or a strong threat that discussed the certainty of death from AIDS.[103] Similarly, scare tactics have not been as effective as hoped in getting teenagers to decrease their use of alcohol or drugs. Teens simply tune out the message or deny its relevance to them.[104] On the other hand, a study of adolescent responses to social versus physical threat appeals in drug prevention messages found that social threat is a more effective strategy.[105]

Some of the research on fear appeals may be confusing a threat (the literal content of a message, such as saying "engage in safe sex or die") with fear (an emotional response to the message). According to this argument, greater fear does result in greater persuasion—but not all threats are equally effective because different people will respond differently to the same threat. Therefore, the strongest threats are not always the most persuasive because they may not have the desired impact on the perceiver. For example, raising the specter of AIDS is about the strongest threat that can be delivered to sexually active kids—but this tactic is only effective if the kids believe they will get the disease. Because many young people (especially those

Did you know that the acids which eat away at your teeth and cause decay are most destructive in the twenty minutes immediately after eating?

That's why we brush our teeth in the morning, after breakfast and at night, right after dinner.

Brushing helps remove plaque, a sticky film that sets like glue, trapping acids and bacteria against your teeth.

But, how many of us brush after lunch?

The next thing that gets eaten is your teeth.

According to dental research, less than 10%.

The rest of us are either out of the house or just far too busy, right?

Wrong. We should all have a second toothbrush at work or school.

You'll find brushing after lunch is not only good for your teeth, it's good for your breath as well.

It takes just 3 minutes to brush your teeth properly. That's less time than it takes to make a cup of coffee.

So it's not as inconvenient as you think to make it part of your daily routine.

Remember, if you eat lunch, so does the acid on your teeth.

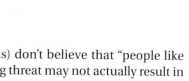

This Australian toothpaste ad uses a mild fear appeal to promote tooth brushing.

who live in fairly affluent suburban or rural areas) don't believe that "people like them" will be exposed to the AIDS virus, this strong threat may not actually result in a high level of fear.[106] The bottom line is that more precise measures of actual fear responses are needed before definitive conclusions can be drawn about the impact of fear appeals on consumption decisions.

The Message as Art Form: Metaphors Be with You

Marketers may be thought of as storytellers who supply visions of reality similar to those provided by authors, poets, and artists. These communications take the form of stories because the product benefits they describe are intangible and must be given tangible meaning by expressing them in a form that is concrete and visible. Advertising creatives rely (consciously or not) on various literary devices to communicate these meanings. For example, characters like Mr. Goodwrench, the Jolly Green Giant, and Charlie the Tuna may personify a product or service. Many ads take the form of an **allegory**, a story told about an abstract trait or concept that has been personified as a person, animal, or vegetable.

A **metaphor** involves placing two dissimilar objects into a close relationship such that "A is B," whereas a **similie** compares two objects, "A is like B." This is accomplished because A and B, however seemingly dissimilar, share some quality that is, in turn, highlighted by the metaphor. Metaphors allow the marketer to activate meaningful images and apply them to everyday events. In the stock market, "white knights" battle "hostile raiders" using "poison pills"; Tony the Tiger allows us to equate cereal with strength, and the Merrill Lynch bull sends the message that the company is "a breed apart."[107]

Life insurance companies often use a fear appeal to motivate consumers to buy policies.

Resonance is another type of literary device that is frequently used in advertising. It is a form of presentation that combines a play on words with a relevant picture. Table 8.3 gives some examples of actual ads that rely on the principle of resonance. Whereas metaphor substitutes one meaning for another by connecting two things that are in some way similar, resonance uses an element that has a double meaning, such as a pun in which there is a similarity in the sound of a word but a difference in meaning. For example, an ad for a diet strawberry shortcake dessert might bear the copy "berried treasure" so that the brand conveys qualities associated with buried treasure—being rich, hidden, and associated with adventurous pirates. Because the text departs from expectations, it creates a state of tension or uncertainty on the part of the viewer until he or she figures out the word play. Once the consumer "gets it," he or she may prefer the ad to a more straightforward message.[108]

为你解开手洗束缚

This Chinese detergent ad uses a handcuff metaphor as it urges the viewer, "Free yourself from the burden of handwash."

Forms of Story Presentation

Just as a story can be told in words or pictures, the way the audience is addressed can also differ. Commercials are structured similarly to other art forms, borrowing conventions from literature and art as they communicate their messages.[109] One important distinction is between a *drama* and a *lecture*.[110] A lecture is like a speech in which the source speaks directly to the audience in an attempt to inform them

TABLE 8.3
SOME EXAMPLES OF ADVERTISING RESONANCE

Product/Headline	Visual
Embassy Suites: "This Year, We're Unwrapping Suites by the Dozen"	Chocolate kisses with hotel names underneath each
Toyota auto parts: "Our Lifetime Guarantee May Come as a Shock"	Man holding a shock absorber
Bucks filter cigarettes: "Herd of These?"	Cigarette pack with a picture of a stag
Bounce fabric softener: "Is There Something Creeping Up Behind You?"	Woman's dress bunched up on her back due to static
Pepsi: "This Year, Hit the Beach Topless"	Pepsi bottle cap lying on the sand
ASICS athletic shoes: "We Believe Women Should Be Running the Country"	Woman jogging in a rural setting

Source: Adapted from Edward F. McQuarne and David Glen Mick. "On Resonance: A Critical Pluralistic Inquiry into Advertising Rhetoric," *Journal of Consumer Research* 19 [September 1992]: 182. Table 1. Reprinted with permission of the University of Chicago Press.

Many products are personified by make-believe characters.

about a product or persuade them to buy it. Because a lecture clearly implies an attempt at persuasion, the audience will regard it as such. Assuming listeners are motivated to do so, the merits of the message will be weighed, along with the credibility of the source. Cognitive responses, such as counterargumentation, will occur. The appeal will be accepted to the extent that it overcomes objections and is congruent with a person's beliefs.

In contrast, a drama is similar to a play or movie. Whereas an argument holds the viewer at arm's length, a drama draws the viewer into the action. The characters only indirectly address the audience; they interact with each other about a product or service in an imaginary setting. Dramas attempt to be experiential—to involve the audience emotionally. In *transformational advertising*, the consumer associates the experience of product usage with some subjective sensation. Thus, ads for the Infiniti attempted to transform the "driving experience" into a mystical, spiritual event.

■ THE SOURCE VERSUS THE MESSAGE: SELL THE STEAK OR THE SIZZLE?

Two major components of the communications model, the source and the message, have been reviewed. Which aspect has the most impact on persuading consumers to change their attitudes? Should marketers worry more about *what* is said, or *how* it's said and *who* says it?

The answer is, it depends. Variations in a consumer's level of involvement, as discussed in Chapter 4, result in the activation of very different cognitive processes when a message is received. Research indicates that this level of involvement will determine which aspects of a communication are processed. The situation appears to resemble a traveler who comes to a fork in the road: One or the other path is chosen, and this choice has a big impact on the factors that will make a difference in persuasion attempts.

■ **FIGURE 8.5** THE ELABORATION LIKELIHOOD MODEL (ELM) OF PERSUASION

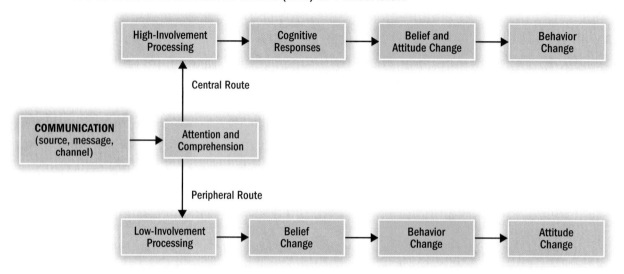

The Elaboration Likelihood Model

The **elaboration likelihood model (ELM)** assumes that once a consumer receives a message he or she begins to process it.[111] Depending on the personal relevance of this information, the receiver will follow one of two routes to persuasion. Under conditions of high involvement, the consumer takes the central route to persuasion. Under conditions of low involvement, a *peripheral route* is taken instead. Figure 8.5 diagrams this model.

The Central Route to Persuasion

When the consumer finds the information in a persuasive message to be relevant or somehow interesting, he or she will carefully attend to the message content. The person is likely to actively think about the arguments presented and generate *cognitive responses* to these arguments. On hearing a radio message warning about drinking while pregnant, an expectant mother might say to herself, "She's right. I really should stop drinking alcohol now that I'm pregnant." Or, she might offer counterarguments, such as "That's a bunch of baloney. My mother had a cocktail every night when she was pregnant with me, and I turned out fine." If a person generates counterarguments in response to a message, it is less likely that he or she will yield to the message, whereas the generation of further supporting arguments by the consumer increases the probability of compliance.[112]

The central route to persuasion is likely to involve the traditional hierarchy of effects, as discussed in Chapter 7. Beliefs are carefully formed and evaluated, and strong attitudes that result will be likely to guide behavior. The implication is that message factors, such as the quality of arguments presented, will be important in determining attitude change. Prior knowledge about a topic results in more thoughts about the message and also increases the number of counterarguments.[113]

The Peripheral Route to Persuasion

In contrast, the peripheral route is taken when the person is not motivated to really think about the arguments presented. Instead, the consumer is likely to use other cues in deciding on the suitability of the message. These cues might include the product's package, the attractiveness of the source, or the context in which the message is presented. Sources of information extraneous to the actual message content are called *peripheral cues* because they surround the actual message.

The peripheral route to persuasion highlights the paradox of low involvement discussed in Chapter 4: When consumers do not care about a product, the stimuli associated with it increase in importance. The implication here is that low-involvement products may be purchased chiefly because the marketer has done a good job in designing a "sexy" package, choosing a popular spokesperson, or perhaps just creating a pleasant shopping environment.

Support for the ELM

The ELM has received a lot of research support.[114] In a typical study, undergraduates were exposed to one of several mock advertisements for Break, a new brand of low-alcohol beer. Using the technique of *thought listing*, they were asked to provide their thoughts about the ads, which were later analyzed by the researcher.[115] Three independent variables crucial to the ELM were manipulated:

1 *Message-processing involvement:* Some subjects were motivated to be highly involved with the ads. They were promised a gift of low-alcohol beer for participating in the study and were told that the brand would soon be available in their area. Low-involvement subjects, who were not promised a gift, were told that the brand would be introduced in a distant area.
2 *Argument strength:* One version of the ad used strong, compelling arguments to drink Break (e.g., "Break contains one-half of the amount of alcohol of regular beers and, therefore, has less calories than regular beer."), whereas the other listed only weak arguments (e.g., "Break is just as good as any other regular beer.")
3 *Source characteristics:* Both ads contained a photo of a couple drinking the beer, but their relative social attractiveness was varied by their dress, their posture and nonverbal expressions, and the background information given about their educational achievements and occupations.

Consistent with the ELM, high-involvement subjects had more thoughts related to the ad messages than did low-involvement subjects, who devoted more cognitive activity to the sources used in the ad. The attitudes of high-involvement subjects were more likely to be swayed by powerful arguments, whereas the attitudes of low-involvement subjects were more likely to be influenced by the ad version using attractive sources. The results of this study, paired with numerous others, indicate that the relative effectiveness of a strong message and a favorable source depends on consumers' level of involvement with the product being advertised.

These results underscore the basic idea that highly involved consumers look for the "steak" (e.g., strong, rational arguments). Those who are less involved are more affected by the "sizzle" (e.g., the colors and images used in packaging or endorsements by famous people). It is important to remember, however, that the same communications variable can be both a central and a peripheral cue, depending on its relation to the attitude object. The physical attractiveness of a model might serve as a peripheral cue in a car commercial, but her beauty might be a central cue for a product such as shampoo, as the product's benefits are directly tied to enhancing attractiveness.[116]

CHAPTER SUMMARY

Persuasion refers to an attempt to change consumers' attitudes.

The communications model specifies the elements needed to transmit meaning. These include a source, message, medium, receiver, and feedback.

The traditional view of communications tends to regard the perceiver as a passive element in the process. Proponents of the uses and gratifications approach instead regard the consumer as an active participant who uses media for a variety of reasons.

New developments in interactive communications highlight the need to consider the active roles a consumer might play in obtaining product information and building a relationship with a company. Advocates of permission marketing argue that it's more effective to send messages to consumers who have already indicated an interest in learning about a product than trying to hit people "cold" with these solicitations.

A product-related communication that directly yields a transaction is a first-order response. Customer feedback in response to a marketing message that is not in the form of a transaction is a second-order response. This may take the form of a request for more information about a good, service, or organization, or perhaps receipt of a "wish list" from the customer that specifies the types of product information he or she would like to get in the future.

Two important characteristics that determine the effectiveness of a source are its attractiveness and credibility. Although celebrities often serve this purpose, their credibility is not always as strong as marketers hope. Marketing messages that consumers perceive as buzz (that are authentic and consumer-generated) tend to be more effective than those they categorize as hype (that are inauthentic, biased, and company-generated).

Some elements of a message that help to determine its effectiveness are whether it is conveyed in words or pictures, whether an emotional or a rational appeal is employed, the frequency with which it is repeated, whether a conclusion is drawn, whether both sides of the argument are presented, and whether the message includes fear, humor, or sexual references.

Advertising messages often incorporate elements from art or literature such as dramas, lectures, metaphors, allegories, and resonance.

The relative influence of the source versus the message depends on the receiver's level of involvement with the communication. The elaboration likelihood model (ELM) specifies that a less-involved consumer will more likely be swayed by source effects, whereas a more involved consumer will more likely attend to and process components of the actual message.

KEY TERMS

Allegory 278
Avatar 265
Buzz 260
Communications model 255
Comparative advertising 271
Corporate Paradox 260
Elaboration likelihood model (ELM) 282

Fear appeals 276
Hype 260
Match-up hypothesis 263
Metaphor 278
Permission marketing 256
Persuasion 254
Refutational argument 269
Resonance 279

Similie 278
Sleeper effect 259
Source attractiveness 261
Source credibility 258
Two-factor theory 268
Uses and gratifications theory 256

CONSUMER BEHAVIOR CHALLENGE

1 A government agency wants to encourage the use of designated drivers by people who have been drinking. What advice could you give the organization about constructing persuasive communications? Discuss some factors that might be important, including the structure of the communications, where they should appear, and who should deliver them. Should fear appeals be used, and if so, how?

2 Discuss some conditions in which it would be advisable to use a comparative advertising strategy.

3 Why would a marketer consider saying negative things about his or her product? When is this strategy feasible? Can you find examples of it?

4 A marketer must decide whether to incorporate rational or emotional appeals in its communications strategy. Describe conditions that are more favorable to using one or the other.

5 Collect ads that rely on sex appeal to sell products. How often are benefits of the actual product communicated to the reader?

6 Observe the process of counterargumentation by asking a friend to talk out loud while watching a commercial. Ask him or her to respond to each point in the ad or to write down reactions to the claims made. How much skepticism regarding the claims can you detect?

7 Make a log of all the commercials shown on one network television channel during a two-hour period. Categorize each according to product category, and whether they are presented as drama or argument. Describe the types of messages used (e.g., two-sided arguments), and keep track of the types of spokespeople (e.g., TV actors, famous people, animated characters). What can you conclude about the dominant forms of persuasive tactics currently employed by marketers?

8 Collect examples of ads that rely on the use of metaphors or resonance. Do you feel these ads are effective? If you were marketing the products, would you feel more comfortable with ads that use a more straightforward, "hard-sell" approach? Why or why not?

9 Create a list of current celebrities whom you feel typify cultural categories (e.g., clown, mother figure, etc.). What specific brands do you feel each could effectively endorse?

10 The American Medical Association encountered a firestorm of controversy when it agreed to sponsor a line of health care products manufactured by Sunbeam (a decision it later reversed). Should trade or professional organizations, journalists, professors, and others endorse specific products at the expense of other offerings?

11 Conduct an "avatar hunt" by going to e-commerce Web sites, online video game sites, and online communities like The Sims or Cybertown that let people select what they want to look like in cyberspace. What seem to be the dominant figures people are choosing? Are they realistic or fantasy characters? Male or female? What types of avatars do you believe would be most effective for each of these different kinds of Web sites and why?

12 Many, many companies rely on celebrity endorsers as communications sources to persuade. Especially when targeting younger people, these spokespeople often are "cool" musicians, athletes, or movie stars. In your opinion, who would be the most effective celebrity endorser today, and why? Who would be the least effective? Why?

NOTES

1. Robert B. Cialdini and Kelton V. L. Rhoads, "Human Behavior and the Marketplace," *Marketing Research* (Fall 2001).
2. Gert Assmus, "An Empirical Investigation into the Perception of Vehicle Source Effects," *Journal of Advertising* 7 (Winter 1978): 4–10. For a more thorough discussion of the pros and cons of different media, see Stephen Baker, *Systematic Approach to Advertising Creativity* (New York: McGraw-Hill, 1979).
3. Alladi Venkatesh, Ruby Roy Dholakia, and Nikhilesh Dholakia, "New Visions of Information Technology and Postmodernism: Implications for Advertising and Marketing Communications," in Walter Brenner and Lutz Kolbe, eds., *The Information Superhighway and Private Households: Case Studies of Business Impacts* (Heidelberg: Physical-Verlag, 1996), 319–37; Donna L. Hoffman and Thomas P. Novak, "Marketing in Hypermedia Computer-Mediated Environments: Conceptual Foundations," *Journal of Marketing* 60, no. 3 (July 1996): 50–68. For an early theoretical discussion of interactivity in communications paradigms, see R. Aubrey Fisher, *Perspectives on Human Communication* (New York: Macmillan, 1978).
4. Seth Godin, *Permission Marketing: Turning Strangers into Friends, and Friends into Customers* (New York: Simon & Schuster, 1999).
5. First proposed by Elihu Katz, "Mass Communication Research and the Study of Popular Culture: An Editorial Note on a Possible Future for this Journal," *Studies in Public Communication* 2 (1959): 1–6. For a recent discussion of this approach, see Stephanie O'Donohoe, "Advertising Uses and Gratifications," *European Journal of Marketing* 28, no. 8/9 (1994): 52–75.
6. O'Donohoe, "Advertising Uses and Gratifications," 66.
7. Brad Stone, "The War for Your TV," *Newsweek* (July 29, 2002): 46–47.
8. This section is adapted from a discussion in Michael R. Solomon and Elnora W. Stuart, *Marketing: Real People, Real Choices*, 3rd ed. (Upper Saddle River, NJ: Prentice Hall, 2002).
9. Carl I. Hovland and W. Weiss, "The Influence of Source Credibility on Communication Effectiveness," *Public Opinion Quarterly* 15 (1952): 635–50.
10. Herbert Kelman, "Processes of Opinion Change," *Public Opinion Quarterly* 25 (Spring 1961): 57–78; Susan M. Petroshius and Kenneth E. Crocker, "An Empirical Analysis of Spokesperson Characteristics on Advertisement and Product Evaluations," *Journal of the Academy of Marketing Science* 17 (Summer 1989): 217–26.
11. Kenneth G. DeBono and Richard J. Harnish, "Source Expertise, Source Attractiveness, and the Processing of Persuasive Information: A Functional Approach," *Journal of Personality and Social Psychology* 55, no. 4 (1988): 541–46.
12. Hershey H. Friedman and Linda Friedman, "Endorser Effectiveness by Product Type," *Journal of Advertising Research* 19, no. 5 (1979): 63–71. For a recent study that looked at *nontarget market effects*—the effects of advertising intended for other market segments—see Jennifer L. Aaker, Anne M. Brumbaugh, and Sonya A. Grier, "Non-Target Markets and Viewer Distinctiveness: The Impact of Target Marketing on Advertising Attitudes," *Journal of Consumer Psychology* 9, no. 3 (2000): 127–40.
13. S. Ratneshwar and Shelly Chaiken, "Comprehension's Role in Persuasion: The Case of Its Moderating Effect on the Persuasive Impact of Source Cues," *Journal of Consumer Research* 18 (June 1991): 52–62.
14. Jagdish Agrawal and Wagner A. Kamakura, "The Economic Worth of Celebrity Endorsers: An Event Study Analysis," *Journal of Marketing* 59 (July 1995): 56–62.
15. Anthony R. Pratkanis, Anthony G. Greenwald, Michael R. Leippe, and Michael H. Baumgardner, "In Search of Reliable Persuasion Effects: III. The Sleeper Effect Is Dead, Long Live the Sleeper Effect," *Journal of Personality and Social Psychology* 54 (1988): 203–18.
16. Herbert C. Kelman and Carl I. Hovland, "Reinstatement of the Communication in Delayed Measurement of Opinion Change," *Journal of Abnormal Psychology* 48, no. 3 (1953): 327–35.
17. Darlene Hannah and Brian Sternthal, "Detecting and Explaining the Sleeper Effect," *Journal of Consumer Research* 11 (September 1984): 632–42.
18. David Mazursky and Yaacov Schul, "The Effects of Advertisement Encoding on the Failure to Discount Information: Implications for the Sleeper Effect," *Journal of Consumer Research* 15 (June 1988): 24–36.
19. Robber Makes It Biggs in Ad," *Advertising Age* (May 29, 1989): 26.
20. Bruce Horovitz, "Gen Y: A Tough Crowd to Sell," *USA Today Online* (April 21, 2002).
21. Deborah Ball, "Half-brother of Osama bin Laden Plans Line of 'Bin Laden' Clothing," *Wall Street Journal Interactive Edition* (January 1, 2002).
22. Robert LaFranco, "MTV Conquers Madison Avenue," *Forbes* (June 3, 1996): 138.
23. Alice H. Eagly, Andy Wood, and Shelly Chaiken, "Causal Inferences about Communicators and Their Effect in Opinion Change," *Journal of Personality and Social Psychology* 36, no. 4 (1978): 424–35.
24. William Dowell, "Microsoft Offers Tips to Agreeable Academics," *Time* (June 1, 1998): 22.
25. Suzanne Vranica and Sam Walker, "Tiger Woods Switches Watches; Branding Experts Disapprove," *Wall Street Journal Interactive Edition* (October 7, 2002).
26. Stuart Elliott, "Celebrity Promoter Says the Words and Has Her Say," *New York Times on the Web* (November 25, 2002).
27. This section is based on a discussion in Michael R. Solomon, *Conquering Consumerspace: Marketing Strategies for a Branded World*

(New York: AMACOM, 2003); see also David Lewis and Darren Bridger, *The Soul of the New Consumer: Authenticity—What We Buy and Why in the New Economy* (London: Nicholas Brealey Publishing, 2000).

28. Hillary Chura, "No Bull: Coke Targets Clubs," *Advertising Age* (December 9, 2002): 3(2).

29. Jeff Neff, "Pressure Points at IPG," *Advertising Age* (December 2001): 4.

30. Melody Petersen, "Suit Says Company Promoted Drug in Exam Rooms, *New York Times on the Web* (May 15, 2002).

31. Melody Petersen, "CNN to Reveal When Guests Promote Drugs for Companies," *New York Times on the Web* (August 23, 2002).

32. Eilene Zimmerman, "Catch the Bug," *Sales and Marketing Management* (February 2001): 78.

33. Becky Ebenkamp, "Guerrilla Marketers of the Year," *Brandweek* (November 13, 2001): 25–32.

34. Wayne Friedman, "Street Marketing Hits the Internet," *Advertising Age* (May 2000): 32; Erin White, "Online Buzz Helps Album Skyrocket to Top of Charts," *Wall Street Journal Interactive Edition* (October 5, 1999).

35. Peter Romeo, "A Restaurateur's Guide to the Web," *Restaurant Business* 95, no. 14 (September 20, 1996): 181.

36. Kruti Trivedi, "Great-Grandson of Artist Renoir Uses His Name for Marketing Blitz," *Wall Street Journal Interactive Edition* (September 2, 1999).

37. Richard Sandomir, "A Pitchman with Punch: George Foreman Sells His Name," *New York Times on the Web* (January 21, 2000).

38. Karen K. Dion, "What Is Beautiful Is Good," *Journal of Personality and Social Psychology* 24 (December 1972): 285–90.

39. Michael J. Baker and Gilbert A. Churchill Jr., "The Impact of Physically Attractive Models on Advertising Evaluations," *Journal of Marketing Research* 14 (November 1977): 538–55; Marjorie J. Caballero and William M. Pride, "Selected Effects of Salesperson Sex and Attractiveness in Direct Mail Advertisements," *Journal of Marketing* 48 (January 1984): 94–100; W. Benoy Joseph, "The Credibility of Physically Attractive Communicators: A Review," *Journal of Advertising* 11, no. 3 (1982): 15–24; Lynn R. Kahle and Pamola M. Homer, "Physical Attractiveness of the Celebrity Endorser: A Social Adaptation Perspective," *Journal of Consumer Research* 11 (March 1985): 954–61; Judson Mills and Eliot Aronson, "Opinion Change as a Function of Communicator's Attractiveness and Desire to Influence," *Journal of Personality and Social Psychology* 1 (1965): 173–77.

40. Leonard N. Reid and Lawrence C. Soley, "Decorative Models and the Readership of Magazine Ads," *Journal of Advertising Research* 23, no. 2 (1983): 27–32.

41. Marjorie J. Caballero, James R. Lumpkin, and Charles S. Madden, "Using Physical Attractiveness as an Advertising Tool: An Empirical Test of the Attraction Phenomenon," *Journal of Advertising Research* (August–September 1989): 16–22.

42. Baker and Churchill Jr., "The Impact of Physically Attractive Models on Advertising Evaluations"; George E. Belch, Michael A. Belch, and Angelina Villareal, "Effects of Advertising Communications: Review of Research," in *Research in Marketing*, no. 9 (Greenwich, CT: JAI Press, 1987): 59–117; A. E. Courtney and T. W. Whipple, *Sex Stereotyping in Advertising* (Lexington, MA: Lexington Books, 1983).

43. Kahle and Homer, "Physical Attractiveness of the Celebrity Endorser."

44. Vranica and Walker, "Tiger Woods Switches Watches; Branding Experts Disapprove."

45. Heather Buttle, Jane E. Raymond, and Shai Danziger, "Do Famous Faces Capture Attention?" paper presented at Association for Consumer Research Conference Columbus, Ohio (October 1999).

46. Michael A. Kamins, "Celebrity and Noncelebrity Advertising in a Two-Sided Context," *Journal of Advertising Research* 29 (June–July 1989): 34; Joseph M. Kamen, A. C. Azhari, and J. R. Kragh, "What a Spokesman Does for a Sponsor," *Journal of Advertising Research* 15, no. 2 (1975): 17–24; Lynn Langmeyer and Mary Walker, "A First Step to Identify the Meaning in Celebrity Endorsers," in Rebecca H. Holman and Michael R. Solomon, eds., *Advances in Consumer Research* 18 (Provo, UT: Association for Consumer Research, 1991): 364–71.

47. Grant McCracken, "Who Is the Celebrity Endorser? Cultural Foundations of the Endorsement Process," *Journal of Consumer Research* 16, no. 3 (December 1989): 310–21.

48. Michael A. Kamins, "An Investigation into the 'Match-Up' Hypothesis in Celebrity Advertising: When Beauty May Be Only Skin Deep," *Journal of Advertising* 19, no. 1 (1990): 4–13; Kahle and Homer, "Physical Attractiveness of the Celebrity Endorser," 954–61.

49. Roberts L. Johnnie, "The Rap of Luxury," *Newsweek* (September 2, 2002): 42–44.

50. David P. Hamilton, "Celebrities Help 'Educate' Public about the Virtues of New Drugs," *Wall Street Journal Interactive Edition* (April 21, 2002).

51. Joel Baglole, "Mascots Are Getting Bigger Role in Corporate Advertising Plans," *Wall Street Journal Interactive Edition* (April 9, 2002).

52. David Germain, "Simone Leading Lady Is Living and Breathing Model," *New York Times* (August 26, 2002): D1.

53. Christopher Lawton, "Virtual Characters Push Cigarettes in New Vending Machine," *Wall Street Journal* (August 6, 2002): B1 (2).

54. Tran T. L. Knanh and Regalado Antonio, "Web Sites Bet on Attracting Viewers with Humanlike Presences of Avatars," *Wall Street Journal Interactive Edition* (January 24, 2001).

55. Olaf Schirm, President, NoDNA GmbH, personal Internet communication, August 13, 2002.

56. David W. Stewart and David H. Furse, "The Effects of Television Advertising Execution on Recall, Comprehension, and Persuasion," *Psychology & Marketing* 2 (Fall 1985): 135–60.

57. R. C. Grass and W. H. Wallace, "Advertising Communication: Print Vs. TV," *Journal of Advertising Research* 14 (1974): 19–23.

58. Elizabeth C. Hirschman and Michael R. Solomon, "Utilitarian, Aesthetic, and Familiarity Responses to Verbal versus Visual Advertisements," in Thomas C. Kinnear, ed., *Advances in Consumer Research* 11 (Provo, UT: Association for Consumer Research, 1984): 426–31.

59. Terry L. Childers and Michael J. Houston, "Conditions for a Picture-Superiority Effect on Consumer Memory," *Journal of Consumer Research* 11 (September 1984): 643–54.

60. Andrew A. Mitchell, "The Effect of Verbal and Visual Components of Advertisements on Brand Attitudes and Attitude toward the Advertisement," *Journal of Consumer Research* 13 (June 1986): 12–24.

61. John R. Rossiter and Larry Percy, "Attitude Change through Visual Imagery in Advertising," *Journal of Advertising Research* 9, no. 2 (1980): 10–16.

62. Jolita Kiselius and Brian Sternthal, "Examining the Vividness Controversy: An Availability-Valence Interpretation," *Journal of Consumer Research* 12 (March 1986): 418–31.

63. Scott B. Mackenzie, "The Role of Attention in Mediating the Effect of Advertising on Attribute Importance," *Journal of Consumer Research* 13 (September 1986): 174–95.

64. Robert B. Zajonc, "Attitudinal Effects of Mere Exposure," *Journal of Personality and Social Psychology* 8 (1968): 1–29.

65. Giles D'Souza and Ram C. Rao, "Can Repeating an Advertisement More Frequently Than the Competition Affect Brand Preference in a Mature Market?" *Journal of Marketing* 59 (April 1995): 32–42.

66. George E. Belch, "The Effects of Television Commercial Repetition on Cognitive Response and Message Acceptance," *Journal of Consumer Research* 9 (June 1982): 56–65; Marian Burke and Julie Edell, "Ad Reactions over Time: Capturing Changes in the Real World," *Journal of Consumer Research* 13 (June 1986): 114–18; Herbert Krugman, "Why Three Exposures May Be Enough," *Journal of Advertising Research* 12 (December 1972): 11–14.

67. Robert F. Bornstein, "Exposure and Affect: Overview and Meta-Analysis of Research, 1968–1987," *Psychological Bulletin* 106, no. 2 (1989): 265–89; Arno Rethans, John Swasy, and Lawrence Marks, "Effects of Television Commercial Repetition, Receiver Knowledge, and Commercial Length: A Test of the Two-Factor Model," *Journal of Marketing Research* 23 (February 1986): 50–61.

68. Curtis P. Haugtvedt, David W. Schumann, Wendy L. Schneier, and Wendy L. Warren, "Advertising Repetition and Variation Strategies: Implications for Understanding Attitude Strength," *Journal of Consumer Research* 21 (June 1994): 176–89.

69. Linda L. Golden and Mark I. Alpert, "Comparative Analysis of the Relative Effectiveness of One- and Two-Sided Communication for Contrasting Products," *Journal of Advertising* 16 (1987): 18–25; Kamins, "Celebrity and Noncelebrity Advertising in a Two-Sided Context"; Robert B. Settle and Linda L. Golden, "Attribution Theory and Advertiser Credibility," *Journal of Marketing Research* 11 (May 1974): 181–85.

70. See Alan G. Sawyer, "The Effects of Repetition of Refutational and Supportive Advertising Appeals," *Journal of Marketing Research* 10 (February 1973): 23–33; George J. Szybillo and Richard Heslin, "Resistance to Persuasion: Inoculation Theory in a Marketing Context," *Journal of Marketing Research* 10 (November 1973): 396–403.

71. Golden and Alpert, "Comparative Analysis of the Relative Effectiveness of One- and Two-Sided Communication for Contrasting Products."

72. Ryan Dezember, "FTC Seeks More Media Policing to Foil Bogus Diet Promotions," *Wall Street Journal Interactive Edition* (September 18, 2002).

73. Belch et al., "Effects of Advertising Communications."

74. Frank R. Kardes, "Spontaneous Inference Processes in Advertising: The Effects of Conclusion Omission and Involvement on Persuasion," *Journal of Consumer Research* 15 (September 1988): 225–33.

75. Belch et al., "Effects of Advertising Communications"; Cornelia Pechmann and Gabriel Esteban, "Persuasion Processes Associated with Direct Comparative and Noncomparative Advertising and Implications for Advertising Effectiveness," *Journal of Consumer Psychology* 2, no. 4 (1994): 403–32.

76. Cornelia Dröge and Rene Y. Darmon, "Associative Positioning Strategies Through Comparative Advertising: Attribute vs. Overall Similarity Approaches," *Journal of Marketing Research* 24 (1987): 377–89; D. Muehling and N. Kangun, "The Multidimensionality of Comparative Advertising: Implications for the FTC," *Journal of Public Policy and Marketing* (1985): 112–28; Beth A. Walker and Helen H. Anderson, "Reconceptualizing Comparative Advertising: A Framework and Theory of Effects," in Rebecca H. Holman and Michael R. Solomon, eds., *Advances in Consumer Research* 18 (Provo, UT: Association for Consumer Research, 1991): 342–47; William L. Wilkie and Paul W. Farris, "Comparison Advertising: Problems and Potential," *Journal of Marketing* 39 (October 1975): 7–15; R. G. Wyckham, "Implied Superiority Claims," *Journal of Advertising Research* (February–March 1987): 54–63.

77. Stephen A. Goodwin and Michael Etgar, "An Experimental Investigation of Comparative Advertising: Impact of Message Appeal, Information Load, and Utility of Product Class," *Journal of Marketing Research* 17 (May 1980): 187–202; Gerald J. Gorn and Charles B. Weinberg, "The Impact of Comparative Advertising on Perception and Attitude: Some Positive Findings," *Journal of Consumer Research* 11 (September 1984): 719–27; Terence A. Shimp and David C. Dyer, "The Effects of Comparative Advertising Mediated by Market Position of Sponsoring Brand," *Journal of Advertising* 3 (Summer 1978): 13–19; R. Dale Wilson, "An Empirical Evaluation of Comparative Advertising Messages: Subjects' Responses to Perceptual Dimensions," in B. B. Anderson, ed., *Advances in Consumer Research* 3 (Ann Arbor, MI: Association for Consumer Research, 1976): 53–57.

78. Allison Fass, "Attack Ads," *Forbes* (October 28, 2002): 60.

79. Dhruv Grewal, Sukumar Kavanoor, Edward F. Fern, Carolyn Costley, and James Barnes, "Comparative versus Noncomparative Advertising: A Meta-Analysis," *Journal of Marketing* 61 (October 1997): 1–15.

80. Fass, "Attack Ads," 60.

81. Dröge and Darmon, "Associative Positioning Strategies through Comparative Advertising: Attribute vs. Overall Similarity Approaches."

82. Jean Halliday, "Survey: Comparative Ads Can Dent Car's Credibility," *Advertising Age* (May 4, 1998): 26.

83. Sarah Ellison and John Carreyrou, "Beauty Battle: Giant L'Oréal Faces off Against Rival P&G," *Wall Street Journal Interactive Edition* (January 9, 2003).

84. Alec Klein, "The Techies Grumbled, but Polaroid's Pocket Turned into a Huge Hit," *Wall Street Journal* (May 2, 2000): A1.

85. Edward F. Cone, "Image and Reality," *Forbes* (December 14, 1987): 226.

86. H. Zielske, "Does Day-After Recall Penalize 'Feeling' Ads?" *Journal of Advertising Research* 22 (1982): 19–22.

87. Allessandra Galloni, "Lee's Cheeky Ads Are Central to New European Campaign," *Wall Street Journal Interactive Edition* (March 15, 2002).

88. John Lichfield, "French Get Bored with Sex," *The Independent* London (July 30, 1997).

89. Belch et al., "Effects of Advertising Communications"; Courtney and Whipple, *Sex Stereotyping in Advertising*; Michael S. LaTour, "Female Nudity in Print Advertising: An Analysis of Gender Differences in Arousal and Ad Response," *Psychology & Marketing* 7, no. 1 (1990): 65–81; B. G. Yovovich, "Sex in Advertising—The Power and the Perils," *Advertising Age* (May 2, 1983): M4–M5. For an interesting interpretive analysis, see Richard Elliott and Mark Ritson, "Practicing Existential Consumption: The Lived Meaning of Sexuality in Advertising," in Frank R. Kardes and Mita Sujan, eds., *Advances in Consumer Behavior* 22 (1995): 740–45.

90. Penny M. Simpson, Steve Horton, and Gene Brown, "Male Nudity in Advertisements: A Modified Replication and Extension of Gender and Product Effects," *Journal of the Academy of Marketing Science* 24, no. 3 (1996): 257–62.

91. Rebecca Gardyn, "Where's the Lovin'?" *American Demographics* (February 2001): 10.

92. Michael S. LaTour and Tony L. Henthorne, "Ethical Judgments of Sexual Appeals in Print Advertising," *Journal of Advertising* 23, no. 3 (September 1994): 81–90.

93. Roger Thurow, "As In-Your-Face Ads Backfire, Nike Finds a New Global Tack," *Wall Street Journal Interactive Edition* (May 5, 1997).

94. Katharine Q. Seelye, "Metamucil Ad Featuring Old Faithful Causes a Stir," *New York Times Online* (January 19, 2003).

95. Marc G. Weinberger and Harlan E. Spotts, "Humor in U.S. versus U.K. TV Commercials: A Comparison," *Journal of Advertising* 18, no. 2 (1989): 39–44.

96. Thomas J. Madden, "Humor in Advertising: An Experimental Analysis" (working paper, no. 83-27, University of Massachusetts, 1984); Thomas J. Madden and Marc G. Weinberger, "The Effects of Humor on Attention in Magazine Advertising," *Journal of Advertising* 11, no. 3 (1982): 8–14; Weinberger and Spotts, "Humor in U.S. versus

U.K. TV Commercials"; see also Ashesh Mukherjee and Laurette Dubé, "The Use of Humor in Threat-Related Advertising," unpublished manuscript, McGill University, June 2002.

97. David Gardner, "The Distraction Hypothesis in Marketing," *Journal of Advertising Research* 10 (1970): 25–30.

98. Funny Ads Provide Welcome Relief During These Gloom and Doom Days," *Marketing News* (April 17, 1981): 3.

99. Ex-Lax Taken off Shelves for Now," *Montgomery Advertiser* (August 30, 1997): 1A.

100. Michael L. Ray and William L. Wilkie, "Fear: The Potential of an Appeal Neglected by Marketing," *Journal of Marketing* 34, no. 1 (1970): 54–62.

101. Brian Sternthal and C. Samuel Craig, "Fear Appeals: Revisited and Revised," *Journal of Consumer Research* 1 (December 1974): 22–34.

102. Punam Anand Keller and Lauren Goldberg Block, "Increasing the Effectiveness of Fear Appeals: The Effect of Arousal and Elaboration," *Journal of Consumer Research* 22 (March 1996): 448–59.

103. Ronald Paul Hill, "An Exploration of the Relationship Between AIDS-Related Anxiety and the Evaluation of Condom Advertisements," *Journal of Advertising* 17, no. 4 (1988): 35–42.

104. Randall Rothenberg, "Talking Too Tough on Life's Risks?" *New York Times* (February 16, 1990): D1.

105. Denise D. Schoenbachler and Tommy E. Whittler, "Adolescent Processing of Social and Physical Threat Communications," *Journal of Advertising* 25, no. 4 (Winter 1996): 37–54.

106. Herbert J. Rotfeld, Auburn University, personal communication, December 9, 1997; Herbert J. Rotfeld, "Fear Appeals and Persuasion: Assumptions and Errors in Advertising Research," *Current Issues & Research in Advertising* 11 (1988) 1: 21–40; Michael S. LaTour and Herbert J. Rotfeld, "There are Threats and (Maybe) Fear-Caused Arousal: Theory and Confusions of Appeals to Fear and Fear Arousal Itself," *Journal of Advertising* 26 (Fall 1997) 3: 45–59.

107. Barbara B. Stern, "Medieval Allegory: Roots of Advertising Strategy for the Mass Market," *Journal of Marketing* 52 (July 1988): 84–94.

108. Edward F. McQuarrie and David Glen Mick, "On Resonance: A Critical Pluralistic Inquiry into Advertising Rhetoric," *Journal of Consumer Research* 19 (September 1992): 180–97.

109. See Linda M. Scott, "The Troupe: Celebrities as Dramatis Personae in Advertisements," in Rebecca H. Holman and Michael R. Solomon, eds., *Advances in Consumer Research* 18 (Provo, UT: Association for Consumer Research, 1991): 355–63; Barbara Stern, "Literary Criticism and Consumer Research: Overview and Illustrative Analysis," *Journal of Consumer Research* 16 (1989): 322–34; Judith Williamson, *Decoding Advertisements* (Boston: Marion Boyars, 1978).

110. John Deighton, Daniel Romer, and Josh McQueen, "Using Drama to Persuade," *Journal of Consumer Research* 16 (December 1989): 335–43.

111. Richard E. Petty, John T. Cacioppo, and David Schumann, "Central and Peripheral Routes to Advertising Effectiveness: The Moderating Role of Involvement," *Journal of Consumer Research* 10, no. 2 (1983): 135–46.

112. Jerry C. Olson, Daniel R. Toy, and Philip A. Dover, "Do Cognitive Responses Mediate the Effects of Advertising Content on Cognitive Structure?" *Journal of Consumer Research* 9, no. 3 (1982): 245–62.

113. Julie A. Edell and Andrew A. Mitchell, "An Information Processing Approach to Cognitive Responses," in S. C. Jain, ed., *Research Frontiers in Marketing: Dialogues and Directions* (Chicago: American Marketing Association, 1978).

114. See Mary Jo Bitner and Carl Obermiller, "The Elaboration Likelihood Model: Limitations and Extensions in Marketing," in Elizabeth C. Hirschman and Morris B. Holbrook, eds., *Advances in Consumer Research* 12 (Provo, UT: Association for Consumer Research, 1985): 420–25; Meryl P. Gardner, "Does Attitude Toward the Ad Affect Brand Attitude Under a Brand Evaluation Set?" *Journal of Marketing Research* 22 (1985): 192–98; C. W. Park and S. M. Young, "Consumer Response to Television Commercials: The Impact of Involvement and Background Music on Brand Attitude Formation," *Journal of Marketing Research* 23 (1986): 11–24; Petty, Cacioppo, and Schumann, "Central and Peripheral Routes to Advertising Effectiveness." For a discussion of how different kinds of involvement interact with the ELM, see Robin A. Higie, Lawrence F. Feick, and Linda L. Price, "The Importance of Peripheral Cues in Attitude Formation for Enduring and Task-Involved Individuals," in Rebecca H. Holman and Michael R. Solomon, eds., *Advances in Consumer Research* 18 (Provo, UT: Association for Consumer Research, 1991): 187–93.

115. J. Craig Andrews and Terence A. Shimp, "Effects of Involvement, Argument Strength, and Source Characteristics on Central and Peripheral Processing in Advertising," *Psychology & Marketing* 7 (Fall 1990): 195–214.

116. Richard E. Petty, John T. Cacioppo, Constantine Sedikides, and Alan J. Strathman, "Affect and Persuasion: A Contemporary Perspective," *American Behavioral Scientist* 31, no. 3 (1988): 355–71.

HE'S THE STRONGEST MAN ON THE INTERNET. LET HIS MUSCLE WORK FOR YOU.

...h Jeeves puts the power of the Web's #1 ranked search engine
... That strength puts your message in the right place, at
... the right people.

...d ad products break through the online clutter and deliver a result 6 times higher
...aditional ads. But that's what you'd expect from someone as mighty as Jeeves.

... JEEVES or contact us at advertise@ask.com

...he moment they're most interested in my product? **Ask**

Consumers as Decision Makers

This section explores how we make consumption decisions and discusses the many influences exerted by others during this process. Chapter 9 focuses on the basic sequence of steps we undergo when making a decision. Chapter 10 considers how the particular situation in which we find ourselves affects these decisions and how we go about evaluating the results of our choices. Chapter 11 provides an overview of group processes and discusses the reasons we are motivated to conform to the expectations of others when we choose and display our purchases. Chapter 12 goes on to consider the many instances in which our purchase decisions are made in conjunction with others, especially coworkers or family members.

■ CHAPTERS AHEAD

CHAPTER 9	CHAPTER 10	CHAPTER 11	CHAPTER 12
Individual Decision Making	Buying and Disposing	Group Influence and Opinion Leadership	Organizational and Household Decision Making

Individual Decision Making

richard has had it. There's only so much longer he can go on watching TV on his tiny, antiquated black-and-white set. It was bad enough trying to listen to the scratchy music in MTV videos and squinting through *Friends.* The final straw was when he couldn't tell the Titans from the Jaguars during NFL football. When he went next door to watch the second half on Mark's home theater setup, he really realized what he had been missing. Budget or not, it was time to act: A man has to have his priorities.

Where to start looking? The Web, naturally. Richard checks out a few comparison-shopping Web sites, including *botspot.com* and *pricingcentral.com.* After narrowing down his options, he ventures out to scope out a few sets in person. He figures he'll probably get a decent selection (and an affordable price) at one of those huge new warehouse stores. Arriving at Zany Zack's Appliance Emporium, Richard heads straight for the Video Zone in the back—barely noticing the rows of toasters, microwave ovens, and stereos on his way. Within minutes, a smiling salesman in a cheap suit accosts him. Even though he could use some help, Richard tells the salesman he's just browsing—he figures these guys don't know what they're talking about, and they're just out to make a sale no matter what.

Richard starts to examine some of the features on the 60-inch color sets. He knew his friend Carol had a set by Prime Wave that she really liked, and his sister Diane had warned him to stay away from the Kamashita. Although Richard finds a Prime Wave model loaded to the max with features such as a sleep timer, on-screen programming menu, cable-compatible tuner, and picture-in-picture, he chooses the less expensive Precision 2000X because it has one feature that really catches his fancy: stereo broadcast reception.

Later that day, Richard is a happy man as he sits in his easy chair, watching India.Arie do her thing on MTV. If he's going to be a couch potato, he's going in style.

■ CONSUMERS AS PROBLEM SOLVERS

A consumer purchase is a response to a problem, which in Richard's case is the perceived need for a new TV. His situation is similar to that encountered by consumers virtually every day of their lives. He realizes that he wants to make a purchase, and he goes through a series of steps in order to make it. These steps can be described as (1) problem recognition, (2) information search, (3) evaluation of alternatives, and (4) product choice. Of course, after the decision is made, the quality of that decision affects the final step in the process, in which learning occurs based on how well the choice worked out. This learning process, of course, influences the likelihood that the same choice will be made the next time the need for a similar decision occurs.

Figure 9.1 provides an overview of this decision-making process. This chapter begins by considering various approaches consumers use when faced with a purchase decision. It then focuses on three of the steps in the decision process: how consumers recognize the problem, or need for a product; their search for information about product choices; and the ways in which they evaluate alternatives to arrive at a decision. Chapter 10 considers influences in the actual purchase situation, as well as the person's satisfaction with the decision.

Because some purchase decisions are more important than others, the amount of effort we put into each one differs. Sometimes the decision-making process is almost automatic; we seem to make snap judgments based on very little information. At other times, coming to a purchase decision begins to resemble a full-time job. A person may literally spend days or weeks thinking about an important purchase such as a new home, even to the point of obsession.

Perspectives on Decision Making

Traditionally, consumer researchers have approached decision makers from a **rational perspective**. In this view, people calmly and carefully integrate as much information as possible with what they already know about a product, painstakingly weigh the pluses and minuses of each alternative, and arrive at a satisfactory decision. This process implies that steps in decision making should be carefully studied by marketing managers to understand how information is obtained, how beliefs are formed, and what product choice criteria are specified by consumers. Products then can be developed that emphasize appropriate attributes, and promotional strategies can be tailored to deliver the types of information most likely to be desired in the most effective formats.[1]

How valid is this perspective? Sure, consumers do follow these decision-making steps when making some purchases, but such a process is not an accurate portrayal of many of our purchase decisions.[2] Consumers simply do not go through this elaborate sequence every time they buy something. If they did, their entire lives would be spent making such decisions, leaving them very little time to enjoy the things they eventually decide to buy. Some of our buying behaviors simply don't seem "rational" because they don't serve a logical purpose (e.g., people in Scotland who break the law to collect the eggs of a rare bird called an Osprey even though they have no monetary value[3]); others are done with virtually no advance planning at all (e.g., impulsively grabbing that tempting candy bar from the rack while waiting to pay for groceries). Still other actions actually are contrary to those predicted

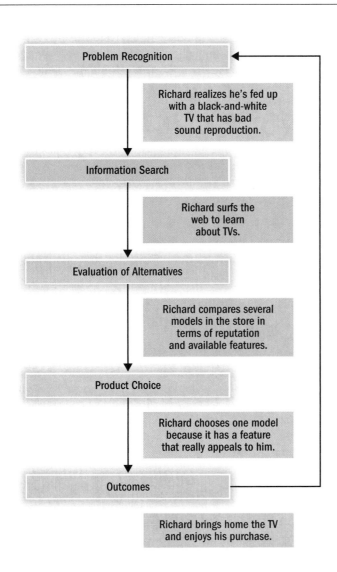

■ FIGURE 9.1
STAGES IN CONSUMER DECISION MAKING

by rational models. For example, **purchase momentum** occurs when these initial impulses actually increase the likelihood that we will buy even more (instead of less as our needs are satisfied), almost as if we get "revved up" and plunge into a spending spree (we've all been there!).[4]

Researchers are now beginning to realize that decision makers actually possess a repertoire of strategies. A consumer evaluates the effort required to make a particular choice, and then he or she chooses a strategy best suited to the level of effort required. This sequence of events is known as *constructive processing*. Rather than using a big club to kill an ant, consumers tailor their degree of cognitive "effort" to the task at hand.[5] When a well-thought-out, rational approach is required, we'll invest the brainpower to do it. Otherwise, we look for shortcuts or fall back on learned responses that "automate" these choices.

Some decisions are made under conditions of low involvement, as discussed in Chapter 4. In many of these situations, the consumer's decision is a learned response to environmental cues (see Chapter 3), as when he or she decides to buy something on impulse that is promoted as a "surprise special" in a store. A concentration on these types of decisions can be described as the **behavioral influence perspective**. Under these circumstances, managers must concentrate on assessing

Net Profit

Marketers continue to seek out strategies that enhance consumers' involvement with their messages and products in order to capture their attention and make it more likely that people will tune in to the information they are presenting. Interactive TV is one new route to achieving this goal. Cable companies, satellite TV, and software giants including Microsoft have made interactive TV a key part of their strategies and are pouring billions into it. So far, Americans are pretty apathetic about interactive, but the concept is gaining critical mass in Europe, particularly in the United Kingdom. British consumers routinely use their TVs to place bets on races, change camera angles while watching sporting events (e.g., "player-cams" that follow specific athletes during soccer games), and interact with game shows. In one cult hit called Banzai, viewers vote by remote control to predict who will win such "sporting events" as Magical Midget Climbs (contestants try to climb a basketball player) and the Old Lady Wheelchair Chicken Challenge where two old ladies careen toward each other until one chickens out.[8]

the characteristics of the environment, such as the design of a retail outlet or whether a package is enticing, that will influence members of a target market.[6]

In other cases, consumers are highly involved in a decision, but still the selections made cannot wholly be explained rationally. For example, the traditional approach is hard-pressed to explain a person's choice of art, music, or even a spouse. In these cases, no single quality is the determining factor. Instead, the **experiential perspective** stresses the *Gestalt*, or totality, of the product or service.[7] Marketers in these areas focus on measuring consumers' affective responses to products or services and develop offerings that elicit appropriate subjective reactions.

Types of Consumer Decisions

One helpful way to characterize the decision-making process is to consider the amount of effort that goes into the decision each time it must be made. Consumer researchers have found it convenient to think in terms of a continuum, which is

This ad for the U.S. Postal Service presents a problem, illustrates the decision-making process, and offers a solution.

anchored on one end by habitual decision making and at the other extreme by extended problem solving. Many decisions fall somewhere in the middle and are characterized by limited problem solving. Figure 9.2 presents this continuum.

Extended Problem Solving

Decisions involving **extended problem solving** correspond most closely to the traditional decision-making perspective. As Table 9.1 indicates, the extended problem-solving process is usually initiated by a motive that is fairly central to the self-concept (see Chapter 5), and the eventual decision is perceived to carry a fair degree of risk. The consumer tries to collect as much information as possible, both from memory (internal search) and from outside sources (external search). Based on the importance of the decision, each product alternative is carefully evaluated. The evaluation is often made by considering the attributes of one brand at a time and seeing how each brand's attributes shape up to some set of desired characteristics.

Limited Problem Solving

Limited problem solving is usually more straightforward and simple. Buyers are not as motivated to search for information or to evaluate each alternative rigorously. People instead use simple *decision rules* to choose among alternatives. These cognitive shortcuts (more about these later) enable them to fall back on general guidelines, instead of having to start from scratch every time a decision is to be made.

Habitual Decision Making

Both extended and limited problem-solving modes involve some degree of information search and deliberation, though they vary in the degree to which these activities are undertaken. At the other end of the choice continuum, however, lies **habitual decision making**—choices made with little to no conscious effort. Many purchase decisions are so routinized that we may not realize we've made them until we look in our shopping carts. We make choices characterized by *automaticity* with minimal effort and without conscious control.[11]

Although this kind of thoughtless activity may seem dangerous or at best stupid, it is actually quite efficient in many cases. The development of habitual, repetitive behavior allows consumers to minimize the time and energy spent on mundane purchase decisions. On the other hand, habitual decision making poses a problem when a marketer tries to introduce a new way of doing an old task. In this case consumers must be convinced to "unfreeze" their former habit and replace it with a new one — perhaps by using an ATM machine instead of a live bank teller, or switching to a self-service gas pump instead of being waited on by an attendant. This is the obstacle now confronting a device called the Personal Valet, a cabinet-size clothes refresher made by Whirlpool that removes odors and wrinkles using a chemical formula developed

Europeans also commonly use *teletext*, a one-way information service that lets them view news headlines, weather reports, movie schedules, flight times, and other tidbits on their TVs. Again, these services are not easily found in the United States, partly because of the higher usage of the Internet. As a result these applications are less likely to rely on coordinated efforts among broadcasters and more on individual pay television providers. In addition, American companies have focused more on technology than content, while European firms have done the opposite. As one American industry executive observed, "Here we were focused on building a better mousetrap. In Europe they were figuring out what the mouse wanted to eat." [9]

However, some U.S. online initiatives have taken up the slack by encouraging Web surfers to contribute their own content. [Outfits like *pseudo.com*, *Bolt.com*, Atomfilms, and the Swatch Groupstream feature original video programming submitted by the audience.] During the 2000 political conventions, ads on *pseudo.com* even allowed viewers to reconfigure the facial features of each party's presidential candidates. *Bolt.com* gave cameras to teen viewers to encourage them to shoot their own spots. New Line Cinema formed a partnership with *garageband.com* to give unknown bands a chance to be included in Adam Sandler's movie *Little Nicky*.[10] When viewers become producers, everyone benefits from the enhanced involvement that results.

■ **FIGURE 9.2** A CONTINUUM OF BUYING DECISION BEHAVIOR

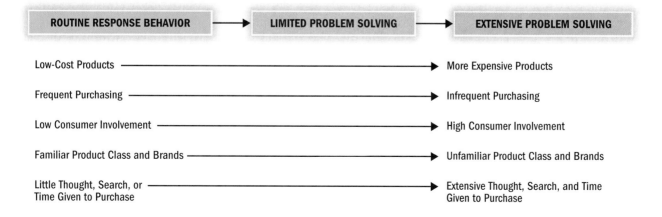

TABLE 9.1
CHARACTERISTICS OF LIMITED VERSUS EXTENDED PROBLEM SOLVING

	Limited Problem Solving	**Extended Problem Solving**
Motivation	Low risk and involvement	High risk and involvement
Information Search	Little search	Extensive search
	Information processed passively	Information process actively
	In-store decision likely	Multiple sources consulted prior to store visits
Alternative Evaluation	Weakly held beliefs	Strongly held beliefs
	Only most prominent criteria used	Many criteria used
	Alternatives perceived as basically similar	Significant differences perceived among alternatives
	Noncompensatory strategy used	Compensatory strategy used
Purchase	Limited shopping time; may prefer self-service	Many outlets shopped if needed
	Choice often influenced by store displays	Communication with store personnel often desirable

by Procter & Gamble. For the product to succeed, the two companies must find a way to "unfreeze" the habit of taking one's clothes to the dry cleaner.[12]

■ PROBLEM RECOGNITION

Problem recognition occurs whenever the consumer sees a significant difference between his or her current state of affairs and some desired or ideal state. The consumer perceives there is a problem to be solved, which may be small or large, simple or complex. A person who unexpectedly runs out of gas on the highway has a problem, as does the person who becomes dissatisfied with the image of his or her car, even though there is nothing mechanically wrong with it. For example, although the quality of Richard's TV had not changed, his *standard of comparison* was altered, and he was confronted with a desire he did not have prior to watching his friend's TV.

Figure 9.3 shows that a problem can arise in one of two ways. As in the case of the person running out of gas, the quality of the consumer's *actual state* can move downward (*need recognition*). On the other hand, as in the case of the person who craves a newer, flashier car, the consumer's *ideal state* can move upward (*opportunity recognition*). Either way, a gulf occurs between the actual state and the ideal state.[13] In Richard's case, a problem was perceived as a result of opportunity recognition; his ideal state in terms of television reception quality was altered.

Need recognition can occur in several ways. The quality of the person's actual state can be diminished simply by running out of a product, by buying a product that turns out not to adequately satisfy needs, or by creating new needs (e.g., buying a house can set off an avalanche of other choices, because many new things are needed to fill the house). Opportunity recognition often occurs when a consumer is exposed to different or better-quality products. This happens because the person's circumstances have somehow changed, as when an individual goes to college or gets a new job. As the person's frame of reference shifts, purchases are made to adapt to the new environment.

Although problem recognition can and does occur naturally, this process is often spurred by marketing efforts. In some cases, marketers attempt to create *primary demand*, in which consumers are encouraged to use a product or service regardless of the brand they choose. Such needs are often encouraged in the early stages of a product's life cycle as, for example, when microwave ovens were first introduced. *Secondary demand*, in which consumers are prompted to prefer a specific brand instead of others, can occur only if primary demand already exists. At

■ **FIGURE 9.3** PROBLEM RECOGNITION: SHIFTS IN ACTUAL OR IDEAL STATES

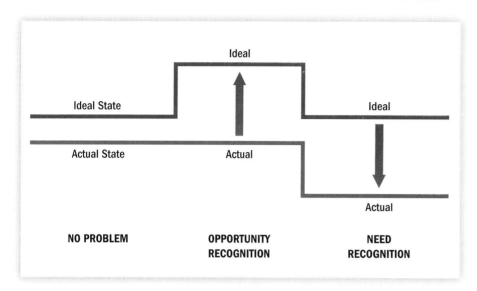

this point, marketers must convince consumers that choosing their brand rather than others in the same category can best solve a problem.

■ INFORMATION SEARCH

Once a problem has been recognized, consumers need adequate information to resolve it. Information search is the process by which the consumer surveys his or her environment for appropriate data to make a reasonable decision. This section will review some of the factors involved in this search.

Types of Information Search

A consumer may recognize a need and then search the marketplace for specific information (a process called *prepurchase search*). On the other hand, many consumers, especially veteran shoppers, enjoy browsing just for the fun of it, or because they like to stay up-to-date on what's happening in the marketplace. They are engaging in *ongoing search*.[14] Table 9.2 describes some differences between these two search modes.

Internal Versus External Search

Information sources can be roughly broken down into two types: internal and external. As a result of prior experience and simply living in a consumer culture, each of us has some degree of knowledge already in memory about many products. When confronted with a purchase decision, we may engage in *internal search* by scanning our own memory banks to assemble information about different product alternatives (see Chapter 3). Usually, though, even those of us who are the most market-savvy need to supplement this knowledge with external search, by which information is obtained from advertisements, friends, or just plain people watching.

Deliberate Versus "Accidental" Search

Our existing knowledge of a product may be the result of *directed learning:* On a previous occasion we had already searched for relevant information or experienced some of the alternatives. A parent who bought a birthday cake for one child last month, for example, probably has a good idea of the best kind to buy for another child this month.

The Tangled Web

Because of the dot-com bust of a few years ago, the Web has lost some of its original luster. Most industry analysts still see a bright future for e-commerce — for example, while holiday retail sales overall were abysmal in 2002, online sales posted strong gains from the year before.[22] What is changing, however, is what we'll see when we visit Web sites and what we do when we get there. Many Web site developers are cutting back on the glitzy "bells and whistles" such as elaborate animations that take forever to load. A lot of Web surfers are more goal-oriented than in the early days of the World Wide Web (that is, a few years ago).

Now many want to use the Web for information search rather than for entertainment (at least when they're not playing online video games). In March 2000, according to a survey by the Pew Internet and American Life Project in Washington, people averaged 90 minutes per online session. A year later, when the same people were polled, that time had dropped to 83 minutes. According to the report, those polled said that they were using the Web more to conduct business than to explore new areas, aiming to get offline as quickly as possible.[23] People also are seeking more control over what they see and what information they access. Research on this process demonstrates that surfers who can provide input into what they see on a site exhibit remember more of the site's contents, exhibit superior knowledge about the domain, and are more confident in their judgments.[24] Indeed, almost 80 percent of Internet users in a 2002 survey said they expect to find the product information they need on a Web site.[25] Web surfing isn't quite as much fun as it used to be, but it's becoming a lot more useful.

TABLE 9.2 A FRAMEWORK FOR CONSUMER INFORMATION SEARCH	
Prepurchase Search	**Ongoing Search**
Determinants	
Involvement in the purchase	Involvement with the product
Market environment	Market environment
Situational factors	Situational factors
Motives	
Making better purchase decisions	Building a bank of information for future use
	Experiencing fun and pleasure
Outcomes	
Increased product and market knowledge	Increased product and market knowledge leading to
Better purchase decisions	• future buying efficiencies
Increased satisfaction with the purchase outcome	• personal influence
	Increased impulse buying
	Increased satisfaction from search and other outcomes

Source: Peter H. Bloch, Daniel L. Sherrell, and Nancy M. Ridgway, "Consumer Search: An Extended Framework," *Journal of Consumer Research* 13 (June 1986): 120. Reprinted with permission of the University of Chicago Press.

Alternatively, we may acquire information in a more passive manner. Even though a product may not be of direct interest to us right now, exposure to advertising, packaging, and sales promotion activities may result in *incidental learning.* Mere exposure over time to conditioned stimuli and observations of others results in the learning of much material that may not be needed for some time after the fact, if ever. For marketers, this result is a benefit of steady, "low-dose" advertising, as product associations are established and maintained until the time they are needed.[18]

In some cases, we may be so expert about a product category (or at least believe we are) that no additional search is undertaken. Frequently, however, our own existing state of knowledge is not sufficient to make an adequate decision, and we must look elsewhere for more information. The sources we consult for advice vary: They may be impersonal and marketer-dominated sources, such as retailers and catalogs; they may be friends and family members; or they may be unbiased third parties such as *Consumer Reports.*[19]

The Economics of Information

The traditional decision-making perspective incorporates the *economics-of-information* approach to the search process; it assumes that consumers will gather as much data as needed to make an informed decision. Consumers form expectations of the value of additional information and continue to search to the extent that the rewards of doing so (what economists call the *utility*) exceed the costs. This utilitarian assumption also implies that the most valuable units of information will be collected first. Additional pieces will be absorbed only to the extent that they are seen to augment what is already known.[20] In other words, people will put themselves out to collect as much information as possible, as long as the process of gathering it is not too onerous or time-consuming.[21]

Variety seeking, the desire to choose new alternatives over more familiar ones, can influence consumers to switch from their favorite product to a less pleasurable item. This can occur even before an individual becomes satiated or tired of her favorite product. Research supports the idea that consumers are willing to trade enjoyment for variety because the unpredictability itself is rewarding.[26]

Do Consumers Always Search Rationally?

As we've seen, consumers don't necessarily engage in a rational search process where they carefully identify every alternative before choosing one they prefer. In fact, the amount of external search for most products is surprisingly small, even when additional information would most likely benefit the consumer. For example, lower-income shoppers, who have more to lose by making a bad purchase, actually search less prior to buying than do more affluent people.[27]

This Singaporean beer ad reminds us that not all product decisions are made rationally.

Like our friend Richard, some consumers typically visit only one or two stores and rarely seek out unbiased information sources prior to making a purchase decision, especially when little time is available to do so.[28] This pattern is especially prevalent for decisions regarding durable goods such as appliances or autos, even when these products represent significant investments. One study of Australian car buyers found that more than a third had made only two or fewer trips to inspect cars prior to buying one.[29]

This tendency to avoid external search is less prevalent when consumers consider the purchase of symbolic items, such as clothing. In those cases, not surprisingly, people tend to do a fair amount of external search, although most of it involves seeking the opinions of peers.[30] Although the stakes may be lower financially, these self-expressive decisions may be seen as having dire social consequences if the wrong choice is made. The level of perceived risk, a concept to be discussed shortly, is high.

In addition, consumers often are observed to engage in *brand switching*, even if their current brand satisfies their needs. For example, researchers for British brewer Bass Export, who were studying the American beer market, discovered a consumer trend toward having a repertoire of two to six favorite brands, rather than sticking to only one. This preference for brand switching led the firm to begin exporting its Tennent's 1885 lager to the United States, positioning the brew as an alternative to young drinkers' usual favorite brands.[31]

Sometimes, it seems that people just plain like to try new things—they are interested in variety seeking, in which the priority is to vary one's product experiences, perhaps as a form of stimulation or to reduce boredom. Variety seeking is especially likely to occur when people are in a good mood, or when there is relatively little stimulation elsewhere in their environment.[32] In the case of foods and beverages, variety seeking can occur due to *sensory-specific satiety*. Put simply, this means the pleasantness of a food item just eaten drops while the pleasantness of uneaten foods remains unchanged.[33] So even though we have favorites, we still like to sample other possibilities. On the other hand, when the decision situation is ambiguous or when there is little information about competing brands, consumers tend to opt for the safe choice by selecting familiar brands and maintaining the status quo. Figure 9.4 shows the brand attributes consumers consider most important when choosing among alternatives, according to a survey conducted by *Advertising Age*.

Biases in the Decision-Making Process

Consider the following scenario: You've been given a free ticket to an important football game. At the last minute, though, a sudden snowstorm makes getting to the stadium somewhat dangerous. Would you still go? Now, assume the same game and snowstorm, except this time you paid handsomely for the ticket. Would you head out in the storm in this case?

Analyses of people's responses to this situation and to other similar puzzles illustrates principles of **mental accounting**, in which decisions are influenced by the way a problem is posed (called *framing*), and by whether it is put in terms of gains or losses.[34] In this case, researchers find that people are more likely to risk their personal safety in the storm if they paid for the football ticket. Only the most die-hard fan would fail to recognize that this is an irrational choice, as the risk to the person is the same regardless of whether he or she got a great deal on the ticket. This decision-making bias is called the *sunk-cost fallacy*—having paid for something makes us reluctant to waste it.

Another bias is known as *loss aversion*. People place much more emphasis on loss than they do on gain. For example, for most people, losing money is more unpleasant than gaining money is pleasant. **Prospect theory**, a descriptive model of how people make choices, finds that utility is a function of gains and losses, and

■ FIGURE 9.4 ADVERTISING AGE POLL: IMPORTANCE OF BRAND ATTRIBUTES

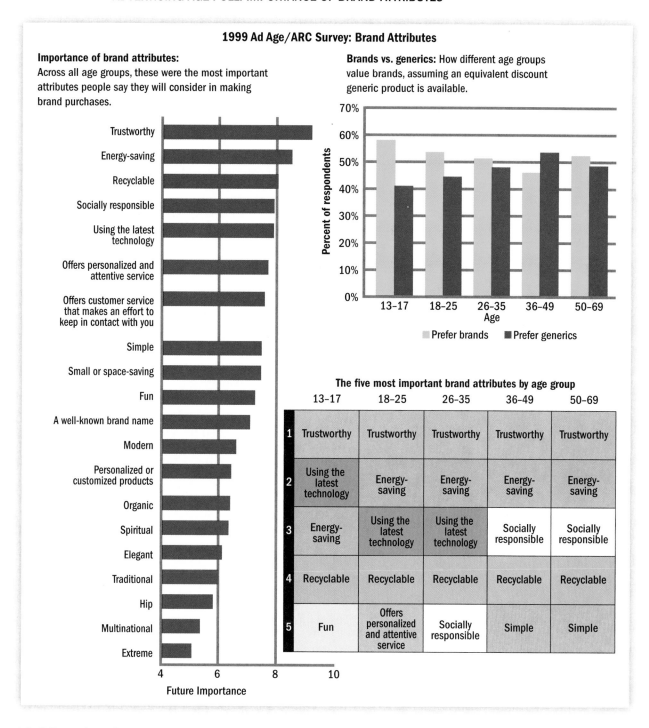

risk differs when the consumer faces options involving gains versus those involving losses.[36]

To illustrate this bias, consider the following choices. For each, would you take the safe bet or choose to gamble?

- *Option 1.* You're given $30 and then offered a chance to flip a coin: Heads you win $9; tails you lose $9.
- *Option 2.* You're given a choice of getting $30 outright, or accepting a coin flip that will win you either $39 or $21.

In one study, 70 percent of those given option 1 chose to gamble, compared to just 43 percent of those offered option 2. Yet, the odds are the same for both options! The difference is that people prefer "playing with the house money"; they are more willing to take risks when they perceive they're using someone else's resources. So, contrary to a rational decision-making perspective, we value money differently depending on where it comes from. This explains, for example, why someone might choose to blow a big bonus on some frivolous purchase, but would never consider taking that same amount out of his or her savings account for this purpose.

Finally, research in mental accounting demonstrates that extraneous characteristics of the choice situation can influence our selections, even though they wouldn't if we were totally rational decision makers. As one example, participants in a survey were provided with one of two versions of this scenario:

> You are lying on the beach on a hot day. All you have to drink is ice water. For the last hour you have been thinking about how much you would enjoy a nice cold bottle of your favorite brand of beer. A companion gets up to go make a phone call and offers to bring back a beer from the only nearby place where beer is sold (either a fancy resort hotel or a small, run-down grocery store, depending on the version you're given). He says that the beer might be expensive and so asks how much you are willing to pay for it. . . . What price do you tell him?

In this survey, the median price given by participants who were in the fancy resort version was $2.65, but those given the grocery store version were only willing to pay $1.50. In both versions the consumption act is the same, the beer is the same, and no "atmosphere" is consumed because the beer is being brought back to the beach.[37] So much for rational decision making!

How Much Search Occurs?

As a general rule, search activity is greater when the purchase is important, when there is a need to learn more about the purchase, or when the relevant information is easily obtained and utilized.[38] Consumers differ in the amount of search they tend to undertake, regardless of the product category in question. All things being equal, younger, better-educated people who enjoy the shopping/fact-finding process tend to conduct more information search. Women are more inclined to search than men are, as are those who place greater value on style and the image they present.[39]

The Consumer's Prior Expertise

Should prior product knowledge make it more or less likely that consumers will engage in search? Product experts and novices use very different procedures during decision making. Novices who know little about a product should be the most motivated to find out more about it. However, experts are more familiar with the product category, so they should be able to better understand the meaning of any new product information they might acquire.

So, who searches more? The answer is neither: Search tends to be greatest among those consumers who are *moderately knowledgeable* about the product. There is an inverted-U relationship between knowledge and external search effort, as shown in Figure 9.5. People with very limited expertise may not feel they are capable of searching extensively. In fact, they may not even know where to start. Richard, who did not spend a lot of time researching his purchase, is representative of this situation. He visited one store, and he only looked at brands with which he was already familiar. In addition, he focused on only a small number of product features.[40]

The *type* of search undertaken by people with varying levels of expertise differs as well. Because experts have a better sense of what information is relevant to the decision, they tend to engage in *selective search*, which means their efforts are more

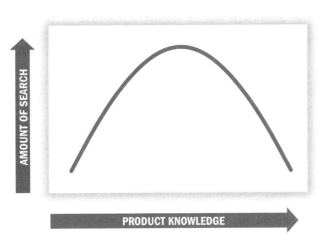

■ **FIGURE 9.5**
THE RELATIONSHIP BETWEEN
AMOUNT OF INFORMATION SEARCH
AND PRODUCT KNOWLEDGE

Minolta features a no-risk guarantee as a way to reduce the perceived risk in buying an office copier.

MAYBE THE BEST WAY TO HANDLE RISK IS TO AVOID IT ALTOGETHER.

That's why Minolta created the No-Risk Guarantee. It takes you out of harm's way by letting you decide whether you're happy with the copier's performance.

Even better, it covers our EP 9760 Pro Series Copier, which was recently voted first overall in productivity in the high-volume class.¹

Here's how it works. If you're not completely satisfied with our copier within the first three years of normal operation, we will replace it with an identical or comparably equipped model, free of charge. In other words, it works or it walks. An award-winning copier combined with an iron-clad guarantee? The only risk involved is passing this opportunity up.

For more information, call 1-800-9-MINOLTA.

NO-RISK COPIERS
ONLY FROM THE MIND OF MINOLTA

MINOLTA

focused and efficient. In contrast, novices are more likely to rely on the opinions of others and on "nonfunctional" attributes, such as brand name and price, to distinguish among alternatives. They may also process information in a "top-down" rather than a "bottom-up" manner, focusing less on details than on the big picture. For instance, they may be more impressed by the sheer amount of technical information presented in an ad than by the actual significance of the claims made.[41]

Perceived Risk

As a rule, purchase decisions that involve extensive search also entail some kind of **perceived risk**, or the belief that the product has potentially negative consequences. Perceived risk may be present if the product is expensive or is complex and hard to understand. Alternatively, perceived risk can be a factor when a product choice is visible to others and we run the risk of embarrassment if the wrong choice is made.[42]

Figure 9.6 lists five kinds of risk—including objective (e.g., physical danger) and subjective factors (e.g., social embarrassment)—as well as the products that tend to be affected by each type. Consumers with greater "risk capital" are less affected by perceived risks associated with the products. For example, a highly self-confident person would be less worried about the social risk inherent in a product, whereas a more vulnerable, insecure consumer might be reluctant to take a chance on a product that peers might not accept.

■ **FIGURE 9.6**
FIVE TYPES OF PERCEIVED RISK

	BUYERS MOST SENSITIVE TO RISK	PURCHASES MOST SUBJECT TO RISK
MONETARY RISK	Risk capital consists of money and property. Those with relatively little income and wealth are most vulnerable.	High-ticket items that require substantial expenditures are most subject to this form of risk.
FUNCTIONAL RISK	Risk capital consists of alternative means of performing the function or meeting the need. Practical consumers are most sensitive.	Products or services whose purchase and use requires the buyer's exclusive commitment are most sensitive.
PHYSICAL RISK	Risk capital consists of physical vigor, health, and vitality. Those who are elderly, frail, or in ill health are most vulnerable.	Mechanical or electrical goods (such as vehicles or flammables), drugs and medical treatment, and food and beverages are most sensitive.
SOCIAL RISK	Risk capital consists of self-esteem and self-confidence. Those who are insecure and uncertain are most sensitive.	Socially visible or symbolic goods, such as clothes, jewelry, cars, homes, or sports equipment are most subject to social risk.
PSYCHO-LOGICAL RISK	Risk capital consists of affiliations and status. Those lacking self-respect or attractiveness to peers are most sensitive.	Expensive personal luxuries that may engender guilt, durables, and services whose use demands self-discipline or sacrifice are most sensitive.

■ EVALUATION OF ALTERNATIVES

Much of the effort that goes into a purchase decision occurs at the stage in which a choice must be made from the available alternatives. After all, modern consumer society abounds with choices. In some cases, there may literally be hundreds of different brands (as in cigarettes) or different variations of the same brand (as in shades of lipstick), each screaming for our attention.

Just for fun, ask a friend to name all of the brands of perfume she can think of. The odds are she will reel off three to five names rather quickly, then stop and think awhile before coming up with a few more. It is likely that she is highly familiar with the first set of brands, and in fact she probably wears one or more of these. The list may also contain one or two brands that she does not like and would perhaps like to forget. Note also that there are many, many more brands on the market she did not name at all.

If your friend were to go to the store to buy perfume, it is likely that she would consider buying some or most of the brands she listed initially. She might also consider a few more possibilities if these were forcefully brought to her attention while at the store—for example, if she is "ambushed" by a representative who is spraying scent samples on shoppers, a common occurrence in some department stores.

Identifying Alternatives

How do we decide which criteria are important, and how do we narrow down product alternatives to an acceptable number and eventually choose one instead of others? The answer varies depending on the decision-making process used. A consumer engaged in extended problem solving may carefully evaluate several brands, whereas someone making a habitual decision may not consider any alternatives to his or her normal brand. Furthermore, some evidence indicates that more extended processing occurs in situations in which negative emotions are aroused due to conflicts among the choices available. This is most likely to occur where difficult trade-offs are involved, as when a person must choose between the risks involved in undergoing a bypass operation versus the potential improvement in his or her life if the operation is successful.[43]

The alternatives actively considered during a consumer's choice process are his or her **evoked set**. The evoked set comprises those products already in memory (the retrieval set), plus those prominent in the retail environment. For example, recall that Richard did not know much about the technical aspects of television sets, and he had only a few major brands in memory. Of these, two were acceptable possibilities and one was not.

Consumers often include a surprisingly small number of alternatives in their evoked set. One study combined results from several large-scale investigations of consumers' evoked sets and found that the number of products included in these sets is limited, although there are some marked variations by product category and across countries. For example, the average evoked set size for American beer consumers was fewer than three, whereas Canadian consumers typically considered seven brands. In contrast, whereas auto buyers in Norway studied two alternatives, American consumers on average looked at more than eight models before making a decision.[44]

For obvious reasons, a marketer who finds that its brand is not in the evoked set of target market has cause to worry. A product is not likely to be placed in the evoked set after it has previously been considered and rejected. Indeed, a new brand is more likely to be added to the evoked set than is an existing brand that was previously considered but passed over, even after additional positive information has been provided for that brand.[45] For marketers, consumers' unwillingness to give a rejected product a second chance underscores the importance of ensuring that it performs well from the time it is introduced.

Marketing Pitfall

Kimberly-Clark Corp., the maker of well-known paper products including Kleenex and Scott tissues, learned the hard way about the perils of product categorization and consumers' resistance to new categories. The company announced "the most significant category innovation since toilet paper first appeared in roll form in 1890." Even Jay Leno covered the news of the new product: Cottonelle Fresh Rollwipes, a roll of moist wipes in a plastic dispenser that clips onto a regular toilet-paper holder. To quiet skeptics who questioned whether Americans would change their habits so dramatically, Kimberly-Clark unveiled its research showing that 63 percent of adults were already in the habit of wetting toilet paper or using a wipe.

Although the company spent more than $100 million to develop the roll and dispenser and guards it with more than 30 patents, high hopes for the product have gone down the toilet. Part of the problem is that the company is dealing with a product most people don't even want to discuss in the first place, and its advertising failed to show consumers what the wipes even do. Its ad agency tried to create a fun image with TV ads showing shots of people splashing in the water from behind with the slogan, "sometimes wetter is better." A print ad with an extreme close-up of a sumo wrestler's derriere didn't go over much better. To make matters worse, the company didn't design a version in small product sizes, so it couldn't pass out free samples. And, the wipes are packaged in a container that is immediately visible in a bathroom—another strike for people already bashful about buying the product.[51]

Product Categorization

Remember that when consumers process product information, they do not do so in a vacuum. Instead, a product stimulus is evaluated in terms of what people already know about a product or things to which it is similar. A person evaluating a particular 35mm camera will most likely compare it to other 35mm cameras rather than to a Polaroid camera, and the consumer would certainly not compare it to a slide projector or DVD. Because the category in which a product is placed determines the other products it will be compared to, *categorization* is a crucial determinant of how a product is evaluated.

The products in a consumer's evoked set are likely to be those that share some similar features. This process can either help or hurt a product, depending upon what people compare it to. For example, in one survey about 25 percent of consumers said they would be less likely to buy a product made of hemp if they know it's derived from the same plant used to obtain marijuana (but without any of the latter's effects). When faced with a new product, consumers refer to their already existing knowledge in familiar product categories to form new knowledge.[46]

It is important to understand how this knowledge is represented in a consumer's cognitive structure, which refers to a set of factual knowledge about products (i.e., beliefs) and the way these beliefs are organized in people's minds.[47] We discussed these knowledge structures in Chapter 4. One reason is that marketers want to ensure that their products are correctly grouped. For example, General Foods brought out a new line of Jell-O flavors, such as Cranberry Orange, that it called Jell-O Gelatin Flavors for Salads. Unfortunately, the company discovered that people would use it only for salad, because the name encouraged them to put the product in their "salad" structure rather than in their "dessert" structure. The product line was dropped.[48]

Levels of Categorization

People group things into categories that occur at different levels of specificity. Typically, a product is represented in a cognitive structure at one of three levels. To understand this idea, consider how someone might respond to these questions about an ice cream cone: What other products share similar characteristics, and which would be considered as alternatives to eating a cone?

These questions may be more complex than they first appear. At one level, a cone is similar to an apple, because both could be eaten as a dessert. At another level, a cone is similar to a piece of pie, because both are eaten for dessert and both are fattening. At still another level, a cone is similar to an ice cream sundae—both are eaten for dessert, are made of ice cream, and are fattening.

It is easy to see that the items a person associates with, say, the category "fattening dessert" influence the choices he or she will make for what to eat after dinner. The middle level, known as a *basic level category*, is typically the most useful in classifying products, because items grouped together tend to have a lot in common with each other but still permit a range of alternatives to be considered. The broader *superordinate category* is more abstract, whereas the more specific *subordinate category* often includes individual brands.[49] Figure 9.7 depicts these three levels.

Of course, not all items fit equally well into a category. Apple pie is a better example of the subordinate category "pie" than is rhubarb pie, even though both are types of pies. Apple pie is more *prototypical*, and would tend to be considered first, especially by category novices. In contrast, pie experts will tend to have knowledge about both typical and atypical category examples.[50]

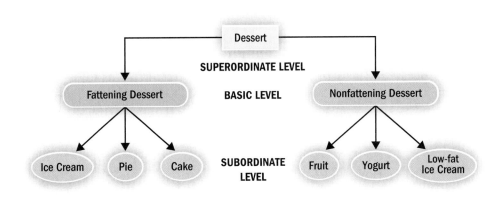

■ **FIGURE 9.7**
LEVELS OF ABSTRACTION IN
DESSERT CATEGORIES

Strategic Implications of Product Categorization

Product categorization has many strategic implications. The way a product is grouped with others has very important ramifications for determining both its competitors for adoption and what criteria will be used to make this choice.

Product Positioning. The success of a *positioning strategy* often hinges on the marketer's ability to convince the consumer that its product should be considered within a given category. For example, the orange juice industry tried to reposition orange juice as a drink that could be enjoyed all day long ("It's not just for breakfast anymore"). On the other hand, soft drink companies are now attempting the opposite by portraying sodas as suitable for breakfast consumption. They are trying to make their way into consumers' "breakfast drink" category, along with orange juice, grapefruit juice, and coffee. Of course, this strategy can backfire, as Pepsi-Cola discovered when it introduced Pepsi A.M. and positioned it as a coffee substitute. The company did such a good job of categorizing the drink as a morning beverage that customers wouldn't drink it at any other time, and the product failed.[52]

Identifying Competitors. At the abstract, superordinate level, many different product forms compete for membership. The category "entertainment" might comprise both bowling and the ballet, but not many people would consider the substitution of one of these activities for the other. Products and services that on the surface are quite different, however, actually compete with each other at a broad level for consumers' discretionary dollars. Although bowling or ballet may not be a likely trade-off for many people, it is feasible, for example, that a symphony might try to lure away season ticket holders to the ballet by positioning itself as an equivalent member of the category "cultural event."[53]

Consumers are often faced with choices between noncomparable categories, in which a number of attributes exist that cannot be directly related to one another (the old problem of comparing apples and oranges). When consumers can derive an overlapping category that encompasses both items (e.g., entertainment, value, usefulness) and then rate each alternative in terms of that superordinate category comparison, the process is easier.[54]

Exemplar Products. As we saw with the case of apple pie versus rhubarb, if a product is a really good example of a category it is more familiar to consumers and is more easily recognized and recalled.[55] Judgments about category attributes tend to be disproportionately influenced by the characteristics of category exemplars.[56] In a sense, brands that are strongly associated with a category get to "call the shots" by defining the criteria that should be used to evaluate all category members.

This ad for Sunkist lemon juice attempts to establish a new category for the product by repositioning it as a salt substitute.

Being a bit less than prototypical is not necessarily a bad thing, however. Products that are moderately unusual within their product category may stimulate more information processing and positive evaluations, because they are neither so familiar that they will be taken for granted nor so discrepant that they will be dismissed.[57] A brand that is strongly discrepant (such as Zima, a clear malt beverage) may occupy a unique niche position, whereas those that are moderately discrepant (e.g., local microbrews) remain in a distinct position within the general category.[58]

Locating Products.   Product categorization also can affect consumers' expectations regarding the places they can locate a desired product. If products do not clearly fit into categories (e.g., is a rug furniture?), consumers' ability to find them or make sense of them may be diminished. For instance, a frozen dog food that had to be thawed and cooked failed in the market, partly because people could not adapt to the idea of buying dog food in the "frozen foods for people" section of their grocery stores.

■ PRODUCT CHOICE: SELECTING AMONG ALTERNATIVES

Once the relevant options from a category have been assembled and evaluated, a choice must be made among them.[59] Recall that the decision rules guiding choice can range from very simple and quick strategies to complicated processes requiring much attention and cognitive processing. Integrating information from sources such as prior experience with the product or a similar one, information present at the time of purchase, and beliefs about the brands that have been created by advertising can influence the choice.[60]

Evaluative Criteria

When Richard was looking at different television sets, he focused on one or two product features and completely ignored several others. He narrowed down his choices by only considering two specific brand names, and from the Prime Wave and Precision models, he chose one that featured stereo capability.

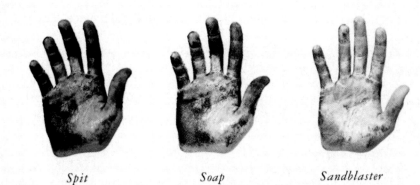

Spit   Soap   Sandblaster   Lava

Hey, your choice.

Lava soap lays out the options and invites us to choose the solution.

Evaluative criteria are the dimensions used to judge the merits of competing options. In comparing alternative products, Richard could have chosen from among any number of criteria, ranging from very functional attributes ("does this TV come with remote control?") to experiential ones ("does this TV's sound reproduction make me imagine I'm in a concert hall?").

Another important point is that criteria on which products *differ* from one another carry more weight in the decision process than do those where the alternatives are *similar*. If all brands being considered rate equally well on one attribute (e.g., if all TVs come with remote control), consumers will have to find other reasons to choose one over another. The attributes actually used to differentiate among choices are **determinant attributes**.

Marketers can play a role in educating consumers about which criteria should be used as determinant attributes. For example, consumer research by Church & Dwight indicated that many consumers view the use of natural ingredients as a determinant attribute. The result was promotion of toothpaste made from baking soda, which the company already manufactured for Church & Dwight's Arm & Hammer brand.[61] And sometimes, the company can even invent a determinant attribute: Pepsi-Cola accomplished this by stamping freshness dates on soda cans. The company spent about $25 million on an advertising and promotional campaign to convince consumers that there's nothing quite as horrible as a stale can of soda—even though it has been estimated that 98 percent of all cans are consumed well before this could be a problem. Six months after introducing the campaign, an independent survey found that 61 percent of respondents felt that freshness dating is an important attribute for a soft drink![62]

The decision about which attributes to use is the result of *procedural learning*, in which a person undergoes a series of cognitive steps before making a choice. These steps include identifying important attributes, remembering whether competing brands differ on those attributes, and so on. In order for a marketer to effectively recommend a new decision criterion, its communication should convey three pieces of information:[63]

- It should point out that there are significant differences among brands on the attribute.
- It should supply the consumer with a decision-making rule, such as if (deciding among competing brands), *then* . . . (use the attribute as a criterion).
- It should convey a rule that can be easily integrated with how the person has made this decision in the past. Otherwise, the recommendation is likely to be ignored because it requires too much mental work.

Cybermediaries

As anyone who's ever typed a phrase like "home theaters" into a search engine like Google knows, the Web delivers enormous amounts of product and retailer information in seconds. In fact, the biggest problem Web surfers face these days is narrowing down their choices, not beefing them up. In cyberspace, simplification is key.

With the tremendous number of Web sites available, and the huge number of people surfing the Web each day, how can people organize information and decide where to click? One type of service that is growing to meet this demand is called a **cybermediary**. This is an intermediary that helps to filter and organize online market information so that customers can identify and evaluate alternatives more efficiently.[64] Cybermediaries take different forms:[65]

- *Directories* and *portals* such as Yahoo! or *fashionmall.com* are general services that tie together a large variety of different sites.
- *Web site evaluators* reduce the risk to consumers by reviewing sites and recommending the best ones. For example, Point Communications selects sites that it designates as Top 5 percent of the Web.
- *Forums, fan clubs,* and *user groups* offer product-related discussions to help customers sift through options (more on these in Chapter 11). Other sites like *about.com* help to narrow alternatives by actually connecting you with human guides that make recommendations. This approach is especially prevalent in the travel industry, in which several sites now connect surfers to travel experts (often volunteers who just like to share their expertise about travel). These sites include *Allexperts.com, BootsnAll.com,* and *Exp.com.*
- *Financial intermediaries* authorize payments from buyer to seller. Payment systems include electronic equivalents to credit card charges (PayPal), writing checks (Checkfree), paying in cash (Digicash), and sending secure electronic mail authorizing a payment (First Virtual).
- *Intelligent agents* are sophisticated software programs that use *collaborative filtering* technologies to learn from past user behavior in order to recommend new purchases. For example, when you let *Amazon.com* suggest a new book, it's using an intelligent agent to propose novels based on what you and others like you have bought in the past. This approach was introduced in 1995 (the Stone Age in Web time!) by Firefly to make recommendations for taste-based products such as music, books, and films.[66] Now, a variety of "shopping robots" (or "bots") are available to act as online purchasing shopping agents, including *mysimon.com*, and Ask Jeeves. Collaborative filtering is still in its infancy. In the next few years, expect to see many new Web-based methods to simplify the con-

Search engines like Ask Jeeves simplify the process of online information search.

sumer decision-making process. Now if only someone could come up with an easier way to pay for all the great stuff you find courtesy of shopping bots!

Heuristics: Mental Shortcuts

Do we actually perform complex mental calculations every time we make a purchase decision? Get a life! To simplify decisions, consumers often employ decision rules that allow them to use some dimensions as substitutes for others. For example, Richard relied on certain assumptions as substitutes for prolonged information search. In particular, he assumed the selection at Zany Zack's would be more than sufficient, so he did not bother to shop any of Zack's competitors. This assumption served as a shortcut to more extended information processing.[67]

Especially when limited problem solving occurs prior to making a choice, consumers often fall back on **heuristics**, or mental rules-of-thumb that lead to a speedy decision. These rules range from the very general (e.g., "higher-priced products are

Consumers often simplify choices by using heuristics such as automatically choosing a favorite color or brand.

i want everything at my party to be yellow. i want yellow balloons, yellow cups, and yellow icing on my cake because yellow is the prettiest color ever. except for pink. i want everything at my party to be pink.

www.iparty.com > birthdays > basics > pink > cups/plates/napkins/favors > order

i want. i click. iparty.com

aol keyword: iparty

higher-quality products" or "buy the same brand I bought last time") to the very specific (e.g., "buy Domino, the brand of sugar my mother always bought").[68]

Sometimes these shortcuts may not be in consumers' best interests. A consumer who personally knows one or two people who have had problems with a particular make of car, for example, might assume he or she would have similar trouble with it and thus overlook the model's overall excellent repair record.[69] The influence of such assumptions may be enhanced if the product has an unusual name, which makes it and the experiences with it more distinctive.[70]

Relying on a Product Signal

One frequently used shortcut is the tendency to infer hidden dimensions of products from observable attributes. The aspect of the item that is visible acts as a **product signal** that communicates some underlying quality. Such inferences explain why someone trying to sell a used car takes great pains to be sure the car's exterior is clean and shiny: Potential buyers often judge the vehicle's mechanical condition by its appearance, even though this means they may drive away in a shiny, clean clunker.[71]

When product information is incomplete, judgments are often derived from beliefs about *covariation,* or perceived associations among events that may or may not actually influence one another.[72] For example, a consumer may form an association between product quality and the length of time a manufacturer has been in business. Other signals or attributes believed to coexist with good or bad products include well-known brand names, country of origin, price, and the retail outlets that carry the product.

Unfortunately, consumers tend to be poor estimators of covariation. Their beliefs persist despite evidence to the contrary. In a process similar to the consistency principle discussed in Chapter 7, people tend to see what they are looking for. They will look for product information that confirms their guesses. In one experiment, consumers sampled four sets of products to determine if price and quality were related. Those who believed in this relationship prior to the study elected to sample higher-priced products, thus creating a sort of self-fulfilling prophecy.[73]

Market Beliefs: Is It Better If I Pay More for It?

Consumers often form assumptions about companies, products, and stores. These market beliefs then become the shortcuts that guide their decisions—whether or not they are accurate.[74] Recall, for instance, that Richard chose to shop at a large "electronics supermarket" because he *assumed* the selection would be better there than at a specialty store. A large number of **market beliefs** have been identified. Table 9.3 lists some of these—how many do you share?

TABLE 9.3
COMMON MARKET BELIEFS

Brand	All brands are basically the same.
	Generic products are just name brands sold under a different label at a lower price.
	The best brands are the ones that are purchased the most.
	When in doubt, a national brand is always a safe bet.
Store	Specialty stores are great places to familiarize yourself with the best brands; but once you figure out what you want, it's cheaper to buy it at a discount outlet.
	A store's character is reflected in its window displays.
	Salespeople in specialty stores are more knowledgeable than other sales personnel.
	Larger stores offer better prices than small stores.
	Locally owned stores give the best service.
	A store that offers a good value on one of its products probably offers good values on all of its items.
	Credit and return policies are most lenient at large department stores.
	Stores that have just opened usually charge attractive prices.
Prices/Discounts/Sales	Sales are typically run to get rid of slow-moving merchandise.
	Stores that are constantly having sales don't really save you money.
	Within a given store, higher prices generally indicate higher quality.
Advertising and Sales Promotion	"Hard-sell" advertising is associated with low-quality products.
	Items tied to "giveaways" are not a good value (even with the freebee).
	Coupons represent real savings for customers because they are not offered by the store.
	When you buy heavily advertised products, you are paying for the label, not for higher quality.
Product/Packaging	Largest-sized containers are almost always cheaper per unit than smaller sizes.
	New products are more expensive when they're first introduced; prices tend to settle down as time goes by.
	When you are not sure what you need in a product, it's a good idea to invest in the extra features, because you'll probably wish you had them later.
	In general, synthetic goods are lower in quality than goods made of natural materials.
	It's advisable to stay away from products when they are new to the market; it usually takes the manufacturer a little time to work the bugs out.

Source: Adapted from Calvin P. Duncan, "Consumer Market Beliefs: A Review of the Literature and an Agenda for Future Research," in Marvin E. Goldberg, Gerald Gorn, and Richard W. Pollay, eds., *Advances in Consumer Research* 17 (Provo, UT: Association for Consumer Research, 1990): 729–35.

Do higher prices mean higher quality? The assumption of a *price–quality relationship* is one of the most pervasive market beliefs.[75] Novice consumers may in fact consider price as the only relevant product attribute. Experts also consider this information, although in these cases price tends to be used for its informational value, especially for products (e.g., virgin wool) that are known to have wide quality variations in the marketplace. When this quality level is more standard or strictly regulated (e.g., Harris Tweed sport coats), experts do not weigh price in their decisions. For the most part, this belief is justified; you do tend to get what you pay for. However, let the buyer beware: The price–quality relationship is not always justified.[76]

Country-of-Origin as a Product Signal

Modern consumers choose among products made in many countries. Americans may buy Brazilian shoes, Japanese cars, clothing imported from Taiwan, or microwave ovens built in South Korea. Consumers' reactions to these imports are mixed. In some cases, people have come to assume that a product made overseas is of better quality (e.g., cameras, cars), whereas in other cases the knowledge that a product has been imported tends to lower perceptions of product quality (e.g.,

A product's country-of-origin in some cases is an important piece of information in the decision making process. Certain items are strongly associated with specific countries, and products from those countries often attempt to benefit from these linkages.

apparel).[77] In general, people tend to rate their own country's products more favorably than do people who live elsewhere, and products from industrialized countries are rated better than are those from developing countries.

Roper Starch Worldwide interviewed 30,000 customers in 30 countries regarding their feelings about different cultures around the world.[78] The firm categorized people in terms of their attachment to their own culture versus affinity for other cultures. Among the segments identified were:

- *Nationalists* (26 percent of the sample): They feel close to their own culture, and their key personal values include duty, respect for ancestors, status, and social stability. These consumers tend to be somewhat older and are likely to be either female homemakers or blue-collar men.
- *Internationalists* (15 percent of the sample): They feel close to three or more outside cultures. Their key personal values include open-mindedness, learning, creativity, and freedom. They are more likely to be male, well educated, and upscale.
- *Disengaged* (7 percent of the sample): These people did not feel great attachment to any culture, including their own. They are bored and disenchanted, and tend to be younger and less educated.

A product's **country-of-origin** in some cases is an important piece of information in the decision-making process.[79] Certain items are strongly associated with specific countries, and products from those countries often attempt to benefit from these linkages. Country-of-origin can function as a **stereotype**—a knowledge structure based on inferences across products. These stereotypes are often biased or inaccurate, but they do play a constructive role in simplifying complex choice situations.[80]

One study showed college students in Ireland, the United States, and Australia photographs of "Irish pubs" taken in each of those three countries and asked them to guess which were the authentic ones from Ireland. Most respondents were more likely to pick the bars that were not actually the Irish ones; the bars in the United States and Australia tended to contain more stereotypical Irish decorations like four-leaf clovers, which you're not as likely to find in the original article.[81]

Recent evidence indicates that learning of a product's country-of-origin is not necessarily good or bad. Instead, it has the effect of stimulating the consumer's

The growing popularity of faux Irish pubs around the world attests to the power of country stereotypes to influence consumers' preferences. About 800 Irish-themed pubs have been opened in countries including South Africa, Italy, China, and Russia. The Irish brewer Guinness PLC encourages the establishment of these outputs, since an Irish pub is mere blarney without Guinness on tap. The company helps owners design the pub and even assists in locating Irish bar staff to dispense its thick brew. As one Guinness executive explained, "We've created a mythology of an Irish ambience." Since Guinness launched its Irish Pub Concept in 1992 it has helped over 1,250 entrepreneurs in 36 countries establish their own Irish pubs. Aspiring Publicans can choose from five pre-set designs: Victorian Dublin, Irish Brewery Pub, Irish Pub Shop, Irish Country Cottage, or Gaelic.

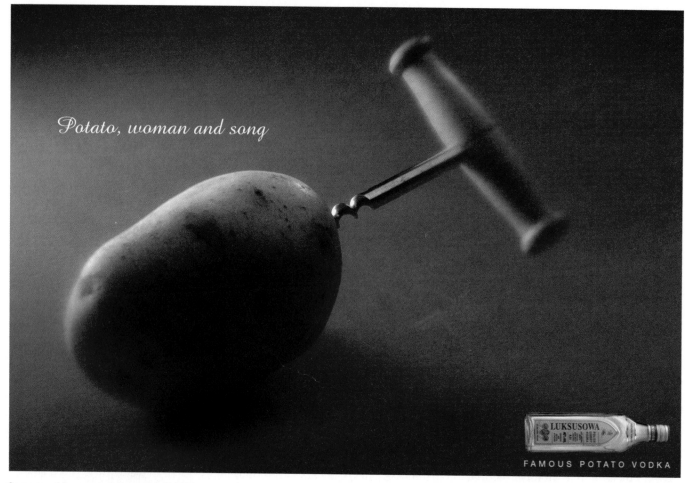

Potato, woman and song

LUKSUSOWA

FAMOUS POTATO VODKA

Some countries are strongly associated with certain types of alcoholic products. This Polish ad plays on these stereotypes.

interest in the product to a greater degree. The purchaser thinks more extensively about the product and evaluates it more carefully.[82] The origin of the product thus can act as a product attribute that combines with other attributes to influence evaluations.[83] In addition, the consumer's own expertise with the product category moderates the effects of this attribute. When other information is available, experts tend to ignore country-of-origin information, whereas novices continue to rely on it. However, when other information is unavailable or ambiguous, both experts and novices will rely on this attribute to make a decision.[84]

The tendency to prefer products or people of one's own culture to those of other countries is called **ethnocentrism**. Ethnocentric consumers are likely to feel it is wrong to buy products from other countries, particularly because of the negative effect this may have on the domestic economy. Marketing campaigns stressing the desirability of "buying American" are more likely to appeal to this consumer segment. This trait has been measured on the Consumer Ethnocentrism Scale (CETSCALE) that was devised for this purpose: The scale identifies ethnocentric consumers by their extent of agreement with statements such as:

- Purchasing foreign-made products is un-American.
- Curbs should be put on all imports.
- American consumers who purchase products made in other countries are responsible for putting their fellow Americans out of work.[85]

This advertisement positions the Macanudo cigar as part of Americana, even though it's imported from the Dominican Republic.

Of course, Americans are not the only people who display ethnocentrism. Citizens of many countries tend to feel that their native products are superior (just ask a Frenchman to choose between French and California wines!). Many Canadians are concerned about the dilution of their culture due to a strong U.S. influence. In one poll, 25 percent of the country's citizens identified "life, liberty, and the pursuit of happiness" as a Canadian constitutional slogan rather than an American one![86] Canadian nationalism was stoked by a commercial for Molson Canadian beer called "The Rant" that almost overnight became an unofficial anthem in Canada. A flannel-shirted young Canadian walks onto a stage and calmly begins explaining away Canadian stereotypes: "I'm not a lumberjack or a fur trader. I don't live in an igloo or eat blubber or own a dog sled . . . My name is Joe and I . . . AM . . . CANADIAN! . . . " In the six weeks after the ad started airing, the Molson brand gained almost two points in market share.[87]

Choosing Familiar Brand Names: Loyalty or Habit?

Branding is a marketing strategy that often functions as a heuristic. People form preferences for a favorite brand, and then they literally may never change their minds in the course of a lifetime. A study by the Boston Consulting Group of the market leaders in 30 product categories found that 27 of the brands that were number one in 1930 (such as Ivory Soap and Campbell's Soup) remained at the top over 50 years later.[88]

THE GLOBAL LOOKING GLASS

In a bid to break the monopoly of U.S. brands, a soft drink aimed at the Muslim community has been launched in the United Kingdom. A Derby-based company launched Qibla Cola to provide an alternative to Muslims and consumers who do not want to patronize U.S.-based cola companies. For every two-liter bottle of Qibla Cola sold, 10 percent of the profits will go to Muslim charity organization

Islamic Aid. The Qibla Cola Company, founded by Bradford-born Pakistani businesswoman Zahida Parveen, hopes to make a significant contribution to Muslim charities from product sales. Its product carries the tag-line "Liberate your taste."

Now, orders for the liter-and-a-half bottles with labels whose bright red and sweeping white script evoke those of Coke are pouring in from around the world—from Britain, Belgium and Germany—together with bids from companies wanting to become local distributors.

A spokesman for the Coca-Cola company responded: "We have built a production facility in the Palestinian Authority Area. It employs over 200 Palestinians. "We're the biggest investor there, creating jobs and supporting livelihoods. We strongly believe that our approach in supporting economic development there through our local business model is the more credible one."

Source: Adapted from ***www.rediff.com***, February 25, 2003.

Marketers treasure a brand commanding fierce loyalty, and for good reason. Brands that dominate their markets are as much as 50 percent more profitable than their nearest competitors.[89] Small wonder, then, that companies work very hard to cultivate loyalty. When the Disney Channel failed to appear on Teenage Research Unlimited's survey of the 50 coolest teen brands, the company tried to spice up its image to attract a loyal adolescent following. The channel began to play music videos—even if it meant doctoring some of the lyrics to maintain its clean-cut image. For example, the lyrics to "Genie in a Bottle" by Christina Aguilera were changed from "My body's saying let's go" to "My friends are saying let's go," and "I'm a genie in a bottle, baby, you gotta rub me the right way" became "You gotta treat me the right way."[90]

Even musical groups understand the value of catering to their loyal following: For example, touring bands like the New Orleans Cajun rock band The Radiators work with travel agencies to offer packages covering airfare, lodging, and meals to hard-core groupies. Fanatic followers of jam bands like The String Cheese Incident and Phish descend upon hotels in the tradition of The Grateful Dead, who encouraged bootleg recordings of their extended musical sets but prospered by selling concert paraphernalia to hard-core fans.[91]

Inertia: The Lazy Customer

Many people tend to buy the same brand just about every time they go to the store. This consistent pattern is often due to **inertia**—a brand is bought out of habit merely because less effort is required. If another product comes along that is for some reason easier to buy (e.g., it is cheaper or the original product is out of stock), the consumer will not hesitate to do so. A competitor who is trying to change a buying pattern based on inertia often can do so rather easily, because little resistance to brand switching will be encountered if the right incentive is offered. When there is little to no underlying commitment to a particular brand, promotional tools such as point-of-purchase displays, extensive couponing, or noticeable price reductions may be sufficient to "unfreeze" a consumer's habitual pattern.

Brand Loyalty: A "Friend," Tried-and-True

This kind of fickleness will not occur if true brand loyalty exists. In contrast to inertia, brand loyalty is a form of repeat purchasing behavior reflecting a conscious decision to continue buying the same brand.[92] For brand loyalty to exist, a pattern of repeat purchase must be accompanied by an underlying positive attitude toward the brand. Brand loyalty may be initiated by customer preference based on objective reasons, but after the brand has been around for a long time and is heavily advertised it can also engender an emotional attachment, either by being incorporated into the consumer's self-image or because it is associated with prior experiences.[93] Purchase decisions based on brand loyalty also become habitual over time, though in these cases the underlying commitment to the product is much firmer.

Compared to an inertia situation in which the consumer passively accepts a brand, a brand-loyal consumer is actively (sometimes passionately) involved with his or her favorite. Because of the emotional bonds that can come about between brand-loyal consumers and products, "true-blue" users react more vehemently when these products are altered, redesigned, or eliminated.[94] For example, when Coca-Cola replaced its tried-and-true formula with New Coke in the 1980s, a firestorm of national call-in campaigns, boycotts, and other protests occurred.

A decade ago, marketers struggled with the problem of *brand parity*, which refers to consumers' beliefs that there are no significant differences among brands. For example, one survey at that time found that more than 70 percent of consumers worldwide believed that all paper towels, soaps, and snack chips are alike.[95] Some analysts even proclaimed the death of brand names, predicting that private label or generic products that offer the same value for less money would kill off the tried-and-true products.

However, these gloomy predictions turned out to be wrong as major brands made a dramatic comeback. In the early part of the twenty-first century, branding is King! Some attribute this renaissance to information overload—with too many alternatives (many of them unfamiliar names) to choose from, people seem to be looking for clear signals of quality. Branded products are in demand today—but sophisticated shoppers are less picky about where they buy them. Old stigmas about shopping in discount stores seems to have largely vanished as consumers figure out that in many cases they can get the same brand-name products at retailers like Target or Kohl's as they can at Macy's. As one retail executive put it, "You could be at a dinner party on Fifth Avenue and millionaires will be talking about what they got at Wal-Mart."[96]

In fact, some brands are so sought after that people are literally willing to wait for years to obtain the right one. Here is a sampling of waiting lists for select products:[97]

- Season tickets for the N.Y. Giants football team: 18 years
- Aston Martin V12 Vanquish: 2 years
- Harley-Davidson Softtail Deuce: 6–18 months
- Remede Sweet (marble-based facial scrub): 3 months
- Padron Millennium cigars: 3–12 weeks
- Silver Oak Napa Valley Cabernet: indefinite

Decision Rules

Consumers consider sets of product attributes by using different rules, depending on the complexity of the decision and the importance of the decision to them. As we have seen, in some cases these rules are quite simple: People simply rely on a "shortcut" to make a choice. In other cases, though, more effort and thought is put into carefully weighing alternatives before coming to a decision.

One way to differentiate among decision rules is to divide them into those that are *compensatory* and those that are *noncompensatory*. To aid the discussion of some of these rules, Table 9.4 summarizes the attributes of the TV sets that Richard considered. Now, let's see how some of these rules result in different brand choices.

Noncompensatory Decision Rules

Noncompensatory decision rules are choice shortcuts where a product with a low standing on one attribute cannot make up for this position by being better on another attribute. In other words, people simply eliminate all options that do not

Net Profit

Brand loyalty lives—online. Many brand fans create personal Web pages that trumpet their allegiance to one or more favorite products. These pages may take the form of passionate essays or perhaps photo albums that show in vivid detail the ways the page creator uses the product. Many of them include external links that provide reams of additional details about the featured products. A study of these personal Web pages found that the brands referenced range from common software and Internet application products to entertainment/entertainers (fan sites), clothing, financial/governmental/political organizations, restaurants, and even household goods. Some of the Web site owners profiled in this study include:

- Kevin, a 28-year-old managing partner in an interior design firm, has a personal site that prominently features the KitchenAid logo and hyperlink to the brand site. The connection to the manufacturer is based on his pride in renovating his own kitchen with KitchenAid appliances and on his success in using the brand in clients' homes. He claims the logo and link "communicate quality . . . like Toyota does for cars." It is also "practical, not artistic, or trendy."
- Tina, a 28-year-old saleswoman for Victoria's Secret, actively invokes the meaning of the product—a feminine, playful, still respectable sexuality. Tina's site contains professionally produced boudoir photographs of herself wearing lingerie. A hyperlink to the Victoria's Secret home page appears near her photographs.

In addition to providing a fascinating glimpse into how far people will go to express their allegiance to favorite products (yes, even to appliances!), these personal online "shrines" to favorite products potentially are a great untapped resource for marketers that want to locate brand-loyal followers who will help them to spread the word in cyberspace.[98]

TABLE 9.4
HYPOTHETICAL ALTERNATIVES FOR A TV SET

Attribute	Importance Ranking	Brand Ratings		
		Prime Wave	Precision	Kamashita
Size of screen	1	Excellent	Excellent	Excellent
Stereo broadcast capability	2	Poor	Excellent	Good
Brand reputation	3	Excellent	Excellent	Poor
Onscreen programming	4	Excellent	Poor	Poor
Cable-ready capability	5	Good	Good	Good
Sleep timer	6	Excellent	Poor	Good

meet some basic standards. A consumer such as Richard who uses the decision rule, "Only buy well-known brand names," would not consider a new brand, even if it were equal or superior to existing ones. When people are less familiar with a product category or are not very motivated to process complex information, they tend to use simple, noncompensatory rules, which are summarized here.[99]

The Lexicographic Rule. When the *lexicographic rule* is used, the brand that is the best on the most important attribute is selected. If two or more brands are seen as being equally good on that attribute, the consumer then compares them on the second most important attribute. This selection process goes on until the tie is broken. In Richard's case, because both the Prime Wave and Precision models were tied on his most important attribute (a 60-inch screen), the Precision was chosen because of its rating on this second most important attribute—its stereo capability.

The Elimination-by-Aspects Rule. Using the *elimination-by-aspects rule*, brands are also evaluated on the most important attribute. In this case, though, specific cutoffs are imposed. For example, if Richard had been more interested in having a sleep timer on his TV (i.e., if it had a higher importance ranking), he might have stipulated that his choice "must have a sleep timer." Because the Prime Wave model had one and the Precision did not, the Prime Wave would have been chosen.

The Conjunctive Rule. Whereas the two former rules involve processing by attribute, the *conjunctive rule* entails processing by brand. As with the elimination-by-aspects procedure, cutoffs are established for each attribute. A brand is chosen if it meets all of the cutoffs, but failure to meet any one cutoff means it will be rejected. If none of the brands meet all of the cutoffs, the choice may be delayed, the decision rule may be changed, or the cutoffs may be modified.

If Richard had stipulated that all attributes had to be rated "good" or better, he would not have been able to choose any of the options. He might then have modified his decision rule, conceding that it was not possible to attain these high standards in the price range he was considering. In this case, perhaps Richard could decide that he could live without on-screen programming, so the Precision model could again be considered.

Compensatory Decision Rules

Unlike noncompensatory decision rules, **compensatory decision rules** give a product a chance to make up for its shortcomings. Consumers who employ these rules tend to be more involved in the purchase and thus are willing to exert the effort to consider the entire picture in a more exacting way. The willingness to let good and bad product qualities balance out can result in quite different choices. For example, if Richard were not concerned about having stereo reception, he might have chosen the Prime Wave model. But because this brand doesn't feature this highly ranked attribute, it doesn't stand a chance when he uses a noncompensatory rule.

Researchers have identified two basic types of compensatory rules. When using the *simple additive rule*, the consumer merely chooses the alternative that has the largest number of positive attributes. This choice is most likely to occur when his or her ability or motivation to process information is limited. One drawback to this approach for the consumer is that some of these attributes may not be very meaningful or important. An ad containing a long list of product benefits may be persuasive, despite the fact that many of the benefits included are actually standard within the product class and aren't determinant attributes at all.

The more complex version is known as the *weighted additive rule*.[100] When using this rule, the consumer also takes into account the relative importance of positively rated attributes, essentially multiplying brand ratings by importance weights. If this process sounds familiar, it should. The calculation process strongly resembles the multiattribute attitude model described in Chapter 7.

CHAPTER SUMMARY

Consumers are constantly faced with the need to make decisions about products. Some of these decisions are very important and entail great effort, whereas others are made on a virtually automatic basis.

Perspectives on decision making range from a focus on habits that people develop over time to novel situations involving a great deal of risk in which consumers must carefully collect and analyze information prior to making a choice. Many of our decisions are highly automated and made largely by habit. This trend is accelerating as marketers begin to introduce smart products that enable silent commerce where some purchases are made automatically by the products themselves (e.g., a malfunctioning appliance that contacts the repair man directly).

A typical decision process involves several steps. The first is problem recognition, in which the consumer first realizes that some action must be taken. This realization may be prompted in a variety of ways, ranging from the actual malfunction of a current purchase to a desire for new things based on exposure to different circumstances or advertising that provides a glimpse into what is needed to "live the good life."

Once a problem has been recognized and is seen as sufficiently important to warrant some action, information search begins. This search may range from simply scanning memory to determine what has been done to resolve the problem in the past to extensive fieldwork in which the consumer consults a variety of sources to amass as much information as possible. In many cases, people engage in surprisingly little search. Instead, they rely on various mental shortcuts, such as brand names or price, or they may simply imitate others.

In the evaluation of alternatives stage, the product alternatives that are considered comprise the individual's evoked set. Members of the evoked set usually share some characteristics; they are categorized similarly. The way products are mentally grouped influences which alternatives will be considered, and some brands are more strongly associated with these categories than are others (i.e., they are more prototypical).

The World Wide Web has changed the way many consumers search for information. Today, the problem often is weeding out excess detail rather than searching for more. Comparative search sites and intelligent agents help to filter and guide the search process. Cybermediaries such as Web portals may be relied upon to sort through massive amounts of information to simplify the decision-making process.

Research in the field of behavioral economics illustrates that decision making is not always strictly rational. Principles of mental accounting demonstrate that decisions can be influenced by the way a problem is posed (called framing) and whether it is put in terms of gains or losses.

When the consumer eventually must make a product choice from among alternatives, a number of decision rules may be used. Noncompensatory rules eliminate alternatives that are deficient on any of the criteria the consumer has chosen to use. Compensatory rules, which are more likely to be applied in high-involvement situations, allow the decision maker to consider each alternative's good and bad points more carefully to arrive at the overall best choice.

Very often, heuristics, or mental rules-of-thumb, are used to simplify decision making. In particular, people develop many market beliefs over time. One of the most common beliefs is that price is positively related to quality. Other heuristics rely on well-known brand names or a product's country-of-origin as signals of product quality. When a brand is consistently purchased over time, this pattern may be due to true brand loyalty, or simply to inertia because it's the easiest thing to do.

KEY TERMS

Behavioral influence perspective   293
Compensatory decision rules   321
Country-of-origin   315
Cybermediary   310
Determinant attributes   309
Ethnocentrism   316
Evaluative criteria   309
Evoked set   305
Experiential perspective   294

Extended problem solving   295
Habitual decision making   295
Heuristics   311
Inertia   318
Limited problem solving   295
Market beliefs   313
Mental accounting   300
Noncompensatory decision rules   319
Perceived risk   304

Problem recognition   296
Product signal   312
Prospect theory   300
Purchase momentum   293
Rational perspective   292
Silent commerce   297
Stereotype   315
Variety seeking   298

CONSUMER BEHAVIOR CHALLENGE

1 If people are not always rational decision makers, is it worth the effort to study how purchasing decisions are made? What techniques might be employed to understand experiential consumption and to translate this knowledge into marketing strategy?

2 List three product attributes that can be used as quality signals and provide an example of each.

3 Why is it difficult to place a product in a consumer's evoked set after it has already been rejected? What strategies might a marketer use in an attempt to accomplish this goal?

4 Define the three levels of product categorization described in this chapter. Diagram these levels for a health club.

5 Discuss two different noncompensatory decision rules and highlight the difference(s) between them. How might the use of one rule versus another result in a different product choice?

6 Choose a friend or parent who grocery shops on a regular basis and keep a log of their purchases of common consumer products during the term. Can you detect any evidence of brand loyalty in any categories based on consistency of purchases? If so, talk to the person about these purchases. Try to determine if his or her choices are based on true brand loyalty or on inertia. What techniques might you use to differentiate between the two?

7 Form a group of three. Pick a product and develop a marketing plan based on each of the three approaches to consumer decision making: rational, experiential, and behavioral influence. What are the major differences in emphasis among the three perspectives? Which is the most likely type of problem-solving activity for the product you have selected? What characteristics of the product make this so?

8 Locate a person who is about to make a major purchase. Ask that person to make a chronological list of all the information sources consulted prior to making a decision. How would you characterize the types of sources used (i.e., internal versus external, media versus personal, etc.)? Which sources appeared to have the most impact on the person's decision?

9 Perform a survey of country-of-origin stereotypes. Compile a list of five countries and ask people what products they associate with each. What are their evaluations of the products and likely attributes of these different products? The power of a country stereotype can also be demonstrated in another way. Prepare a brief description of a product, including a list of features, and ask people to rate it in terms of quality, likelihood of purchase, and so on. Make several versions of the description, varying only the country from which it comes. Do ratings change as a function of the country-of-origin?

10 Ask a friend to "talk through" the process he or she used to choose one brand rather than others during a recent purchase. Based on this description, can you identify the decision rule that was most likely employed?

11 Technology has the potential to make our lives easier by reducing the amount of clutter we need to work through in order to access the information on the Internet that really interests us. On the other hand, perhaps intelligent agents that make recommendations based only on what we and others like us have chosen in the past limit us—they reduce the chance that we will stumble on something (e.g., a book on a topic we've never heard of, or a music group that's different from the style we usually listen to). Will the proliferation of "shopping bots" make our lives too predictable by only giving us more of the same? If so, is this a problem?

12 Give one of the scenarios described in the section on biases in decision making to 10 to 20 people. How do the results you obtain compare with those reported in this chapter?

13 Think of a product you recently shopped for online. Describe your search process. How did you become aware that you wanted/needed the product? How did you evaluate alternatives? Did you wind up buying online? Why or why not? What factors would make it more or less likely that you would buy something online versus in a traditional store?

NOTES

1. John C. Mowen, "Beyond Consumer Decision Making," *Journal of Consumer Marketing* 5, no. 1 (1988): 15–25.
2. Richard W. Olshavsky and Donald H. Granbois, "Consumer Decision Making—Fact or Fiction," *Journal of Consumer Research* 6 (September 1989): 93–100.
3. Chris Marks, "As Two Osprey Nests Are Raided, Fears That Thieves See Scotland as a Soft Option," *Daily Mail* (May 14, 2002).
4. Ravi Dhar, Joel Huber, and Uzma Khan, "The Shopping Momentum Effect," paper presented at the Association for Consumer Research, Atlanta, October 2002.
5. James R. Bettman, "The Decision Maker Who Came in from the Cold" (presidential address), in Leigh McAllister and Michael Rothschild, eds., *Advances in Consumer Research* 20 (Provo, UT: Association for Consumer Research, (1993): 7–11; John W. Payne, James R. Bettman, and Eric J. Johnson, "Behavioral Decision Research: A Constructive Processing Perspective," *Annual Review of Psychology* 4 (1992): 87–131. For an overview of recent developments in individual choice models, see Robert J. Meyer and Barbara E. Kahn, "Probabilistic Models of Consumer Choice Behavior," in Thomas S. Robertson and Harold H. Kassarjian, eds., *Handbook of Consumer Behavior* (Upper Saddle River, NJ: Prentice Hall, 1991), 85–123.
6. Mowen, "Beyond Consumer Decision Making."
7. The Fits-Like-a-Glove (FLAG) framework is a new decision-making perspective that views consumer decisions as a holistic process shaped by the person's unique context; cf. Douglas E. Allen, "Toward a Theory of Consumer Choice as Sociohistorically Shaped Practical Experience: The Fits-Like-a-Glove (FLAG) Framework," *Journal of Consumer Research* 28 (March 2002): 515–532.
8. Jennifer Lee, "In the U.S., Interactive TV Still Awaits an Audience," *New York Times* (December 31, 2001): C1.
9. Ibid., C8.
10. Laurie Freeman, "User-Created Ads Catch On," *Advertising Age* (September 18, 2000): 84.
11. Joseph W. Alba and J. Wesley Hutchinson, "Dimensions of Consumer Expertise," *Journal of Consumer Research* 13 (March 1988): 411–54.
12. Julian E. Barnes, "Whirlpool Trying to Change Consumer Habits," *New York Times on the Web* (March 16, 2001).
13. Gordon C. Bruner III and Richard J. Pomazal, "Problem Recognition: The Crucial First Stage of the Consumer Decision Process," *Journal of Consumer Marketing* 5, no. 1 (1988): 53–63.
14. Peter H. Bloch, Daniel L. Sherrell, and Nancy M. Ridgway, "Consumer Search: An Extended Framework," *Journal of Consumer Research* 13 (June 1986): 119–26.
15. Kevin Maney, "Tag It: Tiny Wireless Wonders Improve Convenience," *Montgomery Advertiser* (May 6, 2002): D1.
16. Ibid.
17. Thomas Maeder "What Barbie Wants, Barbie Gets," *Wired* (January 2002): 4.
18. Girish Punj, "Presearch Decision Making in Consumer Durable Purchases," *Journal of Consumer Marketing* 4 (Winter 1987): 71–82.
19. H. Beales, M. B. Jagis, S. C. Salop, and R. Staelin, "Consumer Search and Public Policy," *Journal of Consumer Research* 8 (June 1981): 11–22.
20. Itamar Simonson, Joel Huber, and John Payne, "The Relationship between Prior Brand Knowledge and Information Acquisition Order," *Journal of Consumer Research* 14 (March 1988): 566–78.
21. John R. Hauser, Glen L. Urban, and Bruce D. Weinberg, "How Consumers Allocate Their Time When Searching for Information," *Journal of Marketing Research* 30 (November 1993): 452–66; George J. Stigler, "The Economics of Information," *Journal of Political Economy* 69 (June 1961): 213–25. For a set of studies focusing on online search costs, see John G. Lynch Jr. and Dan Ariely, "Wine Online: Search Costs and Competition on Price, Quality, and Distribution" *Marketing Science* 19 (1) (2000): 83–103.
22. "Holidays Look Merry for Online Retailers," *Wall Street Journal Interactive Edition* (December 24, 2002).

23. Lisa Guernsey, "As the Web Matures, Fun Is Hard to Find," *New York Times on the Web* (March 28, 2002).

24. Dan Ariely, "Controlling the Information Flow: Effects on Consumers' Decision Making and Preferences," *Journal of Consumer Research* 27 (September 2000): 233–48.

25. "Survey Cites Use of Internet to Gather Data," *New York Times on the Web* (December 30, 2002).

26. Rebecca K. Ratner, Barbara E. Kahn, and Daniel Kahneman, "Choosing Less-Preferred Experiences for the Sake of Variety," *Journal of Consumer Research* 26 (June 1999): 1–15.

27. Cathy J. Cobb and Wayne D. Hoyer, "Direct Observation of Search Behavior," *Psychology & Marketing* 2 (Fall 1985): 161–79.

28. Sharon E. Beatty and Scott M. Smith, "External Search Effort: An Investigation across Several Product Categories," *Journal of Consumer Research* 14 (June 1987): 83–95; William L. Moore and Donald R. Lehmann, "Individual Differences in Search Behavior for a Nondurable," *Journal of Consumer Research* 7 (December 1980): 296–307.

29. Geoffrey C. Kiel and Roger A. Layton, "Dimensions of Consumer Information Seeking Behavior," *Journal of Marketing Research* 28 (May 1981): 233–39; see also Narasimhan Srinivasan and Brian T. Ratchford, "An Empirical Test of a Model of External Search for Automobiles," *Journal of Consumer Research* 18 (September 1991): 233–42.

30. David F. Midgley, "Patterns of Interpersonal Information Seeking for the Purchase of a Symbolic Product," *Journal of Marketing Research* 20 (February 1983): 74–83.

31. Cyndee Miller, "Scotland to U.S.: 'This Tennent's for You'," *Marketing News* (August 29, 1994): 26.

32. Satya Menon and Barbara E. Kahn, "The Impact of Context on Variety Seeking in Product Choices," *Journal of Consumer Research* 22 (December 1995): 285–95; Barbara E. Kahn and Alice M. Isen, "The Influence of Positive Affect on Variety Seeking among Safe, Enjoyable Products," *Journal of Consumer Research* 20 (September 1993): 257–70.

33. J. Jeffrey Inman, "The Role of Sensory-Specific Satiety in Consumer Variety Seeking among Flavors" (unpublished manuscript, A. C. Nielsen Center for Marketing Research, University of Wisconsin–Madison, July 1999).

34. Gary Belsky, "Why Smart People Make Major Money Mistakes," *Money* (July 1995): 76; Richard Thaler and Eric J. Johnson, "Gambling with the House Money or Trying to Break Even: The Effects of Prior Outcomes on Risky Choice," *Management Science* 36 (June 1990): 643–60; Richard Thaler, "Mental Accounting and Consumer Choice," *Marketing Science* 4 (Summer 1985): 199–214.

35. Examples provided by Dr. William Cohen, personal communication, October 1999.

36. Daniel Kahneman and Amos Tversky, "Prospect Theory: An Analysis of Decision under Risk," *Econometrica* 47 (March 1979): 263–91; Timothy B. Heath, Subimal Chatterjee, and Karen Russo France, "Mental Accounting and Changes in Price: The Frame Dependence of Reference Dependence," *Journal of Consumer Research* 22, no. 1 (June 1995): 90–97.

37. Richard Thaler, "Mental Accounting and Consumer Choice," *Marketing Science* 4 (Summer 1985): 199–214, quoted on p. 206.

38. Girish N. Punj and Richard Staelin, "A Model of Consumer Search Behavior for New Automobiles," *Journal of Consumer Research* 9 (March 1983): 366–80.

39. Cobb and Hoyer, "Direct Observation of Search Behavior"; Moore and Lehmann, "Individual Differences in Search Behavior for a Nondurable"; Punj and Staelin, "A Model of Consumer Search Behavior for New Automobiles."

40. James R. Bettman and C. Whan Park, "Effects of Prior Knowledge and Experience and Phase of the Choice Process on Consumer Decision Processes: A Protocol Analysis," *Journal of Consumer Research* 7 (December 1980): 234–48.

41. Alba and Hutchinson, "Dimensions of Consumer Expertise"; Bettman and Park, "Effects of Prior Knowledge and Experience and Phase of the Choice Process on Consumer Decision Processes"; Merrie Brucks, "The Effects of Product Class Knowledge on Information Search Behavior," *Journal of Consumer Research* 12 (June 1985): 1–16; Joel E. Urbany, Peter R. Dickson, and William L. Wilkie, "Buyer Uncertainty and Information Search," *Journal of Consumer Research* 16 (September 1989): 208–15.

42. For a discussion of "collective risk," where consumers experience a reduction in perceived risk by sharing their exposure with others who are also using the product or service, see an analysis of Hotline, an online file-sharing community, in Markus Geisler, "Collective Risk," working paper, Northwestern University, March 2003.

43. Mary Frances Luce, James R. Bettman, and John W. Payne, "Choice Processing in Emotionally Difficult Decisions," *Journal of Experimental Psychology: Learning, Memory, and Cognition* 23 (March 1997): 384–405; example provided by Prof. James Bettman, personal communication, December 17, 1997.

44. John R. Hauser and Birger Wernerfelt, "An Evaluation Cost Model of Consideration Sets," *Journal of Consumer Research* 16 (March 1990): 393–408.

45. Robert J. Sutton, "Using Empirical Data to Investigate the Likelihood of Brands Being Admitted or Readmitted into an Established Evoked Set," *Journal of the Academy of Marketing Science* 15 (Fall 1987): 82.

46. Cyndee Miller, "Hemp is Latest Buzzword," *Marketing News* (March 17, 1997): 1.

47. Alba and Hutchison, "Dimensions of Consumer Expertise"; Joel B. Cohen and Kunal Basu, "Alternative Models of Categorization: Toward a Contingent Processing Framework," *Journal of Consumer Research* 13 (March 1987): 455–72.

48. Robert M. McMath, "The Perils of Typecasting," *American Demographics* (February 1997): 60.

49. Eleanor Rosch, "Principles of Categorization," in E. Rosch and B. B. Lloyd, eds., *Recognition and Categorization* (Hillsdale, NJ: Erlbaum, 1978).

50. Michael R. Solomon, "Mapping Product Constellations: A Social Categorization Approach to Symbolic Consumption," *Psychology & Marketing* 5, no. 3 (1988): 233–58.

51. Emily Nelson, "Moistened Toilet Paper Wipes Out after Launch for Kimberly-Clark," *Wall Street Journal Interactive Edition* (April 15, 2002).

52. McMath, "The Perils of Typecasting," 60.

53. Elizabeth C. Hirschman and Michael R. Solomon, "Competition and Cooperation among Culture Production Systems," in Ronald F. Bush and Shelby D. Hunt, eds., *Marketing Theory: Philosophy of Science Perspectives* (Chicago: American Marketing Association, 1982), 269–72.

54. Michael D. Johnson, "The Differential Processing of Product Category and Noncomparable Choice Alternatives," *Journal of Consumer Research* 16 (December 1989): 300–39.

55. Mita Sujan, "Consumer Knowledge: Effects on Evaluation Strategies Mediating Consumer Judgments," *Journal of Consumer Research* 12 (June 1985): 31–46.

56. Rosch, "Principles of Categorization."

57. Joan Meyers-Levy and Alice M. Tybout, "Schema Congruity as a Basis for Product Evaluation," *Journal of Consumer Research* 16 (June 1989): 39–55.

58. Mita Sujan and James R. Bettman, "The Effects of Brand Positioning Strategies on Consumers' Brand and Category Perceptions: Some Insights from Schema Research," *Journal of Marketing Research* 26 (November 1989): 454–67.

59. See William P. Putsis Jr. and Narasimhan Srinivasan, "Buying or Just Browsing? The Duration of Purchase Deliberation," *Journal of Marketing Research* 31 (August 1994): 393–402.

60. Robert E. Smith, "Integrating Information from Advertising and Trial: Processes and Effects on Consumer Response to Product Information," *Journal of Marketing Research* 30 (May 1993): 204–19.

61. Jack Trout, "Marketing in Tough Times," *Boardroom Reports* 2 (October 1992): 8.

62. Stuart Elliott, "Pepsi-Cola to Stamp Dates for Freshness on Soda Cans," *New York Times* (March 31, 1994): D1; Emily DeNitto, "Pepsi's Gamble Hits Freshness Dating Jackpot," *Advertising Age* (September 19, 1994): 50.

63. Amna Kirmani and Peter Wright, "Procedural Learning, Consumer Decision Making and Marketing Communication," *Marketing Letters* 4, no. 1 (1993): 39–48.

64. Michael Porter, *Competitive Advantage* (New York: Free Press, 1985).

65. Material in this section adapted from Michael R. Solomon and Elnora W. Stuart, *Welcome to* Marketing.com*: The Brave New World of E-Commerce* (Englewood Cliffs, NJ: Prentice Hall, 2001).

66. Phil Patton, "Buy Here, and We'll Tell You What You Like," *New York Times on the Web* (September 22, 1999).

67. Robert A. Baron, *Psychology: The Essential Science* (Boston: Allyn & Bacon, 1989); Valerie S. Folkes, "The Availability Heuristic and Perceived Risk," *Journal of Consumer Research* 15 (June 1989): 13–23; Kahneman and Tversky, "Prospect Theory: An Analysis of Decision Under Risk," 263–91.

68. Wayne D. Hoyer, "An Examination of Consumer Decision Making for a Common Repeat Purchase Product," *Journal of Consumer Research* 11 (December 1984): 822–29; Calvin P. Duncan, "Consumer Market Beliefs: A Review of the Literature and an Agenda for Future

Research," in Marvin E. Goldberg, Gerald Gorn, and Richard W. Pollay, eds., *Advances in Consumer Research* 17 (Provo, UT: Association for Consumer Research, 1990): 729–35; Frank Alpert, "Consumer Market Beliefs and Their Managerial Implications: An Empirical Examination," *Journal of Consumer Marketing* 10, no. 2 (1993): 56–70.

69. Michael R. Solomon, Sarah Drenan, and Chester A. Insko, "Popular Induction: When Is Consensus Information Informative?" *Journal of Personality* 49, no. 2 (1981): 212–24.

70. Folkes, "The Availability Heuristic and Perceived Risk."

71. Beales et al., "Consumer Search and Public Policy."

72. Gary T. Ford and Ruth Ann Smith, "Inferential Beliefs in Consumer Evaluations: An Assessment of Alternative Processing Strategies," *Journal of Consumer Research* 14 (December 1987): 363–71; Deborah Roedder John, Carol A. Scott, and James R. Bettman, "Sampling Data for Covariation Assessment: The Effects of Prior Beliefs on Search Patterns," *Journal of Consumer Research* 13 (June 1986): 38–47; Gary L. Sullivan and Kenneth J. Berger, "An Investigation of the Determinants of Cue Utilization," *Psychology & Marketing* 4 (Spring 1987): 63–74.

73. John et al., "Sampling Data for Covariation Assessment."

74. Duncan, "Consumer Market Beliefs."

75. Chr. Hjorth-Andersen, "Price as a Risk Indicator," *Journal of Consumer Policy* 10 (1987): 267–81.

76. David M. Gardner, "Is There a Generalized Price–Quality Relationship?" *Journal of Marketing Research* 8 (May 1971): 241–43; Kent B. Monroe, "Buyers' Subjective Perceptions of Price," *Journal of Marketing Research* 10 (1973): 70–80.

77. Durairaj Maheswaran, "Country of Origin as a Stereotype: Effects of Consumer Expertise and Attribute Strength on Product Evaluations," *Journal of Consumer Research* 21 (September 1994): 354–65; Ingrid M. Martin and Sevgin Eroglu, "Measuring a Multi-Dimensional Construct: Country Image," *Journal of Business Research* 28 (1993): 191–210; Richard Ettenson, Janet Wagner, and Gary Gaeth, "Evaluating the Effect of Country of Origin and the 'Made in the U.S.A.' Campaign: A Conjoint Approach," *Journal of Retailing* 64 (Spring 1988): 85–100; C. Min Han and Vern Terpstra, "Country-of-Origin Effects for Uni-National and Bi-National Products," *Journal of International Business* 19 (Summer 1988): 235–55; Michelle A. Morganosky and Michelle M. Lazarde, "Foreign-Made Apparel: Influences on Consumers' Perceptions of Brand and Store Quality," *International Journal of Advertising* 6 (Fall 1987): 339–48.

78. Thomas A. W. Miller, "Cultural Affinity, Personal Values Factors in Marketing," *Advertising Age* (August 16, 1999): H22.

79. See Richard Jackson Harris, Bettina Garner-Earl, Sara J. Sprick, and Collette Carroll, "Effects of Foreign Product Names and Country-of-Origin Attributions on Advertisement Evaluations," *Psychology & Marketing* 11 (March–April 1994): 129–45; Terence A. Shimp, Saeed Samiee, and Thomas J. Madden, "Countries and Their Products: A Cognitive Structure Perspective," *Journal of the Academy of Marketing Science* 21 (Fall 1993): 323–30.

80. Durairaj Maheswaran, "Country of Origin as a Stereotype: Effects of Consumer Expertise and Attribute Strength on Product Evaluations," *Journal of Consumer Research* 21 (September 1994): 354–65.

81. Caroline K. Lego, Natalie T. Wood, Stephanie L. McFee, and Michael R. Solomon, "A Thirst for the Real Thing in Themed Retail Environments: Consuming Authenticity in Irish Pubs," *Journal of Foodservice Business Research* 5, no. 2 (2003): 61–75.

82. Sung-Tai Hong and Robert S. Wyer Jr., "Effects of Country-of-Origin and Product-Attribute Information on Product Evaluation: An Information Processing Perspective," *Journal of Consumer Research* 16 (September 1989): 175–87; Marjorie Wall, John Liefeld, and Louise A. Heslop, "Impact of Country-of-Origin Cues on Consumer Judgments in Multi-Cue Situations: A Covariance Analysis," *Journal of the Academy of Marketing Science* 19, no. 2 (1991): 105–13.

83. Wai-Kwan Li and Robert S. Wyer Jr., "The Role of Country of Origin in Product Evaluations: Informational and Standard-of-Comparison Effects," *Journal of Consumer Psychology* 3, no. 2 (1994): 187–212.

84. Maheswaran, "Country of Origin as a Stereotype."

85. Items excerpted from Terence A. Shimp and Subhash Sharma, "Consumer Ethnocentrism: Construction and Validation of the CETSCALE," *Journal of Marketing Research* 24 (August 1987): 282.

86. Roger Ricklefs, "Canada Fights to Fend off American Tastes and Tunes," *Wall Street Journal Interactive Edition* (September 24, 1998).

87. Adam Bryant, "Message in a Beer Bottle," *Newsweek* (May 29, 2000): 43.

88. Richard W. Stevenson, "The Brands with Billion-Dollar Names," *New York Times* (October 28, 1988): A1.

89. Ronald Alsop, "Enduring Brands Hold Their Allure by Sticking Close to Their Roots," *Wall Street Journal*, centennial ed. (1989): B4.

90. Bruce Orwall, "Some Hip Hopes: Disney Channel Spices Up Its Image for Teenagers," *Wall Street Journal Interactive Edition* (October 13, 1999).

91. Jennifer Ordonez, "Travel Packages That Let Devotees Join Rock Bands on the Road Can Cause Jams," *Wall Street Journal Interactive Edition* (December 11, 2001).

92. Jacob Jacoby and Robert Chestnut, *Brand Loyalty: Measurement and Management* (New York: Wiley, 1978).

93. Anne B. Fisher, "Coke's Brand Loyalty Lesson," *Fortune* (August 5, 1985): 44.

94. Jacoby and Chestnut, *Brand Loyalty.*

95. Ronald Alsop, "Brand Loyalty Is Rarely Blind Loyalty," *Wall Street Journal* (October 19, 1989): B1.

96. Constance L. Hays, "One-Word Shoppers' Lexicon: Price," *New York Times* (December 26, 2002): C1 (2).

97. "Playing Hard to Get," *Forbes* (April 16, 2001): 204.

98. Hope Jensen Schau and Mary C. Gilly, "We are What We Post: The Presentation of Self in Personal Webspace," *Journal of Consumer Research* (forthcoming 2003); Hope Schau, Temple University, personal communication, March 2003.

99. C. Whan Park, "The Effect of Individual and Situation-Related Factors on Consumer Selection of Judgmental Models," *Journal of Marketing Research* 13 (May 1976): 144–51.

100. Joseph W. Alba and Howard Marmorstein, "The Effects of Frequency Knowledge on Consumer Decision Making," *Journal of Consumer Research* 14 (June 1987): 14–25.

Buying and Disposing

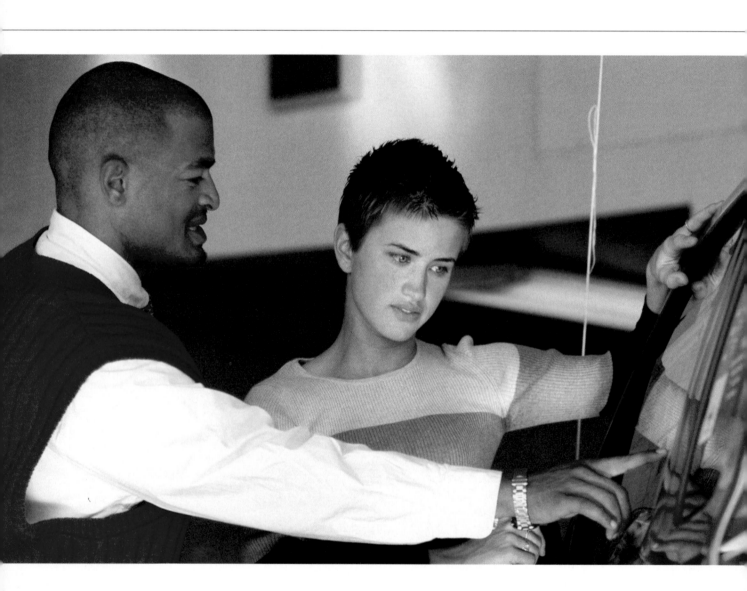

rob is really psyched. The big day has actually arrived: He's going to buy a car! He's had his eye on that silver 1998 Camaro parked in the lot of Russ's Auto-Rama for weeks now. Although the sticker says $2,999, Rob figures he can probably get this baby for a cool $2,000—Russ's looks like just the kind of place where they're hungry to move some cars. Besides, he's already done his homework on the Web. First he found out the wholesale value of similar used Camaros from the Kelley Blue Book (*kbb.com*), and then he scouted out some cars for sale in his area at *autobytel.com*. So, Rob figures he's coming in loaded for bear—he's going to show these guys they're not dealing with some rube.

Unlike some of the newer, flashy car showrooms he's been in lately, this place is a real nuts-and-bolts operation—it's so dingy and depressing he can't wait to get out of there and take a shower. Rob dreads the prospect of haggling over the price, but he hopes to convince the salesman to take his offer because he knows the real market value of the car he wants. At the Auto-Rama lot, big signs on all the cars proclaim that today is Russ's Auto-Rama Rip Us Off Day! Things look better than Rob expected—maybe he can get the Camaro for even less than he had planned. He's a bit surprised when a salesperson comes over to him and introduces herself as Rhoda. He had expected to be dealing with a middle-aged man in a loud sport coat (a stereotype he has about used-car salespeople), but this is more good luck: He figures he won't have to be so tough when dealing with a woman who looks to be about his age.

Rhoda laughs when he offers her $1,800 for the Camaro, pointing out that she can't take such a low bid for such a sweet car to her boss or she'll lose her job. Rhoda's enthusiasm for the car convinces him all the more that he has to have it. When he finally writes a check for $2,700, he's exhausted from all the haggling. What an ordeal! In any case, Rob reminds himself that he at least convinced Rhoda to sell him the car for less than the sticker price—and maybe he can fix it up and sell it for even more in a year or two. That Web surfing really paid off—he's a tougher negotiator than he thought.

■ SITUATIONAL EFFECTS ON CONSUMER BEHAVIOR

Many consumers dread the act of buying a car. In fact, a survey by Yankelovich Partners found that buying a car is the most anxiety-provoking and least-satisfying of any retail experience.[1] But, change is in the wind because the car showroom is being transformed. Car shoppers like Rob are logging onto Internet buying services, calling auto brokers who negotiate for them, buying cars at warehouse clubs, and visiting giant auto malls where they can comparison shop.

Rob's experience in buying a car illustrates some of the concepts to be discussed in this chapter. Making a purchase is often not a simple, routine matter of going to a store and quickly picking out something. As illustrated in Figure 10.1, a consumer's choices are affected by many personal factors, such as his or her mood, whether there is time pressure to make the purchase, and the particular situation or context for which the product is needed. In some situations, such as the purchase of a car or a home, the salesperson or realtor plays a pivotal role in the final selection. And today people are using the Web to arm themselves with product and price information before they even enter a dealership or a store, which puts added pressure on retailers to deliver the value they expect.

But the sale doesn't end at the time of purchase. A lot of important consumer activity occurs after a product has been brought home. After using a product, the consumer must decide whether he is satisfied with it. The satisfaction process is especially important to savvy marketers who realize that the key to success is not selling a product one time, but rather forging a relationship with the consumer so that he will continue to buy one's products in the future. Finally, just as Rob thought about the resale value of his car, we must also consider how consumers go about disposing of products and how secondary markets (e.g., used-car dealers) often play a pivotal role in product acquisition. This chapter considers many issues related to purchase and postpurchase phenomena.

A *consumption situation* is defined by factors beyond characteristics of the person and of the product that influence the buying and/or using of products and services. Situational effects can be behavioral (e.g., entertaining friends) or perceptual (e.g., being depressed or feeling pressed for time).[2] Common sense tells us that people tailor their purchases to specific occasions, and that the way we feel at a specific

■ **FIGURE 10.1**
ISSUES RELATED TO PURCHASE
AND POSTPURCHASE ACTIVITIES

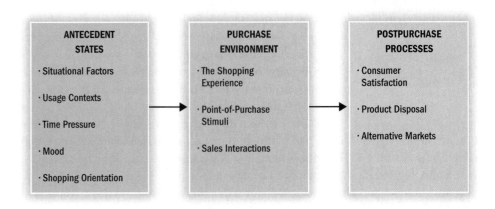

point in time affects what we feel like buying or doing. Smart marketers understand these patterns and tailor their efforts to coincide with situations in which people are most prone to buy. For example, book clubs invest heavily in promotional campaigns in June because many people are looking to stock up on "beach books" to read during the summer.[3]

In addition to the functional relationships between products and usage situation, though, another reason to take environmental circumstances seriously is that the role a person plays at any one time is partly determined by his or her *situational self-image*—he or she basically asks: "Who am I right *now*?" (see Chapter 5).[4] Someone trying to impress his date by playing the role of "man-about-town" may spend more lavishly, ordering champagne instead of beer, and buy flowers—purchases he would never consider when he is hanging out with his friends, slurping beer, and playing the role of "one of the boys." Let's see how these dynamics affect the way people think about what they buy.

By systematically identifying important usage situations, market segmentation strategies can position products that will meet the specific needs arising from these

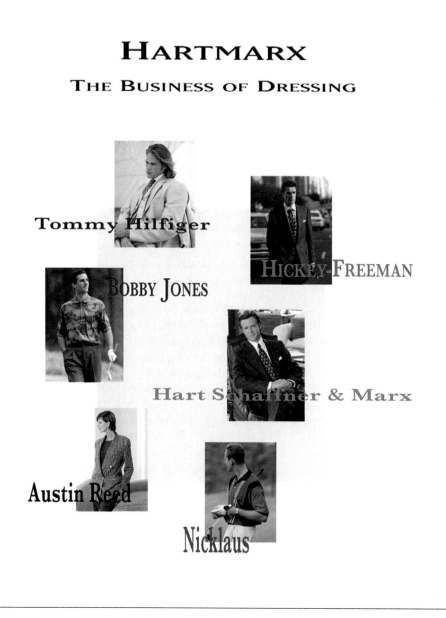

Net Profit

Technology is allowing marketers to fine-tune their messages to the consumption situation in exciting new ways. McDonald's is testing a digital signage system that automatically updates its menu boards as environmental conditions change. In the morning, customers are greeted with animated photos of steaming hash browns and Egg McMuffins that abruptly change to fries, Big Macs, and ice-cold sodas at 10 A.M. when breakfast service is over. Enter the restaurant in a snowstorm, and those sodas will be replaced by hot cups of coffee.[5]

Even highway billboards can be flexible if a plan now being tested by an entrepreneur in San Francisco is successful. Sensors on the billboards can detect which radio stations most drivers are listening to as they pass by. This information is matched to the demographic profiles of the people who listen to these stations. Then, the billboards will display an advertisement targeted to that profile. For example, if the majority of drivers at a certain time are listening to a radio station known to have an affluent audience, the board might select an ad for a luxury product or service.[6]

Clothing choices often are heavily influenced by the situation in which they need to be worn.

TABLE 10.1
A PERSON-SITUATION-SEGMENTATION MATRIX FOR SUNTAN LOTION

Situation	Young Children Fair Skin	Young Children Dark Skin	Teenagers Fair Skin	Teenagers Dark Skin	Adult Women Fair Skin	Adult Women Dark Skin	Adult Men Fair Skin	Adult Men Dark Skin	Benefits /Features
Beach/boat sunbathing	Combined insect repellent				Summer perfume				a. Product serves as windburn protection b. Formula and container can stand heat c. Container floats and is distinctive (not easily lost)
Home-poolside sunbathing					Combined moisturizer				a. Product has large pump dispenser b. Product won't stain wood, concrete, furnishings
Sunlamp bathing					Combined moisturizer and massage oil				a. Product is designed specifically for type of lamp b. Product has an artificial tanning ingredient
Snow skiing					Winter perfume				a. Product provides special protection from special light rays and weather b. Product has antifreeze formula
Person benefit/ features	Special protection a. Protection is critical b. Formula is non-poisonous		Special protection a. Product fits in jean pocket b. Product used by opinion leaders		Special protection Female perfume		Special protection Male perfume		

Source: Adapted from Peter R. Dickson, "Person-Situation: Segmentation's Missing Link," *Journal of Marketing* 46 (Fall 1982): 62. By permission of American Marketing Association.

situations. Many product categories are amenable to this form of segmentation. For example, consumers' furniture choices are often tailored to specific settings. We prefer different styles for a city apartment, beach house, or an executive suite. Similarly, motorcycles can be distinguished in terms of what riders use them for, including commuting, riding them as dirt bikes, using them on a farm versus highway travel, and so on.[7]

Table 10.1 gives one example of how situations can be used to fine-tune a segmentation strategy. By listing the major contexts in which a product is used (e.g., snow skiing and sunbathing for a suntan lotion) and the different users of the product, a matrix can be constructed that identifies specific product features that should be emphasized for each situation. For example, during the summer a lotion manufacturer might promote the fact that the bottle floats and is hard to lose, but tout its nonfreezing formula during the winter season.

■ SOCIAL AND PHYSICAL SURROUNDINGS

A consumer's physical and social environment affects her motives for product usage and how she evaluates products. Important cues include the person's physical surroundings, as well as the amount and type of other consumers also present in that situation. Dimensions of the physical environment, such as decor, odors, and even tem-

The ultimate *habitat* for those who like to sleep between meals.

When you're not sitting up dining on some of the finest cuisine in the sky (vegetarians included) and enjoying a glass or two of something very special, you can lie back in the only 6'6" sleeper bed to Australia or New Zealand. Qantas First Class, it's a niche thing. Call your travel agent or Qantas at (800) 227 4500. www.qantas.com

QANTAS
THE SPIRIT OF AUSTRALIA

Many stores and services (like airlines) try to differentiate themselves in terms of the physical environments they offer, touting such amenities as comfort.

perature can significantly influence consumption. One study even found that pumping certain odors into a Las Vegas casino actually increased the amount of money patrons fed into slot machines![8] We'll take a closer look at some of these factors a bit later in the chapter, when considering strategic issues related to store design.

In addition to physical cues, though, groups or social settings significantly affect many of a consumer's purchase decisions. In some cases, the sheer presence or absence of **co-consumers**, the other patrons in a setting, actually can function as a product attribute, as when an exclusive resort or boutique promises to provide privacy to privileged customers. At other times, the presence of others can have positive value. A sparsely attended ball game or an empty bar can be depressing sights.

The presence of large numbers of people in a consumer environment increases arousal levels, so a consumer's subjective experience of a setting tends to be more intense. This boost, however, can be positive or negative—the experience depends on the consumer's *interpretation* of this arousal. It is important to distinguish

Net Profit

Along with the increase in time poverty, researchers also are noting a rise in *polychronic activity*, or *multitasking*, a phenomenon in which consumers do more than one thing at a time.[16] This type of activity is especially prevalent in eating. Consumers often do not allocate a specific time for dining, but instead eat on the run. In a recent poll, 64 percent of respondents said they usually do something else while eating. As one food industry executive commented, "We've moved beyond grazing and into gulping."[17] The food industry is racing to meet consumers' desires to eat on the run. Here are a few on-the-go products soon to turn up at a grocery store near you:

- General Mills is turning its Yoplait yogurt into a meal with Nouriche, a nonfat yogurt smoothie fortified with 20 vitamins and minerals. A television commercial proclaims, "No time for a meal? Nouriche yourself."
- Kraft Foods is launching Nabisco Go-Paks, cupholder-ready contour packages featuring mini versions of its cookies and crackers, similar to the Frito-Lay Go Snacks already on the market.
- Tubes to squeeze on the run are the next big things: Look for Hershey's Portable Pudding in tubes as well as Jolly Rancher Gel Snacks.[18]

between *density* and *crowding* for this reason. The former term refers to the actual number of people occupying a space, while the psychological state of crowding exists only if a negative affective state occurs as a result of this density.[9] For example, 100 students packed into a classroom designed for 75 may result in an unpleasant situation for all concerned, but the same number of people jammed together at a party occupying a room of the same size might just make for a great rave.

In addition, the *type* of consumers who patronize a store or service or who use a product can influence evaluations. We often infer something about a store by examining its customers. For this reason, some restaurants require men to wear a jacket for dinner (and supply a rather tacky one if they don't), and bouncers at some "hot" nightspots handpick people waiting in line based on whether they have the right "look" for the club. To paraphrase the comedian Groucho Marx, "I would never join a club that would have me for a member!"

Temporal Factors

Time is one of consumers' most precious resources. We talk about "making time" or "spending time" and we frequently are reminded that "time is money." Common sense tells us that more careful information search and deliberation occurs when we have the luxury of taking our time. A meticulous shopper who would normally price an item at three different stores before buying might be found sprinting through the mall at 9:00 P.M. on Christmas Eve, furiously scooping up anything left on the shelves that might serve as a last-minute gift.

Economic Time

Time is an economic variable; it is a resource that must be divided among activities.[10] Consumers try to maximize satisfaction by allocating time to the appropriate combination of tasks. Of course, people's allocation decisions differ; we all know people who seem to play all of the time, and others who are workaholics. An individual's priorities determine his or her *timestyle*.[11] People in different countries also "spend" this resource at different rates. A social scientist compared the pace of life in 31 cities around the world as part of a study on timestyles.[12] He and his assistants timed how long it takes pedestrians to walk 60 feet and the time taken by postal clerks to sell a stamp. Based on these responses, he claims that the fastest and slowest countries are:

Fastest Countries: (1) Switzerland, (2) Ireland, (3) Germany, (4) Japan, (5) Italy
Slowest Countries: (31) Mexico, (30) Indonesia, (29) Brazil, (28) El Salvador (27) Syria

Many consumers believe they are more pressed for time than ever before, a feeling called **time poverty**. This feeling appears to be due more to perception than to fact. People may just have more options for spending their time and feel pressured by the weight of all of these choices. The average working day at the turn of the twentieth century was 10 hours (six days per week), and women did 27 hours of housework per week, compared to less than five hours weekly now. Of course, in some cases husbands are sharing these burdens more, and in some families maintaining an absolutely spotless home may not be as important as it used to be.[13] Still, about a third of Americans report always feeling rushed—up from 25 percent of the population in 1964.[14]

This sense of time poverty has made consumers very responsive to marketing innovations that allow them to save time. For example, rush hour commuters in Hong Kong no longer need to stand in line to buy subway tokens. Instead, a scanner automatically reads an Octopus card and automatically deducts the fare from their accounts. The card doesn't even require contact to be read, so women can just pass their entire handbag over the scanner and race to catch their trains.[15] In the United States, a new kind of vending machine called InstyMeds now being tested in a

Minneapolis hospital even dispenses prescription drugs after a patient enters a security code and swipes his credit card.[19]

Psychological Time

"Time flies when you're having fun," but other situations (like some classes?) seem to last forever. Our experience of time is very subjective and is influenced by our immediate priorities and needs. The fluidity of time is important for marketers to understand, because we're more likely to be in a consuming mood at some times than at others. We can identify time categories in terms of when people are likely to be receptive to marketing messages:[20]

● *Flow time:* As we saw in Chapter 4, in a flow state we become so absorbed in an activity we notice nothing else. Not a good time to be hitting people with ads.

Recognizing that modern women have many time pressures, Spiegel brings retailing to the office.

Time poverty is creating opportunities for many new products (like portable soups) that let people multitask.

- *Occasion time:* Special moments when something monumental occurs, such as a birth or an important job interview. Ads clearly relevant to the situation will be given our undivided attention.
- *Deadline time:* When we're working against the clock. This is the worst time to catch someone's attention.
- *Leisure time:* During downtime, we are more likely to notice ads and perhaps try new things.
- *Time to kill:* Waiting for something to happen such as catching a plane or sitting in a waiting room. This is bonus time, where we feel we have the luxury to focus on extraneous things. As a result we are more receptive to commercial messages, even for products we don't normally use.

Like you,
it does four
different jobs
at once.

Multitasking has become a way of life for many of us.

Our experience of time is largely a result of our culture, because different societies have varying perspectives on this experience. To most Western consumers, time is a neatly compartmentalized thing: We wake up in the morning, go to school or work, come home, eat dinner, go out, go to sleep . . . wake up and do it all over again. This perspective is called *linear separable time;* events proceed in an orderly sequence and different times are well-defined: "There's a time and a place for everything." There is a clear sense of past, present, and future. Many activities are performed as the means to some end that will occur later, as when people "save for a rainy day."

This perspective seems "natural" to us, but not all others share it. Some cultures run on *procedural time* and ignore the clock completely—people simply decide to do something "when the time is right." Much of the world appears to live on "event time"; for example, in Burundi people might arrange to meet when the cows return from the watering hole. If you ask someone in Madagascar how long it takes to get to the market, you will get an answer like, "in the time it takes to cook rice."

Alternatively, in *circular* or *cyclic* time, people are governed by natural cycles, such as the regular occurrence of the seasons (a perspective found in many Hispanic cultures). To these consumers, the notion of the future does not make sense, because that time will be much like the present. Because the concept of future value does not exist, these consumers often prefer to buy an inferior product that is available now rather than wait for a better one that may be available later. Also, it is hard to convince people who function on circular time to buy insurance or save for a rainy day when they do not think in terms of a linear future.

When groups of college students were asked to draw a picture of time, the resulting sketches in Figure 10.2 illustrate some of these different temporal perspectives.

■ FIGURE 10.2
DRAWINGS OF TIME

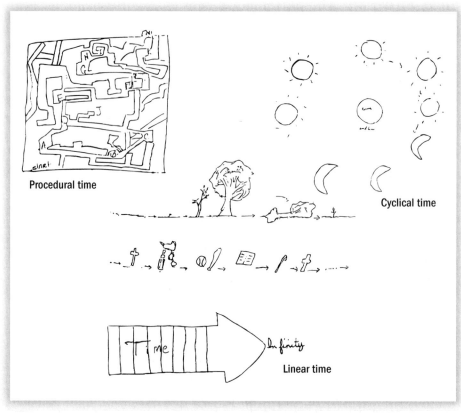

Source: Esther S. Page-Wood, Carol J. Kaufman, and Paul M. Lane, "The Art of Time." *Proceedings of the Academy of Marketing Science* (1990).

The drawing at the top left represents procedural time; there is lack of direction from left to right and little sense of past, present, and future. The three drawings in the middle denote cyclical time, with regular cycles designated by markers. The bottom drawing represents linear time, with a segmented time line moving from left to right in a well-defined sequence.[21]

The psychological dimension of time—how it is actually experienced—is an important factor in **queuing theory**, the mathematical study of waiting lines. A consumer's experience of waiting can radically influence his or her perceptions of service quality. Although we assume that something must be pretty good if we have to wait for it, the negative feelings aroused by long waits can quickly turn off customers.[22]

Marketers have adopted a variety of "tricks" to minimize psychological waiting time. These techniques range from altering customers' perceptions of a line's length to providing distractions that divert attention away from waiting.[23]

● One hotel chain, after receiving excessive complaints about the wait for elevators, installed mirrors near the elevator banks. People's natural tendency to check their appearance reduced complaints, even though the actual waiting time was unchanged.
● Airline passengers often complain about waiting to claim their baggage. In one airport, they would walk one minute from the plane to the baggage carousel and then wait seven minutes for their luggage. By changing the layout so that the walk to the carousel took six minutes and bags arrived two minutes after that, complaints were almost entirely eliminated.[24]

● Restaurant chains are scrambling to put the fast back into fast food, especially for drive-through lanes, which now account for 65 percent of revenues. In a study that ranked the speed of 25 fast food chains, cars spent an average of 203.6 seconds from the menu board to departure. Wendy's was clocked the fastest at 150.3 seconds. To speed things up and eliminate spills, McDonald's created a salad that comes in a container to fit into car cup holders. Arby's is working on a "high viscosity" version of its special sauce that's less likely to spill. Burger King is testing see-through bags so customers can quickly check their orders before speeding off.[25]

Antecedent States: If It Feels Good, Buy It . . .

A person's mood or physiological condition at the time of purchase can have a big impact on what she buys or how she evaluates her purchases.[26] One reason is that behavior is directed toward certain goal states, as was discussed in Chapter 4. If you don't believe it, try grocery shopping on an empty stomach!

A consumer's mood can have a big impact on purchase decisions. For example, stress can impair information-processing and problem-solving abilities.[27] Two dimensions, *pleasure* and *arousal,* determine if a shopper will react positively or negatively to a consumption environment. A person can enjoy or not enjoy a situation, and he or she can feel stimulated or not. As Figure 10.3 indicates, different combinations of pleasure and arousal levels result in a variety of emotional states. For example, an arousing situation can be either distressing or exciting, depending on whether the context is positive or negative (e.g., a street riot versus a street festival). Maintaining an "up" feeling in a pleasant context is one factor behind the success of theme parks such as Disney World, which try to provide consistent doses of carefully calculated stimulation to visitors.[28]

A specific mood is some combination of pleasure and arousal. For example, the state of happiness is high in pleasantness and moderate in arousal, whereas elation is high on both dimensions.[29] A mood state (either positive or negative) biases judgments of products and services in that direction.[30] Put simply, consumers give more positive evaluations when they are in a good mood (this explains the popularity of the business lunch!).

Moods can be affected by store design, the weather, or other factors specific to the consumer. In addition, music and television programming can affect mood, which has important consequences for commercials.[31] When consumers hear

■ **FIGURE 10.3**
DIMENSIONS OF EMOTIONAL STATES

happy music or watch happy programs, they have more positive reactions to commercials and products, especially when the marketing appeals are aimed at arousing emotional reactions.[32] When in positive moods, consumers process ads with less elaboration. They pay less attention to specifics of the message and rely more on heuristic processing (see Chapter 9).[33]

■ SHOPPING: A JOB OR AN ADVENTURE?

Some people shop even though they do not necessarily intend to buy anything at all, whereas others have to be dragged to a mall. Shopping is a way to acquire needed products and services, but social motives for shopping also are important. Thus, shopping is an activity that can be performed for either utilitarian (functional or tangible) or hedonic (pleasurable or intangible) reasons.[34] Indeed, some researchers suggest that most women "shop to love" while most men "shop to win." In this view, women find emotional fulfillment in the act of buying while men seek to demonstrate their expertise or ability to procure status items.[35] Obviously, there are many exceptions to this viewpoint, but nonetheless it's clear that the reasons we shop are more complex than may appear on the surface.

Reasons for Shopping

Do people hate to shop or love it? It depends. Consumers can be segmented in terms of their **shopping orientation**, or general attitudes about shopping. These orientations may vary depending on the particular product categories and store types considered. Rob hates to shop for a car, but he may love to browse in record stores. Our feelings about shopping also are influenced by the culture in which we live. In a survey of women around the world, more than 60 percent of women said they enjoy shopping for clothes in every country except Hong Kong, where only 39 percent responded so positively. The "shopping" prize goes to Latin Americans; more than 80 percent of women in countries like Brazil and Colombia agree that clothes shopping is a favorite activity. Other high-scoring countries include France, Italy, and Japan.[36]

The diversity of shopping motives is illustrated by scale items researchers use to assess people's underlying reasons for shopping. One item that measures hedonic value is "During the trip, I felt the excitement of the hunt." When that type of sentiment is compared to a functionally related statement such as, "I accomplished just what I wanted to on this shopping trip," the contrast between these two dimensions is clear.[37] Hedonic shopping motives can include the following:[38]

- *Social experiences:* The shopping center or department store has replaced the traditional town square or county fair as a community gathering place. Many people (especially in suburban or rural areas) may have no place else to go to spend their leisure time.
- *Sharing of common interests:* Stores frequently offer specialized goods that allow people with shared interests to communicate.
- *Interpersonal attraction:* Shopping centers are a natural place to congregate. The shopping mall has become a central "hangout" for teenagers. It also represents a controlled, secure environment for the elderly, and many malls now feature "mall walkers' clubs" for early morning workouts.
- *Instant status:* As every salesperson knows, some people savor the experience of being waited on, even though they may not necessarily buy anything. One men's clothing salesman offered this advice: "Remember their size, remember what you sold them last time. Make them feel important! If you can make people feel important, they are going to come back. Everybody likes to feel important!"[39]

THE GLOBAL LOOKING GLASS

The purpose of the "International Buy Nothing Day" is to raise consciousness about the grave costs that consumer culture has on people and the environment, by convincing people to abstain from shopping for just one day.

The advertising campaign against Western and in particular American inspired consumerism was a 30-second television commercial of an animated pig superimposed on a map of North America. Smacking its lips, the pig said, "The average North American consumes five times more than a Mexican, 10 times more than a Chinese person, and 30 times more than a person from India. . . Give it a rest."

In fact Westinghouse Electric Corporation's CBS, in a letter rejecting the commercial, went as far as saying that Buy Nothing Day is, "in opposition to the current economic policy in the United States." However, it may be worth noting that the amount spent on advertising convincing Americans to consume is higher than the gross domestic product of sub-Saharan Africa. In Brazil, Caio Lazzuri is an advertising student who got active because of his belief that, ". . . there's something killing the world like a cancer-economic growth." He writes that the one day of no shopping helps us all to see how mindless we become through advertisements and consumerism, especially third world countries such as Brazil "which is treated like a kitchen of the United States."

Source: Adapted from Romana King, "Buying Nothing Around the World," *The Courier* (Centennial College), *www.ddh.nl/nwd/1999/romana2911.*

- *The thrill of the hunt:* Some people pride themselves on their knowledge of the marketplace. Unlike our car-buying friend Rob, they may relish the process of haggling and bargaining, viewing it almost as a sport.

E-Commerce: Clicks Versus Bricks

As more and more Web sites pop up to sell everything from refrigerator magnets to Mack trucks, marketers continue to debate how the online world will affect the way they conduct business.[40] In particular, many are losing sleep wondering whether e-commerce is destined to replace traditional retailing, work in concert with it, or perhaps even fade away to become another fad your kids will laugh about someday. The latter is unlikely: Forrester Research predicts that by 2004, 49 million U.S. households will shop online and spend $184 billion. That's on top of huge numbers of consumers elsewhere. The European online buying population alone will be well over 100 million in just a few years.[41]

For marketers, the growth of online commerce is a sword that cuts both ways: On the one hand, they can reach customers around the world even if they're physically located 100 miles from nowhere. On the other hand, their competition now comes not only from the store across the street, but from thousands of Web sites spanning the globe. A second problem is that offering products directly to consumers has the potential to cut out the middleman—the loyal, store-based retailers who carry the firm's products and who sell them at a marked-up price.[42] The clicks-versus-bricks dilemma is raging in the marketing world.

So, what makes e-commerce sites successful? According to a survey by NPD Online, 75 percent of online shoppers surveyed said that good customer service would make them shop at the site again.[43] And many successful e-tailers are learning that using technology to provide extra value is attracting and keeping customers. For example, Eddie Bauer (*eddiebauer.com*) offers customers a virtual dressing room. The Cover Girl makeup site (*covergirl.com*) allows women to find colors that match their skin and hair types or to design a total look that's right for their lifestyle. Soon MTV viewers will be able to use their remote controls to purchase the CDs that go with the music videos they are seeing.

However, all is not perfect in the virtual world. E-commerce does have its limitations. Security is one important concern. We hear horror stories of consumers whose credit cards and other identity information have been stolen. Although an

ARRÊTEZ LA MUSCU DU SAMEDI.

houra.fr
LE CYBERMARCHÉ

Oui, c'est de la paresse et alors!

Many online shopping sites offer time-saving convenience. This French ad for a shopping/home delivery Web site says, "Stop the muscle training on Saturdays. . . Yes, this is total laziness. But so what?"

individual's financial liability in most theft cases is limited to $50, the damage to one's credit rating can last for years. Some shady companies are making money by prying and then selling personal information to others—one company promotes itself as "an amazing new tool that allows you to find out EVERYTHING you ever wanted to know about your friends, family, neighbors, employees, and even your boss!"[44] Pretty scary. Almost daily we hear of hackers getting into a business or even a government Web site and causing havoc. Businesses risk the loss of trade secrets and other proprietary information. Many must spend significant amounts to maintain security and conduct regular audits to ensure the integrity of their sites.

Other limitations of e-commerce relate to the actual shopping experience. Although it may be satisfactory to buy a computer or a book on the Internet, buying clothing and other items in which touching the item or trying it on is essential may be less attractive. Even though most companies have very liberal return policies, consumers can still get stuck with large delivery and return shipping charges for items that don't fit or simply aren't the right color. Table 10.2, on page 342, summarizes some of the pros and cons of e-commerce. It's clear that traditional shopping isn't quite dead yet—but bricks-and-mortar retailers do need to work harder to give shoppers something they can't get (yet anyway) in the virtual world—a stimulating or pleasant environment in which to browse. Now let's consider how they're doing that.

E-commerce sites like bluefly give shoppers the option of shopping without leaving home.

Retailing as Theater

The competition for customers is becoming even more intense as nonstore alternatives, from Web sites and print catalogs to TV shopping networks and home shopping parties, continue to multiply. With all of these shopping alternatives available, how can a traditional store compete? Shopping malls have tried to gain the loyalty of shoppers by appealing to their social motives as well as providing access to desired goods.

In many communities shopping centers are like the town squares of years past. They are the centers of communities, where residents gather to socialize. Many malls are becoming giant entertainment centers, almost to the point that their traditional retail occupants seem like an afterthought. As one retailing executive put it, "Malls are becoming the new mini-amusement parks."[45] It is now typical to find

TABLE 10.2
PROS AND CONS OF E-COMMERCE

Benefits of E-Commerce	Limitations of E-Commerce
For the Consumer	**For the Consumer**
Shop 24 hours a day	Lack of security
Less traveling	Fraud
Can receive relevant information in seconds from any location	Can't touch items
	Exact colors may not reproduce on computer monitors
More choices of products	Expensive to order and then return
More products available to less-developed countries	Potential breakdown of human relationships
Greater price information	
Lower prices so that less affluent can purchase	
Participate in virtual auctions	
Fast delivery	
Electronic communities	
For the Marketer	**For the Marketer**
The world is the marketplace	Lack of security
Decreases costs of doing business	Must maintain site to reap benefits
Very specialized business can be successful	Fierce price competition
	Conflicts with conventional retailers
Real-time pricing	Legal issues not resolved

Source: Adapted from Michael R. Solomon and Elnora W. Stuart, *Welcome to Marketing.Com: The Brave New World of E-Commerce* (Upper Saddle River, NJ: Prentice Hall, 2001).

such features as carousels, miniature golf, and batting cages in a suburban mall. Hershey opened a make-believe factory smack in the middle of Times Square. It features four steam machines, 380 feet of neon lighting, plus a moving message board that can be programmed for consumers who want to flash messages to surprise their loved ones.[46] The goal is to provide an experience that will draw people to stores, and this motivates innovative marketers like the chocolate manufacturer to blur the line between shopping and theater.[47]

The quest to entertain means that many stores are going all out to create imaginative environments that transport shoppers to fantasy worlds or provide other kinds of stimulation. This strategy is called **retail theming**. Innovative merchants today use four basic kinds of theming techniques:

- *Landscape themes* rely upon associations with images of nature, Earth, animals, and the physical body. Bass Pro Shops, for example, creates a simulated outdoor environment including pools stocked with fish.
- *Marketscape themes* build upon associations with man-made places. An example is The Venetian hotel in Las Vegas that lavishly recreates parts of the Italian city.
- *Cyberspace themes* are built around images of information and communications technology. eBay's retail interface instills a sense of community among its vendors and traders.
- *Mindscape themes* draw on abstract ideas and concepts, introspection and fantasy, and often possess spiritual overtones. The Kiva day spa in downtown Chicago offers health treatments based on a theme of Native American healing ceremonies and religious practices.[48]

Store Image

With so many stores competing for customers, how do consumers pick one over another? As with products (see Chapter 6), we can think of stores as having "personalities." Some stores have very clearly defined images (either good or bad). Others tend to blend into the crowd. They may not have anything distinctive about them and may be overlooked for this reason. This personality, or **store image**, is composed of many different factors. Store features, coupled with such consumer characteristics as shopping orientation, help to predict which shopping outlets people will prefer.[49] Some of the important dimensions of a store's profile are location, merchandise suitability, and the knowledge and congeniality of the sales staff.[50]

These features typically work together to create an overall impression. When shoppers think about stores, they may not say, "Well, that place is fairly good in terms of convenience, the salespeople are acceptable, and services are good." They are more likely to say, "That place gives me the creeps," or "I always enjoy shopping there." Consumers often evaluate stores using a general evaluation, and this overall feeling may have more to do with intangibles such as interior design and the types of people one finds in the store than with aspects such as return policies or credit availability. As a result, some stores are likely to consistently be in consumers' evoked sets (see Chapter 9), whereas others will never be considered.[51]

A recent makeover of FedEx retail outlets illustrates the crucial role design can play in communicating a desirable store image. As shown in the before and after shots in Figure 10.4, consumer research conducted by Ziba Design for FedEx indicated that compared to its main competitors, the firm's brand personality was more innovative, leading-edge, and outgoing—but this impression was certainly not reinforced by its cluttered storefront locations where customers go to drop off packages for delivery. The designers used colors and shapes associated with these attributes to make over the stores.

Atmospherics

Because a store's image is now recognized as a very important aspect of the retailing mix, store designers pay a lot of attention to **atmospherics**, or the "conscious designing of space and its various dimensions to evoke certain effects in buyers."[52] These dimensions include colors, scents, and sounds. For example, stores done in red tend to make people tense, whereas a blue decor imparts a calmer feeling.[53] As Chapter 2 noted, some preliminary evidence indicates that odors (olfactory cues) also can influence evaluations of a store's environment.[54] A store's atmosphere in turn affects purchasing behavior—one recent study reported that the extent of pleasure reported by shoppers five minutes after entering a store was predictive of the amount of time spent in the store as well as the level of spending there.[55]

Marketing Opportunity

The recognition that a store, hotel, or restaurant's audio environment can be a key driver of its personality has created a new niche. Numerous companies including W Hotels, GAP, Structure, Au Bon Pain, Starbucks, and even Lane Bryant now are selling their own musical collections so that customers can recreate the store's vibes at home. While companies have long known that ambient music affects shoppers—from subliminally discouraging theft to putting people in the mood to buy—only recently did they think to package background music as a product itself. The soundtracks are a newly discovered source of free advertising that even provides a modest profit.[56]

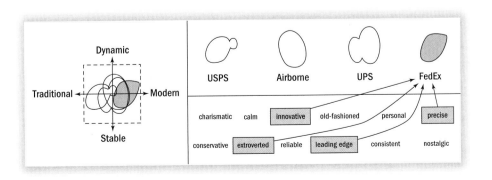

■ **FIGURE 10.4**
FEDEX BRAND IMAGE CONSUMER RESEARCH: BRAND POSITION

The FedEx makeover: Before and after.

Many elements of store design can be cleverly controlled to attract customers and produce desired effects on consumers. Light colors impart a feeling of spaciousness and serenity, and signs in bright colors create excitement. In one subtle but effective application, fashion designer Norma Kamali replaced fluorescent lights with pink ones in department store dressing rooms. The light had the effect of flattering the face and banishing wrinkles, making female customers more willing to try on (and buy) the company's bathing suits.[57] Wal-Mart found that sales were higher in areas of a prototype store lit in natural daylight compared to the more typical artificial light.[58] One study found that brighter in-store lighting influenced people to examine and handle more merchandise.[59]

In addition to visual stimuli, all sorts of cues can influence behaviors.[60] For example, patrons of country-and-western bars drink more when the jukebox music is slower. According to a researcher, "Hard drinkers prefer listening to slower-paced, wailing, lonesome, self-pitying music."[61] Similarly, music can affect eating habits. Another study found that diners who listened to loud, fast music ate more food. In contrast, those who listened to Mozart or Brahms ate less and more slowly. The researchers concluded that diners who choose soothing music at mealtimes can increase weight loss by at least five pounds a month![62]

Expo-Xplore, part of a new shopping complex near Durban, South Africa, is the next wave in retail and entertainment design. The courtyard, lined with retailers selling clothes and gear for a variety of outdoor adventure sports, leads to Planet Blue, the ocean-themed heart of the project, with stores oriented around scuba diving, boating, surfing, and other water sports.

In-Store Decision Making

Despite all their efforts to "pre-sell" consumers through advertising, marketers increasingly recognize that many purchases are strongly influenced by the store environment. Women tell researchers, for example, that store displays are one of the major information sources they use to decide what clothing to buy.[63] This influence is even stronger when we shop for food—it's estimated that about two out of every three supermarket purchases are decided in the aisles. And, people with lists are just as likely to make spontaneous purchases as those without them.[64]

Marketers are scrambling to engineer purchasing environments in order to increase the likelihood they will be in contact with consumers at the exact time they make a decision. This strategy even applies to drinking behavior: Diageo, the world's largest liquor company, discovered that 60 percent of bar customers don't know what they will drink until seconds before they place their orders. To make it more likely that the customer's order will include Smirnoff vodka, Johnnie Walker Scotch, or one of its other brands, Diageo launched its Drinks Invigoration Team to increase what it calls its "share of throat." The Dublin-based team experiments with bar "environments," bottle-display techniques, and how to match drinks to customers' moods. For example, the company researchers discovered that bubbles stimulate the desire for spirits, so it's developing bubble machines to put in back of bars. Diageo has even categorized bars into types and is identifying the types of drinkers—and the drinks they prefer—who frequent each. These include "style bars," where cutting-edge patrons like to sip fancy fresh-fruit martinis, and "buzz bars," where the clientele is receptive to a drink made of Smirnoff and energy brew Red Bull.[65]

Spontaneous Shopping

When a shopper is prompted to buy something in the store, one of two different processes may be at work: *Unplanned buying* may occur when a person is unfamiliar with a store's layout or perhaps when under some time pressure; or, a person may be

Smart retailers recognize that many purchase decisions are made at the time the shopper is in the store. That's one reason why grocery carts sometimes resemble billboards on wheels.

reminded to buy something by seeing it on a store shelf. About one-third of unplanned buying has been attributed to the recognition of new needs while within the store.[66]

In contrast, **impulse buying** occurs when the person experiences a sudden urge that he or she cannot resist. The tendency to buy spontaneously is most likely to result in a purchase when the consumer believes acting on impulse is appropriate, such as purchasing a gift for a sick friend or picking up the tab for a meal.[67] To cater to these urges, so-called *impulse items* such as candy and gum are conveniently placed near the checkout.

Similarly, many supermarkets have installed wider aisles to encourage browsing, and the widest tend to contain products with the highest profit margins. Low markup items that are purchased regularly tend to be stacked high in narrower aisles to allow shopping carts to speed through.[68] A more recent high-tech tool has been added to encourage impulse buying: A device called the Portable Shopper is a personal scanning gun that allows customers to ring up their own purchases as they shop. The gun was initially developed for Albert Hejin, the Netherlands' largest grocery chain, to move customers through the store more quickly. It's now in use in more than 150 grocery stores worldwide.[69]

Shoppers can be categorized in terms of how much advance planning they do. *Planners* tend to know what products and specific brands they will buy beforehand. *Partial planners* know they need certain products, but do not decide on specific brands until they are in the store, whereas *impulse purchasers* do no advance planning whatsoever.[70] A consumer who was asked to sketch a typical impulse purchaser, participating in a study on consumers' shopping experiences, drew Figure 10.5.

■ **FIGURE 10.5**
ONE CONSUMER'S IMAGE OF AN IMPULSE BUYER

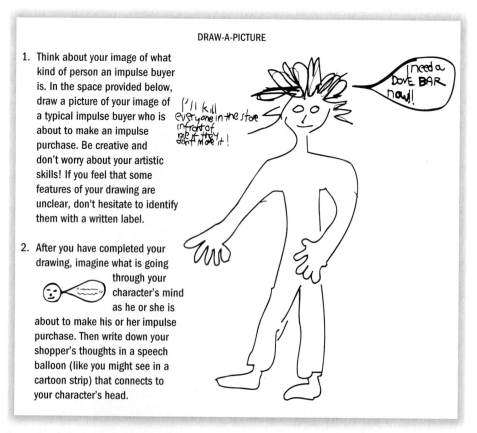

Source: Dennis Rook. "Is Impulse Buying (Yet) a Useful Marketing Concept?" (unpublished manuscript. University of Southern California. Los Angeles. 1990): Fig. 7-A.

Point-of-Purchase Stimuli

Displays can boost impulse purchases by as much as 10 percent. That explains why U.S. companies spend more than $13 billion each year on **point-of-purchase stimuli (POP)**. A POP can be an elaborate product display or demonstration, a coupon-dispensing machine, or even someone giving out free samples of a new cookie in the grocery aisle. Some of the more dramatic POP displays have included:[71]

- *Timex:* A ticking watch sits in the bottom of a filled aquarium.
- *Kellogg's Corn Flakes:* A button with a picture of Cornelius the Rooster is placed within the reach of children near Corn Flakes. When a child presses the button, he hears the rooster cock-a-doodle-doo.
- *Elizabeth Arden:* The company introduced "Elizabeth," a computer and video makeover system that allows customers to test out their images with different shades of makeup without having to actually apply the products first.
- *Tower Records:* A music sampler allows customers to hear records before buying them and to custom-design their own recordings by mixing and matching singles from assorted artists.
- *Trifari:* This company offered paper punch-out versions of its jewelry so that customers can "try on" the pieces at home.
- *Charmin:* Building on the familiar "Please don't squeeze the Charmin" theme, the company deployed the Charmin Squeeze Squad. Employees hid behind stacks of the toilet tissue and jumped out and blew horns at any "squeezers" they caught in the aisles.
- *The Farnam Company:* As somber music plays in the background, a huge plastic rat draped in a black shroud lies next to a tombstone to promote the company's "Just One Bite" rat poison.

The Salesperson

One of the most important in-store factors is the salesperson.[72] This influence can be understood in terms of **exchange theory**, which stresses that every interaction involves an exchange of value. Each participant gives something to the other and hopes to receive something in return.[73]

Music samplers that allow shoppers to check out the latest music tunes before buying have become a fixture in many stores. New versions allow listeners to select files, record them onto a CD, and even select the cover and clip art to personalize it.

Marketing Pitfall

Not all sales interactions are positive, but some *really* stand out. Here are a few incidents that make the rest of them easier to swallow:

- A woman sued a car dealer in Iowa, claiming that a salesperson persuaded her to climb into the trunk of a Chrysler Concorde to check out its spaciousness. He then slammed the trunk shut and bounced the car several times, apparently to the delight of his co-workers. This bizarre act apparently came about because the manager offered a prize of $100 to the salesperson who could get a customer to climb in.[87]
- A Detroit couple filed a $100 million lawsuit against McDonald's, alleging three McDonald's employees beat them after they tried to return a watery milkshake.
- In Alabama a McDonald's employee was arrested on second degree assault charges after stabbing a customer in the forehead with a ballpoint pen. The victim's attorney observed, "There was a great deal of profanity coming out of the employee prior to the stabbing."[88]

What "value" does the customer look for in a sales interaction? There are a variety of resources a salesperson might offer. For example, he or she might offer expertise about the product to make the shopper's choice easier. Alternatively, the customer may be reassured because the salesperson is a likable person whose tastes are similar and who is seen as someone who can be trusted.[75] Rob's car purchase, for example, was strongly influenced by the age and sex of Rhoda, the salesperson with whom he negotiated. In fact, a long stream of research attests to the impact of a salesperson's appearance on sales effectiveness. In sales, as in much of life, attractive people appear to hold the upper hand.[76] In addition, it's not unusual for service personnel and customers to form fairly warm personal relationships; these have been termed *commercial friendships* (think of all those patient bartenders who double as therapists for many people). Researchers have found that commercial friendships are similar to other friendships in that they can involve affection, intimacy, social support, loyalty, and reciprocal gift giving. They also work to support marketing objectives such as satisfaction, loyalty, and positive word of mouth.[77]

A buyer/seller situation is like many other dyadic encounters (two-person groups); it is a relationship in which some agreement must be reached about the roles of each participant: A process of *identity negotiation* occurs.[78] For example, if Rhoda immediately establishes herself as an expert (and Rob accepts this position), she is likely to have more influence over him through the course of the relationship. Some of the factors that help to determine salespersons' roles (and relative effectiveness) are their age, appearance, educational level, and motivation to sell.[79]

In addition, more effective salespersons usually know their customers' traits and preferences better than do ineffective salespersons because this knowledge allows them to adapt their approach to meet the needs of the specific customer.[80] The ability to be adaptable is especially vital when customers and salespeople differ in terms of their *interaction styles*.[81] Consumers, for example, vary in the degree of assertiveness they bring to interactions. At one extreme, nonassertive people believe that complaining is not socially acceptable and they may be intimidated in sales situations. Assertive people are more likely to stand up for themselves in a firm but nonthreatening way. Aggressives may resort to rudeness and threats if they do not get their way.[82]

■ POSTPURCHASE SATISFACTION

Consumer satisfaction/dissatisfaction (CS/D) is determined by the overall feelings, or attitude, a person has about a product after it has been purchased. Consumers engage in a constant process of evaluating the things they buy as they integrate these products into their daily consumption activities.[83] Despite evidence that customer satisfaction is steadily declining in many industries, good marketers are constantly on the lookout for sources of dissatisfaction so that they can improve.[84] For example, when United Airlines' advertising agency set out to identify specific aspects of air travel that were causing problems, they gave frequent fliers crayons and a map showing different stages in a long-distance trip and asked them to fill in colors using hot hues to symbolize areas causing stress and anger and cool colors for parts of the trip associated with satisfaction and calm feelings. Although jet cabins tended to be filled in with a serene aqua color, lo and behold, ticket counters were colored orange, and terminal waiting areas were fire-red. This research led the airline to focus more on overall operations instead of just in-flight experiences, and the "United Rising" campaign was born.[85]

Perceptions of Product Quality

Just what do consumers look for in products? That's easy: They want quality and value. Especially because of foreign competition, claims of product quality have become strategically crucial to maintaining a competitive advantage.[86] Consumers

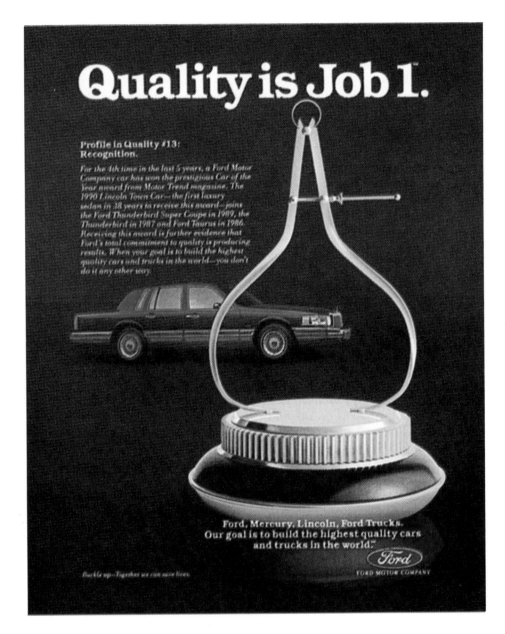

This ad for Ford relies on a common claim about quality.

use a number of cues to infer quality, including brand name, price, and even their own estimates of how much money has been put into a new product's advertising campaign.[89] These cues, as well as others such as product warranties and follow-up letters from the company, are often used by consumers to alleviate perceived risk and assure themselves that they have made smart purchase decisions.[90]

Although everyone wants quality, it is not clear exactly what it means. Certainly, many manufacturers claim to provide it. The Ford Motor Company emphasizes, "Quality is Job 1." Similar claims that have been made at one time or another by car manufacturers include the following:[91]

- *Lincoln-Mercury:* "the highest quality cars of any major American car company"
- *Chrysler:* "quality engineered to be the best"
- *GMC Trucks:* "quality built yet economical"
- *Oldsmobile:* "fulfilling the quality needs of American drivers"
- *Audi:* "quality backed by our outstanding new warranty"

Marketing Pitfall

Consumers are not the only ones who are angry. Many employees have an axe to grind as well. At a Web site put up by a disgruntled former employee of a certain fast-food franchise, we share the pain of this ex-burger flipper: "I have seen the creatures that live at the bottom of the dumpster. I have seen the rat by the soda machine. I have seen dead frogs in the fresh salad lettuce."[96] Fries with that?

A Web site called **customerssuck.com** gets 1,200 hits a day. This is a forum for restaurant and store workers who have to grin and bear it all day. Once off the clock, they can share their frustrations about the idiocy, slovenliness, and insensitivity of their customers. Some contributors to the Web site share stupid questions their customers ask, such as "How much is a 99-cent cheeseburger?" while others complain about working conditions and having to be nice to not-so-nice people. The slogan of the site is "the customer is never right."[97] Clearly, there are a lot of unhappy campers on both sides of the register.

Quality Is What We Expect It to Be

In the book *Zen and the Art of Motorcycle Maintenance*, a cult hero of college students in an earlier generation literally went crazy trying to figure out the meaning of quality.[92] Marketers appear to use the word "quality" as a catchall term for "good." Because of its wide and imprecise usage, the attribute of "quality" threatens to become a meaningless claim. If everyone has it, what good is it?

To muddy the waters a bit more, satisfaction or dissatisfaction is more than a reaction to the actual performance quality of a product or service. It is influenced by prior expectations regarding the level of quality. According to the *expectancy disconfirmation model*, consumers form beliefs about product performance based on prior experience with the product and/or communications about the product that imply a certain level of quality.[93] When something performs the way we thought it would, we may not think much about it. If, on the other hand, it fails to live up to expectations, negative affect may result. Furthermore, if performance happens to exceed our expectations, we are satisfied and pleased.

To understand this perspective, think about different types of restaurants. People expect to be provided with sparkling clear glassware at fancy restaurants, and they might become upset if they discover a grimy glass. On the other hand, they may not be surprised to find fingerprints on a beer mug at a local greasy spoon; they may even shrug it off because it contributes to the place's "charm." An important lesson for marketers: Don't overpromise if you can't deliver.[94]

This perspective underscores the importance of *managing expectations*— customer dissatisfaction is usually due to expectations exceeding the company's ability to deliver. Figure 10.6 illustrates the alternative strategies a firm can choose in these situations. When confronted with unrealistic expectations about what it can do, the firm can either accommodate these demands by improving the range or quality of products it offers, alter the expectations, or perhaps even choose to abandon the customer if it is not feasible to meet his or her needs.[95] Expectations are altered, for example, when waiters tell patrons in advance that the portion size they have ordered will not be very big, or when new-car buyers are warned of strange odors they will experience during the break-in period. A firm also can underpromise, as when Xerox inflates the time it will take for a service rep to visit. When the rep arrives a day earlier, the customer is impressed.

The power of quality claims is most evident when a company's product fails. Here, consumers' expectations are dashed and dissatisfaction results. In these situations, marketers must immediately take steps to reassure customers. When the company confronts the problem truthfully, consumers are often willing to forgive and forget, as was the case for Tylenol (product tampering), Chrysler (disconnecting odometers on executives' cars and reselling them as new), or Perrier (traces of benzene found in the water). When the company appears to be dragging its heels or covering up, on the other hand, consumer resentment will grow, as occurred

■ **FIGURE 10.6** CUSTOMER EXPECTATION ZONES

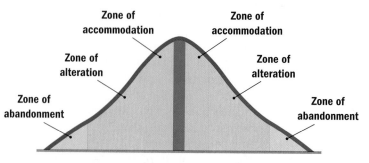

Legend:
- Firm's performance level
- Realistic expectations
- Unrealistic expectations
- Extremely discrepant expectations

Zone of accommodation — Zone of accommodation
Zone of alteration — Zone of alteration
Zone of abandonment — Zone of abandonment

during Union Carbide's chemical disaster in India, the massive Alaskan oil spill caused by the tanker *Exxon Valdez*, or the recent corporate scandals such as the collapse of Enron.

Acting on Dissatisfaction

If a person is not happy with a product or service, what can be done? A consumer has three possible courses of action (more than one can be taken):[98]

1 *Voice response:* The consumer can appeal directly to the retailer for redress (e.g., a refund).
2 *Private response:* Express dissatisfaction about the store or product to friends and/or boycott the store. As will be discussed in Chapter 11, negative word of mouth (WOM) can be very damaging to a store's reputation.
3 *Third-party response:* The consumer can take legal action against the merchant, register a complaint with the Better Business Bureau, or perhaps write a letter to the newspaper.

In one study, business majors wrote complaint letters to companies. Those who were sent a free sample in response indicated their image of the company significantly improved, but those who received only a letter of apology did not change their evaluations of the company. However, students who got no response reported an even more negative image than before, indicating that some form of response is better than none.[99]

A number of factors influence which route is eventually taken. The consumer may be a generally assertive or meek person. Action is more likely to be taken for expensive products such as household durables, cars, and clothing than for inexpensive products.[100] In addition, consumers who are satisfied with a store are more likely to complain; they take the time to complain because they feel connected to the store. Older people are more likely to complain, and are much more likely to believe the store will actually resolve the problem. Shoppers who get their problems resolved feel even *better* about the store than if nothing had gone wrong.[101] On the other hand, if the consumer does not believe that the store will respond well to a complaint, the person will be more likely to simply switch than fight.[102] Ironically, marketers should actually *encourage* consumers to complain to them: People are more likely to spread the word about unresolved negative experiences to their friends than they are to boast about positive occurrences.[103]

TQM: Going to the Gemba

Many analysts who study consumer satisfaction, or who are trying to design new products or services to increase it, recognize that it is crucial to understand how people actually interact with their environment in order to identify potential problems. These investigations typically are done in focus groups where a small set of consumers comes into a facility to try a new item while being observed by company personnel. However, some researchers advocate a more up-close and personal approach that allows them to watch people in the actual environment where the item is consumed. The Japanese approach to Total Quality Management (TQM), a complex set of management and engineering procedures aimed at reducing errors and increasing quality, has influenced this perspective.

To help attain this objective, researchers can *go to the gemba*. The **gemba** means the one true source of information. According to this philosophy, it's essential to send marketers and designers to the precise place where the product or service is being used rather than asking consumers to interact with it in a simulated environment. Figure 10.7 illustrates this idea in practice. Host Foods, which operates food concessions in major airports, sent a team to the *gemba*—in this case, an airport cafeteria—to identify problem areas. Employees watched as

The Tangled Web

Many dissatisfied customers and disgruntled former employees have been inspired to create their own Web sites just to share their tales of woe with others. For example, a Web site for people to complain about the Dunkin' Doughnuts chain got to be so popular the company bought it in order to control the bad press it was getting. A customer initially created the site to express his outrage over the fact that he was unable to get skim milk for his coffee.[104] As a media lawyer observed, "The person who, 20 years ago, was confined to walking up and down outside Chase Bank with a placard can now publish to millions of people with the click of a button."[105] Indeed, a single individual can do a lot of damage in cyberspace. One famous hacker who went by the *nom de guerre* of Pimpshiz hacked into more than 200 Web sites to insert a message supporting Napster before he was finally arrested.[106]

The Web is a very efficient staging ground for mass demonstrations. Political activists protesting corporate policies are able to mobilize large numbers of consumers by touting their causes online. Some Web sites like *fightback.com*, maintained by consumer activist David Horowitz focus on a range of consumerism issues; while others like *mcspotlight.org*, chronicle the ostensible misdeeds of a specific company like McDonald's. Indeed, while their life spans often are brief, at any point in time there are a surprising number of Web pages out there devoted to trashing specific companies, such as *walmartsucks.com*, *NorthWorstAir.org*, *chasebanksucks.com*, and *starbucked.com*.

Some entrepreneurs have been inspired to turn lemons into lemonade by compiling consumer complaints and providing feedback to companies so they can clean up their acts and improve satisfaction. PlanetFeedback.com has forwarded over 750,000 consumer feedback letters (including compliments, complaints, suggestions, and questions) to companies, brands, and corporations to help them find consumer trends, problem areas, marketing opportunities, and product ideas—among other things.

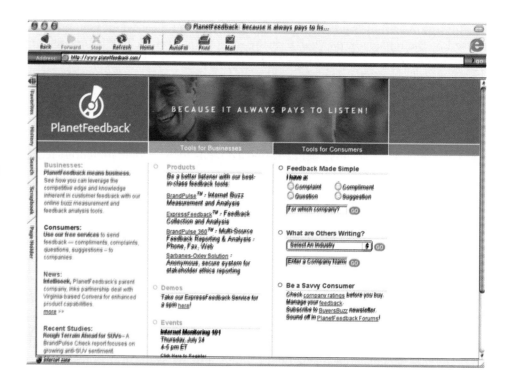

customers chose (or didn't) to enter the facility, then followed them as they inspected the menu, procured silverware, paid, and found a table. The findings were crucial to Host's redesign of the facility to make it easier to use. For example, the team hadn't realized the problem caused by having to put down one's luggage to enter the food line and not being able to keep an eye on valuables during the process.[107]

■ **FIGURE 10.7**
GOING TO THE GEMBA

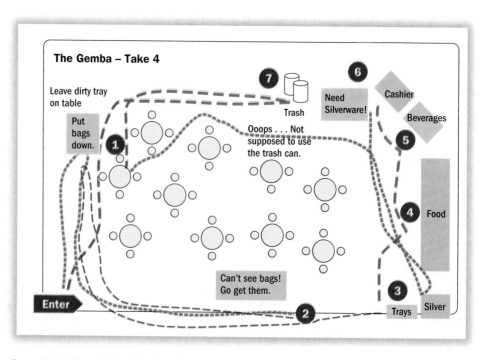

Source: Used with permission of the Quality Function Deployment Institute.

■ PRODUCT DISPOSAL

Because people often do form strong attachments to products, the decision to dispose of something may be a painful one. One function performed by our possessions is that they serve as anchors for our identities: Our past lives on in our things.[108] This attachment is exemplified by the Japanese, who ritually "retire" worn-out sewing needles, chopsticks, and even computer chips by burning them as thanks for good service.[109]

Although some people have more trouble than others in discarding things, even a "pack rat" does not keep everything. Consumers must often dispose of things, either because they have fulfilled their designated functions, or possibly because they no longer fit with consumers' view of themselves. Concern about the environment coupled with a need for convenience has made ease of product disposal a key attribute in categories from razors to diapers.

Disposal Options

When a consumer decides that a product is no longer of use, several choices are available. The person can either (1) keep the item, (2) temporarily dispose of it, or (3) permanently dispose of it. In many cases, a new product is acquired even though the old one still functions. Some reasons for this replacement include a desire for new features, a change in the person's environment (e.g., a refrigerator is the wrong color for a freshly painted kitchen), or a change in the person's role or self-image.[110] Figure 10.8 provides an overview of consumers' disposal options.

The issue of product disposition is doubly vital because of its enormous public policy implications. We live in a throwaway society, which creates problems for the environment and also results in a great deal of unfortunate waste. In a survey, 15 percent of adults admit they are pack rats and another 64 percent say they are

This British ad promotes the use of recycled paper.

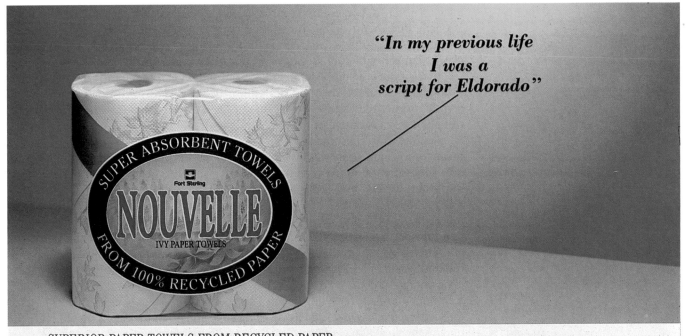

SUPERIOR PAPER TOWELS FROM RECYCLED PAPER

■ FIGURE 10.8 CONSUMERS' DISPOSAL OPTIONS

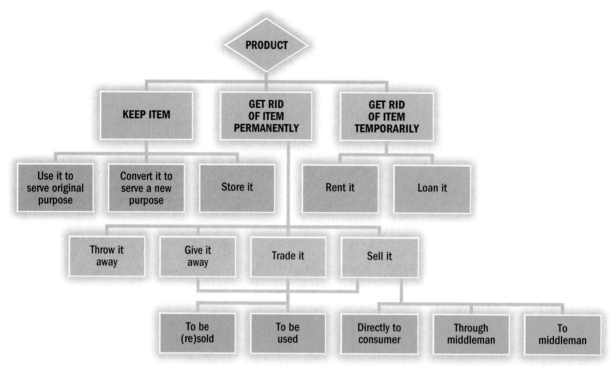

Source: Jacob Jacoby, Carol K. Berning, and Thomas F. Dietvorst, "What about Disposition?" *Journal of Marketing* 41 (April 1977): 23. By permission of American Marketing Association.

selective savers. In contrast, 20 percent say they throw out as much garbage as they can. The consumers most likely to save things are older people and single households.[111]

Training consumers to recycle has become a priority in many countries. Japan recycles about 40 percent of its garbage, and this relatively high rate of compliance is partly due to the social value the Japanese place on recycling: Citizens are encouraged by garbage trucks that periodically rumble through the streets playing classical music or children's songs.[112] Companies continue to search for ways to use resources more efficiently, often at the prompting of activist consumer groups. For example, McDonald's restaurants bowed to pressure by eliminating the use of Styrofoam packages, and its outlets in Europe are experimenting with edible breakfast platters made of maize.[113]

A study examined the relevant goals consumers have in recycling. It used a means–end chain analysis of the type described in Chapter 4 to identify how specific instrumental goals are linked to more abstract terminal values. The most important lower-order goals identified were "avoid filling up landfills," "reduce waste," "reuse materials," and "save the environment." These were linked to the terminal values of "promote health/avoid sickness," "achieve life-sustaining ends," and "provide for future generations." Another study reported that the perceived effort involved in recycling was the best predictor of whether people would go to the trouble—this pragmatic dimension outweighed general attitudes toward recycling and the environment in predicting intention to recycle.[114] By applying such techniques to study recycling and other product disposal behaviors, it will be easier for social marketers to design advertising copy and other messages that tap into the underlying values that will motivate people to increase environmentally responsible behavior.[115]

Lateral Cycling: Junk Versus "Junque"

Interesting consumer processes occur during **lateral cycling**, in which already-purchased objects are sold to others or exchanged for still other things. Many secondhand purchases are made. The reuse of other people's things is especially important in our throwaway society because, as one researcher put it, "there is no longer an 'away' to throw things to."[116]

Flea markets, garage sales, classified advertisements, bartering for services, hand-me-downs, and the black market all represent important alternative marketing systems that operate alongside the formal marketplace. These outlets provide consumers with opportunities to buy and sell items related to popular culture events and people to which they have long-term attachments. For example,

This Dutch ad says, "And when you've had enough of it, we'll clear it away nicely."

Marketing Pitfall

As if other kinds of waste weren't bad enough, one consequence of our infatuation with new technology is figuring out what to do with the stuff that quickly becomes obsolete. Now even discarded cell phones are becoming a problem as customers rapidly switch among mobile services and upgrade to new models. One popular solution seems to be to ship unwanted electronic waste such as old computer monitors and circuit boards to the Third World. As much as 50 to 80 percent of electronics waste collected for recycling in the United States is placed on container ships and sent to China, India, Pakistan, or other developing countries, where it is reused or recycled under largely unregulated conditions. Recycling industries in these places often use young children to handle cathode ray tubes filled with lead and other toxic substances. The European Union is so concerned about the problem that it is moving toward requiring manufacturers to take cradle-to-grave responsibility for their products.[117]

Flea markets are an important form of lateral cycling.

demand for rock 'n' roll memorabilia from icons like The Beatles or Buddy Holly remains strong. A buyer recently paid $850,000 for a guitar that formerly belonged to the Grateful Dead's Jerry Garcia.[118]

The Internet has revolutionized the lateral cycling process, as millions of people flock to eBay to buy and sell their "treasures." This phenomenally successful online auction site started as a trading post for Beanie Babies and other collectibles. Now two-thirds of the site's sales are for practical goods. eBay expects to sell $2 billion worth of used cars and $1 billion worth of computers a year. Coming next are event tickets, food, industrial equipment, and real estate.[119]

Ironically, an economic slowdown is good news for auction sites like eBay, because it's the kind of business that prospers when other businesses aren't doing well. As one analyst explained, "The interesting thing about eBay is that it may benefit because some people may choose not to buy something new, like a computer or consumer electronics." Hobbies and crafts also are selling strongly, which may be due to the number of people staying home rather than traveling.

Despite its success, there's sometimes a bittersweet quality to eBay. Some of the sellers are listing computers, fancy cars, jewelry, and other luxury items because they desperately need the money. As one vendor explained when he described the classic convertible he wanted to sell, "I am out of money and need to pay my rent, so my toys have to be sold." The site witnessed a particularly strong surge in these kinds of messages following 9/11, when many people got laid off in the wake of a sluggish economy. In the words of an accountant who lost his job, "Things were bad before, and then they got really bad after the bombings. Everything completely dried up." Noting that he used to sell merchandise on eBay as a hobby but now he's forced to sell some of his own possessions including his BMW and his wife's jewelry, he commented, "If it weren't for eBay, I'm not sure what I'd be doing. We definitely would not be able to pay the bills."[120]

Although traditional marketers have not paid much attention to used-product sellers, factors such as concern about the environment, demands for quality, and cost and fashion consciousness are conspiring to make these "secondary" markets more important.[121] In fact, economic estimates of this **underground economy** range from 3 percent to 30 percent of the Gross National Product of the United States and up to 70 percent of the GDP of other countries. Trade publications such

The used recording market is alive and well.

as *Yesteryear, Swap Meet Merchandising, Collectors Journal, The Vendor Newsletter,* and *The Antique Trader* offer reams of practical advice to consumers who want to bypass formal retailers and swap merchandise.

In the United States alone, there are more than 3,500 flea markets—including at least a dozen huge operations such as the 60-acre Orange County Marketplace in California—that operate nationwide to produce upwards of $10 billion in gross sales.[122] Other growth areas include student markets for used computers and text-books, as well as ski swaps, at which millions of dollars worth of used ski equipment is exchanged. A new generation of secondhand storeowners is developing markets for everything from used office equipment to cast-off kitchen sinks. Many are non-profit ventures started with government funding. A trade association called the Reuse Development Organization *(redo.org)* encourages them. These efforts remind us that recycling is actually the last step in the familiar mantra of the environmental movement: Reduce, reuse, and recycle.[123]

CHAPTER SUMMARY

The act of purchase can be affected by many factors. These include the consumer's antecedent state (e.g., his/her mood, time pressure, or disposition toward shopping). Time is an important resource that often determines how much effort and search will go into a decision. Mood can be affected by the degree of pleasure and arousal a store environment creates.

The usage context of a product can be a basis for segmentation; consumers look for different product attributes, depending on the use to which they intend to put their purchase. The presence or absence of other people (co-consumers)—and the types of people they are—can also affect a consumer's decisions.

The shopping experience is a pivotal part of the purchase decision. In many cases, retailing is like theater—the consumer's evaluation of stores and products may depend on the type of "performance" he or she witnesses. The actors (e.g., salespeople), the setting (the store environment), and props (e.g., store displays) influence this evaluation. A *store image,* like a brand personality, is determined by a number of factors such as perceived convenience, sophistication, expertise of salespeople, and so on. With increasing competition from nonstore alternatives, the creation of a positive shopping experience has never been more important. Online shopping is growing in importance, and this new way to acquire products has both good (e.g., convenience) and bad (e.g., security) aspects.

Because many purchase decisions are not made until the time the consumer is actually in the store, *point-of-purchase (POP)* stimuli are very important sales tools. These include product samples, elaborate package displays, place-based media, and in-store promotional materials such as "shelf talkers." POP stimuli are particularly useful in stimulating impulse buying, in which a consumer yields to a sudden urge for a product.

The consumer's encounter with a salesperson is a complex and important process. The outcome can be affected by such factors as the salesperson's similarity to the customer and his or her perceived credibility.

Consumer satisfaction is determined by the person's overall feeling toward the product after purchase. Many factors influence perceptions of product quality, including price, brand name, and product performance. Satisfaction is often determined by the degree to which a product's performance is consistent with the consumer's prior expectations of how well it will function.

Product disposal is an increasingly important problem. Recycling is one option that will continue to be stressed as consumers' environmental awareness grows. *Lateral cycling* occurs when objects are bought and sold secondhand, fenced, or bartered in an increasingly important underground economy.

KEY TERMS

Atmospherics   343
Co-consumers   331
Consumer satisfaction/
   dissatisfaction (CS/D)   348
Exchange theory   347

Gemba   351
Impulse buying   346
Lateral cycling   355
Point-of-purchase stimuli (POP)   347
Queuing theory   336

Retail theming   342
Shopping orientation   338
Store image   343
Time poverty   332
Underground economy   356

1 Discuss some of the motivations for shopping described in this chapter. How might a retailer adjust its strategy to accommodate these motivations?

2 Court cases in recent years have attempted to prohibit special interest groups from distributing literature in shopping malls. Mall managements claim that these centers are private property. On the other hand, these groups argue that the mall is the modern-day version of the town square and as such is a public forum. Find some recent court cases involving this free-speech issue, and examine the arguments pro and con. What is the current status of the mall as a public forum? Do you agree with this concept?

3 What are some positive and negative aspects of requiring employees who interact with customers to wear some kind of uniform or of mandating a dress code in the office?

4 Think about exceptionally good and bad salespeople you have encountered in the past. What qualities seem to differentiate them?

5 Discuss the concept of "timestyle." Based on your own experiences, how might consumers be segmented in terms of their timestyles?

6 Compare and contrast different cultures' conceptions of time. What are some implications for marketing strategy within each of these frameworks?

7 The movement away from a "disposable consumer society" toward one that emphasizes creative recycling creates many opportunities for marketers. Can you identify some?

8 Conduct naturalistic observation at a local mall. Sit in a central location and observe the activities of mall employees and patrons. Keep a log of the nonretailing activity you observe (e.g., special performances, exhibits, socializing, etc.). Does this activity enhance or detract from business conducted at the mall? As malls become more like high-tech game rooms, how valid is the criticism that shopping areas are only encouraging more loitering by teenage boys, who don't spend a lot in stores and simply scare away other customers?

9 Select three competing clothing stores in your area and conduct a store image study for them. Ask a group of consumers to rate each store on a set of attributes and plot these ratings on the same graph. Based on your

findings, are there any areas of competitive advantage or disadvantage you could bring to the attention of store management?

10 Using Table 10.1 as a model, construct a person/situation segmentation matrix for a brand of perfume.

11 What applications of queuing theory can you find employed among local services? Interview consumers who are waiting in lines to determine how this experience affects their satisfaction with the service.

12 The store environment is heating up as more and more companies put their promotional dollars into point-of-purchase efforts. Shoppers are now confronted by videos at the checkout counter, computer monitors attached to their shopping carts, and so on. We're increasingly exposed to ads in nonshopping environments. Recently, a health club in New York was forced to remove TV monitors that showed advertising on the Health Club Media Networks, claiming that they interfered with workouts. Do you feel that these innovations are overly intrusive? At what point might shoppers "rebel" and demand some peace and quiet while shopping? Do you see any market potential in the future for stores that "countermarket" by promising a "hands-off" shopping environment?

13 New interactive tools are being introduced that allow surfers on sites such as *landsend.com* to view apparel product selections on virtual models in full, 360-degree rotational view. In some cases the viewer can modify the bodies, face, skin coloring, and the hairstyles of these models. In others, the consumer can project his or her *own* likeness into the space by scanning a photo into a "makeover" program. *Boo.com* plans to offer 3-D pictures that can be rotated for close looks, even down to the stitching on a sweater, as well as online mannequins that will incorporate photos of shoppers and mimic voice patterns.[124] Visit *landsend.com* or another site that offers a personalized mannequin. Surf around. Try on some clothes. How was your experience—how helpful was this mannequin? When you shop for clothes online, would you rather see how they look on a body with dimensions the same as yours, or on a different body? What advice can you give Web site designers who are trying to personalize these shopping environments by creating life-like models to guide you through the site?

NOTES

1. Keith Naughton, "Revolution in the Showroom," *BusinessWeek* (February 19, 1996): 70.
2. Pradeep Kakkar and Richard J. Lutz, "Situational Influence on Consumer Behavior: A Review," in Harold H. Kassarjian and Thomas S. Robertson, eds., *Perspectives in Consumer Behavior*, 3rd ed. (Glenview, IL: Scott, Foresman, 1981): 204–14.
3. Ibid.
4. Carolyn Turner Schenk and Rebecca H. Holman, "A Sociological Approach to Brand Choice: The Concept of Situational Self-Image," in Jerry C. Olson, ed., *Advances in Consumer Research* 7 (Ann Arbor, MI: Association for Consumer Research, 1980): 610–14.
5. Kenneth Hein, "Was That a Big Mac or a McNugget? The Latest in Technology," *Brandweek* (February 25, 2002): 21.
6. Matt Richtel, "New Billboards Sample Radios as Cars Go By, Then Adjust," *New York Times on the Web* (December 27, 2002).
7. Peter R. Dickson, "Person–Situation: Segmentation's Missing Link," *Journal of Marketing* 46 (Fall 1982): 56–64.
8. Alan R. Hirsch, "Effects of Ambient Odors on Slot-Machine Usage in a Las Vegas Casino," *Psychology & Marketing* 12 (October 1995): 585–94.
9. Daniel Stokols, "On the Distinction between Density and Crowding: Some Implications for Future Research," *Psychological Review* 79 (1972): 275–77.
10. Carol Felker Kaufman, Paul M. Lane, and Jay D. Lindquist, "Exploring More than 24 Hours a Day: A Preliminary Investigation of Polychronic Time Use," *Journal of Consumer Research* 18 (December 1991): 392–401.
11. Laurence P. Feldman and Jacob Hornik, "The Use of Time: An Integrated Conceptual Model," *Journal of Consumer Research* 7 (March 1981): 407–19; see also Michelle M. Bergadaa, "The Role of Time in the Action of the Consumer," *Journal of Consumer Research* 17 (December 1990): 289–302.
12. Alan Zarembo, "What if There Weren't Any Clocks to Watch?" *Newsweek* (June 30, 1997): 14; based on research reported in Robert Levine, *A Geography of Time: The Temporal Misadventures of a Social Psychologist, or How Every Culture Keeps Time Just a Little Bit Differently* (New York: Basic Books, 1997).
13. Robert J. Samuelson, "Rediscovering the Rat Race," *Newsweek* (May 15, 1989): 57.
14. John P. Robinson, "Time Squeeze," *Advertising Age* (February 1990): 30–33.
15. "Plugged In: Hong Kong Embraces the Octopus Card," *New York Times on the Web* (June 8, 2002).
16. Lane, Kaufman, and Lindquist, "Exploring More than 24 Hours a Day."
17. Dena Kleiman, "Fast Food? It Just Isn't Fast Enough Anymore," *New York Times* (December 6, 1989): C12.
18. Stephanie Thompson, " 'To Go' Becoming the Way to Go," *Advertising Age* (May 13, 2002): 73.
19. "Instant Refills," *Wired* (June 2002): 36.
20. David Lewis and Darren Bridger, *The Soul of the New Consumer: Authenticity — What We Buy and Why in the New Economy* (London: Nicholas Brealey Publishing, 2000).
21. Robert J. Graham, "The Role of Perception of Time in Consumer Research," *Journal of Consumer Research* 7 (March 1981): 335–42; Esther S. Page-Wood, Paul M. Lane, and Carol J. Kaufman, "The Art of Time," *Proceedings of the 1990 Academy of Marketing Science Conference*, ed. B. J. Dunlap, Vol. XIII, Cullowhee, NC: Academy of Marketing Science (1990): 56–61.
22. See Shirley Taylor, "Waiting for Service: The Relationship between Delays and Evaluations of Service," *Journal of Marketing* 58 (April 1994): 56–69.
23. David H. Maister, "The Psychology of Waiting Lines," in John A. Czepiel, Michael R. Solomon, and Carol F. Surprenant, eds., *The Service Encounter: Managing Employee/Customer Interaction in Service Businesses* (Lexington, MA: Lexington Books, 1985): 113–24.
24. David Leonhardt, "Airlines Using Technology in a Push for Shorter Lines," *New York Times on the Web* (May 8, 2000).
25. Jennifer Ordonez, "An Efficiency Drive: Fast-Food Lanes, Equipped with Timers, Get Even Faster," *Wall Street Journal Interactive Edition* (May 18, 2000).
26. Laurette Dube and Bernd H. Schmitt, "The Processing of Emotional and Cognitive Aspects of Product Usage in Satisfaction Judgments," in Rebecca H. Holman and Michael R. Solomon, eds., *Advances in Consumer Research* 18 (Provo, UT: Association for Consumer Research, 1991): 52–56; Lalita A. Manrai and Meryl P. Gardner, "The Influence of Affect on Attributions for Product Failure," in Rebecca H. Holman and Michael R. Solomon, eds., *Advances in Consumer Research* 18 (Provo, UT: Association for Consumer Research, 1991): 249–54.
27. Kevin G. Celuch and Linda S. Showers, "It's Time to Stress Stress: The Stress–Purchase/Consumption Relationship," in Rebecca H. Holman and Michael R. Solomon, eds., *Advances in Consumer Research* 18 (Provo, UT: Association for Consumer Research, 1991): 284–89; Lawrence R. Lepisto, J. Kathleen Stuenkel, and Linda K. Anglin, "Stress: An Ignored Situational Influence," in Rebecca H. Holman and Michael R. Solomon, eds., *Advances in Consumer Research* 18 (Provo, UT: Association for Consumer Research, 1991): 296–302.
28. See Eben Shapiro, "Need a Little Fantasy? A Bevy of New Companies Can Help," *New York Times* (March 10, 1991): F4.
29. John D. Mayer and Yvonne N. Gaschke, "The Experience and Meta-Experience of Mood," *Journal of Personality and Social Psychology* 55 (July 1988): 102–11.
30. Meryl Paula Gardner, "Mood States and Consumer Behavior: A Critical Review," *Journal of Consumer Research* 12 (December 1985): 281–300; Scott Dawson, Peter H. Bloch, and Nancy M. Ridgway, "Shopping Motives, Emotional States, and Retail Outcomes," *Journal of Retailing* 66 (Winter 1990): 408–27; Patricia A. Knowles, Stephen J. Grove, and W. Jeffrey Burroughs, "An Experimental Examination of Mood States on Retrieval and Evaluation of Advertisement and Brand Information," *Journal of the Academy of Marketing Science* 21 (April 1993): 135–43; Paul W. Miniard, Sunil Bhatla, and Deepak Sirdeskmuhk, "Mood as a Determinant of Postconsumption Product Evaluations: Mood Effects and Their Dependency on the Affective Intensity of the Consumption Experience," *Journal of Consumer Psychology* 1, no. 2 (1992): 173–95; Mary T. Curren and Katrin R. Harich, "Consumers' Mood States: The Mitigating Influence of Personal Relevance on Product Evaluations," *Psychology & Marketing* 11 (March–April 1994): 91–107; Gerald J. Gorn, Marvin E. Rosenberg, and Kunal Basu, "Mood, Awareness, and Product Evaluation," *Journal of Consumer Psychology* 2, no. 3 (1993): 237–56.
31. Gordon C. Bruner, "Music, Mood, and Marketing," *Journal of Marketing* 54 (October 1990): 94–104; Basil G. Englis, "Music Television and Its Influences on Consumers, Consumer Culture, and the Transmission of Consumption Messages," in Rebecca H. Holman and Michael R. Solomon, eds., *Advances in Consumer Research* 18 (Provo, UT: Association for Consumer Research, 1991): 111–14.
32. Marvin E. Goldberg and Gerald J. Gorn, "Happy and Sad TV Programs: How They Affect Reactions to Commercials," *Journal of Consumer Research* 14 (December 1987): 387–403; Gorn, Goldberg, and Basu, "Mood, Awareness, and Product Evaluation"; Curren and Harich, "Consumers' Mood States."
33. Rajeev Batra and Douglas M. Stayman, "The Role of Mood in Advertising Effectiveness," *Journal of Consumer Research* 17 (September 1990): 203; John P. Murry Jr. and Peter A. Dacin, "Cognitive Moderators of Negative-Emotion Effects: Implications for Understanding Media Context," *Journal of Consumer Research* 22 (March 1996): 439–47; see also Curren and Harich, "Consumers' Mood States"; Gorn, Goldberg, and Basu, "Mood, Awareness, and Product Evaluation."
34. For a scale that was devised to assess these dimensions of the shopping experience, see Barry J. Babin, William R. Darden, and Mitch Griffin, "Work and/or Fun: Measuring Hedonic and Utilitarian Shopping Value," *Journal of Consumer Research* 20 (March 1994): 644–56.
35. Cele Otnes and Mary Ann McGrath, "Perceptions and Realities of Male Shopping Behavior," *Journal of Retailing* 77 (Spring 2001): 111–37.
36. "A Global Perspective . . . on Women and Women's Wear," *Lifestyle Monitor* 14 (Winter 1999–2000): 8–11.
37. Babin, Darden, and Griffin, "Work and/or Fun."
38. Edward M. Tauber, "Why Do People Shop?" *Journal of Marketing* 36 (October 1972): 47–48.
39. Robert C. Prus, *Making Sales: Influence as Interpersonal Accomplishment* (Newbury Park, CA: Sage Publications, 1989), 225.
40. Some material in this section was adapted from Michael R. Solomon and Elnora W. Stuart, *Welcome to Marketing.Com: The Brave New World of E-Commerce* (Upper Saddle River, NJ: Prentice Hall, 2001).
41. Seema Williams, David M. Cooperstein, David E. Weisman, and Thalika Oum, "Post-Web Retail," *The Forrester Report*, Forrester

Research, Inc., September 1999; Catherine Arnold, "Across the Pond," *Marketing News* (October 28, 2002): 3.

42. Rebecca K. Ratner, Barbara E. Kahn, and Daniel Kahneman, "Choosing Less-Preferred Experiences for the Sake of Variety," *Journal of Consumer Research* 26 (June 1999): 1–15.

43. Jennifer Gilbert, "Customer Service Crucial to Online Buyers," *Advertising Age* (September 13, 1999): 52.

44. Timothy L. O'Brien, "Aided by Internet, Identity Theft Soars," *New York Times on the Web* (April 3, 2000).

45. Jacquelyn Bivins, "Fun and Mall Games," *Stores* (August 1989): 35.

46. Vanessa O'Connell, "Fictional Hershey Factory Will Send Kisses to Broadway," *Wall Street Journal Interactive Edition* (August 5, 2002).

47. Sallie Hook, "All the Retail World's a Stage: Consumers Conditioned to Entertainment in Shopping Environment," *Marketing News* 21 (July 31, 1987): 16.

48. Millie Creighton, "The Seed of Creative Lifestyle Shopping: Wrapping Consumerism in Japanese Store Layouts," in John F. Sherry Jr., ed., *Servicescapes: The Concept of Place in Contemporary Markets* (Lincolnwood, IL: NTC Business Books, 1998), 199–228.

49. Susan Spiggle and Murphy A. Sewall, "A Choice Sets Model of Retail Selection," *Journal of Marketing* 51 (April 1987): 97–111; William R. Darden and Barry J. Babin, "The Role of Emotions in Expanding the Concept of Retail Personality," *Stores* 76, no. 4 (April 1994): RR7–RR8.

50. Most measures of store image are quite similar to other attitude measures, as discussed in Chapter 5. For an excellent bibliography of store image studies, see Mary R. Zimmer and Linda L. Golden, "Impressions of Retail Stores: A Content Analysis of Consumer Images," *Journal of Retailing* 64 (Fall 1988): 265–93.

51. Spiggle and Sewall, "A Choice Sets Model of Retail Selection."

52. Philip Kotler, "Atmospherics as a Marketing Tool," *Journal of Retailing* (Winter 1973–74): 10; Anna Mattila and Jochen Wirtz "Congruency of Scent and Music as a Driver of In-Store Evaluations and Behavior," *Journal Of Retailing* 77 (2) 2001: 273–289; J. Duncan Herrington, "An Integrative Path Model of the Effects of Retail Environments on Shopper Behavior," in Robert L. King, ed., *Marketing: Toward the Twenty-First Century* (Richmond, VA: Southern Marketing Association, 1991), 58–62; see also Ann E. Schlosser, "Applying the Functional Theory of Attitudes to Understanding the Influence of Store Atmosphere on Store Inferences," *Journal of Consumer Psychology* 7, no. 4 (1998): 345–69.

53. Joseph A. Bellizzi and Robert E. Hite, "Environmental Color, Consumer Feelings, and Purchase Likelihood," *Psychology & Marketing* 9 (September–October 1992): 347–63.

54. See Eric R. Spangenberg, Ayn E. Crowley, and Pamela W. Henderson, "Improving the Store Environment: Do Olfactory Cues Affect Evaluations and Behaviors?" *Journal of Marketing* 60 (April 1996): 67–80, for a study that assessed olfaction in a controlled, simulated store environment.

55. Robert J. Donovan, John R. Rossiter, Gilian Marcoolyn, and Andrew Nesdale, "Store Atmosphere and Purchasing Behavior," *Journal of Retailing* 70, no. 3 (1994): 283–94.

56. Julie Flaherty, "Ambient Music Has Moved to Record Store Shelves," *New York Times on the Web* (July 4, 2001).

57. Deborah Blumenthal, "Scenic Design for In-Store Try-ons," *New York Times* (April 9, 1988): N9.

58. John Pierson, "If Sun Shines in, Workers Work Better, Buyers Buy More," *Wall Street Journal* (November 20, 1995): B1.

59. Charles S. Areni and David Kim, "The Influence of In-Store Lighting on Consumers' Examination of Merchandise in a Wine Store," *International Journal of Research in Marketing* 11, no. 2 (March 1994): 117–25.

60. Jean-Charles Chebat, Claire Gelinas Chebat, and Dominique Vaillant, "Environmental Background Music and In-store Selling," *Journal of Business Research* 54 (2001): 115–23; Judy I. Alpert and Mark I. Alpert, "Music Influences on Mood and Purchase Intentions," *Psychology & Marketing* 7 (Summer 1990): 109–34.

61. "Slow Music Makes Fast Drinkers," *Psychology Today* (March 1989): 18.

62. Brad Edmondson, "Pass the Meat Loaf," *American Demographics* (January 1989): 19.

63. "Through the Looking Glass," *Lifestyle Monitor* 16 (Fall–Winter 2002).

64. Jennifer Lach, "Meet You in Aisle Three," *American Demographics* (April 1999): 41.

65. Ernest Beck, "Diageo Attempts to Reinvent the Bar in an Effort to Increase Spirits Sales," *Wall Street Journal* (February 23, 2001).

66. Easwar S. Iyer, "Unplanned Purchasing: Knowledge of Shopping Environment and Time Pressure," *Journal of Retailing* 65 (Spring 1989): 40–57; C. Whan Park, Easwar S. Iyer, and Daniel C. Smith, "The

67. Dennis W. Rook and Robert J. Fisher, "Normative Influences on Impulsive Buying Behavior," *Journal of Consumer Research* 22 (December 1995): 305–13; Francis Piron, "Defining Impulse Purchasing," in Rebecca H. Holman and Michael R. Solomon, eds., *Advances in Consumer Research* 18 (Provo, UT: Association for Consumer Research, 1991): 509–14; Dennis W. Rook, "The Buying Impulse," *Journal of Consumer Research* 14 (September 1987): 189–99.

68. Michael Wahl, "Eye POPping Persuasion," *Marketing Insights* (June 1989): 130.

69. "Zipping Down the Aisles," *New York Times Magazine* (April 6, 1997): 30.

70. Cathy J. Cobb and Wayne D. Hoyer, "Planned versus Impulse Purchase Behavior," *Journal of Retailing* 62 (Winter 1986): 384–409; Easwar S. Iyer and Sucheta S. Ahlawat, "Deviations from a Shopping Plan: When and Why Do Consumers Not Buy as Planned," in Melanie Wallendorf and Paul Anderson, eds., *Advances in Consumer Research* 14 (Provo, UT: Association for Consumer Research, 1987): 246–49.

71. Lisa Bertagnoli, "Signposts: The Power of Point-of-Purchase," *Marketing News* 21 (May 2001): 3; Michael Janofsky, "Using Crowing Roosters and Ringing Business Cards to Tap a Boom in Point-of-Purchase Displays," *New York Times* (March 21, 1994): D9.

72. See Robert B. Cialdini, *Influence: Science and Practice,* 2nd ed. (Glenview, IL: Scott, Foresman, 1988).

73. Richard P. Bagozzi, "Marketing as Exchange," *Journal of Marketing* 39 (October 1975): 32–39; Peter M. Blau, *Exchange and Power in Social Life* (New York: Wiley, 1964); Marjorie Caballero and Alan J. Resnik, "The Attraction Paradigm in Dyadic Exchange," *Psychology & Marketing* 3, no. 1 (1986): 17–34; George C. Homans, "Social Behavior as Exchange," *American Journal of Sociology* 63 (1958): 597–606; Paul H. Schurr and Julie L. Ozanne, "Influences on Exchange Processes: Buyers' Preconceptions of a Seller's Trustworthiness and Bargaining Toughness," *Journal of Consumer Research* 11 (March 1985): 939–53; Arch G. Woodside and J. W. Davenport, "The Effect of Salesman Similarity and Expertise on Consumer Purchasing Behavior," *Journal of Marketing Research* 8 (1974): 433–36.

74. Sally Beatty, "Bank of America Places Ads in ATMs to Offset Expenses," *Wall Street Journal Interactive Edition* (July 25, 2002); David L. Margulus, "Going to the A.T.M. for More than a Fistful of Twenties," *New York Times on the Web* (January 17, 2002).

75. Paul Busch and David T. Wilson, "An Experimental Analysis of a Salesman's Expert and Referent Bases of Social Power in the Buyer-Seller Dyad," *Journal of Marketing Research* 13 (February 1976): 3–11; John E. Swan, Fred Trawick Jr., David R. Rink, and Jenny J. Roberts, "Measuring Dimensions of Purchaser Trust of Industrial Salespeople," *Journal of Personal Selling and Sales Management* 8 (May 1988): 1.

76. For a study in this area, see Peter H. Reingen and Jerome B. Kernan, "Social Perception and Interpersonal Influence: Some Consequences of the Physical Attractiveness Stereotype in a Personal Selling Setting," *Journal of Consumer Psychology* 2 (1993): 25–38.

77. Linda L. Price and Eric J. Arnould, "Commercial Friendships: Service Provider–Client Relationships in Context," *Journal of Marketing* 63 (October 1999): 38–56.

78. Mary Jo Bitner, Bernard H. Booms, and Mary Stansfield Tetreault, "The Service Encounter: Diagnosing Favorable and Unfavorable Incidents," *Journal of Marketing* 54 (January 1990): 7–84; Robert C. Prus, *Making Sales* (Newbury Park, CA: Sage Publications, 1989); Arch G. Woodside and James L. Taylor, "Identity Negotiations in Buyer–Seller Interactions," in Elizabeth C. Hirschman and Morris B. Holbrook, eds., *Advances in Consumer Research* 12 (Provo, UT: Association for Consumer Research, 1985): 443–49.

79. Barry J. Babin, James S. Boles, and William R. Darden, "Salesperson Stereotypes, Consumer Emotions, and Their Impact on Information Processing," *Journal of the Academy of Marketing Science* 23, no. 2 (1995): 94–105; Gilbert A. Churchill Jr., Neil M. Ford, Steven W. Hartley, and Orville C. Walker Jr., "The Determinants of Salesperson Performance: A Meta-Analysis," *Journal of Marketing Research* 22 (May 1985): 103–18.

80. Siew Meng Leong, Paul S. Busch, and Deborah Roedder John, "Knowledge Bases and Salesperson Effectiveness: A Script-Theoretic Analysis," *Journal of Marketing Research* 26 (May 1989): 164; Harish Sujan, Mita Sujan, and James R. Bettman, "Knowledge Structure Differences Between More Effective and Less Effective Salespeople," *Journal of Marketing Research* 25 (February 1988): 81–86; Robert Saxe

Effects of Situational Factors on In-Store Grocery Shopping," *Journal of Consumer Research* 15 (March 1989): 422–33.

and Barton Weitz, "The SOCCO Scale: A Measure of the Customer Orientation of Salespeople," *Journal of Marketing Research* 19 (August 1982): 343–51; David M. Szymanski, "Determinants of Selling Effectiveness: The Importance of Declarative Knowledge to the Personal Selling Concept," *Journal of Marketing* 52 (January 1988): 64–77; Barton A. Weitz, "Effectiveness in Sales Interactions: A Contingency Framework," *Journal of Marketing* 45 (Winter 1981): 85–103.

81. Jagdish M. Sheth, "Buyer-Seller Interaction: A Conceptual Framework," in *Advances in Consumer Research* Ud. 3 (Cincinnati, OH: Association for Consumer Research, 1976): 382–86; Kaylene C. Williams and Rosann L. Spiro, "Communication Style in the Salesperson-Customer Dyad," *Journal of Marketing Research* 22 (November 1985): 434–42.

82. Marsha L. Richins, "An Analysis of Consumer Interaction Styles in the Marketplace," *Journal of Consumer Research* 10 (June 1983): 73–82.

83. Rama Jayanti and Anita Jackson, "Service Satisfaction: Investigation of Three Models," in Rebecca H. Holman and Michael R. Solomon, eds., *Advances in Consumer Research* 18 (Provo, UT: Association for Consumer Research, 1991): 603–10; David K. Tse, Franco M. Nicosia, and Peter C. Wilton, "Consumer Satisfaction as a Process," *Psychology & Marketing* 7 (Fall 1990): 177–93. For a recent treatment of satisfaction issues from a more interpretive perspective, see Susan Fournier and David Mick, "Rediscovering Satisfaction," *Journal of Marketing* 63 (October 1999): 5–23.

84. Constance L. Hayes, "Service Takes a Holiday," *New York Times* (December 23, 1998): C1.

85. Leslie Kaufman, "Enough Talk," *Newsweek* (August 18, 1997): 48–49.

86. Robert Jacobson and David A. Aaker, "The Strategic Role of Product Quality," *Journal of Marketing* 51 (October 1987): 31–44. For a review of issues regarding the measurement of service quality, see J. Joseph Cronin Jr. and Steven A. Taylor, "Measuring Service Quality: A Reexamination and Extension," *Journal of Marketing* 56 (July 1992): 55–68.

87. Calmetta Y. Coleman, "A Car Salesman's Bizarre Prank May End up Backfiring in Court," *Wall Street Journal* (May 2, 1995): B1.

88. "Woman Stabbed Over McDonald's Meal Dispute," *Opelika/Auburn News* (April 13, 2002).

89. Anna Kirmani and Peter Wright, "Money Talks: Perceived Advertising Expense and Expected Product Quality," *Journal of Consumer Research* 16 (December 1989): 344–53; Donald R. Lichtenstein and Scot Burton, "The Relationship Between Perceived and Objective Price-Quality," *Journal of Marketing Research* 26 (November 1989): 429–43; Akshay R. Rao and Kent B. Monroe, "The Effect of Price, Brand Name, and Store Name on Buyers' Perceptions of Product Quality: An Integrative Review," *Journal of Marketing Research* 26 (August 1989): 351–57.

90. Shelby Hunt, "Post-Transactional Communication and Dissonance Reduction," *Journal of Marketing* 34 (January 1970): 46–51; Daniel E. Innis and H. Rao Unnava, "The Usefulness of Product Warranties for Reputable and New Brands," in Rebecca H. Holman and Michael R. Solomon, eds., *Advances in Consumer Research* 18 (Provo, UT: Association for Consumer Research, 1991): 317–22; Terence A. Shimp and William O. Bearden, "Warranty and Other Extrinsic Cue Effects on Consumers' Risk Perceptions," *Journal of Consumer Research* 9 (June 1982): 38–46.

91. Morris B. Holbrook and Kim P. Corfman, "Quality and Value in the Consumption Experience: Phaedrus Rides Again," in Jacob Jacoby and Jerry C. Olson, eds., *Perceived Quality: How Consumers View Stores and Merchandise* (Lexington, MA: Lexington Books, 1985): 31–58.

92. Holbrook and Corfman, "Quality and Value in the Consumption Experience"; Robert M. Pirsig, *Zen and the Art of Motorcycle Maintenance: An Inquiry into Values* (New York: Bantam Books, 1974).

93. Gilbert A. Churchill Jr. and Carol F. Surprenant, "An Investigation into the Determinants of Customer Satisfaction," *Journal of Marketing Research* 19 (November 1983): 491–504; John E. Swan and I. Frederick Trawick, "Disconfirmation of Expectations and Satisfaction with a Retail Service," *Journal of Retailing* 57 (Fall 1981): 49–67; Peter C. Wilton and David K. Tse, "Models of Consumer Satisfaction Formation: An Extension," *Journal of Marketing Research* 25 (May 1988): 204–12. For a discussion of what may occur when customers evaluate a new service for which comparison standards do not yet exist, see Ann L. McGill and Dawn Iacobucci, "The Role of Post-Experience Comparison Standards in the Evaluation of Unfamiliar Services," in John F. Sherry Jr. and Brian Sternthal, eds., *Advances in Consumer Research* 19 (Provo, UT: Association for Consumer Research, 1992): 570–78; William Boulding, Ajay Kalra, Richard Staelin, and Valarie A. Zeithaml, "A Dynamic Process Model of Service Quality: From Expectations to Behavioral Intentions," *Journal of Marketing Research* 30 (February 1993): 7–27.

94. John W. Gamble, "The Expectations Paradox: The More You Offer Customers, the Closer You Are to Failure," *Marketing News* (March 14, 1988): 38.

95. Jagdish N. Sheth and Banwari Mittal, "A Framework for Managing Customer Expectations," *Journal of Market Focused Management* 1 (1996): 137–58.

96. www.protest.net, accessed June 17, 2000.

97. Keith Naughton, "Tired of Smile-Free Service," *Newsweek* (March 6, 2000): 44–45.

98. Mary C. Gilly and Betsy D. Gelb, "Post-Purchase Consumer Processes and the Complaining Consumer," *Journal of Consumer Research* 9 (December 1982): 323–28; Diane Halstead and Cornelia Droge, "Consumer Attitudes Toward Complaining and the Prediction of Multiple Complaint Responses," in Rebecca H. Holman and Michael R. Solomon, eds., *Advances in Consumer Research* 18 (Provo, UT: Association for Consumer Research, 1991): 210–16; Jagdip Singh, "Consumer Complaint Intentions and Behavior: Definitional and Taxonomical Issues," *Journal of Marketing* 52 (January 1988): 93–107.

99. Gary L. Clark, Peter F. Kaminski, and David R. Rink, "Consumer Complaints: Advice on How Companies Should Respond Based on an Empirical Study," *Journal of Services Marketing* 6 (Winter 1992): 41–50.

100. Alan Andreasen and Arthur Best, "Consumers Complain—Does Business Respond?" *Harvard Business Review* 55 (July–August 1977): 93–101.

101. Tibbett L. Speer, "They Complain Because They Care," *American Demographics* (May 1996): 13–14.

102. Ingrid Martin, "Expert-Novice Differences in Complaint Scripts," in Rebecca H. Holman and Michael R. Solomon, eds., *Advances in Consumer Research* 18 (Provo, UT: Association for Consumer Research, 1991): 225–31; Marsha L. Richins, "A Multivariate Analysis of Responses to Dissatisfaction," *Journal of the Academy of Marketing Science* 15 (Fall 1987): 24–31.

103. John A. Schibrowsky and Richard S. Lapidus, "Gaining a Competitive Advantage by Analyzing Aggregate Complaints," *Journal of Consumer Marketing* 11 (1994): 15–26.

104. "Dunkin' Donuts Buys Out Critical Web Site," *New York Times on the Web* (August 27, 1999).

105. Jan McCallum, "I Hate You, and Millions Know It," *BRW* (July 7, 2000): 84.

106. S. McManis, "An Internet Outlaw Goes on Record: Pleasant Hill Student Tells of His 'Hacktivism'," *San Francisco Chronicle* (February 24, 2002): A21.

107. Material adapted from a presentation by Glenn H. Mazur, QFD Institute, 2002.

108. Russell W. Belk, "The Role of Possessions in Constructing and Maintaining a Sense of Past," in Marvin E. Goldberg, Gerald Gorn, and Richard W. Pollay, eds., *Advances in Consumer Research* 17 (Provo, UT: Association for Consumer Research, 1989): 669–76.

109. David E. Sanger, "For a Job Well Done, Japanese Enshrine the Chip," *New York Times* (December 11, 1990): A4.

110. Jacob Jacoby, Carol K. Berning, and Thomas F. Dietvorst, "What About Disposition?" *Journal of Marketing* 41 (April 1977): 22–28.

111. Jennifer Lach, "Welcome to the Hoard Fest," *American Demographics* (April 2000): 8–9.

112. Mike Tharp, "Tchaikovsky and Toilet Paper," *U.S. News and World Report* (December 1987): 62; B. Van Voorst, "The Recycling Bottleneck," *Time* (September 14, 1992): 52–54; Richard P. Bagozzi and Pratibha A. Dabholkar, "Consumer Recycling Goals and Their Effect on Decisions to Recycle: A Means-End Chain Analysis," *Psychology & Marketing* 11 (July/August 1994): 313–40.

113. "Finally, Something at McDonald's You Can Actually Eat," *UTNE Reader* (May–June 1997): 12.

114. Debra J. Dahab, James W. Gentry, and Wanru Su, "New Ways to Reach Non-Recyclers: An Extension of the Model of Reasoned Action to Recycling Behaviors" (paper presented at the meetings of the Association for Consumer Research, 1994).

115. Bagozzi and Dabholkar, "Consumer Recycling Goals and Their Effect on Decisions to Recycle"; see also L. J. Shrum, Tina M. Lowrey, and John A. McCarty, "Recycling as a Marketing Problem: A Framework for Strategy Development," *Psychology & Marketing* 11 (July–August 1994): 393–416; Dahab, Gentry, and Su, "New Ways to Reach Non-Recyclers."

116. John F. Sherry Jr., "A Sociocultural Analysis of a Midwestern American Flea Market," *Journal of Consumer Research* 17 (June 1990): 13–30.

117. John Markoff, "Technology's Toxic Trash Is Sent to Poor Nations," *New York Times on the Web* (February 25, 2002); "Recycling Phones to Charities, Not Landfills," *New York Times on the Web* (October 26, 2002).

118. Alex Markels,"Collectors Shake, Rattle and Watch Those Bankrolls," *New York Times on the Web* (October 13, 2002).

119. Saul Hansell, "Meg Whitman and eBay, Net Survivors," *New York Times on the Web* (May 5, 2002).

120. Stephanie Stoughton, "Unemployed Americans Turn to *E-Bay* to Make Money," *The Boston Globe* (October 16, 2001).

121. Allan J. Magrath, "If Used Product Sellers Ever Get Organized, Watch Out," *Marketing News* (June 25, 1990): 9; Kevin McCrohan and James D. Smith, "Consumer Participation in the Informal Economy," *Journal of the Academy of Marketing Science* 15 (Winter 1990): 62.

122. John F. Sherry Jr., "Dealers and Dealing in a Periodic Market: Informal Retailing in Ethnographic Perspective," *Journal of Retailing* 66 (Summer 1990): 174.

123. New Kind of Store Getting More Use out of Used Goods," *Montgomery Advertiser* (December 12, 1996): 7A.

124. William Echison, "Designers Climb onto the Virtual Catwalk," *BusinessWeek* (October 11, 1999): 164.

Group Influence
and Opinion Leadership

Zachary leads a secret life. During the week, he is a straight-laced stock analyst for a major investment firm. The weekend is another story. Come Friday evening, it's off with the Brooks Brothers suit and on with the black leather, as he trades in his BMW for his treasured Harley-Davidson motorcycle. A dedicated member of HOG (Harley Owners Group), Zachary belongs to the faction of Harley riders known as "RUBs" (rich urban bikers). Everyone in his group wears expensive leather vests with Harley insignias and owns customized "Low Riders." Just this week, Zack finally got his new Harley belt buckle when he logged onto The Genuine Harley-Davidson Roadstore at *Harley-Davidson.com*. Surfing around the site makes him realize the lengths some of his fellow enthusiasts go to make sure others know they are HOG riders. As one of the Harley Web pages observed, "It's one thing to have people buy your products. It's another thing to have them tattoo your name on their bodies." Zack had to restrain himself from buying more Harley stuff; there were jackets, vests, eyewear, belts, buckles, scarves, watches, jewelry, even housewares ("home is the road") for sale. He settled for a set of Harley salt-and-pepper shakers that would be perfect for his buddy Soren's new crib.

Zack has spent a lot of money on his bike and on outfitting himself to be like the rest of the group. But it's worth it. He feels a real sense of brotherhood with his fellow RUBs. The group rides together in two-column formation to bike rallies that sometimes attract up to 300,000 cycle enthusiasts. What a sense of power he feels when they're all cruising together—it's them against the world!

Of course, an added benefit is the business networking he's been able to accomplish during his weekend jaunts with his fellow professionals who also wait for the weekend to "ride on the wild side."[1] Sometimes sharing a secret can pay off in more ways than one.

■ REFERENCE GROUPS

Humans are social animals. We all belong to groups, try to please others, and take cues about how to behave by observing the actions of those around us. In fact, some people's desire to "fit in" or to identify with desirable individuals or groups is the primary motivation for many of their purchases and activities. There are those who go to great lengths to please the members of a group whose acceptance they covet.[2]

Zachary's biker group is an important part of his identity, and this membership influences many of his buying decisions. He has spent many thousands of dollars on parts and accessories since acquiring his identity as a RUB. His fellow riders are united by their consumption choices, so total strangers feel an immediate bond with each other when they meet. The publisher of *American Iron*, an industry magazine, observed, "You don't buy a Harley because it's a superior bike, you buy a Harley to be a part of a family."[3]

Zachary doesn't model himself after just *any* biker—only the people with whom he really identifies can exert that kind of influence on him. For example, Zachary's group doesn't have much to do with outlaw clubs, which are primarily composed of blue-collar riders sporting Harley tattoos. The members of his group also have only polite contact with "Ma and Pa" bikers, whose bikes are the epitome of comfort, featuring such niceties as radios, heated handgrips, and floorboards. Essentially, only the RUBs comprise Zachary's *reference group*.

A **reference group** is "an actual or imaginary individual or group conceived of having significant relevance upon an individual's evaluations, aspirations, or behavior."[4] Reference groups influence consumers in three ways. These influences, *informational*, *utilitarian*, and *value-expressive*, are described in Table 11.1. This chapter focuses on how other people, whether fellow bikers, co-workers, friends, family, or just casual acquaintances, influence our purchase decisions. It considers how our preferences are shaped by our group memberships, by our desire to please or be accepted by others, or even by the actions of famous people whom we've never met. Finally, it explores why some people are more influential than others in affecting consumers' product preferences and how marketers go about finding those people and enlisting their support in the persuasion process.

When Reference Groups Are Important

Reference group influences are not equally powerful for all types of products and consumption activities. For example, we are not as likely to take others' preferences into account when choosing products that are not very complex, that are low in perceived risk, or that can be tried prior to purchase.[5] In addition, the specific impact of reference groups may vary. At times knowing what others prefer may determine the use of certain products rather than others (e.g., owning or not owning a computer, eating junk food versus health food), whereas at other times this knowledge may exert specific effects on brand decisions within a product category (e.g., wearing Levi's jeans versus Diesel jeans, or smoking Marlboro cigarettes rather than Virginia Slims).

Two dimensions that influence the degree to which reference groups are important are whether the purchase is to be consumed publicly or privately and whether it is a luxury or a necessity. As a rule, reference group effects are more

TABLE 11.1
THREE FORMS OF REFERENCE GROUP INFLUENCE

Information Influence	• The individual seeks information about various brands from an association of professionals or independent group of experts.
	• The individual seeks information from those who work with the product as a profession.
	• The individual seeks brand-related knowledge and experience (such as how Brand A's performance compares to Brand B's) from those friends, neighbors, relatives, or work associates who have reliable information about the brands.
	• The brand the individual selects is influenced by observing a seal of approval of an independent testing agency (such as *Good Housekeeping*).
	• The individual's observation of what experts do (such as observing the type of car that police drive or the brand of television that repairmen buy) influences his or her choice of a brand.
Utilitarian Influence	• So that he or she satisfies the expectations of fellow work associates, the individual's decision to purchase a particular brand is influenced by their preferences.
	• The individual's decision to purchase a particular brand is influenced by the preferences of people with whom he or she has social interaction.
	• The individual's decision to purchase a particular brand is influenced by the preferences of family members.
	• The desire to satisfy the expectations that others have of him or her has an impact on the individual's brand choice.
Value-Expressive Influence	• The individual feels that the purchase or use of a particular brand will enhance the image others have of him or her.
	• The individual feels that those who purchase or use a particular brand possess the characteristics that he or she would like to have.
	• The individual sometimes feels that it would be nice to be like the type of person that advertisements show using a particular brand.
	• The individual feels that the people who purchase a particular brand are admired or respected by others.
	• The individual feels that the purchase of a particular brand would help show others what he or she is or would like to be (such as an athlete, successful business person, good parent, etc.).

Source: Adapted from G. Whan Park and V. Parker Lessig, "Students and Housewives: Differences in Susceptibility to Reference Group Influence," *Journal of Consumer Research* 4 (September 1977): 102. Reprinted with permission of The University of Chicago Press.

robust for purchases that are (1) luxuries rather than necessities (e.g., sailboats), because products that are purchased with discretionary income are subject to individual tastes and preferences, whereas necessities do not offer this range of choices; and (2) socially conspicuous or visible to others (e.g., living room furniture or clothing), because consumers do not tend to be swayed as much by the opinions of others if their purchases will never be observed by anyone but themselves.[6] The relative effects of reference group influences on some specific product classes are shown in Figure 11.1.

Why are reference groups so persuasive? The answer lies in the potential power they wield over us. **Social power** refers to "the capacity to alter the actions of others."[7] To the degree to which you are able to make someone else do something, whether they do it willingly or not, you have power over that person. The following classification of power bases can help us to distinguish among the reasons a person can exert power over another, the degree to which the influence is allowed voluntarily, and whether this influence will continue to have an effect in the absence of the power source.[8]

 Referent power: If a person admires the qualities of a person or a group, he or she will try to imitate those qualities by copying the referent's behaviors (e.g., choice of clothing, cars, leisure activities) as a guide to forming consumption preferences, just as Zack's fellow bikers affected his preferences. Prominent people in all walks of life can affect people's consumption behaviors by virtue of product endorsements (e.g., Michael Jordan for Air Nike), distinctive fashion statements (e.g., Madonna's use of lingerie as outerwear), or championing causes (e.g., Jerry Lewis' work for muscular dystrophy). **Referent power** is

■ FIGURE 11.1
RELATIVE REFERENCE GROUPS'
INFLUENCE ON PURCHASE INTENTION

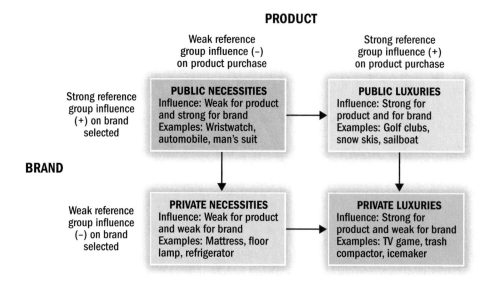

important to many marketing strategies because consumers voluntarily change behaviors to please or identify with a referent.

● *Information power:* A person can have power simply because he or she knows something others would like to know. Editors of trade publications such as *Women's Wear Daily* often possess power due to their ability to compile and disseminate information that can make or break individual designers or companies. People with **information power** are able to influence consumer opinion by virtue of their (assumed) access to the "truth."

● *Legitimate power:* Sometimes power is granted to people by virtue of social agreements, such as the authority we give to policemen, soldiers, and yes, sometimes even professors. The **legitimate power** conferred by a uniform is recognized in many consumer contexts, including teaching hospitals, in which medical students don white coats to enhance their aura of authority with patients, and banks, in which tellers' uniforms communicate trustworthiness.[9] Marketers may "borrow" this form of power to influence consumers. For example, an ad featuring a model wearing a white doctor's coat can add an aura of legitimacy or authority to the presentation of the product ("I'm not a doctor, but I play one on TV").

● *Expert power:* To attract the casual Internet user, U.S. Robotics signed up British physicist Stephen Hawking to endorse its modems. A company executive commented, "We wanted to generate trust. So we found visionaries who use U.S. Robotics technology, and we let them tell the consumer how it makes their lives more productive." Hawking, who has Lou Gehrig's disease and speaks via a synthesizer, said in one TV spot, "My body may be stuck in this chair, but with the Internet my mind can go to the end of the universe."[10] **Expert power** such as Hawking has is derived from possessing specific knowledge about a content area; it helps to explain the weight many of us assign to reviews of restaurants, books, movies, cars, and so on, by critics who specialize in evaluating products on our behalf.[11]

● *Reward power:* When a person or group has the means to provide positive reinforcement (see Chapter 3), that entity will have **reward power** over a consumer to the extent that this reinforcement is valued or desired. The reward may be tangible, as occurs when an employee is given a raise. Or, the reward may be intangible: Social approval or acceptance is often what is exchanged in return for molding one's behavior to a group or buying the products expected of group members.

A physician has expert power, and a white coat reinforces this expertise by conferring legitimate power.

- *Coercive power:* A threat is often effective in the short term, but it does not tend to produce permanent attitudinal or behavioral change. **Coercive power** refers to influencing a person by social or physical intimidation. Fortunately, this type of power is rarely employed in marketing situations, unless you count those annoying calls from telemarketers! However, elements of this power base are evident in fear appeals, intimidation in personal selling, and some campaigns that emphasize the negative consequences that might occur if people do not use a product.

Types of Reference Groups

Although two or more people are normally required to form a group, the term *reference group* is often used a bit more loosely to describe *any* external influence that provides social cues.[12] The referent may be a cultural figure and have an impact on many people (e.g., Osama bin Laden) or a person or group whose influence is confined to the consumer's immediate environment (e.g., Zachary's biker club). Reference groups that affect consumption can include parents, fellow motorcycle enthusiasts, the Democratic Party, or even the Chicago Bears, the Dave Matthews Band, or Spike Lee.

A reference group can take the form of a large, formal organization that has a recognized structure, complete with a charter, regular meeting times, and officers. Or it can be small and informal, such as a group of friends or students living in a dormitory. Marketers tend to be more successful at influencing formal groups because they are more easily identifiable and accessible. However, as a rule it is small, informal groups that exert a more powerful influence on individual consumers. Small, informal groups tend to be more a part of our day-to-day lives and to be more important to us, because they are high in normative influence. Larger,

Fellow college students may act as a reference group.

formal groups tend to be more product- or activity-specific and thus are high in comparative influence.[13]

Obviously, some groups and individuals exert a greater influence than others and affect a broader range of consumption decisions. For example, our parents may play a pivotal role in forming our values on many important issues, such as attitudes about marriage or where to go to college. This type of influence is **normative influence**—that is, the reference group helps to set and enforce fundamental standards of conduct. In contrast, a Harley-Davidson club might exert **comparative influence,** whereby decisions about specific brands or activities are affected.[14]

Brand Communities and Tribes

Some marketing researchers are embracing a new perspective on reference groups as they identify groups built around shared allegiance to a product or activity. A **brand community** is a set of consumers who share a set of social relationships based upon usage or interest in a product. Unlike other kinds of communities, these members typically don't live near each other—except when they may meet for brief periods at organized events called *brandfests*, such as those sponsored by Jeep, Saturn, or Harley-Davidson. These brandfests help owners to "bond" with fellow enthusiasts and strengthen their identification with the product as well as with others whom they meet that share their passion.

Researchers find that people who participate in these events feel more positive about the products as a result and this enhances brand loyalty. They are more forgiving than others of product failures or lapses in service quality, and less likely to switch brands even if they learn that competing products are as good or better. Furthermore, these community members become emotionally involved in the company's welfare, and they often serve as brand missionaries by carrying its marketing message to others.[15]

The notion of a **consumer tribe** is similar, because this refers to a group of people who share a lifestyle and who can identify with each other because of a shared allegiance to an activity or a product. Although these tribes are often unstable and short-lived, at least for a time members identify with others through shared emo-

Brandfests sponsored by companies like Harley-Davidson help to create strong brand communities.

tions, moral beliefs, styles of life, and of course the products they jointly consume as part of their tribal affiliation. The challenge of **tribal marketing** is to link one's product to the needs of a group as a whole. Many tribes devoted to activities like skateboarding or basketball are youth-oriented, and we'll talk more about these in Chapter 15. However, there also are plenty of tribes with older members, such as car enthusiasts who gather to celebrate such cult products (see Chapter 4) as the Citroën and Mini Cooper in Europe and the Ford Mustang in the United States, or "foodies" who share their passion about cooking with other Wolfgang Puck wannabes around the world.[16]

Many products, especially those targeted to young people, are often touted as a way to take the inside track to popularity. This Brazilian ad lets us know about people who don't like a certain shoe.

Marketing Opportunity

Members of reference groups have a huge influence on our tastes and desires, but connecting with like-minded people in the first place can be a challenge in today's hectic world. Numerous online matchmaking services have sprung up to search for that perfect (or at least not gross) date including sites such as Lava Life in the United States and uDate in the United Kingdom. One site called *Match.com* alone boasts over three million members worldwide. And once you find that perfect someone you can even check out his or her background by using sites like *repcheck.com* that provide reports about a person's reputation.[22]

Of course, if you're even too shy to meet prospective mates this way you can always try the Lovegety, a Japanese product. It works this way: Boy sees girl. Boy is too shy to talk to girl. Instead he flicks on his male Lovegety and sends out an infrared signal. If the girl's Lovegety is within five meters of his, it starts to chirp with delight. Depending on her interest, she can send back one of three responses: talk, karaoke, and friend. Wow, nothing like a little romantic karaoke to set the mood![23]

Membership Versus Aspirational Reference Groups

Some reference groups consist of people the consumer actually knows; others are composed of either people the consumer can identify with or admire. Not surprisingly, many marketing efforts that specifically adopt a reference group appeal concentrate on highly visible, widely admired figures (such as well-known athletes or performers). These **aspirational reference groups** comprise idealized figures such as successful business people, athletes, or performers. For example, one study that included business students who aspired to the "executive" role found a strong relationship between products they associated with their *ideal selves* (see Chapter 5) and those they assumed would be owned or used by executives.[17]

Because people tend to compare themselves to those who are similar, often knowing what others who are like them are doing—and buying—can influence their own preferences. For this reason, many promotional strategies include "ordinary" people whose consumption activities provide informational social influence. The likelihood that people will become part of a consumer's **membership reference group** is affected by several factors, including the following:

- *Propinquity:* As physical distance between people decreases and opportunities for interaction increase, relationships are more likely to form. Physical nearness is called *propinquity*. An early study on friendship patterns in a housing complex showed this factor's strong effects: Residents were much more likely to be friends with the people next door than with those who lived only two doors away. Furthermore, people who lived next to a staircase had more friends than those at the ends of a hall (presumably, they were more likely to "bump into" people using the stairs).[18] Physical structure has a lot to do with whom we get to know and how popular we are.
- *Mere exposure:* We come to like persons or things simply as a result of seeing them more often, which is known as the *mere exposure phenomenon*.[19] Greater frequency of contact, even if unintentional, may help to determine one's set of local referents. The same effect holds when evaluating works of art or even political candidates.[20] One study predicted 83 percent of the winners of political primaries solely by the amount of media exposure given to candidates.[21]
- *Group cohesiveness:* Cohesiveness refers to the degree to which members of a group are attracted to each other and value their group membership. As the value of the group to the individual increases, so too does the likelihood that the group will guide consumption decisions. Smaller groups tend to be more cohesive because in larger groups the contributions of each member are usually less important or noticeable. By the same token, groups often try to restrict membership to a select few, which increases the value of membership to those who are admitted. Exclusivity of membership is a benefit often touted by credit card companies, book clubs, and so on, even though the actual membership base might be fairly large.

Positive Versus Negative Reference Groups

Reference groups may exert either a positive or a negative influence on consumption behaviors. In most cases, consumers model their behavior to be consistent with what they think the group expects of them. In some cases, though, consumers may try to distance themselves from other people or groups that function as *avoidance groups*. They may carefully study the dress or mannerisms of a disliked group (e.g., "nerds," "druggies," or "preppies") and scrupulously avoid buying anything that might identify them with that group. For example, rebellious adolescents often resent parental influence and may deliberately do the opposite of what their parents would like as a way of making a statement about their independence.

The motivation to distance oneself from a negative reference group can be as powerful or more powerful than the desire to please a positive group.[24] That's why advertisements occasionally show an undesirable person using a competitor's product to subtly make the point that the target of the message can avoid winding up like *that* kind of person by staying away from the products he or she buys. As a once-popular book reminded us, "Real men *don't* eat quiche!"[25] Today, others have adapted this avoidance group appeal to point out the ways we define ourselves by not consuming some products or services. For example, a T-shirt for sale on a computer-oriented Web site proudly proclaims, "Real Men Don't Click Help."

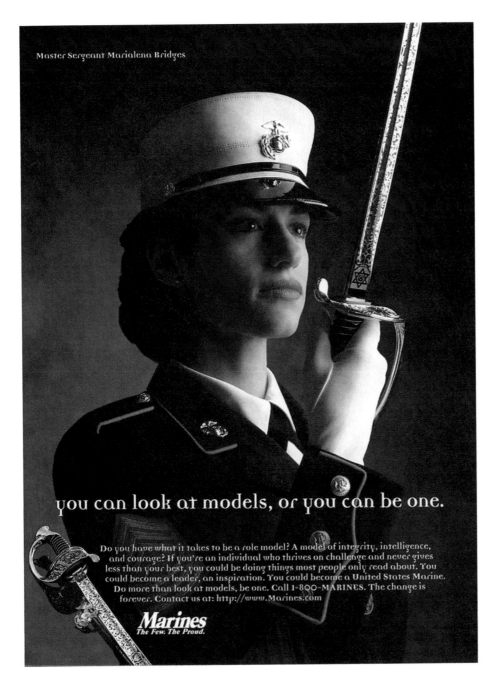

This recruiting ad presents a compelling role model for young women contemplating a career in the armed forces.

Exclusive nightclubs have referent power because they determine who is cool enough to be admitted.

■ CONSUMERS DO IT IN GROUPS

With more people in a group, it becomes less likely any one member will be singled out for attention. People in larger groups or those in situations in which they are likely to be unidentified tend to focus less attention on themselves, so normal restraints on behavior are reduced. You may have observed that people sometimes behave more wildly at costume parties or on Halloween than they do normally. This phenomenon is known as **deindividuation**, a process in which individual identities become submerged within a group.

Social loafing refers to the fact that people do not devote as much to a task when their contribution is part of a larger group effort.[27] Waitresses are painfully aware of social loafing: People who eat in groups tend to tip less per person than when they are eating alone.[28] For this reason, many restaurants automatically tack on a fixed gratuity for groups of six or more.

There is some evidence that decisions made by groups differ from those that would be made by each individual. In many cases, group members show a greater willingness to consider riskier alternatives following group discussion than they would if members made their own decisions with no discussion. This change is known as the **risky shift.**[29]

Several explanations have been advanced to explain this increased riskiness. One possibility is that something similar to social loafing occurs. As more people are involved in a decision, each individual is less accountable for the outcome, resulting in *diffusion of responsibility.*[30] The practice of placing blanks in at least one of the rifles used by a firing squad is one way of diffusing each soldier's responsibility for the death of a prisoner. Another explanation is termed the *value hypothesis.* In this case, riskiness is a culturally valued characteristic, and social pressures operate on individuals to conform to attributes valued by society.[31]

Evidence for the risky shift is mixed. A more general effect appears to be that group discussion tends to increase **decision polarization.** Therefore whichever direction the group members were leaning toward before discussion began (whether a risky choice or a conservative choice) becomes even more extreme in that direction after discussion. Group discussions regarding product purchases tend to create a risky shift for low-risk items, but they yield even more conservative group decisions for high-risk products.[32]

Even shopping behavior changes when people do it in groups. For example, people who shop with at least one other person tend to make more unplanned purchases, buy more, and cover more areas of a store than those who go alone.[33] These effects are due to both normative and informational social influence. Group members may be convinced to buy something to gain the approval of the others, or they may simply be exposed to more products and stores by pooling information with the group. For these reasons, retailers are well-advised to encourage group shopping activities.

Home shopping parties, as epitomized by the Tupperware party, capitalize on group pressures to boost sales.[34] A company representative makes a sales presentation to a group of people who have gathered in the home of a friend or acquaintance. This format is effective because of informational social influence: Participants model the behavior of others who can provide them with information

Marketing Pitfall

College parties sometimes illustrate the dark side of deindividuation when students are encouraged by their peers to consume almost superhuman volumes of alcohol in group settings. About 4.5 million young people are estimated to be alcohol-dependent or problem drinkers. Binge drinking among college students is reaching epidemic proportions. In a two-week period, 42 percent of all college students engage in binge drinking (more than five drinks at a time) versus 33 percent of their noncollege counterparts. One in three students drinks primarily to get drunk, including 35 percent of college women. For most, social pressure to throw inhibitions aside is the culprit.[26]

Costumes hide our true identities and encourage deindividuation.

Marketing Pitfall

Norms change slowly over time, but there is general agreement within a society about which ones should be obeyed, and we adjust our way of thinking to conform to these norms. A powerful example is the change in American society's attitude toward smoking since the 1960s, when this practice was first linked with health concerns such as cancer and emphysema. By the mid-1990s, some communities even outlawed smoking in public places. Even New York City did this in 2002.

Much of the motivation to begin smoking at an early age is due to peer pressure; the alluring advertising images of smokers as cool, sexy, or mature help to convince many young people that beginning the habit is a path to social acceptance. Because the power of advertising to influence attitudes is widely recognized, some groups have tried to fight fire with fire by creating antismoking ads that depict smoking as an ugly habit that turns people off.

Are these ads effective? One study of nonsmoking seventh graders by a pair of consumer researchers examined the kids' perceptions of smokers after being exposed to both cigarette ads and antismoking ads. Results were promising: The researchers found that kids who saw the antismoking ads were more likely to rate smokers lower in terms of both personal appeal and common sense. These findings imply that it is possible to use advertising to debunk myths about the glamour of smoking, especially if used in tandem with other health education efforts.[37]

about how to use certain products, especially because the home party is likely to be attended by a relatively homogeneous group (e.g., neighborhood homemakers) that serves as a valuable benchmark. Normative social influence also operates because actions are publicly observed. Pressures to conform may be particularly intense and may escalate as more and more group members begin to "cave in" (this process is sometimes termed the "bandwagon effect").

In addition, deindividuation and/or the risky shift may be activated: As consumers get caught up in the group, they may find themselves willing to try new products they would not normally consider. These same dynamics underlie the latest wrinkle on the Tupperwear home selling technique: the Botox party. The craze for Botox injections that paralyze facial nerves to reduce wrinkles (for three to six months anyway) is being fueled by gatherings where dermatologists or plastic surgeons redefine the definition of house calls. For patients, mixing cocktail hour with cosmetic injections takes some of the anxiety out of the procedure. Egged on by the others at the party, as many as 10 patients can be dewrinkled in an hour. An advertising executive who worked on the Botox marketing strategy explained that the membership reference group appeal is more effective than the traditional route of using a celebrity spokesperson to tout the injections in advertising: "We think it's more persuasive to think of your next-door neighbor using it."[35] The only hitch is that after you get the injections your face is so rigid your friends can't tell if you're smiling!

Conformity

The early bohemians who lived in Paris around 1830 made a point of behaving, well, differently from others. One flamboyant figure of the time became famous for walking a lobster on a leash through the gardens of the Royal Palace. His friends drank wine from human skulls, cut their beards in strange shapes, and slept in tents on the floors of their garrets.[36]

Women at a home Tupperware party.

Group pressure often influences our clothing choices.

Although in every age there certainly are those who "march to their own drummers," most people tend to follow society's expectations regarding how they should act and look (with a little improvisation here and there, of course). **Conformity** refers to a change in beliefs or actions as a reaction to real or imagined group pressure. In order for a society to function, its members develop **norms**, or informal rules that govern behavior. Without these rules, chaos would result. Imagine the confusion if a simple norm such as stopping for a red traffic light did not exist.

We conform in many small ways everyday—even though we don't always realize it. Unspoken rules govern many aspects of consumption. In addition to norms regarding appropriate use of clothing and other personal items, we conform to rules that include gift-giving (we expect birthday presents from loved ones and get upset if they do not materialize), sex roles (men often are expected to pick up the check on a first date), and personal hygiene (we are expected to shower regularly to avoid offending others).

Factors Influencing the Likelihood of Conformity

Conformity is not an automatic process, and many factors contribute to the likelihood that consumers will pattern their behavior after others.[38] Among the factors that affect the likelihood of conformity are the following:

- *Cultural pressures:* Different cultures encourage conformity to a greater or lesser degree. The American slogan "Do your own thing" in the 1960s reflected a movement away from conformity and toward individualism. In contrast, Japanese society is characterized by the dominance of collective well-being and group loyalty over individuals' needs.
- *Fear of deviance:* The individual may have reason to believe that the group will apply *sanctions* to punish behavior that differs from the group's. It is not unusual to observe adolescents shunning a peer who is "different" or a corporation or university passing over a person for promotion because he or she is not a "team player."

- *Commitment:* The more people are dedicated to a group and value membership in it, the more motivated they will be to follow the dictates of the group. Rock groupies and followers of TV evangelists may do anything that is asked of them, and terrorists may be willing to die for the good of their cause. According to the *principle of least interest*, the person or group that is least committed to staying in a relationship has the most power, because that party won't be susceptible to threatened rejection.[39]

- *Group unanimity, size, and expertise:* As groups gain in power, compliance increases. It is often harder to resist the demands of a large number of people than just a few, and this difficulty is compounded when the group members are perceived to know what they are talking about.

- *Susceptibility to interpersonal influence:* This trait refers to an individual's need to identify or enhance his or her image in the opinion of significant others. This enhancement process is often accompanied by the acquisition of products the person believes will impress his or her audience and by the tendency to learn about products by observing how others use them.[40] Consumers who are low on this trait have been called *role-relaxed*; they tend to be older, affluent, and to have high self-confidence. Based on research identifying role-relaxed consumers, Subaru created a communications strategy to reach these people. In one commercial, a man is heard saying, "I want a car. . . . Don't tell me about wood paneling, about winning the respect of my neighbors. They're my neighbors. They're not my heroes."

Social Comparison: "How'm I Doing?"

Sometimes we look to the behavior of others to provide a yardstick about reality. **Social comparison theory** asserts that this process occurs as a way to increase the stability of one's self-evaluation, especially when physical evidence is unavailable.[41] Social comparison even applies to choices for which there are no objectively correct answers. Stylistic decisions such as tastes in music and art are assumed to be a matter of individual choice, yet people often assume that some choices are "better" or more "correct" than others.[42] If you have ever been responsible for choosing the music to play at a party, you can probably appreciate the social pressure involved in choosing the right "mix."

Although people often like to compare their judgments and actions to those of others, they tend to be selective about precisely whom they will use as benchmarks. Similarity between the consumer and others used for social comparison boosts confidence that the information is accurate and relevant (though we may find it more threatening to be outperformed by someone similar to ourselves).[43] We tend to value the views of obviously dissimilar others only when we are reasonably certain of our own.[44]

In general people tend to choose a *co-oriented peer,* or a person of equivalent standing, when performing social comparison. For example, a study of adult cosmetics users found that women were more likely to seek information from and trust the judgments of similar others about product choices, to reduce uncertainty.[45] The same effects have been found for evaluations of products as diverse as men's suits and coffee.[46]

Resisting Conformity

Many people pride themselves on their independence, unique style, or ability to resist the best efforts of salespeople and advertisers to buy products.[47] Indeed, individuality should be encouraged by the marketing system: Innovation creates change and demand for new products and styles.

It is important to distinguish between *independence* and *anticonformity;* in anticonformity, defiance of the group is the actual object of behavior.[48] Some people will go out of their way *not* to buy whatever happens to be in at the moment. Indeed, they may spend a lot of time and effort to ensure that they will not be caught "in style." This behavior is a bit of a paradox, because in order to be vigilant about not doing what is expected, one must always be aware of what is expected. In contrast, truly independent people are oblivious to what is expected; they "march to their own drummers."

In addition, people have a deep-seated need to preserve freedom of choice. When they are threatened with a loss of this freedom, they try to overcome this loss. As Romeo and Juliet discovered, nothing makes a dating partner more attractive than a little parental opposition. **Reactance** is the negative emotional state that results when we are deprived of our freedom to choose.[49] This feeling can drive us to value forbidden things even if they wouldn't be that interesting to us otherwise. Many efforts to censor books, television shows, or music lyrics that some people find objectionable ironically result in an increased desire for these products.[50] Similarly, extremely overbearing promotions that tell consumers they must or should use a product may wind up losing more customers in the long run, even those who were already loyal to the advertised brand!

■ WORD-OF-MOUTH COMMUNICATION

An obscure, 200-year-old breath mint called Altoids is all the rage these days, even though the manufacturer did virtually no advertising for most of the brand's history. How did this happen? The revival began when the mint began to attract a devoted following among smokers and coffee drinkers who hung out in the blossoming Seattle club scene during the 1980s. Until 1993, when manufacturer Callard & Bowers was bought by Kraft, only those "in the know" bought the mints. At that point, the brand's marketing manager persuaded this bigger company to hire advertising agency Leo Burnett to develop a modest promotional effort. The agency decided to publicize the candy by using subway posters sporting retro imagery and other " low-tech" media to avoid making the product seem mainstream—that would turn off the original audience.[51] As the product was shared among young people, its popularity mushroomed.

As the Altoids success story illustrates, people convey a lot of product information to others on an informal basis. **Word-of-mouth (WOM)** is product information transmitted by individuals to individuals. Because we get the word from people we know, WOM tends to be more reliable and trustworthy than recommendations we get through more formal marketing channels. And unlike advertising, WOM often is backed up by social pressure to conform to these recommendations.[52] Ironically, despite all of the money pumped into creating lavish advertisements, WOM is far more powerful: It's estimated to influence two-thirds of all consumer-goods sales.[53]

If you think carefully about the content of your own conversations in the course of a normal day, you will probably agree that much of what you discuss with friends, family members, or co-workers is product-related: Whether you compliment someone on her dress and ask her where she bought it, recommend a new restaurant to a friend, or complain to your neighbor about the shoddy treatment you got at the bank, you are engaging in WOM. Recall, for example, that many of Zachary's biker purchases were directly initiated by comments and suggestions from his fellow RUBs. Marketers have been aware of the power of WOM for many years, but recently they've been more aggressive about trying to promote and control it instead of sitting back and hoping people will like their products enough to talk about them. In addition to Altoids, recent WOM success stories encompass products as diverse as cars (the VW Beetle), dolls (Beanie Babies), and cult movies (*The Blair Witch Project*).

As far back as the Stone Age (well, the 1950s, anyway), communications theorists began to challenge the assumption that advertising is the primary determinant

The Tangled Web

There is a long and "honored" tradition of people inventing fake stories to see who will swallow them—like the one in 1824 when a man convinced 300 New Yorkers to sign up for a construction project. He claimed all the new building in the lower part of Manhattan (what is now the Wall Street area) was making the island bottom-heavy. As a result it needed to be sawed off and towed out to sea or all of New York City would tip over!

The Web is a perfect medium for spreading rumors and hoaxes, and we can only guess how much damage this "project" would cause today if construction crews were recruited via e-mail! Modern-day hoaxes abound; many of these are in the form of e-mail chain letters promising instant riches if you pass the message on to 10 friends. Your professor will love one variation of this hoax: In a scam called "Win Tenure Fast" academics were told to add their names to a document and then cite it in their own research papers. The idea is that everyone who gets the letter cites the professor's name and with so many citations you're guaranteed to get tenure! If only it were that easy.

Other hoaxes involve major corporations. A popular one promised that if you try Microsoft products you would win a free trip to Disneyland. Nike received several hundred pairs of old sneakers a day after the rumor spread that you would get a free pair of new shoes in exchange for your old, smelly ones (pity the delivery people who had to cart these packages to the company!). Procter & Gamble received more than 10,000 irate calls after a rumor began spreading on news-groups that its Febreze fabric softener kills dogs. [In a preemptive strike, the company registered numerous Web site names such as *febrezekillspet.com*, *febrezesucks.com*, and *ihateprocterandgamble.com* to be sure angry consumers didn't use them.] The moral: Don't believe everything you click on.

The U.S. Postal Service hopes to create a buzz via word of mouth.

of purchases. It is now generally accepted that advertising is more effective at reinforcing existing product preferences than at creating new ones.[54] Studies in both industrial and consumer purchase settings underscore the idea that although information from impersonal sources is important for creating brand awareness, word of mouth is relied upon in the later stages of evaluation and adoption.[55] The more positive information consumers get about a product from peers, the more likely they will be to adopt the product.[56]

The influence of others' opinions is at times even more powerful than one's own perceptions. In one study of furniture choices, consumers' estimates of how much their friends would like the furniture was a better predictor of purchase than their *own* evaluations.[57] In addition, consumers may find their own reasons to push a brand that take the manufacturer by surprise: That's what happened with Mountain Dew, whose popularity among younger consumers can be traced to the "buzz" about the soda's high caffeine content. As an advertising executive explained, "The caffeine thing was not in any of Mountain Dew's television ads. This drink is hot by word-of-mouth."[58]

Hoaxkill.com is a Web site dedicated to tracking hoaxes and debunking product rumors.

WOM is especially powerful when the consumer is relatively unfamiliar with the product category. Such a situation would be expected in the case of new products (e.g., medications to prevent hair loss) or those that are technologically complex (e.g., CD players). One way to reduce uncertainty about the wisdom of a purchase is to talk about it. Talking gives the consumer an opportunity to generate more supporting arguments for the purchase and to garner support for this decision from others. As one example, the strongest predictor of a person's intention to buy a residential solar water-heating system was found to be the number of solar-heat users the person knows.[59]

Product-related conversations can be motivated by a number of factors:[60]

- A person might be highly involved with a type of product or activity and get pleasure in talking about it. Computer hackers, avid bird watchers, and "fashion plates" seem to share the ability to steer a conversation toward their particular interests.
- A person might be knowledgeable about a product and use conversations as a way to let others know it. Thus, word-of-mouth communication sometimes enhances the ego of the individual who wants to impress others with his or her expertise.
- A person might initiate such a discussion out of genuine concern for someone else. We are often motivated to ensure that people we care about buy what is good for them, do not waste their money, and so on.

Negative WOM and the Power of Rumors

Word-of-mouth is a two-edged sword that can cut both ways for marketers. Informal discussions among consumers can make or break a product or store. Furthermore, consumers weigh **negative word-of-mouth** more heavily than they do positive comments. According to a study by the White House Office of Consumer Affairs, 90 percent of unhappy customers will not do business with a company again. Each of these people is likely to share his or her grievance with at least nine other people, and 13 percent of these disgruntled customers will go on to tell more than 30 people of their negative experience.[61]

Especially when she is considering a new product or service, the consumer is likely to pay more attention to negative information than positive information and to relate news of this experience to others.[62] Negative WOM has been shown to reduce the credibility of a firm's advertising and to influence consumers' attitudes toward a product as well as their intention to buy it.[63] And, negative WOM is even easier to spread online. Many dissatisfied customers and disgruntled former employees have been "inspired" to create Web sites just to share their tales of woe with others. For example, a Web site for people to complain about the Dunkin' Donuts chain got to be so popular the company bought it in order to control the bad press it was getting. It grew out of a complaint by the original owner because he could not get skim milk for his coffee.[64]

A rumor, even if it has no basis in fact, can be a very dangerous thing. In the 1930s, "professional rumormongers" were hired to organize word-of-mouth campaigns to promote clients' products and criticize those of competitors.[65] More recently, Bio Business International, a small Canadian company that markets 100 percent cotton non-chlorine-bleached tampons under the name Terra Femme, encouraged women to spread a message that tampons made by its

■ **FIGURE 11.2**
THE TRANSMISSION OF MISINFORMATION: THESE DRAWINGS PROVIDE A CLASSIC EXAMPLE OF THE DISTORTIONS THAT CAN OCCUR AS INFORMATION IS TRANSMITTED FROM PERSON TO PERSON. AS EACH PARTICIPANT REPRODUCED THE FIGURE, IT GRADUALLY CHANGED FROM AN OWL TO A CAT.

American competitors contain dioxin. There is very little evidence to support the claim that these products are dangerous, but as a result of this rumor Procter & Gamble received thousands of complaints about its feminine hygiene products.[66]

As information is transmitted among consumers, it tends to change. The resulting message usually does not at all resemble the original. Social scientists who study rumors have examined the process by which information gets distorted. The British psychologist Frederic Bartlett used the method of *serial reproduction* to examine this phenomenon. As in the game of "Telephone," a subject is asked to reproduce a stimulus, such as a drawing or a story. Another subject is given this reproduction and asked to copy that, and so on. This technique is shown in Figure 11.2. Bartlett found that distortions almost inevitably follow a pattern: They tend to change from ambiguous forms to more conventional ones as subjects try to make them consistent with preexisting schemas. This process, known as *assimilation*, is characterized by *leveling*, in which details are omitted to simplify the structure, or *sharpening*, in which prominent details are accentuated.

Cutting-Edge WOM Strategies

As marketers increasingly recognize the power of WOM to make or break a new product, they are coming up with new ways to get consumers to help them sell. Let's review three successful strategies.

A German ad for an Internet dating service: "Finds only true matches."

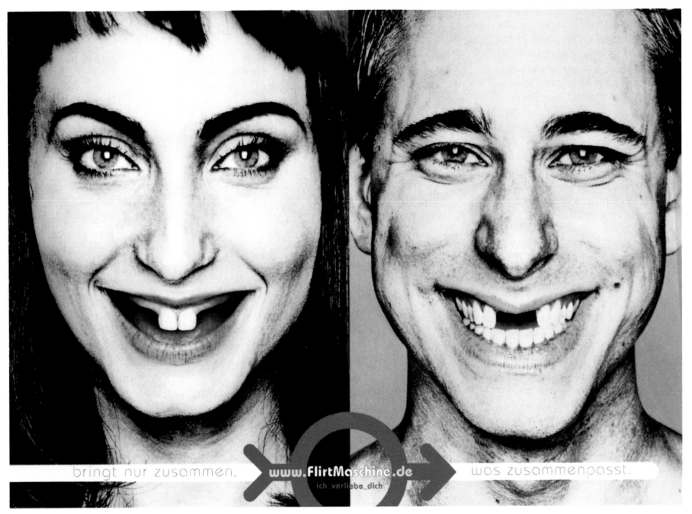

Net Profit

The emergence of gaming as an online, shared experience opens new vistas to marketers. Consider this: Toyota's digital racing game called Tundra Madness attracts 8,000 consumers who spend an average of eight minutes on the site daily. The company's research showed that the campaign raised brand awareness by 28 percent and intent to purchase by 5 percent. Heartened by the success of this experiment, Toyota launched games to promote other models. To target first-time car buyers the company created the Matrix Video Mixer game, which it promoted through sites like *RollingStone.com*, *GetMusic.com*, and *Launch.com*. The effort was tied to a Gravity Games sponsorship and an in-theater commercial campaign. About 3 in 10 registered users forwarded videos created through the game to their friends; 65 percent of those e-mails were opened.[72]

The secret behind the appeal of this format is the huge chunks of time people spend immersed in these games. The average online player logs 17 hours per week, and firms like Sony, Microsoft, and Sega are building their own virtual worlds to get a piece of the action. As one game company executive put it, "This is not a genre of game but a break-through new medium. It provides a completely new social, collaborative shared experience. We're basically in the Internet community business."[73]

Sony Online's EverQuest is among the most successful of the new breed of Massively Multiplayer Online Role-Player Games that allow people to live shadow lives. More than 430,000 registered players worldwide belong to "guilds" in a never-ending journey to slay monsters and earn points. EverQuest combines the stunning graphics of advanced gaming with the social scene of a chat room. Like The Sims, players create a character as a virtual alter ego, which may be a wise elf or a back-stabbing rogue. Some players sell powerful characters on eBay for $1,000 or more.

Virtual Communities

In ancient times (that is, before the Web was widely accessible), most membership reference groups consisted of people who had face-to-face contact. Now, it's possible to share interests with people whom you've never met—and probably never will. Consider the case of Widespread Panic. The band has never had a music video on MTV or cracked the Billboard Top 200. But, it's one of the top 40 touring bands in the United States. How did it get to be so successful? Simple—the group built a virtual community of fans and opened itself up to them. It enlisted listeners to help promote the group in exchange for free tickets and backstage passes. Then, it went virtual: The band lets fans send messages to its recording studio, and hard-core followers can find out vital information such as what band members ate for lunch via regular updates on their Web sites.[67]

A **virtual community of consumption** is a collection of people whose online interactions are based upon shared enthusiasm for and knowledge of a specific consumption activity. Like the brand communities we discussed earlier, these groups form around a shared love for a product, whether it's Barbie dolls or Blackberry PDAs. However, members remain anonymous because they only interact with each other in cyberspace.

Virtual communities are a huge global phenomenon. Forrester Research estimates that 400,000 communities exist on the Internet and 27 percent of the online audience are community users.[68] Another study conducted by Pew Internet and the American Life foundation found that 84 percent of all Internet users have been in contact with an online group, 79 percent have kept in contact with a particular group, and 23 million Internet users exchange e-mails with other group members several times a week.[69]

Virtual communities come in many different forms:[70]

- *Multi-User Dungeons (MUD):* Originally, these were environments in which players of fantasy games met. Now they refer to any computer-generated environment in which people socially interact through the structured format of role and game playing. Online gaming is catching on in a big way: Sony Online Entertainment's gaming Web site, The Station (*www.station.com*), has more than 12 million registered users, while Microsoft's Gaming Zone (*www.zone.com*) boasts a membership of 29 million.[71]
- *Rooms, rings, and lists:* These include internet relay chat (IRC), otherwise known as *chat rooms. Rings* are organizations of related home pages, and *lists* are groups of people on a single mailing list who share information.
- *Boards:* Online communities organized around interest-specific electronic bulletin boards. Active members read and post messages sorted by date and subject. There are boards devoted to musical groups, movies, wind, cigars, cars, comic strips, even fast-food restaurants.
- *Blogs:* The newest and fastest growing form of online community is the **weblog**, or *blog*. These online personal journals are building an avid following among Internet users who like to dash off a few random thoughts, post them on a Web site, and read similar musings by others. Although these sites are similar to Web pages offered by Geocities and other free services, they employ a different technology that lets people upload a few sentences without going through the process of updating a Web site built with conventional home page software. For example, one site (*www.livejournal.com*) has signed up 690,000 registered users in four years and is adding another 1,100 every day. Bloggers can fire off thoughts on a whim, click a button, and quickly have them appear on a site. Weblogs frequently look like online diaries, with brief musings about the days' events, and perhaps a link or two of interest. A new blogger puts in his or her two cents every 40 seconds, so this burgeoning **Blogosphere** (the name given to the universe of active Weblogs) is starting to look like a force to be reckoned with. Already, one media giant is smelling blood: Recognizing that many thousands of

Brazilians are getting into blogging, *Globo.com* is licensing blogger software and is posting blogs from Brazilian *telenovela* (soap opera) stars like Boris, an 800-year-old vampire who wears armor and a horned helmet.[77]

How do people get drawn into consumption communities? Internet users tend to progress from asocial information gathering ("lurkers" are surfers who like to watch but don't participate) to increasingly affiliative social activities. At first they will merely browse the site, but later they may well be drawn into active participation.

The intensity of identification with a virtual community depends on two factors. The first is that the more central the activity is to a person's self-concept, the more likely he will be to pursue an active membership in a community. The second is that the intensity of the social relationships the person forms with other members of the virtual community helps to determine the extent of his involvement. As Figure 11.3 shows, combining these two factors creates four distinct member types:

1 *Tourists* lack strong social ties to the group, and maintain only a passing interest in the activity.
2 *Minglers* maintain strong social ties, but are not very interested in the central consumption activity.
3 *Devotees* express strong interest in the activity, but have few social attachments to the group.
4 *Insiders* exhibit both strong social ties and strong interest in the activity.

Devotees and insiders are the most important targets for marketers who wish to leverage communities for promotional purposes. They are the heavy users of virtual communities. And, by reinforcing usage, the community may upgrade tourists and minglers to insiders and devotees.[78] But marketers have only scratched the surface of this intriguing new virtual world.

Guerrilla Marketing

Lyor Cohen, a partner in the Def Jam hip-hop label, built his business using street marketing tactics. To promote hip-hop albums, Def Jam and other labels start building a buzz months before a release, leaking advance copies to deejays who put

The game is also the center of an active social scene. Players can travel around in groups of six. In many cases they settle into a regular group and spend two to three hours each night online with the same people.[74] They may also mingle offline; Fan Faires attracts several thousand people who often dress as their game characters.[75] The average EverQuest subscriber spends about 20 hours a week living in this virtual world. Some view it as a possible addiction; EverCrack is a popular nickname for the game. One factor that makes it hard to kick the habit may be peer pressure, because when a player logs off this may hurt his guild's chances of advancing in the game.[76]

Role-playing computer games involve thousands of players worldwide in interactive, online communities.

The Tangled Web

Virtual consumption communities hold great promise, but there is also great potential for abuse if members can't trust that other visitors are behaving ethically. Many hard-core community members are sensitive to interference from companies and react negatively when they suspect that another member may in fact be a shill of a marketer who wants to influence evaluations of products on the site. One of the reasons for the success of the eBay auction site is that buyers rate the quality and trustworthiness of sellers, so a potential bidder can get a pretty good idea of what she's dealing with before participating. In some cases even this system has fallen flat as unscrupulous people find ways to violate the bond of trust.

More generally, e-commerce sites know that consumers give more weight to the opinions of real people, so they are finding ways to let these opinions be included on their Web sites. This trend of posting customer reviews was started by **Amazon.com** way back in 1995. Now, sellers of computers and other high-priced products post customer reviews. A great idea—but in a highly publicized lawsuit Amazon was accused of charging publishers to post positive reviews on the site. The company had to offer refunds for all books it recommended and now Amazon tells customers when a publisher has paid for a prominent display on its site. Similarly, some online investment forums have had to hire patrols to keep an eye out for stock promoters who have been hired by companies to create a buzz about their stocks. The Motley Fool site (**fool.com**), for example, employs 20 full-time "community strollers" who monitor its message boards on America Online and the Web.[79]

■ **FIGURE 11.3** VIRTUAL COMMUNITIES

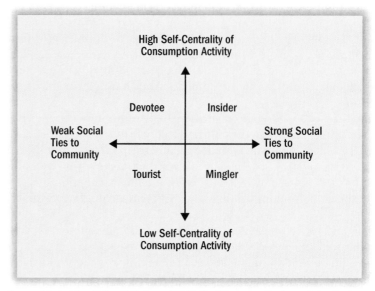

Source: Adapted from Robert V. Kozinets, " E-Tribalized Marketing: The Strategic Implications of Virtual Communities of Consumption," *Eurpean Management Journal* 17, 3 (June 1999): 252–264.

together "mix tapes" to sell on the street. If the kids seem to like a song, *street teams* then push it to club deejays. As the official release date nears, these groups of fans start slapping up posters around the inner city. They plaster telephone poles, sides of buildings, and car windshields with promotions announcing the release of new albums by artists such as Public Enemy, DMX, or L. L. Cool J.[80]

These streetwise strategies started in the mid-1970s, when pioneering deejays like Kool DJ Herc and Afrika Bambaataa promoted their parties through graffiti-style flyers. This type of grassroots effort epitomizes **guerrilla marketing**; promotional strategies that use unconventional locations and intensive word-of-mouth campaigns to push products. As Ice Cube observed, "Even though I'm an established artist, I still like to leak my music to a kid on the street and let him duplicate it for his homies before it hits radio."[81] As CD sales decline (partly due to Internet piracy), these street campaigns are more essential than ever. For example, the popular hiphip group B2K got its start by appearing at schools and malls accompanied by hype generated by street teams, and the rapper Jay-Z peddled his music on the streets before achieving commercial success.[82]

Today, big companies are buying into guerrilla marketing strategies big time. Coca-Cola did it for a Sprite promotion, and Nike did it to build interest in a new shoe model.[83] Here are some guerrilla campaigns that successfully generated a buzz among consumers:

● To promote its Blucaos (pronounced "blue chaos") liqueur as a shot drink to young people, Amaretto di Saronno created strike teams that were literally to loudly call for "order" in GenX-favored bars, then blow whistles and scream for "chaos!" This attention-getting yell was followed by the distribution of Nerf balls (blue, of course), T-shirts, caps, and tattoos. It was hoped that all this mayhem by blue-bodysuited strike teams would soon have the crowd following suit and echoing the cry to "order chaos." Branching out, strike teams on in-line skates took to the streets to distribute Blucaos tattoos. Print ads followed the word-of-mouth campaign in the next year after the label had gained ground with its target audience.[84]

Ads painted on sidewalks are one form of guerrilla marketing.

● In Singapore, the EMI Group PLC gave fans of Gorillaz, a popular rock group of four cartoon characters, the opportunity to exchange text messages over their mobile phones with the band member of their choice. Each member has a distinctive look and personality, and after selecting a favorite character its cartoon face was sent to the recipient's mobile phone. These phone numbers are, of course, a potential gold mine for EMI, as they'll allow the company to communicate with music fans at will. EMI chose Gorillaz because its fan base is young, hip, and devoted. As the company's managing director observed, "For a very cool band like Gorillaz, the last thing you want to do is go mainstream." That explains why the text messages used in the promotion were distinctly anti-corporate: A typical one read, "Greedy record company wants me 2 tell U 2 buy Gorillaz album. Record people suck. Buy or don't buy, up to you."[85]

● A growing number of marketers are experimenting with using human beings as *brand ambassadors* who pop up in eye-catching outfits to announce a new brand or service. AT&T sent its ambassadors to high-traffic areas of California and New Jersey, doing random favors such as handing dog biscuits to people walking their dogs and providing binoculars to concertgoers to promote its new AT&T Local Service. Hyatt Hotels unleashed 100 bellhops in Manhattan, who spent the day opening doors, carrying packages, and handing out pillow mints to thousands of consumers. Dewar's is training a squad of men in the Scotch brand's lore and traditions so they can play the role of the "Dewar Highlander, who roams bars and restaurants teaching patrons and bartenders how to enjoy whiskey and mix cocktails with Dewar's."[86]

Net Profit

The Internet provides a new way for consumers to share their opinions, and share them they do. Indeed, Roper Starch Worldwide and Burston-Marsteller identified a group called **e-fluentials.** These persuasive folks number approximately 11 million people but influence the purchasing decisions of another 155 million American consumers both offline and online. In the course of a year, e-fluentials share an estimated 88 million opinions about companies and 73 million on products. They are asked for their advice three times more often than is the average online user. They also share their views without being prompted; on average they notify 17 individuals about negative company experiences and 11 others about positive encounters. Ninety-three percent tell individuals in person or on the phone about their experiences, and 87 percent e-mail their friends with the news. Men typically offer and seek advice concerning technology-related products, whereas women focus on health-, beauty-, and food-related products. E-fluential advice is usually well researched in that 85 percent of these consumers visit company Web sites, 62 percent read online magazines, and 55 percent visit opinion Web sites; and a large majority double-check their information.[94]

Viral Marketing

Many students are big fans of Hot Mail, a free e-mail service. But, there's no such thing as a free lunch: Hot Mail inserts a small ad on every message sent, making each user a salesperson. The company had five million subscribers in its first year and continues to grow exponentially.[87] **Viral marketing** refers to the strategy of getting customers to sell a product on behalf of the company that creates it. This approach is particularly well-suited to the Web because e-mails circulate so easily. According to a study by Jupiter Communications, only 24 percent of consumers say they learn about new Web sites in magazine or newspaper ads. Instead, they rely on friends and family for new site recommendations, so viral marketing is their main source of information about new sites. The chief executive of *Gazooba.com*, a company that creates viral marketing promotions, observed, "the return mail address of a friend is a brand that you trust."[88]

- Viral marketing for an oil? Pretty slick. WD-40 quadrupled visitors to its fan club Web site by offering 1,000 AM/FM radios in the shape of oil cans to individuals who signed up 10 other members.[89]
- The movie *A.I.* (Artificial Intelligence) launched an elaborative viral marketing campaign by listing a credit at the end of the film for Jeanine Salla, who was described as a "sentient machine therapist." Curious viewers who typed her name into the Google search engine got back a list of Web addresses and they eventually got drawn into a futuristic murder mystery where characters (including robots) from the film e-mailed and voice-mailed them with clues. The campaign generated more than 3 million sessions, and 28 percent of the visitors remained online for more than half an hour. [90]
- To promote its new Pocket Paks oral breath care strips, Listerine created a "Germinator" game on the brand's Web site. Players are encouraged to e-mail their scores to friends to goad them into playing.[91]

■ OPINION LEADERSHIP

Although consumers get information from personal sources, they do not tend to ask just *anyone* for advice about purchases. If you decide to buy a new stereo, you will most likely seek advice from a friend who knows a lot about sound systems. This friend may own a sophisticated system, or she may subscribe to specialized magazines such as *Stereo Review* and spend free time browsing through electronics stores. On the other hand, you may have another friend who has a reputation for being stylish and who spends his free time reading *Gentleman's Quarterly* and shopping at trendy boutiques. You might not bring up your stereo problem with him, but you may take him with you to shop for a new fall wardrobe.

The Nature of Opinion Leadership

Everyone knows people who are knowledgeable about products and whose advice is taken seriously by others. These individuals are **opinion leaders.** An opinion leader is a person who is frequently able to influence others' attitudes or behaviors.[92] Clearly, some people's recommendations carry more weight than others.

Opinion leaders are extremely valuable information sources for a number of reasons:

- They are technically competent and thus convincing because they possess expert power.[93]
- They have prescreened, evaluated, and synthesized product information in an unbiased way, so they possess knowledge power.[95] Unlike commercial endorsers, opinion leaders do not actually represent the interests of one company. Thus, they are more credible because they have no "axe to grind."

Opinion leadership is a big factor in the marketing of athletic shoes. Many styles first become popular in the inner city and then spread by word-of-mouth.

- They tend to be socially active and highly interconnected in their communities.[96] They are likely to hold offices in community groups and clubs and to be active outside of the home. As a result, opinion leaders often have legitimate power by virtue of their social standing.

- They tend to be similar to the consumer in terms of their values and beliefs, so they possess referent power. Note that although opinion leaders are set apart by their interest or expertise in a product category, they are more convincing to the extent that they are *homophilous* rather than *heterophilous*. **Homophily** refers to the degree to which a pair of individuals is similar in terms of education, social status, and beliefs.[97] Effective opinion leaders tend to be slightly higher in terms of status and educational attainment than those they influence, but not so high as to be in a different social class.

- Opinion leaders are often among the first to buy new products, so they absorb much of the risk. This experience reduces uncertainty for others who are not as courageous. Furthermore, whereas company-sponsored communications tend to focus exclusively on the positive aspects of a product, the hands-on experience of opinion leaders makes them more likely to impart *both* positive and negative information about product performance.

How Influential Is an Opinion Leader?

When marketers and social scientists initially developed the concept of the opinion leader, it was assumed that certain influential people in a community would exert an overall impact on group members' attitudes. Later work, however, began to question the assumption that there is such a thing as a *generalized opinion leader*, somebody whose recommendations are sought for all types of purchases. Very few people are capable of being expert in a number of fields. Sociologists distinguish between those who are *monomorphic*, or expert in a limited field, and those who are *polymorphic*, or expert in several fields.[98] Even opinion leaders who are polymorphic, however, tend to concentrate on one broad domain, such as electronics or fashion.

Research on opinion leadership generally indicates that although opinion leaders do exist for multiple product categories, expertise tends to overlap across similar categories. It is rare to find a generalized opinion leader. An opinion leader for home appliances is likely to serve a similar function for home cleaners but not for cosmetics. In contrast, a fashion opinion leader whose primary influence is on clothing choices may also be consulted for recommendations on cosmetics purchases, but not necessarily on microwave ovens.[99]

Types of Opinion Leaders

Early conceptions of the opinion leader role also assumed a static process: The opinion leader absorbs information from the mass media and in turn transmits data to opinion receivers. This view has turned out to be overly simplified; it confuses the functions of several different types of consumers.

Opinion leaders may or may not be purchasers of the products they recommend. As we will see in Chapter 17, early purchasers are known as *innovators*. Opinion leaders who also are early purchasers have been termed *innovative communicators*. One study identified a number of characteristics of college men who were innovative communicators for fashion products. These men were among the first to buy new fashions, and other students were likely to follow their lead when they made their own purchases. Other characteristics of the men included the following:[100]

- They were socially active.
- They were appearance-conscious and narcissistic (i.e., they were quite fond of themselves and self-centered).
- They were involved in rock culture.
- They were heavy magazine readers, including *Playboy* and *Sports Illustrated*.
- They were likely to own more clothing, and a broader range of styles, than other students.

Opinion leaders also are likely to be *opinion seekers*. They are generally more involved in a product category and actively search for information. As a result, they are more likely to talk about products with others and to solicit others' opinions as well.[101] Contrary to the static view of opinion leadership, most product-related conversation does not take place in a "lecture" format in which one person does all of the talking. A lot of product-related conversation is prompted by the situation and occurs in the context of a casual interaction rather than as formal instruction.[102] One study, which found that opinion seeking is especially high for food products, revealed that two-thirds of opinion seekers also view themselves as opinion leaders.[103] Figure 11.4 contrasts this updated view of interpersonal product communication with the traditional view.

The Market Maven

Consumers who are expert in a product category may not actively communicate with others, whereas other consumers may have a more general interest in being involved in product discussions. A consumer category called the **market maven** describes people who are actively involved in transmitting marketplace information of all types. Market mavens are not necessarily interested in certain products and may not necessarily be early purchasers of products; they're just into shopping and staying on top of what's happening in the marketplace. They come closer to the function of a generalized opinion leader because they tend to have a solid overall knowledge of how and where to procure products. The following scale items, to which respondents indicate how much they agree or disagree, have been used to identify market mavens:[104]

TRADITIONAL MODEL

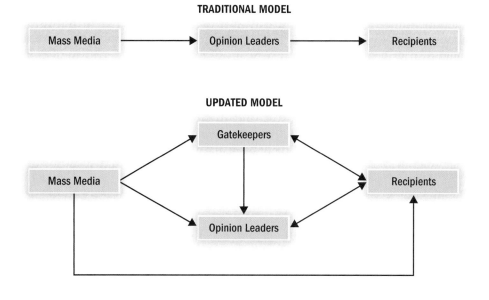

■ **FIGURE 11.4**
PERSPECTIVES ON THE
COMMUNICATIONS PROCESS

UPDATED MODEL

1 I like introducing new brands and products to my friends.
2 I like helping people by providing them with information about many kinds of products.
3 People ask me for information about products, places to shop, or sales.
4 If someone asked me where to get the best buy on several types of products, I could tell him or her where to shop.
5 My friends think of me as a good source of information when it comes to new products or sales.

Think about a person who has information about a variety of products and likes to share this information with others. This person knows about new products, sales, stores, and so on, but does not necessarily feel he or she is an expert on one particular product. How well would you say this description fits you?

Fashion opinion leaders tend to be knowledgeable about clothing and highly motivated to stay on top of fashion trends.

The Surrogate Consumer

In addition to everyday consumers who are instrumental in influencing others' purchase decisions, a class of marketing intermediary called the **surrogate consumer** is an active player in many categories. A surrogate consumer is a person who is hired to provide input into purchase decisions. Unlike the opinion leader or market maven, the surrogate is usually compensated for his or her advice.

Interior decorators, stockbrokers, professional shoppers, or college consultants can all be thought of as surrogate consumers. Whether or not they actually make the purchase on behalf of the consumer, surrogates' recommendations can be enormously influential. The consumer in essence relinquishes control over several or all decision-making functions, such as information search, evaluation of alternatives, or the actual purchase. For example, a client may commission an interior decorator to redo her house, and a broker may be entrusted to make crucial buy/sell decisions on behalf of investors. The involvement of surrogates in a wide range of purchase decisions tends to be overlooked by many marketers, who may be mistargeting their communications to end consumers instead of to the surrogates who are actually sifting through product information.[105]

Identifying Opinion Leaders

Because opinion leaders are so central to consumer decision making, marketers are quite interested in identifying influential people for a product category. In fact, many ads are intended to reach these influentials rather than the average consumer, especially if the ads contain a lot of technical information. For example, CBS sent a CD-ROM to 10,000 critics, affiliates, advertising agencies, and others it had identified as "influencers" in order to plug the network's prime-time shows.[106]

Unfortunately, because most opinion leaders are everyday consumers and are not formally included in marketing efforts, they are harder to find. A celebrity or an influential industry executive is by definition easy to locate. He or she has national or at least regional visibility or may be listed in published directories. In contrast, opinion leaders tend to operate at the local level and may influence 5 to 10 consumers rather than an entire market segment.

In some cases, companies have tried to identify influentials and involve them directly in their marketing efforts, hoping to create a "ripple effect" as these consumers sing the company's praises to their friends. To promote the film *Crouching Tiger, Hidden Dragon*, the producers enlisted a core group of celebrities ranging from rapper Ghostface Killah to feminist author Naomi Wolf to attend early screenings, hoping they would fan out and create a sort of party-circuit dialogue about the film.[107] Similarly, Walt Disney Co. set up screenings for orchestra leaders, music teacher associations, and instrument makers to get expert WOM going about the movie *Mr. Holland's Opus*, where actor Richard Dreyfuss plays a music teacher.

Because of the difficulties involved in identifying specific opinion leaders in a large market, most attempts to do so focus instead on exploratory studies through which the characteristics of representative opinion leaders can be identified and then generalized to the larger market. This knowledge helps marketers target their product-related information to appropriate settings and media. For example, one attempt to identify financial opinion leaders found that these consumers were more likely to be involved in managing their own finances and tended to use a computer to do so. They also were more likely to follow their investments on a daily basis and to read books and watch television shows devoted to financial issues.[108]

The Self-Designating Method

The most commonly used technique to identify opinion leaders is simply to ask individual consumers whether they consider themselves to be opinion leaders.

■ **FIGURE 11.5** A REVISED AND UPDATED VERSION OF THE OPINION LEADERSHIP SCALE

Please rate yourself on the following scales relating to your interactions with friends and neighbors regarding _____.

1. In general, do you talk to your friends and neighbors about _____:

very often				never
5	4	3	2	1

2. When you talk to your friends and neighbors about _____ do you:

give a great deal of information				give very little information
5	4	3	2	1

3. During the past six months, how many people have you told about a new _____?

told a number of people				told no one
5	4	3	2	1

4. Compared with your circle of friends, how likely are you to be asked about new _____?

very likely to be asked				not at all likely to be asked
5	4	3	2	1

5. In discussion of new _____, which of the following happens most?

you tell your friends about _____				your friends tell you about _____
5	4	3	2	1

6. Overall in all of your discussions with friends and neighbors are you:

often used as a source of advice				not used as a source of advice
5	4	3	2	1

Sources: Adapted from Terry L. Childers, "Assessment of the Psychometric Properties of an Opinion Leadership Scale," *Journal of Marketing Reasearch* 23 (May 1986): 184–88; and Leisa Reinecke Flynn, Ronald E. Goldsmith, and Jacqueline K. Eastman, "The King and Summers Opinion Leadership Scale: Revision and Refinement," *Journal of Business Research* 31 (1994): 55–64.

Although respondents who report a greater degree of interest in a product category are more likely to be opinion leaders, the results of surveys intended to identify *self-designated opinion leaders* must be viewed with some skepticism. Some people have a tendency to inflate their own importance and influence, whereas others who really are influential might not admit to this quality or be conscious of it.[109]

The fact that we transmit advice about products does not mean other people *take* that advice. For someone to be considered a *bona fide* opinion leader, his or her advice must actually be heard and heeded by opinion seekers. An alternative is to select certain group members (*key informants*) who in turn are asked to identify opinion leaders. The success of this approach hinges on locating those who have accurate knowledge of the group and on minimizing their response biases (e.g., the tendency to inflate one's own influence on the choices of others).

The self-designating method is not as reliable as a more systematic analysis (in which individual claims of influence can be verified by asking others whether the person is really influential), but it does have the advantage of being easy to apply to a large group of potential opinion leaders. In some cases not all members of a community are surveyed. Figure 11.5 shows one of the measurement scales developed for self-designation of opinion leaders.

Sociometry

The popular play *Six Degrees of Separation* is based upon the premise that everyone on the planet indirectly knows everyone else—or at least knows people who know them. Indeed, it is estimated that the average person has 1,500 acquaintances and that five to six intermediaries could connect any two people in the United States.[110] A popular game challenges players to link the actor Kevin Bacon with other actors in much the same way.

Sociometric methods trace communication patterns among members of a group. These techniques allow researchers to systematically map out the interactions that take place among group members. By interviewing participants and asking them to whom they go for product information, researchers can identify those who tend to be sources of product-related information. This method is the most precise, but it is very difficult and expensive to implement because it involves very close study of interaction patterns in small groups. For this reason, sociometric techniques are best applied in a closed, self-contained social setting, such as in hospitals, prisons, and army bases, where members are largely isolated from other social networks.

Many professionals and services marketers depend primarily on word-of-mouth to generate business. In many cases consumers recommend a service provider to a friend or co-worker, and in other cases business people will make recommendations to their customers. For example, only 0.2 percent of respondents in one study reported choosing a physician based on advertising. Advice from family and friends was the most widely used criterion.[111]

Sociometric analyses can be used to better understand *referral behavior* and to locate strengths and weaknesses in terms of how one's reputation is communicated through a community.[112] *Network analysis* focuses on communication in social systems, considers the relations among people in a *referral network*, and measures the *tie strength* among them. Tie strength refers to the nature of the bond between people. It can range from strong primary (e.g., one's spouse) to weak secondary (e.g., an acquaintance that one rarely sees). A strong tie relationship may be thought of as a primary reference group; interactions are frequent and important to the individual.

Although strong ties are important, weak ties can perform a *bridging function*. This type of connection allows a consumer access between subgroups. For example, you might have a regular group of friends who serve as a primary reference group (strong ties). If you have an interest in tennis, say, one of these friends might introduce you to a group of people in her dorm who play on the tennis team. As a result, you gain access to their valuable expertise through this bridging function. This referral process demonstrates the strength of weak ties. One study using this method examined similarities in brand choice among members of a college sorority. The researchers found evidence that subgroups, or *cliques*, within the sorority were likely to share preferences for various products. In some cases, even choices of "private" (i.e., socially inconspicuous) products were shared, possibly because of structural variables such as shared bathrooms in the sorority house.[113]

CHAPTER SUMMARY

Consumers belong to or admire many different groups and are often influenced in their purchase decisions by a desire to be accepted by others.

Individuals have influence in a group to the extent that they possess social power; types of social power include information power, referent power, legitimate power, expert power, reward power, and coercive power.

Brand communities unite consumers who share a common passion for a product. Brandfests organized by companies to encourage this kind of community can build brand loyalty and reinforce group membership.

We conform to the desires of others for two basic reasons: (1) People who model their behavior after others because they take others' behavior as evidence of the correct way to act are conforming because of informational social influence, and (2) those who conform to satisfy the expectations of others or to be accepted by the group are affected by normative social influence.

Group members often do things they would not do as individuals because their identities become merged with the group; they become deindividuated.

Individuals or groups whose opinions or behavior are particularly important to consumers are reference groups. Both formal and informal groups influence the individual's purchase decisions, although the impact of reference group influence is affected by such factors as the conspicuousness of the product and the relevance of the reference group for a particular purchase.

The Web has greatly amplified consumers' abilities to be exposed to numerous reference groups. Virtual consumption communities are composed of people who are united by a common bond—enthusiasm about or knowledge of a specific product or service.

Opinion leaders who are knowledgeable about a product and whose opinions are highly regarded tend to influence others' choices. Specific opinion leaders are somewhat hard to identify, but marketers who know their general characteristics can try to target them in their media and promotional strategies.

Other influencers include market mavens, who have a general interest in marketplace activities, and surrogate consumers, who are compensated for their advice about purchases.

Much of what we know about products is learned through word-of-mouth communication (WOM) rather than formal advertising. Product-related information tends to be exchanged in casual conversations. Guerrilla marketing strategies try to accelerate the WOM process by enlisting consumers to help spread the word.

Although WOM often is helpful for making consumers aware of products, it can also hurt companies when damaging product rumors or negative WOM occurs.

Emerging marketing strategies try to leverage the potential of the Web to spread information from consumer to consumer extremely quickly. Viral marketing techniques enlist individuals to tout products, services, Web sites, and so on, to others on behalf of companies. A new mode of online communication called blogging allows consumers to easily post their thoughts about products for others to see.

Sociometric methods are used to trace referral patterns. This information can be used to identify opinion leaders and other influential consumers.

KEY TERMS

CONSUMER BEHAVIOR CHALLENGE

1 Compare and contrast the five bases of power described in the text. Which are most likely to be relevant for marketing efforts?

2 Why is referent power an especially potent force for marketing appeals? What factors help to predict whether reference groups will or will not be a powerful influence on a person's purchase decisions?

3 Evaluate the strategic soundness of the concept of guerrilla marketing. For what types of product categories is this strategy most likely to be a success?

4 Discuss some factors that determine the amount of conformity likely to be observed among consumers.

5 Under what conditions are we more likely to engage in social comparison with dissimilar others versus similar others? How might this dimension be used in the design of marketing appeals?

6 Discuss some reasons for the effectiveness of home shopping parties as a selling tool. What other products might be sold this way?

7 Discuss some factors that influence whether membership groups will have a significant influence on a person's behavior.

8 Why is word-of-mouth communication often more persuasive than advertising?

9 Is there such a thing as a generalized opinion leader? What is likely to determine if an opinion leader will be influential with regard to a specific product category?

10 The adoption of a certain brand of shoe or apparel by athletes can be a powerful influence on students and other fans. Should high school and college coaches be paid to determine what brand of athletic equipment their players will wear?

11 The power of unspoken social norms often becomes obvious only when these norms are violated. To witness this result firsthand, try one of the following: stand facing the back wall in an elevator; serve dessert before the main course; offer to pay cash for dinner at a friend's home; wear pajamas to class; or tell someone not to have a nice day.

12 Identify a set of avoidance groups for your peers. Can you identify any consumption decisions that are made with these groups in mind?

13 Identify fashion opinion leaders on your campus. Do they fit the profile discussed in this chapter?

14 Conduct a sociometric analysis within your dormitory or neighborhood. For a product category such as music or cars, ask each individual to identify other individuals with whom they share information. Systematically trace all of these avenues of communication, and identify opinion leaders by locating individuals who are repeatedly named as providing helpful information.

15 The strategy of *viral marketing* gets customers to sell a product to other customers on behalf of the company. That often means convincing your friends to climb on the bandwagon, and sometimes you get a cut if they wind up buying something.[114] Some might argue that means you're selling out your friends (or at least selling to your friends) in exchange for a piece of the action. Others might say you're just sharing the wealth with those you care about. Have you been involved in viral marketing by passing along names of your friends or sending them to a Web site such as ***hotmail.com***? If so, what happened? How do you feel about this practice?

NOTES

1. Details adapted from John W. Schouten and James H. McAlexander, "Market Impact of a Consumption Subculture: The Harley-Davidson Mystique," in Fred van Raaij and Gary Bamossy, eds., *Proceedings of the 1992 European Conference of the Association for Consumer Research* (Amsterdam, 1992); John W. Schouten and James H. McAlexander, "Subcultures of Consumption: An Ethnography of the New Bikers," *Journal of Consumer Research* 22 (June 1995): 43–61. See also Kelly Barron, "Not So Easy Riders," *Forbes* (May 15, 2000).

2. Joel B. Cohen and Ellen Golden, "Informational Social Influence and Product Evaluation," *Journal of Applied Psychology* 56 (February 1972): 54–59; Robert E. Burnkrant and Alain Cousineau, "Informational and Normative Social Influence in Buyer Behavior," *Journal of Consumer Research* 2 (December 1975): 206–15; Peter H. Reingen, "Test of a List Procedure for Inducing Compliance with a Request to Donate Money," *Journal of Applied Psychology* 67 (1982): 110–18.

3. Dyan Machan, "Is the Hog Going Soft?" *Forbes* (March 10, 1997): 114–19.

4. C. Whan Park and V. Parker Lessig, "Students and Housewives: Differences in Susceptibility to Reference Group Influence," *Journal of Consumer Research* 4 (September 1977): 102–10.

5. Jeffrey D. Ford and Elwood A. Ellis, "A Re-examination of Group Influence on Member Brand Preference," *Journal of Marketing Research* 17 (February 1980): 125–32; Thomas S. Robertson, *Innovative Behavior and Communication* (New York: Holt, Rinehart and Winston, 1980): Chapter 8.

6. William O. Bearden and Michael J. Etzel, "Reference Group Influence on Product and Brand Purchase Decisions," *Journal of Consumer Research* 9 (1982): 183–94.

7. Kenneth J. Gergen and Mary Gergen, *Social Psychology* (New York: Harcourt Brace Jovanovich, 1981): 312.

8. J. R. P. French Jr. and B. Raven, "The Bases of Social Power," in D. Cartwright, ed., *Studies in Social Power* (Ann Arbor, MI: Institute for Social Research, 1959): 150–67.

9. Michael R. Solomon, "Packaging the Service Provider," *The Service Industries Journal* 5 (March 1985): 64–72.

10. Tamar Charry, "Advertising: Hawking, Wozniak Pitch Modems for U.S. Robotics," *New York Times News Service* (February 5, 1997).

11. Patricia M. West and Susan M. Broniarczyk, "Integrating Multiple Opinions: The Role of Aspiration Level on Consumer Response to Critic Consensus," *Journal of Consumer Research* 25 (June 1998): 38–51.

12. Gergen and Gergen, *Social Psychology*.

13. For a recent study that compared the relative potency of the two types, see Julie Tinson and John Ensor, "Formal and Informal Referent Groups: An Exploration of Novices and Experts in Maternity Services," *Journal of Consumer Behaviour* 1, no. 2 (November 2001): 174–183.

14. Harold H. Kelley, "Two Functions of Reference Groups," in Harold Proshansky and Bernard Siedenberg, eds., *Basic Studies in Social Psychology* (New York: Holt, Rinehart and Winston, 1965): 210–14.

15. James H. McAlexander, John W. Schouten, and Harold F. Koenig, "Building Brand Community," *Journal of Marketing* 66 (January 2002): 38–54; Albert Muniz and Thomas O'Guinn, "Brand Community," *Journal of Consumer Research* (March 2001): 412–32.

16. Veronique Cova and Bernard Cova, "Tribal Aspects of Postmodern Consumption Research: The Case of French In-Line Roller Skaters," *Journal Of Consumer Behavior* 1 (June 2001): 67–76.

17. A. Benton Cocanougher and Grady D. Bruce, "Socially Distant Reference Groups and Consumer Aspirations." *Journal of Marketing Research* 8 (August 1971): 79–81.

18. L. Festinger, S. Schachter, and K. Back, *Social Pressures in Informal Groups: A Study of Human Factors in Housing* (New York: Harper, 1950).

19. R. B. Zajonc, H. M. Markus, and W. Wilson, "Exposure Effects and Associative Learning," *Journal of Experimental Social Psychology* 10 (1974): 248–63.

20. D. J. Stang, "Methodological Factors in Mere Exposure Research," *Psychological Bulletin* 81 (1974): 1014–25; R. B. Zajonc, P. Shaver, C. Tavris, and D. Van Kreveid, "Exposure, Satiation and Stimulus Discriminability," *Journal of Personality and Social Psychology* 21 (1972): 270–80.

21. J. E. Grush, K. L. McKeogh, and R. F. Ahlering, "Extrapolating Laboratory Exposure Research to Actual Political Elections," *Journal of Personality and Social Psychology* 36 (1978): 257–70.

22. www.repcheck.com, accessed December 31, 2002.

23. "BT Openworld Hooks up with uDate," *New Media Age* (December 5, 2002); "iVillage enters the Dating Arena with Match.Com," *New Media Age* (August 22, 2002): 7; "Virtual Valentines?" *Yahoo! Internet Life* (February 1, 2002); Jon Herskovitz, "Japanese Look for Love," *Advertising Age International* (July 13, 1998): 6.

24. Basil G. Englis and Michael R. Solomon, "To Be and Not to Be: Reference Group Stereotyping and *The Clustering of America*," *Journal of Advertising* 24 (Spring 1995): 13–28; Michael R. Solomon and Basil G. Englis, "I Am Not, Therefore I Am: The Role of Anti-Consumption in the Process of Self-Definition" (Special Session at the Association for Consumer Research meetings, October 1996, Tucson, Arizona).

25. Bruce Feirstein, *Real Men Don't Eat Quiche* (New York: Pocket Books, 1982); www.auntiefashions.com, accessed December 31, 2002.

26. J. Craig Andrews and Richard G. Netemeyer, "Alcohol Warning Label Effects: Socialization, Addiction, and Public Policy Issues," in Ronald P. Hill, ed., *Marketing and Consumer Research in the Public Interest* (Thousand Oaks, CA: Sage, 1996): 153–75; "National Study Finds Increase in College Binge Drinking," *Alcoholism & Drug Abuse Weekly* (March 27, 2000): 12–13.

27. B. Latane, K. Williams, and S. Harkins, "Many Hands Make Light the Work: The Causes and Consequences of Social Loafing," *Journal of Personality and Social Psychology* 37 (1979): 822–32.

28. S. Freeman, M. Walker, R. Borden, and B. Latane, "Diffusion of Responsibility and Restaurant Tipping: Cheaper by the Bunch," *Personality and Social Psychology Bulletin* 3 (1975): 584–87.

29. Nathan Kogan and Michael A. Wallach, "Risky Shift Phenomenon in Small Decision-Making Groups: A Test of the Information Exchange Hypothesis," *Journal of Experimental Social Psychology* 3 (January 1967): 75–84; Nathan Kogan and Michael A. Wallach, *Risk Taking* (New York: Holt, Rinehart and Winston, 1964); Arch G. Woodside and M. Wayne DeLozier, "Effects of Word-of-Mouth Advertising on Consumer Risk Taking," *Journal of Advertising* (Fall 1976): 12–19.

30. Kogan and Wallach, *Risk Taking*.

31. Roger Brown, *Social Psychology* (New York: The Free Press, 1965).

32. David L. Johnson and I. R. Andrews, "Risky Shift Phenomenon Tested with Consumer Product Stimuli," *Journal of Personality and Social Psychology* 20 (1971): 382–85; see also Vithala R. Rao and Joel H. Steckel, "A Polarization Model for Describing Group Preferences," *Journal of Consumer Research* 18 (June 1991): 108–18.

33. Donald H. Granbois, "Improving the Study of Customer In-Store Behavior," *Journal of Marketing* 32 (October 1968): 28–32.

34. Len Strazewski, "Tupperware Locks in New Strategy," *Advertising Age* (February 8, 1988): 30.

35. Melanie Wells, "Smooth Operator," *Forbes* (May 13, 2002): 167–68.

36. Luc Sante, "Be Different! (Like Everyone Else!)" *New York Times Magazine* (October 17, 1999).

37. Cornelia Pechmann and S. Ratneshwar, "The Effects of Antismoking and Cigarette Advertising on Young Adolescents' Perceptions of Peers Who Smoke," *Journal of Consumer Research* 21 (September 1994): 236–51.

38. For a study attempting to measure individual differences in proclivity to conformity, see William O. Bearden, Richard G. Netemeyer, and Jesse E. Teel, "Measurement of Consumer Susceptibility to Interpersonal Influence," *Journal of Consumer Research* 15 (March 1989): 473–81.

39. John W. Thibaut and Harold H. Kelley, *The Social Psychology of Groups* (New York: Wiley, 1959); W. W. Waller and R. Hill, *The Family, a Dynamic Interpretation* (New York: Dryden, 1951).

40. Bearden, Netemeyer, and Teel, "Measurement of Consumer Susceptibility to Interpersonal Influence," 473–81; Lynn R. Kahle, "Observations: Role-Relaxed Consumers: A Trend of the Nineties," *Journal of Advertising Research* (March–April 1995): 66–71; Lynn R. Kahle and Aviv Shoham, "Observations: Role-Relaxed Consumers: Empirical Evidence," *Journal of Advertising Research* (May–June 1995): 59–62.

41. Leon Festinger, "A Theory of Social Comparison Processes," *Human Relations* 7 (May 1954): 117–40.

42. Chester A. Insko, Sarah Drenan, Michael R. Solomon, Richard Smith, and Terry J. Wade, "Conformity as a Function of the Consistency of Positive Self-Evaluation with Being Liked and Being Right," *Journal of Experimental Social Psychology* 19 (1983): 341–58.

43. Abraham Tesser, Murray Millar, and Janet Moore, "Some Affective Consequences of Social Comparison and Reflection Processes: The Pain and Pleasure of Being Close," *Journal of Personality and Social Psychology* 54, no. 1 (1988): 49–61.

44. L. Wheeler, K. G. Shaver, R. A. Jones, G. R. Goethals, J. Cooper, J. E. Robinson, C. L. Gruder, and K. W. Butzine, "Factors Determining the Choice of a Comparison Other," *Journal of Experimental Social Psychology* 5 (1969): 219–32.

45. George P. Moschis, "Social Comparison and Informal Group Influence," *Journal of Marketing Research* 13 (August 1976): 237–44.

46. Robert E. Burnkrant and Alain Cousineau, "Informational and Normative Social Influence in Buyer Behavior," *Journal of Consumer Research* 2 (December 1975): 206–15; M. Venkatesan, "Experimental Study of Consumer Behavior Conformity and Independence," *Journal of Marketing Research* 3 (November 1966): 384–87.

47. Gergen and Gergen, *Social Psychology*.

48. L. J. Strickland, S. Messick, and D. N. Jackson, "Conformity, Anticonformity and Independence: Their Dimensionality and Generality," *Journal of Personality and Social Psychology* 16 (1970): 494–507.

49. Jack W. Brehm, *A Theory of Psychological Reactance* (New York: Academic Press, 1966).

50. R. D. Ashmore, V. Ramchandra, and R. Jones, "Censorship as an Attitude Change Induction" (paper presented at meeting of Eastern Psychological Association, New York, 1971); R. A. Wicklund and J. Brehm, *Perspectives on Cognitive Dissonance* (Hillsdale, NJ: Erlbaum, 1976).

51. Pat Wechsler, "A Curiously Strong Campaign," *BusinessWeek* (April 21, 1997): 134.

52. Johan Arndt, "Role of Product-Related Conversations in the Diffusion of a New Product," *Journal of Marketing Research* 4 (August 1967): 291–95.

53. John Gaffney, "Enterprise: Marketing: The Cool Kids Are Doing It. Should You?" *Asiaweek* (November 23, 2001): 1.

54. Elihu Katz and Paul F. Lazarsfeld, *Personal Influence* (Glencoe, IL: Free Press, 1955).

55. John A. Martilla, " Word-of-Mouth Communication in the Industrial Adoption Process," *Journal of Marketing Research* 8 (March 1971): 173–78; see also Marsha L. Richins, "Negative Word-of-Mouth by Dissatisfied Consumers: A Pilot Study," *Journal of Marketing* 47 (Winter 1983): 68–78.

56. Arndt, "Role of Product-Related Conversations in the Diffusion of a New Product."

57. James H. Myers and Thomas S. Robertson, "Dimensions of Opinion Leadership," *Journal of Marketing Research* 9 (February 1972): 41–46.

58. Ellen Neuborne, "Generation Y," *BusinessWeek* (February 15, 1999): 86.

59. Dorothy Leonard-Barton, "Experts as Negative Opinion Leaders in the Diffusion of a Technological Innovation," *Journal of Consumer Research* 11 (March 1985): 914–26.

60. James F. Engel, Robert J. Kegerreis, and Roger D. Blackwell, "Word-of-Mouth Communication by the Innovator," *Journal of Marketing* 33 (July 1969): 15–19.

61. Chip Walker, "Word-of-Mouth," *American Demographics* (July 1995): 38–44.

62. Richard J. Lutz, "Changing Brand Attitudes through Modification of Cognitive Structure," *Journal of Consumer Research* 1 (March 1975): 49–59. For some suggested remedies to bad publicity, see Mitch Griffin, Barry J. Babin, and Jill S. Attaway, "An Empirical Investigation of the Impact of Negative Public Publicity on Consumer Attitudes and Intentions," in Rebecca H. Holman and Michael R. Solomon, eds., *Advances in Consumer Research* 18 (Provo, UT: Association for Consumer Research, 1991): 334–41; Alice M. Tybout, Bobby J. Calder, and Brian Sternthal, "Using Information Processing Theory to Design Marketing Strategies," *Journal of Marketing Research* 18 (1981): 73–79; see also Russell N. Laczniak, Thomas E. DeCarlo, and Sridhar N. Ramaswami, "Consumers' Responses to Negative Word-of-Mouth Communication: An Attribution Theory Perspective," *Journal of Consumer Psychology*, in press.

63. Robert E. Smith and Christine A. Vogt, "The Effects of Integrating Advertising and Negative Word-of-Mouth Communications on Message Processing and Response," *Journal of Consumer Psychology* 4, no. 2 (1995): 133–51; Paula Fitzgerald Bone, "Word-of-Mouth Effects on Short-Term and Long-Term Product Judgments," *Journal of Business Research* 32 (1995): 213–23.

64. "Dunkin' Donuts Buys Out Critical Web Site," *New York Times on the Web* (August 27, 1999). For a discussion of ways to assess negative WOM online, see David M. Boush and Lynn R. Kahle, "Evaluating Negative Information in Online Consumer Discussions: From Qualitative Analysis to Signal Detection," *Journal of EuroMarketing* 11, no. 2 (2001): 89–105.

65. Charles W. King and John O. Summers, "Overlap of Opinion Leadership across Consumer Product Categories," *Journal of Marketing Research* 7 (February 1970): 43–50.

66. Michael Fumento, "Tampon Terrorism," *Forbes* (May 17, 1999): 170.

67. Greg Jaffe, "No MTV for Widespread Panic, Just Loads of Worshipful Fans," *Wall Street Journal Interactive Edition* (February 17, 1999).

68. Christina Le Beau, "Cracking the Niche," *American Demographics* (June 2000): 38–40.

69. Kim Folstad, "A Chat Room of One's Own" [Web site] (Cox News Service, February, 2002 [cited April 27, 2002]); available from www.e-fluentials.com/news; INTERNET.

70. This typology is adapted from material presented in Robert V. Kozinets, "E-Tribalized Marketing: The Strategic Implications of Virtual Communities of Consumption," *European Management Journal* 17 (June 1999): 252–64. See also Miriam Catterall and Pauline Maclaran, "Researching Consumers in Virtual Worlds: A Cyberspace Odyssey," *Journal of Consumer Behavior* 1, no. 3 (February 2000): 228–37.

71. Hassan Fattah and Pamela Paul, "Gaming Gets Serious," *American Demographics* (May 2002): 39–43.

72. Ibid.

73. Marc Gunther, "The Newest Addiction," *Fortune* (August 2, 1999): 123.

74. Tom Weber, "Net's Hottest Game Brings People Closer," *Wall Street Journal Interactive Edition* (March 20, 2000).

75. David Kushner, "Where Warriors and Ogres Lock Arms Instead of Swords," *New York Times on the Web* (August 9, 2002).

76. Martha Irvine, "Mother Blames Internet Game for Son's Suicide," *Montgomery Advertiser* (May 26, 2002): 6(A).

77. Bob Tedeschi, "Is Weblog Technology Here to Stay or Just Another Fad?" *New York Times on the Web* (February 25, 2002); Steven Levy, "Living in the Blog-Osphere," *Newsweek* (August 26, 2002): 42–44; David F. Gallagher, "Free Weblog Service and a Vampire, Too," *New York Times on the Web* (August 26, 2002); David F. Gallagher, "A Site to Pour Out Emotions, and Just about Anything Else," *New York Times on the Web* (September 5, 2002).

78. Kozinets, "E-Tribalized Marketing: The Strategic Implications of Virtual Communities of Consumption," 252–64.

79. Glyn Moody, "Gold in Amazon's Box of Tricks," *Computer Weekly* (July 18, 2002): 27; "Shopping (online consumer ratings)," *Yahoo! Internet Life* (July 1, 2002); Bob Tedeschi, "Online Retailers Find that Customer Reviews Build Loyalty," *New York Times on the Web* (September 6, 1999); "Bookseller Offers Refunds for Advertised Books," *Opelika-Auburn [Alabama] News* (February 11, 1999): A11; Jason Anders, "When It Comes to Promoters, Boards Say, 'Reader Beware'," *Wall Street Journal Interactive Edition* (July 25, 1998).

80. Sonia Murray, "Street Marketing Does the Trick," *Advertising Age* (March 20, 2000): S12.

81. "Taking to the Streets," *Newsweek* (November 2, 1998): 70–73.

82. Lynette Holloway, "Declining CD Sales Spur Labels to Use Street Marketing Teams," *New York Times on the Web* (September 30, 2002).

83. Constance L. Hays, "Guerrilla Marketing Is Going Mainstream," *New York Times on the Web* (October 7, 1999).

84. Betsy Spethmann, "X Marks Target For Blucaos Booming Shooter," *Brandweek* (September 24, 1994): 3.

85. Gabriel Kahn, "Virtual Rock Band Corresponds with Fans via Text Messaging," *Wall Street Journal Interactive Edition* (April 19, 2002).

86. Kate Fitzgerald, "Branding Face to Face," *Advertising Age* (October 21, 2002): 47.

87. Jared Sandberg, "The Friendly Virus," *Newsweek* (April 12, 1999): 65–66.

88. Karen J.Bannan, "Marketers Try Infecting the Internet," *New York Times on the Web* (March 22, 2000).

89. Sitelab's Execution of Viral Marketing Campaign for WD-40 Helps Net Nearly 40,000 Fans" *BusinessWire* (January 14, 2002): 279.

90. Peter Landau, "A.I. Promotion," *Mediaweek* (November 12, 2001).

91. Jeff Neff, "Pressure Points at IPG," *Advertising Age* (December 2001): 4.

92. Everett M. Rogers, *Diffusion of Innovations*, 3rd ed. (New York: Free Press, 1983).

93. Leonard-Barton, "Experts as Negative Opinion Leaders in the Diffusion of a Technological Innovation"; Rogers, *Diffusion of Innovations*.

94. Burson-Marsteller, "The E-fluentials: 2000," Retrieved April 23, 2002, from "The E-fluentials: 2000," [online magazine] [cited April 23, 2002] Burson Marsteller; available from http://bm.com; S. Khodarahmi, "Pass It On"[online magazine] [cited April 26, 2002] DotCEO; available from www.dotceo.com; Seana Mulcahy, "Selling to E-fluentials" [online magazine] [cited April 27, 2002]; *ClickZ Today* (January 3, 2002); available from www. e-fluentials.com/news.

95. Herbert Menzel, "Interpersonal and Unplanned Communications: Indispensable or Obsolete?" in Edward B. Roberts, ed., *Biomedical Innovation* (Cambridge, MA: MIT Press, 1981), 155–63.

96. Meera P. Venkatraman, "Opinion Leaders, Adopters, and Communicative Adopters: A Role Analysis," *Psychology & Marketing* 6 (Spring 1989): 51–68.

97. Rogers, *Diffusion of Innovations*.

98. Robert Merton, *Social Theory and Social Structure* (Glencoe, IL: Free Press, 1957).

99. King and Summers, "Overlap of Opinion Leadership across Consumer Product Categories"; see also Ronald E. Goldsmith, Jeanne R. Heitmeyer, and Jon B. Freiden, "Social Values and Fashion Leadership," *Clothing and Textiles Research Journal* 10 (Fall 1991): 37–45; J. O. Summers, "Identity of Women's Clothing Fashion Opinion Leaders," *Journal of Marketing Research* 7 (1970): 178–85.

100. Steven A. Baumgarten, "The Innovative Communicator in the Diffusion Process," *Journal of Marketing Research* 12 (February 1975): 12–18.

101. Laura J. Yale and Mary C. Gilly, "Dyadic Perceptions in Personal Source Information Search," *Journal of Business Research* 32 (1995): 225–37.

102. Russell W. Belk, "Occurrence of Word-of-Mouth Buyer Behavior as a Function of Situation and Advertising Stimuli," in Fred C. Allvine, ed., *Combined Proceedings of the American Marketing Association*, series no. 33 (Chicago: American Marketing Association, 1971): 419–22.

103. Lawrence F. Feick, Linda L. Price, and Robin A. Higie, "People Who Use People: The Other Side of Opinion Leadership," in Richard J. Lutz, ed., *Advances in Consumer Research* 13 (Provo, UT: Association for Consumer Research, 1986): 301–5.

104. For discussion of the market maven construct, see Lawrence F. Feick and Linda L. Price, "The Market Maven," *Managing* (July 1985): 10; scale items adapted from Lawrence F. Feick and Linda L. Price, "The Market Maven: A Diffuser of Marketplace Information," *Journal of Marketing* 51 (January 1987): 83–87.

105. Michael R. Solomon, "The Missing Link: Surrogate Consumers in the Marketing Chain," *Journal of Marketing* 50 (October 1986): 208–18.

106. CBS Extends Its High-Tech Reach: CD-ROM Goes to 'Influencers'," *PROMO: The International Magazine for Promotion Marketing* (October 1994): 59.

107. John Lippman, "Sony's Word-of-Mouth Campaign Creates Buzz for 'Crouching Tiger'," *Wall Street Journal* (January 11, 2001).

108. Stern and Gould, "The Consumer as Financial Opinion Leader."

109. William R. Darden and Fred D. Reynolds, "Predicting Opinion Leadership for Men's Apparel Fashions," *Journal of Marketing Research* 1 (August 1972): 324–28. A modified version of the opinion leadership scale with improved reliability and validity can be found in Terry L. Childers, "Assessment of the Psychometric Properties of an Opinion Leadership Scale," *Journal of Marketing Research* 23 (May 1986): 184–88.

110. Dan Seligman, "Me and Monica," *Forbes* (March 23, 1998): 76.

111. "Referrals Top Ads as Influence on Patients' Doctor Selections," *Marketing News* (January 30, 1987): 22.

112. Peter H. Reingen and Jerome B. Kernan, "Analysis of Referral Networks in Marketing: Methods and Illustration," *Journal of Marketing Research* 23 (November 1986): 370–78.

113. Peter H. Reingen, Brian L. Foster, Jacqueline Johnson Brown, and Stephen B. Seidman, "Brand Congruence in Interpersonal Relations: A Social Network Analysis," *Journal of Consumer Research* 11 (December 1984): 771–83; see also James C. Ward and Peter H. Reingen, "Sociocognitive Analysis of Group Decision-making among Consumers," *Journal of Consumer Research* 17 (December 1990): 245–62.

114. Thomas E. Weber, "Viral Marketing: Web's Newest Ploy May Make You an Unpopular Friend," *The Wall Street Journal Interactive Edition* (September 13, 1999).

Organizational and Household Decision Making

amanda is about as nervous as she can be. Tonight she and her partner are throwing their first party in their new apartment, and it's really coming down to the wire. Some of her friends and family who were skeptical about Amanda's plan to move out of her parents' house and to live with a man will have the chance to say "I told you so" if this debut of her new living arrangement self-destructs.

Life hasn't exactly been a bed of roses since she and Orlando moved in together. It's a bit of a mystery—although his desk is tidy and organized at the publishing company where they both work, his personal habits are another story. Orlando's really been making an effort to clean up his act, but Amanda has still been forced to take on more than her share of cleaning duties—partly out of self-defense because they have to share a bathroom! And, she's learned the hard way not to trust Orlando to do the grocery shopping—he goes to the store with a big list of staples and returns with beer and junk food. You would think that a man who is responsible for buying the firm's multimillion-dollar computer network would have a bit more sense when it comes to sticking to a budget and picking out the right household supplies. What's even more frustrating is that although Orlando can easily spend a week digging up information about the new big-screen TV they're buying (with her bonus!), she has to virtually drag him by the ear to look at dining room furniture. Then, to add insult to injury, he's quick to criticize her choices—especially if they cost too much.

401

So, how likely is it that while she's at work Orlando has been home cleaning up the apartment and making some hors d'oeuvres as he promised? Amanda did her part by downloading a recipe for crabmeat salad and wasabi caviar from the entertaining section on *epicurious.com*. She even jotted down some adorable table setting ideas such as napkin holders made out of homegrown bamboo at *marthastewart.com*. The rest is up to him—at this point she'd be happy if Orlando remembers to pick up his underwear from the living room couch. This soiree could turn out to be a real proving ground for their relationship. Amanda sighs as she walks into an editors' meeting. She sure has learned a lot about relationships since setting up a new household . . . living together is going to be a lot bumpier than it's made out to be in romance novels.

■ ORGANIZATIONAL DECISION MAKING

Amanda's trials and tribulations with Orlando illustrate that many consumer decisions are made jointly. The individual decision making process described in detail in Chapter 9 is, in many cases, overly simplistic because more than one person may be involved in any stage of the problem-solving sequence, from initial problem recognition and information search to evaluation of alternatives and product choice. To further complicate matters, these decisions often involve two or more people who may not have the same level of investment in the outcome, the same tastes and preferences, or the same consumption priorities.

This chapter examines issues related to *collective decision making*, a process in which more than one person is involved in the purchasing process for products or services that may be used by multiple consumers. The first part of the chapter looks at organizational decision making, where purchases are made on behalf of a larger group. We then move on to focus more specifically on one of the most important organizations to which most of us claim membership—the family unit. We'll consider how members of a family negotiate among themselves and how important changes in modern family structure are affecting this process. This chapter concludes by focusing on how "new employees"—children—learn how to be consumers. First, though, let's focus on decision making that occurs when people leave their families at home and go to work.

Many employees of corporations or other organizations make purchase decisions on a daily basis. **Organizational buyers** are people like Orlando who purchase goods and services on behalf of companies for use in the process of manufacturing, distribution, or resale. These individuals buy from **business-to-business marketers**, who specialize in meeting the needs of organizations such as corporations, government agencies, hospitals, and retailers. In terms of sheer volume, *B2B marketing* is where the action is: Roughly $2 trillion worth of products and services change hands among organizations, which is actually *more* than is purchased by end consumers.

Organizational buyers have a lot of responsibility. They must decide on the vendors with whom they want to do business and what specific items they require from these suppliers. The items they consider can range in price and significance from paper clips to that multimillion-dollar computer system Orlando has to worry about. Obviously, there is a lot at stake in understanding how these important decisions are made.

The organizational buyer's perception of the purchase situation is influenced by a number of factors. These include his *expectations* of the supplier (e.g., product quality, the competence and behavior of the firm's employees, and prior experiences in dealing with that supplier), the *organizational climate* of his own company (i.e., perceptions regarding how the company rewards performance and what it values), and the buyer's *assessment* of his own performance (e.g., whether he believes in taking risks).[1]

In the Information Age, organizational decision makers must stay on top of clients' complex needs.

Like other consumers, organizational buyers engage in a learning process in which members of the firm share information with one another and develop an "organizational memory" consisting of shared beliefs and assumptions about the proper course of action.[2] Just as a buyer is influenced by "market beliefs" when he goes shopping with the family on the weekend (see Chapter 9), the same person is also an information processor at the office. He (perhaps with fellow employees) attempts to solve problems by searching for information, evaluating alternatives, and making decisions.[3] There are, of course, some important differences between the two situations.

Organizational Decision Making Versus Consumer Decision Making

Many factors distinguish organizational and industrial purchase decisions from individual consumer decisions. Some of these differences are as follows:[4]

- Purchase decisions made by companies frequently involve many people, including those who do the actual buying, those who directly or indirectly influence this decision, and the employees who will actually use the product or service.
- Organizational and industrial products are often bought according to precise, technical specifications that require a lot of knowledge about the product category.
- Impulse buying is rare (industrial buyers do not suddenly get an "urge to splurge" on lead pipe or silicon chips). Because buyers are professionals, their decisions are based on past experience and a careful weighing of alternatives.

- Decisions often are risky, especially in the sense that a buyer's career may be riding on his demonstration of good judgment.
- The dollar volume of purchases is often substantial, dwarfing most individual consumer grocery bills or mortgage payments. One hundred to 250 organizational customers often account for more than half of a supplier's sales volume, which gives the buyers a lot of influence over the supplier.
- Business-to-business marketing often involves more of an emphasis on personal selling than on advertising or other forms of promotion. Dealing with organizational buyers typically requires more face-to-face contact than is necessary in the case of end consumers.

We must consider these important features when we try to understand the purchasing decisions made by organizations. Still, there are actually more similarities between organizational buyers and ordinary consumers than many people realize. True, organizational purchase decisions do tend to have a higher economic or functional component compared to individual consumer choices, but emotional aspects enter the scene as well. For example, although organizational buyers may appear to the outsider to be models of rationality, their decisions are sometimes guided by brand loyalty, by long-term relationships they have established with particular suppliers or salespeople, or even by aesthetic concerns.

Intel's development of the hugely successful "Intel Inside" campaign illustrates how important issues such as branding and product image can be in industrial contexts. Competitors had been using Intel's numerical sequencing to label their computer chips since the company had introduced its 286 model. These labels did not, however, guarantee that the rival versions possessed the same architecture as Intel's version, so this created confusion in the marketplace. After trying unsuccessfully to trademark the "286" name, the firm developed the "Intel Inside" logo and persuaded 240 manufacturers to include the new logo in their packaging. In a three-year period, Intel invested more than $500 million in promotional programs and advertising to build recognition of the Intel brand name.[5] This "commodity branding" strategy continues to pay off for the chipmaker.

How Do Organizational Buyers Operate?

Like end consumers, organizational buyers are influenced by both internal and external stimuli. Internal stimuli include the buyer's unique psychological characteristics such as willingness to make risky decisions and job experience and training. External stimuli include the nature of the organization for which the buyer works as well as the overall economic and technological environment in which the industry is operating. Another set of factors is cultural; vastly different norms for doing business can be found in different countries. For example, Americans tend to be less formal in their interactions than are many of their European or Asian counterparts.

Type of Purchase

The type of item to be purchased influences the organizational buyer's decision-making process. As with consumer purchases, the more complex, novel, or risky the decision, the greater the amount of information search and effort will be devoted to evaluating alternatives. On the other hand, reliance on a fixed set of suppliers for routine purchases is one strategy that greatly reduces the information search and effort in evaluating competing alternatives that would otherwise be required.[6]

Typically, more complex organizational decisions also tend to be made by a group of people (members of a **buying center**) who play different roles in the decision. As we will see later on, this joint involvement is somewhat similar to family decision making, in which more family members are likely to be involved in more important purchases.

Executives devote substantial effort to processing information from business media.

The Buyclass Framework

Organizational buying decisions can be divided into three types, which range from the most to the least complex. This classification scheme is called the buyclass theory of purchasing, and it uses three decision making dimensions to describe the purchasing strategies of an organizational buyer:[7]

1   The level of information that must be gathered prior to making a decision
2   The seriousness with which all possible alternatives must be considered
3   The degree to which the buyer is familiar with the purchase

In practice, these three dimensions relate to how much cognitive effort will be expended in making a purchase decision. Three types of "buyclasses," or strategies based on these dimensions encompass most organizational decision situations.[8] Each type of purchase corresponds to one of the three types of decisions discussed

TABLE 12.1 **TYPES OF ORGANIZATIONAL BUYING DECISIONS**			
Buying Situation	**Extent of Effort**	**Risk**	**Buyers Involved**
Straight rebuy	Habitual decision making	Low	Automatic reorder
Modified rebuy	Limited problem solving	Low to moderate	One or a few
New task	Extensive problem solving	High	Many

Source: Adapted from Patrick J. Robinson, Charles W. Faris, and Yoram Wind, *Industrial Buying and Creative Marketing* [Boston: Allyn & Bacon, 1967].

in Chapter 9: habitual decision making, limited problem solving, and extensive problem solving. Table 12.1 summarizes these strategies.

A **straight rebuy** is like a habitual decision. It is an automatic choice, as when an inventory level reaches a preestablished reorder point. Most organizations maintain an approved vendor list, and as long as experience with the vendor is satisfactory there is little or no ongoing information search or evaluation.

A **modified rebuy** situation involves limited decision making. It occurs when an organization wants to repurchase a product or service, but with some minor modifications. This decision might involve a limited search for information, most likely by speaking to a few vendors. One or a few people will probably make the final decision.

A **new task** involves extensive problem solving. Because the decision has not been made before, there is often a serious risk that the product won't perform as it should or that it will be too costly. The organization designates a buying center with assorted specialists to evaluate the purchase, and they typically gather a lot of information before coming to a decision.

Decision Roles

A number of specific roles are played when a collective decision must be made, either by members of a household or by individuals in an organizational buying center.[9] Depending on the decision, some or all of the group members may be involved, and one person may play any number (or even all) of these roles. These roles include:

- *Initiator:* The person who brings up the idea or need.
- *Gatekeeper:* The person who conducts the information search and controls the flow of information available to the group. In organizational contexts the gatekeeper identifies possible vendors and products for the rest of the group to consider.
- *Influencer:* The person who tries to sway the outcome of the decision. Some people may be more motivated than others to get involved, and participants also differ in terms of the amount of power they have to convince others of their choice. In organizations, engineers are often influencers for product information, whereas purchasing agents play a similar role when the group evaluates the vendors that supply these items.
- *Buyer:* The person who actually makes the purchase. The buyer may or may not actually use the product. This person may pay for the item, actually procure it, or both.
- *User:* The person who winds up using the product or service.

B2B E-Commerce

The Web is radically changing the way organizational buyers learn about and select products for their companies. **Business-to-business (B2B) e-commerce** refers to Internet interactions between two or more businesses or organizations. This includes exchanges of information, products, services, or payments. A majority of U.S. firms plan to be transacting business on the Web if they're not doing so already.

In the simplest form of B2B e-commerce, the Internet provides an online catalog of products and services needed by businesses. Companies like Dell Computer have found their Internet site is important for delivering online technical support, product information, order status information, and customer service to corporate customers. Early on, Dell discovered that it could serve the needs of its customers more effectively by tailoring its Internet presence to different customer segments. Dell's Internet site allows shoppers to get recommendations based on their customer segment (home, home office, government, small business, and education). The company saves millions of dollars a year by replacing hard copy manuals with electronic downloads. For its larger customers, Dell provides customer-specific, password-protected pages that allow business customers to obtain technical support or to place an order.

■ THE FAMILY

It is not unusual to read in newspapers and magazines about the death of the family unit. Although it is true that the proportion of people living in a traditional family structure consisting of a married couple with children living at home continues to decline, many other types of families are growing rapidly. Indeed, some experts have argued that as traditional family living arrangements have waned, people are placing even greater emphasis on siblings, close friends, and other relatives in providing companionship and social support.[10] Some people are even joining "intentional families": groups of unrelated people who meet regularly for meals and who spend holidays together.[11]

Defining the Modern Family

The **extended family** was once the most common family unit. It consists of three generations living together and often includes grandparents, aunts, uncles, and cousins. As evidenced by the Cleavers of *Leave It to Beaver* and other TV families of the 1950s, the **nuclear family**—a mother and a father and one or more children (perhaps with a sheepdog thrown in for good measure)—became the model family unit over time. However, many changes have occurred since the days of Beaver Cleaver. Although people may continue to conjure up an image of the typical American family based on old TV shows, demographic data show that this ideal image of the family is no longer a realistic picture.

Just What Is a Household?

When it conducts the national census every 10 years, the U.S. Census Bureau regards any occupied housing unit as a household regardless of the relationships among people living there. A **family household**, as defined by the Census Bureau, contains at least two people who are related by blood or marriage. The Census Bureau and other survey firms compile a massive amount of data on family households, but certain categories are of particular interest to marketers.

There's no doubt that the way we think of family is evolving. Changes in consumers' family structures, such as the upheaval caused by divorce, often represent opportunities for marketers as normal purchasing patterns become unfrozen and

Net Profit

The Web is revolutionizing the way companies communicate with other firms and even the way they share information with their own people. Roughly half of B2B e-commerce transactions take the form of auctions, bids, and exchanges where numerous suppliers and purchasers interact.[12] Experts expect the worldwide market for these kinds of supply chain services to reach nearly $483 billion by 2005.[13] For example, the 62 major retailers that belong to the Worldwide Retail Exchange use this online resource to cut costs as they develop new products and identify suppliers.[14] Working in cyberspace facilitates the creative process as well: Product designers at apparel manufacturers like VF Corp. can log into the firm's intranet and play with product samples and colors in a database as they come up with new clothing ideas. Don't like that color or the way that button looks? A click of a button gives you a new one. In the old days, a new sample would have to be physically produced and evaluated, but now design ideas can be selected and the materials needed to produce them can be located on the desktop.[15] That's business at light speed.

CERTE COSE SONO DIFFICILI DA MANDARE GIÙ.

QUANDO SERVE, CITROSODINA ANTIACIDO. **CITROSODINA** A STAR BENE C È PIÙ GUSTO.

Family structures continue to evolve, but some basic conflicts remain the same. This Italian ad for an antacid product says, "Certain things are hard to swallow."

people make new choices about products and brands.[16] More than one million couples divorce in a typical year. In the United States approximately 20 million children under 18 live with just one parent, and in 84 percent of these cases that parent is the mother.[17] Divorces and separations are an accepted part of our culture, and marital breakups are an ever-present theme in books, music, and movies.[18] Reflecting the prevalence of this situation, a few years ago a Canadian entrepreneur created DivorceX, a digital imaging service that removes ex-spouses from family pictures![19]

Ironically, although many people proclaim that the traditional family is dead, it appears to be making a bit of a comeback among young couples now. A recent study found that a surprisingly small percentage of female business school graduates over the past 20 years are currently working full-time. And, U.S. Census figures show that after rising steadily for a quarter-century, the number of women with children under age one in the workforce dropped from a record high of 59 percent in 1998 to 55 percent in 2000.

This trend of taking time off from work to raise small children is concentrated among the best-educated and highest-achieving women—those in their thirties and forties who have college degrees. Federal Reserve data show that nearly half of households earning $250,000 to $499,999 now have just one breadwinner, up from 38 percent in the early 1990s. This stay-at-home idea is appealing to those who have the luxury to do it. People in this age group consider the balancing of home and

This ad for Family Circle magazine humorously emphasizes that some traditional family values persist among young people today.

work their biggest challenge, and they also see it as a higher priority than earning a mega-income or an impressive title.[20]

Family Size

Family size depends on such factors as educational level, the availability of birth control, and religion.[21] The **fertility rate** is determined by the number of births per year per 1,000 women of childbearing age. Marketers keep a close eye on the population's birth rate to gauge how the pattern of births will affect demand for products in the future. The U.S. fertility rate increased dramatically in the late 1950s and early 1960s, when the parents of so-called baby boomers began to reach childrearing age. It declined in the 1970s and began to climb again in the 1980s as baby boomers began to have their own children in a new "baby boomlet."

Worldwide, surveys show that almost all women want smaller families today. This trend is a problem for European countries whose fertility rates have plummeted over the last decades. Ironically, while populations are booming in many underdeveloped parts of the world, industrialized countries face future crises because there will be relatively fewer young people to support their elders. In order for population levels to remain constant, this rate needs to be 2.0 so that the two children can replace their parents. That's not happening in places like Spain, Sweden, Germany, and Greece, where the fertility rate is 1.4 or lower. By contrast, the United States had a 2.0 rate, which demographers attribute to greater immigration.

Folger's Coffee addresses an important need by allowing single people to brew one cup of coffee at a time.

Some countries are considering a variety of measures to encourage people to have more children. For example, Spain is weighing cheaper utility bills for large families, assistance for young couples trying to afford homes, and the creation of hundreds of thousands of new preschools and nursery schools. The Italian government provides mothers with nearly full salary compensation for about a half year of maternity leave, but women are stubbornly refusing to have more kids.

There are many reasons for this shift from past eras where heavily Catholic countries tended to have large families: Contraception and abortion are more readily available, divorce is more common, and older people who used to look after grandchildren now are pursuing other activities such as travel. And, some experts cite the fact that many Italian men live with their mothers into their thirties so when they do get married they're not prepared to help out at home. One analyst commented, "Even the most open-minded guy—if you scratch with the nail a little bit, there's the mother who did everything for him. I hate the mothers of these men. These mothers are a disaster."[22]

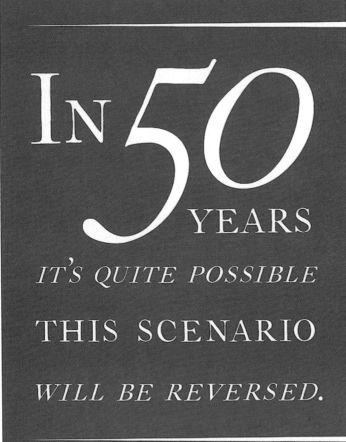

Something quite wonderful is happening. We're all getting older. And living longer. Consider that, for the first time ever, the fastest growing segment of the U.S. population is over ninety years old. Or that by the year 2020, less than 30 years from now, one-in-three of us will be over the age of fifty.

Consider also that sometime in the not-too-distant future you could find yourself being called upon to provide for your parents, just as they once provided for you. Perhaps all that will be needed are a few words of love and reassurance. Perhaps something more.

Now consider a forward-looking company with a clear vision of what all this change means and how it will impact our lives. A company universally looked to as the leader in disability insurance. A company that has taken the next logical step by pioneering new approaches in long term care coverage to protect a lifetime of savings. And when you stop and think about it—well, it could be quite a lifetime.

Heck, we're 145 years old ourselves. Here's to a long life.

UNUM
We see farther

This insurance ad reminds us that people in the "sandwich generation" often must care for their parents in addition to their children.

Nontraditional Family Structures

The U.S. Census Bureau regards any occupied housing unit as a household, regardless of the relationships among people living there. Thus, one person living alone, three roommates, or two lovers (whether straight or gay) constitute households. Indeed, same-sex households are increasingly common and as a result more marketers are targeting them as a family unit. *Gayweddings.com* and *twobrides.com* offers wedding decorations and gifts. Conventional companies that make products like baby food and children's clothing are even starting to advertise in *And Baby*, a gay parenting magazine.[23]

Many people share a living arrangement the government calls *POSSLQ*, which stands for Persons of Opposite Sex Sharing Living Quarters. Like Amanda and Orlando, this situation is increasingly common. Nearly half of Americans aged 25 to 40 have at some point lived with a person of the opposite sex.[24] These changes are part of a broader shift toward nonfamily and childless households. It is projected that by 2010 there will be an increase of 7.4 million childless married-couple households, 6.4 new single-person households, 2.4 million more mixed-family situations, 1.2 million more single parents, 1.1 million more roommate households, and a decrease of 1.5 million married couples with children under 18.[25]

The National Center of Health Statistics confirms that the percentage of women of childbearing age who define themselves as *voluntarily childless* is on the rise: from 2.4 percent in 1982, to 4.3 percent in 1990, to 6.6 percent in 1995 (the most recent available figure). Childless couples are an attractive market segment

Marketing Opportunity

Coca-Cola executives in the U.K. realized that many of their hard-core consumers don't live in traditional families. The company's research found that a majority of British households were either childless couples or single people, many of them sharing a home with a roommate because of rising housing costs. To meet this need, Coke introduced a "share-size" bottle (1.25 liter) to make it easier for two roommates to share their soft drinks in the same way a traditional family would share a larger bottle. A clever advertising campaign depicts people sharing various products. One poster shows a young man and woman wearing a huge, stretched pair of underwear while another features two middle-aged men sharing a slimy-looking toupee. The ads read, "New share size Coke. For those who like to share."[34]

for some companies (obviously not for others like Gerber Baby Food). Two-income couples without children are better educated than two-income couples with children. According to the U.S. Census Bureau, 30 percent of childless couples consist of two college graduates, compared with 17 percent of those with kids. The childless are more likely to have professional or managerial occupations (24 percent versus 16 percent of dual-employed couples with children). Dave and Buster's, a Dallas-based restaurant chain, caters to this group by enforcing strict policies meant to deter families with small children. However, many childless couples feel they are snubbed by a child-oriented society. In recent years, they have formed several networking organizations such as Child-Free by Choice (*www.childfree.net*) and No Kidding! to support this lifestyle choice.[26]

Who's Living at Home?

Although traditional families are shrinking, ironically in other cases the traditional extended family is very much a reality. Many adults are caring for their own parents as well as for their children. In fact, Americans on average spend 17 years caring for children, but 18 years assisting aged parents.[27] Middle-aged people have been termed "the sandwich generation" because they must attend to those above and below them in age. In addition to dealing with live-in parents, many adults are surprised to find that their children are living with them longer or are moving back in well after their "lease" has expired.[28] As an Argentinean jeans ad asked, "If you are over 20 and still live with your parents, this is wrong. Isn't it high time you started looking for an apartment for them?"

Demographers call these returnees **boomerang kids**. The number of children between 18 and 34 living at home is growing dramatically, and today more than one-fifth of 25-year-old Americans still live with their parents. Young adults who do leave the nest to live by themselves are relatively unlikely to return, whereas those who move in with roommates are more likely to come back. And, young people who move in with a romantic partner are more likely than average to end up back home if the relationship fails![29] If this trend continues, it will affect a variety of markets as boomerang kids spend less on housing and staples and more on discretionary purchases like entertainment.

Animals Are People Too! Nonhuman Family Members

Companion animals often are treated as family members. Many people assume pets share our emotions—perhaps that helps to explain why more than three-quarters of domestic cats and dogs receive presents on holidays and birthdays.[30] More than half of all U.S. households (62 percent) have at least one pet—92 percent of pet owners consider their furry friends to be members of the family—and 83 percent call themselves "Mommy" or "Daddy" when talking to their animals.[31]

In fact, lawmakers in Colorado are pushing legislation that would elevate the status of cats and dogs from property to companions—if it passes, pet owners could sue veterinarians and animal abusers for "loss of companionship" for up to $100,000. The state is among 14 in the United States that already legally recognize cats and dogs as beneficiaries, allowing people to leave their money and property to their furry friends.[32]

Americans spend about $29 billion per year to make these family members happy. Following are some ways they're doing it.

- Some manufacturers recognize that pet owners consider themselves parents, so they're looking to human children's playthings for inspiration. Hasbro, a toy company, teamed up with pet superstore PetSmart to launch a line of products called Paws 'N More, which includes such toys as Puppy's First Key Teether and Catch-a-Fish Mobile for Cats.[33]
- The Los Angeles Kennel Club pampers pets in a theme-decorated cottage with a bed, a TV, and a VCR stocked with doggie videos. Pets can also mingle with other

This Spanish public service ad promotes pet sterilization via a fake ad for dog condoms.

dogs for story time and a pupcorn snack. Exercise classes and massage are also available. And what should the well-turned-out pet wear to the kennel? At the Petigree shop operated by Macy's department store, you can buy pink satin party dresses and black dinner jackets for the proper pooch.

● Car manufacturers are figuring out that people like to travel with their animals in tow. Saab offers a full line of pet-friendly accessories including seat-belt restraints and a travel bowl that prevents spilling. General Motors is developing its Pet Pro concept for the GMC Envoy. The SUV will feature rear storage units customized for pet supplies and an integrated vacuum cleaner and dog ramp that slides out of the rear cargo area to help older dogs who may have difficulty climbing aboard.

● And what happens when that companion goes to the great kennel in the sky? One trend is to freeze-dry the departed pet rather than bury it or cremate it. The bereaved say turning furry friends into perma-pets helps them deal with loss and maintain a connection to their former companions. Once dried, the animal's body doesn't decay, so it can continue to occupy that special place on the couch.

The Family Life Cycle

A family's needs and expenditures are affected by factors such as the number of people (children and adults) in the family, their ages, and whether one, two, or more adults are employed outside of the home. Two important factors that determine how a couple spends time and money are: (1) whether they have children; and (2) whether the woman works.

   Recognizing that family needs and expenditures change over time, marketers apply the **family life cycle (FLC)** concept to segment households. The FLC combines trends in income and family composition with the changes in demands placed upon this income. As we age, our preferences and needs for products and activities tend to change. Households headed by twentysomethings spend less than

Motorola recognizes the new, mobile lifestyles of many modern families. The company positions its paging products to meet the needs of on-the-go parents.

Choices of living environments provide a useful reflection of changing patterns and preferences in everyday life. The average new single-family home in the United States grew from 1,645 sq. ft. in 1975 to 2,095 sq. ft. in 1995. Americans increasingly prefer homes with privacy, but common living space in the home is growing in popularity. People do more of their living in the kitchen, and formal areas are losing ground. These are being replaced by great rooms that accommodate multiple family activities in one location. When people are asked to design their dream home, common responses include a state-of-the-art kitchen, fireplace, in-ground pool, and Jacuzzi. Women want walk-in closets; men want a game/billiard room, a workshop, or a high-tech entertainment center.

average on most products and services because their households are small and their incomes are low. Income levels tend to rise (at least until retirement), so that people can afford more over time. Older consumers spend more per capita on luxury items like gourmet foods and upscale home furnishings.[35] In addition, many purchases that must be made at an early age do not have to be repeated very often. For example, we tend to accumulate durable goods such as large appliances and only replace them as necessary.

A life-cycle approach to the study of the family assumes that pivotal events alter role relationships and trigger new stages of life that alter our priorities. These events include couples such as Amanda and Orlando moving in together, the birth of a first child, the departure of the last child from the house, the death of a spouse, retirement of the principal wage earner, and possibly divorce.[36] Movement through these life stages is indeed accompanied by significant changes in expenditures in leisure, food, durables, and services, even after the figures have been adjusted to reflect changes in income.[37]

FLC Models

This focus on longitudinal changes in priorities is particularly valuable in predicting demand for specific product categories over time. For example, the money spent by a couple with no children on dinners out and vacations will probably be diverted for quite different purchases after the birth of a child. Ironically, although the entertainment industry focuses on winning the hearts and wallets of young consumers, it's the senior citizens who have become America's true party animals. The average household headed by a 65- to 74-year-old spends more on entertainment than does the average household headed by a person under age 25.[38]

A number of models have been proposed to describe family life-cycle stages, but their usefulness has been limited because in many cases they have failed to take into account such important social trends as the changing role of women, the acceleration of alternative lifestyles, childless and delayed-child marriages, and single-parent households.

This ad by a furniture manufacturer specifically refers to stages in the family life cycle.

Four variables are necessary to adequately describe these changes: (1) age; (2) marital status; (3) the presence or absence of children in the home; and (4) the ages of children, if present. In addition, our definition of marital status must be relaxed to include any couple living together in a long-term relationship. Thus, although roommates might not be considered "married," a man and woman who have established a household would be, as would two homosexual men who have a similar understanding.

When these changes are considered, this approach allows us to identify a set of categories that include many more types of family situations.[39] Figure 12.1 shows that these categories divide consumers into groups in terms of age, whether there is more than one adult present, and whether there are children at home. For example, it makes a distinction between the consumption needs of people in the Full Nest I category (in which the youngest child is less than six), the Full Nest II category (in which the youngest child is older than six), the Full Nest III category (in which the youngest child is older than six and the parents are middle-aged), and the Delayed Full Nest (in which the parents are middle-aged but the youngest child is younger than six).

■ **FIGURE 12.1** FAMILY LIFE CYCLE

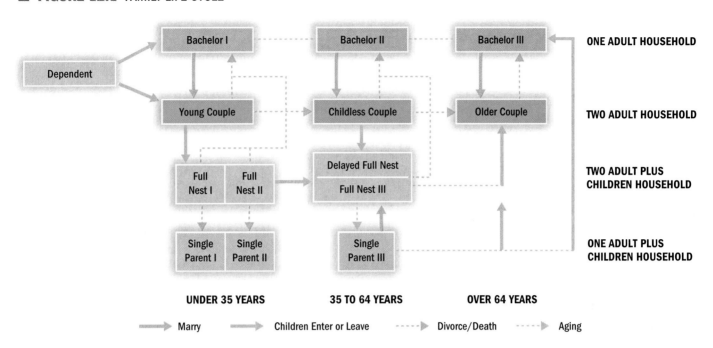

Source: Robert E. Wilkes, "Household Life-cycle Stages, Transitions, and Product Expenditures," *Journal of Consumer Research 22* (June 1995): 29. Published by the University of Chicago Press. Used with permission.

Life-Cycle Effects on Buying

Consumers classified into these categories show marked differences in consumption patterns. Young bachelors and newlyweds have the most "modern" sex-role attitudes, are the most likely to exercise, to go out to bars, concerts, movies, and restaurants, and to drink alcohol. Although people in their twenties account for less than 4 percent of all household spending in the United States, their expenditures are well above average in such categories as apparel, electronics, and gasoline.[40] Families with young children are more likely to consume health foods such as fruit, juice, and yogurt; those made up of single parents and older children buy more junk foods. The dollar value of homes, cars, and other durables is lowest for bachelors and single parents, but increases as people go through the full nest and childless couple stages. Perhaps reflecting the bounty of wedding gifts, newlyweds are the most likely to own appliances such as toaster ovens and electric coffee grinders. Babysitter and day care usage is, of course, highest among single-parent and full nest households, whereas home maintenance services (e.g., lawn mowing) are most likely to be employed by older couples and bachelors. Now, let's review how these different households make all of these decisions in the first place.

■ THE INTIMATE CORPORATION: FAMILY DECISION MAKING

The decision process within a household unit resembles a business conference. Certain matters are put on the table for discussion, different members may have different priorities and agendas, and there may be power struggles to rival any tale of corporate intrigue. In just about every living situation, whether a conventional family, students sharing a sorority house or apartment, or some other nontraditional arrangement, group members seem to take on different roles just as purchasing agents, engineers, account executives, and others do within a company.

Household Decisions

An understanding of household decision making dynamics is important for marketers. For example, when Chevrolet wanted to win drivers over to its new Venture minivan, the company sent teams of anthropologists to observe families in their natural habitats. Conventional wisdom says that minivan buyers are practical; they care about affordability, lots of features, and plenty of room. But these researchers discovered a different story: People see the vehicles as part of the family. When consumers were asked to identify the best metaphor for a minivan, many picked a photo of a hang glider because it represents freedom and families on the go. The advertising slogan for the Venture became: "Let's go."[41]

Families make two basic types of decisions.[42] In a **consensual purchase decision**, members agree on the desired purchase, differing only in terms of how it will be achieved. In these circumstances, the family will most likely engage in problem solving and consider alternatives until the means for satisfying the group's goal is found. For example, a household considering adding a dog to the family but concerned about who will take care of it might draw up a chart assigning individuals to specific duties.

Unfortunately, life is not always so easy. In an **accommodative purchase decision**, group members have different preferences or priorities and cannot agree on a purchase that will satisfy the minimum expectations of all involved. It is here that bargaining, coercion, compromise, and the wielding of power are all likely to be used to achieve agreement on what to buy or who gets to use it. Conflict occurs when there is not complete correspondence in family members' needs and preferences. Although money is the most common source of conflict between marriage partners, TV-viewing choices come in a close second![43] In general, decisions will involve conflict among family members to the extent that they are somehow important or novel, or if individuals have strong opinions about good and bad alternatives. The degree to which these factors generate conflict determines the type of decision the family will make.[44] Some specific factors determining the degree of family decision conflict include the following:[45]

- *Interpersonal need* (a person's level of investment in the group): A teenager may care more about what his or her family buys for the house than will a college student who is temporarily living in a dorm.
- *Product involvement and utility* (the degree to which the product in question will be used or will satisfy a need): A family member who is an avid coffee drinker will obviously be more interested in the purchase of a new coffeemaker than a similar expenditure for some other item.
- *Responsibility* (for procurement, maintenance, payment, and so on): People are more likely to have disagreements about a decision if it entails long-term consequences and commitments. For example, a family decision about getting a dog may involve conflict regarding who will be responsible for walking it and feeding it.
- *Power* (or the degree to which one family member exerts influence over the others in making decisions): In traditional families, the husband tends to have more power than the wife, who in turn has more than the oldest child, and so on. In family decisions, conflict can arise when one person continually uses the power he or she has within the group to satisfy his or her priorities. For example, if a child believed that his life would end if he did not receive an XBox for his birthday, he might be more willing to resort to extreme tactics to influence his parents, perhaps by throwing a tantrum or refusing to participate in family chores.

Sex Roles and Decision Making Responsibilities

Who "wears the pants" in the family? Sometimes it's not obvious which spouse makes the decisions. Indeed, although many men still wear the pants, it's women who buy them. When Haggar's research showed that nearly half of married women bought pants for their husbands without them being present, the firm started advertising its menswear products in women's magazines.[46] When one family member chooses a product, this is called an **autonomic decision**. In traditional households, for example, men often have sole responsibility for selecting a car, whereas decorating choices fall to women. **Syncratic decisions**, such as choosing a vacation destination, are made jointly. According to a study conducted by Roper Starch Worldwide, wives still tend to have the most say when buying groceries, children's toys, clothes, and medicines. Syncratic decisions are common for cars, vacations, homes, appliances, furniture, home electronics, interior design, and long-distance phone services. As the couple's education increases, more decisions are likely to be made together.[47] Roper sees signs of a shift in marital decision making toward more compromise and turn-taking. For example, the survey firm finds that wives tend to win out in arguments about how the house is kept while husbands get control of the remote![48]

In any case, spouses typically exert significant influence on decision making—even after one of them has died. An Irish study found that many widows claim to sense the continued presence of their dead husbands, and to conduct "conversations" with them about household matters![49] Comments from married women who participated in focus groups conducted for *Redbook* magazine illustrate some of the dynamics of autonomic versus syncratic decision making:

- "We just got our steps done and that was a big project. The contractor would talk (to my husband) and not talk to me. And I said, 'Excuse me, I'm here, too.'"
- "We are looking for a house now, and we're making decisions on which side of town we want it on, what size house do we want, and it's a together decision. That's never how my mother did it."
- "My husband did not want a van, because we have just one child, but I said, 'I want a van. And it's not because everyone else has a van. I want comfort.' He wanted a convertible. And we got a van."[50]

Identifying the Decision Maker

Figuring out who makes buying decisions is an important issue for marketers because this information tells them who to target and whether they need to reach both spouses to influence a choice. For example, when marketing research in the 1950s indicated that women were playing a larger role in household purchasing decisions, lawn mower manufacturers began to emphasize the rotary mower over other power mowers. Rotary mowers, which conceal the cutting blades and engine, were shown in ads featuring young women and smiling grandmothers cutting the grass, to downplay fears of injuries.[51]

Researchers have paid special attention to which spouse plays the role of the **family financial officer (FFO)**, the individual who keeps track of the family's bills and decides how any surplus funds will be spent. Among newlyweds, this role tends to be played jointly, and then over time one spouse or the other takes over these responsibilities.[52] In traditional families (and especially those with low educational levels), women are primarily responsible for family financial management—the man makes it, and the woman spends it. Each spouse "specializes" in certain activities.[53]

The pattern is different among families in which spouses adhere to more modern sex-role norms. These couples believe that there should be shared participation in family maintenance activities. In these cases, husbands assume more responsibility for laundering, housecleaning, grocery shopping, and so on, in addition to such traditionally "male" tasks as home maintenance and garbage removal.[54] Shared decision making is becoming the norm for most American couples today—a recent Roper poll reported that 94 percent of partnered women say they make the decision or share equally in home furnishings selections (not a huge surprise), but in addition, 81 percent said the same for financial savings/investments and 74 percent participate in deciding what car to buy.[55]

In the **female** the ability to match colors comes at an early age.

In the **male** it comes when he marries a female.

The City Casuals three-button, crepe jacket, 100% cotton, French-yarn shirt, Bedford cord pants, and a touch of color.

HAGGAR
Stuff you can work with.

Although many men still wear the pants in the family, it's women who buy them. Haggar is redirecting $8 million worth of advertising to target women who shop for and with men. The apparel manufacturer placed menswear ads in about a dozen women's magazines after its research found that women exert tremendous influence over men's clothing choices. In a survey, nearly half of the females polled had purchased men's pants without the man present, and 41 percent said they accompanied the man when he bought pants. Female influence is strongest for decisions involving the matching of colors and the mixing/matching of separates.

Decision-making responsibilities continue to evolve, especially as women continue to work outside the home and have less time to do the duties traditionally assigned to them. These working mothers often struggle with what one researcher has called the "juggling lifestyle," a frenzied, guilt-ridden compromise between conflicting cultural ideals of motherhood and professionalism.[56] Figure 12.2 shows four distinct mother types identified in a study by LeoShe, a unit of the Leo Burnett advertising agency that focuses on marketing to women.[57]

● *June Cleaver, the Sequel:* Women who maintain the traditional roles of stay-at-home moms. They are mostly white, highly educated, and upscale.
● *Tug of War:* Women who are forced to work but who aren't happy about it. They tend to be strapped for time, so they buy well-known brand names to make shopping easier.
● *Strong Shoulders:* Women who are in lower-income levels but who have a positive view of themselves and their future. More than one-third of the women in this segment are single moms. LeoShe concludes that they are good candidates to try new brands that will help them express themselves.
● *Mothers of Invention:* These women enjoy motherhood and also work out of the home. One reason for their contentment is that their husbands pitch in a lot.

Cultural background plays a big role in determining whether husbands or wives are dominant in the family unit. For example, husbands tend to be more dominant in decision making among couples with a strong Hispanic ethnic identification. Vietnamese-Americans also are more likely to adhere to the traditional model: The man makes the decision for any large purchase, whereas the woman is given a budget to manage the home. In a study comparing marital decision making in the United States and China, American women reported more "wife decides" sit-

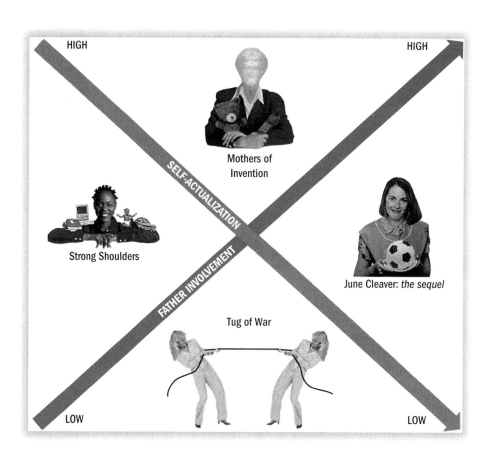

■ **FIGURE 12.2**
LEO MOTHER TYPES

Source: Cristina Merrill, "Mother's Work is Never Done," *American Demographics* (September 1999): 30. Reprinted with permission from *American Demographics*.

uations than did the Chinese. Assumptions about "who's the boss" often are reflected in advertising and marketing strategies. Following are a few examples to illustrate some cross-cultural differences.[58]

● The Coca-Cola Company developed a campaign to appeal to Latin American women based on a big research project the company conducted in Brazil. It found that a motherly female kangaroo was most likely to appeal to women shopping for their families—who happen to account for 80 percent of Coke's $3.5 billion Brazilian sales. The ads were themed "Mom knows everything," after women in focus groups said they felt the media neglected them even though they were responsible for purchasing all the products in their households.

● A program in India called Butterfly enlists village medicine men to convince local women to take birth control pills. A big obstacle is that women are not accustomed to making these decisions for themselves. The response of one village resident is typical: "I have never taken contraceptives. My husband is my master—he will decide."

● The traditional sex-role norms prevalent in India also influenced a commercial Procter & Gamble produced for its Ariel laundry detergent. A man named Ravi is shown doing the laundry, which is highly unusual in that country. A female voice questions, "Where's the wife? Are you actually going to wash them? . . . a man should not wash clothes . . . [he is] sure to fail."

● Ads showing men doing housework are risky in Asia as well, even though more Asian women are working outside the home. A South Korean vacuum cleaner ad showed a woman lying on the floor giving herself a facial with slices of cucumber while her husband vacuums around her. Women there didn't appreciate this ad. As a local ad executive put it, they regarded the ad a challenge to "the leadership of women in the home."

TABLE 12.2
DIVISION OF HOUSEHOLD TASKS IN THE UNITED KINGDOM

Division of Household Tasks, 1994	Always the Woman	Usually the Woman	About Equal or Both Together	Usually the Man	Always the Man	All Couples
Washing and ironing	47	32	18	1	1	100
Deciding what to have for dinner	27	32	35	3	1	100
Looking after sick family members	22	26	45	–	–	100
Shopping for groceries	20	21	52	4	1	100
Small repairs around the house	2	3	18	49	25	100

Source: Nicholas Timmins, "New Man Fails to Survive into the Nineties," *The Independent*, January 25, 1996.

Four factors appear to determine the degree to which decisions will be made jointly or by one or the other spouse:[59]

- *Sex-role stereotypes:*   Couples who believe in traditional sex-role stereotypes tend to make individual decisions for sex-typed products (i.e., those considered to be "masculine" or "feminine").
- *Spousal resources:*   The spouse who contributes more resources to the family has the greater influence.
- *Experience:*   Couples who have gained experience as a decision-making unit make individual decisions more frequently.
- *Socioeconomic status:*   Middle-class families make more joint decisions than do either higher- or lower-class families.

With many women now working outside of the home, men are participating more in housekeeping activities. In one-fifth of American homes, men do most of the shopping, and nearly one-fifth of men do at least seven loads of laundry a week.[60] Still, as Amanda discovered to her chagrin, women continue to do the lion's share of household chores. Ironically, this even appears to be true when the woman's outside income actually exceeds that of her husband's![61]

On the other hand, recent evidence indicates that women are gaining more influence in the decision-making process overall.[62] As shown in Table 12.2, a similar situation exists in other Western countries such as the United Kingdom. Overall, the degree to which a couple adheres to traditional sex-role norms determines how much their allocation of responsibilities, including consumer decision making, will fall along traditional lines.

Despite recent changes in decision-making responsibilities, women are still primarily responsible for the continuation of the family's **kin-network system**: They perform the rituals intended to maintain ties among family members, both immediate and extended. This function includes activities such as coordinating visits among relatives, calling and writing family members, sending greeting cards, and arranging social engagements.[63] This organizing role means that women often make important decisions about the family's leisure activities, and they are more likely to decide with whom the family will socialize.

Heuristics in Joint Decision Making

The **synoptic ideal** calls for the husband and wife to take a common view and act as joint decision makers. According to this ideal, they would very thoughtfully weigh alternatives, assign one another well-defined roles, and calmly make mutually ben-

Women often manage many tasks within the family that pull them in many directions.

eficial consumer decisions. The couple would act rationally, analytically, and use as much information as possible to maximize joint utility. In reality, however, spousal decision making is often characterized by the use of influence or methods that are likely to reduce conflict. A couple "reaches" rather than "makes" a decision. Researchers simply describe this process as "muddling through."[64]

One common technique for simplifying the decision making process is the use of *heuristics* (see Chapter 9). Some decision-making patterns frequently observed when a couple makes decisions in buying a new house illustrate the use of heuristics:

1 The couple's areas of common preference are based on salient, objective dimensions rather than subtler, hard-to-define cues. For example, a couple may easily agree on the number of bedrooms they need in the new home, but will have more difficulty achieving a common view of how the home should look.

2 The couple agrees on a system of *task specialization* in which each is responsible for certain duties or decision areas and does not interfere on the other's "turf." For many couples, these assignments are likely to be influenced by their perceived sex roles. For example, the wife may scout out houses that meet their requirements in advance, and the husband determines whether the couple can obtain a mortgage.

3 Concessions are based on the intensity of each spouse's preferences. One spouse will yield to the influence of the other in many cases simply because his or her level of preference for a certain attribute is not particularly intense, whereas in other situations he or she will be willing to exert effort to obtain a favorable decision.[65] In cases where intense preferences for different attributes exist, rather than attempt to influence each other, spouses will "trade off" a less-intense preference for a more strongly felt one. For example, a husband who is somewhat indifferent about kitchen design may give in to his wife, but expect that in turn he will be allowed to design his own garage workshop.

■ CHILDREN AS DECISION MAKERS: CONSUMERS-IN-TRAINING

It's hard to find an adult in Helsinki (home to the Finnish company Nokia) who doesn't have a cell phone—92 percent of its households have at least one, if not several. But, while the phones have been an accepted part of daily life for grownups and teenagers for over a decade, the latest boom in phone use is occurring among little kids. Many of them get their first phone at age seven or so when they start to engage in activities like soccer practice where their parents aren't present.

Now, there's an expanding market for accessories like phone covers decorated with pictures of Donald Duck or Star Wars characters, even though Finland has very strict laws about how products can be pitched to children. Because they are forbidden to market directly to kids, companies try to convince their parents that the phones are an essential child-rearing tool in a society where most parents work. They argue that "mobile parenting" lets Mom or Dad keep track of their kids by telephone rather than in person and in return Finnish kids get a head start on using an adult product.[66]

The Finns are not the only ones who bend over backwards to please their kids with loads of "stuff." Anyone who has had the "delightful" experience of grocery shopping with children in tow knows that kids often have a say (sometimes a loud, whiney one) in what their parents buy.[67] Children make up three distinct markets.[68]

Primary Market. Kids spend a lot on their own wants and needs. In 1991 the typical allowance of a 10-year-old was $4.20 a week, and by 1997 this weekly stipend had risen to $6.13. And, on average an allowance is only 45 percent of a kid's income. The rest comes from money earned for doing household chores and gifts from relatives. About one-third of this goes to food and beverages with the balance spent on toys, apparel, movies, and games. When marketers at M&Ms candy figured out who was actually buying a lot of their products, they redesigned vending machines with coin slots lower to the ground to accommodate shorter people, and sales went up dramatically. Even hip-hop artists are getting into the action: A new children's book and CD series titled "Hip-Kid Hop" features rhyming stories by LL Cool J and Doug E. Fresh.[69]

Influence Market. **Parental yielding** occurs when a parental decision maker is influenced by a child's request and "surrenders."[70] This is a key driver of product selections because about 90 percent of requests to a parent are by brand name. In recognition of this influence, Mrs. Butterworth's Syrup created a $6 million campaign to target kids directly with humorous ads that show the lengths adults will go to get the syrup bottle

**TABLE 12.3
KIDS' INFLUENCE ON HOUSEHOLD PURCHASES**

Top 10 Selected Products	Industry Sales (Billions)	Influence Factor (%)	Sales Influence (Billions)
Fruit snacks	0.30	80	0.24
Frozen novelties	1.40	75	1.05
Kids' beauty aids	1.20	70	0.84
Kids' fragrances	0.30	70	0.21
Toys	13.40	70	9.38
Canned pasta	0.57	60	0.34
Kids' clothing	18.40	60	11.04
Video games	3.50	60	2.10
Hot cereals	0.74	50	0.37
Kids' shoes	2.00	50	1.00

Source: "Charting the Children's Market," *Adweek* [February 10, 1992]: 42. Reprinted with permission of James U. McNeal, Texas A&M University, College Station, Texas.

to talk to them. An executive who worked on the campaign explained, "We needed to create the nag factor [where kids demand their parents buy the product]."[71]

The likelihood that yielding will occur partly depends upon the dynamics within a particular family. As we all know, parental styles range from permissive to strict, and they also vary in terms of the amount of responsibility children are given to make decisions.[72] One study documented the strategies kids use to request purchases. Although most children simply asked for things, some other common tactics included saying they had seen it on TV, saying that a sibling or friend has it, or doing chores in return. Other actions were less innocuous; they included directly placing the object in the cart and continuous pleading—often a "persuasive" behavior![73] In addition, the amount of influence children have over consumption is culturally determined. Children who live in individualistic cultures such as the United States have more direct influence, whereas kids in collective cultures like Japan get their way more indirectly.[74] Table 12.3 documents kids' influence in 10 different product categories.

Future Market. Kids have a way of growing up to be adults (eventually), and savvy marketers try to lock in brand loyalty at an early age. That explains why Kodak is working so hard to encourage kids to become photographers. Currently, only 20 percent of children aged 5 to 12 own cameras, and they shoot an average of just one roll of film a year. The company produces ads that portray photography as a cool pursuit and as a form of rebellion. Cameras are packaged with an envelope to mail the film directly back so parents can't see the photos.

Indeed, many of the allegiances we form to products as children do stay with us as we age. This tendency is especially pronounced in Japan, where the culture encourages adults to act like kids. The Japanese are obsessed with "cute" images and products that may strike some Americans as a bit, well, juvenile. All Nippon Airways spent about $1 million in licensing fees and paint to decorate the exterior of three of its 747s with 24-foot-high pocket monsters from Pokémon. Cute characters abound in Japan, including the image of Miffy the bunny on Asahi Bank ATM cards and Hello Kitty charm bags at Shinto shrines. When a Japanese baseball player hits a home run, he is awarded a stuffed animal. Some explain this obsession by noting that the Japanese miss childhood because adulthood in Japan is so demanding and there is such pressure to conform.[75]

The Tangled Web

The number of children under age 12 who have access to the Internet will grow to 26.9 million by 2005.[83] There's certainly nothing wrong with that, but the big question is what are they doing once they leave the playground for cyberspace? In late 2002, Congress passed legislation creating a special Internet domain called *kids.us.* Companies wishing to register there would have to agree to display only child-friendly material; they would be prohibited from linking to Internet sites outside the children's area and instant messaging or chat rooms also would be banned unless they are certified as safe.[84]

That's a positive step, but it only addresses part of the problem: Adults have been concerned about violent kids' games for a long time, but now the debate is intensifying as children as young as six spend their leisure time in arcades called PC rooms playing games like *Half-Life: Counter-Strike* with others around the world using high-speed Internet connections. PC rooms let kids compete in teams, and form little armies that search, strategize, and destroy. These locales typically don't check players' ages or limit their access to games like *Half-Life* that are supposed to be restricted to players 17 and older. The rooms began to pop up in the United States a few years ago after first catching on in a big way in Asia. The earliest ones were makeshift; kids would gather at warehouses and hook their computers together to play.

Now, there are hundreds of PC rooms around the country, with the heaviest concentration in tech-savvy Los Angeles and San Francisco. So far, efforts to police the games are about as successful as those trying to restrict kids from buying games with inappropriate content—a Federal Trade Commission study that was based on an undercover survey found that 78 percent of unaccompanied customers aged 13 to 16 who tried to buy M-rated (mature) games at retail outlets were successful.[85]

Consumer Socialization

We've seen that kids are responsible for a lot of marketplace activity, but how do they know what they like and want? Children do not spring from the womb with consumer skills already in memory. **Consumer socialization** is the process "by which young people acquire skills, knowledge, and attitudes relevant to their functioning in the marketplace."[76] Where does this knowledge come from? Friends and teachers certainly participate in this process. For instance, children talk to one another about consumer products, and this tendency increases with age.[77] Especially for young children, though, the two primary socialization sources are the family and the media.

Influence of Parents

Parents' influences in consumer socialization are both direct and indirect. They deliberately try to instill their own values about consumption in their children ("You're going to learn the value of a dollar"). Parents also determine the degree to which their children will be exposed to other information sources, such as television, salespeople, and peers.[78] Cultural expectations regarding the involvement of children in purchase decisions influence when and how parents socialize their kids as consumers. For example, parents in traditional cultures like Greece and India hold later development timetables for consumer-related skills and understanding advertising practices than do American and Australian parents.[79]

Grownups also serve as significant models for observational learning (see Chapter 3). Children learn about consumption by watching their parents' behavior and imitating it. Marketers encourage this process by packaging adult products in child versions. This "passing down" of product preferences helps to create brand loyalty; researchers find evidence of intergenerational influence when they study the product choices of mothers and their daughters.[80]

The process of consumer socialization begins with infants, who accompany their parents to stores where they are initially exposed to marketing stimuli. Within the first two years, children begin to make requests for desired objects. As kids learn to walk, they also begin to make their own selections when they are in stores. By around the age of five, most kids are making purchases with the help of parents and grandparents, and by eight most are making independent purchases and have become full-fledged consumers.[81] Figure 12.3 summarizes the sequence of steps involved in turning kids into consumers.

Three dimensions combine to produce different "segments" of parental styles. Parents characterized by certain styles have been found to socialize their children differently.[82] For example, "authoritarian parents" are hostile, restrictive, and emotionally uninvolved. They do not have warm relationships with their children, they censor the types of media to which their children are exposed, and they tend to have negative views about advertising. "Neglecting parents" also do not have warm relationships, but they are more detached from their children and do not exercise much control over what their children do. In contrast, "indulgent parents" communicate more with their children about consumption-related matters and are less restrictive. They believe that children should be allowed to learn about the marketplace without much interference.

Television: "The Electric Babysitter"

Advertising's influence over us begins at a very early age. As we've seen, many marketers start to push their products on kids to encourage them to build a habit at an early age. One recent, controversial exception recently occurred in France, where a McDonald's ad placed in the magazine *Femme Actuelle* actually encouraged parents to limit kids' visits to its outlets by proclaiming, "there is no reason to eat excessive amounts of junk food, nor go more than once a week to McDonald's." A spokesman for McDonald's in the United States said the company did not agree with the views expressed in the ad.[87] This anti-consumption message is certainly a notable exception to the barrage of messages aimed at kids, especially on television. Because the media teach people about a culture's values, the more a child is exposed to television, whether the show is *The Osbournes* or *SpongeBob Squarepants,* the more he or she will accept the images depicted there as real.[88] A British TV show called *Teletubbies* targets viewers from three months to two years old. The show has become a national obsession, attracting viewers from more than 20 countries every weekday morning. A Teletubbie record even sold enough copies to make it to the number one spot on the British charts.[89]

In addition to the large volume of programming targeted directly to children, kids are also exposed to idealized images of what it is like to be an adult. Because children over the age of six do about a quarter of their television viewing during prime time, they are affected by programs and commercials targeted to adults. For example, young girls exposed to adult lipstick commercials learn to associate lipstick with beauty.[90]

Sex-Role Socialization

Children pick up on the concept of gender identity (see Chapter 5) at an earlier age than was previously believed—perhaps as young as age one or two. By the age of three, most children categorize driving a truck as masculine and cooking and cleaning as feminine.[91] Even cartoon characters portrayed as helpless are more likely to wear frilly or ruffled dresses.[92] Toy companies perpetuate these stereotypes by promoting gender-linked toys with commercials that reinforce sex-role expectations through their casting, emotional tone, and copy.[93]

One function of child's play is to rehearse for adulthood. Children "act out" different roles they might assume later in life and learn about the expectations others have of them. The toy industry provides the props children use to perform these roles.[94] Depending on which side of the debate you're on, these toys either reflect or teach children about what society expects of males and females. Preschool boys

Marketing Opportunity

Many retailers are trying to attract parents by offering environments where kids and grownups can feel at home. Home Depot conducts weekly workshops for kids. About 30 Starbucks coffee shops nationwide have built kids' play areas to encourage Moms to gather there and drink coffee. Providing a place for kids to jump around while parents relax can pay off: A survey of Burger King customers found that 9 of 10 parents said they would return to Burger King so their children could play there.[86]

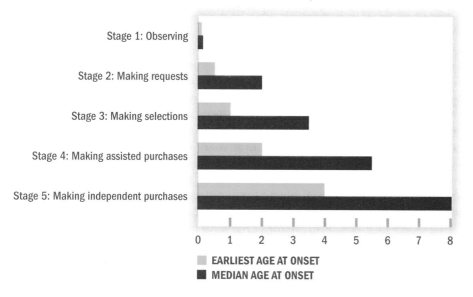

A CONSUMER IS BORN

Children start accompanying parents to the marketplace as early as one month old and begin to make independent purchases as early as four years old.

- Stage 1: Observing
- Stage 2: Making requests
- Stage 3: Making selections
- Stage 4: Making assisted purchases
- Stage 5: Making independent purchases

0 1 2 3 4 5 6 7 8

■ EARLIEST AGE AT ONSET
■ MEDIAN AGE AT ONSET

■ **FIGURE 12.3**
FIVE STAGES OF CONSUMER DEVELOPMENT BY EARLIEST AGE AT ONSET AND MEDIAN AGE AT ONSET

Marketing Pitfall

Are marketers robbing kids of their childhood? Young children have become the target of grown-up designers. As a spokesperson for Donna Karan observed, "These seven-year-olds are going on 30. A lot of them have their own sense of style." Maybe so, but perhaps one of the consequences is that they are forced to adopt adult values earlier than they should. One author of a book about kids complains, "We are seeing the deliberate teening of childhood. Parents are giving their kids a lot more choices on what to wear at ever younger ages. The advertisers know this, and they are exploiting the kids' longing to seem sophisticated and grown-up.... One of the great things about childhood in the U.S. used to be that kids were protected by the market and allowed to grow their own ideas. Now there is no time to be a kid separate from those pressures. You may have always had kids who are little princesses, but now there are eight-year-old boys that are extremely uptight if they don't get the right Abercrombie & Fitch sweatshirt." Maybe that explains why preteens now account for $200 million of the $3 billion mass-market sales of makeup; a survey of 8- to 12-year-old girls found that two-thirds regularly used cosmetics. So much for the Age of Innocence.[102]

and girls do not exhibit many differences in toy preferences, but after the age of five they part company: Girls tend to stick with dolls, whereas boys gravitate toward "action figures" and high-tech diversions.

Industry critics charge that this is because males dominate the toy industry, but toy company executives counter that they are simply responding to kids' natural preferences.[95] Indeed, after two decades of working to avoid boy-versus-girl stereotypes, many companies seem to have decided that differences are inevitable. Toys "R" Us unveiled a new store design after interviewing 10,000 customers, and the chain now has separate sections called Girls' World and Boys' World. According to the president of Fox Family Channel, "Boys and girls are different, and it's great to celebrate what's special about each."[96] Boys tend to be more interested in battle and competition; girls are more interested in creativity and relationships. This is what experts refer to as "male and female play patterns." Because kids in day care are exposed to other kids earlier than in the past, these patterns are being observed in younger children than used to be the case.[97]

Recognizing the powerful role toys play in consumer socialization, doll manufacturers are creating characters they hope will teach little girls about the real world—not the fantasy "bimbo" world that many dolls represent. Recently, a group of California entrepreneurs brought out a line of dolls called Smartees. These characters include Ashley the attorney, Emily the entrepreneur, and Destiny the doctor. A paperback tells each doll's story and includes a sample resume for a person who might have that job in real life. Not to be outdone, Barbie's recent rebirth as a career woman illustrates how a firm can take concerns about socialization to heart. Although the Barbie doll was introduced as an astronaut in 1964 and as an airline pilot in 1999, there was never much detail about the careers themselves—girls bought the uniform and accessories but they never learned about the professions represented. Now a Working Woman Barbie is on the market as the result of a partnership between Mattel and *Working Woman* magazine. She comes with a miniature computer and cell phone as well as a CD-ROM with information about understanding finances. She is dressed in a grey suit, but the skirt reverses to a red dress to be worn with red platform shoes for her after-work adventures with Ken.[98]

Cognitive Development

The ability of children to make mature, "adult" consumer decisions obviously increases with age (not that grown-ups always make mature decisions). Kids can be segmented by age in terms of their **stage of cognitive development**, or ability to comprehend concepts of increasing complexity. Some evidence indicates that very young children are able to learn consumption-related information surprisingly well.[99]

The foremost proponent of the idea that children pass through distinct stages of cognitive development was the Swiss psychologist Jean Piaget, who believed that each stage is characterized by a certain cognitive structure the child uses to handle information.[100] In one classic demonstration of cognitive development, Piaget poured the contents of a short, squat glass of lemonade into a taller, thinner glass. Five-year-olds, who still believed that the shape of the glass determined its contents, thought this glass held more liquid than the first glass. They are in what Piaget termed a *preoperational stage of development*. In contrast, six-year-olds tended to be unsure, but seven-year-olds knew the amount of lemonade had not changed.

Many developmental specialists no longer believe that children necessarily pass through these fixed stages at the same time. An alternative approach regards children as differing in information-processing capability, or ability to store and retrieve information from memory (see Chapter 3). The following three segments have been identified by this approach:[101]

- *Limited:* Below the age of six, children do not employ storage and retrieval strategies.
- *Cued:* Children between the ages of 6 and 12 employ these strategies, but only when prompted.
- *Strategic:* Children 12 and older spontaneously employ storage and retrieval strategies.

This sequence of development underscores the notion that children do not think in the same way adults do, and they cannot be expected to use information the same way. It also reminds us that they do not necessarily form the same conclusions as adults do when presented with product information. For example, kids are not as likely to realize that something they see on TV is not "real," and as a result they are more vulnerable to persuasive messages.

Marketing Research and Children

Despite children's buying power, relatively little real data on their preferences or influences on spending patterns is available. Compared to adults, kids are difficult subjects for market researchers. They tend to be undependable reporters of their own behavior, they have poor recall, and they often do not understand abstract questions.[103] This problem is compounded in Europe, where some countries restrict marketers' ability to interview children. Still, market research can pay off, and many companies, as well as a number of specialized firms, have been successful in researching some aspects of this segment.[104]

Product Testing

A particularly helpful type of research with children is product testing. Young subjects can provide a valuable perspective on what products will succeed with other kids. These insights are obtained either by watching kids play with toys or by involving them in focus groups. For example, the Fisher-Price Company maintains a nursery known as the Playlab. Children are chosen from a waiting list of 4,000 to play with new toys while staff members watch from behind a one-way mirror.[105]

Marketing Opportunity

Several new business ventures illustrate that using sound principles of consumer psychology can also make good financial sense. The trend started a long time ago with public television's *Sesame Street*, but today the for-profit networks are getting into the game as well. The first successful foray into the preschool market was *Blues' Clues* in 1996, which turned into a huge hit as viewers abandoned the smarmy *Barney & Friends* to share in the learning experiences.

Now, when millions of preschoolers tune into Nickelodeon's hit show *Dora the Explorer*, they don't realize that they are responding to content based upon "multiple-intelligence theory," an influential perspective first advanced in 1983 that argues for other types of intelligence, such as athletic prowess or musical ability, beyond the traditional math and verbal skills used to measure IQ. Thus, when Dora consults her map, she is promoting "spatial" skills. And when Dora asks her young viewers to help her count planks to build a bridge, she is building "interpersonal intelligence." To get on the educational bandwagon, Disney is launching a new channel called Playhouse Disney, built around what it calls the "whole-child curriculum" that promotes emotional, social, and cognitive development.[106] *P* is for profits.

Lego did research to learn how boys and girls play with its building toys. When executives watched girls play with the toys they noticed they were more likely to build living areas while boys tended to build cars. The company introduced a new version of its product called Paradisa to entice girls to buy more Legos. This set emphasizes the ability to build "socially oriented structures" such as homes, swimming pools, and stables. Sales to girls picked up, though the company still sells most of its sets to boys.

Family Fun magazine sponsors an annual Toy of the Year award to help the toy industry predict which new entries will be a hit or a bust. To do this, 100 children are selected to fill out questionnaires about toys they like and then are shown new toys in focus groups. Finally, the most popular toys are sent to day care centers, where other kids cast secret ballots.[107] This process works well; in the past the kids have successfully identified hot new toys including the huge hit Tickle Me Elmo.

Message Comprehension

Because children differ in their abilities to process product-related information, many serious ethical issues are raised when advertisers try to appeal directly to them.[108] Children's advocacy groups argue that kids under the age of seven do not understand the persuasive intent of commercials and younger children can not readily distinguish between a commercial and programming. Kids' cognitive defenses are not yet sufficiently developed to filter out commercial appeals, so in a sense altering their brand preferences may be likened to "shooting fish in a barrel," as one critic put it.[109] Beginning in the 1970s the Federal Trade Commission took some action to protect children, such as limiting commercials during "children's" programming (most often Saturday morning television) and requiring "separators" to help children discern when a program ended and a commercial began (e.g., "We'll be right back after these commercial messages"). The FTC reversed itself in the early 1980s during the deregulatory, pro-business climate of the Reagan administration. Although some of the restrictions were restored with the passage of the 1990 Children's Television Act, the new model of the child consumer that some have termed "kid kustomer" is not someone to be sheltered from the market, but one who should engage in its pleasures.[110] Figure 12.4 shows one attempt to assess whether kids can tell that a commercial is trying to persuade them.

■ **FIGURE 12.4**
THE SKETCHES USED TO MEASURE CHILDREN'S PERCEPTION OF THE INTENT OF COMMERCIALS

CHAPTER SUMMARY

- More than one person actually makes many purchasing decisions. Collective decision making occurs whenever two or more people are involved in evaluating, selecting, or using a product or service.

- Organizational buyers are people who make purchasing decisions on behalf of a company or other group. Although these buyers are influenced by many of the same factors that affect how they make decisions in their personal lives, organizational buying decisions tend to be more rationally based. They are also likely to involve more financial risk, and as they become more complex it is probable that a greater number of people will be involved in making the decision.

- The amount of cognitive effort that goes into organizational decisions is influenced by internal factors, such as the individuals' psychological characteristics, and by external factors, such as the company's willingness to tolerate risk. One of the most important determinants is the type of purchase being considered: The extent of problem solving required depends on whether the product or service to be procured is simply to be reordered (a straight rebuy), ordered with minor modifications (modified rebuy), or if it has never been purchased before or is complex and risky (new task). Online purchasing sites are revolutionizing the way organizational decision makers collect and evaluate product information in business-to-business (B2B) e-commerce.

- In organizations and in families, several different roles must be played during the decision-making process. These roles include the gatekeeper, influencers, buyers, and users.

- Demographics are statistics that measure a population's characteristics. Some of the most important of these relate to family structure (e.g., the birth rate, the marriage rate, and the divorce rate).

- A household is an occupied housing unit. The number and type of U.S. households is changing in many ways, including delays in getting married and having children, and in the composition of family households, which are increasingly headed by a single parent. New perspectives on the family life cycle, which focuses on how people's needs change as they move through different stages in their lives, are forcing marketers to more seriously consider consumer segments such as homosexuals, divorced persons, and childless couples when they develop targeting strategies.

- Families must be understood in terms of their decision-making dynamics. Spouses in particular have different priorities and exert varying amounts of influence in terms of effort and power. Children are also increasingly influential during a widening range of purchase decisions.

- Children undergo a process of socialization, whereby they learn how to be consumers. Parents and friends instill some of this knowledge, but a lot of it comes from exposure to mass media and advertising. Because children are in some cases so easily persuaded, the ethical aspects of marketing to them are hotly debated among consumers, academics, and marketing practitioners.

KEY TERMS

Accommodative purchase
  decision   418
Autonomic decision   419
Boomerang kids   412

Business-to-business (B2B)
  e-commerce   407
Business-to-business marketers   402
Buying center   404

Consensual purchase decision   418
Consumer socialization   426
Extended family   407
Family financial officer (FFO)   419

CONSUMER BEHAVIOR CHALLENGE

1 Do you think market research should be performed with children? Give the reasons for your answer.

2 What do you think of the practice of companies and survey firms collecting public data (e.g., from marriage licenses, birth records, or even death announcements) to compile targeted mailing lists? State your opinion from both a consumer's and a marketer's perspective.

3 Marketers have been criticized for donating products and services to educational institutions in exchange for free promotion. Is this a fair exchange, in your opinion, or should corporations be prohibited from attempting to influence youngsters in school?

4 For each of the following five product categories—groceries, automobiles, vacations, furniture, and appliances—describe the ways in which you believe a married couple's choices would be affected if they had children.

5 In identifying and targeting newly divorced couples, do you think marketers are exploiting these couples' situations? Are there instances in which you think marketers may actually be helpful to them? Support your answers with examples.

6 Arrange to interview two married couples, one younger and one older. Prepare a response form listing five product categories—groceries, furniture, appliances, vacations, and automobiles—and ask each spouse to indicate, without consulting the other, whether purchases in each category are made by joint or unilateral decisions, and to indicate whether the unilateral decisions are made by the husband or the wife. Compare each couple's responses for agreement between husbands and wives relative to who makes the decisions, and compare both couples' overall responses for differences relative to the number of joint versus unilateral decisions. Report your findings and conclusions.

7 Collect ads for three different product categories in which the family is targeted. Find another set of ads for different brands of the same items in which the family is not featured. Prepare a report comparing the probable effectiveness of the two approaches. Which specific categories would most likely benefit from a family emphasis?

8 Observe the interactions between parents and children in the cereal section of a local grocery store. Prepare a report on the number of children who expressed preferences, how they expressed their preferences, and how parents responded, including the number who purchased the child's choice.

9 Watch three hours of children's programming on commercial television stations. Evaluate the marketing techniques used in the commercials in terms of the ethical issues raised in the final section of this chapter. Report your findings and conclusions.

10 Select a product category, and using the life-cycle stages given in this chapter, list the variables that will affect a purchase decision for the product by consumers in each stage of the cycle.

11 Consider three important changes in modern family structure. For each, find an example of a marketer who has attempted to be conscious of this change as reflected in product communications, retailing innovations, or other aspects of the marketing mix. If possible, also try to find examples of marketers who have failed to keep up with these developments.

12 Industrial purchase decisions are totally rational. Aesthetic or subjective factors don't—and shouldn't—play a role in this process. Do you agree?

13 College students living away from home can be thought of as having a substitute "family." Whether you live with your parents, with a spouse, or with other students, how are decisions made in your college residence "family?" Do some people take on the role of mother or father or children? Give a specific example of a decision that had to be made and the roles that were played.

NOTES

1. See J. Joseph Cronin Jr. and Michael H. Morris, "Satisfying Customer Expectations; the Effect on Conflict and Repurchase Intentions in Industrial Marketing Channels," *Journal of the Academy of Marketing Science* 17 (Winter 1989): 41–49; Thomas W. Leigh and Patrick F. McGraw, "Mapping the Procedural Knowledge of Industrial Sales Personnel: A Script-Theoretic Investigation," *Journal of Marketing* 53 (January 1989): 16–34; William J. Qualls and Christopher P. Puto, "Organizational Climate and Decision Framing: An Integrated Approach to Analyzing Industrial Buying," *Journal of Marketing Research* 26 (May 1989): 179–92.

2. James M. Sinkula, "Market Information Processing and Organizational Learning," *Journal of Marketing* 58 (January 1994): 35–45.

3. Allen M. Weiss and Jan B. Heide, "The Nature of Organizational Search in High Technology Markets," *Journal of Marketing Research* 30 (May 1993): 220–33; Jennifer K. Glazing and Paul N. Bloom, "Buying Group Information Source Reliance," *Proceedings of the American Marketing Association Educators' Conference* (Summer 1994): 454.

4. B. Charles Ames and James D. Hlaracek, *Managerial Marketing for Industrial Firms* (New York: Random House Business Division, 1984); Edward F. Fern and James R. Brown, "The Industrial/Consumer Marketing Dichotomy: A Case of Insufficient Justification," *Journal of Marketing* 48 (Spring 1984): 68–77.

5. Kevin Keller, *Strategic Brand Management* (Upper Saddle River, NJ: Prentice Hall, 1998); Michael R. Solomon and Elnora W. Stuart, *Marketing: Real People, Real Choices*, 2nd ed. (Upper Saddle River, NJ: Prentice Hall, 2000).

6. Daniel H. McQuiston "Novelty, Complexity, and Importance as Causal Determinants of Industrial Buyer Behavior," *Journal of Marketing* 53 (April 1989): 66–79.

7. Patrick J. Robinson, Charles W. Faris, and Yoram Wind, *Industrial Buying and Creative Marketing* (Boston: Allyn & Bacon, 1967).

8. Erin Anderson, Wujin Chu, and Barton Weitz, "Industrial Purchasing: An Empirical Examination of the Buyclass Framework," *Journal of Marketing* 51 (July 1987): 71–86.

9. Fred E. Webster and Yoram Wind, *Organizational Buying Behavior* (Upper Saddle River, NJ: Prentice Hall, 1972).

10. Robert Boutilier, "Targeting Families: Marketing to and Through the New Family," *American Demographics Marketing Tools* (Ithaca, NY: 1993): 4–6; W. Bradford Fay, "Families in the 1990s: Universal Values, Uncommon Experiences," *Marketing Research: A Magazine of Management & Applications* 5 (Winter 1993): 47.

11. Ellen Graham, "Craving Closer Ties, Strangers Come Together as Family," *Wall Street Journal* (March 4, 1996): B1.

12. Steven J. Kafka, Bruce D. Temkin, Matthew R. Sanders, Jeremy Sharrard, and Tobias O. Brown, "eMarketplaces Boost B2B Trade," *The Forrester Report* (Forrester Research, Inc., February 2000).

13. B2B Supply Chain: How Companies Are Using the Web to Cut Costs," *Supply Chain* (November 2001).

14. www.worldwideretailexchange.org, accessed January 8, 2003.

15. Alison Hardy, "Designing Time and Sampling Money," *Apparel Industry Magazine* (May 2000): 22.

16. Alan R. Andreasen, "Life Status Changes and Changes in Consumer Preferences and Satisfaction," *Journal of Consumer Research* 11 (December 1984): 784–94; James H. McAlexander, John W. Schouten, and Scott D. Roberts, "Consumer Behavior and Divorce," *Research in Consumer Behavior* 6 (1993): 153–84.

17. Randolph E. Schmid, "Most Americans Still the Marrying Kind, Statistics Show; Trend: The Percentage of Adults Who Are Wed and Living with Their Spouse Is Declining, but Still the Majority," *Los Angeles Times* (January 17, 1999): 9.

18. Study Finds Why Marriage Is on the Decline," *Jet 96* (July 26, 1999): 16–19.

19. Wendy Bounds, "An Easy Way to Get an Ex out of the Picture—and No Lawyer!" *Wall Street Journal* (June 16, 1994): B1.

20. "Mommy Is Really Home from Work," *BusinessWeek* (November 25, 2002): 101–2.

21. Karen Hardee-Cleaveland, "Is Eight Enough?" *American Demographics* (June 1989): 60.

22. Frank Bruni, "Persistent Drop in Fertility Reshapes Europe's Future," *New York Times on the Web* (December 26, 2002).

23. Ronald Alsop, "Businesses Market to Gay Couples as Same Sex Households Increases," *Wall Street Journal Interactive Edition* (August 8, 2002).

24. Brad Edmondson, "Inside the New Household Projections," *The Number News* (July 1996).

25. Brad Edmondson, "Inside the New Household Projections."

26. P. Paul, "Childless by Choice," *American Demographics* (November 2001): 45–48, 50.

27. "Mothers Bearing a Second Burden," *New York Times* (May 14, 1989): 26.

28. Thomas Exter, "Disappearing Act," *American Demographics* (January 1989): 78; see also Keren Ami Johnson and Scott D. Roberts, "Incompletely-Launched and Returning Young Adults: Social Change, Consumption, and Family Environment," in Robert P. Leone and V. Kumar, eds., *Enhancing Knowledge Development in Marketing* (Chicago: American Marketing Association), 249–54; John Burnett and Denise Smart, "Returning Young Adults: Implications for Marketers," *Psychology & Marketing* 11 (May–June 1994): 253–69.

29. Marcia Mogelonsky, "The Rocky Road to Adulthood," *American Demographics* (May 1996): 26.

30. For a review, see Russell W. Belk, "Metaphoric Relationships with Pets," *Society and Animals* 4, no. 2 (1996): 121–46.

31. Rebecca Gardyn, "Animal Magnetism," *American Demographics* (May 2002): 31–37.

32. "Colorado Proposal Would Recognize Pets as Companions Rather than Property," *Montgomery Advertiser* (February 10, 2003): 4A.

33. Rebecca Gardyn, "Animal Magnetism"; Anne S. Lewis, "Fancy Fidos Check in at Pet Palazzi," *Wall Street Journal Interactive Edition* (August 27, 1999); Jeffrey Krasner, "Freeze-drying Pets Soothes Owners and the Profits Are 'Phenomenal'," *Wall Street Journal Interactive Edition* (January 9, 2001).

34. Erin White and Betsy McKay, "Coke's New Twist: A Bottle for Two," *Wall Street Journal* (May 17, 2002): B2.

35. Brad Edmondson, "Do the Math," *American Demographics* (October 1999): 50–56.

36. Mary C. Gilly and Ben M. Enis, "Recycling the Family Life Cycle: A Proposal for Redefinition," in Andrew A. Mitchell, ed., *Advances in Consumer Research* 9 (Ann Arbor, MI: Association for Consumer Research, 1982): 271–76.

37. Charles M. Schaninger and William D. Danko, "A Conceptual and Empirical Comparison of Alternative Household Life Cycle Models," *Journal of Consumer Research* 19 (March 1993): 580–94; Robert E. Wilkes, "Household Life-Cycle Stages, Transitions, and Product Expenditures," *Journal of Consumer Research* 22 (June 1995): 27–42.

38. Cheryl Russell, "The New Consumer Paradigm," *American Demographics* (April 1999): 50.

39. These categories are an adapted version of an FLC model proposed by Gilly and Enis (1982). Based on a recent empirical comparison of several competing models, Schaninger and Danko found that this framework outperformed others, especially in terms of its treatment of nonconventional households, though they recommend several improvements to this model as well. See Gilly and Enis, "Recycling the Family Life Cycle"; Schaninger and Danko, "A Conceptual and Empirical Comparison of Alternate Household Life Cycle Models"; Scott D. Roberts, Patricia K. Voli, and Kerenami Johnson, "Beyond the Family Life Cycle: An Inventory of Variables for Defining the Family as a Consumption Unit," in Victoria L. Crittenden, ed., *Developments In Marketing Science* 15 (Coral Gables, FL: Academy of Marketing Science, 1992): 71–75.

40. Brad Edmondson, "Do the Math," 50–56.

41. Jennifer Lach, "Intelligence Agents," *American Demographics* (March 1999): 52–60.

42. Harry L. Davis, "Decision Making within the Household," *Journal of Consumer Research* 2 (March 1972): 241–60; Michael B. Menasco and David J. Curry, "Utility and Choice: An Empirical Study of Wife/Husband Decision Making," *Journal of Consumer Research* 16 (June 1989): 87–97; Conway Lackman and John M. Lanasa, "Family Decision Making Theory: An Overview and Assessment," *Psychology & Marketing* 10 (March–April 1993): 81–94.

43. Shannon Dortch, "Money and Marital Discord," *American Demographics* (October 1994): 11.

44. For research on factors affecting how much influence adolescents exert in family decision making, see Ellen Foxman, Patriya Tansuhaj, and Karin M. Ekstrom, "Family Members' Perceptions of Adolescents' Influence in Family Decision Making," *Journal of Consumer Research* 15 (March 1989): 482–91; Sharon E. Beatty and Salil Talpade, "Adolescent Influence in Family Decision Making: A Replication with Extension," *Journal of Consumer Research* 21 (September 1994): 332–41.

45. Daniel Seymour and Greg Lessne, "Spousal Conflict Arousal: Scale Development," *Journal of Consumer Research* 11 (December 1984): 810–21.

46. Robert Lohrer, "Haggar Targets Women with $8M Media Campaign," *Daily News Record* (January 8, 1997): 1.

47. Diane Crispell, "Dual-Earner Diversity," *American Demographics* (July 1995): 32–37.

48. Marriage: The Art of Compromise," *American Demographics* (February 1998): 41.

49. Darach Turley, "Dialogue with the Departed," *European Advances in Consumer Research* 2 (1995): 10–13.

50. "Wives and Money," *American Demographics* (December 1997): 34.

51. Thomas Hine, *Populuxe* (New York: Knopf, 1986).

52. Robert Boutilier, "Targeting Families: Marketing to and Through the New Family."

53. Dennis L. Rosen and Donald H. Granbois, "Determinants of Role Structure in Family Financial Management," *Journal of Consumer*

Research 10 (September 1983): 253–58; Robert F. Bales, *Interaction Process Analysis: A Method for the Study of Small Groups* (Reading, MA: Addison-Wesley, 1950). For a cross-gender comparison of food-shopping strategies, see Rosemary Polegato and Judith L. Zaichkowsky, "Family Food Shopping: Strategies Used by Husbands and Wives," *Journal of Consumer Affairs* 28, no. 2 (1994): 278–99.

54. Alma S. Baron, "Working Parents: Shifting Traditional Roles," *Business* 37 (January–March 1987): 36; William J. Qualls, "Household Decision Behavior: The Impact of Husbands' and Wives' Sex Role Orientation," *Journal of Consumer Research* 14 (September 1987): 264–79; Charles M. Schaninger and W. Christian Buss, "The Relationship of Sex-Role Norms to Household Task Allocation," *Psychology & Marketing* 2 (Summer 1985): 93–104.

55. "Tailor-Made," *Advertising Age* (September 23, 2002): 14.

56. Craig J. Thompson, "Caring Consumers: Gendered Consumption Meanings and the Juggling Lifestyle," *Journal of Consumer Research* 22 (March 1996): 388–407.

57. Cristina Merrill, "Mother's Work Is Never Done," *American Demographics* (September 1999): 29–32.

58. Miriam Jordan, "India's Medicine Men Market an Array of Contraceptives," *Wall Street Journal Interactive Edition* (September 21, 1999); Patricia Winters Lauro, "Sports Geared to Parents Replace Stodgy with Cool," *New York Times on the Web* (January 3, 2000); Cynthia Webster, "Effects of Hispanic Ethnic Identification on Marital Roles in the Purchase Decision Process," *Journal of Consumer Research* 21 (September 1994): 319–31. For a recent study that examined the effects of family depictions in advertising among Hispanic consumers, see Gary D. Gregory and James M. Munch, "Cultural Values in International Advertising: An Examination of Familial Norms and Roles in Mexico," *Psychology & Marketing* 14 (March 1997): 99–120; John Steere, "How Asian-Americans Make Purchase Decisions," *Marketing News* (March 13, 1995): 9; John B. Ford, Michael S. LaTour, and Tony L. Henthorne, "Perception of Marital Roles in Purchase Decision Processes: A Cross-Cultural Study," *Journal of the Academy of Marketing Science* 23 (Spring 1995): 120–31; Chankon Kim and Hanjoon Lee, "A Taxonomy of Couples Based on Influence Strategies: The Case of Home Purchase," *Journal of Business Research* 36 (June 1996): 157–68; Claudia Penteado, "Coke Taps Maternal Instinct with New Latin American Ads," *Advertising Age International* (January 1997): 15.

59. Gary L. Sullivan and P. J. O'Connor, "The Family Purchase Decision Process: A Cross-Cultural Review and Framework for Research," *Southwest Journal of Business & Economics* (Fall 1988): 43; Marilyn Lavin, "Husband-Dominant, Wife-Dominant, Joint," *Journal of Consumer Marketing* 10, no. 3 (1993): 33–42.

60. Diane Crispell, "Mr. Mom Goes Mainstream," *American Demographics* (March 1994): 59; Gabrielle Sándor, "Attention Advertisers: Real Men Do Laundry," *American Demographics* (March 1994): 13.

61. Tony Bizjak, "Chore Wars Rage On—Even When Wife Earns the Most," *The Sacramento Bee* (April 1, 1993): A1.

62. Michael A. Belch and Laura A. Willis, "Family Decision at the Turn of the Century: Has the Changing Structure of Households Impacted the Family Decision Making Process," *Journal of Consumer Behavior* 2 (2001): 111–24.

63. Micaela DiLeonardo, "The Female World of Cards and Holidays: Women, Families, and the Work of Kinship," *Signs* 12 (Spring 1942): 440–53.

64. C. Whan Park, "Joint Decisions in Home Purchasing: A Muddling-Through Process," *Journal of Consumer Research* 9 (September 1982): 151–62; see also William J. Qualls and Francoise Jaffe, "Measuring Conflict in Household Decision Behavior: Read My Lips and Read My Mind," in John F. Sherry Jr. and Brian Sternthal, eds., *Advances in Consumer Research* 19 (Provo, UT: Association for Consumer Research, 1992): 522–31.

65. Kim P. Corfman and Donald R. Lehmann, "Models of Cooperative Group Decision Making and Relative Influence: An Experimental Investigation of Family Purchase Decisions," *Journal of Consumer Research* 14 (June 1987): 1–13.

66. Sarah Lyall, "Jacks? Dolls? Yo-Yos? No, They Want Cellphones," *New York Times on the Web* (October 24, 2002).

67. Charles Atkin, "Observation of Parent-Child Interaction in Supermarket Decision Making," *Journal of Marketing* 42 (October 1978): 41–45. For more information related to children and consumption, see the government Web site, www.childstats.gov.

68. James U. McNeal, "Tapping the Three Kids' Markets," *American Demographics* (April 1998): 3, 737–41.

69. Harris Curtis, "Making Kids Street Smart," *Newsweek* (September 16, 2002): 10.

70. Kay L. Palan and Robert E. Wilkes, "Adolescent-Parent Interaction in Family Decision Making," *Journal of Consumer Research* 24 (September 1997): 159–69.

71. Stephanie Thompson, "Mrs. Butterworth's Changes Her Target," *Advertising Age* (December 20, 1999): 44.

72. Les Carlson, Ann Walsh, Russell N. Laczniak, and Sanford Grossbart, "Family Communication Patterns and Marketplace Motivations, Attitudes, and Behaviors of Children and Mothers," *Journal of Consumer Affairs* 28, no. 1 (1994): 25–53; see also Roy L. Moore and George P. Moschis, "The Role of Family Communication in Consumer Learning," *Journal of Communication* 31 (Autumn 1981): 42–51.

73. Leslie Isler, Edward T. Popper, and Scott Ward, "Children's Purchase Requests and Parental Responses: Results from a Diary Study," *Journal of Advertising Research* 27 (October–November 1987): 28–39.

74. Gregory M. Rose, "Consumer Socialization, Parental Style, and Development Timetables in the United States and Japan," *Journal of Marketing* 63, no. 3 (1999): 105–19.

75. Mary Roach, "Cute Inc.," *Wired* (December 1999): 330–43.

76. Scott Ward, "Consumer Socialization," in Harold H. Kassarjian and Thomas S. Robertson, eds., *Perspectives in Consumer Behavior* (Glenview, IL: Scott, Foresman, 1980): 380.

77. Thomas Lipscomb, "Indicators of Materialism in Children's Free Speech: Age and Gender Comparisons," *Journal of Consumer Marketing* (Fall 1988): 41–46.

78. George P. Moschis, "The Role of Family Communication in Consumer Socialization of Children and Adolescents," *Journal of Consumer Research* 11 (March 1985): 898–913.

79. Gregory M. Rose, Vassilis Dalakas, and Fredric Kropp, "A Five-Nation Study of Developmental Timetables, Reciprocal Communication and Consumer Socialization," *Journal of Business Research* 55 (2002): 943–49.

80. Elizabeth S. Moore, William L. Wilkie, and Richard J. Lutz, "Passing the Torch: Intergenerational Influences as a Source of Brand Equity," *Journal of Marketing* 66 (April 2002): 17–37.

81. James U. McNeal and Chyon-Hwa Yeh, "Born to Shop," *American Demographics* (June 1993): 34–39.

82. See Les Carlson, Sanford Grossbart, and J. Kathleen Stuenkel, "The Role of Parental Socialization Types on Differential Family Communication Patterns Regarding Consumption," *Journal of Consumer Psychology* 1, no. 1 (1992): 31–52.

83. Hassan Fattah, "Hollywood, the Internet, and Kids," *American Demographics* (May 2001): 50–55.

84. Congress Creates Kids' Internet Area," *New York Times on the Web* (November 15, 2002).

85. Matt Richtel, "PC Rooms: Rated M for Mockery," *New York Times on the Web* (September 5, 2002).

86. Bruce Horovitz, "Targeting the Kindermarket," *USA Today* (March 3, 2000): B1.

87. Marian Burros, "McDonald's France Puts Its Mouth Where Its Money Is," *New York Times on the Web* (October 30, 2002).

88. See Patricia M. Greenfield, Emily Yut, Mabel Chung, Deborah Land, Holly Kreider, Maurice Pantoja, and Kris Horsley, "The Program-Length Commercial: A Study of the Effects of Television/Toy Tie-Ins on Imaginative Play," *Psychology & Marketing* 7 (Winter 1990): 237–56 for a study on the effects of commercial programming on creative play.

89. Marina Baker, "Teletubbies say 'Eh Oh . . . It's War!' " *The Independent* (March 6, 2000): 7; "A Trojan Horse for Advertisers" *BusinessWeek* (April 3, 2000): 10.

90. Gerald J. Gorn and Renee Florsheim, "The Effects of Commercials for Adult Products on Children," *Journal of Consumer Research* 11 (March 1985): 962–67. For a recent study that assessed the impact of violent commercials on children, see V. Kanti Prasad and Lois J. Smith, "Television Commercials in Violent Programming: An Experimental Evaluation of Their Effects on Children," *Journal of the Academy of Marketing Science* 22, no. 4 (1994): 340–51.

91. Glenn Collins, "New Studies on 'Girl Toys' and 'Boy Toys'," *New York Times* (February 13, 1984): D1.

92. Susan B. Kaiser, "Clothing and the Social Organization of Gender Perception: A Developmental Approach," *Clothing and Textiles Research Journal* 7 (Winter 1989): 46–56.

93. D. W. Rajecki, Jill Ann Dame, Kelly Jo Creek, P. J. Barrickman, Catherine A. Reid, and Drew C. Appleby, "Gender Casting in Television Toy Advertisements: Distributions, Message Content Analysis, and Evaluations," *Journal of Consumer Psychology* 2, no. 3 (1993): 307–27.

94. Lori Schwartz and William Markham, "Sex Stereotyping in Children's Toy Advertisements," *Sex Roles* 12 (January 1985): 157–70.

95. Joseph Pereira, "Oh Boy! In Toyland, You Get More if You're Male," *Wall Street Journal* (September 23, 1994): B1; Joseph Pereira, "Girls Favorite Playthings: Dolls, Dolls, and Dolls," *Wall Street Journal* (September 23, 1994): B1.

96. Lisa Bannon, "More Kids' Marketers Pitch Number of Single-Sex Products," *Wall Street Journal Interactive Edition* (February 14, 2000).

97. Ibid.

98. Constance L. Hays, "A Role Model's Clothes: Barbie Goes Professional," *New York Times on the Web* (April 1, 2000).

99. Laura A. Peracchio, "How Do Young Children Learn to Be Consumers? A Script-Processing Approach," *Journal of Consumer Research* 18 (March 1992): 425–40; Laura A. Peracchio, "Young Children's Processing of a Televised Narrative: Is a Picture Really Worth a Thousand Words?" *Journal of Consumer Research* 20 (September 1993): 281–93; see also M. Carole Macklin, "The Effects of an Advertising Retrieval Cue on Young Children's Memory and Brand Evaluations," *Psychology & Marketing* 11 (May–June 1994): 291–311.

100. Jean Piaget, "The Child and Modern Physics," *Scientific American* 196, no. 3 (1957): 46–51; see also Kenneth D. Bahn, "How and When Do Brand Perceptions and Preferences First Form? A Cognitive Developmental Investigation," *Journal of Consumer Research* 13 (December 1986): 382–93.

101. Deborah L. Roedder, "Age Differences in Children's Responses to Television Advertising: An Information-Processing Approach," *Journal of Consumer Research* 8 (September 1981): 144–53; see also Deborah Roedder John and Ramnath Lakshmi-Ratan, "Age Differences in Children's Choice Behavior: The Impact of Available Alternatives," *Journal of Marketing Research* 29 (May 1992): 216–26; Jennifer Gregan-Paxton and Deborah Roedder John, "Are Young Children Adaptive Decision Makers? A Study of Age Differences in Information Search Behavior," *Journal of Consumer Research* 21, no. 4 (1995): 567–80.

102. Kay Hymovitz, quoted in Leslie Kaufman, "New Style Maven: 6 Years Old and Picky," *New York Times on the Web* (September 7, 1999); Tara Parker-Pope, "Cosmetics Industry Takes Look at the Growing Preteen Market," *Wall Street Journal Interactive Edition* (December 4, 1998).

103. Janet Simons, "Youth Marketing: Children's Clothes Follow the Latest Fashion," *Advertising Age* (February 14, 1985): 16.

104. Horst Stipp, "Children as Consumers"; see Laura A. Peracchio, "Designing Research to Reveal the Young Child's Emerging Competence," *Psychology & Marketing* 7 (Winter 1990): 257–76, for details regarding the design of research on children.

105. Laura Shapiro, "Where Little Boys Can Play with Nail Polish," *Newsweek* (May 28, 1990): 62.

106. Sally Beatty, "Multiple Intelligence Theory Lets TV Appeal to Both Parents, Preschoolers," *Wall Street Journal Interactive Edition* (April 1, 2002).

107. Joseph Pereira, "Pint-Size Judges Make Their Picks for Holiday Favorites This Season," *Wall Street Journal Interactive Edition* (December 17, 1997); Tom McGee, "Getting Inside Kids' Heads," *American Demographics* (January 1997): 53.

108. Gary Armstrong and Merrie Brucks, "Dealing with Children's Advertising: Public Policy Issues and Alternatives," *Journal of Public Policy and Marketing* 7 (1988): 98–113.

109. Bonnie Reece, "Children and Shopping: Some Public Policy Questions," *Journal of Public Policy and Marketing* (1986): 185–94.

110. Daniel Cook, University of Illinois, personal communication, December 2002; and "Contradictions and Conundrums of the Child Consumer: The Emergent Centrality of an Enigma in the 1990s" (paper presented at the Association for Consumer Research, October 2002).

L'original

Consumers and Subcultures

The chapters in this section consider some of the social influences that help to determine who we are, with an emphasis on the subcultures that help to determine each of our unique identities. Chapter 13 focuses on factors that define social class, and how membership in a social class exerts a strong pull on what we want to buy with the money we make. Chapter 14 discusses the ways that our ethnic, racial, and religious identifications help to stamp our social identities. Chapter 15 considers how the bonds we share with others who were born at roughly the same time unite us.

■ CHAPTERS AHEAD

CHAPTER 13	CHAPTER 14	CHAPTER 15
Income and Social Class	Ethnic, Racial, and Religious Subcultures	Age Subcultures

Income and Social Class

finally, the big day has come! Phil is going home with Marilyn to meet her parents. Phil had been doing some contracting work at the securities firm where Marilyn works, and it was love at first sight. Even though Phil had attended the "School of Hard Knocks" on the streets of Brooklyn and Marilyn was fresh out of Princeton, somehow they knew they could work things out despite their vastly different backgrounds. Marilyn's been hinting that her family has money, but Phil doesn't feel intimidated. After all, he knows plenty of guys from his old neighborhood who have wheeled-and-dealed their way into six figures. He guesses he can handle one more big shot in a silk suit, flashing a roll of bills and showing off his expensive modern furniture with mirrors and gadgets everywhere you look.

When they arrive at the family estate in Connecticut, Phil looks for a Rolls-Royce parked in the circular driveway, but he only sees a beat-up Jeep Cherokee, which must belong to one of the servants. Once inside, Phil is surprised by how simply the house is decorated and by how shabby everything seems. The hall entryway is covered with a faded Oriental rug, and all of the furniture looks really old.

Phil is even more surprised when he meets Marilyn's father, Mr. Caldwell. He had half expected him to be wearing a tuxedo and holding a large brandy snifter like the people he's seen in the movies. In fact, Phil had put on his best shiny Italian suit in anticipation, and he wore his large cubic zirconium pinky ring so this guy would know that he had some money too. When Marilyn's father emerges from his study wearing an old rumpled cardigan sweater and tennis sneakers, Phil realizes he's definitely not one of those guys from the old neighborhood.

■ CONSUMER SPENDING AND ECONOMIC BEHAVIOR

As Phil's eye-opening experience at the Caldwells' house suggests, there are many ways to spend money, and a wide gulf exists between those who have it and those who don't. Perhaps an equally wide one exists between those who have had it for a long time and those who "made it the hard way—by earning it!" This chapter begins by briefly considering how general economic conditions affect the way consumers allocate their money. Then, reflecting the adage that says "The rich are different," we'll explore how people who occupy different positions in society consume in very different ways.

Luxury items like diamond engagement rings are valued as status symbols the world over, as this Brazilian ad for a jeweler reminds us.

Whether a skilled worker like Phil or a child of privilege like Marilyn, a person's social class has a profound impact on what he does with money and on how consumption choices reflect his "place" in society. As this chapter illustrates, these choices serve another purpose as well. The specific products and services we buy are often intended to make sure other people know what our social standing is—or what we would like it to be. Products are frequently bought and displayed as markers of social class; they are valued as **status symbols**. This is especially true in large, modern societies where behavior and reputation can no longer be counted on to convey one's position in a community.

Income Patterns

Many Americans would probably say that they don't make enough money, but in reality the average American's standard of living continues to improve. These income shifts are linked to two key factors: a shift in women's roles and increases in educational attainment.[1]

Woman's Work

One reason for this increase in income is that there has also been a larger proportion of people of working age participating in the labor force. Mothers with preschool children are the fastest-growing segment of working people. Furthermore, many of these jobs are in high-paying occupations such as medicine and architecture, which used to be dominated by men. Although women are still a minority in most professional occupations, their ranks continue to swell. The steady increase in the numbers of working women is a primary cause of the rapid growth of middle- and upper-income families. There are now more than 18 million married couples making over $50,000 a year—but in almost two-thirds of these families, it is the wife's paycheck that is propelling the couple up the income ladder.[2]

Yes, It Pays to Go to School!

Another factor that determines who gets a bigger piece of the pie is education. Although picking up the tab for college often entails great sacrifice, it still pays off in the long run. College graduates earn about 50 percent more than those who have only gone through high school during the course of their lives. Women without a high school diploma earn only 40 percent as much as women who have a college degree.[3] So, hang in there!

Education is strongly linked to a higher standard of living. People who earn a college degree are likely to earn much more during their lives than those who do not.

To Spend or Not to Spend, That Is the Question

Consumer demand for goods and services depends on both ability to buy and willingness to buy. Whereas demand for necessities tends to be stable over time, other expenditures can be postponed or eliminated if people don't feel that now is a good time to spend money.[4] For example, a person may decide to "make do" with his current clunker for another year rather than buy a new car right away.

Discretionary Spending

Discretionary income is the money available to a household over and above that required for a comfortable standard of living. American consumers are estimated to wield about $400 billion a year in discretionary spending power. People aged 35 to 55, whose incomes are at a peak, account for about half of this amount. As the population ages and income levels rise, the typical U.S. household is changing the way it spends its money. The most noticeable change is that a much larger share of the budget is spent on shelter and transportation, and less on food and apparel. These shifts are due to factors such as an increase in the prevalence of home ownership (the number of homeowners rose by more than 80 percent during the last three decades) and in the need for working wives to pay commuting costs. On a more cheerful note, households are spending more now on entertainment, reading, and education than in the past.

Individual Attitudes Toward Money

Especially in the wake of 9/11, many consumers are experiencing doubts about their individual and collective futures, and they are anxious about holding on to what they have. Of course, not everyone has the same attitudes about money and its importance. Table 13.1 summarizes seven distinct types of money personalities.

A consumer's anxieties about money are not necessarily related to how much he or she actually has: Acquiring and managing money is more a state of mind than of wallet. For example, we all know people who are "tightwads" with their money and others whose cash seems to burn a hole in their wallets until they part with it. In recent years being frugal has become a passion for some people, who consider it a point of honor not to pay more than they have to for anything. There is even a publication called *The Tightwad Gazette* that offers its readers advice on buying in bulk, buying used goods, reusing products, and even timing showers to save on water bills.[5]

Money has a variety of complex psychological meanings; it can be equated with success or failure, social acceptability, security, love, or freedom.[6] There are even therapists who specialize in treating money-related disorders, and they report that some people even feel guilty about their success and deliberately make bad investments to reduce this feeling! Some other clinical conditions include *atephobia* (fear of being ruined), *harpaxophobia* (fear of becoming a victim of robbers), *peniaphobia* (fear of poverty), and *aurophobia* (fear of gold).[7]

Consumer Confidence

The field of **behavioral economics**, or economic psychology, is concerned with the "human" side of economic decisions (including the biases in decision making we examined in Chapter 9). Beginning with the pioneering work of psychologist George Katona, this discipline studies how consumers' motives and their expectations about the future affect their current spending, and how these individual decisions add up to affect a society's economic well-being.[8]

Consumers' beliefs about what the future holds is an indicator of **consumer confidence**, which reflects the extent to which people are optimistic or pessimistic about the future health of the economy and how they will fare down the road. These

TABLE 13.1
MONEY PERSONALITIES

	Types						
	The Hunter	**The Gatherer**	**The Protector**	**The Splurger**	**The Striver**	**The Nester**	**The Idealist**
Percent of population	13	19	16	14	13	14	10
Mean income	$44,000	$35,000	$36,000	$33,000	$29,000	$31,000	$30,000
Exemplar	Bill Gates (CEO Microsoft)	Warren Buffet (Nebraska-based investor)	Paul Newman (actor and entrepreneur)	Elizabeth Taylor (movie star)	Tonya Harding (disgraced figure skater)	Roseanne (comedienne/actress)	Allen Ginsberg (deceased poet)
Profile	Takes risks to get ahead	Is better safe than sorry	Puts others first	Travels first class or not at all	Is controlled by money	Needs just enough to take care of self	Believe there's more to life than money
Characteristics	Is aggressive and equates money with happiness and achievement; is likely to have unstable personal life	Is a conservative investor with traditional values; tends to be thrifty and tries to minimize borrowing	Believes money is a means of protecting loved ones; tends to be predominantly women; is most likely married	Is self-indulgent; prefers to buy luxury items rather than practical items; is self-centered and not a good planner	Believes money makes the world go round; equates money with power; tends not to be well educated and most likely is divorced	Is not very interested in money; mostly concerned about meeting immediate needs	Mostly believes that money is the root of all evil; is not very interested in material things

Source: Adapted from Robert Sultivan, "Americans and Their Money," *Worth* (June 1994): 60, based on a survey of approximately 2,000 American consumers conducted by Roper/Starch Worldwide. Reprinted by permission of *Worth* magazine.

beliefs influence how much money they will pump into the economy when making discretionary purchases.

Many businesses take forecasts about anticipated spending very seriously, and periodic surveys attempt to "take the pulse" of the American consumer. The Conference Board conducts a survey of consumer confidence, as does the Survey Research Center at the University of Michigan. The following are the types of questions posed to consumers in these surveys:[9]

- Would you say that you and your family are better off or worse off financially than a year ago?
- Will you be better off or worse off a year from now?
- Is now a good time or a bad time for people to buy major household items, such as furniture or a refrigerator?
- Do you plan to buy a car in the next year?

When people are pessimistic about their prospects and about the state of the economy, they tend to cut back their spending and take on less debt. On the other hand, when they are optimistic about the future, they tend to reduce the amount they save, take on more debt, and buy discretionary items. Thus the overall savings rate is influenced by: (1) individual consumers' pessimism or optimism about their personal circumstances such as a sudden increase in personal wealth after buying a high-tech stock; (2) world events such as the conflict in the Persian Gulf;

and (3) cultural differences in attitudes toward saving (e.g., the Japanese have a much higher savings rate than do Americans).[10]

■ SOCIAL CLASS

All societies can be roughly divided into the "haves" and the "have-nots" (though sometimes having is a question of degree). The United States is a place where "all men are created equal," but even so some people seem to be "more equal than others." As Phil's encounter with the Caldwells suggests, a consumer's standing in society—his social class—is determined by a complex set of variables, including income, family background, and occupation.

The place one occupies in the social structure is an important determinant not only of *how much* money is spent, but also *how* it is spent. Phil was surprised that the Caldwells, who clearly had a lot of money, did not seem to flaunt it. This understated way of living is a hallmark of so-called "old money." People who have had it for a long time don't need to prove they've got it. In contrast, consumers who are relative newcomers to affluence might allocate the same amount of money very differently.

A Universal Pecking Order

In many animal species, a social organization is developed whereby the most assertive or aggressive animals exert control over the others and have the first pick of food, living space, and even mating partners. Chickens, for example, develop a clearly defined *dominance–submission hierarchy*. Within this hierarchy, each hen has a position in which she is submissive to all of the hens above her and dominates all of the ones below her (hence, the origin of the term *pecking order*).[11]

People are not much different. They also develop a pecking order in which they are ranked in terms of their relative standing in society. This standing determines their access to such resources as education, housing, and consumer goods. People try to improve their ranking by moving up in the social order whenever possible. This desire to improve one's lot in life, and often to let others know that one has done so, is at the core of many marketing strategies.

Social Class Affects Access to Resources

Just as marketers try to carve society into groups for segmentation purposes, sociologists have developed ways to describe meaningful divisions of society in terms of people's relative social and economic resources. Some of these divisions involve political power, whereas others revolve around purely economic distinctions. Karl Marx, the nineteenth-century economic theorist, felt that position in a society was determined by one's relationship to the *means of production*. Some people (the haves) control resources, and they use the labor of others to preserve their privileged positions. The have-nots lack control and depend on their own labor for survival, so these people have the most to gain by changing the system. Distinctions among people that entitle some to more than others are perpetuated by those who will benefit by doing so.[12] The German sociologist Max Weber showed that the rankings people develop are not one-dimensional. Some involve prestige or "social honor" (he called these *status groups*), some rankings focus on power (or *party*), and some revolve around wealth and property (*class*).[13]

Social Class Affects Taste and Lifestyles

The term **social class** is now used more generally to describe the overall rank of people in a society. People who are grouped within the same social class are approximately equal in terms of their social standing in the community. They work in roughly similar occupations, and they tend to have similar lifestyles by virtue of their income levels and common tastes. These people tend to socialize with one another and share many

This ad implies that there are social class differences in leisure activities and preferred beverages.

ideas and values regarding the way life should be lived.[14] Indeed, "birds of a feather do flock together." We tend to marry people in a similar social class to ours; a tendency sociologists call **homogamy** or "assortative mating." In 2000, 94 percent of married high school dropouts were wed to someone who was also a dropout or who had only a high school diploma. On the other side of the spectrum, less than one percent of the most highly educated Americans have a spouse who did not complete high school.[15]

Social class is as much a state of being as it is of having: As Phil saw, class is also a matter of what one *does* with one's money and how one defines his or her role in society. Although people may not like the idea that some members of society are better off or "different" from others, most consumers do acknowledge the existence of different classes and the effect of class membership on consumption. As one wealthy woman observed when asked to define social class,

> I would suppose social class means where you went to school and how far. Your intelligence. Where you live. . . Where you send your children to school. The hobbies you have. Skiing, for example, is higher than the snowmobile. . . It can't be [just] money, because nobody ever knows that about you for sure.[16]

Social Stratification

In school, it always seems that some kids get all the breaks. They have access to many resources, such as special privileges, fancy cars, large allowances, or dates with other popular classmates. At work, some people are put on the fast track and are promoted to high-prestige jobs, given higher salaries, and perhaps perks such as a parking space, a large office, or the keys to the executive washroom.

In virtually every context, some people seem to be ranked higher than others. Patterns of social arrangements evolve whereby some members get more resources than others by virtue of their relative standing, power, or control in the group.[17] The phenomenon of **social stratification** refers to this creation of artificial divisions in a society: "those processes in a social system by which scarce and valuable resources are distributed unequally to status positions that become more or less permanently ranked in terms of the share of valuable resources each receives."[18]

Achieved Versus Ascribed Status

Think back to groups to which you've belonged. You'll probably agree that in many instances some members seem to get more than their fair share of goodies, whereas other individuals are not so lucky. Some of these resources may have gone to people who earned them through hard work or diligent study. This allocation is due to *achieved status*. Other rewards may have been obtained because the person was lucky enough to be born with "a silver spoon in her mouth." Such good fortune reflects *ascribed status*.

Whether rewards go to the "best and the brightest" or to someone who happens to be related to the boss, allocations are rarely equal within a social group. Most groups exhibit a structure, or **status hierarchy,** in which some members are somehow better off than others. They may have more authority or power, or they are simply better liked or respected.

In our society, wealth is more likely to be earned than inherited.

Some people still inherit wealth, the rest of us have no choice but to earn it.

The good news is, a lot of us know how. But then what? Phoenix has been showing people innovative new directions for 150 years. We understand that making money—and knowing what to do with it—are two different skills. It's one reason high-net-worth people and their advisors turn to Phoenix for help. To learn more about how Phoenix could be helping you, contact your financial advisor or visit www.phoenixwm.com.

Money. It's just not what it used to be.

PHOENIX
WEALTH MANAGEMENT

Class Structure in the United States

The United States supposedly does not have a rigid, objectively defined class system. Nevertheless, America has tended to maintain a stable class structure in terms of income distribution. Unlike other countries, however, what *does* change are the groups (ethnic, racial, and religious) that have occupied different positions within this structure at different times.[19] The most influential and earliest attempt to describe American class structure was proposed by W. Lloyd Warner in 1941. Warner identified six social classes:[20]

1 Upper Upper
2 Lower Upper
3 Upper Middle
4 Lower Middle
5 Upper Lower
6 Lower Lower

Note that these classifications imply (in ascending order) some judgment of desirability in terms of access to resources such as money, education, and luxury goods. Variations on this system have been proposed over the years, but these six levels summarize fairly well the way social scientists think about class. Figure 13.1 provides one view of the American status structure.

Class Structure Around the World

Every society has some type of hierarchical class structure, which determines people's access to products and services. The Chinese are a great example—an economic boom is rapidly creating a middle class estimated at more than 130 million people, which is projected to grow to more than 400 million in 10 years. Because costs are low, a family with an annual income below the U.S. poverty threshold of about $14,000 can enjoy middle-class comforts, including stylish clothes, Chinese-made color televisions, DVD players, and cell phones.[21] Of course, the specific "markers" of success depend on what is valued in each culture. For the Chinese, one marker of success is hiring a bodyguard to protect oneself and one's newly acquired possessions.[22]

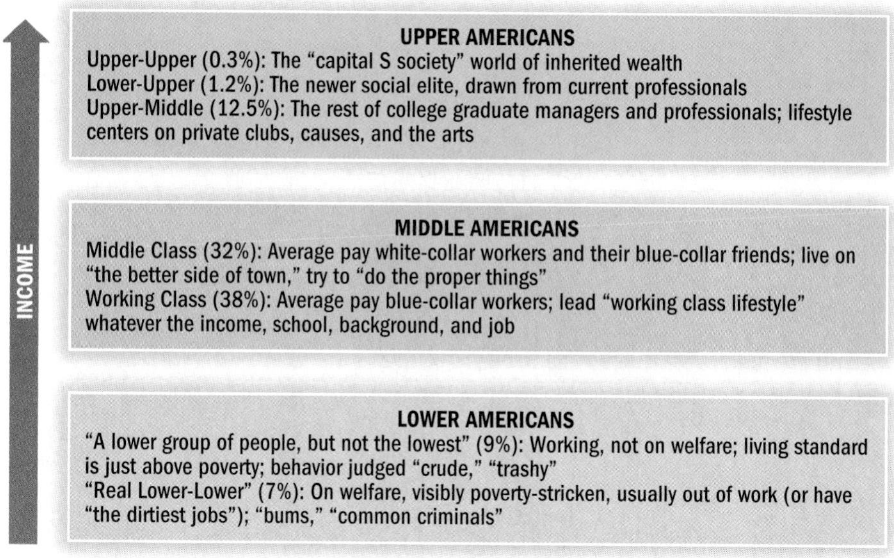

INCOME →

UPPER AMERICANS
Upper-Upper (0.3%): The "capital S society" world of inherited wealth
Lower-Upper (1.2%): The newer social elite, drawn from current professionals
Upper-Middle (12.5%): The rest of college graduate managers and professionals; lifestyle centers on private clubs, causes, and the arts

MIDDLE AMERICANS
Middle Class (32%): Average pay white-collar workers and their blue-collar friends; live on "the better side of town," try to "do the proper things"
Working Class (38%): Average pay blue-collar workers; lead "working class lifestyle" whatever the income, school, background, and job

LOWER AMERICANS
"A lower group of people, but not the lowest" (9%): Working, not on welfare; living standard is just above poverty; behavior judged "crude," "trashy"
"Real Lower-Lower" (7%): On welfare, visibly poverty-stricken, usually out of work (or have "the dirtiest jobs"); "bums," "common criminals"

■ **FIGURE 13.1**
A CONTEMPORARY VIEW OF THE AMERICAN CLASS STRUCTURE

Marketing Opportunity

As the old saying goes, "The rich get richer, and the poor get poorer." Both the top and bottom ends of American income levels are swelling. Since 1980 the wealthiest fifth of the population has increased its income by 21 percent, while wages for the bottom 60 percent have stagnated or dipped. America's most powerful brands, from Levi's jeans to Ivory soap, were built on a mass-marketing premise, but now that's changing. Stores such as Wal-Mart and Tiffany are reporting big earnings, whereas middle-class outlets such as JCPenney have weak sales. The positioning strategy called *chic discount* is very successful. Target's bright-red bull's eye logo has become a fashion statement for affordable style. Referred to as "tar-jay" by its many fans, it is a Kmart for yuppies.

This trend has led some companies to try to have their cake and eat it too by developing a two-tiered marketing strategy where they separately target upscale and downscale consumers. For example, Walt Disney's Winnie the Pooh can be purchased as an original line-drawn figure on fine china or on pewter spoons in upscale specialty and department stores, whereas a plump, cartoon-like Pooh is available on plastic key chains and polyester bed sheets at Wal-Mart. GAP is remodeling its Banana Republic stores to make them more upscale and simultaneously offers its Old Navy stores for the low end.[26]

Japan is a highly status-conscious society where upscale, designer labels are quite popular, and people are constantly seeking new forms of status. To the Japanese, a traditional rock garden, formerly a vehicle for leisure and tranquility, has become a sought-after item. Possession of a rock garden implies inherited wealth, because historically aristocrats were patrons of the arts. In addition, considerable assets are needed to afford the required land in a country in which real estate is extraordinarily costly. The scarcity of land also helps to explain why the Japanese are fanatic golfers: Because a golf course takes up so much space, membership in a golf club is extremely expensive.[23]

On the other side of the world, there is always the United Kingdom. England is also an extremely class-conscious country, and at least until recently, consumption patterns were preordained in terms of one's inherited position and family background. Members of the upper class were educated at schools such as Eaton and Oxford and they spoke like Henry Higgins in *My Fair Lady*. Remnants of this rigid class structure can still be found. "Hooray Henrys" (wealthy young men) play polo at Windsor and hereditary peers still dominate the House of Lords.

The dominance of inherited wealth appears to be fading in Britain's traditionally aristocratic society. According to a survey, 86 of the 200 wealthiest people in England made their money the old-fashioned way: They earned it. Even the sanctity of the royal family, which epitomizes the aristocracy, has been diluted through tabloid exposure and the antics of younger family members who have been transformed into celebrities more like rock stars than royalty. As one observer put it, "the royal family has gone down-market . . . to the point that it sometimes resembles soap opera as much as grand opera."[24] Following the harsh criticism of the royal family following Princess Diana's death, there are changes afoot. Whether the changes heralding a "New Britain" will be more substance than form remains to be seen.

Social Mobility

To what degree do people tend to change their social classes? In some societies, such as India, one's social class is very difficult to change, but America is reported to be a country in which "any man (or woman?) can grow up to be president." **Social mobility** refers to the "passage of individuals from one social class to another."[25]

Golf is a high-status game in Japan, where land is scarce and greens fees are extremely high.

Whether it's a swift horse, a smart hound or an agile car, the English have long known the importance of good breeding.

This Jaguar ad uses a blatant appeal to status.

This passage can be upward, downward, or even horizontal. *Horizontal mobility* refers to movement from one position to another roughly equivalent in social status; for instance, becoming a nurse instead of an elementary school teacher. *Downward mobility* is, of course, not very desirable, but this pattern is unfortunately quite evident in recent years as farmers and other displaced workers have been forced to go on welfare rolls or have joined the ranks of the homeless. A conservative estimate is that 2 million Americans are homeless on any given day.[27]

Despite that discouraging trend, demographics in fact decrees that there must be *upward mobility* in our society. The middle and upper classes reproduce less (i.e., have fewer children per family) than the lower classes (an effect known as *differential fertility*), and they tend to restrict family size below replacement level (i.e., often having only one child). Therefore, so the reasoning goes, positions of higher status over time must be filled by those of lower status.[28] Overall, though, the offspring of blue-collar consumers tend also to be blue-collar, whereas the offspring of white-collar consumers also tend to wind up as white-collar.[29] People tend to improve their positions over time, but these increases are not usually dramatic enough to catapult them from one social class to another. The exception is when a person marries someone considerably richer. This "Cinderella fantasy" is a popular theme in our society that gets played out in movies (*Pretty Woman* or *Maid in Manhattan*) and popular TV shows like *Joe Millionaire*, where women are duped into courting a rich bachelor only to find out later that in reality he's a construction worker.

Components of Social Class

When we think about a person's social class, there are a number of pieces of information we may consider. Two major ones are occupation and income. A third important factor is educational attainment, which is strongly related to income and occupation.

This ad for *US* Magazine uses a strategy that relies on cultural tastes of consumers in different social classes.

Occupational Prestige

In a system in which (like it or not) a consumer is defined to a great extent by what he or she does for a living, *occupational prestige* is one way to evaluate the "worth" of people. Hierarchies of occupational prestige tend to be quite stable over time, and they also tend to be similar across different societies. Similarities in occupational prestige have been found in countries as diverse as Brazil, Ghana, Guam, Japan, and Turkey.[30]

A typical ranking includes a variety of professional and business occupations at the top (e.g., CEO of a large corporation, physician, and college professor), whereas jobs hovering near the bottom include shoe shiner, ditch digger, and garbage collector. Because a person's occupation tends to be strongly linked to his or her use of leisure time, allocation of family resources, political orientation, and so on, this variable is often considered to be the single best indicator of social class.

Income

The distribution of wealth is of great interest to social scientists and to marketers because it determines which groups have the greatest buying power and market potential. Wealth is by no means distributed evenly across the classes. The top fifth of the population controls about 75 percent of all assets.[31] As we have seen, income *per se* is not often a very good indicator of social class because the way money is spent is more telling than how much is spent. Still, people need money to obtain the goods and services that they need to express their tastes, so obviously income is still very important. American consumers are getting both wealthier and older, and these changes will continue to influence consumption preferences.

The Relationship Between Income and Social Class

Although consumers tend to equate money with class, the precise relationship between other aspects of social class and income is not clear and has been the subject of debate among social scientists.[32] The two are by no means synonymous, which is why many people with a lot of money try to use it to upgrade their social class.

One problem is that even if a family increases household income by adding wage earners, each additional job is likely to be of lower status. A homemaker who gets a part-time job is not as likely to get one that is of equal or greater status than the primary wage earner's full-time job. In addition, the extra money earned is often not pooled toward the common good of the family. Instead, the individual uses it for his or her own personal spending. More money does not then result in increased status or changes in consumption patterns because it tends to be devoted to buying more of the usual rather than upgrading to higher-status products.[33]

The following general conclusions can be made regarding the relative value of social class (i.e., place of residence, occupation, cultural interests, etc.) versus income in predicting consumers' choices of products that are bought for functional reasons versus those bought primarily for symbolic reasons (e.g., to convey a desired impression to others).

- Social class appears to be a better predictor of purchases that have symbolic aspects, but low to moderate prices (e.g., cosmetics, liquor).
- Income is a better predictor of major expenditures that do not have status or symbolic aspects (e.g., major appliances).
- Both social class and income data are needed to predict purchases of expensive, symbolic products (e.g., cars, homes).

Measuring Social Class

Because social class is a complex concept that depends on a number of factors, it is not surprising that it has proven difficult to measure. Early measures included the Index of Status Characteristics developed in the 1940s and the Index of Social Position developed in the 1950s.[34] These indices used various combinations of individual characteristics (e.g., income, type of housing) to arrive at a label of class standing. The accuracy of these composites is still a subject of debate among researchers; a study claimed that for segmentation purposes, raw education and income measures work as well as composite status measures.[35] Figure 13.2 shows one measurement instrument.

American consumers generally have little difficulty placing themselves in either the working class (lower-middle class) or middle class. Also, the number that rejects the idea that such categories exist is rather small.[36] The proportion of consumers identifying themselves as working class tended to rise until about 1960, but it has been declining since then.

Blue-collar workers with relatively high-prestige jobs still tend to view themselves as working class, even though their income levels may be equivalent to many white-collar workers.[37] This fact reinforces the idea that the labels of "working class" or "middle class" are very subjective. Their meanings say at least as much about self-identity as they do about economic well-being.

■ **FIGURE 13.2** EXAMPLE OF A COMPUTERIZED INDEX

Interviewer circles code numbers (for the computer) that in his/her judgment best fit the respondent and family. Interviewer asks for detail on occupation, then makes rating. Interviewer often asks the respondent to describe neighborhood in own words. Interviewer asks respondent to specify income—a card is presented to the respondent showing the eight brackets—and records R's response. If interviewer feels this is overstatement or understatement, a "better judgment" estimate should be given, along with an explanation.

EDUCATION:	Respondent	Respondent's Spouse
Grammar school (8 yrs or less)	-1	-1
Some high school (9 to 11 yrs)	-2	-2
Graduated high school (12 yrs)	-3	-3
Some post high school (business, nursing, technical, 1 yr college)	-4	-4
Two, three years of college—possibly Associate of Arts degree	-5	-5
Graduated four-year college (B.A./B.S.)	-7	-7
Master's or five-year professional degree	-8	-8
Ph.D. or six/seven-year professional degree	-9	-9

Respondent: R's Age ___
Respondent's Spouse: Spouse's Age ___

OCCUPATION PRESTIGE LEVEL OF HOUSEHOLD HEAD: Interviewer's judgment of how head of household rates in occupational status.

(Respondent's description—asks for previous occupation if retired, or if R. is widow, asks husband's: _____)

Chronically unemployed—"day" laborers, unskilled; on welfare	-0
Steadily employed but in marginal semiskilled jobs; custodians, minimum pay factory help, service workers (gas attendants, etc.)	-1
Average-skill assembly-line workers, bus and truck drivers, police and firefighters, route deliverymen, carpenters, brickmasons	-2
Skilled craftsmen (electricians), small contractors, factory foremen, low-pay salesclerks, office workers, postal employees	-3
Owners of very small firms (2–4 employees), technicians, salespeople, office workers, civil servants with average-level salaries	-4
Middle management, teachers, social workers, lesser professionals	-5
Lesser corporate officials, owners of middle-sized businesses (10–20 employees), moderate-success professionals (dentists, engineers, etc.)	-7
Top corporate executives, "big successes" in the professional world (leading doctors and lawyers), "rich" business owners	-9

AREA OF RESIDENCE: Interviewer's impressions of the immediate neighborhood in terms of its reputation in the eyes of the community.

Slum area: people on relief, common laborers	-1
Strictly working class: not slummy but some very poor housing	-2
Predominantly blue-collar with some office workers	-3
Predominantly white-collar with some well-paid blue-collar	-4
Better white-collar area: not many executives, but hardly any blue-collar either	-5
Excellent area: professionals and well-paid managers	-7
"Wealthy" or "society"-type neighborhood	-9

TOTAL SCORE _____

TOTAL FAMILY INCOME PER YEAR:

Under $5,000	-1	$20,000 to $24,999	-5
$5,000 to $9,999	-2	$25,000 to $34,999	-6
$10,000 to $14,999	-3	$35,000 to $49,999	-7
$15,000 to $19,999	-4	$50,000 and over	-8

Estimated Status _____

(Interviewer's estimate: _____ and explanation _____)

R's MARITAL STATUS: Married ____ Divorced/Separated ____ Widowed ____ Single ____ (CODE: ____)

Problems with Measures of Social Class

Market researchers were among the first to propose that people from different social classes can be distinguished from each other in important ways. Some of these class distinctions still exist, but others have changed.[38] Unfortunately, many of these measures are badly dated and are not as valid today for a variety of reasons.[39]

One reason is that most measures of social class were designed to accommodate the traditional nuclear family, with a male wage earner in the middle of his career and a female full-time homemaker. Such measures have trouble accounting for two-income families, young singles living alone, or households headed by women, which are so prevalent in today's society (see Chapter 12).

Another problem with measuring social class is attributable to the increasing anonymity of our society. Earlier studies relied on the *reputational method*, in which extensive interviewing was done within a community to determine the reputations and backgrounds of individuals (see the discussion of sociometry in Chapter 11). This information, coupled with the tracing of interaction patterns among people, provided a very comprehensive view of social standing within a community. However, this approach is virtually impossible to implement in most communities today. One compromise is to interview individuals to obtain demographic data and to combine these data with the subjective impressions of the interviewer regarding the person's possessions and standard of living.

An example of this approach appears in Figure 13.2. Note that the accuracy of this questionnaire relies largely on the interviewer's judgment, especially regarding the quality of the respondent's neighborhood. These impressions are in danger of being biased by the interviewer's own circumstances, which may affect his or her standard of comparison. Furthermore, the characteristics are described by highly subjective and relative terms: "Slummy" and "excellent" are not objective measures. These potential problems highlight the need for adequate training of interviewers, as well as for some attempt to cross-validate such data, possibly by employing multiple judges to rate the same area.

One problem with assigning any group of people to a social class is that they may not be equal in their standing on all of the relevant dimensions. A person might come from a low-status ethnic group but have a high-status job, whereas another may live in a fancy part of town but may not have finished high school. The concept of **status crystallization** was developed to assess the impact of inconsistency on the self and social behavior.[40] The logic behind this idea is that because the rewards from each part of such an "unbalanced" person's life would be variable and unpredictable, stress would result. People who exhibit such inconsistencies tend to be more receptive to social change than are those whose identities are more firmly rooted.

A related problem occurs when a person's social-class standing creates expectations that are not met. Some people find themselves in the not-unhappy position of making more money than is expected of those in their social class. This situation is known as an *overprivileged* condition and is usually defined as an income that is at least 25 to 30 percent greater than the median for one's class.[41] In contrast, *underprivileged* consumers, who earn at least 15 percent less than the median, must often allocate a big chunk of their income toward maintaining the impression that they occupy a certain status.

Lottery winners are examples of consumers who become overprivileged virtually overnight. As attractive as winning is to many people, it has its problems. Consumers with a certain standard of living and level of expectations may have trouble adapting to sudden affluence and engage in flamboyant and irresponsible displays of wealth. Ironically, it is not unusual for lottery winners to report feelings of depression in the months after cashing in. They may have trouble adjusting to an unfamiliar world, and they frequently experience pressure from friends, relatives, and businesspeople to "share the wealth."

The traditional assumption is that husbands define a family's social class, whereas wives must live it. Women achieve their social status through their husbands.[42] Indeed, the evidence indicates that physically attractive women tend to "marry up" (*hierogamy*) in social class to a greater extent than attractive men do. Women trade the resource of sexual appeal, which historically has been one of the few assets they were allowed to possess, for the economic resources of men.[43]

Lottery winners who experience sudden wealth may have trouble adapting to their new social status.

The accuracy of this assumption in today's world must be questioned. Many women now contribute equally to the family's well-being, and they work in positions of comparable or even greater status than their spouses. Employed women tend to average both their own and their husband's positions when estimating their own subjective status.[44] Nevertheless, a prospective spouse's social class is often an important "product attribute" when evaluating alternatives in the interpersonal marketplace (as Phil and Marilyn were to find out).

Problems with Social Class Segmentation: A Summary

Social class remains an important way to categorize consumers. Many marketing strategies do target different social classes. However, marketers have failed to use social class information as effectively as they could for the following reasons:

- They have ignored status inconsistency.
- They have ignored intergenerational mobility.
- They have ignored subjective social class (i.e., the class a consumer identifies with rather than the one he or she objectively belongs to).
- They have ignored consumers' aspirations to change their class standing.
- They have ignored the social status of working wives.

■ HOW SOCIAL CLASS AFFECTS PURCHASE DECISIONS

Different products and stores are perceived by consumers to be appropriate for certain social classes.[45] Working-class consumers tend to evaluate products in more utilitarian terms such as sturdiness or comfort rather than style or fashionability. They are less likely to experiment with new products or styles, such as modern furniture or colored appliances.[46] In contrast, more affluent people who live in the suburbs tend to be concerned about appearance and body image, so they are more avid consumers of diet foods and drinks compared to people in more downscale small towns. These differences mean that social class standing can be used to segment markets for soft drinks and other similar products.[47]

Class Differences in Worldview

A major social class difference involves the *worldview* of consumers. The world of the working class (i.e., the lower middle class) is more intimate and constricted. For example, working-class men are likely to name local sports figures as heroes and are less likely to take long vacation trips to out-of-the-way places.[48] Immediate needs, such as a new refrigerator or TV, tend to dictate buying behavior for these consumers, whereas the higher classes tend to focus on more long-term goals, such as saving for college tuition or retirement.[49] Working-class consumers depend heavily on relatives for emotional support and tend to orient themselves in terms of the community rather than the world at large. They are more likely to be conservative and family-oriented. Maintaining the appearance of one's home and property is a priority, regardless of the size of the house.

Although they would like to have more in the way of material goods, working-class people do not necessarily envy those who rank above them in social standing.[50] The maintenance of a high-status lifestyle is sometimes not seen as worth the effort. As one blue-collar consumer commented, "Life is very hectic for those people. There are more breakdowns and alcoholism. It must be very hard to sustain the status, the clothes, and the parties that are expected. I don't think I'd want to take their place."[51]

This person may be right. Although good things appear to go hand-in-hand with higher status and wealth, the picture is not that clear. The social scientist Émile Durkheim observed that suicide rates are much higher among the wealthy; he wrote in 1897, "The possessors of most comfort suffer most."[52] Durkheim's wisdom may still be accurate today. Many well-off consumers seem to be stressed or unhappy despite or even because of their wealth, a condition sometimes termed *affluenza*.[53] In a *New York Times*/CBS News poll, kids aged 13 to 17 were asked to compare their lives with what their parents experienced growing up. Forty-three percent said they were having a harder time, and upper-income teenagers were the most likely to say that their lives were harder and subject to more stress. Apparently, they feel the pressure to get into elite schools and to maintain the family's status.[54]

Taste Cultures, Codes, and Cultural Capital

A **taste culture** differentiates people in terms of their aesthetic and intellectual preferences. This concept helps to illuminate the important yet sometimes subtle distinctions in consumption choices among the social classes.[55] For example, a comprehensive analysis of social class differences using data from 675,000 households suggests that differences in consumption patterns for mass-marketed products have largely disappeared between the upper and upper-middle classes and between the middle and working classes. However, strong differences still emerge in terms of how consumers spend their discretionary income and leisure time. Upper- and upper-middle-class people are more likely to visit museums and attend live theater, and middle-class consumers are more likely to go camping and fishing. The upper class are more likely to listen to all-news programs, whereas the middle classes are more likely to tune in to country music.[56]

Although analyses based on distinguishing taste cultures have met with criticism due to the implicit value judgments involved, they are valuable because they recognize the existence of groupings based on shared tastes in literature, art, music,

People in the upper classes are more likely to share tastes in the arts as well. They spend relatively more of their leisure time attending the symphony, museums, the theater, and so on.

leisure activities, and home decoration. In one of the classic studies of social differences in taste, researchers cataloged homeowners' possessions as they were asking them about income and occupation. Clusters of furnishings and decorative items that seemed to appear together with some regularity were identified, and different clusters were found depending on the consumer's social status (see Figure 13.3). For example, religious objects, artificial flowers, and still-life portraits tended to be found together in relatively lower-status living rooms, whereas a cluster containing abstract paintings, sculptures, and modern furniture was more likely to appear in a higher-status home.[57]

Another approach to social class focuses on differences in the types of *codes* (the ways meanings are expressed and interpreted by consumers) used within different social strata. Discovery of these codes is valuable to marketers because this knowledge allows them to communicate to markets using concepts and terms most likely to be understood and appreciated by specific consumers. Marketing appeals constructed with class differences in mind will result in quite different messages. For example, a life insurance ad targeted to a lower-class person might depict in simple, straightforward terms a hard-working family man who feels good immediately after purchasing a policy. A more upscale appeal might depict a more affluent older couple surrounded by photos of their children and grandchildren. It might include extensive copy emphasizing the satisfaction that comes from planning for the future and highlighting the benefits of a whole-life insurance policy.

The nature of these codes varies among social classes. **Restricted codes** are dominant among the working class, whereas **elaborated codes** tend to be used by the middle and upper classes. Restricted codes focus on the content of objects, not on relationships among objects. Elaborated codes, in contrast, are more complex and depend on a more sophisticated worldview. These code differences extend to the way consumers approach basic concepts such as time, social relationships, and objects. Table 13.2 summarizes some differences between these two code types.

■ **FIGURE 13.3** LIVING ROOM CLUSTERS AND SOCIAL CLASS

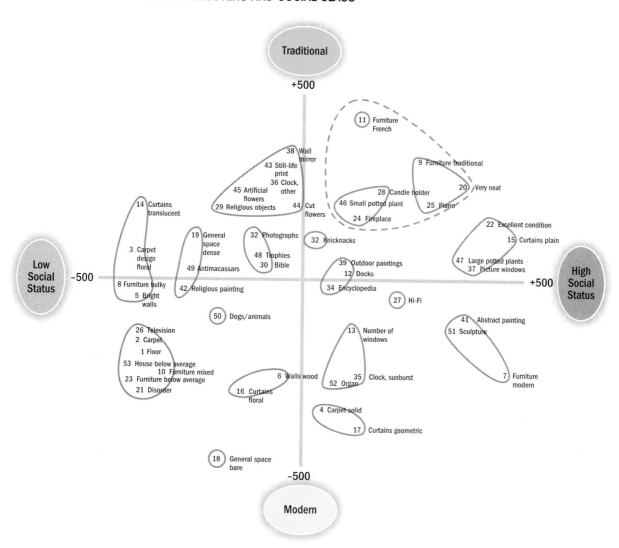

Clearly, not all taste cultures are created equal. The upper classes have access to resources that enable them to perpetuate their privileged position in society. A French theorist named Pierre Bourdieu has written at length about the process by which people compete for resources, or *capital*. These include *economic capital* (financial resources) and *social capital* (organizational affiliations and networks). The importance of access to social capital is demonstrated by the legions of aspiring professionals who in recent years have taken up golf because so much business is conducted on the greens.

Bourdieu also reminds us of the importance of **cultural capital**. This refers to a set of distinctive and socially rare tastes and practices—knowledge of "refined" behavior that admits a person into the realm of the upper class.[58] The elites in a society collect a set of skills that enable them to hold positions of power and authority, and they pass these on to their children (think etiquette lessons and debutante balls). These resources gain in value because access to them is restricted. That's part of the reason why people compete so fiercely for admission to elite colleges. Much as we hate to admit it, the rich *are* different.

Bourdieu closely linked lifestyle to social class by showing how the way we make sense of the world and put things into categories is influenced by our economic and social backgrounds. He called this the **habitus**, which refers to the ways we classify

TABLE 13.2
EFFECTS OF RESTRICTED VERSUS ELABORATED CODES

	Restricted Codes	**Elaborated Codes**
General characteristics	Emphasize description and contents of objects	Emphasize analysis and interrelationship between objects; i.e., hierarchical organization and instrumental connections
	Have implicit meanings (context dependent)	Have explicit meanings
Language	Use few qualifiers, i.e., few adjectives or adverbs	Have language rich in personal, individual qualifiers
	Use concrete, descriptive, tangible symbolism	Use large vocabulary, complex conceptual hierarchy
Social relationships	Stress attributes of individuals over formal roles	Stress formal role structure, instrumental relationships
Time	Focus on present; have only general notion of future	Focus on instrumental relationship between present activities and future rewards
Physical space	Locate rooms, spaces in context of other rooms and places: e.g., "front room," "corner store"	Identify rooms, spaces in terms of usage; formal ordering of spaces; e.g., "dining room," "financial district"
Implications for marketers	Stress inherent product quality, contents (or trustworthiness, goodness of "real-type"), spokesperson	Stress differences, advantages vis-à-vis other products in terms of some autonomous evaluation criteria
	Stress implicit of fit of product with total lifestyle	Strees product's instrumental ties to distant benefits
	Use simple adjectives, descriptions	Use complex adjectives, descriptors

Source: Adapted from Jeffrey F. Durgee, "How Consumer Sub-Cultures Code Reality: A Look at Some Code Types," in Richard J. Lutz, ed., *Advances in Consumer Research,* 13 (Provo, UT: Association of Consumer Research, 1986): 332.

experiences as a result of our socialization processes. Bourdieu demonstrated how cultural capital determines people's tastes and lifestyles in French society.[59]

More recently, an attempt has been made to translate Bourdieu's terms into a relatively simple lifestyle categorization scheme.[60] Based on Bourdieu's notions of economic capital (income and wealth) and cultural capital (education plus the ability to distinguish between cultural styles), this model proposed four different but fundamental consumer types (see Figure 13.4).[61] So far, the model has only been used in Denmark, but it is likely to apply to other countries as well.

This approach is based upon the **grid-group theory** developed by anthropologist Mary Douglas. The distinction between grid and group refers to an individual's relation to his or her own social group and to the general social system (or grid). So, the model distinguishes between people with high and low group identification

■ FIGURE 13.4
A THEORETICALLY BASED LIFESTYLE MODEL

High cultural capital High economic capital Low group High grid	High cultural capital Low economic capital High group Low grid
Low cultural capital High economic capital Low group Low grid	Low cultural capital Low economic capital High group High grid

Source: Adapted from Henrik Dahl, *Hvis din nabo var en bil* (Copenhagen Akademisk Forlag, 1997).

and a more or less affirmative (high and low) relation to the organization of society (the grid). The model ends up with the following segments:

- *First quadrant:* Professional, career-oriented people, with higher education and income, and with a rather individualistic attitude and an accepting attitude toward the social organization (they are responsible for much of it anyway). Their search for meaning is characterized by ambition for power and wealth.
- *Second quadrant:* Well-educated intellectuals with less well-paid career opportunities (many university professors here), with a high degree of identification with their professional group, but with a critical attitude toward society. Their search for meaning lies in the realization of their own intellectual ideals.
- *Third quadrant:* Relatively wealthy people, with low education or not so culturally interested (the stereotypical self-made (wo)man). They are not very engaged with the larger society and they may even tend to consider the rest of society (and everything strange) as relatively hostile.
- *Fourth quadrant:* Low on both types of capital, money and education, but with strong group affiliation and a relatively affirmative attitude toward society, these people tend to be locally oriented. The search for meaning is rooted in their daily activities and daily lives.

Targeting the Poor

About 14 percent of Americans live below the poverty line, and most marketers largely ignore this segment. Still, although poor people obviously have less to spend than do rich ones, they have the same basic needs as everyone else. Low-income families purchase staples such as milk, orange juice, and tea at the same rates as average-income families. Minimum wage–level households spend more than average on out-of-pocket health care costs, rent, and food eaten at home.[62] Unfortunately, these resources are harder to obtain due to the reluctance of many businesses to locate in lower-income areas. On average, residents of poor neighborhoods must travel more than two miles to have the same access to supermarkets, large drug stores, and banks as do residents of more affluent areas.[63]

The unemployed tend to feel alienated in a consumer society because they are unable to obtain many of the items that our culture tells us we "need" to be successful. However, idealized advertising portrayals don't appear to bother low-end consumers who have been interviewed by researchers. Apparently, one way to preserve self-esteem is by placing themselves outside of the culture of consumption and emphasizing the value of a simple way of life with less emphasis on materialism. In some cases, they enjoy the advertising as entertainment without actually yearning for the products; a comment by one 32-year-old British woman is typical, "They're not aimed at me, definitely not. It's fine to look at them, but they're not aimed at me so in the main I just pass over them."[64]

Targeting the Rich

We live in a time where one can purchase a Pink Splendor Barbie complete with crystal jewelry and a bouffant gown sewn with 24-karat threads.[65] To dress a "living doll," Victoria's Secret offers its Million Dollar Miracle Bra, with more than 100 carats of real diamonds.[66] *Somebody* is buying this stuff!

Many marketers try to target affluent, upscale markets. This practice often makes sense, because these consumers obviously have the resources to expend on costly products (often with higher profit margins). However, it is a mistake to assume that everyone with a high income should be placed into the same market segment. As noted earlier, social class involves more than absolute income. It is also a way of life, and affluent consumers' interests and spending priorities are significantly affected by factors such as where they got their money, how they got it, and how long they have had it.[67]

Marketing Opportunity

Some promising (although scattered) efforts to target lower-income people are taking shape. For example, Hewlett-Packard recently launched an initiative called World e-Inclusion, which aims to sell, lease, or donate a billion dollars' worth of satellite-powered computer products and services to underserved markets in Africa, Asia, Eastern Europe, Latin America, and the Middle East.

These activities appeal to the self-interest of organizations who understand they can turn a profit while having a positive effect on society—and sow the seeds for future growth by getting entrenched in markets that may well gain wealth over time. This movement has been dubbed **B2-4B (Business to Four Billion)**, reflecting the estimated size of the lower-income market worldwide. Investing in future potential looks like a smart move—according to the World Bank, economic growth rates for developing countries are about twice that of developed nations.

We can find one success story in India, where Hindustan Lever decided in the 1990s to introduce products for low-income Indians. The firm's engineers developed extremely low-cost packaging material and other innovations that allowed the company to distribute high-quality products in single-use sachets costing the equivalent of pennies instead of the US$4 to US$5 that the regular-size containers cost. Good things do come in small packages.[68]

Despite our stereotype of rich people living it up, one study found the typical millionaire is a 57-year-old man who is self-employed, earns a median household income of $131,000, has been married to the same wife for most of his adult life, has children, has never spent more than $399 on a suit or more than $140 for a pair of shoes, and drives a Ford Explorer. Interestingly, many affluent people don't consider themselves to be rich. One tendency noticed by many researchers is that they indulge in luxury goods while pinching pennies on everyday items—buying shoes at Neiman Marcus and deodorant at Wal-Mart, for example.[69]

SRI Consulting Business Intelligence (the research firm that developed VALS2 as discussed in Chapter 6) divides consumers into three groups based on their attitudes toward luxury:

1 *Luxury is Functional:* These consumers use their money to buy things that will last and have enduring value. They conduct extensive pre-purchase research and make logical decisions rather than emotional or impulsive choices

2 *Luxury is a Reward:* These consumers tend to be younger than the first group but older than the third group. They often use luxury goods to say, "I've made it." The desire to be successful and to demonstrate their success to others motivates these consumers to purchase conspicuous luxury items, such as high-end automobiles and homes in exclusive communities.

3 *Luxury is Indulgence:* This group is the smallest of the three, and tends to include younger consumers and slightly more males than the other two groups. To these consumers, the purpose of owning luxury is to be extremely lavish and self-indulgent. This group is willing to pay a premium for goods that express their individuality and make others take notice. These consumers have a more emotional approach to luxury spending, and are more likely than the other two groups to make impulse purchases.[70]

Old Money

"Old money" families (e.g., the Rockefellers, DuPonts, Fords, etc.) live primarily on inherited funds.[71] One commentator called this group "the class in hiding."[72] Following the Great Depression of the 1930s, monied families became more discreet about exhibiting their wealth. Many fled from mansions such as those found in Manhattan to hideaways in Virginia, Connecticut, and New Jersey.

Merely having wealth is not sufficient to achieve social prominence in these circles. Money must be accompanied by a family history of public service and philanthropy, which is often manifested in tangible markers that enable these donors to achieve a kind of immortality (e.g., Rockefeller University or the Whitney Museum).[73] "Old money" consumers tend to make distinctions among themselves in terms of ancestry and lineage rather than wealth.[74] Old money people (like the Caldwells) are secure in their status. In a sense, they have been trained their whole lives to be rich.

The Nouveau Riches

Today there are many people—including high-profile billionaires such as Bill Gates, Steve Jobs, and Richard Branson—who can be thought of as "the working wealthy."[75] The Horatio Alger myth, where a person goes from "rags to riches" through hard work and a bit of luck, is still a powerful force in American society. That's why a commercial showing the actual garage where the two co-founders of Hewlett-Packard first worked strikes a chord in so many.

Although many people do in fact become "self-made millionaires," they often encounter a problem (although not the worst problem one could think of!) after they have become wealthy and change their social status: Consumers who have achieved extreme wealth and have relatively recently become members of upper social classes are known as the *nouveau riches*, a term that is usually used in a derogatory manner to describe newcomers to the world of wealth.

Alas, many nouveau riches are plagued by *status anxiety.* They monitor the cultural environment to ensure that they are doing the "right" thing, wearing the "right" clothes, being seen at the "right" places, using the "right" caterer, and so on.[76] Flamboyant consumption can thus be viewed as a form of *symbolic self-completion*, whereby the excessive display of symbols thought to denote "class" is used to make up for an internal lack of assurance about the "correct" way to behave.[77] In major Chinese cities like Shanghai, some people have taken to wearing pajamas in public as a way to flaunt their newfound wealth. As one consumer explained, "Only people in cities can afford clothes like this. In farming villages, they still have to wear old work clothes to bed."[78]

Advertising directed to this group often plays on these insecurities by emphasizing the importance of "looking the part." Clever merchandising supplies these consumers with the props necessary to masquerade by playing the role of old money people. For example, ads for *Colonial Homes* magazine feature consumers who "have worked very hard to make it look like they never had to." A housing development near Santa Monica, California, epitomizes the demand for ready-made affluent lifestyles. It features completely furnished mansions (complete with linens, dishes, even artwork) and each residence also includes four-car garages, hot tubs, fake boulders doubling as outdoor speaker enclosures, and a built-in computer network. IBM Home Director software controls the lighting and the coffeemaker and even phones you anywhere in the world if the temperature gets too high in the wine cellar (don't you just *hate* when that happens?). Buyers choose from one of four different pre-fab lifestyle fantasies: English Country Estate, Tuscan Villa, French Regency, or New York Penthouse.[79] These little gems can be had for as low as $10 million, so don't waste any time putting in your offer!

■ STATUS SYMBOLS

The "understated" homes described above clearly are meant to showcase their owners' ability to afford them. People have a deep-seated tendency to evaluate themselves, their professional accomplishments, and their material well-being relative to others. The popular phrase "keeping up with the Joneses" (in Japan it's "keeping up with the Satos") refers to the comparison between one's standard of living and that of one's neighbors. Many consumers like to feel as if they are special, wealthy, accomplished, and even famous. Maybe that explains the success of Tinseltown Studios, a dinner theater in Anaheim, California, that lets patrons pretend they are movie stars. Enter the gates, and immediately light bulbs flash and autograph seekers close in. Follow the red carpet and watch yourself being interviewed on a giant screen.[80]

However, often it's not enough to have wealth or fame—what matters is that you have more of it than others. A major motivation for the purchase and display of products is not to enjoy them, but rather to let others know that we can afford them. In other words, these products function as status symbols. The desire to accumulate these "badges of achievement" is summarized by the popular bumper sticker slogan, "He who dies with the most toys, wins." Status-seeking is a significant source of motivation to procure appropriate products and services that the user hopes will let others know that he or she has "made it."

The particular products that count as status symbols of course vary across cultures and locales. For example, owning one's own private helicopter is a must for well-to-do Brazilians, who are dogged by traffic snarls and kidnappers. There are more than 400 of these choppers prowling the skies of São Paulo.[81] Journey to

Marketing Pitfall

Traditionally, designer brands are a popular antidote to status anxiety—if you're not sure about your own taste, cover your bet by buying a well-known label and display it prominently. This solution seems to be falling out of favor, as shoppers increasingly turn to house-brand bargain clothes from stores like Target and Kohl's. Some analysts attribute this trend to the glut of imitation products that have eroded the value of designer goods, while others cite 9/11 as the motivation for a return to simplicity (see Chapter 4). According to one retail analyst, "They don't want to look like anybody else and they don't want to have somebody's else's name plastered on their things."[82]

A recent survey asked 7,500 apparel customers whether their desires for specific status brands and trademarks had diminished recently. Over half said that logos and labels were less important to them. And, loyalty to designers diminishes as we age: Sixty-nine percent of consumers aged 45 to 59 said logos factor "much less" or "less" in their buying habits, compared with 41 percent of respondents aged 21 to 34.[83]

Status symbols are always in flux. At one time, having very pale skin was the mark of an upper social class because it indicated that the person did not have to work in the fields. Today, a suntan is equated with leisure time and consumers go to great lengths to get one naturally or with "help."

China, where children are status symbols (partly because couples are strongly discouraged from having more than one baby). Parents want to show off their pampered child and are eager to surround their "little emperors" with luxury goods. Chinese families spend one-third to one-half of their disposable income on their children.[84]

Conspicuous Consumption

The social analyst Thorstein Veblen first discussed the motivation to consume for the sake of consuming at the turn of the last century. Veblen felt that a major role of products was for **invidious distinction**—they are used to inspire envy in others through display of wealth or power. To understand how this works, consider the recent trend in men's fashion to weave real gold into clothing. Ties made with 18-karat gold thread are selling for $260. One man spent $9,000 for a black silk tuxedo and a bow tie and cummerbund set flecked with gold thread. Others are buying pinstriped suits priced from $10 to $20 thousand.[85] Presumably these clothes are dry clean only.

Veblen coined the term **conspicuous consumption** to refer to people's desire to provide prominent visible evidence of their ability to afford luxury goods. His work was motivated by the excesses of his time. Veblen wrote in the era of the "Robber Barons," where the likes of J. P. Morgan, Henry Clay Frick, and William Vanderbilt were building massive financial empires and flaunting their wealth by throwing lavish parties. Some of these events of excess became legendary, as described in this account:

> There were tales, repeated in the newspapers, of dinners on horseback; of banquets for pet dogs; of hundred-dollar bills folded into guests' dinner napkins; of a hostess who attracted attention by seating a chimpanzee at her table; of centerpieces in which lightly clad living maidens swam in glass tanks, or emerged from huge pies; of parties at which cigars were ceremoniously lighted with flaming banknotes of large denominations.[86]

Sounds like they really lived it up back in the old days, right? Well, maybe the more things change, the more they stay the same: The recent wave of corporate scandals involving companies like Enron, WorldCom, and Tyco infuriated many consumers as they discovered that some top executives were living it up even as

Armored cars are a status symbol in Brazil. This ad for an armored-car maker uses an egg carton metaphor to illustrate the security it offers.

Marketing Opportunity

Is that a phone in your pocket, or are you just glad to see me? The quest for status influences both kids and adults, though the symbols we choose to pursue vary as we age. However, the cell phone is emerging as a new status symbol that cuts across age groups.

Young people view a cell phone as a necessity, not a luxury. It's their primary means of staying connected with others. But a cell phone is not just a means of communication. It is an accessory, a fashion statement, an instant messenger, a toy, and a social prop. It is a symbol of independence second only to the car, and an extension of their personality, many teenagers say. Phone manufacturers are scrambling to provide what kids want. The companies have their sights set on young people for good reason: Since only 38 percent of American teenagers have cell phones, the market has plenty of room for growth. Some firms are retooling existing phone models, adding features like an FM radio or even access to AOL Instant Messenger. As we saw in Chapter 1, others like Wildseed are offering customizable faceplates to let users express their unique identity.

Adults aren't immune to the status appeal of a mobile, and some research suggests that men are especially susceptible to its lure. Researchers at the University of Liverpool in the United Kingdom were inspired to investigate this phenomenon after reading newspaper accounts about night clubs in South America that began requiring patrons to check their cell phones at the door. The clubs' managers soon discovered that a huge percentage of the phones were fake. To see how people were really using their phones as social props, the researchers observed patrons at an upscale pub frequented by lawyers, entrepreneurs, and other single professionals. They discovered that men had a markedly different

For young people, the cell phone has become a primary mode of communication.

other employees were being laid off. One account of a $1 million birthday party thrown by the chief executive of Tyco for his wife sounds eerily familiar to the shindigs thrown by those old Robber Barons: The party reportedly had a gladiator theme and included an ice sculpture of Michelangelo's David with vodka streaming from his penis into crystal glasses. The company also furnished the executive's New York apartment with such essentials as a $6,000 shower curtain, a $2,200 gilt wastebasket, and a $17,100 "traveling toilet box."[87]

The Billboard Wife

This phenomenon of conspicuous consumption was, for Veblen, most evident among what he termed the *leisure class*, people for whom productive work is taboo. In Marxist terms, such an attitude reflects a desire to link oneself to ownership or control of the means of production, rather than to the production itself. Any evidence that one actually has to labor for a living is to be shunned, as suggested by the term the "idle rich."

This analysis also included wives: Veblen criticized the "decorative" role women were often forced to play as they were showered with expensive clothes, pretentious homes, and a life of leisure as a way to advertise the wealth of their husbands—a sort of "walking billboard." Fashions such as high-heeled shoes, tight

DIFFERENT RINGS FOR DIFFERENT BOYFRIENDS. TECHNOLOGY CAN BE SO NAUGHTY.

LG

Assign individual CMX MIDI melodies to the people you want to hear from most. It's just one of the things about the new, ultra-compact, super-light LG 08525 that will make you smile. Other features include: Voice Recording/Memo/Playback, Phone Book, Vibration Alert, Scheduler, Voice Activated Dialing, CMX MIDI Sound for Ringer and Games, 4-Way Navigation Key, Two Games. VISIT WWW.LGINFOCOMM.COM

corsets, billowing trains on dresses, and elaborate hairstyles all conspired to ensure that wealthy women could barely move without assistance, much less perform manual labor. Similarly, the Chinese practice of foot-binding prevented women from walking, and they had to be carried from place to place.

Veblen was inspired by anthropological studies of the Kwakiutl Indians, who lived in the Pacific Northwest. At a ceremony called a *potlatch*, the host showed off his wealth and gave extravagant presents to the guests. The more one gave away, the better one looked to the others. Sometimes, the host would use an even more radical strategy to flaunt his wealth. He would publicly *destroy* some of his property just to demonstrate how much he had.

This ritual was also used as a social weapon: Because guests were expected to reciprocate, a poorer rival could be humiliated by inviting him to a lavish potlatch. The need to give away as much as the host, even though he could not afford it, would essentially force the hapless guest into bankruptcy. If this practice sounds "primitive," think for a moment about many modern weddings. Parents commonly invest huge sums of money to throw a lavish party and compete with others for the distinction of giving their daughter the "best" or most extravagant wedding, even if they have to dip into their retirement savings to do it.

Like the potlatch ritual, the desire to convince others that one has a surplus of resources creates the need to display evidence of this abundance. Accordingly, priority is given to consumption activities that use up as many resources as possible in nonconstructive pursuits. This *conspicuous waste* in turn shows others that one has the assets to spare. Veblen wrote, "we are told of certain Polynesian chiefs, who, under the stress of good form, preferred to starve rather than carry their food to their mouths with their own hands."[90]

Parody Display

As the competition to accumulate status symbols escalates, sometimes the best tactic is to switch gears and go in reverse. One way to do this is to deliberately avoid status symbols—that is, to seek status by mocking it. This sophisticated form of conspicuous consumption has been termed **parody display**.[91]

A good example of parody display is the home furnishing style known as High Tech that was in vogue a few years ago. This motif incorporated the use of industrial

relationship to their cell phones than did women. The female customers generally kept their phones in their purses and retrieved them only as needed, but the men would take their phones out of their jacket pockets or briefcases upon sitting down and place them on the bar counter or table for all to see.

The authors of this study propose that men are using their mobile phones as peacocks use their plumage or male bullfrogs use their croaks—to advertise their status to available mates. They noted that the amount of time the men spent toying with and displaying their phones increased significantly as the number of men relative to women increased—just as male peacocks fan open their feathers more vigorously as the number of competing suitors increases.[88]

And, even the phone numbers assigned to cell phones appear to function as status symbols for some. Numbers ending in "00" or "000" are hot and in demand even though (or because?) most phone companies charge extra to assign them. Independent sales agents who sell new phone accounts report customers frequently ask for these coveted numbers. As one observed, "People used to want their names spelled out. Now the most requested and hardest thing to get is a triple or a double zero number."[89] That's status calling.

THE GLOBAL LOOKING GLASS

Patrick Stewart, the British actor who achieved international fame as the French captain of the *USS Enterprise* in *Star Trek: The Next Generation*, says that "A lot of America's global actions stink." He finds it "laughable that the United States considers itself the land of opportunity" and asks "How can you be truly free when there is so much poverty and poor education?" That's a funny question since it was America, after all, that made both Stewart and his son, an actor on *Third Rock from the Sun*, stinking rich. But Stewart is simply practicing the America bashing that has become fashionable all around the world.

Rarely does a week go by that an anti-American protest doesn't sprout up somewhere around the globe. One week protestors make ruckuses in South Korea and Haiti. The next week, it could be Mexico City or Beijing. And nowhere in the world does America bashing have more elite respectability than France, where some of the most popular books have titles like *Who Is Killing France? The American Strategy, American Totalitarianism* and the best-seller *No Thanks, Uncle Sam*, written by a member of the French Parliament, who concludes, "It is appropriate to be downright anti-American."

Most of this anti-Americanism is based quite simply on snobbish jealousy of the success of American popular culture around the globe. What bothers Europeans is not so much that Americans make bad films, books, and food; but that average Europeans love our films, books, and food. Half the spots on the French best-seller list are taken by translations of American books. American films repeatedly dominate the top-10 box-office hits throughout Europe and the world.

Source: Excerpted from Jonah Goldberg, "*America Bashing Becomes International Pastime,*" **Yrock.Com** (Young Republicans Online Community Network), April 28, 2003.

Ripped jeans (especially the pricey kind that come that way when you buy them) are an example of parody display.

equipment (e.g., floors were covered with plates used on the decks of destroyers), and pipes and support beams were deliberately exposed.[92] This decorating strategy is intended to show that one is so witty and "in the know" that status symbols aren't necessary. Hence, the popularity of old, ripped blue jeans, and "utility" vehicles such as Jeeps among the upper classes (like the Caldwells). Thus, "true" status is shown by the adoption of product symbolism that is deliberately not fashionable.

CHAPTER SUMMARY

The field of behavioral economics considers how consumers decide what to do with their money. In particular, discretionary expenditures are made only when people are able and willing to spend money on items above and beyond their basic needs. Consumer confidence—the state of mind consumers have about their own personal situation, as well as their feelings about their overall economic prospects—helps to determine whether they will purchase goods and services, take on debt, or save their money.

A consumer's social class refers to his or her standing in society. It is determined by a number of factors, including education, occupation, and income.

Virtually all groups make distinctions among members in terms of relative superiority, power, and access to valued resources. This social stratification creates a status hierarchy in which some goods are preferred over others and are used to categorize their owners' social class.

Although income is an important indicator of social class, the relationship is far from perfect. Social class is also determined by factors such as place of residence, cultural interests, and worldview.

Purchase decisions are sometimes influenced by the desire to "buy up" to a higher social class or to engage in the process of conspicuous consumption, through which one's status is flaunted by the deliberate and nonconstructive use of valuable resources. This spending pattern is a characteristic of the nouveau riches, whose relatively recent acquisition of income, rather than ancestry or breeding, is responsible for their increased social mobility.

Products often are used as status symbols to communicate real or desired social class. Parody display occurs when consumers seek status by deliberately avoiding fashionable products.

KEY TERMS

B2–4B   459
Behavioral economics   442
Conspicuous consumption   463
Consumer confidence   442
Cultural capital   457
Discretionary income   442
Elaborated codes   456

Grid-group theory   458
Habitus   457
Homogamy   445
Invidious distinction   462
Parody display   465
Restricted codes   456
Social class   444

Social mobility   448
Social stratification   446
Status crystallization   453
Status hierarchy   446
Status symbols   441
Taste culture   455

CONSUMER BEHAVIOR CHALLENGE

1 Sears, JCPenney and, to a lesser degree, Kmart have made concerted efforts in recent years to upgrade their images and appeal to higher-class consumers. How successful have these efforts been? Do you believe this strategy is wise?

2 What are some of the obstacles to measuring social class in today's society? Discuss some ways to get around these obstacles.

3 What consumption differences might you expect to observe between a family characterized as underprivileged and one whose income is average for its social class?

4 When is social class likely to be a better predictor of consumer behavior than mere knowledge of a person's income?

5 How do you assign people to social classes, or do you at all? What consumption cues do you use (e.g., clothing, speech, cars, etc.) to determine social standing?

6 Thorstein Veblen argued that women were often used as "trophy wives" to display their husbands' wealth. Is this argument still valid today?

7 Given present environmental conditions and dwindling resources, what is the future of "conspicuous waste?" Can the desire to impress others with affluence ever be eliminated? If not, can it take on a less dangerous form?

8 Many designers today are reacting to consumers' growing desires for understated elegance by downplaying the logos that were so prominent on products in the 1990s. Some people argue that status symbols are dead. Do you agree?

9 Using the Status Index presented in Figure 13.3, compute a social class score for people you know, including their parents, if possible. Ask several friends (preferably from different places) to compile similar information for people they know. How closely do your answers compare? If you find differences, how can you explain them?

10 Compile a list of occupations and ask a sample of students in a variety of majors (both business and nonbusiness) to rank the prestige of these jobs. Can you detect any differences in these rankings as a function of students' majors?

11 Compile a collection of ads that depict consumers of different social classes. What generalizations can you make about the reality of these ads and about the media in which they appear?

12 This chapter observes that some marketers are finding "greener pastures" by targeting low-income people. How ethical is it to single out consumers who cannot afford to waste their precious resources on discretionary items? Under what circumstances should this segmentation strategy be encouraged or discouraged?

13 Status symbols are products that are valued because they show others how much money or prestige a person has, such as Rolex watches or expensive sports cars. Do you believe that your peer group values status symbols? Why or why not? If yes, what are the products that you think are regarded as status symbols now for consumers your age?

NOTES

1. Data in this section adapted from Fabian Linden, *Consumer Affluence: The Next Wave* (New York: The Conference Board, 1994). For additional information about U.S. income statistics, access Occupational Employment and Wage Estimates at www.bls.gov/oes/oes_data.htm.

2. Sylvia Ann Hewlett, "Feminization of the Workforce," *New Perspectives Quarterly* 98 (July 1, 1998): 66–70.

3. Mary Bowler, "Women's Earnings: An Overview," *Monthly Labor Review* 122 (December 1999): 13–22.

4. Christopher D. Carroll, "How Does Future Income Affect Current Consumption?" *Quarterly Journal of Economics* 109 (February 1994): 111–47.

5. For a scale that measures consumer frugality, see John L. Lastovicka, Lance A. Bettencourt, Renee Shaw Hughner, and Ronald J. Kuntze, "Lifestyle of the Tight and Frugal: Theory and Measurement," *Journal of Consumer Research* 26 (June 1999): 85–98.

6. José F. Medina, Joel Saegert, and Alicia Gresham, "Comparison of Mexican-American and Anglo-American Attitudes toward Money," *The Journal of Consumer Affairs* 30, no. 1 (1996): 124–45.

7. Kirk Johnson, "Sit Down. Breathe Deeply. This Is Really Scary Stuff," *New York Times* (April 16, 1995): F5.

8. Fred van Raaij, "Economic Psychology," *Journal of Economic Psychology* 1 (1981): 1–24.

9. Richard T. Curtin, "Indicators of Consumer Behavior: The University of Michigan Surveys of Consumers," *Public Opinion Quarterly* (1982): 340–52.

10. George Katona, "Consumer Saving Patterns," *Journal of Consumer Research* 1 (June 1974): 1–12.

11. Floyd L. Ruch and Philip G. Zimbardo, *Psychology and Life,* 8th ed. (Glenview, IL: Scott Foresman, 1971).

12. Jonathan H. Turner, *Sociology: Studying the Human System*, 2nd ed. (Santa Monica, CA: Goodyear, 1981).

13. Ibid.

14. Richard P. Coleman, "The Continuing Significance of Social Class to Marketing," *Journal of Consumer Research* 10 (December 1983): 265–80; Turner, *Sociology: Studying the Human System*.

15. Rebecca Gardyn, "The Mating Game," *American Demographics* (July–August 2002): 33–34.

16. Richard P. Coleman and Lee Rainwater, *Standing in America: New Dimensions of Class* (New York: Basic Books, 1978), 89.

17. Coleman and Rainwater, *Standing in America: New Dimensions of Class.*

18. Turner, *Sociology: Studying the Human System.*

19. James Fallows, "A Talent for Disorder (Class Structure)," *U.S. News & World Report* (February 1, 1988): 83.

20. Coleman, "The Continuing Significance of Social Class to Marketing"; W. Lloyd Warner and Paul S. Lunt, eds., *The Social Life of a Modern Community* (New Haven, CT: Yale University Press, 1941).

21. J. David Lynch, "Emerging Middle Class Reshaping China," *USA Today* (November 12, 2002): 13A.

22. Nicholas D. Kristof, "Women as Bodyguards: In China, It's All the Rage," *New York Times* (July 1, 1993): A4.

23. James Sterngold, "How Do You Define Status? A New BMW in the Drive. An Old Rock in the Garden," *New York Times* (December 28, 1989): C1.

24. Robin Knight, "Just You Move Over, 'Enry 'Iggins; A New Regard for Profits and Talent Cracks Britain's Old Class System," *U.S. News & World Report* 106 (April 24, 1989): 40.

25. Turner, *Sociology: Studying the Human System*, 260.

26. Leslie Kaufman, "Deluxe Dilemma: To Sell Globally or Sell Haughtily?" *New York Times on the Web* (September 22, 1999).

27. See Ronald Paul Hill and Mark Stamey, "The Homeless in America: An Examination of Possessions and Consumption Behaviors," *Journal of Consumer Research* 17 (December 1990): 303–21; estimate provided by Dr. Ronald Hill, personal communication, December 1997.

28. Joseph Kahl, *The American Class Structure* (New York: Holt, Rinehart and Winston, 1961).

29. Leonard Beeghley, *Social Stratification in America: A Critical Analysis of Theory and Research* (Santa Monica, CA: Goodyear, 1978).

30. Coleman and Rainwater, *Standing in America: New Dimensions of Class*, 220.

31. Turner, *Sociology: Studying the Human System.*

32. See Coleman, "The Continuing Significance of Social Class to Marketing"; Charles M. Schaninger, "Social Class versus Income Revisited: An Empirical Investigation," *Journal of Marketing Research* 18 (May 1981): 192–208.

33. Coleman, "The Continuing Significance of Social Class to Marketing."

34. August B. Hollingshead and Fredrick C. Redlich, *Social Class and Mental Illness: A Community Study* (New York: Wiley, 1958).

35. John Mager and Lynn R. Kahle, "Is the Whole More Than the Sum of the Parts? Re-evaluating Social Status in Marketing," *Journal of Business Psychology* 10 (Fall 1995): 3–18.

36. Beeghley, *Social Stratification in America: A Critical Analysis of Theory and Research.*

37. R. Vanneman and F. C. Pampel, "The American Perception of Class and Status," *American Sociological Review* 42 (June 1977): 422–37.

38. Donald W. Hendon, Emelda L. Williams, and Douglas E. Huffman, "Social Class System Revisited," *Journal of Business Research* 17 (November 1988): 259.

39. Coleman, "The Continuing Significance of Social Class to Marketing."

40. Gerhard E. Lenski, "Status Crystallization: A Non-Vertical Dimension of Social Status," *American Sociological Review* 19 (August 1954): 405–12.

41. Richard P. Coleman, "The Significance of Social Stratification in Selling," in Martin L. Bell, ed., *Marketing: A Maturing Discipline: Proceedings of the American Marketing Association 43rd National Conference* (Chicago: American Marketing Association, 1960), 171–84.

42. E. Barth and W. Watson, "Questionable Assumptions in the Theory of Social Stratification," *Pacific Sociological Review* 7 (Spring 1964): 10–16.

43. Zick Rubin, "Do American Women Marry Up?" *American Sociological Review* 33 (1968): 750–60.

44. K. U. Ritter and L. L. Hargens, "Occupational Positions and Class Identifications of Married Working Women: A Test of the Asymmetry Hypothesis," *American Journal of Sociology* 80 (January 1975): 934–48.

45. J. Michael Munson and W. Austin Spivey, "Product and Brand-User Stereotypes Among Social Classes: Implications for Advertising Strategy," *Journal of Advertising Research* 21 (August 1981): 37–45.

46. Stuart U. Rich and Subhash C. Jain, "Social Class and Life Cycle as Predictors of Shopping Behavior," *Journal of Marketing Research* 5 (February 1968): 41–49.

47. Thomas W. Osborn, "Analytic Techniques for Opportunity Marketing," *Marketing Communications* (September 1987): 49–63.

48. Coleman, "The Continuing Significance of Social Class to Marketing."

49. Jeffrey F. Durgee, "How Consumer Sub-Cultures Code Reality: A Look at Some Code Types," in Richard J. Lutz, ed., *Advances in Consumer Research* 13 (Provo, UT: Association for Consumer Research, 1986): 332–37.

50. David Halle, *America's Working Man: Work, Home, and Politics Among Blue-Collar Owners* (Chicago: University of Chicago Press, 1984); David Montgomery, "America's Working Man," *Monthly Review* (1985): 1.

51. Coleman and Rainwater, *Standing in America: New Dimensions of Class*, 139.

52. Roger Brown, *Social Psychology* (New York: Free Press, 1965).

53. Kit R. Roane, "Affluenza Strikes Kids," *U.S. News & World Report* (March 20, 2000): 55.

54. Tamar Lewin, "Next to Mom and Dad: It's a Hard Life (or Not)," *New York Times on the Web* (November 7, 1999).

55. Herbert J. Gans, "Popular Culture in America: Social Problem in a Mass Society or Social Asset in a Pluralist Society?" in Howard S. Becker, ed., *Social Problems: A Modern Approach* (New York: Wiley, 1966).

56. Eugene Sivadas, George Mathew, and David J. Curry, "A Preliminary Examination of the Continuing Significance of Social Class to Marketing: A Geodemographic Replication," *Journal of Consumer Marketing* 41, no. 6 (1997): 463–79.

57. Edward O. Laumann and James S. House, "Living Room Styles and Social Attributes: The Patterning of Material Artifacts in a Modern Urban Community," *Sociology and Social Research* 54 (April 1970): 321–42; see also Stephen S. Bell, Morris B. Holbrook, and Michael R. Solomon, "Combining Esthetic and Social Value to Explain Preferences for Product Styles with the Incorporation of Personality and Ensemble Effects," *Journal of Social Behavior and Personality* 6 (1991): 243–74.

58. Pierre Bourdieu, *Distinction: A Social Critique of the Judgement of Taste* (Cambridge, UK: Cambridge University Press, 1984); see also Douglas B. Holt, "Does Cultural Capital Structure American Consumption?" *Journal of Consumer Research* 1 (June 1998): 1–25.

59. Pierre Bourdieu, *La Distinction. Critique Social du Jugement* (Paris: Editions de Minuit, 1979). English translation 1984.

60. Henrik Dahl, *Hvis Din Nabo Var En Bil* (Copenhagen: Akademisk Forlag, 1997): 55–81.

61. Mary Douglas, *Natural Symbols* (New York: Random House, 1973).

62. Paula Mergenhagen, "What Can Minimum Wage Buy?" *American Demographics* (January 1996): 32–36.
63. Linda F. Alwitt and Thomas D. Donley, "Retail Stores in Poor Urban Neighborhoods," *The Journal of Consumer Affairs* 31, no. 1 (1997): 108–27.
64. Richard Elliott, "How Do the Unemployed Maintain Their Identity in a Culture of Consumption?" *European Advances in Consumer Research* 2 (1995): 3. For a discussion of coping strategies used by impoverished consumers to combat the consequences of limited product availability and restricted income sources, see Ronald R. Hill and Debra L. Stephens, "Impoverished Consumer and Consumer Behavior: The Case of the AFDC Mothers," *Journal of Macromarketing* (Fall 1997): 32–48.
65. Cyndee Miller, "New Line of Barbie Dolls Targets Big, Rich Kids," *Marketing News* (June 17, 1996): 6.
66. Cyndee Miller, "Baubles Are Back," *Marketing News* (April 14, 1997): 1.
67. Reading the Buyer's Mind," *U.S. News & World Report* (March 16, 1987): 59.
68. D. James, "B2–4B Spells Profits," *Marketing News* (November 5, 2001): 1.
69. Shelly Reese, "The Many Faces of Affluence," *Marketing Tools* (November–December 1997): 44–48.
70. Rebecca Gardyn, "Oh, the Good Life," *American Demographics* (November 2002): 34.
71. Paul Fussell, *Class: A Guide through the American Status System* (New York: Summit Books, 1983): 29.
72. Ibid., 30.
73. Elizabeth C. Hirschman, "Secular Immortality and the American Ideology of Affluence," *Journal of Consumer Research* 17 (June 1990): 31–42.
74. Coleman and Rainwater, *Standing in America: New Dimensions of Class*, 150.
75. Kerry A. Dolan, "The World's Working Rich," *Forbes* (July 3, 2000): 162.
76. Jason DeParle, "Spy Anxiety: The Smart Magazine that Makes Smart People Nervous about Their Standing," *Washingtonian Monthly* (February 1989): 10.
77. For a recent examination of retailing issues related to the need for status, see Jacqueline Kilsheimer Eastman, Leisa Reinecke Flynn, and Ronald E. Goldsmith, "Shopping for Status: The Retail Managerial Implications," *Association of Marketing Theory and Practice* (Spring 1994): 125–30.
78. Martin Fackler, "Pajamas: Not Just for Sleep Anymore," *Opelika-Auburn News* (September 13, 2002): 7A.
79. Jerry Adler and Tara Weingarten, "Mansions off the Rack," *Newsweek* (February 14, 2000): 60.
80. Debra Goldman, "Paradox of Pleasure," *American Demographics* (May 1999): 50–53.
81. Seth Lubove, "Copter Crazy," *Forbes* (May 13, 2002): 50.
82. Tracie Rozhon, "Dropping Logos that Shout, Luxury Sellers Try Whispers," *New York Times on the Web* (September 15, 2002).
83. Shelly Branch, "What's in a Name? Not Much, According to Clothes Shoppers," *Wall Street Journal Interactive Edition* ((July 16, 2002).
84. Western Companies Compete to Win Business of Chinese Babies," *Wall Street Journal Interactive Edition* (May 15, 1998).
85. Susan Carey, "Not All that's Gold Glitters in a $14,000 Pinstriped Suit," *Wall Street Journal Interactive Edition* (December 13, 1999).
86. John Brooks, *Showing off in America* (Boston: Little, Brown, 1981), 13.
87. Naughton Keith, "The Perk Wars," *Newsweek* (September 30, 2002): 42–46.
88. Natalie Angier, "Cell Phone or Pheronome? New Props for Mating Game," *New York Times on the Web* (November 7, 2000).
89. Shell Branch, "To Some, You're Simply a Zero without 0's in Your Cell Number," *Wall Street Journal Interactive Edition* ((August 28, 2002).
90. Thorstein Veblen, *The Theory of the Leisure Class* (1899; reprint, New York: New American Library, 1953), 45.
91. Brooks, *Showing Off in America*.
92. Ibid., 31–32.

Ethnic, Racial, and Religious Subcultures

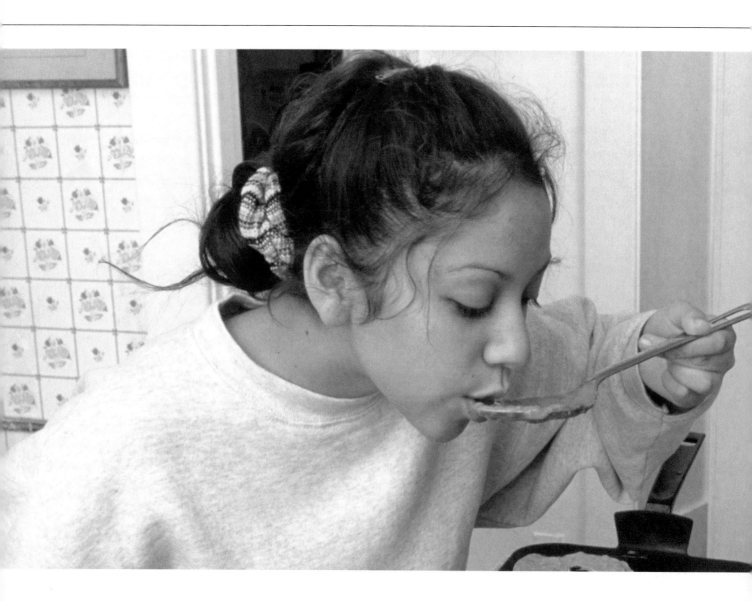

maria wakes up early on Saturday morning and braces herself for a long day of errands and chores. As usual, her mother is at work and expects Maria to do the shopping and help prepare dinner for the big family gathering tonight. Of course, her older brother José would never be asked to do the grocery shopping or help out in the kitchen—these are women's jobs.

Family gatherings make a lot of work, and Maria wishes that her mother would use prepared foods once in a while, especially on a Saturday when Maria has an errand or two of her own to do. But no, her mother insists on preparing most of her food from scratch. She rarely uses any convenience products, to ensure that the meals she serves are of the highest quality.

Resigned, Maria watches a *telenovela* (soap opera) on Univision while she's getting dressed, and then she heads down to the *carnicería* (small grocery store) to buy a newspaper—there are almost 40 different Spanish newspapers published in her area, and she likes to pick up new ones occasionally. Then Maria buys the grocery items her mother wants; the list is full of well-known brand names that she gets all the time, such as Casera and Goya, so she's able to finish quickly. With any luck, she'll have a few minutes to go to the *mercado* (shopping center) to pick up that new CD by Gloria Trevi that was written up at *Quepasa.com*. She'll listen to it in the kitchen while she chops, peels, and stirs.

Maria smiles to herself: Los Angeles is a great place to live and what could be better than spending a lively, fun evening with *la familia.*

■ SUBCULTURES AND CONSUMER IDENTITY

Yes, Maria lives in Los Angeles, not Mexico City. More than one in four Californians are Hispanic, and overall the state has more nonwhite than white residents. In fact, the most-watched TV network in L.A. is Spanish-language Univision.[1] If current trends continue, demographers say the entire United States will have a nonwhite majority by the year 2050.[2]

Maria and other Hispanic Americans have much in common with members of other racial and ethnic groups who live in the United States. They observe the same national holidays, their expenditures are affected by the country's economic health, and they may join in rooting for Team USA in the Olympics. Nonetheless, American citizenship may provide the raw material for some consumption decisions, but others are profoundly affected by the enormous variations in the social fabric of the United States. The United States truly is a "melting pot" of hundreds of diverse and interesting groups, from Italian and Irish Americans to Mormons and Seventh-Day Adventists. Consider that students speak more than 100 languages in some American school systems, including New York City, Chicago, and Los Angeles![3]

Consumers' lifestyles are affected by group memberships *within* the society-at-large. These groups are known as **subcultures**, whose members share beliefs and common experiences that set them apart from others. Every consumer belongs to many subcultures. These memberships can be based on similarities in age, race or ethnic background, place of residence, or even a strong identification with an activity or art form. Whether "Dead Heads," "Netizens," or skinheads, each group

Contemporary Mountain Men share a strong sense of identity and community.

exhibits its own unique set of norms, vocabulary, and product insignias (such as the skulls and roses that signify the Grateful Dead subculture). A recent study of contemporary Mountain Men in the western United States illustrates the binding influence of a subculture on its members. Researchers found that members of this group shared a strong sense of identity, and these ties were reinforced by such items as tipis, buffalo robes, buckskin leggings, and beaded moccasins that created a sense of community among fellow Mountain Men.[4]

These "communities" can even gel around fictional characters and events. Many devotees of *Star Trek*, for example, immerse themselves in a make-believe world of starships, phasers, and Vulcan mind melds. Gene Roddenberry, *Star Trek*'s creator, realized early on that people who identify with the show would also value products that identify them as members of this subculture. Sure enough, sales of *Star Trek* merchandise top $1 billion, and approximately 3 million people attend the more than 3,000 *Star Trek* conventions that are held each year. Some Trekkers have even formed more specialized subcultures within the larger one. One group of fans is devoted to the Klingons, an aggressive warrior race that battles the Federation. These loyal followers boast their own language (*tlhIngan*, which was created by a linguist for one of the *Star Trek* movies), fan magazines, food, and even a summer camp.[5]

Our subcultures often play a key role in defining the extended self (see Chapter 5) and typically command fierce loyalty. *Star Trek* fans are notorious for their devotion to the cause. The negative stereotype of the dweeb wearing fake Spock ears even surfaced on a classic *Saturday Night Live* skit, where ex-star William Shatner asks two hapless attendees at a Trekkie convention if they have ever kissed a girl. This stigma seems to only fuel the fire and unite fans as a dedicated subculture. An excerpt from a fan's e-mail illustrates this devotion:

> I have to admit to keeping pretty quiet about my devotion to the show for many years simply because people do tend to view a *Trek* fan as weird or crazy . . . . [after attending her first convention she says]. . . . Since then I have proudly worn my Bajoran earring and not cared about the looks I get from others. . . . I have also met . . . other *Trek* fans and some of these people have become very close friends. We have a lot in common and have had some of the same experiences as concerns our love of *Trek*.[6]

The *Star Trek* subculture continues to attract loyal members.

Net Profit

King for a day? Sure, the Internet allows people to form their own subcultures—but how about your own nation? Numerous "micronations" exist in cyberspace, some complete with their own monarchs and constitutions. Here's a sampler of these cybersubcultures:[7]

- *www.talossa.com:* The King of Talossa lives with his father and sister near the University of Wisconsin–Milwaukee campus. At age 14 (more than 20 years ago), he proclaimed his bedroom a sovereign nation. The name of the country comes from a Finnish word meaning "inside the house." The roughly 60 citizens of Talossa have a body of law, four political parties, an online journal, local holidays, and even a flag. They also have their own language and maintain a dictionary with 28,000 entries.

- *www.freedonia.org:* This micronation is a collective of libertarians based in Boston. Its monarch is a Babson College student who goes by the name of Prince John I. Members have minted their own line of currency, but for now the capital of the country is Prince John's house.

- *www.new-utopia.com:* This micronation proposes to build a chain of islands in international waters and sells citizenship bonds over the Web for $1,500. The country's founder goes by the name of Prince Lazarus Long. Buyer beware: The Prince does not have the best of diplomatic relations with the Securities Exchange Commission due to these sales.

Star Trek is a merchandising empire that continues to beam up millions of dollars in revenues. Needless to say, it's not alone in this regard. Numerous other subcultures are out there, thriving on their collective worship of mythical and not-so-mythical worlds and characters ranging from Phish to Hello Kitty.

■ ETHNIC AND RACIAL SUBCULTURES

Ethnic and religious identity is a significant component of a consumer's self-concept. An **ethnic subculture** is a self-perpetuating group of consumers who are held together by common cultural or genetic ties, and is identified both by its members and by others as being a distinguishable category.[8]

In some countries, Japan, for instance, ethnicity is almost synonymous with the dominant culture because most citizens claim the same homogenous cultural ties (although even Japan has sizeable minority populations, most notably people of Korean ancestry). In a heterogenous society such as the United States, many different cultures are represented, and consumers may expend great effort to keep their subcultural identification from being submerged into the mainstream of the dominant society.

Marketers cannot ignore the stunning diversity of cultures that are reshaping mainstream society. Ethnic minorities spend more than $600 billion a year on products and services, so firms must devise products and communications strategies tailored to the needs of these subcultures. And this vast market is growing all the time: Immigrants now make up 10 percent of the U.S. population and will account for 13 percent by 2050.[9]

Almost half of all *Fortune* 1,000 companies have an ethnic marketing program up and running. For example, AT&T sponsors Chinese Dragon Boat Festival races and Cuban folk festivals; it also airs advertisements that are aimed at 30 different cultures, including messages in languages such as Tagalog, spoken by Filipinos, and Twi, a West African dialect. As AT&T's director of multicultural marketing observed, "Marketing today is part anthropology."[10] It makes good business sense to cater to these segments by (literally) speaking their language when promoting products and services: Surveys repeatedly show that members of ethnic groups get much of their product information from specialized ethnic media; one found that 63 percent of ethnic Californians watch native-language TV daily and a third of them also read an ethnic newspaper at least once a week.[11]

Ethnicity and Marketing Strategies

Although some people feel uncomfortable with the notion that people's racial and ethnic differences should be explicitly taken into account when formulating marketing strategies, the reality is that these subcultural memberships are frequently paramount in shaping people's needs and wants. Research indicates, for example, that members of minority groups are likely to find an advertising spokesperson from their own group more trustworthy, and this enhanced credibility in turn translates into more positive brand attitudes.[12]

Membership in ethnic subcultures often is predictive of consumer variables such as level and type of media exposure, food and apparel preferences, political behavior, leisure activities, and even willingness to try new products. For example, a diary study of 8,000 respondents that asked people to note how they allocated their time found that African Americans spent the most time on religious activities, Caucasians put in the most hours on housework, and Asian Americans devoted the most time to education.[13]

In addition, the way marketing messages should be structured depends on subcultural differences in how meanings are communicated. Sociologists make a distinction between *high-context cultures* and *low-context cultures*. In a **high-context**

Tex-Mex cuisine is popular in Scandinavia. This ad appeared in a Swedish magazine.

culture, group members tend to be tightly knit, and they are likely to infer meanings that go beyond the spoken word. Symbols and gestures, rather than words, carry much of the weight of the message. Compared to Anglos, many minority cultures are high-context and have strong oral traditions, so perceivers will be more sensitive to nuances in advertisements that go beyond the message copy.[14]

Is Ethnicity a Moving Target?

Although ethnic marketing is in vogue with many firms, the process of actually defining and targeting members of a distinct ethnic group is not always so easy in our "melting pot" society. The popularity of golfer Tiger Woods illuminates the complexity of ethnic identity in the United States. Although Woods has been lauded as an African American role model, in reality he is a model of multiracialism. His mother is Thai, and he also has Caucasian and Indian ancestry. Other popular cultural figures are also multiracial, including actor Keanu Reeves (Hawaiian, Chinese, and Caucasian), singer Mariah Carey (black Venezuelan and white), and Dean Cain of Superman fame (Japanese and Caucasian). Indeed, 70 to 90 percent of people

Marketing Pitfall

The mass merchandising of ethnic products is widespread and growing. Aztec Indian designs appear on sweaters, gym shoes are sold trimmed in *kente* cloth from an African tribe, and greeting cards bear likenesses of Native American sand paintings. However, many people are concerned about the borrowing—and in some cases, misinterpretation—of distinctive symbolism. Consider, for example, the storm of protest from the international Islamic community a few years ago over what started as a simple dress design for the House of Chanel. In a fashion show, supermodel Claudia Schiffer wore a strapless evening gown designed by Karl Lagerfeld. The dress included Arabic letters that the designer believed spelled out a love poem. Instead, the message was a verse from the Koran, the Muslim holy book. To add insult to injury, the word "God" happened to appear over the model's right breast. Both the designer and the model received death threats, and the controversy subsided only after the three versions of the dress that had been made (and priced at almost $23,000) were burned.[22] Some industry experts feel that it's acceptable to appropriate symbols from another culture even if the buyer does not know their original meaning. They argue that even in the host society there is often disagreement about these meanings. What do you think?

who call themselves African Americans actually are of mixed lineage, and the same is true of many Caucasians.[15] In the 2000 U.S. Census, some 7 million people identified with two or more races, refusing to describe themselves as only white, black, Asian, Korean, Samoan or one of the other categories listed.[16]

This trend toward the blurring of ethnic and racial boundaries will only increase over time—the number of married couples of different races or ethnic groups has doubled since 1980. These couples tend to be upscale, well educated, and young. For example, fully two-thirds of Hispanics with some college education outmarry. Intermarriage rates are highest among people of Asian descent; approximately 12 percent of Asian men and 25 percent of Asian women marry non-Asians.[17]

Multicultural households are attractive targets: A study of consumer spending revealed that they exceeded white households in five categories, including groceries, entertainment, personal care products, clothing, and education. They also outspend whites on more expensive goods, such as cars and homes.[18] Still, portraying mixed couples in advertising is a risky business because there is resentment in some minority communities toward people who outmarry. That explains why Philips Electronics decided to focus on a diverse "tribe" of multicultural young people rather than depicting mixed-race couples in its advertising campaign.[19]

Products that are marketed with an ethnic appeal are not necessarily intended for consumption only by the ethnic subculture from which they originate. **De-ethnicization** refers to the process whereby a product formerly associated with a specific ethnic group is detached from its roots and marketed to other subcultures. This process is illustrated by bagels, a bread product formerly associated with Jewish culture and now mass marketed. Recent variations include jalapeño bagels, blueberry bagels, and even a green bagel for St. Patrick's Day.[20] Bagels now account for three to six percent of all American breakfasts, and bagel franchisers such as Bruegger's Corporation and the Einstein/Noah Bagel Corporation are opening hundreds of stores in cities that had never heard of a bagel just a few years ago.[21] A similar attempt to assimilate ethnic products into mainstream culture is underway by Goya Foods, a major marketer of Hispanic food products. As one company executive noted, "Several food items such as tacos

Tiger Woods' multiracial background illustrates the complexity of ethnic identity in the United States.

Bagels have been de-ethnicized and are now part of mainstream culture.

. . . and burritos were once considered the domain of an ethnic group, and now they're mainstream."[23] To underscore this evolution, consider the fact that salsa is now the most popular condiment in the United States, outselling ketchup by $40 million.[24]

The "Big Three" American Subcultures

Three groups that account for much of America's current growth are African Americans, Hispanic Americans, and Asian Americans. In 2000, the U.S. Census showed that the Hispanic population is now the largest ethnic subculture, with 12.5 percent of Americans claiming this background.[25] Asian Americans, though much smaller in absolute numbers with only 3.6 percent of the population, are the fastest-growing racial group. This growth is largely due to immigration; each year more Asians arrive in the United States as immigrants than are born in the country.[26]

New Ethnic Groups

The dominant American culture has historically exerted pressure on immigrants to divest themselves of their origins and to become absorbed into mainstream society. As President Theodore Roosevelt put it in the early part of the last century, "We welcome the German or the Irishman who becomes an American. We have no use for the German or the Irishman who remains such."[27] Indeed, there is a tendency for ethnic groups with a relatively longer history of settling in the United States to view themselves as more mainstream and relax their identification with their country of origin. When the 2000 Census asked respondents to write up to two ancestries that defined their background, the results showed a clear decline in the number of people identifying themselves as Irish, German, and other European ancestries. Compared to other subcultures, more people from these countries simply choose to call themselves "American."[28]

■ **FIGURE 14.1** AMERICA'S NEWEST MARKETS

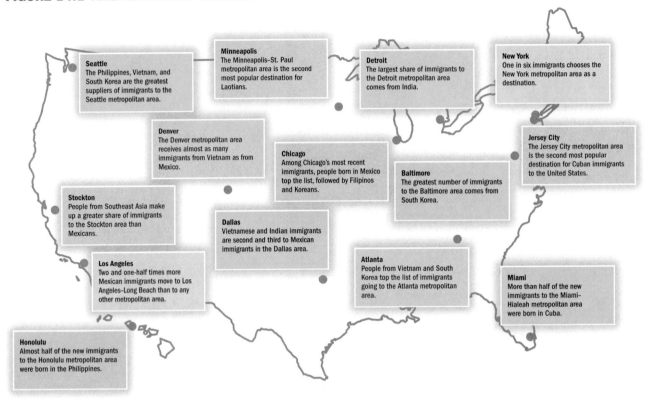

Seattle
The Philippines, Vietnam, and South Korea are the greatest suppliers of immigrants to the Seattle metropolitan area.

Minneapolis
The Minneapolis–St. Paul metropolitan area is the second most popular destination for Laotians.

Detroit
The largest share of immigrants to the Detroit metropolitan area comes from India.

New York
One in six immigrants chooses the New York metropolitan area as a destination.

Denver
The Denver metropolitan area receives almost as many immigrants from Vietnam as from Mexico.

Chicago
Among Chicago's most recent immigrants, people born in Mexico top the list, followed by Filipinos and Koreans.

Baltimore
The greatest number of immigrants to the Baltimore area comes from South Korea.

Jersey City
The Jersey City metropolitan area is the second most popular destination for Cuban immigrants to the United States.

Stockton
People from Southeast Asia make up a greater share of immigrants to the Stockton area than Mexicans.

Dallas
Vietnamese and Indian immigrants are second and third to Mexican immigrants in the Dallas area.

Los Angeles
Two and one-half times more Mexican immigrants move to Los Angeles–Long Beach than to any other metropolitan area.

Atlanta
People from Vietnam and South Korea top the list of immigrants going to the Atlanta metropolitan area.

Miami
More than half of the new immigrants to the Miami–Hialeah metropolitan area were born in Cuba.

Honolulu
Almost half of the new immigrants to the Honolulu metropolitan area were born in the Philippines.

The bulk of American immigrants historically came from Europe, but immigration patterns have shifted dramatically. New immigrants are much more likely to be Asian or Hispanic. As these new waves of immigrants settle in the United States, marketers are attempting to track their consumption patterns and adjust their strategies accordingly. These new arrivals—whether Arabs, Asians, Russians, or people of Caribbean descent—are best marketed to in their native languages. They tend to cluster together geographically, which makes them easy to reach. The local community is the primary source for information and advice, so word of mouth is especially important (see Chapter 11). Figure 14.1 shows how new waves of immigrants are changing the ethnic composition of major American cities.

One striking example is the rising numbers of American consumers who have immigrated from India. This group is relatively affluent and is growing. Many Indian Americans live in urban portions of New York and New Jersey, but the largest numbers reside in California. The first wave of an immigrant group often consists of relatively well-off people, and that is the case here. In 1990, 30 percent of Indian Americans were employed in professional specialty occupations, compared to 13 percent of the general population. These consumers also own a large number of businesses, partly because family networks allow the businesses to grow—it is common for residents to pool resources and form associations enabling them to buy in bulk and sell at lower prices. This segment places great value on education and financial security, has a very high savings rate, and buys a lot of insurance. A growing number of Indo-American magazines such as *Masala*, *Onward*, and *Hum* have sprung up to straddle two cultures and appeal to young people.[29]

Ethnic and Racial Stereotypes

A controversial Taco Bell television commercial illustrates how marketers (intentionally or not) use ethnic and racial stereotypes to craft promotional communications. The spot for the restaurant's Wild Burrito featured dark-skinned "natives" with painted faces who danced around in loincloths. Following an uproar in the African American community, the ad was withdrawn.[30]

Many subcultures have powerful stereotypes associated with them. Members of a subgroup are assumed to possess certain traits, even though these assumptions are often erroneous. The same trait can be cast either positively or negatively, depending on the communicator's intentions and biases. For example, the Scottish stereotype in the United States is largely positive, so the supposed frugality of this ethnic group is viewed favorably. 3M used Scottish imagery to denote value (e.g., Scotch tape), as does a motel chain called Scotch Inns that offers inexpensive lodging. However, invoking the Scottish "personality" might carry quite different connotations to consumers in Britain or Ireland. One person's "thrifty" is another's "stingy."

In the past, marketers have used ethnic symbolism as shorthand to connote certain product attributes. The images employed were often crude and unflattering. Blacks were depicted as subservient, Mexicans as bandits.[31] As the Civil Rights movement gave more power to minority groups and their rising economic status commanded respect from marketers, these negative stereotypes began to disappear. Frito-Lay responded to protests by the Hispanic community and stopped using the Frito Bandito character in 1971, and Quaker Foods gave Aunt Jemima a makeover in 1989.

The use of subtle (and sometimes not so subtle) ethnic stereotypes in movies illustrates how the media can perpetuate assumptions about ethnic or racial groups. In 1953, the Disney animated feature *Peter Pan* caricatured Native Americans as tomahawk-wielding savages (absurdly led by a blonde, blue-eyed Tiger Lily!), but in the more recent movie *Pocahontas*, the company tried to be more sensitive to stereotypes. Still, objections were raised about the historical accuracy of this feature: Disney turned the 12-year-old heroine into a more mature, older character because it was felt that a 12-year-old in love with a 27-year-old man would not be received well by modern audiences.[32] Disney also drew fire from the Arab American community about the movie *Aladdin*, and some controversial lyrics were changed when the movie was released on video.

■ AFRICAN AMERICANS

African Americans comprise a significant racial subculture and accounted for 12.3 percent of the U.S. population in the 2000 Census.[33] Although black consumers do differ in important ways from whites, the African American market is hardly as homogenous as many marketers seem to believe. Indeed, some commentators have argued that black–white differences are largely illusory. With some exceptions, the overall spending patterns of blacks and whites are roughly similar. Both blacks and whites spend about two-thirds of their incomes on housing, transportation, and food.[34]

Different consumption behaviors are more likely due to differences in income, the relatively high concentration of African Americans in urban areas, and other dimensions of social class. And, these differences will continue to diminish as black consumers continue to move up the economic ladder. While still lower than the white majority, median household income is hitting historic highs, an improvement that can be traced directly to a steady increase in educational attainment. African Americans had a median household income of $30,439 in 2000, up from $18,676 in 1990. By the end of the decade, more than 51 percent of married African Americans had incomes at $50,000 or above.[35]

Marketing Opportunity

Consumers often learn about a foreign subculture through their stomachs; ethnic food is very popular. Restaurants featuring Chinese, Italian, or other cuisines are a fixture in most American communities. Now, Thai food has become one of America's fastest-growing cuisines, along with Indian, Vietnamese, and Cajun. But, the Thai government has decided to throw fuel on the fire by bankrolling the country's delicacies in an unusual experiment. It plans to launch a chain of more than 3,000 Thai restaurants worldwide over the next five years, with the largest number, more than 1,000, slated for the United States. This gastronomical assault will take three forms, as plans include the development of eating places targeted to different lifestyles. The restaurants, which will go by the names Elephant Jump for the fast-food branches, Cool Basil for mid-priced restaurants, and Golden Leaf for upscale eateries, are believed to be the first ever launched by a government.[36]

Marketing Opportunity

Although African Americans represent slightly more than 10 percent of the online population, as of now they don't seem to be spending their time on the Web buying from virtual stores; they account for only 4 percent of online shoppers. But, e-commerce executives are hopeful that this situation is going to change because Web surfers generally don't start to participate in e-commerce until they have been online for 18 months to three years. Internet usage among this ethnic group is growing at the highest rate of all such segments, and some predict that as African Americans spend more time online they will start to open their wallets as well.[37]

L'original

Many national brands routinely use African American models.

Nonetheless, there clearly are some differences between blacks and whites in consumption priorities and marketplace behaviors that demand marketers' attention.[38] Sometimes these differences are subtle but still can be important. When Coffee-mate discovered that African Americans tend to drink their coffee with sugar and cream much more than Caucasians do, the company mounted a promotional blitz using black media and in return benefited from double-digit increases in sales volume and market share for this segment.[39] Volvo North America created its first advertising campaign targeting African Americans after research showed that car crashes are the leading cause of death among African American children, who are half as likely to use seat belts as other children.[40]

■ HISPANIC AMERICANS

The umbrella term "Hispanic" describes people of many different backgrounds. According to the 2000 Census, nearly 60 percent of Hispanic Americans are of Mexican descent. The next largest group, Puerto Ricans, make up just fewer than 10 percent of Hispanics. Other groups counted in this category include Central Americans, Dominicans, South Americans, and Cubans.[41]

The Hispanic subculture is a sleeping giant that until recently was largely ignored by many U.S. marketers. The growth and increasing affluence of this group has now made it impossible to overlook, and major corporations avidly court Hispanic consumers like Maria and her family. Marketers especially like the fact that Hispanics tend to be brand loyal. In one study, about 45 percent reported that they always buy their usual brand, whereas only one in five said they frequently switch brands.[42] Another study found that Hispanics who strongly identify with their ethnic origin are more likely to seek Hispanic vendors, to be loyal to brands used by family and friends, and to be influenced by Hispanic media.[43] This segment is also highly concentrated geographically by country of origin, which makes them relatively easy to reach. More than 50 percent of all Hispanic Americans live in the Los Angeles, New York, Miami, San Antonio, San Francisco, and Chicago metropolitan areas.[44]

Many initial efforts to market to Hispanic Americans were, to say the least, counterproductive. Companies bumbled in their efforts to translate advertising adequately or to compose copy that could capture desired nuances. These mistakes do not occur so much anymore as marketers are more sophisticated in dealing with this segment and tend to involve Hispanics in advertising production to ensure they are getting it right. The following are some translation mishaps that have slipped through in the past:[45]

- The Perdue slogan, "It takes a tough man to make a tender chicken," was translated as "It takes a sexually excited man to make a chick affectionate."
- Budweiser was promoted as the "queen of beers."
- A burrito was called a *burrada*, which means "big mistake."
- Braniff, promoting the comfortable leather seats on its airplanes, used the headline, *Sentado en cuero*, which was interpreted as "Sit naked."
- Coors beer's slogan to "get loose with Coors" appeared in Spanish as "get the runs with Coors."

Nike made history in 1993 by running the first Spanish-language commercial ever broadcast in prime time on a major American network. The spot, which ran during the All-Star baseball game, featured boys in tattered clothes playing ball in the *Dominican Republic*, or *La Tierra de Mediocampistas* (the Land of Shortstops). This title refers to the fact that more than 70 Dominicans have played for major league ball clubs, many of whom started at the shortstop position. This groundbreaking spot also laid bare some of the issues involved in marketing to Hispanics: Many found the commercial condescending (especially the ragged look of the actors), and felt that it promoted the idea that Hispanics don't really want to assimilate into mainstream Anglo culture.[46]

If nothing else, though, this commercial by a large corporation was a wake-up call for many companies. Many are rushing to sign Hispanic celebrities, such as Daisy Fuentes and Rita Moreno, to endorse their products.[47] Others are working hard to add more Hispanic consumers; CBS recently introduced Spanish-speaking characters on its soap opera *The Bold and the Beautiful*.[48] Even the well-known movie star Raquel Welch is now "repositioning" herself by reclaiming her Hispanic heritage. After starring in several movies and TV shows featuring Hispanic characters, Jo-Raquel Tejada (her real name) recently proclaimed, "Latinos are here to stay."[49] The president of an ad agency specializing in the Latino market refers to this phenomenon as "Hispanization—or the Ricky Martin effect." She notes that firms are consciously using Hispanic references because these are cool and hip now. That's the thinking behind the new Dulce de Leche caramel variety of M&Ms, for example.[50]

Some firms are developing separate Spanish-language campaigns, often with entirely different emphases calculated to appeal to the unique characteristics of this market. For example, the California Milk Processor Board discovered that its hugely successful "Got milk?" campaign was not well received by Hispanics because biting, sarcastic humor is not part of the Hispanic culture. In addition, the notion of milk deprivation is not funny to the Hispanic homemaker because running out of milk means she has failed her family. To make matters worse, "Got milk?" translates as "Are you lactating?", so Spanish-language versions were tailored to Latino moms by saying instead, "And you, have you given them enough milk today?" with tender scenes centered around cooking flan in the family kitchen.[51]

Marketing Pitfall

Critics of ethnic market segmentation often point to a famous example to illustrate the ethical pitfalls of this strategy. This controversy occurred when R.J. Reynolds Tobacco announced plans to test-market a menthol cigarette, called Uptown, specifically to black consumers in the Philadelphia area. Although the marketing of cigarettes to minorities is not a novel tactic, it was the first time a company explicitly acknowledged the strategy. Many people attacked the proposal, arguing that the campaign would exploit poor blacks—especially as black people suffer from a higher incidence of tobacco-related diseases than any other group. For its part, Reynolds claimed that its actions were a natural result of shrinking markets and the need to more finely target increasingly small segments. Unlike other ethnic groups that do not seem to display marked cigarette preferences, the tastes of African American consumers are easy to pinpoint. According to Reynolds, 69 percent of black consumers at the time preferred menthol, more than twice the rate of smokers overall. After market research indicated that blacks tend to open cigarette packs from the bottom, the company decided to pack Uptowns with the filters facing down. Following a storm of criticism by both private health groups and government officials (including the Secretary of Health and Human Services), the company announced that it was canceling its test-marketing plans. But the story's not over: In 1999, Philip Morris announced plans to test yet another new menthol cigarette, Marlboro Mild, in order to break into the minority-dominated menthol market now monopolized by Lorillard's Newport.[52]

Net Profit

Public policy experts worry that ethnic minorities will get left behind as the general population continues to go online in record numbers. In fact, Hispanics are narrowing this "digital divide" by buying computers at a rate much greater than that of the general population. A 2000 survey found that 42 percent of the nation's Hispanic households have a computer, which is a 68 percent increase over 1998. A 2001 study found that Hispanics in the United States are more likely to be online at home than Caucasians and African Americans. It estimates that U.S. ethnic groups will spend $3.1 billion on Internet access by 2005. Several Hispanic Web portals are operating, including *Quepasa.com*, *StarMedia.com*, *ElSitio.com* (country-specific content), *YupiMSN.com*, and *Terra.com*. Univision, the Spanish-speaking network that controls 91 percent of the U.S. Hispanic television market, is also trying to capture a big Web audience.[58]

Some major corporations have figured out that surfing the Web is a popular pastime for these consumers. Proctor & Gamble opened a whole new market when it crafted a campaign for its Head & Shoulders shampoo targeted directly at Hispanic youth. The promotion included an online game surfers could play with others that was placed on Web portals. The effort was so successful that P&G is planning several promotions for other brands including Cover Girl cosmetics.[59]

Rock en Español: Distinguishing Characteristics of the Hispanic Market

One of the most notable characteristics of the Hispanic market is its youth: The median age of Hispanic Americans is 23.6, compared with the U.S. average of 32. Many of these consumers are "young biculturals" who bounce back and forth between hip-hop and *Rock en Español*, blend Mexican rice with spaghetti sauce, and spread peanut butter and jelly on tortillas.[53] Latino youth are changing mainstream culture. By the year 2020, the U.S. Census Bureau estimates that the number of Hispanic teens will grow by 62 percent compared with 10 percent growth in teens overall. They are looking for spirituality, stronger family ties, and more color in their lives—three hallmarks of Latino culture. Music cross-overs are leading the trend, including musicians like Shakira and Big Pun, the first Latino hip-hop artist to go platinum. In recognition of this growing market, music retailer Wherehouse Entertainment opened a separate division called Tu Musica (Your Music).[54]

A second notable characteristic of this market is that family size tends to be large. The average Hispanic household contains 3.5 people, compared to only 2.7 for other U.S. households. These differences obviously affect the overall allocation of income to various product categories. For example, Hispanic households spend 15 to 20 percent more of their disposable income than the national average on groceries.[55] That helps to explain why General Mills developed a breakfast cereal called Buñuelitos specifically for this market. The brand name is an adaptation of *buñuelos*, a traditional Mexican pastry served on holidays.[56]

The importance of the family to Hispanics like Maria cannot be overstated. Preferences to spend time with family influence the structure of many consumption activities. As one illustration, the act of going to the movies has a different meaning for many Hispanics, who tend to regard this activity as a family outing. One study found that 42 percent of Hispanic moviegoers attend in groups of three or more, as compared with only 28 percent of Anglo consumers.[57]

Music crossovers like Shakira are giving mainstream music an Hispanic flavor.

Behaviors that underscore one's ability to provide well for the family are reinforced in this subculture. Clothing one's children well is regarded in particular as a matter of pride. In contrast, convenience and a product's ability to save time are not terribly important to the Hispanic homemaker. Women like Maria's mother are willing to purchase labor-intensive products if it means that their families will benefit. For this reason, a time-saving appeal short-circuited for Quaker Foods, which found that Hispanic women tend to cook Instant Quaker Oats on the stove as if it were regular oatmeal, refrigerate it, and serve it later as a pudding.[60] Similarly, telephone company promotions that emphasize cheaper rates for calling family members would offend many Hispanic consumers, who would view deterring a phone call home just to save money as an insult![61] This orientation also explains why generic products do not tend to do well in the Hispanic market; these consumers value the quality promised by well-known brand names.

Levels of Acculturation: Understanding Hispanic Identity

Acculturation refers to the process of movement and adaptation to one country's cultural environment by a person from another country.[62] This factor is especially important when considering the Hispanic market because the degree to which these consumers are integrated into the American way of life varies widely. For instance, about 38 percent of all Hispanics live in *barrios*, or predominantly Hispanic neighborhoods, which tend to be somewhat insulated from mainstream society.[63] Table 14.1 describes one attempt to segment Hispanic consumers in terms of degree of acculturation.

Native language and culture are important components of Hispanic identity and self-esteem (about three-quarters of Hispanics still speak Spanish at home), and these consumers are very sympathetic to marketing efforts that acknowledge and emphasize the Hispanic cultural heritage.[64] More than 40 percent of Hispanic consumers say they deliberately attempt to buy products that show an interest in the Hispanic consumer, and this number jumps to more than two-thirds for Cuban Americans.[65] Indeed, although a lot of Hispanic food, music, and athletes are crossing over into the mainstream, many Hispanics are starting to go in the other direction. Today many younger Hispanics are searching for their roots and rediscovering the value of ethnic identity.[66]

The behavior profile of the Hispanic consumer includes a need for status and a strong sense of pride. A high value is placed on self-expression and familial devotion. Some campaigns have played to Hispanics' fear of rejection and apprehension about loss of control and embarrassment in social situations. Conventional wisdom

TABLE 14.1
SEGMENTING THE HISPANIC AMERICAN SUBCULTURE BY DEGREE OF ACCULTURATION

Segment	Size	Status	Description	Characteristics
Established adapters	17%	Upwardly mobile	Older, U.S.-born; assimilated into U.S. culture	Relatively low identification with Hispanic culture
Young strivers	16%	Increasingly important	Younger, born in U.S.; highly motivated to succeed; adaptable to U.S. culture	Movement to reconnect with Hispanic roots
Hopeful loyalists	40%	Largest but shrinking	Working class; attached to traditional values	Slow to adapt to U.S. culture; Spanish is dominant language
Recent seekers	27%	Growing	Newest; very conservative with high aspirations	Strongest identification with Hispanic background; little use of non-Hispanic media

Source: Adapted from a report by Yankelovich Clancy Shulman, described in "A Subculture with Very Different Needs," *Adweek* (May 11, 1992): 44. By permission of Yankelovich Partners, Inc.

recommends creating action-oriented advertising and emphasizing a problem-solving atmosphere. Assertive role models who are cast in nonthreatening situations are effective.[67]

A study of Mexican immigrants that used the research technique of *ethnography* probed their acculturation as they adapt to life in the United States.[68] Interviews and observations of recent arrivals in natural settings revealed that immigrants feel a lot of ambivalence about their move. On the one hand, they are happy about the improvements in the quality of their lives due to greater job availability and educational opportunities for their children. On the other hand, they report bittersweet feelings about leaving Mexico. They miss their friends, their holidays, their food, and the comfort that comes from living in familiar surroundings.

The nature of the transition process is affected by many factors, as shown in Figure 14.2. Individual differences, such as whether the person speaks English, influence how rocky the adjustment will be. The person's contact with **acculturation agents**—people and institutions that teach the ways of a culture, are also crucial. Some of these agents are aligned with the *culture of origin* (in this case, Mexico), including family, friends, the church, local businesses, and Spanish-language media that keep the consumer in touch with her country of origin. Other agents are associated with the *culture of immigration* (in this case, America), and help the consumer to learn how to navigate in the new environment. These include public schools, English-language media, and government agencies.

As immigrants adapt to their new surroundings, several processes come into play. *Movement* refers to the factors motivating people to physically uproot themselves from one location and go to another. In this case, people leave Mexico because of the scarcity of jobs and the desire to provide a good education for their children. On arrival, immigrants encounter a need for *translation*. This means attempting to master a set of rules for operating in the new environment, whether learning how to decipher a different currency or figuring out the social meanings of unfamiliar clothing styles. This cultural learning leads to a process of *adaptation*, by which new consumption patterns are formed. For example, some of the Mexican women interviewed started to wear shorts and pants since settling in the United States, although this practice is frowned upon in Mexico.

■ **FIGURE 14.2**
A MODEL OF CONSUMER
ACCULTURATION

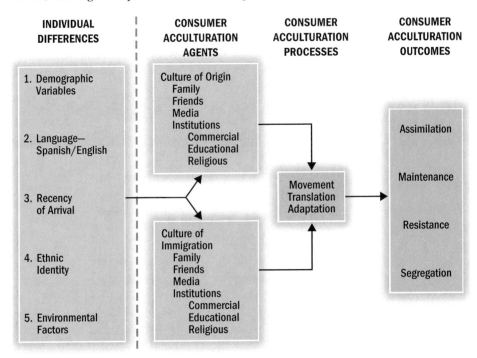

Source: Lisa Peñaloza, "Atravesando Fronteras/Border Crossings: A Critical Ethnographic Exploration of the Consumer Acculturation of Mexican Immigrants," *Journal of Consumer Research* (June 1994): 32–54.

During the acculturation process, many immigrants undergo *assimilation*, where they adopt products, habits, and values that are identified with the mainstream culture. At the same time, there is an attempt at *maintenance* of practices associated with the culture of origin. Immigrants stay in touch with people in their country and, like Maria, many continue to eat Spanish foods and read Spanish newspapers. Their continued identification with Mexican culture may cause *resistance*, as they resent the pressure to submerge their Mexican identities and take on new roles. Finally, immigrants (voluntarily or not) tend to exhibit *segregation*; they are likely to live and shop in places that are physically separated from mainstream Anglo consumers.

These processes illustrate that ethnicity is a fluid concept, and the boundaries of a subculture are constantly being re-created. An **ethnic pluralism** perspective argues that ethnic groups differ from the mainstream in varying degrees, and that adaptation to the larger society occurs selectively. Research evidence refutes the idea that assimilation necessarily involves losing identification with the person's original ethnic group. One study found, for example, that many French Canadians show a high level of acculturation, yet still retain a strong ethnic affiliation. The best indicator of ethnic assimilation, these researchers argue, is the extent to which members of an ethnic group have social interactions with members of other groups in comparison to their own.[69]

The acculturation of Hispanic consumers can be understood in terms of the **progressive learning model**. This perspective assumes that people gradually learn a new culture as they increasingly come in contact with it. Thus, we would expect the consumer behavior of Hispanic Americans to be a mixture of practices taken from their original culture and those of the new or *host culture*.[70] Research has generally obtained results that support this pattern when factors such as shopping orientation, the importance placed on various product attributes, media preference, and brand loyalty are examined.[71] When the intensity of ethnic identification is taken into account, consumers who retain a strong ethnic identification differ from their more assimilated counterparts in the following ways:[72]

- They have a more negative attitude toward business in general (probably caused by frustration due to relatively low income levels).
- They are higher users of Spanish-language media.
- They are more brand loyal.
- They are more likely to prefer brands with prestige labels.
- They are more likely to buy brands specifically advertised to their ethnic group.

■ ASIAN AMERICANS

Realtors who do business in areas with a high concentration of Asian American buyers are learning to adapt to some unique cultural traditions. Asians are very sensitive to the design and location of a home, especially as these aspects affect the home's *chi*—an invisible energy current that is believed to bring good or bad luck. Asian homebuyers are concerned about whether a prospective house offers a good *feng shui* environment (translated literally as "the wind and the water"). One home developer in San Francisco sold up to 80 percent of its homes to Asian customers after making a few minor design changes, such as reducing the number of "T" intersections in the houses and adding rounded rocks to the garden—harmful *chi* travels in a straight line, whereas gentle *chi* travels on a curved path.[73]

Although their numbers are still relatively small, Asian Americans are the fastest-growing minority group in the United States. Marketers are just beginning to recognize their potential as a unique market segment, and some are beginning to adapt their products and messages to reach this group. The problems encountered by American marketers when they first tried to reach the Hispanic market also occurred when they initially went after Asian Americans:[74]

Net Profit

The affluent Asian immigrant population in the United States is creating a new market for Asian products. For example, the Chinese music industry is benefiting from the demand in the Asian American community for the mix of syrupy ballads known as Mandarin Pop. Music idols such as Andy Lau and Jacky Cheung tour the United States, and Chinese record companies are using the Web to build a bigger following overseas. *RockaCola.com* is one of the largest Chinese music labels in Taiwan and Hong Kong, and another site called *YesAsia.com* gets 1.68 million visits a month.[83]

- Coca-Cola's slogan, "Coke Adds Life" was translated as "Coke brings your ancestors back from the dead" in Japanese.
- Kentucky Fried Chicken described its chicken as "finger-lickin' good" to the Chinese, who don't think licking your fingers is very polite.
- A footwear ad depicted Japanese women performing foot binding, a practice done exclusively in China.

Now, the American advertising industry is spending between $200 million and $300 million to court these consumers.[75] Ford set up a toll-free consumer hotline staffed by operators fluent in three Asian languages, and JCPenney holds one-day sales in stores in Asian communities during certain holidays such as the moon festival.[76] WonderBra even launched a special line sized for the slimmer Asian body.[77]

Why all the interest? Asians not only make up the fastest-growing population group, but they are generally the most affluent, best educated, and most likely to hold technology jobs of any ethnic subculture. Indeed, Asian Americans are much more likely than average Americans to buy high-tech gadgets. They are almost three times as likely to own a digital camcorder and twice as likely to have an MP3 player.[78] About 32 percent of Asian households have incomes of more than $50,000 compared to 29 percent in the entire U.S. population. Estimates put this segment's buying power at $253 billion annually. That explains why the brokerage firm Charles Schwab now employs more than 300 people who speak Chinese, Korean, and Vietnamese at its call centers.[79]

Despite its potential, this group is hard to market to because it actually is composed of subgroups that are culturally diverse and speak many different languages and dialects. The term "Asian" refers to 20 ethnic groups, with Chinese being the largest and Filipino and Japanese second and third, respectively.[80] Filipinos are the only Asians who predominantly speak English among themselves; most Asians prefer media in their own languages.[81] The most frequently spoken languages among Asian Americans are Mandarin Chinese, Korean, Japanese, and Vietnamese.[82]

On the other hand, as one Asian American advertising executive noted, "Prosperous Asians tend to be very status-conscious and will spend their money on premium brands, such as BMW and Mercedes-Benz, and the best French cognac

YesAsia.com gives Asian Americans access to music, videos, and all sorts of entertainment products from several Asian countries.

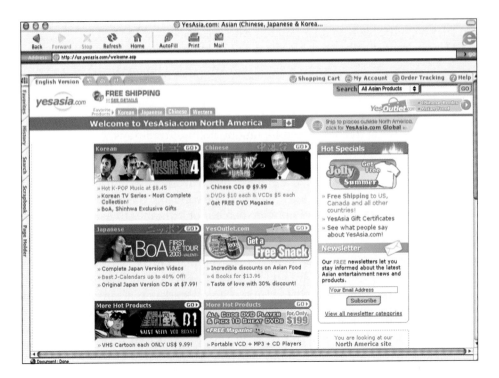

and Scotch whiskey."[84] Advertising that features Asian celebrities can be particularly effective. When Reebok used tennis star Michael Chang in one advertisement, shoe sales among Asian Americans soared.[85]

■ RELIGIOUS SUBCULTURES

Spirituality was already on the rise in the United States, and the events surrounding 9/11 threw even more fuel on the fire. For example, more than two-thirds of respondents in a survey of business travelers said they were taking steps to lead more spiritual lives. The poll sponsor pointed out that "When we're out in the world, we just feel more vulnerable. . . . We ask ourselves, 'If this is the last day of our lives, do we know where we're going?' We tend to have a lot of time on our hands to think about those kinds of things when we travel."[86]

The Rise of Spirituality

In recent years we've witnessed an explosion of religion and spirituality in popular culture. For example, the tremendous success of the movie *Titanic* was partly due to its spiritual overtones (yes, Leonardo is good-looking too). Jack is Rose's spiritual guide—he stands for values such as freedom, art, and love—and he gives up his life to save hers. Her immersion in the sea is a kind of baptism, cleansing her of her false self. The popularity of this movie is consistent with the popularity of such books as *The Celestine Prophecy*, movements such as the Promise Keepers, the very high percentage of Americans who believe in angels, and the growth of self-help groups such as Alcoholics Anonymous, which proclaim belief in a higher power.[87] American Greetings introduced a Rainbows of Faith line of religious cards, and Hallmark Cards has a similar Morning Light line.[88]

This quest for meaning is influencing mainstream churches as well. They are evolving with the times, and many are adopting an aggressive marketing orientation. In the United States there are approximately 400 *megachurches*, each serving 2,000 or more congregants per week (some actually attract more than 20,000 to Sunday services!), with a combined annual income of $1.85 billion.[89] Christian bookstores now make less than 40 percent of their sales in books and Bibles, as consumers buy religion-oriented merchandise including apparel (such as a clothing line for born-again Christians called Witness Wear, that sells more than $1 million worth of apparel per year), framed art, and inspirational gifts.[90] In fact, sales of Christian merchandise now exceed $3 billion per year. As a church marketing consultant observes, "Baby boomers think of churches like they think of supermarkets. They want options, choices, and convenience. Imagine if Safeway was open only one hour a week, had only one product, and didn't explain it in English."[91] Clearly, religion is big business.

Marketing Opportunity

Because many consumers are more comfortable when interacting with others like themselves, some companies that rely on personal selling are instituting programs to penetrate closed religious subcultures. *Multilevel marketing* companies that rely upon individual distributors to sell their wares find that sales momentum builds quickest among tightly knit groups. That's why Salt Lake City–based Nu Skin Enterprises enlists thousands of Mormons to promote its products. Shaklee excels at recruiting salespeople from groups most companies would consider unrecruitable, including the Amish, Mennonites, and Hasidim, a movement within ultra-Orthodox Judaism that began in Eastern Europe in the eighteenth century. Shaklee succeeds by accommodating the special needs of such highly insular communities. For the Amish and Mennonite sales force, Shaklee awards "bonus buggies" instead of cars. For the Hasidim, company representatives hold separate meetings before the Sabbath and find synagogues for husbands to pray in during convention trips.[92]

THE GLOBAL LOOKING GLASS

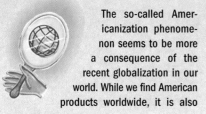

The so-called Americanization phenomenon seems to be more a consequence of the recent globalization in our world. While we find American products worldwide, it is also increasingly common to find Asian products in the United States. In one day in San Francisco, or Seattle, or Houston, we can buy Shiseido cosmetics from Japan at the Galleria Mall, have sushi and sashimi in one of the many Japanese restaurants in the city, go to the cinema and enjoy the beautiful American-Chinese movie *Crouching Tiger, Hidden Dragon*, and take home *spring rolls* from one of the many Chinese restaurants in town.

Source: Excerpted from Yara Berg, "Asianization: The Influence of Asia on America," http://staff.uscolo. edu/peterssl/topics/globalization/asianization.htm, accessed April 28, 2003

Net Profit

The Web is exerting a big impact on religious practice, as numerous Web sites and portals spring up to meet the needs of spiritual surfers. Indeed, 16 percent of teenagers say that the Internet will substitute for their current church-based religious experience in the next five years. More adult Americans use the Internet for religious purposes than for gambling, banking, or trading stocks. Of the 100 million Americans online, 25 percent used the Internet for religious purposes each month, mainly to communicate on e-mail or chat rooms about religious ideas or experiences. Some big religious portals such as *Beliefnet.com* and *SpiritChannel.com* hope to attract people from many different religions. According to one participant, "The Internet is an invitation for people who are skeptical. They feel released and can ask the religious questions they want to explore. I've received e-mails at 3 A.M. from people who haven't stepped inside a church in years." Pray for wide bandwidth.[97]

Ironically, despite this frenzy of faith, the number of adults who attend religious services in the United States and other advanced nations is slipping. However, weekly church attendance in the United States still is far higher than in most other developed nations, according to the World Values Survey conducted by Michigan's Institute for Social Research. More than 90 percent of Americans say they believe in God. About 44 percent of Americans attend church once a week (excluding funerals and Christenings), compared to 27 percent of Britons, 21 percent of the French, 4 percent of Swedes, and 3 percent of Japanese.[93]

Old and New Religions

What are the dominant religions worldwide? The Barna Research Group estimates that there are 2 billion Christians, 1.2 billion people practicing Islam, 900 million are Hindus, 315 million are Buddhists, 15 million are Jews, and a category it terms Primal Indigenous makes up another 190 million. In addition, there are 750,000 practicing Scientologists and 700,000 Rastafarians. Among Americans, the majority (57 percent) is Protestant; one-quarter is Catholic. Muslims, Hindus, and Buddhists make up 5 percent of the population, and Jews are another 2 percent. About 12 percent of Americans have no religious preference.[94] Figure 14.3 summarizes some of the demographic characteristics of many different religious subcultures.

In addition to these established religions, a major survey of 113,000 people on religious attitudes highlights the emergence of new affiliations. For example, it found that there are more Scientologists than Fundamentalists, and also sizable numbers of followers of Wicca (witchcraft) and New Age faiths.[95] Something for everybody.[96]

Indeed, there is an astonishing variety of flourishing new religious movements, most of which are largely unrecognized in the West. One of these came into prominence in 2003, when a cult called The Raelians claimed to have cloned several human babies. Rael, a French race-car journalist formerly known as Claude

Some U.S. megachurches have more than 20,000 members.

■ FIGURE 14.3 THE DEMOGRAPHICS OF RELIGIOUS SUBCULTURES

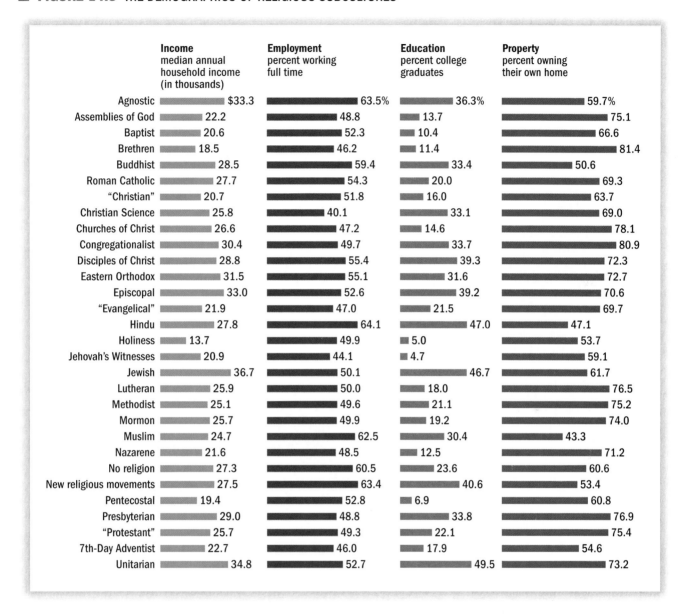

	Income median annual household income (in thousands)	Employment percent working full time	Education percent college graduates	Property percent owning their own home
Agnostic	$33.3	63.5%	36.3%	59.7%
Assemblies of God	22.2	48.8	13.7	75.1
Baptist	20.6	52.3	10.4	66.6
Brethren	18.5	46.2	11.4	81.4
Buddhist	28.5	59.4	33.4	50.6
Roman Catholic	27.7	54.3	20.0	69.3
"Christian"	20.7	51.8	16.0	63.7
Christian Science	25.8	40.1	33.1	69.0
Churches of Christ	26.6	47.2	14.6	78.1
Congregationalist	30.4	49.7	33.7	80.9
Disciples of Christ	28.8	55.4	39.3	72.3
Eastern Orthodox	31.5	55.1	31.6	72.7
Episcopal	33.0	52.6	39.2	70.6
"Evangelical"	21.9	47.0	21.5	69.7
Hindu	27.8	64.1	47.0	47.1
Holiness	13.7	49.9	5.0	53.7
Jehovah's Witnesses	20.9	44.1	4.7	59.1
Jewish	36.7	50.1	46.7	61.7
Lutheran	25.9	50.0	18.0	76.5
Methodist	25.1	49.6	21.1	75.2
Mormon	25.7	49.9	19.2	74.0
Muslim	24.7	62.5	30.4	43.3
Nazarene	21.6	48.5	12.5	71.2
No religion	27.3	60.5	23.6	60.6
New religious movements	27.5	63.4	40.6	53.4
Pentecostal	19.4	52.8	6.9	60.8
Presbyterian	29.0	48.8	33.8	76.9
"Protestant"	25.7	49.3	22.1	75.4
7th-Day Adventist	22.7	46.0	17.9	54.6
Unitarian	34.8	52.7	49.5	73.2

Vorilhon, founded the group in 1973. He claims that while he was in the dish of a French volcano, he was taken onto a flying saucer, where he met a four-foot humanoid extraterrestrial with olive-colored skin, almond-shaped eyes, and long dark hair. Rael supposedly learned that the human race was cloned from beings known as the *Elohim*, a word he claims was mistranslated in the Bible as "God," that actually means "those who came from the sky."[98]

Although this sect has gotten the lion's share of publicity, there are other, much larger ones that claim the allegiance of consumers around the world. These include:[99]

● *The Ahmadis:* A messianic Muslim sect based in Pakistan, with perhaps 8 million members in 70 countries. Muslims consider members of the movement to be heretics and they are barred entry to Mecca. In the Ahmadi version of religious history, Jesus escaped the cross and made his way to India, where he died at the age of 120.

● *The Brahma Kumaris World Spiritual University:* A mostly female movement based in India with about 500,000 members. It was established to give self-determination

Marketing Pitfall

Religious sensibilities vary around the world, and big trouble can result if marketers violate taboo subjects in other cultures. Here are some recent examples:[101]

- A Lipton ad won the prestigious Gold Lion award in Cannes, but the company had to decline the honor in the face of objections. The ad mocked the Catholic Church by showing a man standing in the communion line with a bowl of onion dip in his hand.

- In Salt Lake City, a proposed billboard for a beer called Polygamy Porter aroused the ire of Mormons worldwide. The billboard company under contract with the brewery refused to erect the ad. The board, which was going to feature a picture of a scantily clad man, cherubs, and a six-pack of spouses, advises drinkers to "take some home for the wives." It was rejected for being in "bad taste" in a state where the Mormon Church once sanctioned the practice of marrying multiple women.

- American restaurants in the Middle East must adapt to local customs. The rules about the mixing of the sexes and the consumption of alcohol are quite strict. Chili's Grill & Bar is known simply as Chili's, and the chain offers a midnight buffet during Ramadan season. McDonald's in Saudi Arabia offers separate dining areas for single men and women and children. Booths must have screens because women can't be seen eating meat.

and self-esteem to Indian women. Members wear white, abstain from meat and sex, and are committed to social welfare projects.

- *Cao Dai:* A Vietnam-based religion with more than 3 million members in 50 countries, Coa Dia combines the teachings of Confucianism, Taoism, and Buddhism. Its institutional structure is based on the Catholic Church, including a pope, cardinals, and priests. Its "Three Saints" are Sun Yat-sen, a sixteenth-century Vietnamese poet named Trang Trihn, and Victor Hugo.

- *Soka Gakkai International:* A form of Buddhism based in Japan that claims 18 million members in 115 countries. Members believe that true Buddhists should celebrate earthly experience rather than avoid it. Early members were criticized for their goal of worldwide conversion and their aggressive approach to evangelism; a strategy referred to as *shakubuku*, or "break through and overcome."

- *The Toronto Blessing:* A new evangelical Christian Charismatic movement, based in Canada. Services often induce "a move of the Holy Spirit" that tends to cause behaviors including uncontrollable laughter, apparent drunkenness, and barking like a dog.

- *Umbanda:* A spirit worship movement based in Brazil, with approximately 20 million members in 22 countries, Umbanda combines traditional African religion with native South American beliefs and elements of Catholicism.

The Impact of Religion on Consumption

Religion has not been studied extensively in marketing, possibly because it is seen as a taboo subject.[100] Indeed, big companies know they need to tread lightly when they try to appeal to specific religious beliefs. Recently, Chevrolet came under fire

Especially since 9/11, many people are thirsting for religious experiences. This photo was taken at the 2002 Burning Man Festival described in Chapter 4.

Source: Photo courtesy of Professor Robert Kozinets, Northwestern University.

because the car company sponsored the Come Together and Worship Tour, a 16-city event for evangelical Christians that includes contemporary Christian music and a sermon by a pastor.[102]

However, the little evidence that has been accumulated indicates that religious affiliation has the potential to be a valuable predictor of consumer behavior.[103] In some cases dietary or dress requirements create demand for certain products, and these items then may gain in popularity among other groups. For example, less than a third of the 6 million consumers who buy kosher products are Jewish. Seventh-Day Adventists and Muslims have very similar dietary requirements, and other people simply believe that kosher food is of higher quality. That's why some of the nation's largest manufacturers get involved. About two-thirds of Pepperidge Farm's products, for example, are kosher.[104]

Religious subcultures in particular may exert a significant impact on consumer variables such as personality, attitudes toward sexuality, birthrates and household formation, income, and political attitudes. Church leaders can encourage consumption, but more importantly, they can discourage it—sometimes with powerful effects. The Disney Corporation discovered how effective these movements could

- An ad for Levi's jeans produced in London shows a young man buying condoms from a pharmacist and hiding them in the small side pocket of his jeans. When he goes to pick up his date, he discovers that her father is the same pharmacist. The commercial was a hit in the United Kingdom, but in a strongly Catholic country like Italy or Spain it was not appreciated.

- A Brazilian ad for Pirelli tires drew heat from religious leaders. The ad shows a soccer superstar with his arms spread and a tire tread on the sole of his foot standing in place of the Christ the Redeemer statue that overlooks Rio de Janeiro.

- An ad in a Danish campaign for the French car manufacturer Renault had to be withdrawn after protests from the Catholic community. The ad described a dialogue during confession between a Catholic priest and a repenting man. The man atones for his sins by praying *Ave Marias* until he confesses to having scratched the paint of the priest's new Renault—then the priest shouts "heathen" and orders the man to pay a substantial penalty to the church.

- Burger King had to modify a commercial it aired on U.S. black radio stations in which a coffeehouse poet reads an ode to a Whopper with bacon. In the original spot the person's name is Rasheed and he uses a common Islamic greeting. A Muslim group called the Council on American–Islamic Relations issued a press release noting that Islam prohibits the consumption of pork products. In the new version the poet was introduced as Willie.

For the Contemporary Muslim Woman

AZIZAH.®

FALL 2001

Addressing the Media's Portrayal of Muslim Women

Angels – Instruments of Allah's Will
Celebrating Motherhood
Digging For Our History – Unearthing Islamic Artifa

US$8.50

Specialized ethnic media, like this magazine for Muslim women, are springing up to meet the needs of underserved American subcultures.

Source: Lorraine Ali, "A Magazine of Their Own," *Newsweek* (May 27, 2002): 62.

Religious groups can influence companies' decisions by encouraging their members to boycott products or stage protests.

be when the Southern Baptist Convention voted to persuade all its members to boycott its operations.[103] This edict included all of the Disney Company theme parks, ABC television, Disney Studios, ESPN, Dimension films, Miramax films, and Disney's *Go.com* Web site. The anti-Mickey rebellion was instituted because of the "Gay Days" held at the theme parks and a view that Disney had a radical homosexual agenda that it promoted through its broadcasts. Soon other organizations joined the cause, including the American Family Association, the General Council of the Assemblies of God, Congregational Holiness Church, the Catholic League for Religious and Civil Rights, and the Free Will Baptists.[104] The fallout from the boycott was significant, resulting in a layoff of 4,000 employees. One year after the boycott, Disney theme parks saw business drop by 8 percent from the previous year's corresponding quarter and ABC television and Disney Studios also announced cuts because releases failed to achieve expected profits.[105]

CHAPTER SUMMARY

Consumers identify with many groups that share common characteristics and identities. These large groups that exist within a society are subcultures, and membership in them often gives marketers a valuable clue about individuals' consumption decisions. A large component of a person's identity is often determined by his or her ethnic origins, racial identity, and religious background.

The three largest ethnic and racial subcultures are African Americans, Hispanic Americans, and Asian Americans, but consumers with many diverse backgrounds are beginning to be considered by marketers as well. Indeed, the growing numbers of people who claim multiethnic backgrounds is beginning to blur the traditional distinctions drawn among these subcultures.

African Americans are a very important market segment. In some respects the market expenditures of these consumers do not differ that much from whites, but blacks are above-average consumers in such categories as personal care products.

Hispanic Americans and Asian Americans are other ethnic subcultures that marketers are courting actively. The sizes of both groups are increasing rapidly, and in the coming years one or the other will dominate some major markets. Asian Americans on the whole are extremely well educated, and the socioeconomic status of Hispanics is increasing as well.

Key issues for reaching the Hispanic market are consumers' degree of acculturation into mainstream American society and the recognition of important cultural differences among Hispanic subgroups (e.g., Puerto Ricans, Cubans, Mexicans).

Both Asian Americans and Hispanic Americans tend to be extremely family-oriented and are receptive to advertising that understands their heritage and reinforces traditional family values.

The quest for spirituality is influencing demand in product categories including books, music, and cinema. Although the impact of religious identification on consumer behavior is not clear, some differences among religious subcultures do emerge. The sensibilities of believers must be considered carefully when marketers use religious symbolism to appeal to members of different denominations.

KEY TERMS

Acculturation 483
Acculturation agents 484
De-ethnicization 476

Ethnic pluralism 485
Ethnic subculture 474
High-context culture 474–75

Progressive learning model 485
Subcultures 472

CONSUMER BEHAVIOR CHALLENGE

1 R.J. Reynolds' controversial plan to test-market a cigarette to black consumers raises numerous ethical issues about segmenting subcultures. Does a company have the right to exploit a subculture's special characteristics, especially to increase sales of a harmful product such as cigarettes? What about the argument that virtually every business that follows the marketing concept designs a product to meet the needs and tastes of a preselected segment?

2 Describe the progressive learning model and discuss why this perspective is important when marketing to subcultures.

3 Born-again Christian groups have been instrumental in organizing boycotts of products advertised on shows they find objectionable, especially those that they feel undermine family values. Do religious groups have a right or a responsibility to dictate what advertising a network should carry?

4 Can you locate any current examples of marketing stimuli that depend on an ethnic stereotype to communicate a message? How effective are these appeals?

5 To understand the power of ethnic stereotypes, conduct your own poll. For a set of ethnic groups, ask people to anonymously provide attributes (including personality traits and products) most likely to characterize each group using the technique of free association. How much agreement do you obtain across respondents? To what extent do the characteristics derive from or reflect negative stereotypes? Compare the associations for an ethnic group between actual members of that group and nonmembers.

6 Locate one or more consumers (perhaps family members) who have immigrated from another country. Interview them about how they adapted to their host culture. In particular, what changes did they make in their consumption practices over time?

7 Religious symbolism increasingly is being used in advertising, even though some people object to this practice. For example, a French Volkswagen ad for the relaunch of the Golf showed a modern version of the Last Supper with the tagline, "Let us rejoice, my friends, for a new Golf has been born."[108] A group of clergy in France sued the company and the ad had to be removed from 10,000 billboards. One of the bishops involved in the suit said, "Advertising experts have told us that ads aim for the sacred in order to shock, because using sex does not work anymore." Do you agree? Should religion be used to market products? Do you find this strategy effective or offensive? When and where is this appropriate, if at all?

NOTES

1. Jaime Mejia and Gabriel Sama, "Media Players Say 'Si' to Latino Magazines," *Wall Street Journal Interactive Edition* (May 15, 2002).
2. Pui-Wing Tam, "The Growth in Ethnic Media Usage Poses Important Business Decisions," *Wall Street Journal Interactive Edition* (April 23, 2002).
3. "The Numbers Game," *Time* (Fall 1993): 17.
4. Russell W. Belk and Janeen Arnold Costa, "The Mountain Man Myth: A Contemporary Consuming Fantasy," *Journal of Consumer Research* 25 (1998): 218–40.
5. Erik Davis, "tlhIngan Hol Dajatlh'a' (Do You Speak Klingon?)," *Utne Reader* (March–April 1994): 122–29; additional material provided by personal communication, Professor Robert V. Kozinets, Northwestern University, October 1997; and adapted from Philip Kotler, Gary Armstrong, Peggy H. Cunningham, and Robert Warren, *Principles of Marketing*, 3rd Canadian ed. (Scarborough, Ontario: Prentice Hall Canada, 1997): 96.
6. Robert V. Kozinets, "Utopian Enterprise: Articulating the Meanings of *Star Trek*'s Culture of Consumption," *Journal of Consumer Research* 28 (June 2001): 74.
7. Alex Blumberg, "It's Good to Be King," *Wired* (March 2000): 132–49; Web sites accessed February 8, 2003.
8. See Frederik Barth, *Ethnic Groups and Boundaries: The Social Organization of Culture Difference* (London: Allen and Unwin, 1969); Janeen A. Costa and Gary J. Bamossy, "Perspectives on Ethnicity, Nationalism, and Cultural Identity," in J. A. Costa and G. J. Bamossy, eds., *Marketing in a Multicultural World: Ethnicity, Nationalism, and Cultural Identity* (Thousand Oaks, CA: Sage, 1995), 3–26; Michel Laroche, Annamma Joy, Michael Hui, and Chankon Kim, "An Examination of Ethnicity Measures: Convergent Validity and Cross-Cultural Equivalence," in Rebecca H. Holman and Michael R. Solomon, eds., *Advances in Consumer Research* 18 (Provo, Utah: Association for Consumer Research, 1991): 150–57; Melanie Wallendorf and Michael Reilly, "Ethnic Migration, Assimilation, and Consumption," *Journal of Consumer Research* 10 (December 1983): 292–302; Milton J. Yinger, "Ethnicity," *Annual Review of Sociology* 11 (1985): 151–80.
9. D'Vera Cohn, "2100 Census Forecast: Minorities Expected to Account for 60% of U.S. Population," *Washington Post* (January 13, 2000): A5. For interactive demographic graphics, visit www.understandingusa.com.
10. Thomas McCarroll, "It's a Mass Market No More," *Time* (Fall 1993): 80–81.
11. Pui-Wing Tam, "The Growth in Ethnic Media Usage Poses Important Business Decisions," *Wall Street Journal Interactive Edition* (April 23, 2002).
12. Rohit Deshpandé and Douglas M. Stayman, "A Tale of Two Cities: Distinctiveness Theory and Advertising Effectiveness," *Journal of Marketing Research* 31 (February 1994): 57–64.
13. John Robinson, Bart Landry, and Ronica Rooks, "Time and the Melting Pot," *American Demographics* (June 1998): 18–24.
14. Steve Rabin, "How to Sell across Cultures," *American Demographics* (March 1994): 56–57.
15. John Leland and Gregory Beals, "In Living Colors," *Newsweek* (May 5, 1997): 58.
16. J. Raymond, "The Multicultural Report," *American Demographics* (November 2001): S3, S4, S6.
17. Linda Mathews, "More Than Identity Rides on a New Racial Category," *New York Times* (July 6, 1996): 1.
18. Tom Maguire, "Ethnics Outspend in Areas," *American Demographics* (December 1998): 12–15.
19. Roberto Suro, "Mixed Doubles," *American Demographics* (November 1999): 57–62.
20. Eils Lotozo, "The Jalapeño Bagel and Other Artifacts," *New York Times* (June 26, 1990): C1.
21. Dana Canedy, "The Shmeering of America," *New York Times* (December 26, 1996): D1.
22. Karyn D. Collins, "Culture Clash," *Asbury Park Press* (October 16, 1994): D1.
23. Cara S. Trager, "Goya Foods Tests Mainstream Market's Waters," *Advertising Age* (February 9, 1987): S20.
24. Molly O'Neill, "New Mainstream: Hot Dogs, Apple Pie and Salsa," *New York Times* (March 11, 1992): C1.
25. U.S. Census Bureau, *Census 2000 Brief: Overview of Race and Hispanic Origin* (U.S. Department of Commerce, Economics and Statistics Administration, March 2001).
26. Robert Pear, "New Look at the U.S. in 2050: Bigger, Older and Less White," *New York Times* (December 4, 1992): A1.
27. Peter Schrag, *The Decline of the WASP* (New York: Simon and Schuster, 1971), 20.
28. "Nation's European Identity Falls by the Wayside," *Montgomery Advertiser* (June 8, 2002): A5.
29. Marcia Mogelonsky, "Asian-Indian Americans," *American Demographics* (August 1995): 32–38.
30. McCarroll, "It's a Mass Market No More," 80–81.
31. Marty Westerman, "Death of the Frito Bandito," *American Demographics* (March 1989): 28.
32. Betsy Sharkey, "Beyond Tepees and Totem Poles," *New York Times* (June 11, 1995): H1; Paula Schwartz, "It's a Small World . . . and Not Always P.C.," *New York Times* (June 11, 1995): H22.
33. U.S. Census Bureau, *Census 2000 Brief: Overview of Race and Hispanic Origin*.
34. William O'Hare, "Blacks and Whites: One Market or Two?" *American Demographics* (March 1987): 44–48.
35. Raymond, "The Multicultural Report," S3, S4, S6.
36. Frank Robert, "Thai Government Plans 3,000 Restaurants in U.S. and Elsewhere to Promote Nation," *Wall Street Journal* (February 6, 2001).
37. Bob Tedeschi, "Ethnic Focus for Online Merchants," *New York Times on the Web* (January 13, 2003).
38. For studies on racial differences in consumption, see Robert E. Pitts, D. Joel Whalen, Robert O'Keefe, and Vernon Murray, "Black and White Response to Culturally Targeted Television Commercials: A Values-Based Approach," *Psychology & Marketing* 6 (Winter 1989): 311–28; Melvin T. Stith and Ronald E. Goldsmith, "Race, Sex, and Fashion Innovativeness: A Replication," *Psychology & Marketing* 6 (Winter 1989): 249–62.
39. Bob Jones, "Black Gold," *Entrepreneur* (July 1994): 62–65.
40. Jean Halliday, "Volvo to Buckle Up African-Americans," *Advertising Age* (February 14, 2000): 28.
41. Raymond, "The Multicultural Report," S3, S4, S6.
42. Joe Schwartz, "Hispanic Opportunities," *American Demographics* (May 1987): 56–59.
43. Naveen Donthu and Joseph Cherian, "Impact of Strength of Ethnic Identification on Hispanic Shopping Behavior," *Journal of Retailing* 70, no. 4 (1994): 383–93. For another study that compared shopping behavior and ethnicity influences among six ethnic groups, see Joel Herce and Siva Balasubramanian, "Ethnicity and Shopping Behavior," *Journal of Shopping Center Research* 1 (Fall 1994): 65–80.
44. Howard LaFranchi, "Media and Marketers Discover Hispanic Boom," *Christian Science Monitor* (April 20, 1988): 1.
45. Schwartz, "Hispanic Opportunities."
46. Michael Janofsky, "A Commercial by Nike Raises Concerns about Hispanic Stereotypes," *New York Times* (July 13, 1993): D19.
47. Kelly Shermach, "Infomercials for Hispanics," *Marketing News* (March 17, 1997): 1.
48. Eduardo Porter, "CBS Hopes It Can Lure a Latino Audience with New Characters, Bilingual Broadcast," *Wall Street Journal Interactive Edition* (April 17, 2001).
49. Mireya Navarro, "Raquel Welch Is Reinvented as a Latina," *New York Times on the Web* (June 11, 2002).

50. Stephanie Thompson, "Foods Appeal to 2 Palates," *Advertising Age* (November 19, 2001): 10.

51. Rick Wartzman, "When You Translate 'Got Milk' for Latinos, What Do You Get?" *Wall Street Journal Interactive Edition* (June 3,1999).

52. "Plans for Test Marketing Cigarette Canceled," *The Asbury Park Press* (January 1990): 20; Anthony Ramirez, "A Cigarette Campaign Under Fire," *New York Times* (January 12, 1990): D1; Brad Bennett, "Smoke Signals," *The Asbury Park Press* (July 24, 1994): A1; Suein L. Hwang, "Philip Morris Tests Menthol Type of Marlboros, Targeting Minorities," *Wall Street Journal Interactive Edition* (July 26, 1999).

53. Wartzman, "When You Translate 'Got Milk' for Latinos, What Do You Get?"

54. Jeffery D. Zbar, "'Latinization' Catches Retailers' Ears," *Advertising Age* (November 16, 1998): S22.

55. Cheryl Russell, *Racial Ethnic Diversity: Asians, Blacks, Hispanics, Native Americans, and Whites*, 2nd ed. May (Ithaca, NY: American Demographics, 1998).

56. Beth Enslow, "General Mills: Baking New Ground," *Forecast* (November–December 1993): 18.

57. "'Cultural Sensitivity' Required When Advertising *to Hispanics*," *Marketing News* (March 19, 1982): 45.

58. "What Digital Divide? Hispanic and Asian Households Are More Likely to Be Online," www.insight-corp.com/2_15_01.html, February 15, 2001, accessed January 18, 2003; www.starmedia.com, accessed January 18, 2003; www.elsitio.com, accessed January 18, 2003; Katie Hafner, "Hispanics Are Narrowing the Digital Divide," *New York Times on the Web* (April 6, 2000); Ronald Grover, "Univision Peers into Cyberspace," *BusinessWeek* (January 17, 2000): 74.

59. Hassan Fattah and Pamela Paul, "Gaming Gets Serious," *American Demographics* (May 2002): 39–43.

60. Westerman, "Death of the Frito Bandito."

61. Stacy Vollmers and Ronald E. Goldsmith, "Hispanic-American Consumers and Ethnic Marketing," *Proceedings of the Atlantic Marketing Association* (1993): 46–50.

62. See Lisa Peñaloza, "*Atravesando Fronteras*/Border Crossings: A Critical Ethnographic Exploration of the Consumer Acculturation of Mexican Immigrants," *Journal of Consumer Research* 21 (June 1994): 32–54; Lisa Peñaloza and Mary C. Gilly, "Marketer Acculturation: The Changer and the Changed," *Journal of Marketing* 63 (July 1999): 84–104.

63. Sigfredo A. Hernandez and Carol J. Kaufman, "Marketing Research in Hispanic Barrios: A Guide to Survey Research," *Marketing Research* (March 1990): 11–27.

64. "Dispel Myths Before Trying to Penetrate Hispanic Market," *Marketing News* (April 16, 1982): 1.

65. Schwartz, "Hispanic Opportunities."

66. "'Born Again' Hispanics: Choosing What to Be," *Wall Street Journal Interactive Edition* (November 3, 1999).

67. "'Cultural Sensitivity' Required When Advertising to Hispanics," 45.

68. Peñaloza, "*Atravesando Fronteras*/Border Crossings."

69. Michael Laroche, Chankon Kim, Michael K. Hui, and Annamma Joy, "An Empirical Study of Multidimensional Ethnic Change: The Case of the French Canadians in Quebec," *Journal of Cross-Cultural Psychology* 27 (January 1996): 114–31.

70. Wallendorf and Reilly, "Ethnic Migration, Assimilation, and Consumption," 292–302.

71. Ronald J. Faber, Thomas C. O'Guinn, and John A. McCarty, "Ethnicity, Acculturation and the Importance of Product Attributes," *Psychology & Marketing* 4 (Summer 1987): 121–34; Humberto Valencia, "Developing an Index to Measure Hispanicness," in Elizabeth C. Hirschman and Morris B. Holbrook, eds., *Advances in Consumer Research* 12 (Provo, Utah: Association for Consumer Research, 1985): 118–21.

72. Rohit Deshpande, Wayne D. Hoyer, and Naveen Donthu, "The Intensity of Ethnic Affiliation: A Study of the Sociology of Hispanic Consumption," *Journal of Consumer Research* 13 (September 1986): 214–20.

73. Dan Fost, "Asian Homebuyers Seek Wind and Water," *American Demographics* (June 1993): 23–25.

74. Marty Westerman, "Fare East: Targeting the Asian-American Market," *Prepared Foods* (January 1989): 48–51; Eleanor Yu, "Asian-American Market Often Misunderstood," *Marketing News* (December 4, 1989): 11.

75. Greg Johnson and Edgar Sandoval, "Advertisers Court Growing Asian Population: Marketing, Wide Range of Promotions Tied to New Year Typify Corporate Interest in Ethnic Community," *Los Angeles Times* (February 4, 2000): C1.

76. Alice Z. Cuneo and Jean Halliday Ford, "Penney's Targeting California's Asian Populations," *Advertising Age* (January 4, 1999): 28.

77. Dorinda Elliott, "Objects of Desire," *Newsweek* (February 12, 1996): 41.

78. "Made in Japan," *American Demographics* (November 2002): 48.

79. Hassa Fattah, "Asia Rising," *American Demographics* (July–August 2002): 38–43; Raymond, "The Multicultural Report," S3, S4, S6.

80. Donald Dougherty, "The Orient Express," *The Marketer* (July–August 1990): 14; Cyndee Miller, "'Hot' Asian-American Market Not Starting Much of a Fire Yet," *Marketing News* (January 21, 1991): 12.

81. Dougherty, "The Orient Express."

82. Westerman, "Fare East: Targeting the Asian-American Market."

83. Pui-Wing Tam, "Mandarin Pop Is Looking to Penetrate U.S. Markets," *Wall Street Journal Interactive Edition* (March 31, 2000).

84. Dougherty, "The Orient Express," 14.

85. Miller, "'Hot' Asian-Market Not Starting Much of a Fire Yet."

86. Stephen Gregory, "Practicing Religion While on the Go," *New York Times on the Web* (October 15, 2002).

87. Myra Stark, "Titanic Brand Possibilities," *Advertising Age* (March 9, 1998): 36.

88. "Cards Reflect Return to Spiritual Values," *Chain Drug Review* 21 (February 15, 1999).

89. Patricia Leigh Brown, "Megachurches as Minitowns: Full-Service Havens from Family Stress Compete with Communities," *New York Times* (May 9, 2002): D1; Edward Gilbreath "The New Capital of Evangelicalism: Move Over, Wheaton and Colorado Springs—Dallas, Texas, Has More Megachurches, Megaseminaries, and Mega-Christian Activity than Any Other American City," *Christianity Today* (May 21, 2002): 38; Tim W. Ferguson, "Spiritual Reality: Mainstream Media Are Awakening to the Avid and Expanding Interest in Religion in the U.S.," *Forbes* (January 27, 1997): 70.

90. Tim W. Ferguson and Josephine Lee, "Spiritual Reality," *Forbes* (January 27, 1997): 70; Catherine Dressler, "Holy Socks! This Line Sends a Christian Message," *Marketing News* (February 12, 1996): 5.

91. Richard Cimino and Don Lattin, "Choosing My Religion," *American Demographics* (April 1999).

92. H. J. Shrager, "Close Social Networks of Hasidic Women, other Tight Groups, Boost Shaklee Sales," *Wall Street Journal Interactive Edition* (November 19, 2001).

93. Rebecca Gardyn, "Soul Searchers," *American Demographics* (March 2000): 14; Shelly Reese, "Religious Spirit," *American Demographics* (August 1998).

94. Susan Mitchell, *American Attitudes*, 2nd ed. (Ithaca, NY: New Strategist Publications, 1998). (Taken from a sample page off the New Strategist Publications Web page, www.newstrategist.com).

95. Kenneth L. Woodward, "The Rites of Americans," *Newsweek* (November 29, 1993): 80.

96. "Somebody Say Amen!", 72.

97. "Somebody Say Amen!" *American Demographics* (April 2000): 72; MSNBC Online, www.msnbc.com/modules/exports/ct_email.asp?/news/677141.asp, accessed December 26, 2001.; Lori Leibovich, "That Online Religion with Shopping, Too," *New York Times on the Web* (April 6, 2000).

98. www.rickross.com/groups/raelians.html, accessed January 18, 2003.

99. Toby Lester, "Oh, Gods!" *The Atlantic Monthly* (February 2002): 37–45.

100. For a couple of exceptions, see Michael J. Dotson and Eva M. Hyatt, "Religious Symbols as Peripheral Cues in Advertising: A Replication of the Elaboration Likelihood Model," *Journal of Business Research* 48 (2000): 63–68; Elizabeth C. Hirschman, "Religious Affiliation and Consumption Processes: An Initial Paradigm," *Research in Marketing* (Greenwich, CT: JAI Press, 1983): 131–70.

101. Jack Neff, "Dip Ad Stirs Church Ire," *Advertising Age* (July 2, 2001): 8; G. Burton, "Oh, My Heck! Beer Billboard Gets the Boot," *Salt Lake Tribune* (November 6, 2001); "Religion Reshapes Realities for U.S. Restaurants in Middle East," *Nation's Restaurant News* 32 (February 16, 1998); Sarah Ellison, "Sexy-Ad Reel Shows What Tickles in Tokyo Can Fade Fast in France," *Wall Street Journal Interactive Edition* (March 31, 2000); Claudia Penteado, "Brazilian Ad Irks Church," *Advertising Age* (March 23, 2000): 11; "Burger King Will Alter Ad that Has Offended Muslims," *Wall Street Journal Interactive Edition* (March 15, 2000).

102. Stuart Elliot, "G.M. Criticized for Backing Tour of Christian Music Performers," *New York Times on the Web* (October 24, 2002).

103. See for example, Nejet Delener, "The Effects of Religious Factors on Perceived Risk in Durable Goods Purchase Decisions," *Journal of Consumer Marketing* 7 (Summer 1990): 27–38.

104. Yochi Dreazen, "Kosher-Food Marketers Aim More Messages at Non-Jews," *Wall Street Journal Interactive Edition* (July 30, 1999).

105. The Ethics and Religious Liberty Commission, "Resolution on Moral Stewardship and the Disney Company" [Web site] (July 30, 1997) [cited February 12, 2002]; available from www.erlc.com/WhoSBC/Resolutions/1997/97Disney.htm.

106. Family Research Council, "Southern Baptists Offer Terms to End Disney Boycott" [Web site] (June 28, 2001) [cited February 19, 2002]; available from ourworld.compuserve.com.

107. Ibid.

108. Penteado, "Brazilian Ad Irks Church," 11.

Age Subcultures

it's the last week of summer vacation, and Kurt is looking forward to going back to college. It's been a tough summer. He had trouble finding a summer job and seemed to be out of touch with his old friends—and with so much time on his hands just hanging around the house, he and his mother weren't getting along too well. As usual, Kurt is plopped on the couch, aimlessly flipping channels—from *The Osbournes* on MTV, to *Bewitched* on Nickelodeon, to a Sony beach volleyball tournament on ESPN, back to MTV. Suddenly, his mother marches in, grabs the remote, and switches the channel to public television. Yet another documentary is on about Woodstock (the original one, way back in 1969). When Kurt protests, "Come on Pam, get a life. . ." his mom snaps back, "Keep your cool. You might actually learn about what it was like to be in college when it really meant something. And what's with the first name stuff? In my day I would never have dreamed of calling my mom or dad by their first name!"

That's when Kurt loses it. He's tired of hearing about the "good old days" of Woodstock, Berkeley, and 20 other places he doesn't care about. Besides, most of his mom's ex-hippie friends now work for the very corporations they used to protest about—who are they to preach to him about doing something meaningful with his life? In disgust, Kurt storms into his room, puts a John Mayer CD into his Discman, and pulls the covers up over his head. So much for a constructive use of time. What's

497

the difference, anyway—they'll probably all be dead from the "greenhouse effect" by the time he graduates.

■ AGE AND CONSUMER IDENTITY

The era in which a consumer grows up creates a cultural bond with the millions of others who come of age during the same time period. As we grow older, our needs and preferences change, often in concert with others who are close to our own age. For this reason a consumer's age exerts a significant influence on his or her identity. All things being equal, we are more likely to have things in common with others of our own age than with those younger or older. As Kurt found out, this identity may become even stronger when the actions and goals of one generation conflict with those of others—an age-old battle.

A marketer needs to communicate with members of an age group in their own language. For example, Sony finally figured out that it had to sponsor events such as beach volleyball to get the attention of young people. When the electronics giant first entered the U.S. car stereo market, it simply hammered on its usual themes of

Converse courts the youth market with an edgy message.

technical prowess and quality. This got nothing but yawns from the 16- to 24-year-olds who make up half of the consumers who buy these products, and Sony ranked a pitiful seventh in the market after 10 years. Finally, the company got the picture—it totally revamped its approach and eventually doubled its car stereo revenues.[1]

Now, Sony Electronics is reorganizing its entire internal marketing organization so that it can target products to consumers' different life stages. Instead of assigning managers to products, they are in charge of age-related segments like Gen Y (under age 25), Young Professionals/D.I.N.K.s (double income no kids, 25–34), Families (35–54) and Zoomers (55+).[2] In this chapter, we'll explore some of the important characteristics of some key age groups and consider how marketing strategies must be modified to appeal to diverse age subcultures.

An **age cohort** consists of people of similar ages who have undergone similar experiences. They share many common memories about cultural heroes (e.g., John Wayne versus Brad Pitt, or Frank Sinatra versus Kurt Cobain), important historical events (e.g., World War II versus the 2001 terrorist attacks), and so on. Although there is no universally accepted way to divide up people into age cohorts, each of us seems to have a pretty good idea of what we mean when we refer to "my generation."

Marketers often target products and services to a specific age cohort, and our possessions play a key role in letting us identify with others of a certain age as well as expressing the priorities and needs we encounter at each life stage.[3] A recent ad campaign for Saturn features a set of commercials that represent stages in life from childhood and high school to college and marriage. As four friends drive around in the new Saturn Ion, they come upon populations composed only of kids playing on swing sets, students on prom night, partying fraternity members, and young marrieds in tuxedos and wedding gowns. The campaign intends to reinforce the idea that the car is designed to take its owner through each life stage.[4]

As shown in Figure 15.1, although middle-aged people make the most money, there's plenty of market potential attached to other age groups as well. The same offering will probably not appeal to people of different ages, nor will the language and images used to reach them. In some cases separate campaigns are developed

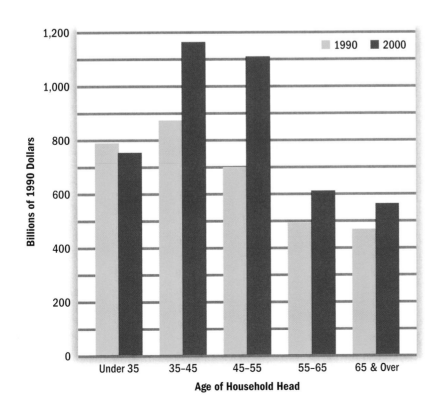

■ **FIGURE 15.1**
HOUSEHOLD INCOME BY AGE

Marketing Opportunity

A *reunion* is an event based on a shared age cohort. People who were not necessarily fond of each other in high school or college come together to celebrate the common experience of having been in school at the same time and place. More than 150,000 reunions are held in the United States each year, attended by 22 million people (the 10-year high school reunion is the most heavily attended). In addition to the boon this nostalgia provides to caterers and professional reunion organizers, some marketers realize that the people who attend reunions represent a valuable customer base. They are self-selected to be fairly successful, because the "failures" tend not to show up. Some companies use reunion-goers to test new products, and travel-related businesses interview attendees about their trips or provide special promotional packages for returning. So, rent that limo, drop those unwanted extra pounds, print up some impressive business cards, and have a great time.[7]

TABLE 15.1
THE NOSTALGIA SCALE

Scale Items

They don't make 'em like they used to.
Things used to be better in the good old days.
Products are getting shoddier and shoddier.
Technological change will ensure a brighter future (reverse coded).
History involves a steady improvement in human welfare (reverse coded).
We are experiencing a decline in the quality of life.
Steady growth in GNP has brought increased human happiness (reverse coded).
Modern business constantly builds a better tomorrow (reverse coded).

Note: Items are presented on a nine-point scale ranging from strong disagreement (1) to strong agreement [9], and responses are summed.

Source: Morris B. Holbrook and Robert M. Schindler, "Age, Sex, and Attitude toward the Past as Predicters of Consumers' Aesthetic Tastes for Cultural Products," *Journal of Marketing Research* 31 (August 1994): 416. Reprinted by permission of the American Marketing Association.

to attract consumers of different ages. For example, Norelco found that younger men are far less likely to use electric shavers than are its core customer base of older men. The company launched a two-pronged effort to convince younger men, on the one hand, to switch from wet shaving to electric, and on the other hand, to maintain loyalty among its older following. Ads for Norelco's Speedrazor, aimed at males aged 18 to 35, ran on late-night TV and in *GQ* and *Details*. Messages about the company's triple-head razors, geared to men over 35, ran instead in publications that attract older readers, such as *Time* and *Newsweek*.

Because consumers within an age group confront crucial life changes at roughly the same time, the values and symbolism used to appeal to them can evoke powerful feelings of nostalgia (see Chapter 3). Adults over 30 are particularly susceptible to this phenomenon.[5] However, references to their past influence young people as well as old. In fact, research indicates that some people are more disposed to be nostalgic than others, regardless of age. Table 15.1 shows a scale that has been used to measure the impact of nostalgia on individual consumers.

■ THE TEEN MARKET: GEN Y LIKE TOTALLY RULES

In 1956, the label "teenage" first entered the general American vocabulary when Frankie Lymon and the Teenagers became the first pop group to identify themselves with this new subculture. Believe it or not, the concept of a teenager is a fairly new idea. Throughout most of history a person simply made the transition from child to adult (often accompanied by some sort of ritual or ceremony, as we'll see in the next chapter). The magazine *Seventeen*, born in 1944, was based on the revelation that young women didn't want to look just like Mom. Following World War II, the teenage conflict between rebellion and conformity began to unfold, pitting Elvis Presley with his slicked hair and suggestive pelvis swivels against the wholesome Pat Boone with his white bucks (see Figure 15.2). Now, this rebellion is often played out for so-called **Generation Y** kids (those born between 1977 and 1994 who are the younger siblings of Generation X, which we'll discuss later) by teen idols such as hip-hop star Eminem or by the confused, sullen teens appearing daily on Ricki Lake and other daytime talk shows.[6]

■ **FIGURE 15.2** THE U.S. TEEN POPULATION

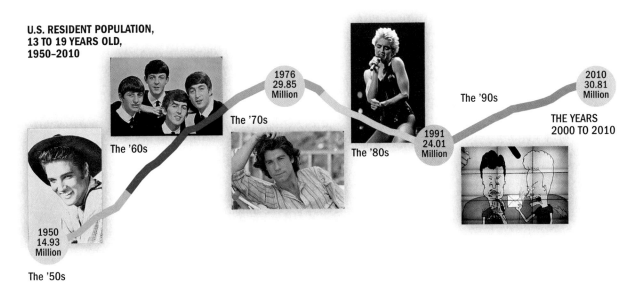

U.S. RESIDENT POPULATION,
13 TO 19 YEARS OLD,
1950–2010

The '60s

1976
29.85
Million

The '70s

The '80s

The '90s

2010
30.81
Million

THE YEARS
2000 TO 2010

1991
24.01
Million

1950
14.93
Million

The '50s

Gen Y makes up over 20 percent of the population and the proportion of people this age is expected to increase at twice the rate of the rest of the population over the next decade. Generation Y is an ethnically diverse generation. While minorities make up 24 percent of their parents' age cohort (Baby Boomers, which we'll discuss later in the chapter), they form 34 percent of Generation Y. Unlike their cynical Gen X predecessors (which we'll also get to), Gen Yers tend to be more upbeat about their lives and their prospects. Alcohol consumption among high school seniors is dropping steadily, and drug usage, pregnancy, and homicide rates among teens also are declining. There is a bit of a renaissance of family and religious values, and sociologists are predicting a surge in younger marriages and bigger families as these kids come into their own in a few years.[8]

Teen Values, Conflicts, and Desires

As anyone who has been there knows, the process of puberty and adolescence can be both the best of times and the worst of times. Many exciting changes happen as individuals leave the role of child and prepare to assume the role of adult. These changes create a lot of uncertainty about the self, and the need to belong and to find one's unique identity as a person becomes extremely important. At this age, choices of activities, friends, and clothes are often crucial to social acceptance. Teens actively search for cues for the "right" way to look and behave from their peers and from advertising. Advertising geared to teens is typically action-oriented and depicts a group of "in" teens using the product.

Consumers in this age subculture have a number of needs, including experimentation, belonging, independence, responsibility, and approval from others. Product usage is a significant medium through which to express these needs. For example, many kids view smoking cigarettes as a status activity because of the numerous movies they've seen that glorify this practice. In one study, ninth graders watched original movie footage with either smoking scenes or control footage with the smoking edited out. Sure enough, when the young viewers saw the actors smoking, this enhanced their perceptions of smokers' social stature and increased their own intent to smoke (the good news: when kids were shown an antismoking advertisement before the film these effects canceled out).[9]

Teenagers in every culture grapple with fundamental developmental issues as they make the transition from childhood to adult. Teenagers throughout history

Net Profit

Teens use products to express their identities, to explore the world and their newfound freedoms in it, and also to rebel against the authority of their parents and other socializing agents. A thriving Internet subculture has developed among many teens to serve this purpose. The Internet is the preferred method of communication for many young people because its anonymity makes it easier to talk to people of the opposite sex or of different ethnic and racial groups.[13] The Web also provides a forum for experimentation that appeals to teens grappling with identity issues. Researchers report that teens value privacy when surfing the Web because they view it as a way to express their individuality—that's why it's common for them to have multiple e-mail accounts, each with a different "personality."[14] Indeed, many teens are using the Web to experiment with different identities. More than half have more than one screen name or e-mail address. Nearly a quarter of this multi-monikered group keep at least one name secret so they can go online without being recognized by friends. And, 24 percent of teens who use e-mail, instant messaging (IM), or chat rooms pretend to be someone else.[15]

have had to cope with insecurity, parental authority, and peer pressure. According to Teenage Research Unlimited, today the five most important social issues for teens are AIDS, race relations, child abuse, abortion, and the environment. Today's teens often have to cope with additional family responsibilities as well, especially if they live in nontraditional families in which they must take significant responsibility for shopping, cooking, and housework. It's hard work being a teen in the modern world. Research by the Saatchi & Saatchi advertising agency identified four basic conflicts common to all teens:

- *Autonomy versus belonging:* Teens need to acquire independence, so they try to break away from their families. On the other hand, they need to attach themselves to a support structure, such as peers, to avoid being alone. One survey of teens found that only 11 percent view themselves as "popular."[10]
- *Rebellion versus conformity:* Teens need to rebel against social standards of appearance and behavior, yet they still need to fit in and be accepted by others. Cult products that cultivate a rebellious image are prized for this reason. Hot Topic, a retail chain based in Pomona, California, caters to this need by selling $44 million per year of such "in-your-face" items as nipple rings, tongue barbells, and purple hair dye.[11]
- *Idealism versus pragmatism:* Teens tend to view adults as hypocrites, whereas they see themselves as being sincere. They have to struggle to reconcile their view of how the world should be with the realities they perceive around them.
- *Narcissism versus intimacy:* Teens are often obsessed with their own appearance and needs. On the other hand, they also feel the desire to connect with others on a meaningful level.[12]

A growing number of marketers are capitalizing on the ritual of Spring Break to reach college students.

Appealing to the Youth Market

Collectively, American teens spent $172 billion in 2001—that's a lot of Slurpees![16] The spending power of American teens is well known, and lately European companies also are appreciating the vast economic clout of the young. Euroteens also have plenty of cash to spend; a survey of Germans aged 16 to 18 by *Yomag.net*, an online magazine for European teens, found that 60 percent had a job and 92 percent received an allowance, with a significant number receiving both. Another *Yomag.net* survey of teens from other European countries showed that they received a monthly allowance of about €36.74 (one euro having roughly the same value as a dollar). That figure doesn't compare with the $22.68 *weekly* average that U.S. teens receive, but it's still more than chump change![17] Indeed, the potential of the global youth market is massive, representing about $100 billion in spending power! This is because of the huge proportion of people in many countries who are very young. For example, consider that while 21 percent of U.S. residents are 14 or younger, these are the corresponding percentages in some other countries:[18]

- China: 25 percent
- Argentina: 27 percent
- Brazil: 29 percent
- India: 33 percent
- Iran: 33 percent
- Malaysia: 35 percent
- Philippines: 37 percent

Learning from their parents, many young consumers have figured out that they don't even need to have cash on hand: 42 percent of teens aged 18 and 19 already have a credit card in their own name. Another 11 percent say they have access to a parent's credit card.[19] Debit cards like Splash Plastic and Smartcreds further encourage teen spending.[20] Much of this money goes toward "feel-good" products: cosmetics, posters, and fast food—with the occasional nose ring thrown in as well. Because they are so interested in many different products and have the resources to obtain them, many marketers avidly court the teen market.

Indeed, some major corporations are figuring out the value of teaming with very dissimilar players to develop youth-based products. For example, Nike and Polaroid have formed a partnership that lets teens personalize their sneakers by inserting pictures they take with the I-Zone camera directly into the shoes.[21] Toyota created a special marketing unit called Genesis Group just to reach young adults. Genesis launched its first campaign to support Toyota's new crop of youth-oriented models like the Echo.[22] The company is teaming with fashionable surfwear maker Roxy to create a surf-friendly version of its Echo sedan for the young female market, complete with water-resistant, neoprene-covered seats, a Yakima roof rack, and wet-gear storage bins. If this lifestyle strategy works, Toyota plans to roll out a male-oriented sport wagon or pickup linked to the trendy Quiksilver name.[23]

Tweens

Marketers use the term **tweens** to describe the 27 million children aged 8 to 14 who spend $14 billion *dollars* a year on clothes, CDs, movies, and other "feel good" products. Tweens are "between" childhood and adolescence and exhibit characteristics of both age groups. As one tween commented, "When we're alone we get weird and crazy and still act like kids. But in public we act cool, like teenagers."[24] One of the biggest tween success stories of all is the meteoric rise of Mary-Kate and Ashley Olsen, who made their acting debut as little girls on the TV series *Full House*. Today, the Olsen twins are a brand name to be reckoned with. They have become the most financially successful child stars in history, generating over $500 million in retail sales in just one year. They have been television, video, and film stars, editors-in-chief of

Marketing Pitfall

Although teens have the "rep" of always questioning authority, it's also important to keep in mind that one person's rebellion is another's disobedience—there are strong cultural differences when it comes to the desirability of revolting against the establishment. Teen rebellion is a new phenomenon in Japan, a country known for rigid conformity and constant pressure to achieve. Now, more and more teenagers seem to be making up for lost time. The dropout rate among Japanese students in junior and senior high school increased by 20 percent in a two-year period. More than 50 percent of girls have had intercourse by their senior year of high school.[25]

Elsewhere in Asia, however, things are different: Many Asian teens don't necessarily value rebellion against a middle class that they are just now starting to join. An MTV executive commented, "Asian youth are schizophrenic. They lead double lives, almost. On one hand, they've got their earrings, belly-button rings and ponytails, but on the other hand, they're completely conformist." In Singapore, Coca-Cola discovered that teen-oriented ads it had used successfully elsewhere, such as a shirtless guy bodysurfing at a rock concert or recklessly riding a grocery cart down a store aisle, just didn't make it with local kids who thought the ads were too unruly. One 18-year-old Singaporean's reactions to a scene showing kids head-banging sums up this feeling: "They look like they're on drugs constantly. And if they're on drugs, then how can they be performing at school?"

In some cases, advertisers have to walk a fine line: For example, an ad for Bajaj Auto, India's largest scooter and motorcycle maker, features an Indian boy and his Caucasian girlfriend cruising around on a bike. This is a provocative image in a country where most marriages are still arranged in line with strict caste codes. But then the couple arrives at a temple, and the boy respectfully covers the girl's head with a shawl to show there are limits to pushing the envelope.[26]

Car manufacturers are developing new models that appeal to youth subcultures.

their own magazine, fashion designers, recording artists, executive producers, authors, and even videogame heroines.[27]

Tweens like to talk on the phone and in chat rooms, they squeal and shout when Britney Spears takes the stage—and they've definitely got marketers' attention. For example, Kodak made a $75 million, five-year commitment to convince tween girls to buy its single-use Kodak Max cameras. According to internal research, this segment is 50 percent more likely than boys of the same age to own a camera. When girls are asked to name their most prized possession, 15 percent said photographs, whereas only 4 percent of their male counterparts put photos at the top of their lists. Kodak discovered that a majority of girls keep journals, collect quotes, and maintain online bulletin boards, and the company is betting that this desire to share experiences with friends will turn into a picture-perfect marketing strategy.[28]

THE GLOBAL LOOKING GLASS

In a reflection of how advertising often parallels current sensibilities, some marketers here are spoofing American manners and behavior at a time when many in Europe are criticizing U.S. foreign policy. . . The commercials mirror Europeans' complex, changing attitudes toward the United States, say some marketing consultants. "People have gone through the love affair with Americana and they're coming out of the other side," says Marie Ridgley, an executive at Added Value, a strategic marketing consulting

firm owned by Britain's WPP Group PLC. "It's not necessarily totally anti-Americanism going on, but it's a reappraisal of that relationship. We've gone through the stage where we buy into the T.G.I. Friday's, we buy into McDonald's, we buy into Nike hook, line, and sinker."

Mother, the agency behind the I-Can't-Believe-It's-Not-Butter commercials, has gotten a lot of mileage out of American spoofs. It also created ads for Dr Pepper and a publicly traded Internet banking firm called Egg PLC that plays on American stereotypes. One spot for Dr Pepper shows an American school cheerleader offering Dr Pepper to a handsome young

man. He tries it and spills some. Spotting a bit of tissue paper popping out of her shirt, he grabs it and unwittingly pulls a trail of tissue paper out of her stuffed bra. Mortified, she runs off, ending any romantic opportunities. The playful tagline: "Dr Pepper. What's the worst that could happen?" "The whole thing is *Scary Movie* meets *Scream* meets *Porky's*," Mr. Calcraft of Mother says. "Global teen culture is very, very American."

Source: Excerpted from Erin White, "National Lampoon: U.K. Ads Satirize American Demeanor," *Wall Street Journal Online Edition*, April 28, 2003.

Speaking to Teens in Their Language

Because modern teens were raised on TV and tend to be more "savvy" than older generations, marketers must tread lightly in attempts to reach them. In particular, the messages must be seen as authentic and not condescending. As one researcher observed, "they have a B.S. alarm that goes off quick and fast. . . . They walk in and usually make up their minds very quickly about whether it's phat or not phat, and whether they want it or don't want it. They know a lot of advertising is based on lies and hype."[29]

So what are the rules of engagement when it comes to young consumers?[30]

Rule 1: Don't Talk Down. Younger consumers want to feel they are drawing their own conclusions about products. In the words of one teen: "I don't like it when someone tells me what to do. Those drugs and sex commercials preach. What do

Marketers often influence public policy by creating messages to influence behaviors like smoking or drug use. This mosaic was used to promote Lorillard Tobacco's Youth Smoking Prevention Program.

they know? Also, I don't like it when they show a big party and say come on and fit in with this product. That's not how it works."

Rule 2: Don't Try to Be What You're Not. Stay True to Your Brand Image. Kids value straight talk. Firms that back up what they say impress them. Procter & Gamble appealed to this value by including a money-back guarantee on its Old Spice High Endurance deodorant with an invitation to phone 1–800–PROVEIT.

Rule 3: Entertain Them. Make It Interactive and Keep the Sell Short. Gen Y kids like to find brands in unexpected places. The prospect of catching appealing ads is part of the reason they're watching that TV show in the first place. If they want to learn more, they'll check out your Web site.

Rule 4: Show That You Know What They're Going Through, but Keep It Light. In a commercial for Hershey's Ice Breakers mints, the brand's product benefit is tied to a guy's stress at approaching a strange girl at a club. "I'm wearing my lucky boxers," he reassures himself. "Don't trip. Don't drool. Relax. How's my breath?"

Youth Tribes

We talked about the emergence of consumer tribes in Chapter 11. As we said then, this phenomenon is most pronounced among young consumers. The essence of tribal consumption is that these products and services reinforce the notion of belonging regardless of the commitment level of the individual. Whether the tribal member is deeply committed or is just a novice, each person attains a sense of belonging embracing the trappings and rituals of the tribe.[31] The tribal idea is picking up speed among marketers. Mattel is introducing a line of My Scene dolls, including a more approachable and multicultural Barbie aimed at older girls. As a Mattel executive explains, "They really pick up on this notion there are various tribes girls want to belong to."[32]

In-line roller skaters in France are a great example of the tribal phenomenon at work. There are about 2 million in-line skaters in France today, divided equally by gender. This group has its "in-groups" and "out-groups" within the tribe, but all are connected by their shared skating experience. These urban skaters hold national gatherings in Paris that attract as many as 15,000 people, many of whom belong to associations like Roller et Coquillages and Paris Roller. Specialized Web sites for members of the skating tribe let them meet to chat and to exchange information. Small tribal divisions exist (e.g., fitness skaters versus stunt skaters), but all identify with the skating tribe.

Tribal gatherings provide manufacturers with an opportunity to strengthen the group bond by offering accessories such as shoes, key chains, belts and hats, backpacks, sunglasses, T-shirts, and other goodies that reinforce membership. Although many brands of skates are available including K2, Razors, Oxygen, Tecnica, and Nike, the original Rollerblade product retains cult status within the tribe. A company like Tatoo, the pager arm of France Telecom, builds on tribal bonds with in-line skaters by sponsoring Tatoo Roller Skating in Paris and similar events around the country. Specialized magazines like *Crazy Roller, Urban,* and *Roller Saga* carry informational articles as well as celebrity spots.

Closer to home, an American sneaker company called And 1 appeals to members of a basketball tribe that sets admission standards based on the ability to blow by a defender on the court. The company carefully cultivates a trash-talking street image (distributing shirts with slogans like "I'm sorry. I thought you could play") and it recruits street players to match its renegade brand image. This group, known as The Entertainers Tour, puts on shows of hoops and music at playgrounds and appears in And 1's TV advertising. Footage from the events was blended with some unreleased rap music to produce a video that was handed out at playgrounds, parks, and clubs by street teams to spread the word about this upstart company. [33]

The tribal phenomenon is perhaps most pronounced in Japan, where teenagers invent, adopt, and discard fads with lightning speed. Teenage girls in Japan exhibit what science fiction writer William Gibson (who invented the term *cyberspace*) calls "techno-cultural suppleness"—a willingness to grab something new and use it for their own ends—matched by no other group on earth. According to one estimate, cell phones sit in the purses and pockets of about 95 percent of all Japanese teenage girls. Unlike American phones, these devices are connected constantly to the Internet and plug these girls into a massive network. Index, a Tokyo software start-up company, offers a Net-phone service called God of Love. For about $1.40 per month, users can tap the birth date of a potential mate into their phones and receive a computerized prediction of the relationship's future.[34]

Researching the Youth Market

Research firms are coming up with innovative ways to tap the desires of teens, many of whom don't respond well to traditional survey techniques. Pizza Hut invites teens into to its boardroom to have lunch with company executives and share their opinions about the perfect pie.[35] Some research companies give teens video cameras and ask them to record a "typical" day at school—along with play-by-play commentary to help interpret what's going on.

Japanese teens aren't the only ones who are wired. The average American kid spends 11.3 hours a week online.[36] It hasn't taken long for marketers to accept that the Internet is the medium for targeting Generation Y—the generation that has grown up with computers. Teen-oriented Web portals like Alloy Online, **Bolt.com**, and **Snowball.com** are thriving. Although research shows that teens spend most of their time online in scholastic pursuits such as research for papers, most admit that at least a quarter of their online time is spent checking out or buying items like music, books, or concert tickets. E-commerce spending among online teens and young adults currently accounts for 13 percent of their total spending—a figure that is more than four times the rate of e-commerce spending among all adults.[37]

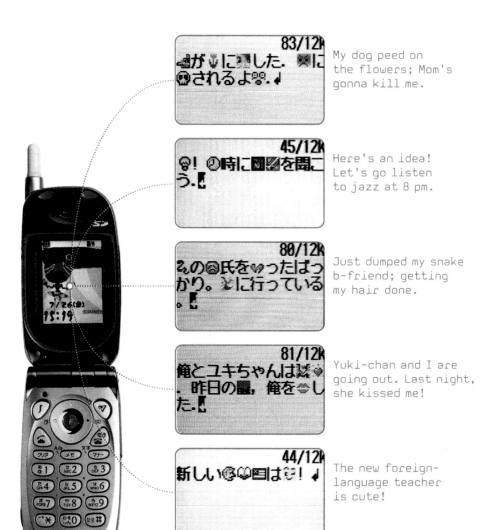

My dog peed on the flowers; Mom's gonna kill me.

Here's an idea! Let's go listen to jazz at 8 pm.

Just dumped my snake b-friend; getting my hair done.

Yuki-chan and I are going out. Last night, she kissed me!

The new foreign-language teacher is cute!

Hip Japanese kids have invented a new way to send cell phone messages. A graphics-based language called *emoji* uses tiny images instead of words. Each cell provider features its own set of emoticons.

Marketing Pitfall

Calvin Klein's strategy of using adolescent sexuality to sell the company's products dates way back to 1980, when Brooke Shields proclaimed, "Nothing comes between me and my Calvins." Later, ads featuring singer Marky Mark in his underwear sparked a new fashion craze. A few years ago Klein took this approach one very daring step further, when the company unveiled a controversial advertising campaign featuring young-looking models in situations dripping with sexual innuendo. In one spot, an old man with a gravelly voice says to a scantily clad young boy who's lying down in a seedy-looking basement, "You got a real nice look. How old are you? Are you strong? You think you could rip that shirt off of you? That's a real nice body. You work out? I can tell." The campaign ended when the chairman of Dayton Hudson asked that the stores' names be removed from the ads, and *Seventeen* refused to carry them. By that time, of course, Klein had reaped invaluable volumes of free publicity as teens and adults hotly debated the appropriateness of these images.[44]

Firms like Sputnik employ **coolhunters**; kids in major markets like New York, Los Angeles, or London who roam the streets to report back on cutting-edge trends. Other companies send researchers to "live with the natives" and observe how they *really* use products in their daily lives. One firm sends researchers to spend the night with respondents so they can observe them up-close and personal. During the evening they talk about important stuff such as their skin care routines, but then in the morning the interviewer watches to see what they actually do in the bathroom while primping before school.[38] When the Leo Burnett advertising agency was revamping Heinz ketchup's image to make it cool, the account research team took teens to dinner to see how they actually used ketchup. These meals opened their eyes; new ads focus on teens' need for control by showing ketchup smothering fries "until they can't breathe" and touting new uses for the condiment on pizza, grilled cheese, and potato chips.[39]

Procter & Gamble goes to the Web to learn what kids are thinking. The company built two teen community Web sites to identify emerging trends. One of them, ***tremor.com***, recruits teen members and rewards them with merchandise for spreading the word about products, while ***toejam.com*** (which stands for Teens Openly Expressing Just About Me) lets members preview new products and critique ads before they are widely distributed.[40]

This research is all about defining what is cool to teens—the Holy Grail of youth marketing. One study asked young people in the United States and the Netherlands to write essays about what is "cool" and "uncool" and to create visual collages representing things that represent being cool to them.[41] The researchers found that being cool has several meanings, though there were a lot of similarities between the two cultures when kids use this term. Some of the common dimensions include having charisma, being in control, and being a bit aloof. And many of the respondents agreed that being cool is a moving target: The harder you try to be cool, the more uncool you are! Some of their actual responses are listed here:

- "Cool means being relaxed, to nonchalantly be the boss of every situation, and to radiate that" (Dutch female).
- "Cool is the perception from others that you've got 'something' which is macho, trendy, hip, etc." (Dutch male).
- "Cool has something stand-offish, and at the same time, attractive." (Dutch male).
- "Being different, but not too different. Doing your own thing, and standing out, without looking desperate while you're doing it" (American male).
- "When you are sitting on a terrace in summer, you see those machos walk by, you know, with their mobile [phones] and their sunglasses. I always think, 'Oh please, come back to earth!' These guys only want to impress. That is just so uncool." (Dutch female).
- "When a person thinks he is cool, he is absolutely uncool" (Dutch female).
- "To be cool we have to make sure we measure up to it. We have to create an identity for ourselves that mirrors what we see in magazines, on TV, and with what we hear on our stereos" (American male).

Marketers view teens as "consumers-in-training" because brand loyalty often develops during adolescence. A teenager who is committed to a brand may continue to purchase it for many years to come. Such loyalty creates a barrier-to-entry for other brands that were not chosen during these pivotal years. Thus, advertisers sometimes try to "lock in" consumers so that in the future they will buy their brands more or less automatically. As one teen magazine ad director observed, "We . . . always say it's easier to start a habit than stop it."[42]

Teens also exert a big influence on the purchase decisions of their parents (see Chapter 12).[43] In addition to providing "helpful" advice to parents, teens are increasingly buying products on behalf of the family. The majority of mothers are employed outside the home today, so they have less time to shop for the family. This fundamental change in family structure has altered the way marketers must conceive of teenage consumers. Although teens are still a good market for discretionary items, in recent years their spending on such "basics" as groceries is even larger than for nonessentials. Marketers are beginning to respond to these changes—the next time you are leafing through a magazine like *Seventeen*, notice the large number of ads for food products.

Big (Wo)Man on Campus: We're Talking to You!

Advertisers spend approximately $100 million a year on campus to woo college students, and with good reason: Overall, students spend more than $11 billion a year on snacks and beverages, $4 billion on personal care products, and $3 billion on CDs and tapes.[45] Many students have plenty of extra cash and free time (not you, of course. . . .): On an average day the average student spends 1.7 hours in class and another 1.6 hours studying. This "average" student (or are all students above average?) has about $287 to spend on discretionary items per month. As one marketing executive observed, "This is the time of life where they're willing to try new products. . . . This is the time to get them in your franchise."[46] The college market is also attractive to many companies because these novice consumers are away from home for the first time, so they have yet to form unshakeable brand loyalty to products such as cleaning supplies.

Nevertheless, college students pose a special challenge for marketers, because they are hard to reach via conventional media like newspapers. Of course, online advertising is very effective: Fully 99 percent of college students go online at least a few times per week and 90 percent do so daily. In addition, enterprises like College Television Network (CTN) and Burley Bear Network are blossoming because they reach students where they live and play. Burley is sent directly to dorm rooms at 600 colleges and universities through cable television, while CTN places monitors in high traffic areas on college campuses like cafeterias and fitness centers that are watched by over seven million students every week.[47] These specialized networks are providing college students with irreverent programming designed to appeal to their sense of humor, with such shows as "Bridget the Midget" that follows the life of a three-foot-tall former porn star who is now an aspiring rock singer, and an anti–Martha Stewart cooking show called "Half Baked" that features celebrities like Shaquille O'Neal and Lisa Loeb sharing recipes.[48]

Other strategies to reach students include the widespread distribution of sampler boxes containing a variety of personal care products in student centers and dormitories and the use of posters (termed *wall media*). In addition, a growing number of marketers are capitalizing on the ritual of Spring Break to reach college students; it is estimated that about 40 percent of students now make the annual trek to points south. Beach promotions used to be dominated by suntan lotion and beer companies, but now firms such as Chanel, Hershey, Chevrolet, Procter & Gamble, and Columbia Pictures join them.[49]

Baby Busters: "Generation X"

The cohort of consumers born between 1966 and 1976 consists of 46 million Americans. This group was labeled "**Generation X**" following the best-selling 1991 novel of that name. They have also been called "slackers" or "baby busters" because of their supposed alienation and laziness, and these stereotypes pervade popular culture in movies such as *Clueless* or in the music of groups such as Marilyn Manson.[50]

In the past, advertisers fell all over themselves trying to create messages that would not turn off the worldly Generation X cohort. Many of these efforts involved references to old TV shows such as *Gilligan's Island* or vignettes featuring disheveled actors in turned-around baseball caps doing their best to appear blasé. This approach actually turned off a lot of busters because it implies that they have

Marketing Opportunity

In the old days, new college students would stock up on "essentials" like popcorn makers, linens, or blue jeans when they went off to school. Today, the boring stuff won't cut it: Dorm rooms are becoming fashion hubs as students are adding faux-fur blankets, multicolored pillows, Zen lamps, and yoga mats to their must-have lists. Funky dorm products from designers like Todd Oldham are the rage. Delia's offers its "Roomwares" line of home décor that features the same patterns and materials that appear in the clothing it sells. Bed Bath & Beyond appeals to parents who want to make the transition to college as stress-free as possible. The chain created a shopping list to guide the first-time buyer, conveniently divided into four basic categories—sleep, eat, wash, and study (seems like they may have left out a few things?).[51] So, tear down those ratty old Phish posters and get with the program!

nothing else to do but sit around and watch old television reruns. Subaru sponsored one of the first commercials of this genre. It showed a sloppily dressed young man who described the Impreza model as "like punk rock" while denouncing the competition as "boring and corporate." The commercial did not play well with its intended audience, and Subaru eventually switched advertising agencies.

Perhaps one reason marketing appeals to Xers with messages of alienation, cynicism, and despair have not succeeded is that many busters turned out not to be so depressed after all! Generation Xers actually are quite a diverse group—they don't all wear reversed baseball caps and work as burger flippers. A CNN/Time study found that 60 percent want to be their own bosses, and another study revealed that Xers are already responsible for 70 percent of new start-up businesses in the United States. One industry expert observed, "Today's Gen Xer is both values-oriented and value-oriented. This generation is really about settling down." Many people in this segment seem to be determined to have stable families after being latchkey children themselves. Seven out of 10 regularly save some portion of their income, a rate comparable to that of their parents. Xers tend to view the home as an expression of individuality rather than material success. More than half are involved in home improvement and repair projects.[52] They don't sound all that lazy.

■ BABY BOOMERS

The **baby boomer** age segment (people born between 1946 and 1965) consists of people whose parents established families following the end of World War II and during the 1950s when the peacetime economy was strong and stable (as a general rule, when people feel confident about how things are going in the world, they are more likely to decide to have children). The sheer size of this age cohort has helped to make it the source of many fundamental cultural and economic changes.[53]

As teenagers in the 1960s and 1970s, the "Woodstock Generation" created a revolution in style, politics, and consumer attitudes. As they have aged, their collective will has been behind cultural events as diverse as the Free Speech movement and hippies in the 1960s to Reaganomics and yuppies in the 1980s. Now that they are older, they continue to influence popular culture in important ways.

This generation is much more active and physically fit than its predecessors; baby boomers are six percent more likely than the national average to be involved in some type of sporting activity.[54] And boomers are now in their peak earning years. As one commercial for VH1, the music-video network that caters to those who are a bit too old for MTV, pointed out, "The generation that dropped acid to escape reality . . . is the generation that drops antacid to cope with it."

Levi Strauss is a good example of a company that built its core business on the backs (or backsides) of boomers. More recently, though, the apparel maker faced the challenge of keeping aging baby boomers in their franchise as former jeans-wearing hippies got older and lost interest in traditional styles. Levi Strauss answered this challenge by creating a new product category, "New Casuals," that would be more formal than jeans but less casual than dress slacks. The target audience was men aged 25 to 49 with higher-than-average education and income, who worked in white-collar jobs in major metropolitan areas. The Dockers line was born.[55]

Consumers aged 35 to 44 spend the most on housing, cars, and entertainment. Baby boomers are "feathering their nests"; they account for roughly 40 percent of all the money spent on household furnishings and equipment.[56] In addition, consumers aged 45 to 54 spend the most of any age category on food (30 percent above average), apparel (38 percent above average), and retirement programs (57 percent above average). To appreciate the impact middle-aged consumers have and will have on our economy, consider this: At current spending levels, a one percent

now it's Pepsi–for those who think young

Thinking young is a wholesome attitude, an enthusiastic outlook. It means getting the most out of life, and everyone can join in. This is the life for Pepsi —light, bracing, clean-tasting Pepsi. Think young. Say "Pepsi, please!"

ENJOY THE STEVE ALLEN SHOW PRESENTED BY PEPSI WEEKLY ON ABC-TV

This 1962 Pepsi ad highlights the emphasis on youth power that began to shape our culture as baby boomers came of age in the 1960s.

increase in the population of householders aged 35 to 54 results in an additional $8.9 billion in consumer spending.

In addition to the direct demand for products and services created by this age group, these consumers have also created a new baby boom of their own to keep marketers busy in the future. Because fertility rates have dropped, this new boom is not as big as the one that created the baby boom generation; the new upsurge in the number of children born in comparison can best be described as a *baby boomlet*. Many boomer couples postponed getting married and having children because of the new opportunities and options for women. They began having babies in their late twenties and early thirties, resulting in fewer (but perhaps more pampered) children per family. This new emphasis on children and the family has created opportunities for products such as cars (e.g., the success of the SUV concept among "soccer Moms"), services (e.g., the day care industry, as exemplified by the KinderCare chain), and media (e.g., magazines such as *Working Mother*).

Many Boomers are interested in maintaining a youthful appearance and will go to great lengths to preserve it. Botox injections are the newest craze.

It took forty years to get it.

And ten minutes to do something about it.

Welcome to the age of Botox® Cosmetic. Finally, a simple, non-surgical procedure that can dramatically reduce even your toughest wrinkle within days. One ten-minute treatment - a few tiny injections - relaxes the muscles between your brows that cause lines to form. And keeps them relaxed up to four months. Botox® Cosmetic has been widely tested. And now it's approved by the FDA. So it's really up to you. You can choose to live with wrinkles. Or you can choose to live without them.

Untouched clinical photos taken while frowning before and after Botox® Cosmetic. In clinical trials, 89% of patients rated improvement in frown lines as moderate or better. Individual results may vary.

Ask your dermatologist, ophthalmologist, or plastic surgeon about Botox® Cosmetic. Or call toll-free or visit our website for a listing of Botox® Cosmetic Network physicians.

The most common side effects are headache, respiratory infection, flu syndrome, temporary eyelid droop, and nausea. Botox® Cosmetic should not be used if there is an infection at injection site.

Please see additional important information on the following page.

It's not magic, it's

BOTOX®
—Cosmetic
Botulinum Toxin Type A

1-800-BotoxMD
www.BotoxCosmetic.com

Botox® and the Botox® Cosmetic logo are registered trademarks owned by Allergan, Inc.

■ THE GRAY MARKET

The old woman sits alone in her dark apartment while the television blares out a soap opera. Once every couple of days, she slowly and painfully opens her triple-locked door with arthritic hands and ventures out to the corner store to buy essentials such as tea, milk, and cereal, always being sure to pick the least expensive brand. Most of the time she sits in her rocking chair, thinking sadly of her dead husband and the good times she used to have.

Is this the image you have of a typical elderly consumer? Until recently, many marketers did. As a result, they largely neglected the elderly in their feverish pursuit of the baby boomer market. But as our population ages and people are living longer and healthier lives, the game is rapidly changing. A lot of businesses are beginning to replace the old stereotype of the poor recluse. The newer, more accurate image is of an older person who is active, interested in what life has to offer, and is an enthusiastic consumer with the means and willingness to buy many goods and services.

For example, as we saw earlier in this chapter, Sony is now targeting "Zoomers," after the company discovered that about a third of its sales are coming from consumers age 50 and older. And, this market is growing even as we speak: An American turns 50 every seven seconds.[58]

Gray Power: Seniors' Economic Clout

Think about this: By the year 2010, one of every seven Americans will be 65 or older. And, by 2100 the number of Americans who are at least 100 years old will jump from 65,000 now to more than 5 million.[59] None of us may be around to see that, but we can already see the effects of the **gray market** today as seniors impact the marketplace. Older adults control more than 50 percent of discretionary income and spend more than $60 billion annually in the United States alone.[60] The mature market is the second-fastest-growing market segment in the United States, lagging only behind the baby boomers. Such dramatic growth can largely be explained by healthier lifestyles, improved medical diagnoses and treatment, and the resulting increase in life expectancy.

Given the economic clout of senior consumers, it's often surprising how many marketers ignore them in favor of younger buyers. This is certainly true in the world of television advertising, where most companies are anxious to attract the 18 to 34 segment. This is true even though people over the age of 50 account for half of all the discretionary spending in the United States. Although they watch more television, go to more movies, and buy more CDs than young people do, Americans over 50 are the focus of less than 10 percent of the advertising![61]

And, the economic health of older consumers is good and getting better. Some of the important areas that stand to benefit from the surging gray market include exercise facilities, cruises and tourism, cosmetic surgery and skin treatments, and "how-to" books and university courses that offer enhanced learning opportunities. In many product categories seniors spend their money at an even greater rate than other age groups: Householders aged 55 to 64 spend 15 percent more than average per capita. They shell out 56 percent more than the average consumer on women's clothing, and as new grandparents they actually spring for more toys and playground equipment than people aged 25 to 44.[62] In fact, the average grandparent spends an average of about $500 per year on gifts for grandchildren—have you called yours today?[63]

Understanding Seniors

Researchers have identified a set of key values that are relevant to older consumers. For marketing strategies to succeed, they should be related to one or more of these factors:[64]

- *Autonomy:* Mature consumers want to lead active lives and to be self-sufficient. The advertising strategy for Depends, undergarments for incontinent women made by Kimberly-Clark, is centered on senior celebrities like actress June Allyson, who plays golf and goes to parties without worrying about her condition.
- *Connectedness:* Mature consumers value the bonds they have with friends and family. Quaker Oats successfully tapped into this value with its ads featuring actor Wilford Brimley, who dispenses grandfatherly advice to the younger generation about eating right.
- *Altruism:* Mature consumers want to give something back to the world. Thrifty Car Rental found in a survey that more than 40 percent of older consumers would select a rental car company if it sponsored a program that gives van discounts to senior citizens' centers. Based on this research, the company launched its highly successful program, "Give a Friend a Lift."

Marketing Opportunity

Seniors are fueling a leisure travel boom as they seek out exotic experiences such as a cruise to Antarctica or an expedition to see Incan ruins. The explanation is simple: Until we reach middle age, we tend to spend most of our income on acquiring possessions—feathering our nests. After the little birds have flown, however, it's a different matter and people tend to think about going to places they've never been or having new experiences. That explains why Americans aged 55 to 64 are spending $17 billion a year on travel-related goods and services. So be alert—the person holding the bungee cord next to you may be your grandmother.[65]

Echoing the saying, "You're only as old as your feel," these ads remind us that a person's perceived age often does not correspond to his or her chronological age.

Perceived Age: You're Only as Old as You Feel

Market researchers who work with older consumers often comment that people think of themselves as being 10 to 15 years younger than they actually are. In fact, research confirms the popular wisdom that age is more a state of mind than of body. A person's mental outlook and activity level have a lot more to do with his or her longevity and quality of life than does *chronological age*, the actual number of years lived.

A better yardstick to categorize seniors is **perceived age**, or how old a person feels as opposed to his or her chronological age. Perceived age can be measured on several dimensions, including "feel-age" (i.e., how old a person feels) and "look-age" (i.e., how old a person looks).[66] The older consumers get, the younger they feel relative to actual age. For this reason, many marketers emphasize product benefits rather than age-appropriateness in marketing campaigns because many consumers will not relate to products targeted to their chronological age.[67]

Segmenting Seniors

The senior subculture is an extremely large market: The number of Americans 65 and older exceeds the entire population of Canada.[68] The elderly market is particularly well suited for segmentation because older consumers are easy to identify by age and stage in the family life cycle. Most receive Social Security benefits, so they can be located without much effort, and many belong to organizations such as the American Association of Retired Persons (*aarp.org*), which boasts more than 12 million dues-paying members. AARP's main publication, *Modern Maturity*, has the largest circulation of any American magazine.

In addition to chronological age, marketers segment the elderly along such dimensions as the particular years a person came of age (age cohort), current marital status (e.g., widowed versus married), and a person's health and outlook on life.[69] For example, one ad agency devised a segmentation scheme for American women over the age of 65 using two dimensions: self-sufficiency and perceived opinion leadership.[70] The study discovered many important differences among the groups. For example, the self-sufficient group was found to be more independent, cosmopolitan, and outgoing. Compared to the other seniors, these women were more likely to read a book, attend concerts and sporting events, and dine out.

Several segmentation approaches begin with the premise that a major determinant of elderly marketplace behavior is the way a person deals with being old.[71] **Social aging theories** try to understand how society assigns people to different roles across the life span. For example, when people retire they may reflect society's expectations for someone at this life stage—this is a major transition point when people exit from many relationships.[72] Some people become depressed, withdrawn, and apathetic as they age; some are angry and resist the thought of aging; and others accept the new challenges and opportunities this period of life has to offer. Table 15.2 summarizes some selected findings from one segmentation approach called **gerontographics**, which divides the mature market into groups based on both level of physical well-being and social conditions such as becoming a grandparent or losing a spouse.

Net Profit

The Internet can be a godsend for the elderly, especially those seniors who have difficulty leaving the house to go shopping or who are socially isolated. Senior surfers can reduce unnecessary car trips by ordering food to be delivered from companies such as *peapod.com* and arranging for automatic delivery of medications from online pharmacies such as *Drugstore.com* and *PlanetRX.com*. They can also find new friends online and receive important information and reminders. Some other helpful Web sites include:

- *IPing.com*—reminders to take medications
- *PayMyBills.com*—Pay bills online
- *Caregiver.org*—The Family Caregiver Alliance locates Web pals
- *ElderWeb.com*—a network of financial and health care links
- *Seniors-Site.com*—message boards for caregivers and seniors[73]

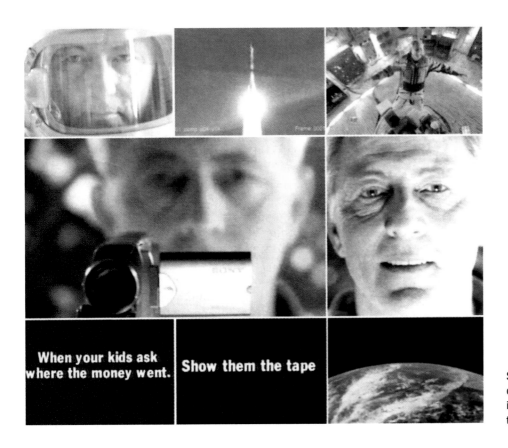

When your kids ask where the money went. Show them the tape

Sony sells about 1/3 of its products to consumers ages 50 and older. The company is targeting mature consumers with ads like this one that celebrate "Zoomers" freedom.

TABLE 15.2
GERONTOGRAPHICS: SELECTED CHARACTERISTICS

Segment	% of 55+ Population	Profile	Marketing Ramifications
Healthy Indulgers	18%	Have experienced the fewest events related to aging, such as retirement or widowhood, and are most likely to behave like younger consumers. Main focus is an enjoying life.	Looking for independent living and are good customers for discretionary services like home cleaning and answering machines.
Healthy Hermits	36%	React to life events like the death of a spouse by becoming withdrawn. Resent that they are expected to behave like old people	Emphasize conformity. They want to know their appearance is socially acceptable, and tend to be comfortable with well-known brands.
Ailing Outgoers	29%	Maintain positive self-esteem despite adverse life events. They accept limitations but are still determined to get the most out of life.	Have health problems that may require a special diet. Special menus and promotions will bring these people into restaurants seen as catering to their needs.
Frail Recluses	17%	Have adjusted their lifestyles to accept old age, but have chosen to cope with negative events by becoming spiritually stronger.	Like to stay put in the same house where they raised their families. Good candidates for remodeling, also for emergency-response systems.

Source: Adapted from George P. Moschis, "Life Stages of the Mature Market," *American Demographics* (September 1996): 44–50.

Selling to Seniors

Most older people lead more active, multidimensional lives than we assume. Nearly 60 percent engage in volunteer activities, one in four seniors aged 65 to 72 still works, and more than 14 million are involved in daily care of a grandchild.[74] And, it is crucial to remember that income alone does not express the spending power of this group. Older consumers are finished with many of the financial obligations that siphon off the income of younger consumers. Eighty percent of consumers past age 65 own their own homes, and 80 percent of those homes are owned outright. In addition, child-rearing costs are over. As evidenced by the popularity of the bumper sticker that proudly proclaims "We're Spending Our Children's Inheritance," many seniors now are more inclined to spend money on themselves rather than skimp for the sake of children and grandchildren.

Still, outdated images of mature consumers persist. The editors of *Modern Maturity* reject about a third of the ads submitted to them because they portray older people in a negative light. In one survey, one-third of consumers over age 55 reported that they deliberately did not buy a product because of the way an older person was stereotyped in the product's advertising.[75] To address these negative depictions, marketers can provide more welcoming environments for seniors. Wal-Mart hires older people as greeters to be sure their senior customers feel at home. A California bank named Home Savings of America went even farther by opening branches catering to seniors. The bank supplies coffee and donuts and encourages its older customers to think of the branches as a convenient meeting place and a venue for social interaction.[76]

Product Adaptations

Many consumer products will encounter a more sympathetic reception from seniors if products and the packages they come in are redesigned to be sensitive to physical limitations. Packages are often awkward and difficult to manage, especially for those who are frail or arthritic. Also, many serving sizes are not geared to smaller families, widows, and other people living alone, and coupons tend to be for family-sized products, rather than for single servings.

Some seniors have difficulty with pull-tab cans and push-open milk cartons. Ziploc packages and clear plastic wrap also can be difficult to handle. Packages need to be easier to read and should be made lighter and smaller. Finally, designers need to pay attention to contrasting colors. A slight yellowing of the eye's lens as one ages can make it harder to see background colors on packages. Discerning between blues, greens, and violets becomes especially difficult. The closer identifying type colors are to the package or ad background color, the less visibility and attention they will command.

Carmakers are at the forefront of adapting their products to the needs of the aged. General Motors formed a group called Paragon Team that studies the needs of aging car buyers, and Ford has a similar group of engineers and designers called the

Marketing Pitfall

Some marketing efforts targeted to older adults have backfired because they reminded people of their advanced age or depicted their age group in an unflattering way. Heinz committed one of the more infamous blunders. A company analyst found that many older people were buying baby food because of the small portions and easy chewing consistency, so Heinz introduced a line of "Senior Foods" made especially for denture wearers. Needless to say, the product failed. Consumers did not want to admit that they required strained foods (even to the supermarket cashier). They preferred to purchase baby foods, which they could pretend they were buying for a grandchild.

"Jockey For Her is the best fitting underwear I've ever worn. It's so comfortable. And now my favorite granddaughters wear Jockey For Girls®. Just Jockey."

Catherine Councell Moll
Grandmother/Banker
Sheboygan, Wisconsin

So Comfortable JOCKEY For Her

For Pantyhose That Fit . . . Wear Jockey For Her Pantyhose with Lycra®

Jockey Apparel is one of many advertisers that is increasingly featuring attractive older models in its ads.

Third Age Suit. GM redesigned some Oldsmobile models to include bigger buttons and clearer dashboard displays, and a Cadillac's rearview mirrors automatically dim when hit with headlights. The Lincoln Town Car (the average age of a Lincoln driver is 67) features two sets of radio and air conditioning controls, one on the dashboard and one on the steering wheel, because some older drivers have trouble shifting attention from controls to the road. Chrysler engineers are experimenting with collision-control systems that sound an alarm when a driver is too close to another car.[77]

Mature Marketing Messages

Older adults respond positively to ads that provide an abundance of information. Unlike other age groups, these consumers usually are not amused, or persuaded, by imagery-oriented advertising. A more successful strategy involves the construction of advertising that depicts the aged as well-integrated, contributing members of society, with emphasis on their expanding their horizons rather than clinging precariously to life. Some basic guidelines for effective advertising to the elderly include the following:[78]

- Keep language simple.
- Use clear, bright pictures.
- Use action to attract attention.
- Speak clearly, and keep the word count low.
- Use a single sales message, and emphasize brand extensions to tap consumers' familiarity.
- Avoid extraneous stimuli (i.e., excessive pictures and graphics can detract from the message).

CHAPTER SUMMARY

People have many things in common with others merely because they are about the same age. Consumers who grew up at the same time share many cultural memories because they belong to a common age cohort, so they may respond well to marketers' nostalgia appeals that remind them of these experiences.

Four important age cohorts are teens, college students, baby boomers, and older adults. Teenagers are making a transition from childhood to adulthood, and their self-concepts tend to be unstable. They are receptive to products that help them to be accepted and enable them to assert their independence. Because many teens earn money but have few financial obligations, they are a particularly important segment for many nonessential or expressive products, ranging from chewing gum to clothing fashions and music. Due to changes in family structure, many teens also are taking more responsibility for their families' day-to-day shopping and routine purchase decisions. College students are an important but hard-to-reach market. In many cases, they are living alone for the first time, so they are making important decisions about setting up a household. Tweens are an increasingly important market segment; kids aged 8 to 14 who are making the transition from childhood to adolescence are influential purchasers of clothing, CDs, and other "feel-good" products. Many young people belong to youth tribes that influence their lifestyles and product preferences.

Baby boomers are the most powerful age segment because of their size and economic clout. As this group ages, its interests have changed and marketing priorities have changed as well. The needs and desires of baby boomers affect demands for housing, childcare, automobiles, clothing, and many other products.

As the population ages, the needs of older consumers will become increasingly influential. Many marketers traditionally have ignored seniors because of the stereotype that they are too inactive and spend too little. This stereotype is no longer accurate. Many older adults are healthy, vigorous, and interested in new products and experiences—and they have the income to purchase them. Marketing appeals to this age subculture should focus on consumers' self-concepts and perceived ages, which tend to be more youthful than their chronological ages. Marketers also should emphasize concrete benefits of products because this group tends to be skeptical of vague, image-related promotions.

KEY TERMS

Age cohort   499
Baby boomer   510
Coolhunters   508
Generation X   509

Generation Y   500
Gerontographics   515
Gray market   513
Perceived age   514

Social aging theories   515
Tweens   503

CONSUMER BEHAVIOR CHALLENGE

1 What are some possible marketing opportunities present at reunions? What effects might attending such an event have on consumers' self-esteem, body image, and so on?

2 What are some of the positives and negatives of targeting college students? Identify some specific marketing strategies that you feel have either been successful or unsuccessful at appealing to this segment. What characteristics distinguish the successes from the failures?

3 Why have baby boomers had such an important impact on consumer culture?

4 How has the baby boomlet changed attitudes toward child-rearing practices and created demand for different products and services?

5 "Kids these days seem content to just hang out, surf the Net, and watch mindless TV shows all day." How accurate is this statement?

6 Is it practical to assume that people age 55 and older constitute one large consumer market? What are some approaches to further segmenting this age subculture?

7 What are some important variables to keep in mind when tailoring marketing strategies to older adults?

8 Find good and bad examples of advertising targeted to older consumers. To what degree does advertising stereotype the elderly? What elements of ads or other promotions appear to determine their effectiveness in reaching and persuading this group?

9 If you were a marketing researcher assigned to study what products are "cool," how would you do this? Do you agree with the definitions of "cool" provided by the young people in this chapter?

10 Marketers of entrenched brands like Nike, Pepsi, and Levi Strauss are tearing their hair out over Gen Y consumers. Image-building campaigns (e.g., Michael Jordan endorsing Nike) are not as effective as they once were. Compared to their predecessors, these young consumers seem to be more interested in individuality than in fitting in. For example, Kodak is successfully marketing its "Sticky Film" to young people who use the product to express themselves in original ways. Perhaps this change is partly due to the amount of time young people spend surfing alone on the Web. As a Nike executive put it, "Television drives homogeneity. The Internet drives diversity."[79] What advice would you give to a marketer who wants to appeal to Gen Y? What are major do's and don'ts? Can you provide some examples of specific marketing attempts targeted to Gen Y that work or don't work?

NOTES

1. Shelly Reese, "The Lost Generation," *Marketing Tools* (April 1997): 50.
2. Toby Elkin, "Sony Marketing Aims at Lifestyle Segments," *Advertising Age* (March 18, 2002): 3.
3. James W. Gentry, Stacey Menzel Baker, and Frederic B. Kraft, "The Role of Possessions in Creating, Maintaining, and Preserving Identity: Variations over the Life Course," in Frank Kardes and Mita Sujan, eds., *Advances in Consumer Research* 22 (1995): 413–18.
4. Stuart Elliot, "Saturn Tries Alternate Worlds to Change Its Image," *New York Times on the Web* (January 8, 2003).
5. Bickley Townsend, "Ou Sont les Reiges Díantan? (Where Are the Snows of Yesteryear?)" *American Demographics* (October 1988): 2.
6. Stephen Holden, "After the War the Time of the Teen-Ager," *New York Times* (May 7, 1995): E4.
7. Paula Mergenhagen, "The Reunion Market," *American Demographics* (April 1996): 30–34.
8. Chantal Liu, "Faces of the New Millennium," [Web site] Northwestern University, 1999 [cited April 6, 2002]; available from pubweb. acns.nwu.edu/~eyc345/final.html.
9. Cornelia Pechmann and Chuan-Fong Shih, "Smoking Scenes in Movies and Antismoking Advertisements Before Movies: Effects on Youth," *Journal of Marketing* 63 (July 1999): 1–13.
10. Maureen Tkacik, "Alternative Teens Are Hip to Hot Topics Mall Stores," *Wall Street Journal Interactive Edition* (February 12, 2002).
11. Mary Beth Grover, "Teenage Wasteland," *Forbes* (July 28, 1997): 44–45.
12. Junu Bryan Kim, "For Savvy Teens: Real Life, Real Solutions," *New York Times* (August 23, 1993): S1.
13. Scott McCartney, "Society's Subcultures Meet by Modem," *Wall Street Journal* (December 8, 1994): B1.
14. Ellen Neuborne, "Generation Y," *BusinessWeek* (February 15, 1999): 83.
15. A. A. Nolan, "Me, Myself, and IM," *Brandweek* (August 13, 2001): 24.
16. "Teens Spent $172 Billion in 2001," in Teenage Research Unlimited [Web site] (Northbrook, IL, 2002 [cited April 6, 2002]); available from www.teenresearch.com.
17. L. Bertagnoli, "Continental Spendthrifts," *Marketing News* (October 22, 2001): 1, 15.
18. Arundhati Parmar, "Global Youth United," *Marketing News* (October 28, 2002): 1–49.
19. "Teens Spent $155 Billion in 2000," in Teenage Research Unlimited [Web site] (Northbrook, IL, 2002 [cited April 6, 2002]); available from www.teenresearch.com/PRview.cfm?edit_id=75; Grover, "Teenage Wasteland," 44–45.
20. David Murphy, "Connecting with Online Teenagers" *Marketing* (September 27, 2001): 31–32.
21. Cara Beardi, "Photo Op: Nike, Polaroid Pair up for Footwear Line," *Advertising Age* (April 2, 2001): 8.
22. F. S. Washington, "Aim Young; No, Younger; Millennial Potential Is Huge as Toyota, Ford Hit the High Notes: Music, Fashion, Fun, Sports, Technology," *Advertising Age* (April 9, 2001): 16.
23. Mark Rechtin, "Surf's up for Toyota's Co-Branded Roxy Echo," *Automotive News* (June 25, 2001): 17.
24. Karen Springen, Ana Figueroa, and Nicole Joseph-Goteiner, "The Truth about Tweens," *Newsweek* (October 18, 1999): 62–72.
25. Howard W. French, "Vocation for Dropouts Is Painting Tokyo Red," *New York Times on the Web* (March 5, 2000).
26. Cris Prystay, "Consumer Firms Temper Ads for Conservative Asian Teens," *Wall Street Journal Interactive Edition* (October 3, 2002).
27. "The Human Truman Show," *Fortune* (July 8, 2002): 96–98.
28. Matthew Grimm, "Snap It, Girlfriend!" *American Demographics* (April 2000): 66–67.
29. Cyndee Miller, "Phat Is Where It's at for Today's Teen Market," *Marketing News* (August 15, 1994): 6; see also Tamara F. Mangleburg and Terry Bristol, "Socialization and Adolescents' Skepticism Toward Advertising," *Journal of Advertising* 27 (Fall 1998): 11; see also Gil McWilliam and John Deighton, "Alloy-com: Marketing to Generation Y," *Journal of Interactive Marketing* 14 (Spring 2000): 74–83.
30. Adapted from Gerry Khermouch, "Didja C that Kewl Ad?" *BusinessWeek* (August 26, 2002): 158–60.
31. Veronique Cova and Bernard Cova, "Tribal Aspects of Postmodern Consumption Research: The Case of French In-Line Roller Skaters," *Journal of Consumer Behavior* 1 (June 2001): 67–76.
32. Kate MacArthur, "Plastic Surgery: Barbie Gets Real Makeover," *Advertising Age* (November 4, 2002): 4.
33. Terry Lefton, "Feet on the Street," *Brandweek* (March 2000): 36–40.
34. C. C. Mann, "Why 14-Year-Old Japanese Girls Rule the World" *Yahoo! Internet Life* (August 2001): 98–105.
35. Dave Carpenter, "Tuning in Teens: Marketers Intensify Pitch for 'Most Savvy' Generation Ever," *Canadian Press* (November 19, 2000).
36. Anthony A. Perkins, "The Rise of the Always-On Generation," *Red Herring* (November 16, 2001).
37. Julia Fien Azoulay, "Cyber Shopping—A Family Affair," *Children's Business* 16 (July 2001): 24.
38. Jane Bainbridge, "Keeping up with Generation Y," *Marketing* (February 18, 1999): 37–38.
39. Daniel McGinn, "Pour on the Pitch," *Newsweek* (May 31, 1999): 50–51.
40. Jack Neff, "P&G Targets Teens via Tremor, Toejam Site," *Advertising Age* (March 5, 2001): 12.
41. Gary J. Bamossy, Michael R. Solomon, Basil G. Englis, and Trinske Antonidies, "You're Not Cool if You Have to Ask: Gender in the Social Construction of Coolness" (paper presented at the Association for Consumer Research Gender Conference, Chicago, June 2000); see also Clive Nancarrow, Pamela Nancarrow, and Julie Page, "An Analysis of the Concept of Cool and its Marketing Implications," *Journal of Consumer Behavior* 1 (June 2002): 311–22.
42. Ellen Goodman, "The Selling of Teenage Anxiety," *Washington Post* (November 24, 1979).
43. Ellen R. Foxman, Patriya S. Tansuhaj, and Karin M. Ekstrom, "Family Members' Perceptions of Adolescents' Influence in Family Decision-making," *Journal of Consumer Research* 15 (March 1989): 482–91.
44. Margaret Carlson, "Where Calvin Crossed the Line," *Time* (September 11, 1995): 64.
45. Rebecca Gardyn, "Educated Consumers," *Demographics* (November 2002): 18.
46. Tibbett L. Speer, "College Come-Ons," *American Demographics* (March 1998): 40–46; Fannie Weinstein, "Time to Get Them in Your Franchise," *Advertising Age* (February 1, 1988): S6.
47. Bernard Stamler, "Advertising: Wooing Collegians on Campus with, What Else, Television," *New York Times on the Web* (June 6, 2001).
48. Laura Randal, "Battle of the Campus TV Networks," *New York Times on the Web* (January 12, 2003).
49. Stuart Elliott, "Beyond Beer and Sun Oil: The Beach-Blanket Bazaar," *New York Times* (March 18, 1992): D17.
50. Laura Zinn, "Move Over, Boomers," *BusinessWeek* (December 14, 1992): 7.
51. Trujillo Melissa, "Retailers Hype Funky Dorm Items," *Associated Press* (September 16, 2002): 48.
52. Robert Scally, "The Customer Connection: Gen X Grows Up, They're in Their 30s Now," *Discount Store News* 38, no. 20 (1999).
53. Brad Edmondson, "Do the Math," *American Demographics* (October 1999): 50–56.
54. John Fetto, "The Wild Ones," *American Demographics* (February 2000): 72.
55. Kevin Keller, *Strategic Marketing Management* (Upper Saddle River, NJ: Prentice Hall, 1998).
56. Edmondson, "Do the Math," 50–56.
57. Blayne Cutler, "Marketing to Menopausal Men," *American Demographics* (March 1993): 49.
58. Elkin Tobi, "Sony Ad Campaign Targets Boomers-Turned-Zoomers," *Advertising Age* (October 21, 2002): 6.
59. D'Vera Cohn, "2100 Census Forecast: Minorities Expected to Account for 60% of U.S. Population," *Washington Post* (January 13, 2000): A5.
60. Catherine A. Cole and Nadine N. Castellano, "Consumer Behavior," in James E. Binnen, ed., *Encyclopedia of Gerontology*, vol. 1 (San Diego, CA: Academic Press, 1996), 329–39.
61. Jonathan Dee, "The Myth of '18 to 34'," *New York Times Magazine* (October 13, 2002); Hillary Chura, "Ripe Old Age," *Advertising Age* (May 13, 2002): 16.
62. Cheryl Russell, "The Ungraying of America," *American Demographics* (July 1997): 12.
63. Jeff Brazil, "You Talkin' to Me?" *American Demographics* (December 1998): 55–59.
64. David B. Wolfe, "Targeting the Mature Mind," *American Demographics* (March 1994): 32–36.
65. Peter Francese, "The Exotic Travel Boom," *American Demographics* (June 2002): 48–49.

66. Benny Barak and Leon G. Schiffman, "Cognitive Age: A Nonchronological Age Variable," in Kent B. Monroe, ed., *Advances in Consumer Research* 8 (Provo, UT: Association for Consumer Research, 1981): 602–6.

67. David B. Wolfe, "An Ageless Market," *American Demographics* (July 1987): 27–55.

68. Lenore Skenazy, "These Days, It's Hip to Be Old," *Advertising Age* (February 15, 1988): 8.

69. L. A. Winokur, "Targeting Consumers," *Wall Street Journal Interactive Edition* (March 6, 2000).

70. Ellen Day, Brian Davis, Rhonda Dove, and Warren A. French, "Reaching the Senior Citizen Market(s)," *Journal of Advertising Research* (December 1987–January 1988): 23–30.

71. Day et al., "Reaching the Senior Citizen Market(s)"; Warren A. French and Richard Fox, "Segmenting the Senior Citizen Market," *Journal of Consumer Marketing* 2 (1985): 61–74; Jeffrey G. Towle and Claude R. Martin Jr., "The Elderly Consumer: One Segment or Many?" in Beverlee B. Anderson, ed., *Advances in Consumer Research* 3 (Provo, UT: Association for Consumer Research, 1976): 463.

72. Catherine A. Cole and Nadine N. Castellano, "Consumer Behavior," *Encyclopedia of Gerontology*, vol. 1 (1996): 329–39.

73. Dolly Setton, "Cyber Granny," *Forbes* (May 22, 2000): 40.

74. Rick Adler, "Stereotypes Won't Work with Seniors Anymore," *Advertising Age* (November 11, 1996): 32.

75. Melinda Beck, "Going for the Gold," *Newsweek* (April 23, 1990): 74.

76. Paco Underhill, "Seniors & Stores," *American Demographics* (April 1996): 44–48.

77. Michelle Krebs, "50-Plus and King of the Road," *Advertising Age* (May 1, 2000): S18; Daniel McGinn and Julie Edelson Halpert, "Driving Miss Daisy—and Selling Her the Car," *Newsweek* (February 3, 1997): 14.

78. J. Ward, "Marketers Slow to Catch Age Wave," *Advertising Age* (May 22, 1989): S1.

79. Ellen Neuborne, "Generation Y," *BusinessWeek* (February 15, 1999): 80 (7), 83.

Consumers and Culture

The final section of this book looks at consumers as members of a broad cultural system, and reminds us that everyday, mundane consumption activities often are rooted in deeper meanings. Chapter 16 looks at some of the basic building blocks of culture and the impact that such underlying processes as myths and rituals exert on "modern" consumers. Chapter 17 focuses on the ways that products spread throughout the members of a culture, and across cultures as well. This final chapter considers the process by which some consumer products succeed while others don't, and also examines how successful Western products influence the consumption practices of people around the world.

■ CHAPTERS AHEAD

Cultural Influences
on Consumer Behavior

Wendy is at her wits' end. It's bad enough that she has a deadline looming on that new Christmas promotion for her gift shop. Now, there's trouble on the home front as well: Her son Ken had to go and flunk his driver's license road exam, and he's just about suicidal because he feels he can't be a "real man" without successfully obtaining his license. To top things off, now her much-anticipated vacation to Disney World with her younger stepchildren will have to be postponed because she just can't find the time to get away.

When Wendy meets up with her buddy Michelle at their local Starbucks for their daily "retreat," her mood starts to brighten. Somehow the calm of the cafe rubs off as she savors her *grande cappuccino*. Michelle consoles her with her usual assurances, and then she prescribes the ultimate remedy to defeat the blues: Go home, take a nice long bath, and then consume a quart of Starbucks Espresso Swirl ice cream. Yes, that's the ticket. It's amazing how the little things in life can make such a big difference. As she strolls out the door, Wendy makes a mental note to get Michelle a really nice Christmas gift this year. She's earned it.

■ UNDERSTANDING CULTURE

Wendy's daily coffee "fix" is mimicked in various forms around the globe, as people participate in activities that allow them to take a break and affirm their relationships with others. Of course, the products that are consumed in the process can range from black Turkish coffee to Indian tea, or from lager beer to hashish.

Starbucks has experienced phenomenal success by turning the coffee break into a cultural event that, for many, has assumed almost cultlike status. The average Starbucks customer visits 18 times a month, and 10 percent of the clientele stops by twice a day.[1] In 2000, Starbucks announced plans to add 450 U.S. stores to its existing base of more than 2,200 coffeehouses and eventually to add 100 locations in Asia and 50 in Britain to its already 300-plus international stores.[2] And, the chain is innovating to create different kinds of coffee break experiences. It opened an experimental restaurant called Circadia in San Francisco that resurrects the feel of 1960s coffee shops in Greenwich Village. It's decorated with vintage furniture but equipped with high-speed Internet connections, credit card swipe machines, and a conference room to accommodate the need of start-up entrepreneurs for meeting places where they can cut power deals.

Culture, a concept crucial to the understanding of consumer behavior, may be thought of as a society's personality. It includes both abstract ideas, such as values and ethics, and material objects and services, such as the automobile, clothing, food, art, and sports, that are produced or valued by a society. Put another way, **culture** is the accumulation of shared meanings, rituals, norms, and traditions among the members of an organization or society.

Consumption choices simply cannot be understood without considering the cultural context in which they are made: Culture is the "lens" through which people view products. Ironically, the effects of culture on consumer behavior are so powerful and far-reaching that their importance is sometimes difficult to grasp. Like a fish immersed in water, we do not always appreciate this power until we encounter a different environment. Suddenly many of the assumptions we had taken for granted about the clothes we wear, the food we eat, the way we address others, and so on no longer seem to apply. The effect of encountering such differences can be so great that the term "culture shock" is not an exaggeration.

The importance of these cultural expectations is often discovered only when they are violated. For example, while on tour in New Zealand, the Spice Girls (remember them?) created a stir among New Zealand's indigenous Maoris by performing a war dance supposed to be done by men only. A tribal official indignantly stated, "It is not acceptable in our culture, and especially by girlie pop stars from another culture."[3] Sensitivity to cultural issues, whether by rock stars or by brand managers, can only come by understanding these underlying dimensions—that is the goal of this chapter.

A consumer's culture determines the overall priorities that the consumer attaches to different activities and products, and it also mandates the success or failure of specific products and services. A product that provides benefits consistent with those desired by members of a culture at any point in time has a much better chance of attaining acceptance in the marketplace. For example, American culture started to emphasize the concept of a fit, trim body as an ideal of appearance in the mid–1970s. The premium placed on this goal, which stemmed from underlying values such as mobility, wealth, and a focus on the self, greatly contributed to the success of Miller Lite beer at that time. However, when Gablinger introduced a low-cal beer in the 1960s the product failed. This beverage was "ahead of its time" because American consumers were not yet interested in cutting down on calories when drinking brew.

The relationship between consumer behavior and culture is a two-way street. On the one hand, products and services that resonate with the priorities of a culture at any given time have a much better chance of being accepted by consumers. On the other hand, the study of new products and innovations in product design successfully produced by a culture at any point in time provides a window into the dominant cultural ideals of that period. Consider, for example, some American products that reflect underlying cultural processes at the time they were introduced:

- The TV dinner, which hinted at changes in family structure and the onset of a new informality in American home life.
- Cosmetics made of natural materials without animal testing, which reflected consumers' apprehensions about pollution, waste, and animal rights.
- Condoms marketed in pastel carrying cases for female buyers, which signaled changes in attitudes toward sexual responsibility and openness.

Culture is not static. It is continually evolving, synthesizing old ideas with new ones. A cultural system consists of these functional areas:[4]

- *Ecology:* The way in which a system is adapted to its habitat. This area is shaped by the technology used to obtain and distribute resources (e.g., industrialized societies versus Third World countries). The Japanese, for example, greatly value products that are designed for efficient use of space because of the cramped conditions in that island nation.[5]
- *Social structure:* The way in which orderly social life is maintained. This includes the domestic and political groups that are dominant within the culture (e.g., the nuclear family versus the extended family; representative government versus dictatorship).
- *Ideology:* The mental characteristics of a people and the way in which they relate to their environment and social groups. This revolves around the notion that members of a society possess a common *worldview* (an idea we introduced in Chapter 13). They share certain ideas about principles of order and fairness. They also share an ethos, or a set of moral and aesthetic principles. A new theme park in Bombay that caters to India's emerging middle class, called Water Kingdom, illustrates how a culture's worldview can be distinctive. Many consumers there are unfamiliar with mixed-sex public activities of this nature, so the park rents swimsuits to women who have never worn one before. No thongs here, though: The suits cover the women from wrists to ankles.[6]

Although every culture is different, four dimensions appear to account for much of this variability:[7]

1 *Power distance:* The way in which interpersonal relationships form when differences in power are perceived. Some cultures emphasize strict, vertical relationships (e.g., Japan), whereas others, such as the United States, stress a greater degree of equality and informality.

2 *Uncertainty avoidance:* The degree to which people feel threatened by ambiguous situations and have beliefs and institutions that help them to avoid this uncertainty (e.g., organized religion).

3 *Masculinity/femininity:* The degree to which sex roles are clearly delineated (see Chapter 5). Traditional societies are more likely to possess very explicit rules about the acceptable behaviors of men and women, such as who is responsible for certain tasks within the family unit.

4 *Individualism:* The extent to which the welfare of the individual versus that of the group is valued (see Chapter 11). Cultures differ in their emphasis on individualism versus collectivism. In **collectivist cultures**, people subordinate their personal goals to those of a stable in-group. In contrast, consumers in **individualist cultures** attach more importance to personal goals, and people are more likely to change memberships when the demands of the group (e.g., workplace, church, etc.) become too costly. Whereas a collectivist society will stress values (see Chapter 4) such as self-discipline and accepting one's position in life, people in individualist cultures emphasize personal enjoyment, excitement, equality, and freedom. Some strongly individualist cultures include the United States, Australia, Great Britain, Canada, and the Netherlands. Venezuela, Pakistan, Taiwan, Thailand, Turkey, Greece, and Portugal are some examples of strongly collectivist cultures.[8]

Values are very general ideas about good and bad goals. From these flow **norms,** or rules dictating what is right or wrong, acceptable or unacceptable. Some norms, called enacted norms, are explicitly decided on, such as the rule that a green traffic light means "go" and a red one means "stop." Many norms, however, are much more subtle. These *crescive norms* are embedded in a culture and are only discovered through interaction with other members of that culture. Crescive norms include the following:[9]

- A **custom** is a norm handed down from the past that controls basic behaviors, such as division of labor in a household or the practice of particular ceremonies.
- A **more** ("mor-ay") is a custom with a strong moral overtone. A more often involves a taboo, or forbidden behavior, such as incest or cannibalism. Violation of a more often meets with strong sanctions from other members of a society.
- **Conventions** are norms regarding the conduct of everyday life. These rules deal with the subtleties of consumer behavior, including the "correct" way to furnish one's house, wear one's clothes, host a dinner party, and so on.

All three types of crescive norms may operate to completely define a culturally appropriate behavior. For example, a more may tell us what kind of food is permissible to eat. These vary across cultures, so a meal of dog may be taboo in the United States, Hindus shun steak, and Muslims avoid pork products. A custom dictates the appropriate hour at which the meal should be served. Conventions tell us how to eat the meal, including such details as the utensils to be used, table etiquette, and even the appropriate apparel to be worn at dinnertime.

We often take these conventions for granted, assuming that they are the "right" things to do (again, until we travel to a foreign country!). It is good to remember that much of what we know about these norms is learned *vicariously* (see Chapter 3) as we observe the behaviors of actors in television commercials, sitcoms, print ads, and other media.

Cultural differences show up in all kinds of daily activities. For example, a Big Boy restaurant that opened in Thailand had difficulty attracting customers. After interviewing hundreds of people the company found out why. Some said the restaurant's "room energy" was bad and that the food was unfamiliar. Others said the Big Boy statue (like the one Dr. Evil rode in the *Austin Powers* movies) made them nervous. One of the restaurant's executives commented, "It suddenly dawned on me that, here I was, trying to get a 3,500-year-old culture to eat 64-year-old food." Now, since the company put some Thai items on the menu, business is picking up.[10] No word yet on the fate of the statue.

■ MYTHS AND RITUALS

Every culture develops stories and practices that help its members to make sense of the world. When we examine these activities in other cultures, they often seem strange or even unfathomable. Yet, our *own* cultural practices appear quite normal—even though a visitor may find them equally bizarre!

To appreciate how "primitive" belief systems that some may consider bizarre, irrational, or superstitious continue to influence our supposedly "modern" rational society, consider the avid interest of many American consumers in magic. Marketers of health foods, anti-aging cosmetics, exercise programs, and gambling casinos often imply that their offerings have "magical" properties that will ward off sickness, old age, poverty, or just plain bad luck. People by the millions play their

FEELING LUCKY?

LuckySurf.com

LuckySurf.com, a free lottery site, puts an interesting twist on the common practice of keeping a lucky rabbit's foot.

"lucky numbers" in the lottery, carry rabbits' feet and other amulets to ward off "the evil eye," and have "lucky" clothing or other products that they believe will bring them good fortune. Sometimes consumers regard "extraordinary" activities like extreme sports as magical. For example, white-water river rafters report that the rites and rituals they practice on their trips have transformed their lives in profound ways.[11] Software developers even supply "wizards" that help guide the uninitiated through their programs!

An interest in the occult tends to be popular when members of a society feel overwhelmed or powerless—magical remedies simplify our lives by giving us "easy" answers. Many consumers even regard a computer with awe as a sort of "electronic magician" with the ability to solve our problems (or in other cases to cause data to magically disappear!).[12] Or, we may go a step farther and believe the object is possessed by the soul of a being, as when kids (and maybe some adults as well) feel that by putting on their Air Nikes they magically absorb some of the athletic ability of Michael Jordan. Preposterous? A recent movie called *Like Mike* was based upon this very storyline. This section will discuss myths and rituals, two aspects of culture common to all societies from the ancients to the modern world.

This Spanish ad melds modern-day athletes with mythical figures.

Myths

A **myth** is a story containing symbolic elements that represent the shared emotions and ideals of a culture. The story often features some kind of conflict between two opposing forces, and its outcome serves as a moral guide for people. In this way, a myth reduces anxiety because it provides consumers with guidelines about their world. Every society possesses a set of myths that define that culture.

Most members of a culture learn these stories, but usually we don't really think about their origins. Consider, for example, a story familiar to all of us: *Little Red Riding Hood.* This myth started as a peasants' tale in sixteenth-century France, where a girl meets a werewolf on her way to granny's house (there is historical evidence for a plague of wolf attacks during this time, including several incidents where men were put on trial for transforming themselves into the deadly animals).

The werewolf has already killed granny, stored her flesh in the pantry and poured her blood in a bottle. Contrary to the version we know, when the girl arrives at the house, she snacks on granny, strips naked and climbs into bed with the wolf! To make the story even more scandalous, some versions refer to the wolf as a "gaffer" (a contraction of "grandfather") implying that incest was involved as well.

This story first appeared in print in 1697; it was intended as a warning to the loose ladies of Louis XIV's court (the author puts her in red in this version because this color symbolizes harlots). Eventually, the Brothers Grimm offered their own version in 1812, but they substituted violence for sex in order to scare kids into behaving. And to reinforce the sex role standards of that time, in the Grimm version a man rescues the girl from the wolf.[13] So, this myth sends vivid messages about such cultural no-nos as cannibalism, incest, and promiscuity.

An understanding of cultural myths is important to marketers, who in some cases (most likely unconsciously) pattern their strategy along a mythic structure. Consider, for example, the way that McDonald's takes on "mythical" qualities.[14] The "golden arches" are a universally recognized symbol, one that is virtually synonymous with American culture. They offer sanctuary to Americans around the world, who know exactly what to expect once they enter. Basic struggles involving good versus evil are played out in the fantasy world created by McDonald's advertising, as when Ronald McDonald confounds the Hamburglar. McDonald's even has a "seminary" (Hamburger University) where inductees go to learn appropriate behavior.

Corporations often have myths and legends as a part of their history, and some make a deliberate effort to be sure newcomers to the organization learn these. Nike designates senior executives as "corporate storytellers" who explain the company's heritage to other employees, including the hourly workers at Nike stores. They tell stories about the founders of Nike, including the coach of the Oregon track team who poured rubber into his family waffle iron to make better shoes for his team—the origin of the Nike waffle sole. The stories emphasize the dedication of runners and coaches involved with the company to reinforce the importance of teamwork. Rookies even visit the track where the coach worked to be sure they grasp the importance of the Nike legends.[15]

The Functions and Structure of Myths

Myths serve four interrelated functions in a culture:[16]

1 *Metaphysical:* They help to explain the origins of existence.
2 *Cosmological:* They emphasize that all components of the universe are part of a single picture.
3 *Sociological:* They maintain social order by authorizing a social code to be followed by members of a culture.
4 *Psychological:* They provide models for personal conduct.

We can analyze myths by examining their underlying structures, a technique pioneered by the French anthropologist Claude Lévi-Strauss (no relation to the blue jeans company). Lévi-Strauss noted that many stories involve **binary opposition**, in which two opposing ends of some dimension are represented (e.g., good versus evil, nature versus technology).[17] Characters, and in some cases products, are often defined by what they are not rather than what they *are* (e.g., "This is *not* your father's Oldsmobile," "I can't believe it's *not* butter").

Recall from the discussion of Freudian theory in Chapter 6 that the ego functions as a kind of "referee" between the opposing needs of the id and the superego. In a similar fashion, the conflict between mythical opposing forces is sometimes resolved by a *mediating figure* that can link the opposites by sharing characteristics of each. For example, many myths contain animals that have human abilities (e.g., a talking snake) to bridge the gap between humanity and nature, just as cars (technology) are often given animal names (nature) such as Cougar, Cobra, or Mustang.

Some advertisements borrow imagery from fairy tales to tell a story about a product. This Reebok ad substitutes an athletic shoe for a glass slipper in a twist on the Cinderella story.

Myths Abound in Modern Popular Culture

We generally associate myths with the ancient Greeks or Romans, but in reality modern popular culture's myths are embodied in comic books, movies, holidays, and yes, even commercials. Researchers report that some people create their own *consumer fairy tales* where they tell stories that include magical agents, donors, and helpers to overcome villains and obstacles as they seek out goods and services in their quest for happy endings.[18]

Comic book superheroes demonstrate how myths can be communicated to consumers of all ages in order to teach a lesson about a culture. For example, Marvel Comics' Spiderman character tells stories about balancing the obligations of being a superhero with the need of his alter ego, Peter Parker, to do his homework.[19] Indeed, some of these fictional figures represent a **monomyth**, a myth that is common to many cultures.[20] The most prevalent monomyth involves a hero such as Superman who emerges from the everyday world with supernatural powers and

This ad for a clothing boutique borrows from a popular fairy tale.

wins a decisive victory over evil forces. He then returns with the power to bestow good things on his fellow men.

Many "blockbuster" movies and hit TV shows draw directly on mythic themes. Although dramatic special effects or attractive stars certainly don't hurt, a number of these movies perhaps also owe their success to their presentation of characters and plot structures, which follow mythic patterns. Three examples of these mythic blockbusters are:[21]

- *Gone with the Wind.* Myths are often set in times of upheaval such as wars. In this story, the North (which represents technology and democracy) is pitted against the South (which represents nature and aristocracy). The movie depicts a romantic era (the antebellum South) in which love and honor were virtues. Following the war, newer values of materialism and industrialization (i.e., modern consumer culture) replace these priorities. The movie depicts a lost era in which man and nature existed in harmony.
- *E.T.: The Extraterrestrial.* E.T. represents a familiar myth involving messianic visitation. The gentle creature from another world visits Earth and performs

This ad for a line of veggie foods borrows the look of World War II propaganda art to imply that eating your broccoli is a heroic act.

miracles (e.g., reviving a dying flower). His "disciples" are neighborhood children, who help him combat the forces of modern technology and an unbelieving secular society. The metaphysical function of myth is served by teaching that the humans chosen by God are pure and unselfish.

● *Star Trek:* The television series and movies documenting the adventures of the starship *Enterprise* are also linked to myths, such as the story of the New England Puritans exploring and conquering a new continent—"the final frontier." Encounters with the Klingons mirror skirmishes with Native Americans. In addition, the quest for paradise was a theme employed in at least 13 out of the original 79 episodes filmed.[22]

Advertisers sometimes call upon mythical comic book superheroes like The Hulk to represent qualities we value in products like strength, ruggedness, or power.

Commercials can also be analyzed in terms of the underlying mythic themes they represent. For example, commercials for Pepperidge Farm ask consumers to "remember" the good old days (lost paradise) when products were wholesome and natural. Both Chrysler and Avis have used the theme of the underdog prevailing over the stronger foe (i.e., David and Goliath).[23] A recent television commercial designed to encourage Hispanic consumers to buy more milk features a female phantom that wails as she walks through a home. She is *La Llorona* (The Crying One), a character in an Hispanic myth who murders her children, commits suicide, and roams for all eternity looking for her lost family. In this version, however, the moaning phantom makes her way to the refrigerator, only to find an empty milk carton. A voice-over then asks the familiar question: "Got Milk?"[24]

Net Profit

For better or worse, the Web is transforming the age-old ritual of buying wedding gifts. Numerous online gift registries take the guesswork out of buying that perfect toaster for the new couple. These sites collect a referral fee from a retailer if a purchase is made. Although registries have been around since the early 1930s, they used to be subtler—Macy's department store used to publish a booklet titled *Hints on Hinting* to help brides offer gentle suggestions to guests.

Competition for the matrimonial market is fierce, so registry sites are scrambling to offer new incentives that will engage the engaged. At ***theknot.com*** the couple can even subsidize their honeymoon airfare: They earn a frequent-flier mile for every dollar their guests spend on them. At ***weddingchannel.com***, the lucky couple creates a personal wedding page on which they post directions and pictures, plan toasts and seating arrangements, and tell stories about how they met. Guests pull up updated versions of a gift registry and purchase from retailers directly through the Web site. The Wedding Channel hopes to track its customers (assuming they stay married) and create registries as they celebrate anniversaries and the arrival of babies (uh oh, need another gift!).

The proliferation of these registries is understandable given that this business now takes in $19 billion a year. Revenues for Williams-Sonoma's registry alone were an estimated $120 million in 2001; the chain has registered more brides online than in all of its 200-plus physical stores combined.[30] Think about the business potential: The average wedding party includes 12 people (including six who get stuck with those awful dresses) plus 150 guests. On average, the bride

Rituals

A **ritual** is a set of multiple, symbolic behaviors that occur in a fixed sequence and that tend to be repeated periodically.[25] Bizarre tribal ceremonies, perhaps involving animal or human sacrifice, may come to mind when people think of rituals, but in reality many contemporary consumer activities are ritualistic. Just think of Wendy's daily "mental health" trip to Starbucks.

Table 16.1 notes that rituals can occur at several levels. Some affirm broad cultural or religious values. Public rituals like the Super Bowl, presidential inaugurations, and graduation ceremonies are communal activities that affirm our membership in the larger group and reassure us that we are reading from the same script as everyone else.[26] Other rituals occur in small groups or even in isolation. Market researchers discovered that for many people (like Wendy) the act of late-night ice cream eating has ritualistic elements, often involving a favorite spoon and bowl![27] And, rituals are not always set in stone; they can be modified to change with the times. For example, when we throw rice at a wedding we are expressing our desire for the couple to be fertile. In recent years many newlyweds have substituted soap bubbles, jingling bells, or butterflies because of the tendency of birds to eat the rice, which can then expand inside their bodies and cause injury or death.[28]

Many businesses owe their livelihoods to their ability to supply **ritual artifacts** to consumers. These are items needed to perform rituals, such as wedding rice, birthday candles, diplomas, specialized foods and beverages (e.g., wedding cakes, ceremonial wine, or even hot dogs at the ball park), trophies and plaques, band uniforms, greeting cards, and retirement watches.[29] In addition, consumers often employ a *ritual script*, which identifies the artifacts, the sequence in which they are used, and who uses them. Examples include graduation programs, fraternity manuals, and etiquette books.

Grooming Rituals

Whether brushing one's hair 100 strokes a day or talking to oneself in the mirror, virtually all consumers have private grooming rituals. These are sequences of behaviors that aid in the transition from the private self to the public self or back again.

The popular *Star Trek* saga is based on myths, including the quest for paradise.

TABLE 16.1
TYPES OF RITUAL EXPERIENCE

Primary Behavior Source	Ritual Type	Examples
Cosmology	Religious	Baptism, meditation, mass
Cultural values	Rites of passage	Graduation, marriage festivals, holidays
	Cultural	(Valentine's Day), Super Bowl
Group learning	Civic	Parades, elections, trials
	Group	Fraternity initiation, business negotiations, office luncheons
	Family	Mealtimes, bedtimes, birthdays, Mother's Day, Christmas
Individual aims and emotions	Personal	Grooming, household rituals

Source: Dennis W. Rook "The Ritual Dimension of Consumer Behavior," *Journal of Consumer Research* 12 (December 1985) 251–64. Reprinted with permission of the University of Chicago Press.

These rituals serve various purposes, ranging from inspiring confidence before confronting the world to cleansing the body of dirt and other impure materials. When consumers talk about their grooming rituals, some of the dominant themes that emerge from these stories reflect the almost mystical qualities attributed to grooming products and behaviors. Many people emphasize a before-and-after phenomenon, whereby the person feels magically transformed after using certain products (similar to the Cinderella myth).[34]

Two sets of binary oppositions expressed in personal rituals are *private/public* and *work/leisure*. Many beauty rituals, for instance, reflect a transformation from a natural state to the social world (as when a woman "puts on her face") or *vice versa*. The bath is viewed as a sacred, cleansing time, a way to wash away the "sins" of the profane world.[35] In these daily rituals, women reaffirm the value placed by their culture on personal beauty and the quest for eternal youth.[36] This focus is obvious in ads for Oil of Olay Beauty Cleanser that proclaim, "And so your day begins. The Ritual of Oil of Olay."

Gift-Giving Rituals

The promotion of appropriate gifts for every conceivable holiday and occasion provides an excellent example of the influence consumer rituals can exert on marketing phenomena. In the **gift-giving ritual**, consumers procure the perfect object, meticulously remove the price tag and carefully wrap it (symbolically changing the item from a commodity to a unique good), and deliver it to the recipient.[37] Gifts can take the form of store-bought objects, homemade items, or services. Some recent research has even made the case that music file-sharing systems like the now-defunct Napster, KaZaa, or Morpheus really are all about gifting![38]

Researchers view gift-giving as a form of *economic exchange*, in which the giver transfers an item of value to a recipient, who in turn is somehow obligated to reciprocate. However, gift-giving also can involve *symbolic exchange*, when a giver like Wendy wants to acknowledge her friend Michelle's intangible support and companionship. Some research indicates that gift-giving evolves as a form of social expression. It is more exchange-oriented (instrumental) in the early stages of a relationship, but becomes more altruistic as the relationship develops.[39] Table 16.2 (on page 540) lists the ways giving a gift can affect a relationship.

and groom register for more than 50 products and they receive an average of 171 wedding gifts. Wedding registries continue to evolve; some couples have become so brazen that they are requesting specific shares of stock, contributions to fund an around-the-world trip, or even mortgage payments on that new dream house (available on a special registry maintained by the U.S. Department of Housing and Urban Development at hud.gov). About half of the couples register at a place they have never shopped before, giving retailers a new customer base. According to the publisher of *Bride's* magazine, "If you can hook this consumer when she is in this life stage, you will fundamentally brand her for life."[31]

Of course, there are downsides to this new efficiency: Because the wedding couple specifies exactly what they want in advance, the giver doesn't really have to know very much about the recipients. Part of gift-giving is developing or reinforcing a symbolic relationship, but now the process is much more automated. As one etiquette expert disdainfully points out, in the old days (pre-Internet) people were supposed to be "zealous with creativity" when selecting a gift. "Now, it's just gimme, gimme, gimme with a dollar amount attached." And in many cases the registry is listed on the invitation itself—a social no-no.[32] Registries also eliminate the likelihood of getting homemade or creative gifts.

The idea of sharing your specific material needs with friends and loved ones is expanding well beyond nuptials. Now a cottage industry of registries is springing up to enable consumers of all stripes to specify their desires online and sit back to wait for the products to roll in. These registries include:[33]

- *Twodaydreamers.com* for doll collectors
- All Nations Stamp and Coin for philatelists and numismatists
- The Wishing Well for motorboat parts and supplies
- Clinique, Prescriptives, and Bobbi Brown for lipstick and cosmetics
- Restoration Hardware and Goodwood for furniture and home supplies
- *OfficeMax.com* for back-to-school shoppers who need to know what teachers are requiring their students to have on the first day of class

Nivea is well-known for its numerous skin care products. Research conducted for the company as it sought to develop a more consistent brand image for all of its lines in the 1990s confirmed the important, yet intangible, functions played by these items for women as they conduct their private grooming rituals. The company found that consumers associated the Nivea image with scenes depicting moisture, freshness, and relaxation.

Every culture prescribes certain occasions and ceremonies for giving gifts, whether for personal or professional reasons. The giving of birthday presents alone is a major undertaking. Each American on average buys about six birthday gifts a year—about one billion gifts in total.[40] Business gifts are an important component in defining professional relationships. Expenditures on business gifts exceed $1.5 billion per year, and givers take great care to ensure that the appropriate gifts are purchased (sometimes with the aid of professional gift consultants). Most executives believe that corporate gift-giving provides both tangible and intangible results, including improved employee morale and higher sales.[41]

The gift-giving ritual has three distinct stages:[42]

1 During *gestation,* the giver is motivated by an event to procure a gift. This event may be either *structural* (i.e., prescribed by the culture, as when people buy Christmas presents) or *emergent* (i.e., the decision is more personal and idiosyncratic).

An online wedding gift registry.

Gift Idea: *Bowls*

Gift purchasing made easy: just go to WeddingChannel.com, enter the bride or groom's name, select their registry and purchase a gift they want from any of these fine stores.

WeddingChannel.com™
The only place you need to go to buy a wedding gift.

Tiffany & Co.	Bloomingdale's
Williams-Sonoma	Macy's
Crate & Barrel	The Bon Marché
Neiman Marcus	Burdines
Pottery Barn	Goldsmith's
Restoration Hardware	Lazarus
REI	Rich's
Gump's	

2 The second stage is *presentation*, or the process of gift exchange. The recipient responds to the gift (either appropriately or not), and the donor evaluates this response.

3 In the third stage, known as *reformulation*, the bonds between the giver and receiver are adjusted (either looser or tighter) to reflect the new relationship that emerges after the exchange is complete. Negativity can arise if the recipient feels the gift is inappropriate or of inferior quality. For example, the hapless husband who gives his wife a vacuum cleaner as an anniversary present is asking for trouble, as is the new suitor who gives his girlfriend intimate apparel. The donor may feel the response to the gift was inadequate or insincere or a violation of the **reciprocity norm**, which obliges people to return the gesture of a gift with one of equal value.[43] Both participants may feel resentful for being "forced" to participate in the ritual.[44]

TABLE 16.2
GIFT GIVING AND RELATIONSHIPS

Relational Effect	Description	Example
Strengthening	Gift-giving improves the quality of a relationship	An unexpected gift such as one given in a romantic situation
Affirmation	Gift-giving validates the positive quality of a relationship	Usually occurs on ritualized occasions such as birthdays
Negligible Effect	Gift-giving has a minimal effect on perceptions of relationship quality	Informal gift occasions and those in which the gift may be perceived as charity or too good for the current state of the relationship
Negative Confirmation	Gift-giving validates a negative quality of a relationship between the gift giver and receiver	The selection of gift is inappropriate indicating a lack of knowledge of the receiver; alternatively, the gift is viewed as a method of controlling the receiver
Weakening	Gift-giving harms the quality of the relationship between giver and receiver	When there are "strings attached" or the gift is perceived as a bribe, a sign of disrespect, or offensive
Severing	Gift-giving harms the relationship between the giver and receiver to the extent that the relationship is dissolved	When the gift forms part of a larger problem, such as in a threatening relationship; also when a relationship is severed through the receipt of a "parting" gift

Source: Adapted from Julie A. Ruth, Cele C. Otnes, and Frederic F. Brunel, "Gift Receipt and the Reformulation of Interpersonal Relationships," *Journal of Consumer Research* 25 (March 1999), 385–402, Table 1, p. 389.

Japanese gift-giving rituals show how tremendously important these acts are in that culture, where the wrapping of a gift is as important (if not more so) than the gift itself. The economic value of a gift is secondary to its symbolic meaning. To the Japanese, gifts are viewed as an important aspect of one's duty to others in one's social group. Giving is a moral imperative (known as *giri*). Highly ritualized gift-giving occurs during the giving of both household/personal gifts and company/professional gifts. Each Japanese has a well-defined set of relatives and friends with which he or she shares reciprocal gift-giving obligations (*kosai*). Personal gifts are given on social occasions, such as at funerals, to people who are hospitalized, to mark movements from one life stage to another (e.g., weddings, birthdays), and as greetings (e.g., when one meets a visitor). Company gifts are given to commemorate the anniversary of a corporation's founding, the opening of a new building, or when new products are announced. In keeping with the Japanese emphasis on saving face, presents are not opened in front of the giver so that it will not be necessary to hide one's possible disappointment with the present.[45]

In addition to expressing their feelings toward others through consumption, people commonly find (or devise) reasons to give themselves something as well. It is common for consumers to purchase *self-gifts* as a way to regulate their behavior. This ritual provides a socially acceptable way of rewarding themselves for good deeds, consoling themselves after negative events, or motivating themselves to accomplish some goal.[46] Indeed, retailers report that it is becoming increasingly common for people to treat themselves while they are ostensibly searching for goodies for others. As one shopper admitted recently, "It's one for them, one for me, one for them."[47]

Holiday Rituals

On holidays consumers step back from their everyday lives and perform ritualistic behaviors unique to those times.[48] Holiday occasions are filled with ritual artifacts and scripts and are increasingly cast as a time for giving gifts by enterprising marketers. The Thanksgiving holiday bursts with rituals for Americans; these scripts include serving (in gluttonous portions) foods such as turkey and cranberry sauce that often are only consumed on that day, complaints about how much one has eaten (yet rising to the occasion to somehow find room for dessert), and (for many) a post-meal trip to the couch for the obligatory football game. On Valentine's Day, standards regarding sex and love are relaxed or altered as people express feelings that may be hidden during the rest of the year (in Japan, it's the women who send gifts to the men).

In addition to established holidays, businesses invent new occasions to capitalize on the need for cards and other ritual artifacts that will then have to be acquired.[49] These cultural events often originate with the greeting card industry, precisely to stimulate demand for more of its products. Some recently invented holidays include Secretaries' Day and Grandparents' Day.

In other cases retailers elevate relatively minor holidays to major ones to provide more merchandising opportunities. Most recently the Mexican holiday of Cinco de Mayo has become an excuse for Caucasians to drink a lot of margaritas. True, the day marks a May 5, 1862 victory by a small army over stronger French forces, but contrary to what many Americans believe, it is *not* Mexican Independence Day. As the president of a Hispanic-American marketing firm notes, "When Mexicans first come to the United States and somebody mentions that they're all excited about some Cinco de Mayo festival, they say, 'What?' It would be like Canadians making a big deal out of the Boston Tea Party. It's a nonevent made into a big deal by marketing." On Cinco de Mayo Americans eat 17 million pounds of avocados (guacamole) and sales jump for tequila and other ethnic products as restaurants and bars catch the fever. Tequila maker Jose Cuervo even dropped a "margarita bar" into the water off Miami to commemorate "Sink-O de Mayo."[50]

Most cultural holidays are based on a myth, and often a historical (e.g., Miles Standish on Thanksgiving) or imaginary (e.g., Cupid on Valentine's Day) character is at the center of the story. These holidays persist because their basic elements appeal to consumers' deep-seated needs.[51] Two of our holidays that are especially rich both in cultural symbolism and in consumption meanings are Christmas and Halloween.

Christmas. The Christmas holiday is built upon myths and rituals, from Santa's adventures at the North Pole to others' adventures under the mistletoe. The meaning of Christmas has evolved quite dramatically during the last few hundred years. In colonial times, Christmas celebrations resembled carnivals and were marked by public rowdiness. Most notable was the tradition of "wassailing" in which packs of poor young people would lay siege to the rich, demanding food and drink. By the end of the 1800s, the mobs were so unruly that Protestant America invented a tradition of families having Christmas gatherings around a tree, a practice "borrowed" from early pagan rites.

THE GLOBAL LOOKING GLASS

There's an unwelcome guest at Vienna's famous Christmas market these days who lurks among stalls that sell hot punch and kitschy baubles, and hands out sweets to children, casting his bulky shadow over the crib that depicts the birth of Jesus. His name is Santa Claus, but to a growing number of resentful Austrians, he might as well be Mickey Mouse or the Marlboro Man.

Some Austrians have formed the "Pro-Christkind Association" to promote their belief that their countrymen should celebrate their own symbol of Christmas, the Christkind, or Christ Child, who, like Santa, also comes noiselessly to leave gifts under the tree on Christmas Eve. Members of the group said the Santa Claus phenomenon has exploded in the last three years. They attribute it to globalization, which brings Christmas television shows and movies to Austria, as well as to worldwide holiday marketing campaigns by American corporations. The same trends turned Halloween, once observed here only as a day to remember the dead, into a major commercial holiday. Santa, it seems, is viewed here as another example of the corrosive global reach of American multinationals.

Sources: Adapted from Mark Landler, "For Austrians, Ho-Ho-Ho Is No Laughing Matter," *New York Times,* (December 12, 2002), International section. pg 1; See also: R. W. Belk, "A Child's Christmas in America: Santa Claus as Deity, Consumption as Religion," *Journal of American Culture,* 10 (1) (Spring 1987): 87–100.

The Santa Claus myth pervades our culture.

In an 1822 poem, Clement Clarke Moore, the wealthy son of a New York Episcopal bishop, invented the modern-day myth of Santa Claus. The Christmas ritual slowly changed to a focus on children and gift-giving.[52] One of the most important holiday rituals still involves Santa, a mythical figure that children eagerly await the world over. Indeed, a recent study conducted in Australia that looked at letters to Santa written by children found that they tend to specify their brand preferences quite carefully and often include sophisticated request strategies to be sure they get what they want from the Big Guy.[53] In opposition to Christ, Santa is a champion of materialism. Perhaps it is no coincidence, then, that he appears in stores and shopping malls—secular temples of consumption. Whatever his origins, the Santa Claus myth socializes children by teaching them to expect a reward when they are good and that people get what they deserve.

Halloween. This holiday evolved from a pagan religious observance to a secular event. However, in contrast to Christmas, the rituals of Halloween (e.g., trick-or-treating and costume parties) primarily involve nonfamily members. Halloween is an unusual holiday, because its rituals are the opposite of many other cultural occasions. In contrast to Christmas, it celebrates evil instead of good and death rather than birth, and it encourages revelers to extort treats with veiled threats of "tricks" rather than rewarding only the good.

Because of these oppositions, we can think of Halloween as an *antifestival*, an event that distorts the symbols associated with other holidays. For example, the Halloween witch can be viewed as an inverted mother figure. The holiday also parodies the meaning of Easter by stressing the resurrection of ghosts and of Thanksgiving by transforming the wholesome symbolism of the pumpkin pie into the evil jack-o-lantern.[54] Furthermore, Halloween provides a ritualized, and therefore socially sanctioned, context in which people can act out uncharacteristic behaviors and try on new roles: Children can go outside after dark, stay up late, and eat all the candy they like for a night. The otherwise geeky guy who always sits in the back of class comes dressed as Elvis and turns out to be the life of the party.

Halloween observances among adults are booming, changing the character of this holiday. Halloween is now the second most popular party night for adults (after New Year's Eve), and one in four grown-ups wears a costume.[55] The holiday is becoming trendy in Europe as well, where the French in particular have discovered it as an occasion for festivities, dancing, and the chance to show off new fashions.[56]

Rites of Passage

What does a dance for recently divorced people have in common with a fraternity Hell Week? Both are examples of modern **rites of passage**, or special times marked by a change in social status. Every society, both primitive and modern, sets aside times at which such changes occur. Some of these changes may occur as a natural part of consumers' life cycles (e.g., puberty or death), whereas others are more individual in nature (e.g., getting divorced and reentering the dating market). As Wendy's son discovered when he bombed his driving test, the importance of a rite of passage becomes more obvious when one fails to undergo it at the prescribed time.

Halloween is evolving from a children's festival to an opportunity for adults to experiment with fantasy roles—and party.

Marketing Pitfall

Even rites of passage associated with death support an entire industry. At *hardiehouse.org* epitaph you can have your epitaph written before you go. There are a number of "virtual cemeteries" where people can remember a loved one in a virtual grave; check out *imminentdomain.com*. However, death is not all fun and games: Survivors must make fairly expensive purchase decisions, often on short notice and driven by emotional and superstitious concerns. Perhaps because of the emotional tone many of these appeals take, women tend to initiate these purchases. The funeral industry is beginning to be more aggressive in its marketing practices and is even targeting younger consumers who are worried about arranging for their aging parents. (The prepayment of funeral and burial expenses is euphemistically known in the industry as "preneed.") The potential for abuse is high; in one case an 80-year-old Florida widow was persuaded months after the death of her husband to purchase more than $125,000 in unneeded goods and services, including a $40,000 casket and a family mausoleum even though she had no family left.[59]

Much like the metamorphosis of a caterpillar into a butterfly, consumers' rites of passage consist of three phases:[57]

1 The first stage, *separation*, occurs when the individual is detached from his or her original group or status (e.g., the college freshman leaves home).
2 *Liminality* is the middle stage, in which the person is literally between statuses (e.g., the new arrival on campus tries to figure out what is happening during orientation week).
3 The last stage, *aggregation*, takes place when the person reenters society after the rite of passage is complete (e.g., the student returns home for Christmas vacation as a college "veteran").

Rites of passage mark many consumer activities, as exemplified by fraternity pledges, recruits at boot camp, or novitiates becoming nuns. We can observe a similar transitional state when people are prepared for certain occupational roles. For example, athletes and fashion models typically undergo a "seasoning" process. They are removed from their normal surroundings (e.g., athletes are taken to training camps, young models are often moved to Paris), indoctrinated into a new subculture, and then returned to the real world in their new roles.

Funeral ceremonies help the living to organize their relationships with the deceased, and action tends to be tightly scripted, down to the costumes (e.g., the ritual black attire, black ribbons for mourners, the body in its best clothes), and specific behaviors (e.g., sending condolence cards or holding a wake). Mourners "pay their last respects," and seating during the ceremony is usually dictated by mourners' closeness to the individual. Even the *cortege* (the funeral motorcade) is accorded special status by other motorists, who recognize its separate, sacred nature by not cutting in as it proceeds to the cemetery.[58]

■ SACRED AND PROFANE CONSUMPTION

As we saw when considering the structure of myths, many types of consumer activities involve the demarcation, or binary opposition, of categories, such as good versus bad, male versus female—or even regular cola versus diet. One of the most important of these sets of categories is the distinction between the sacred and the profane. **Sacred consumption** involves objects and events that are "set apart" from normal activities and are treated with some degree of respect or awe. They may or may not be associated with religion, but most religious items and events tend to be regarded as sacred. **Profane consumption** involves consumer objects and events that are ordinary, everyday objects and events that do not share the "specialness" of sacred ones. (Note that profane does not mean vulgar or obscene in this context.)

Domains of Sacred Consumption

Sacred consumption events permeate many aspects of consumers' experiences. We find ways to "set apart" a variety of places, people, and events. In this section, we'll consider some examples of ways that "ordinary" consumption is sometimes not so ordinary after all.

Sacred Places

Sacred places are "set apart" by a society because they have religious or mystical significance (e.g., Bethlehem, Mecca, Stonehenge) or because they commemorate some aspect of a country's heritage (e.g., the Kremlin, the Emperor's Palace in Tokyo, the Statue of Liberty or, more recently, Ground Zero in Manhattan). The sacredness of these places is due to the property of **contamination**—that is, something sacred happened on that spot, so the place itself takes on sacred qualities.

Still other places are created from the profane world and imbued with sacred qualities. Graumann's Chinese Theater in Hollywood, where movie stars leave their footprints in concrete for posterity, is one such place. Theme parks are a form of mass-produced fantasy that takes on aspects of sacredness. In particular, Disney World and Disneyland (and their outposts in Europe and Japan) are destinations for pilgrimages by consumers around the globe. Disney World displays many characteristics of more traditional sacred places. It is even regarded by some as having healing powers. A trip to the park is the most common "last wish" for terminally ill children.[60]

In many cultures, the home is a particularly sacred place. It represents a crucial distinction between the harsh, external world and consumers' "inner space." Americans spend more than $50 billion a year on interior decorators and home furnishings, and the home is a central part of consumers' identities: After all, as the saying goes, "Home is where the heart is."[61] Consumers all over the world go to great lengths to create a special environment that allows them to create the quality of "homeyness." They do this by personalizing the home as much as possible, using devices such as door wreaths, mantle arrangements, and a "memory wall" for family photos.[62] Even public places, such as Starbucks cafes, strive for a homelike atmosphere that shelters customers from the harshness of the outside world.

Sacred People

People themselves can be sacred when they are idolized and set apart from the masses. Souvenirs, memorabilia, and even mundane items touched or used by sacred people take on special meanings and acquire value in their own right. Indeed, many businesses thrive on consumers' desire for products associated with famous people. There is a thriving market for celebrity autographs, and objects once owned by celebrities, whether Princess Diana's gowns or John Lennon's guitars, are often sold at auction for astronomical prices.

Souvenirs, tacky or otherwise, allow consumers to tangibilize sacred (i.e., out of the ordinary) experiences accumulated as tourists.

Sacred Events

Many consumers' activities have also taken on a special status. Public events in particular resemble sacred, religious ceremonies, as exemplified by the recitation of the "Pledge of Allegiance" before a game or the reverential lighting of matches at the end of a rock concert.[63]

For many people, the world of sports is sacred and almost assumes the status of a religion. The roots of modern sports events can be found in ancient religious rites, such as fertility festivals (e.g., the original Olympics).[64] Indeed, it is not uncommon for teams to join in prayer prior to a game. The sports pages are like the scriptures (and we describe ardent fans as reading them "religiously"), the stadium is a house of worship, and the fans are members of the congregation. Devotees engage in group activities, such as tailgate parties and the "Wave" where sections of the stadium take turns standing up. The athletes that fans come to see are godlike; they are reputed to have almost superhuman powers (especially superstars such as Michael Jordan, who is accorded the ability to fly in his Air Nikes).

Athletes are central figures in a common cultural myth, the hero tale. In these stories, the player must prove himself under strenuous circumstances, and victory is achieved only through sheer force of will. One extremely popular Coke commercial, which featured the football player Mean Joe Greene and an admiring little boy, followed the same plot structure as the fairy tale of *The Lion and the Mouse*. The injured hero has his confidence restored by the humble mouse/boy, allowing his heroic persona to be rejuvenated. He then shows his gratitude to his benefactor.[65]

Tourism is another example of a sacred, nonordinary experience. When people travel on vacation, they occupy sacred time and space. The tourist is continually in search of "authentic" experiences that differ from his or her normal world (think of Club Med's motto, "The antidote to civilization").[66] This traveling experience involves binary oppositions between work and leisure and being "at home" versus "away." Often, everyday (profane) norms regarding appropriate behavior are relaxed as tourists scramble after illicit or adventurous experiences they would not dream of engaging in at home.

Angels are experiencing a renaissance and this ad for a smoke detector uses a guardian angel message to make its point.

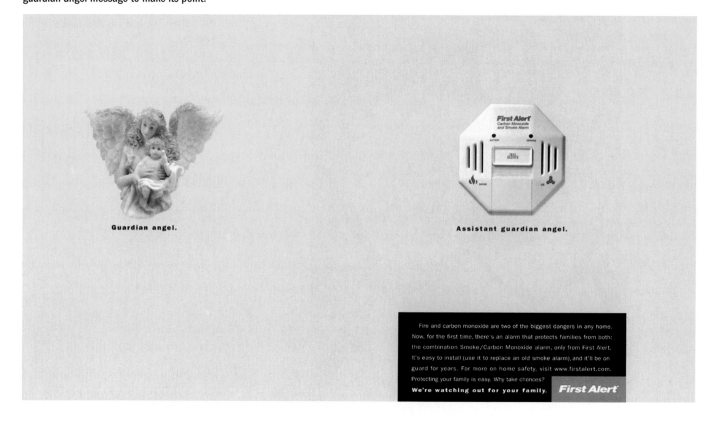

Guardian angel.

Assistant guardian angel.

The desire of travelers to capture these sacred experiences in objects forms the bedrock of the souvenir industry, which may be said to be in the business of selling sacred memories. Whether a personalized matchbook from a wedding or New York City salt-and-pepper shakers, souvenirs represent a tangible piece of the consumer's sacred experience.[67] In addition to personal mementos, such as ticket stubs saved from a favorite concert, the following are other types of sacred souvenir icons:[68]

- Local products (e.g., wine from California)
- Pictorial images (e.g., postcards)
- "Piece of the rock" (e.g., seashells, pine cones)
- Symbolic shorthand in the form of literal representations of the site (e.g., a miniature Statue of Liberty)
- Markers (e.g., Hard Rock Cafe T-shirts)

From Sacred to Profane, and Back Again

Just to make life interesting, in recent times many consumer activities have moved from one sphere to the other: Some things that were formerly regarded as sacred have moved into the realm of the profane, whereas other, everyday phenomena now are regarded as sacred.[69]

Desacralization

Desacralization occurs when a sacred item or symbol is removed from its special place or is duplicated in mass quantities, becoming profane as a result. For example, souvenir reproductions of sacred monuments such as the Washington Monument or the Eiffel Tower, artworks such as the *Mona Lisa* or Michelangelo's *David,* or adaptations of important symbols such as the American flag by clothing designers, eliminate their special aspects by turning them into unauthentic commodities produced mechanically with relatively little value.[70]

Religion itself has to some extent been desacralized. Religious symbols, such as stylized crosses or New Age crystals, have moved into the mainstream of fashion jewelry.[71] Religious holidays, particularly Christmas, are regarded by many (and criticized by some) as having been transformed into secular, materialistic occasions devoid of their original sacred significance. A similar process is occurring in relatively Westernized parts of the Islamic Middle East, where the holy month of Ramadan (traditionally observed by fasting and prayer) is starting to look like Christmas: People are buying lights in the shape of an Islamic crescent moon, sending Ramadan cards to one another, and attending lavish fast-breaking feasts at hotels.[72]

Sacralization

Sacralization occurs when ordinary objects, events, and even people take on sacred meaning to a culture or to specific groups within a culture. As we've seen, events such as the Super Bowl and people such as Elvis Presley now are sacred to some. Virtually anything can become sacred. Skeptical? Consider that a Web site is thriving by selling unlaundered athletic wear worn by members of the Dallas Cowboys football team. Shoes worn by quarterback Troy Aikman sell for $1,999, and an unwashed practice jersey that retains the sweat of an unknown player goes for $99. Used socks are flying out the door at $19.99 a pair. Says the owner, "Fans who have never been able to touch the Cowboys before now have an opportunity."[73]

Objectification occurs when we attribute sacred qualities to mundane items (like smelly socks). One way that this process can occur is through *contamination*, in which objects associated with sacred events or people become sacred in their own right. This explains the desire by many fans for items belonging to, or even touched by, famous people. Even the Smithsonian Institution in Washington, DC, maintains a display featuring such "sacred items" as the ruby slippers from The Wizard of Oz, a phaser from *Star Trek*, and Archie Bunker's chair from the television show *All in the Family*—all reverently protected behind sturdy display glass.

The Tangled Web

The quest to memorialize Elvis has become an industry—about 20,000 people make a pilgrimage to Graceland each year to "worship" his memory. But there are plenty of opportunities for fans to pay homage to The King virtually: There is an official Elvis site: *www.elvis-presley.com*, and many other Web sites devoted to him. Some of the sites are in somewhat poor taste. On one visitors can play a Shockwave game called Gimme That Dang Pill, where the object is to flush the Quaaludes down the toilet before Elvis eats them in order to win a virtual fried peanut butter sandwich (his favorite meal).[74]

In the 1990s, "Swatch fever" infected many people. The company made more than 500 different models, some of which were special editions designed by artists. Although thousands of people still collect the watches, the frenzy has faded.

In addition to museum exhibits displaying rare objects, even mundane, inexpensive things may be set apart in *collections*, where they are transformed from profane items to sacred ones. An item is sacralized as soon as it enters a collection, and it takes on special significance to the collector that outsiders may find hard to comprehend.

Collecting refers to the systematic acquisition of a particular object or set of objects. We can distinguish this activity from *hoarding*, which is merely unsystematic collecting.[75] Collecting typically involves both rational and emotional components; their objects often obsess collectors, but they also carefully organize and exhibit them.[76] Consumers may be ferociously attached to their collections; this passion is exemplified by the comment made in one study by a woman who collects teddy bears: "If my house ever burns down, I won't cry over my furniture, I'll cry over the bears."[77]

Some consumer researchers feel that collectors are motivated to acquire their "prizes" in order to gratify a high level of materialism in a socially acceptable manner. By systematically amassing a collection, the collector is allowed to "worship" material objects without feeling guilty or petty. Another perspective is that collecting is actually an aesthetic experience; for many collectors the pleasure comes from being involved in creating the collection. Whatever the motivation, hard-core collectors often devote a great deal of time and energy to maintaining and expanding their collections, so for many this activity becomes a central component of their extended selves (see Chapter 5).[78]

Name an item, and the odds are that a group of collectors is lusting after it. The contents of collections range from movie posters, rare books, and autographs to *Star Wars* dolls, Elvis memorabilia, old computers, and even junk mail.[79] The 1,200 members of the McDonald's collectors' club trade "prizes" such as sandwich wrappers and

Happy Meal trinkets—rare ones such as the 1987 Potato Head Kids Toys sell for $25.[80] And other consumers collect experiences rather than products: Consider the man who has visited more than 10,000 McDonald's restaurants. He keeps a list of unusual menu items and decor, and he defends his hobby this way: "I'm not an oddball or weirdo. I'm a collector of the McDonald's dining experience. So many issues from the last half of this century can be understood, at least partially, from a seat inside a McDonald's. What could be more quintessentially American?" Supersize that?[81]

CHAPTER SUMMARY

A society's *culture* includes its values, ethics, and the material objects produced by its members. It is the accumulation of shared meanings and traditions among members of a society. A culture can be described in terms of *ecology* (the way people adapt to their habitat), its *social structure*, and its *ideology* (including moral and aesthetic principles).

Myths are stories containing symbolic elements that express the shared ideals of a culture. Many myths involve a *binary opposition*, whereby values are defined in terms of what they are and what they are not (e.g., nature versus technology). Modern myths are transmitted through advertising, movies, and other media.

A *ritual* is a set of multiple, symbolic behaviors that occur in a fixed sequence and that tend to be repeated periodically. Ritual is related to many consumption activities that occur in popular culture. These include holiday observances, gift-giving, and grooming.

A *rite of passage* is a special kind of ritual that involves the transition from one role to another. These passages typically entail the need to acquire products and services, called *ritual artifacts*, to facilitate the transition. Modern rites of passage include graduations, fraternity initiations, weddings, debutante balls, and funerals.

Consumer activities can be divided into *sacred* and *profane* domains. Sacred phenomena are "set apart" from everyday activities or products. *Sacralization* occurs when everyday people, events, or objects become set apart from the ordinary. *Objectification* occurs when sacred qualities are ascribed to products or items owned by sacred people. *Desacralization* occurs when formerly sacred objects or activities become part of the everyday, as when "one-of-a-kind" works of art are reproduced in large quantities.

KEY TERMS

Binary opposition 531	Desacralization 547	Profane consumption 544
Collecting 548	Gift-giving ritual 537	Reciprocity norm 539
Collectivist cultures 527	Individualist cultures 527	Rites of passage 543
Contamination 544	Monomyth 532	Ritual 536
Conventions 528	More 528	Ritual artifacts 536
Culture 526	Myth 529	Sacralization 547
Custom 528	Norms 528	Sacred consumption 544

CONSUMER BEHAVIOR CHALLENGE

1 We can think of culture as a society's personality. If your culture were a person, how would you describe its personality traits?

2 What is the difference between an enacted norm and a crescive norm? Identify the set of crescive norms operating when a man and woman in your culture go out for dinner on a first date. What products and services are affected by these norms?

3 How do the consumer decisions involved in gift-giving differ from other purchase decisions?

4 This chapter argues that not all gift-giving is positive. In what ways can this ritual be unpleasant or negative?

5 What are some of the major motivations for the purchase of self-gifts? Discuss some marketing implications of these.

6 Describe the three stages of the rite of passage associated with graduating from college.

7 Identify the ritualized aspects of football that are employed in advertising.

8 "Christmas has become just another opportunity to exchange gifts and stimulate the economy." Do you agree? Why or why not?

9 Rituals can provide us with a sense of order and security. In a study of the drinking rituals of college students, the researchers found that drinking imposed order in students' daily lives—from the completion of assignments to what and when to eat. In addition, ritualizing an activity such as drinking provided security and fellowship at a time fraught with confusion and turbulent change. Obviously, though, there's a dark side to drinking rituals. Consider the highly publicized death of a Massachusetts Institute of Technology student who died three days after falling into an alcohol-induced coma as the result of a fraternity pledge.[82] Indeed, while binge drinking is probably the most widely practiced ritual among college students, it also has been described as the most significant health hazard on college campuses today.[83] What role does drinking play in the social life on your campus? Based on your experience, how does it fit into rituals of college life? Should these practices be changed? If so, how?

NOTES

1. Bill McDowell, "Starbucks Is Ground Zero in Today's Coffee Culture," *Advertising Age* (December 9, 1996): 1. For a discussion of the act of coffee drinking as ritual, see Susan Fournier and Julie L. Yao, "Reviving Brand Loyalty: A Reconceptualization within the Framework of Consumer–Brand Relationships" (working paper 96-039, Harvard Business School, 1996).

2. Louise Lee, "Now, Starbucks Uses Its Bean," *BusinessWeek* (February 14, 2000): 92–94; Mark Gimein, "Behind Starbucks' New Venture: Beans, Beatniks, and Booze," *Fortune* (May 15, 2000): 80.

3. "Spice Girls Dance into Culture Clash," *Montgomery Advertiser* (April 29, 1997): 2A.

4. Clifford Geertz, *The Interpretation of Cultures* (New York: Basic Books, 1973); Marvin Harris, *Culture, People and Nature* (New York: Crowell, 1971); John F. Sherry Jr., "The Cultural Perspective in Consumer Research," in Richard J. Lutz, ed., *Advances in Consumer Research* 13 (Provo, UT: Association for Consumer Research, 1985): 573–75.

5. William Lazer, Shoji Murata, and Hiroshi Kosaka, "Japanese Marketing: Towards a Better Understanding," *Journal of Marketing* 49 (Spring 1985): 69–81.

6. Celia W. Dugger, "Modestly, India Goes for a Public Swim," *New York Times on the Web* (March 5, 2000).

7. Geert Hofstede, *Culture's Consequences* (Beverly Hills, CA: Sage, 1980); see also Laura M. Milner, Dale Fodness, and Mark W. Speece, "Hofstede's Research on Cross-Cultural Work-Related Values: Implications for Consumer Behavior," in W. Fred van Raaij and Gary J. Bamossy, eds., *European Advances in Consumer Research* (Amsterdam: Association for Consumer Research, 1993), 70–76.

8. Daniel Goleman, "The Group and the Self: New Focus on a Cultural Rift," *New York Times* (December 25, 1990): 37; Harry C. Triandis, "The Self and Social Behavior in Differing Cultural Contexts," *Psychological Review* 96 (July 1989): 506; Harry C. Triandis, Robert Bontempo, Marcelo J. Villareal, Masaaki Asai, and Nydia Lucca, "Individualism and Collectivism: Cross-Cultural Perspectives on Self–Ingroup Relationships," *Journal of Personality and Social Psychology* 54 (February 1988): 323.

9. George J. McCall and J. L. Simmons, *Social Psychology: A Sociological Approach* (New York: The Free Press, 1982).

10. Robert Frank, "When Small Chains Go Abroad, Culture Clashes Require Ingenuity," *Wall Street Journal Interactive Edition* (April 12, 2000).

11. Eric J. Arnould, Linda L. Price, and Cele Otnes, "Making Consumption Magic: A Study of White-Water River Rafting," *Journal of Contemporary Ethnography* 28 (February 1999): 33–68.

12. Molly O'Neill, "As Life Gets More Complex, Magic Casts a Wider Spell," *New York Times* (June 13, 1994): A1.

13. Susannah Meadows, "Who's Afraid of the Big Bad Werewolf?" *Newsweek* (August 26, 2002): 57.

14. Conrad Phillip Kottak, "Anthropological Analysis of Mass Enculturation," in Conrad P. Kottak, ed., *Researching American Culture* (Ann Arbor: University of Michigan Press, 1982), 40–74.

15. Eric Ransdell, "The Nike Story? Just Tell It!" *Fast Company* (January–February 2000): 44.

16. Joseph Campbell, *Myths, Dreams, and Religion* (New York: E. P. Dutton, 1970).

17. Claude Lévi-Strauss, *Structural Anthropology* (Harmondsworth: Peregrine, 1977).

18. Tina Lowrey and Cele C. Otnes, "Consumer Fairy Tales and the Perfect Christmas," in Cele C. Otnes and Tina M. Lowrey, eds. *Contemporary Consumption Rituals: A Research Anthology* (forthcoming, Erlbaum, 2003).

19. Jeff Jensen, "Comic Heroes Return to Roots as Marvel Is Cast as Hip Brand," *Advertising Age* (June 8, 1998): 3.

20. Jeffrey S. Lang and Patrick Trimble, "Whatever Happened to the Man of Tomorrow? An Examination of the American Monomyth and the Comic Book Superhero," *Journal of Popular Culture* 22 (Winter 1988): 157.

21. Elizabeth C. Hirschman, "Movies as Myths: An Interpretation of Motion Picture Mythology," in Jean Umiker-Sebeok, ed., *Marketing and Semiotics: New Directions in the Study of Signs for Sale* (Berlin: Mouton de Gruyter, 1987), 335–74.

22. See William Blake Tyrrell, "Star Trek as Myth and Television as Mythmaker," in Jack Nachbar, Deborah Weiser, and John L. Wright, eds., *The Popular Culture Reader* (Bowling Green, OH: Bowling Green University Press, 1978), 79–88.

23. Bernie Whalen, "Semiotics: An Art or Powerful Marketing Research Tool?" *Marketing News* (May 13, 1983): 8.

24. Eduardo Porter, "New 'Got Milk?' TV Commercials Try to Entice Hispanic Teenagers," *Wall Street Journal Interactive Edition* (December 28, 2001).

25. See Dennis W. Rook, "The Ritual Dimension of Consumer Behavior," *Journal of Consumer Research* 12 (December 1985): 251–64; Mary A. Stansfield Tetreault and Robert E. Kleine III, "Ritual, Ritualized Behavior, and Habit: Refinements and Extensions of the Consumption Ritual Construct," in Marvin Goldberg, Gerald Gorn, and Richard W. Pollay, eds., *Advances in Consumer Research* 17 (Provo, UT: Association for Consumer Research, 1990): 31–38.

26. Virginia Postrel, "From Weddings to Football, the Value of Communal Activities," *New York Times on the Web* (April 25, 2002).

27. Kim Foltz, "New Species for Study: Consumers in Action," *New York Times* (December 18, 1989): A1.

28. For a study that looked at updated wedding rituals in Turkey, see Tuba Ustuner, Guliz Ger, and Douglas B. Holt, "Consuming Ritual: Reframing the Turkish Henna-Night Ceremony," in Stephen J. Hoch and Robert J. Meyers, eds., *Advances in Consumer Research* 27 (Provo, UT: Association for Consumer Research, 2000): 209–14.

29. For a study that looked specifically at rituals pertaining to birthday parties, see Cele Otnes and Mary Ann McGrath, "Ritual Socialization and the Children's Birthday Party: The Early Emergence of Gender Differences," *Journal of Ritual Studies* 8 (Winter 1994): 73–93.

30. "Power of Registries," *Chain Store Age* 77 (October 2001): 41. For a study on how brides use message boards to plan weddings, see Michelle R. Nelson and Cele C. Otnes, "Exploring Cross-Cultural Ambivalence: A Netnography of Intercultural Wedding Message Boards," *Journal of Business Research*, in press.

31. Cyndee Miller, "Nix the Knick-Knacks; Send Cash," *Marketing News* (May 26, 1997): 13.

32. "I Do . . . Take MasterCard," *Wall Street Journal* (June 23, 2000): W1.

33. Debra Allen, "Gift Registries on the Web," *Link-Up* (May–June 2001): 16; Jennifer Gilbert, "New Teen Obsession," *Advertising Age* (February 14, 2000): 8; Jeanne Marie Laskas, "Be Careful What You Wish for,"

Yahoo! Internet Life (Winter 2000): 40; Rutrell Yasin, "Registry Notarizes E-Documents," *Internet Week* (June 5, 2000): 39.

34. Dennis W. Rook and Sidney J. Levy, "Psychosocial Themes in Consumer Grooming Rituals," in Richard P. Bagozzi and Alice M. Tybout, eds., *Advances in Consumer Research* 10 (Provo, UT: Association for Consumer Research, 1983): 329–33.

35. Diane Barthel, *Putting on Appearances: Gender and Advertising* (Philadelphia: Temple University Press, 1988).

36. Barthel, *Putting on Appearances: Gender and Advertising.*

37. Russell W. Belk, Melanie Wallendorf, and John F. Sherry Jr., "The Sacred and the Profane in Consumer Behavior: Theodicy on the Odyssey," *Journal of Consumer Research* 16 (June 1989): 1–38.

38. Markus Giesler and Mali Pohlmann, "The Anthropology of File Sharing: Consuming Napster as a Gift," in Punam Anand Keller and Dennis W. Rook, eds., *Advances in Consumer Research* 30 (Provo, UT: Association for Consumer Research 2003).

39. Russell W. Belk and Gregory S. Coon, "Gift Giving as Agapic Love: An Alternative to the Exchange Paradigm Based on Dating Experiences," *Journal of Consumer Research* 20 (December 1993): 393–417. See also Cele Otnes, Tina M. Lowrey, and Young Chan Kim, "Gift Selection for Easy and Difficult Recipients: A Social Roles Interpretation," *Journal of Consumer Research* 20 (September 1993): 229–44.

40. Monica Gonzales, "Before Mourning," *American Demographics* (April 1988): 19.

41. Alf Nucifora, "Tis the Season to Gift One's Best Clients," *Triangle Business Journal* (December 3, 1999): 14.

42. John F. Sherry Jr., "Gift Giving in Anthropological Perspective," *Journal of Consumer Research* 10 (September 1983): 157–68.

43. Daniel Goleman, "What's Under the Tree? Clues to a Relationship," *New York Times* (December 19, 1989): C1.

44. John F. Sherry Jr., Mary Ann McGrath, and Sidney J. Levy, "The Dark Side of the Gift," *Journal of Business Research* (1993): 225–44.

45. Colin Camerer, "Gifts as Economics Signals and Social Symbols," *American Journal of Sociology* 94 (Supplement 1988): 5, 180–214; Robert T. Green and Dana L. Alden, "Functional Equivalence in Cross-Cultural Consumer Behavior: Gift Giving in Japan and the United States," *Psychology & Marketing* 5 (Summer1988): 155–68; Hiroshi Tanaka and Miki Iwamura, "Gift Selection Strategy of Japanese Seasonal Gift Purchasers: An Explorative Study" (paper presented at the Association for Consumer Research, Boston, October 1994).

46. David Glen Mick and Michelle DeMoss, "Self-Gifts: Phenomenological Insights from Four Contexts," *Journal of Consumer Research* 17 (December 1990): 327; John F. Sherry Jr., Mary Ann McGrath, and Sidney J. Levy, "Monadic Giving: Anatomy of Gifts Given to the Self," in John F. Sherry Jr., ed., *Contemporary Marketing and Consumer Behavior: An Anthropological Sourcebook* (New York: Sage, 1995): 399–432.

47. Cynthia Crossen, "Holiday Shoppers' Refrain: 'A Merry Christmas to Me'," *Wall Street Journal Interactive Edition* (December 11, 1997).

48. See, for example, Russell W. Belk, "Halloween: An Evolving American Consumption Ritual," in Richard Pollay, Jerry Gorn, and Marvin Goldberg, eds., *Advances in Consumer Research* 17 (Provo, UT: Association for Consumer Research, 1990): 508–17; Melanie Wallendorf and Eric J. Arnould, "We Gather Together: The Consumption Rituals of Thanksgiving Day," *Journal of Consumer Research* 18 (June 1991): 13–31.

49. Rick Lyte, "Holidays, Ethnic Themes Provide Built-in F&B Festivals," *Hotel & Motel Management* (December 14, 1987): 56; Megan Rowe, "Holidays and Special Occasions: Restaurants Are Fast Replacing 'Grandma's House' as the Site of Choice for Special Meals," *Restaurant Management* (November 1987): 69; Judith Waldrop, "Funny Valentines," *American Demographics* (February 1989): 7.

50. "Cinco de Mayo, a Yawn for Mexicans, Gives Americans a License to Party," *Wall Street Journal Interactive Edition* (May 5, 2000).

51. Bruno Bettelheim, *The Uses of Enchantment: The Meaning and Importance of Fairy Tales* (New York: Alfred A. Knopf, 1976).

52. Kenneth L. Woodward, "Christmas Wasn't Born Here, Just Invented," *Newsweek* (December 16, 1996): 71.

53. Aron O'Cass and Peter Clarke, "Dear Santa, Do You Have My Brand? A Study of the Brand Requests, Awareness and Request Styles at Christmas Time," *Journal of Consumer Behavior* 2 (September 2002): 37–53.

54. Theodore Caplow, Howard M. Bahr, Bruce A. Chadwick, Reuben Hill, and Margaret M. Williams, *Middletown Families: Fifty Years of Change and Continuity* (Minneapolis: University of Minnesota Press, 1982).

55. Andrea Adelson, "A New Spirit for Sales of Halloween Merchandise," *New York Times* (October 31, 1994): D1.

56. Anne Swardson, "Trick or Treat: In Paris, It's Dress, Dance, Eat," *International Herald Tribune* (October 31, 1996): 2.

57. Arnold Van Gennep, *The Rites of Passage*, trans. Maika B. Vizedom and Shannon L. Caffee (London: Routledge and Kegan Paul, 1960; orig. published 1908); Michael R. Solomon and Punam Anand,

"Ritual Costumes and Status Transition: The Female Business Suit as Totemic Emblem," in Elizabeth C. Hirschman and Morris Holbrook (eds.), *Advances in Consumer Research*, vol. 12 (Washington, DC: Association for Consumer Research, 1995) 315–18.

58. Walter W. Whitaker III, "The Contemporary American Funeral Ritual," in Ray B. Browne, ed., *Rites and Ceremonies in Popular Culture* (Bowling Green, OH: Bowling Green University Popular Press, 1980): 316–25. For a recent examination of funeral rituals, see Larry D. Compeau and Carolyn Nicholson, "Funerals: Emotional Rituals or Ritualistic Emotions" (paper presented at the Association of Consumer Research, Boston, October 1994).

59. "Aggressive Sales Practices in Funeral Industry Decried," *Montgomery Advertiser* (April 11, 2000): 2A.

60. Kottak, "Anthropological Analysis of Mass Enculturation," 40–74.

61. Joan Kron, *Home-Psych: The Social Psychology of Home and Decoration* (New York: Clarkson N. Potter, 1983); Gerry Pratt, "The House as an Expression of Social Worlds," in James S. Duncan, ed., *Housing and Identity: Cross-Cultural Perspectives* (London: Croom Helm, 1981): 135–79; Michael R. Solomon, "The Role of the Surrogate Consumer in Service Delivery," *The Service Industries Journal* 7 (July 1987): 292–307.

62. Grant McCracken, "'Homeyness': A Cultural Account of One Constellation of Goods and Meanings," in Elizabeth C. Hirschman, ed., *Interpretive Consumer Research* (Provo, UT: Association for Consumer Research, 1989): 168–84.

63. Emile Durkheim, *The Elementary Forms of the Religious Life* (New York: Free Press, 1915).

64. Susan Birrell, "Sports as Ritual: Interpretations from Durkheim to Goffman," *Social Forces* 60, no. 2 (1981): 354–76; Daniel Q. Voigt, "American Sporting Rituals," in Browne, ed., *Rites and Ceremonies in Popular Culture.*

65. Alf Walle, "The Epic Hero," *Marketing Insights* (Spring 1990): 63.

66. Dean MacCannell, *The Tourist: A New Theory of the Leisure Class* (New York: Shocken Books, 1976).

67. Belk et al., "The Sacred and the Profane in Consumer Behavior."

68. Beverly Gordon, "The Souvenir: Messenger of the Extraordinary," *Journal of Popular Culture* 20, no. 3 (1986): 135–46.

69. Belk et al., "The Sacred and the Profane in Consumer Behavior."

70. Ibid.

71. Deborah Hofmann, "In Jewelry, Choices Sacred and Profane, Ancient and New," *New York Times* (May 7, 1989).

72. Lee Gomes, "Ramadan, a Month of Prayer, Takes on a Whole New Look," *Wall Street Journal Interactive Edition* (December 4, 2002).

73. J. C. Conklin, "Web Site Caters to Cowboy Fans by Selling Sweaty, Used Socks," *Wall Street Journal Interactive Edition* (April 21, 2000).

74. "Elvis Evermore," *Newsweek* (August 11, 1997): 12.

75. Dan L. Sherrell, Alvin C. Burns, and Melodie R. Phillips, "Fixed Consumption Behavior: The Case of Enduring Acquisition in a Product Category," in Robert L. King, ed., *Developments in Marketing Science* 14 (1991): 36–40.

76. Belk, "Acquiring, Possessing, and Collecting: Fundamental Processes in Consumer Behavior," cf. 74.

77. Ruth Ann Smith, "Collecting as Consumption: A Grounded Theory of Collecting Behavior" (unpublished manuscript, Virginia Polytechnic Institute and State University, 1994): 14.

78. For a discussion of these perspectives, see Smith, "Collecting as Consumption."

79. For an extensive bibliography on collecting, see Russell W. Belk, Melanie Wallendorf, John F. Sherry Jr., and Morris B. Holbrook, "Collecting in a Consumer Culture," in Russell W. Belk, ed., *Highways and Buyways* (Provo, UT: Association for Consumer Research, 1991): 178–215. See also Russell W. Belk, "Acquiring, Possessing, and Collecting: Fundamental Processes in Consumer Behavior," in Ronald F. Bush and Shelby D. Hunt, eds., *Marketing Theory: Philosophy of Science Perspectives* (Chicago: American Marketing Association, 1982): 85–90; Werner Muensterberg, *Collecting: An Unruly Passion* (Princeton, NJ: Princeton University Press, 1994); Melanie Wallendorf and Eric J. Arnould, "'My Favorite Things': A Cross-Cultural Inquiry into Object Attachment, Possessiveness, and Social Linkage," *Journal of Consumer Research* 14 (March 1988): 531–47.

80. Calmetta Y. Coleman, "Just Any Old Thing from McDonald's Can Be a Collectible," *Wall Street Journal* (March 29, 1995): B1; Ken Bensinger, "Recent Boom in Toy Collecting Leads Retailers to Limit Sales," *Wall Street Journal Interactive Edition* (September 25, 1998); "PC Lovers Loyal to Classics," *Montgomery Advertiser* (April 2, 2000): 1.

81. Philip Connors, "Like Fine Wine, a 'Collector' Visits McDonald's for Subtle Differences," *Wall Street Journal Interactive Edition* (August 16, 1999).

82. Debbie Treise, Joyce M. Wolburg, and Cele C. Otnes, "Understanding the 'Social Gifts' of Drinking Rituals: An Alternative Framework for PSA Developers," *Journal of Advertising* 28 (Summer 1999): 17–31.

83. Ibid.

The Creation and Diffusion of Global Consumer Culture

as Alexandra is browsing through the racks at her local Abercrombie & Fitch store in Wichita, Kansas, her friend Chloe yells to her, "Alex, check this out! These leopard-skin Capri pants are so tight!" From watching MTV, Alex knows tight means *cool*, and she agrees. As she takes the pants to the cash register, she's looking forward to wearing them to school the next day. All of her girlfriends in junior high compete with each other to dress just like the women in Destiny's Child and other hot groups—her friends just won't believe their eyes when they see her tomorrow. Maybe some of the younger kids in her school will even think she was fresh off the mean streets of New York City! Even though she has never been east of the Mississippi, Alex just knows she would fit right in with all of the Bronx "sistahs" she reads about in her magazines.

■ THE CREATION OF CULTURE

Even though inner-city teens represent only eight percent of all people in that age group and have incomes significantly lower than their white suburban counterparts, their influence on young people's musical and fashion tastes is much greater than these numbers would suggest. Turn on MTV, and it won't be long before a rap video fills the screen. Go to the newsstand, and magazines such as *Vibe* are waiting for you. Numerous Web sites such as *vibe.com* are devoted to hip-hop culture, and nightclubs let you peek into what's happening online at sites such as *groovetech.com*, *thewomb.com*, and *digitalclubnetwork.com*.[1]

In addition to music, "urban" fashion is spreading into the heartland as major retail chains pick up on the craze and try to lure legions of young middle-class shoppers. Macy's and JC Penney carry FUBU ("for us by us"); although this urban clothing company sells a lot of shiny satin baseball jackets, baggy jeans with loops, and fleece tops in the inner city, 40 percent of its sales are to white customers in the suburbs. Even the aristocratic Polo Jeans by Ralph Lauren started its own line to appeal to the hip-hop nation.[2] How does this subculture influence the mass market in so many ways?

Americans have always been fascinated by outsider heroes—whether John Dillinger, James Dean, or Dr. Dre—who achieve money and fame without being hemmed in by societal constraints. That helps to explain the devotion of many white suburban teens to the urban music scene. As one executive of a firm that researches urban youth noted, "People resonate with the strong anti-oppression messages of rap, and the alienation of blacks."[3]

Ironically, Alex's only experience of "oppression" was being grounded by her parents after her mom found a half-smoked cigarette in her room. She lives in a white middle-class area in the Midwest, but she is able to "connect" symbolically with millions of other young consumers by wearing styles that originated far away—even though the original meanings of those styles have little relevance to her. As a privileged member of "white bread" society, her hip-hop clothes have a very different meaning in her suburban world than they would to street kids in New York City or L.A. In fact, these "cutting-edge" types might even interpret the fact that Alex is wearing a style as a sign that this item is no longer in fashion, and decide it's time to move on to something else.

Big corporations are working hard to capture the next killer fashion being incubated in black urban culture—what is called "flavor" on the streets. For example, Fila, which started as an Italian underwear maker in 1926, initially broke into sportswear by focusing on "lily-white" activities such as skiing and tennis. The company first made a splash by signing Swedish tennis sensation Bjorn Borg as an endorser. Ten years later, the tennis fad faded, but company executives noticed that rap stars such as Heavy D were wearing Fila sweat suits to symbolize their idealized vision of life in white country clubs. Fila switched gears and went with the flow; its share of the sneaker market grew dramatically as a result.[4]

How did hip-hop music and fashions, which began as forms of expression in the black urban subculture, make it to mainstream America? Here's a brief chronology:

- 1968: Bronx DJ Kool Herc invents hip-hop.
- 1973–1978: Urban block parties feature break-dancing and graffiti.
- 1979: A small record company named Sugar Hill becomes the first rap label.
- 1980: Manhattan art galleries feature graffiti artists.
- 1981: Blondie's song "Rapture" hits number one on the charts.
- 1985: Columbia Records buys the Def Jam label.
- 1988: MTV begins *Yo! MTV Raps*, featuring Fab 5 Freddy.
- 1990: Hollywood gets into the act with the hip-hop film *House Party*; Ice-T's rap album is a big hit on college radio stations; amid controversy, white rapper Vanilla Ice hits the big time; NBC launches a new sitcom, *Fresh Prince of Bel Air*.

- 1991: Mattel introduces its Hammer doll (a likeness of the rap star Hammer, formerly known as M. C. Hammer); designer Karl Lagerfeld shows shiny vinyl raincoats and chain belts in his Chanel collection; designer Charlotte Neuville sells gold vinyl suits with matching baseball caps for $800; Isaac Mizrahi features wide-brimmed caps and takeoffs on African medallions; Bloomingdale's launches Anne Klein's rap-inspired clothing line by featuring a rap performance in its Manhattan store.

- 1992: Rappers start to abandon this look, turning to low-fitting baggy jeans, sometimes worn backwards; white rapper Marky Mark appears in a national campaign wearing Calvin Klein underwear, exposed above his hip-hugging pants; composer Quincy Jones launches *Vibe* magazine and it wins over many white readers.[5]

- 1993: Hip-hop fashions and slang continue to cross over into mainstream consumer culture. An outdoor ad for Coca-Cola proclaims, "Get Yours 24–7." The company is confident that many viewers in its target market will know that the phrase is urban slang for "always" (24 hours a day, 7 days a week).[6]

- 1994: The (late) Italian designer Versace pushes oversized overalls favored by urban kids. In one ad, he asks, "Overalls with an oversize look, something like what rappers and homeboys wear. Why not a sophisticated version?"[7]

- 1996: Tommy Hilfiger, a designer who was the darling of the preppie set, turns hip-hop. He gives free wardrobes to rap artists such as Grand Puba and Chef Raekwon, and in return finds his name mentioned in rap songs—the ultimate endorsement. The September 1996 issue of *Rolling Stone* features the Fugees; several band members prominently display the Hilfiger logo. In the same year the designer uses rap stars Method Man and Treach of Naughty by Nature as runway models. Hilfiger's new Tommy Girl perfume plays on his name but also is a reference to the New York hip-hop record label Tommy Boy.[8]

- 1997: Coca-Cola features rapper LL Cool J in a commercial that debuts in the middle of the sitcom *In the House*, a TV show starring the singer.[9]

- 1998: In its battle with Dockers for an increased share of the khaki market, GAP launches its first global ad campaign. One of the commercials, "Khakis Groove," includes a hip-hop dance performance set to music by Bill Mason.[10]

- 1999: Rapper turned entrepreneur Sean (Puffy) Combs introduces an upscale line of menswear he calls "urban high fashion." New companies FUBU, Mecca, and Enyce attain financial success in the multibillion-dollar industry.[11] Lauryn Hill and the Fugees sing at a party sponsored by upscale Italian clothier Emporio Armani and she proclaims, "We just wanna thank Armani for giving a few kids from the ghetto some great suits."[12]

- 2000: *360hip-hop.com*, a Web-based community dedicated to the hip-hop culture, is launched. In addition to promoting the hip-hop lifestyle, the site allows consumers to purchase clothing and music online while watching video interviews with such artists as Will Smith and Busta Rymes.[13]

- 2001: Hip-hop dancing becomes the rage among China's youth, who refer to it as *jiew*, or street dancing.[14]

- 2002–2003: Toy manufacturers mimic the hip-hop practice of using the letter "Z" instead of the letter "S" in names. This trend started with the 1991 film *Boyz N The Hood* (a title that was itself borrowed from a 1989 song by the rap group N.W.A.). It caught on with other hip-hop terms like "skillz," "gangstaz" and "playaz." Musical artists including 504 Boyz, Kidz Bop Kidz, Xzibit, the Youngbloodz, and Smilez incorporated the popular "Z" into their names. During the 2002 Christmas season, Target created a kids' section called "Kool Toyz," where parents can buy dolls with names like Bratz (Girlz and Boyz), Diva Starz, and Trophy Tailz—and a dollhouse to put them in called Dinky Digz. They can find a toy called "Scannerz," a karaoke machine named Loud Lipz, and Marble Moovz, a toddlers' marble set. There's more, including Rescue Rigz, ControlBotz, 4Wheelerz, and the American Patriotz action figures.[15]

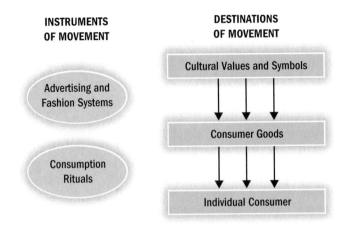

■ FIGURE 17.1
THE MOVEMENT OF MEANING

It's common for mainstream culture to modify symbols identified with "cutting-edge" subcultures and present these to a larger audience. As this occurs, these cultural products undergo a process of **co-optation** by which outsiders transform their original meanings. In this case, rap music was to a large extent divorced from its original connection with the struggles of young African Americans and is now a mainstream entertainment format.[16] One writer sees the white part of the "hip-hop nation" as a series of concentric rings. In the center are those who actually know blacks and understand their culture. The next ring consists of those who have indirect knowledge of this subculture via friends or relatives, but who don't actually rap, spray-paint, or break-dance. Then, there are those a bit further out who simply play hip-hop between other types of music. Finally come the more suburban "wiggers" who are simply trying to catch on to the next popular craze.[17] The spread of hip-hop fashions and music is just one example of what happens when the meanings created by some members of a culture are interpreted and produced for mass consumption.

This chapter considers how the culture in which we live creates the meaning of everyday products and how these meanings move through a society to consumers. As Figure 17.1 shows, the advertising and fashion industries help to transfer meanings by associating functional products with symbolic qualities such as sexiness, sophistication, or just plain "cool." These goods, in turn, impart their meanings to consumers as they use these products to create and express their identities.[18] Recall that in Chapter 1 we learned that "one of the fundamental premises of the modern field of consumer behavior is that people often buy products not for what they *do,* but for what they *mean.*" This closing chapter brings us full circle as we explore how product symbolism evolves and spreads through our culture.

Cultural Selection

Nipple rings. Leopard-skin pants. Sushi. High-tech furniture. Postmodern architecture. Chat rooms. Double decaf cappuccino with a hint of cinnamon. We inhabit a world brimming with different styles and possibilities. The food we eat, the cars we drive, the clothes we wear, the places we live and work, the music we listen to—all are influenced by the ebb and flow of popular culture and fashion.

Consumers may at times feel overwhelmed by the sheer number of choices in the marketplace. A person trying to decide on something as routine as a necktie has many hundreds of alternatives to choose from! Despite this seeming abundance, however, the options available to consumers at any point in time actually represent only a small fraction of the total set of possibilities.

Figure 17.2 shows that the selection of certain alternatives over others—whether automobiles, dresses, computers, recording artists, political candidates, religions, or even scientific methodologies—is the culmination of a complex filtration process resembling a funnel. Many possibilities initially compete for adoption,

CULTURE PRODUCTION PROCESS

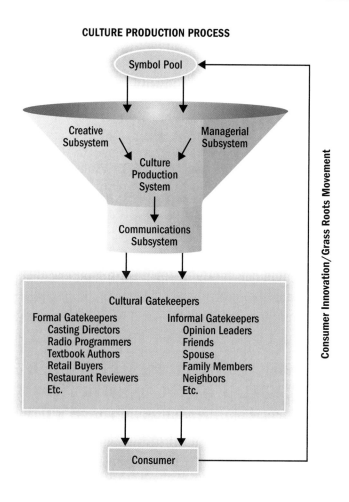

and these are steadily winnowed out as they make their way down the path from conception to consumption in a process of **cultural selection**.

Our tastes and product preferences are not formed in a vacuum. Choices are driven by the images presented to us in mass media, our observations of those around us, and even by our desires to live in the fantasy worlds created by marketers. These options are constantly evolving and changing. A clothing style or type of cuisine that is "hot" one year may be "out" the next.

Alex's emulation of hip-hop style illustrates some of the characteristics of fashion and popular culture:

- Styles are often a reflection of more fundamental societal trends (e.g., politics and social conditions).
- A style begins as a risky or unique statement by a relatively small group of people, and then spreads as others increasingly become aware of the style and feel confident about trying it.
- Styles usually originate as an interplay between the deliberate inventions of designers and business people and spontaneous actions by ordinary consumers who modify styles to suit their own needs. Designers, manufacturers, and merchandisers who can anticipate what consumers want will succeed in the marketplace. In the process, they help to fuel the fire by encouraging mass distribution of the item.
- These cultural products can travel widely, often across countries and even continents.
- Influential people in the media play a large role in deciding which will succeed.
- Most styles eventually wear out as people continually search for new ways to express themselves and marketers scramble to keep up with these desires.

Culture Production Systems

No single designer, company, or advertising agency is totally responsible for creating popular culture. Every product, whether a hit record, a car, or a new clothing style, requires the input of many different participants. The set of individuals and organizations responsible for creating and marketing a cultural product is a **culture production system (CPS)**.[19]

The nature of these systems helps to determine the types of products that eventually emerge from them. Factors such as the number and diversity of competing systems and the amount of innovation versus conformity that is encouraged are important. For example, an analysis of the country/western music industry showed that the hit records it produces tend to be similar to one another during periods when a few large companies dominate the industry, whereas there is more diversity when a greater number of producers are competing within the same market.[20]

The different members of a CPS may not necessarily be aware of or appreciate the roles played by other members, yet many diverse agents work together to create popular culture.[21] Each member does his or her best to anticipate which particular images will be most attractive to a consumer market. Of course, those who are able to consistently forecast consumers' tastes most accurately will be successful over time.

As this AT&T ad demonstrates, many products and styles are destined to become obsolete.

TABLE 17.1
CULTURAL SPECIALISTS IN THE MUSIC INDUSTRY

Specialist	Functions
Songwriter(s)	Compose music and lyrics; must reconcile artistic preferences with estimates of what will succeed in the marketplace
Performer(s)	Interpret music and lyrics; may be formed spontaneously, or may be packaged by an agent to appeal to a predetermined market (e.g., The Monkees, Menudo, and New Kids on the Block)
Teachers and coaches	Develop and refine performers' talents
Agents	Represent performers to record companies
A&R (artist & repertoire) executives	Acquire artists for the record label
Publicists, image consultants, designers, stylists	Create an image for the group that is transmitted to the buying public
Recording technicians, producers	Create a recording to be sold
Marketing executives	Make strategic decisions regarding performer's appearances, ticket pricing, promotional strategies, and so on
Video directors	Interpret the song visually to create a music video that will help to promote the record
Music reviewers	Evaluate the merits of a recording for listeners
Disc jockeys, radio program directors	Decide which records will be given airplay and/or placed in the radio stations' regular rotations
Record store owners	Decide which of the many records produced will be stocked and/or promoted heavily in the retail environment

Components of a CPS

A culture production system has three major subsystems: (1) *a creative subsystem* responsible for generating new symbols and products; (2) *a managerial subsystem* responsible for selecting, making tangible, mass producing, and managing the distribution of new symbols and products; and (3) *a communications subsystem* responsible for giving meaning to the new product and providing it with a symbolic set of attributes that are communicated to consumers.

An example of the three components of a culture production system for a record would be: (1) a singer (e.g., rapper Eminem, a creative subsystem); (2) a company (e.g., Interscope Records, which manufactures and distributes Eminem's CDs, a managerial subsystem); and (3) the advertising and publicity agencies hired to promote the CDs (a communications subsystem). Table 17.1 illustrates some of the many cultural specialists who are required to create a hit CD.

Cultural Gatekeepers

Many judges or "tastemakers" have influence on which products are eventually offered to consumers. These **cultural gatekeepers** are responsible for filtering the overflow of information and materials intended for consumers. Gatekeepers include movie, restaurant, and car reviewers; interior designers; disc jockeys; retail buyers; and magazine editors. Collectively, this set of agents is known as the *throughput sector.*[22]

High Culture and Popular Culture

Do Beethoven and Puff Daddy have anything in common? Although both the famous composer and the rap singer are associated with music, many would argue that the similarity stops there. Culture production systems create many kinds of products, but some basic distinctions can be offered regarding their characteristics.

Arts and Crafts

One distinction is between arts and crafts.[23] An **art product** is viewed primarily as an object of aesthetic contemplation without any functional value. A **craft product**, in contrast, is admired because of the beauty with which it performs some function (e.g., a ceramic ashtray or hand-carved fishing lures). A piece of art is original, subtle, and valuable, and typically is associated with the elite of society. A craft tends to follow a formula that permits rapid production. According to this framework, elite culture is produced in a purely aesthetic context and is judged by reference to recognized classics. It is high culture—"serious art."[24]

One way to appreciate this distinction is to consider the phenomenal success of artist Thomas Kinkade. This painter has sold 10 million digital reproductions of his work. The pictures are manufactured at a factory in California, where a digital photograph of each original is reproduced thousands of times onto thin plastic film that is glued to canvases. Then, technicians called "high-lighters" sit along an assembly line, dabbing oil paint onto set spots. Each of the 10,000 pieces produced in the factory each month is signed in ink containing drops of the artist's blood, although he never actually touched most of these works. Kinkade also has licensed images to appear on coffee mugs, La-Z-Boy recliners, and even a romance-novel cover.[25]

High Art Versus Low Art

As Kinkade's "formula for success" demonstrates, the distinction between high and low culture is not as clear as it used to be. In addition to the possible class bias that drives such a distinction (i.e., we assume that the rich have culture but the poor do not), today high and low culture blend together in interesting ways. Popular culture

As this British ad illustrates, high art merges with popular culture in interesting ways.

At home in the world's great landscapes. Elddis

reflects the world around us; these phenomena touch rich and poor. In Europe, for example, advertising is widely appreciated as an art form. Some advertising executives are public figures in Great Britain. For more than 10 years, people in France have paid up to $30 to watch an all-night program in a movie theater consisting of nothing but television commercials.[26]

The arts are big business. Americans alone spend more than $2 billion per year to attend arts events.[27] All cultural products that are transmitted by mass media become a part of popular culture.[28] Classical recordings are marketed in much the same way as Top 40 albums, and museums use mass-marketing techniques to sell their wares. The Metropolitan Museum of Art has branch gift shops across the United States and some are operated as boutiques within large department stores.

Marketers often incorporate high art imagery to promote products. They may feature works of art on shopping bags or sponsor artistic events to build public goodwill.[29] When observers from Toyota watched customers in luxury car showrooms, the company found that these consumers tended to view a car as an art object. This theme was then used in an ad for the Lexus with the caption, "Until now, the only fine arts we supported were sculpture, painting, and music."[30]

Cultural Formulae

Mass culture, in contrast, churns out products specifically for a mass market. These products aim to please the average taste of an undifferentiated audience and are predictable because they follow certain patterns. As illustrated in Table 17.2, many popular art forms, such as detective stories or science fiction, generally follow a **cultural formula**, in which certain roles and props often occur consistently.[31] Romance novels are an extreme case of a cultural formula. Computer programs even allow users to "write" their own romances by systematically varying certain set elements of the story.

Reliance on these formulae also leads to a *recycling* of images, as members of the creative subsystem reach back through time for inspiration. Thus, young people watch retro shows like *Gilligan's Island* and remakes of *The Brady Bunch*, designers modify styles from Victorian England or colonial Africa, hip-hop DJs sample sound bits from old songs and combine them in new ways, and GAP runs ads featuring now-dead celebrities including Humphrey Bogart, Gene Kelly, and Pablo Picasso dressed in khaki pants. With easy access to VCRs, CD burners, digital cameras, and imaging software, virtually anyone can "remix" the past.[32]

TABLE 17.2
CULTURAL FORMULAE IN PUBLIC ART FORMS

Art Form/Genre	Classic Western	Science Fiction	Hard-Boiled Detective	Family Sitcom
Time	1800s	Future	Present	Anytime
Location	Edge of civilization	Space	City	Suburbs
Protagonist	Cowboy (lone individual)	Astronaut	Detective	Father (figure)
Heroine	Schoolmarm	Spacegal	Damsel in distress	Mother (figure)
Villain	Outlaws, killers	Aliens	Killer	Boss, neighbor
Secondary characters	Townfolk, Indians	Technicians in spacecraft	Cops, underworld	Kids, dogs
Plot	Restore law and order	Repel aliens	Find killer	Solve problem
Theme	Justice	Triumph of humanity	Pursuit and discovery	Chaos and confusion
Costume	Cowboy hat, boots, etc.	High-tech uniforms	Raincoat	Regular clothes
Locomotion	Horse	Spaceship	Beat-up car	Station wagon
Weaponry	Sixgun, rifle	Rayguns	Pistol, fists	Insults

Source: Arthur A. Berger, *Signs in Contemporary Culture: An Introduction to Semiotics* (New York: Longman, 1984): 86. Copyright © 1984. Reissued 1989 by Sheffield Publishing Company, Salem, Wisconsin. Reprinted with permission of the publisher.

This perfume ad recycles imagery from pulp romance novels.

Aesthetic Market Research

Creators of aesthetic products are increasingly adapting conventional marketing methods to fine-tune their mass-market offerings. Market research is used, for example, to test audience reactions to movie concepts. Although testing cannot account for such intangibles as acting quality or cinematography, it can determine if the basic themes of the movie strike a responsive chord in the target audience. This type of research is most appropriate for blockbuster movies, which usually follow one of the formulae described earlier. In some cases research is combined with publicity, as when the producers of the Will Smith movie *Men in Black* showed the first 12 minutes of the film to an advance audience and then let them meet the stars to create a pre-release buzz.[33]

Consumer research even may help to shape a movie's plot. Typically, free invitations to prescreenings are handed out in malls and movie theaters. Attendees are asked a few questions about the movie, and then some are selected to participate in focus groups. Although audience reactions usually result in only minor editing changes, occasionally more drastic effects result. When initial reaction to the ending of *Fatal Attraction* was negative, Paramount Pictures spent an additional $1.3 million to shoot a new one.[34] Of course, this feedback isn't always accurate—before the megahit *E.T.: The Extra-Terrestrial* was released, consumer research indicated that no one over the age of four would go to see the movie![35] Whoever did that research project needs to phone home.

■ REALITY ENGINEERING

The village of Riverside, Georgia, has a colorful history. You can look at the sepia photographs showing the town in the nineteenth century or read excerpts from period novels lauding the settlement's cosmopolitan flair. You'll also discover that the town was used as a Union garrison during the Civil War. There's only one hitch: Riverside didn't exist until 1998. The account of nineteenth-century Riverside is a clever fabrication created to promote a new housing and commercial development. The story "is a figment of our imagination," acknowledges the developer.[36]

Like Riverside, many consumer environments—whether housing developments, shopping malls, sports stadiums, or theme parks—are largely composed of images and characters spawned by marketing campaigns. The director of strategic planning at Saatchi & Saatchi New York predicts, "Any space you can take in visually, anything you hear in the future will be branded, I believe. It's not going to be the Washington Monument. It's going to be the Washington Post Monument."[37]

Reality engineering occurs as marketers appropriate elements of popular culture and convert them for use as promotional vehicles.[38] It's hard to know what's real anymore; even "used jeans" get created by specialists who apply chemical washes, sandpaper, and other techniques to make a new pair of jeans look like they're ready for retirement. The industry even has a term for this practice that sums up the contradiction: *new vintage*![39]

The elements used by reality engineers are both sensory and spatial, whether in the form of products appearing in movies, scents pumped into offices and stores, billboards, theme parks, video monitors attached to shopping carts, TV screens in the backs of taxicabs, ad space being sold on police patrol cars, or even faked "documentaries" like *The Blair Witch Project*.[40] This process is accelerating; historical analyses of Broadway plays, best-selling novels, and the lyrics of hit songs, for example, clearly show large increases in the use of real brand names over time.[41] Some recent reality engineering projects underscore how advertisers are pushing the envelope that defines where we can expect to see marketing messages:

- Television advertisers are waking up to the reality that viewers just won't sit through commercials anymore. Some of them are experimenting with new ways to get their messages across while avoiding that mass exodus for the rest rooms during commercial breaks. A show called *Live from Tomorrow* will showcase new products but will have no commercials. Instead, each hour-long episode will work sponsors' products into variety/news segments.[42] Another new show called *Lost at Home* will integrate brands into the storyline—actor Gregory Hines stars as the head of the advertising agency that handles such real products as Midol, Timberland, and Volvo.[43]
- In Denmark, a media company gives parents of newborns free use of a top-quality baby carriage if they agree to push it around Copenhagen with a corporate sponsor's logo on the buggy's side.[44]
- A pro bowler named Kim Adler sold the rights to her backside on eBay: The winning bidder gets to put an 8-square-inch logo on the TV-camera side of her shorts or skirt. She estimates that an advertiser's logo will get about 20 minutes of screen time during a televised match.[45]

The Tangled Web

A knockoff is a style that has been deliberately copied and modified, often with the intent to sell to a larger or different market. *Haute couture* clothing styles presented by top designers in Paris and elsewhere are commonly "knocked off" by other designers and sold to the mass market. The Web is making it easier than ever for firms to copy these designs—in some cases so quickly that their pirated styles show up in stores at the same time as the originals. Wildcatters such as First View have set up Web sites to show designers' latest creations, sometimes revealing everything from a new collection. Things have gotten so bad that the House of Chanel requires photographers to sign contracts promising their shots will not be distributed on the Internet. But, isn't imitation the sincerest form of flattery?[46]

Marketing Pitfall

One of the most controversial intersections between marketing and society occurs when companies provide "educational materials" to schools. Many firms including Nike, Hershey, Crayola, Nintendo, and Foot Locker provide free book covers swathed in ads. Almost 40 percent of secondary schools in the United States start the day with a video feed from Channel One, which exposes students to commercials in the classroom in exchange for educational programming. Similarly, an Internet company called ZapMe! gives client schools free computers and Internet connections as well as a network of 11,000 educational sites in exchange for a promise to use the computers at least four hours a day. Commercials run continuously on the lower left-hand quarter of the screen, and the company has permission to monitor the students' browsing habits, breaking down the data by age, sex, and zip code. In a few cases companies are contracting with schools to run focus groups with their students during the school day in order to get reactions to new product ideas. Coca-Cola signed a 10-year, $8 million exclusive beverage contract with the Colorado Springs, Colorado, school system. In some schools third graders practice math by counting Tootsie Rolls, and the kids use reading software sporting the logos of Kmart, Coke, Pepsi, and Cap'n Crunch cereal.

Corporate involvement with schools is hardly new—in the 1920s Ivory Soap sponsored soap-carving competitions for students. But, the level of intrusion is sharply increasing, as companies scramble to compensate for the decrease in children's viewership of television on Saturday mornings and weekday afternoons and try to compete with videos and computer games for kids' attention. Many educators argue that these materials are a godsend for resource-poor schools that otherwise could not provide computers and other goodies to their students. On the other hand, a new California law bans the use of textbooks with brand names and company logos. This legislation was prompted by complaints from parents about a middle school math book that uses names like Barbie, Oreos, Nike, and Sony PlayStation in word problems.[58]

● In a promotion dubbed Fake Tourist, an electronics company sent actors and actresses to tourist attractions such as the Empire State Building in New York and the Space Needle in Seattle. Working in teams of two or three and behaving as if they were actual tourists, they asked unsuspecting passersby to take their pictures using a camera built into a cell phone. Then, the actors engage the Good Samaritans in enthusiastic conversation about this new device—but they never identify themselves as employees of the manufacturer. Another team of female models frequents trendy lounges and bars. As a woman makes small talk with a patron, her phone "happens" to ring and the caller's picture pops up on the screen.[47]

Media images, whether of an actor drinking a can of Coke or driving a BMW, appear to significantly influence consumers' perceptions of reality. These depictions affect viewers' notions about what the "real world" is like, including such issues as dating behavior, racial stereotypes, and occupational status.[48] Studies of the **cultivation hypothesis** focus on the media's ability to distort consumers' perceptions of reality. They show that heavy television viewers tend to overestimate how wealthy people are and the likelihood that they will be victims of a violent crime.[49]

The media also exaggerate or distort the frequency of behaviors such as drinking or smoking.[50] A study conducted by the National Partnership for Women and Families illustrates the divergence between life as shown on TV and what occurs in the real world. An analysis of two weeks of prime-time TV shows and movies shown on six broadcast networks revealed several gaps between reality and fantasy. Only 13 of 150 episodes showed a character dealing with stress caused by conflicts between the demands of a job and family. Only 26 of 820 adult TV characters had any caretaking responsibility for an adult relative (one in four U.S. workers actually does). Fourteen percent of adult TV characters are over 50, compared with 38 percent of the U.S. population. Characters shown taking time off for personal problems encountered no resistance from their bosses. In real life, 34 percent of workers find it difficult to get time off to deal with personal matters.[51] Then again, maybe this kind of escape from reality is why people are watching TV in the first place.

Product Placement

Traditionally, networks demanded that brand names be "greeked" (altered) before they could appear in a show, as when a Nokia cell phone was changed to "Nokio" on *Melrose Place*.[52] Nowadays, though, real products pop up everywhere. In many cases, these "plugs" are no accident. **Product placement** refers to the insertion of specific products and the use of brand names in movie and TV scripts. Perhaps the greatest product placement success story was Reese's Pieces; sales jumped by 65 percent after the candy appeared in the film *E.T.*[53]

The success of a product placement strategy in that movie opened the floodgates, and today most major releases are brimming with real products. Directors like to incorporate branded props because they contribute to the film's realism. When Stephen Spielberg did the movie *Minority Report* he used such brands as Nokia, Lexus, Pepsi, Guinness, Reebok, and American Express to lend familiarity to the plot's futuristic settings. Lexus even created a new sports car model called the Maglev just for the film.[54]

Some researchers claim that product placement can aid in consumer decision making because the familiarity of these props creates a sense of cultural belonging while generating feelings of emotional security.[55] One recent study found that consumers are more persuaded by embedded products when they are consistent with the plot.[56] On the other hand, a majority of consumers polled believe the line between advertising and programming is becoming too fuzzy and distracting (though as might be expected, concerns about this blurring of boundaries rose steadily with the age of respondents).[57] For better or worse, products are popping up everywhere:

- In an action series on the TNN cable network called *18 Wheels of Justice,* the Kenworth truck company spent nearly $1 million and also lent trucks to the show. In exchange, the series features multiple shots of the truck, mentions the company by name in the closing credits, and guarantees a minimum of six minutes of screen time in each episode. Although very few consumers are in the market for 18-wheel trucks, the company hopes that the series will improve the trucking industry's image.[59]

- Although IBM sells a lot more computers, Apples are seen in many more TV shows and movies such as *Mission Impossible* and *Independence Day.* Producers like to use the Apple because its image is more hip. But Apple will only let that happen if the brand is identified onscreen.[60]

- Philip Morris paid to place Marlboro cigarettes and signs in *Superman* movies and doled out $350,000 to have Lark cigarettes featured in the James Bond film *License to Kill.*[61]

- The hit CBS show *Survivor* portrayed the adventures of 16 people stranded on a desert island near Borneo for 39 days. They battled for a chance to wear Reeboks, drink Budweiser, and sleep in a Pontiac Aztec sport utility vehicle.[62]

Product placement has been an American phenomenon—until recently. Now, marketers in other countries are discovering the value of placing their brand messages wherever they can.[63] In France, cafes are turning tabletops into billboards for United Airlines, Swatch watches, and other companies. Although some patrons decry the invasion of such commercialism into the "sacred" French practice of lounging at bistros, the owner of a firm that is supplying the ads observes, "We want to make cafes more interesting places for people to visit."[64] *Sacre bleu!*

In China, product placement is emerging as a new way to get noticed. Most commercials on Chinese state-run TV play back-to-back in 10-minute segments, making it difficult for any one 30-second ad to attract attention. So, enterprising marketers are embedding product messages in the shows instead. A soap opera

Product placement refers to the insertion of specific products and/or the use of brand names in movies and TV scripts. The popular sitcom *Seinfeld* includes blatant references to numerous products, from Junior Mints and Kenny Rogers Fried Chicken to Snapple and Pez.

called *Love Talks* features such products as Maybelline lipstick, Motorola mobile phones, and Pond's Vaseline Intensive Care lotion.[65]

In India, the booming Bombay film industry (known as Bollywood) is discovering the potential of movies to expose viewers to brand names (Indian cinema attracts huge local audiences, especially in villages where television is not available). Coca-Cola paid to have its local soft drink, Thums Up, prominently featured in a Hindi-language remake of the Quentin Tarantino classic *Reservoir Dogs*. Just in case the audience misses the placements, in one scene just before bullets start flying a group of slickly dressed gangsters flashes each other the thumbs-up sign.[66]

Advergaming

In the video game *Cool Borders,* three characters ride past Butterfinger candy bar banners and wear Levi's jeans while attempting to beat opponents' times as recorded on Swatch watches. A Sony PlayStation game called Psybadek outfits its main characters in shoes and clothing from Vans. A Sony executive comments, "We live in a world of brands. We don't live in a world of generics. If a kid is bouncing a basketball in a video game, to us it makes sense that it should be a Spalding basketball."[67]

Products are popping up in video games wherever you turn. Even the latest online version of The Sims (see Chapter 6) now lets players purchase Big Macs from McDonald's kiosks.[68] Computer gaming isn't what it used to be. Not long ago, the typical players were scruffy teenage boys shooting at TV screens in their basements. But with the online gaming explosion of recent years, gamers have become a more sophisticated lot, and are now more representative of the general population. More women are participating, as well as older people and professionals. In fact, today over 41 percent of people who frequent gaming sites like GamesSpot, Candystand, and Pogo are women, and 43 percent are ages 25 to 49.[69]

As gaming goes mass market, many marketers are turning on to a new strategy called **advergaming**, where online games merge with interactive advertisements that let companies target specific types of consumers. It's estimated that revenue from advergaming will reach about $3/4 billion by 2006.[70] Why is this new medium so hot? For one thing, compared to a 30-second TV spot, advertisers can get viewers' attention for much longer: Players spend an average of 5 to 7 minutes on an advergame site. Also, the nature of the game and the products in it can be tailored to the profiles of different users. For example, strategy games can be directed to upscale, educated users, while action games can be geared to younger users.

Here are some other success stories that resulted from promotional deals struck between manufacturers and game developers:

- In Activision's new game *Street Hoops,* signs advertising Sprite appear on billboards and passing buses. In exchange, Sprite agreed to distribute 40 million to 50 million bottles and cans with *Street Hoops* logos.
- Activision featured Taco Bell signs and stores in *Tony Hawk's Pro Skater 2* for X Box.
- A shooting game called *Run Like Hell* lets players enhance their health by drinking virtual Bawls, a drink that in real life contains more than twice the caffeine of Coca-Cola.
- The Aston Martin Vanquish driven by James Bond will also star in a video game called *James Bond 007: NightFire.* Gamers embark on several missions while driving the sports car; at one point, it plunges off a ship's deck and is transformed into a submarine.[71]
- In a first for the music industry, the record label Island Def Jam announced in Spring 2003 that it will introduce new songs on a new video game rather than on

the radio. The goal is to lure young, male consumers into buying entire CDs when they are released to stores up to four months later. *Vendetta*, a wrestling game, will contain 12 Def Jam artists, including DMX, Scarface, Method Man, Ghostface Killah, and Ludacris, who will choke-hold and drop-kick their opponents around the ring. The games will allow players to take on the role of their favorite artists in wrestling matches, which will take place against the backdrop of upbeat new singles by each of the artists.[72]

■ THE DIFFUSION OF INNOVATIONS

An **innovation** is any product or service that consumers perceive to be new. Innovations may take the form of a clothing style (e.g., skirts for men); a new manufacturing technique (such as the ability to design your own running shoe at **customatix.com**); a new variation on an existing product (such as Parkay Fun Squeeze Colored Margarine that now comes in electric blue and shocking pink); a new way to deliver a product (such as ordering groceries online and having them delivered to your home by Peapod); or a new way to package a current product (such as Campbell's Soup at Hand Microwaveable Soup that comes in a travel mug).[73]

If an innovation is successful (most are not!), it spreads through the population. First it is bought or used by only a few people who decide to try something new. Then, more and more consumers decide to adopt it, until sometimes it seems that almost everyone has bought or tried the innovation. **Diffusion of innovations** refers to the process whereby a new product, service, or idea spreads through a population. The rate at which a product diffuses varies. For example, within 10 years after its introduction, cable TV was used by 40 percent of U.S. households, compact disks by 35 percent, answering machines by 25 percent, and color TVs by 20 percent. It took radio 30 years to reach 60 million users and TV 15 years to reach this number. In contrast, within 3 years 90 million were surfing the Web.[74]

Adopting Innovations

A consumer's adoption of an innovation resembles the decision-making sequence discussed in Chapter 9. The person moves through the stages of awareness, information search, evaluation, trial, and adoption. The relative importance of each stage may differ, depending on how much is already known about a product, as well as on cultural factors that may affect people's willingness to try new things.[75] A study of 11 European countries found that consumers in individualistic cultures are more innovative than consumers in collective cultures (see Chapter 16).[76] However, even within the same culture, not all people adopt an innovation at the same rate. Some do so quite rapidly, and others never do at all. Consumers can be placed into approximate categories based on their likelihood of adopting an innovation.

As Figure 17.3 shows, roughly one-sixth of the population (innovators and early adopters) are very quick to adopt new products, and one-sixth of the people (**laggards**) are very slow. The other two-thirds, so-called **late adopters**, are somewhere in the middle. These consumers are the mainstream public. They are interested in new things, but they do not want them to be *too* new. In some cases, people deliberately wait to adopt an innovation because they assume that its technological qualities will be improved or that its price will fall after it has been on the market awhile.[77] Keep in mind that the proportion of consumers falling into each category is an estimate; the actual size of each depends on such factors as the complexity of the product, its cost, and how much risk is associated with trying it.

■ **FIGURE 17.3** TYPES OF ADOPTERS

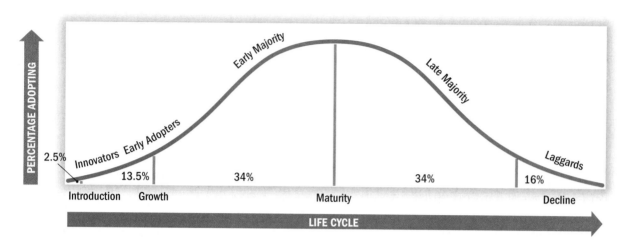

Even though **innovators** represent only about 2.5 percent of the population, marketers are always interested in identifying them. These are the brave souls who are always on the lookout for novel developments and will be the first to try a new offering. Just as generalized opinion leaders do not appear to exist (see Chapter 11), innovators tend to be category-specific as well. A person who is an innovator in one

A laggard.

area may even be a laggard in another. A gentleman who prides himself as being on the cutting edge of fashion may have no conception of new developments in recording technology—he may still stubbornly cling to his antique phonograph albums even as he searches for the latest avant-garde clothing styles in trendy boutiques. Despite this qualification, some generalizations can be offered regarding the profile of innovators.[78] Not surprisingly, for example, they tend to have more favorable attitudes toward taking risks. They also are likely to have higher educational and income levels, and to be socially active.

Early adopters share many of the same characteristics as innovators, but an important difference is their degree of concern for social acceptance, especially with regard to expressive products, such as clothing, cosmetics, and so on. Generally speaking, an early adopter is receptive to new styles because he or she is involved in the product category and values being in fashion. What appears on the surface to be a fairly high-risk adoption (e.g., wearing a skirt three inches above the knee when most people are wearing them below the knee) is actually not that risky. The style change has already been "field-tested" by innovators, who truly took the fashion risk. Early adopters are likely to be found in "fashion-forward" stores featuring the latest "hot" designers. In contrast, true innovators are more likely to be found in small boutiques featuring as-yet-unknown designers.

Behavioral Demands of Innovations

We can categorize innovations in terms of the degree to which they demand changes in behavior from adopters. Three major types of innovations have been identified, though these three categories are not absolutes. They refer, in a relative sense, to the amount of disruption or change they bring to people's lives.

A *continuous innovation* refers to a modification of an existing product, such as when General Mills introduced a Honey Nut version of Cheerios or Levi's promoted shrink-to-fit jeans. This type of change may be used to set one brand apart from its competitors. Most product innovations are of this type; that is, they are evolutionary rather than revolutionary. Small changes are made to position the product, add line extensions, or merely to alleviate consumer boredom.

Consumers may be lured to the new product, but adoption represents only minor changes in consumption habits because innovation perhaps adds to the product's convenience or to the range of choices available. A typewriter company, for example, many years ago modified the shape of its product to make it more "user friendly" to secretaries. One simple change was making the tops of the keys concave, a convention that is carried over on today's computer keyboards. The reason for the change was that secretaries had complained about the difficulty of typing with long fingernails on the flat surfaces.

A *dynamically continuous innovation* is a more pronounced change in an existing product, as represented by self-focusing 35-mm cameras or touch-tone telephones. These innovations have a modest impact on the way people do things, requiring some behavioral changes. When IBM introduced its Selectric typewriter, which uses a typing ball rather than individual keys, the new design permitted secretaries to instantly change the typeface of manuscripts by replacing one Selectric ball with another.

A *discontinuous innovation* creates major changes in the way we live. Major inventions, such as the airplane, the car, the computer, and the television have radically changed modern lifestyles. The personal computer has, in many cases, supplanted the typewriter, and it has created the phenomenon of "telecommuters" by allowing many consumers to work from their homes. Of course, the cycle continues, as new continuous innovations (e.g., new versions of software) are constantly being made for computers; dynamically continuous innovations such as the "mouse" and trackballs compete for adoption, and discontinuous innovations such as wristwatch personal computers start to appear in stores.

Marketing Opportunity

Innovators are a prize catch for marketers who want a heads-up on how their products will fare in the mass market. Indeed, some innovative companies understand the value of involving their most forward-thinking customers in business decisions before the final product is introduced. For example, more than 650,000 customers tested a beta version of Microsoft Windows 2000. Many were even prepared to pay Microsoft a fee to do this because working with the program would help them understand how it could create value for their own businesses. The value of the research and development investment by customers to Microsoft was estimated at more than $500 million. Similarly, Cisco gives its customers open access to its resources and systems so that they can solve the problems encountered by other customers.

This approach is more prevalent in high-tech industries, in which many businesses involve lead users in product development. A **lead user** is an involved, experienced customer who is very knowledgeable about the field. Indeed, it is not unusual for high-tech products to be initially thought of and even prototyped by lead users rather than manufacturers. These customers often experience problems or needs well in advance of others, so their solutions can be applied to other markets. According to one estimate, users rather than manufacturers developed 70 percent of the innovations in the chemical industry! The value of this approach for consumer goods is obvious but has yet to be widely applied.[79]

Prerequisites for Successful Adoption

Regardless of how much behavioral change is demanded by an innovation, several factors are desirable for a new product to succeed.[80]

Compatibility. The innovation should be compatible with consumers' lifestyles. As one illustration shows, a manufacturer of personal care products tried unsuccessfully several years ago to introduce a cream hair remover for men as a substitute for razors and shaving cream. This formulation was similar to what many women use to remove hair from their legs. Although the product was simple and convenient to use, it failed because men were not interested in a product they perceived to be too feminine and thus threatening to their masculine self-concepts.

Trialability. Because high perceived risk accompanies an unknown product, people are more likely to adopt an innovation if they can experiment with it prior to making a commitment. To reduce this risk, companies often choose the expensive strategy of distributing free "trial-size" samples of new products.

Complexity. The product should be low in complexity. All things equal, a product that is easier to understand and use will be chosen over its competitors. This strategy requires less effort from the consumer, and it also lowers perceived risk. Manufacturers of videocassette recorders, for example, have put a lot of effort into simplifying VCR usage (e.g., on-screen programming) to encourage adoption.

Observability. Innovations that are easily observable are more likely to spread because this quality makes it more likely that other potential adopters will become aware of its existence. The rapid proliferation of fanny packs (pouches worn around the waist in lieu of wallets or purses) was due to their high visibility. It was easy for others to see the convenience offered by this alternative.

Relative Advantage. Most importantly, the product should offer relative advantage over other alternatives. The consumer must believe that its use will provide a benefit other products cannot offer. For example, a product called the Bugchaser is a wristband containing insect repellent. Mothers with young children liked it because it is nontoxic and nonstaining—clear advantages over existing alternatives. In contrast, the Crazy Blue Air Freshener, which was added to windshield wiper fluid and emitted a fragrance when the wipers were turned on, fizzled: People didn't see the need for the product and felt there were simpler ways to freshen their cars if they cared to.

■ THE FASHION SYSTEM

The **fashion system** consists of all those people and organizations involved in creating symbolic meanings and transferring these meanings to cultural goods. Although people tend to equate fashion with clothing, it is important to keep in mind that fashion processes affect *all* types of cultural phenomena, including music, art, architecture, and even science (i.e., certain research topics and scientists are "hot" at any point in time). Even business practices are subject to the fashion process; they evolve and change depending on which management techniques are "in vogue," such as total quality management or just-in-time inventory control.

Fashion can be thought of as a *code*, or language, that helps us to decipher these meanings.[81] Unlike a language, however, fashion is *context-dependent*. Different consumers can interpret the same item differently.[82] In semiotic terms (see Chapter 2), the meaning of fashion products often is *undercoded*. There is no one precise meaning, but rather plenty of room for interpretation among perceivers.

At the outset, it may be helpful to distinguish among some confusing terms. **Fashion** is the process of social diffusion by which a new style is adopted by some group(s) of consumers. In contrast, a *fashion* (or style) refers to a particular combination of attributes. And, to be *in fashion* means that some reference group positively evaluates this combination. Thus, the term *Danish Modern* refers to particular characteristics of furniture design (i.e., a fashion in interior design); it does not necessarily imply that Danish Modern is a fashion that consumers currently desire.[83]

Cultural Categories

The meaning that does get imparted to products reflects underlying **cultural categories** that correspond to the basic ways we characterize the world.[84] Our culture makes distinctions between different times, between leisure and work, and between genders. The fashion system provides us with products that signify these categories. For example, the apparel industry gives us clothing to denote certain times (e.g., evening wear, resort wear), differentiates between leisure clothes and work clothes, and promotes masculine and feminine styles.

These cultural categories affect many different kinds of products. As a result, it is common to find that dominant aspects of a culture at any point in time tend to be reflected in the design and marketing of a wide range of items. This concept is a bit hard to grasp, because on the surface a clothing style, say, has little in common with a piece of furniture or a car. However, an overriding concern with a value such as achievement or environmentalism can determine the types of products likely to be accepted by consumers at any point in time. These underlying themes then surface in a product's design. A few examples of this interdependence will help to demonstrate how a dominant fashion *motif* reverberates across industries.

- Costumes worn by political figures or movie and rock stars can affect the fortunes of the apparel and accessory industries. A movie appearance by actor Clark Gable without a T-shirt (unusual at that time) dealt a severe setback to the men's apparel industry, while Jackie Kennedy's famous "pillbox hat" prompted a rush for hats by women in the 1960s. Other cross-category effects include the craze for ripped sweatshirts instigated by the movie *Flashdance*, a boost for cowboy boots from the movie *Urban Cowboy*, and singer Madonna's transformation of lingerie as an acceptable outerwear clothing style.
- The Louvre in Paris was remodeled to include a controversial glass pyramid at the entrance designed by the architect I. M. Pei. Shortly thereafter, several designers unveiled pyramid-shaped clothing at Paris fashion shows.[85]
- In the 1950s and 1960s, much of America was preoccupied with science and technology. This concern with "space-age" mastery was fueled by the Russians' launching of the Sputnik satellite, which prompted fears that America was falling behind in the technology race. The theme of technical mastery of nature and of futuristic design became a motif that cropped up in many aspects of American popular culture—from car designs with prominent tail fins to high-tech kitchen styles.

Remember that creative subsystems within a culture production system attempt to anticipate the tastes of the buying public. Despite their unique talents, members of this subsystem are also members of mass culture. Cultural gatekeepers are drawing from a common set of cultural categories, so it's not that surprising that their choices often converge—even though they compete against one another to offer the consumer something new or different. The process by which certain

A cultural emphasis on science in the 1950s and 1960s affected product designs, as seen in the design of automobiles with large tail fins (to resemble rockets).

symbolic alternatives are chosen over others is termed **collective selection**.[86] As with the creative subsystem, members of the managerial and communications subsystems also seem to develop a common frame of mind. Although products within each category must compete for acceptance in the marketplace, they can usually be characterized by their adherence to a dominant theme or motif—be it "The Western Look," "New Wave," "Danish Modern," or "Nouvelle Cuisine."

Behavioral Science Perspectives on Fashion

Fashion is a very complex process that operates on many levels. At one extreme, it is a societal phenomenon affecting many people simultaneously. At the other, it exerts a very personal effect on individual behavior. A consumer's purchase decisions are often motivated by his or her desire to be in fashion. Fashion products also are aesthetic objects, and their origins are rooted in art and history. For this reason, there are many perspectives on the origin and diffusion of fashion. Although these cannot be described in detail here, we can summarize some major approaches.[87]

Psychological Models of Fashion

Many psychological factors help to explain why people are motivated to be in fashion. These include conformity, variety seeking, personal creativity, and sexual attraction. For example, many consumers seem to have a "need for uniqueness": They want to be different (though not necessarily *too* different!).[88] For this reason, people often conform to the basic outlines of a fashion, but try to improvise and make a personal statement within these general guidelines.

One of the earliest theories of fashion proposed that "shifting *erogenous zones*" (sexually arousing areas of the body) accounted for fashion changes, and that different zones become the object of interest because they reflect societal trends. J. C. Flugel, a disciple of Freud, proposed in the 1920s that sexually charged areas

Some people argue that consumers are at the mercy of fashion designers. What do you think?

wax and wane in order to maintain interest, and that clothing styles change to highlight or hide these parts. For example, it was common for Renaissance-era women to drape their abdomens in fabrics in order to give a swollen appearance—successful childbearing was a priority in the disease-ridden fourteenth and fifteenth centuries. Now, some suggest that the current prevalence of the exposed midriff reflects the premium our society places on fitness.[89] It's important to note, by the way, that until very recently the study of fashion focused almost exclusively on its impact on women. Hopefully, this concentration will broaden as scholars and practitioners begin to appreciate that men are affected by many of the same fashion influences.

Economic Models of Fashion

Economists approach fashion in terms of the model of supply and demand. Items that are in limited supply have high value, whereas those readily available are less desirable. Rare items command respect and prestige.

Veblen's notion of conspicuous consumption proposed that the wealthy consume to display their prosperity, for example by wearing expensive (and at times impractical) clothing. As noted in Chapter 13, this approach is somewhat outdated; upscale consumers often engage in *parody display* where they deliberately adopt formerly low-status or inexpensive products and stores, such as jeans and Wal-Mart. Other factors also influence the demand curve for fashion-related products. These include a *prestige–exclusivity effect,* in which high prices still create high demand, and a *snob effect,* whereby lower prices actually reduce demand ("If it's that cheap, it can't be any good").[90]

This ad for Maidenform illustrates that fashions have accentuated different parts of the female anatomy throughout history.

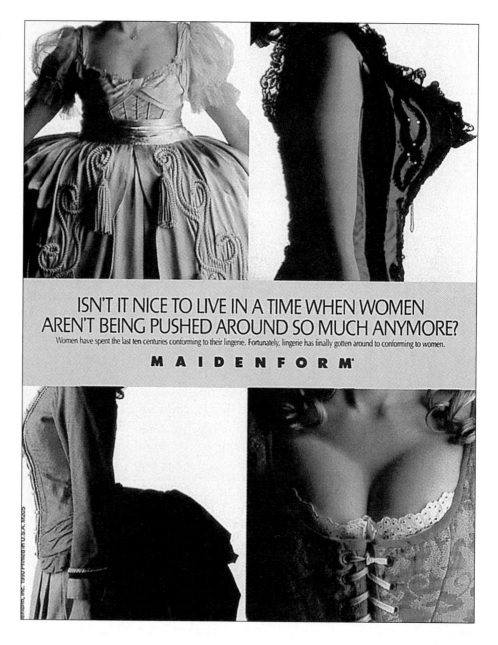

Sociological Models of Fashion

The collective selection model discussed previously is an example of a sociological approach to fashion. This perspective focuses on the initial adoption of a fashion (idea, style, etc.) by a subculture and its subsequent diffusion into society as a whole. Such diffusion often begins with youth subcultures like the hip-hop segment. Another current example is the integration of Goth culture into the mainstream. This fashion started as a mode of expressing rebellion by young outcasts who admire nineteenth-century romantics and who defied conventional styles with their black clothing (often including over-the-top fashion statements like Count Dracula capes, fishnet stockings, studded collars, and black lipstick) and punk music from bands like Siouxsie & the Banshees and Bauhaus. Today, Virgin Megastores sells vampire-girl lunchboxes, mall outlets sell tons of clunky cross jewelry and black lace. You can find a T-shirt that looks like a corset at Kmart. At the Hot Topic Web site, teen surfers can buy a "Multi-Ring Choker." Hard-core Goths are not amused, but hey, that's fashion for you.[91]

Trickle-down theory, first proposed in 1904 by Georg Simmel, has been one of the most influential approaches to understanding fashion. It states that there are two conflicting forces that drive fashion change. First, subordinate groups try to adopt the status symbols of the groups above them as they attempt to climb up the ladder of social mobility. Dominant styles thus originate with the upper classes and trickle down to those below.

However, this is where the second force kicks in: Those people in the superordinate groups are constantly looking below them on the ladder to ensure that they are not imitated. They respond to the attempts of lower classes to "impersonate" them by adopting even newer fashions. These two processes create a self-perpetuating cycle of change—the machine that drives fashion.[92] The integration of hip-hop phrases into our vocabulary illustrates how people who set fashions often resist their adoption by the mainstream. The street elite shunned some slang terms like "bad," fresh, and "jiggy," once they became too mainstream. The rap community even held a funeral (with a eulogy delivered by Rev. Al Sharpton), for the word "Def" once it was included in the *Oxford English Dictionary*.[93]

Trickle-down theory was quite useful for understanding the process of fashion changes when applied to a society with a stable class structure, which permitted the easy identification of lower- versus upper-class consumers. This task is not so easy in modern times. In contemporary Western society, we must modify this approach to account for new developments in mass culture:[94]

- A perspective based on class structure cannot account for the wide range of styles that are simultaneously made available in our society. Modern consumers have a much greater degree of individualized choice than those in the past because of advances in technology. Just as an adolescent like Alex is almost instantly aware of the latest style trends by watching MTV, elite fashion has been largely replaced by *mass fashion* because media exposure permits many groups to become aware of a style at the same time.
- Consumers tend to be more influenced by opinion leaders who are similar to them. As a result each social group has its own fashion innovators who determine fashion trends. It is often more accurate to speak of a *trickle-across effect*, whereby fashions diffuse horizontally among members of the same social group.[95]

Grassroots innovators typically are people who lack prestige in the dominant culture such as urban youth who are the drivers behind the hip-hop craze.

● Finally, current fashions often originate with the lower classes and *trickle up*. Grassroots innovators typically are people who lack prestige in the dominant culture (e.g., urban youth). Because they are less concerned with maintaining the status quo, they are free to innovate and take risks.[96]

A "Medical" Model of Fashion

For years and years, the lowly Hush Puppy was a shoe for nerds. Suddenly—almost overnight—the shoe became a chic fashion statement even though the company did nothing to promote this image. Why did this style diffuse through the population so quickly? **Meme theory** explains this process using a medical metaphor. A *meme* is an idea or product that enters the consciousness of people over time—examples include tunes, catch-phrases ("Is that your final answer?"), or styles such as the Hush Puppy. In this view, memes spread among consumers in a geometric progression just as a virus starts off small and steadily infects increasing numbers of people until it becomes an epidemic. Memes "leap" from brain to brain via a process of imitation.

The memes that survive tend to be distinctive and memorable, and the hardiest ones often combine aspects of prior memes. For example, the *Star Wars* movies evoked prior memes relating to Arthurian legend, religion, heroic youth, and 1930s adventure serials. Indeed, George Lucas studied comparative religion and mythology as he prepared his first draft of the *Star Wars* saga, "The Story of Mace Windu."[97]

The diffusion of many products in addition to Hush Puppies seems to follow the same basic path. A few people initially use the product, but change happens in a hurry when the process reaches the moment of critical mass—which one author has called the **tipping point**. For example, Sharp introduced the first low-priced fax machine in 1984 and sold about 80,000 in that year. There was a slow climb in the number of users for the next three years. Then, suddenly in 1987 enough people had fax machines that it made sense for everyone to have one—Sharp sold a million units that year. Cell phones followed a similar trajectory.[98]

Cycles of Fashion Adoption

In the early 1980s, Cabbage Patch dolls were all the rage among American children. Faced with a limited supply of the product, some retailers reported near-riots among adults as they tried desperately to buy the dolls for their children. A Milwaukee disc jockey jokingly announced that people should bring catcher's mitts to a local stadium because 2,000 dolls were going to be dropped from an airplane. Listeners were instructed to hold up their American Express cards so their numbers could be aerially photographed. More than two dozen anxious parents apparently didn't get the joke; they showed up in subzero weather, mitts in hand.[99]

■ **FIGURE 17.4** A NORMAL FASHION CYCLE

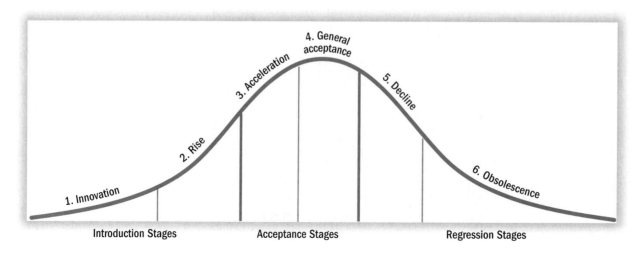

Although the Cabbage Patch craze lasted for a couple of seasons, it eventually died out, and consumers moved on to other things, such as Teenage Mutant Ninja Turtles, which grossed more than $600 million in 1989.[100] The Mighty Morphin Power Rangers eventually replaced the Turtles, and Beanie Babies and Giga Pets in turn deposed them before the invasion of Pokémon.[101] What will be next?

Fashion Life Cycles

Although the longevity of a particular style can range from a month to a century, fashions tend to flow in a predictable sequence. The fashion life cycle is quite similar to the more familiar product life cycle. An item or idea progresses through basic stages from birth to death, as shown in Figure 17.4.

The diffusion process discussed earlier in this chapter is intimately related to the popularity of fashion-related items. To illustrate how this process works, consider how the **fashion acceptance cycle** works in the popular music business. In the *introduction stage,* a song is heard by a small number of music innovators. It may be played in clubs or on "cutting-edge" college radio stations, which is how "grunge rock" groups such as Nirvana got their start. During the *acceptance stage,* the song enjoys increased social visibility and acceptance by large segments of the population. A record may get wide airplay on Top 40 stations, steadily rising up the charts "like a bullet."

In the *regression stage,* the song reaches a state of social saturation as it becomes overused, and eventually it sinks into decline and obsolescence as new songs rise to take its place. A hit record may be played once an hour on a Top 40 station for several weeks. At some point, though, people tend to get sick of it and focus their attention on newer releases. The former hit record eventually winds up in the discount rack at the local record store.

Figure 17.5 illustrates that fashions are characterized by slow acceptance at the beginning, which (if the fashion is to "make it") rapidly accelerates, peaks, and then tapers off. We can identify different classes of fashion by considering the relative length of the fashion acceptance cycle. Many fashions exhibit a moderate cycle, taking several years to work their way through the stages of acceptance and decline; others are extremely long-lived or short-lived.

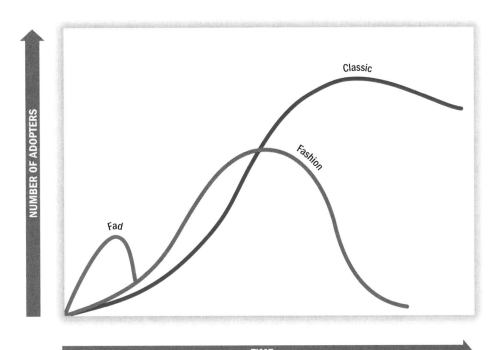

■ **FIGURE 17.5**
COMPARISON OF THE ACCEPTANCE CYCLES OF FADS, FASHIONS, AND CLASSICS

■ FIGURE 17.6 THE BEHAVIOR OF FADS

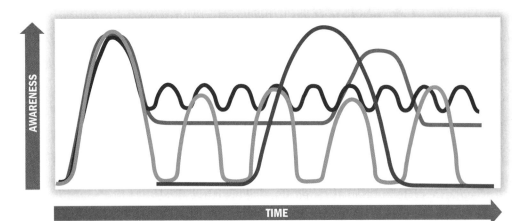

TRUE FAD	CYCLICAL FAD	FAD-TO-FRANCHISE	GENERATIONAL FAD
Life Span: One year or less	**Life Span:** One year or less at each spike	**Life Span:** One to five years	**Life Span:** One year or less at each spike
Top Sources: Toy/ novelty, TV, dance/ music, fashion	**Top Sources:** Toy/ novelty	**Top Sources:** Toy/ novelty, publishing, movies	**Top Sources:** Toy/ novelty
Demographics: All	**Demographics:** All	**Demographics:** All	**Demographics:** Children and nostalgic adults
Example: Pet Rock	**Example:** Yo-yos	**Example:** Barbies	**Example:** Trolls

A **classic** is a fashion with an extremely long acceptance cycle. It is in a sense "antifashion" because it guarantees stability and low risk to the purchaser for a long period of time. Keds sneakers, introduced in 1917, have been successful because they appeal to those who are turned off by the high fashion, trendy appeal of L. A. Gear or Reebok. When consumers in focus groups were asked to imagine what kind of building Keds would be, a common response was a country house with a white picket fence. In other words, the shoes are seen as a stable, classic product. In contrast, people often described Nikes as steel-and-glass skyscrapers, reflecting their more modern image.[102]

A **fad** is a very short-lived fashion. Relatively few people usually adopt a fad product. Adopters may all belong to a common subculture, and the fad "trickles across" members but rarely breaks out of that specific group. Some successful fad products include hula hoops, snap bracelets, and pet rocks; to learn more about these and other "must have" products, visit *badfads.com*. Figure 17.6 illustrates some types of fads have longer life spans than others.

Streaking was a fad that hit college campuses in the mid-1970s. This term referred to students running nude through classrooms, cafeterias, dorms, and sports venues. Although the practice quickly spread across many campuses, it was primarily restricted to college settings. Streaking highlights several of a fad's "naked truths:"[103]

● The fad is nonutilitarian; it does not perform any meaningful function.
● The fad is often adopted on impulse; people do not undergo stages of rational decision making before joining in.
● The fad diffuses rapidly, gains quick acceptance, and is short-lived.

Fad or Trend?

In 1988, a company called Clearly Canadian began testing a clear soft drink, and during the next few years others jumped on board. Colgate-Palmolive spent $6 million developing a clear version of Palmolive dishwashing liquid. By 1992, Colgate was selling clear soap, Coors introduced a clear malt beverage called Zima, and consumers

You always come back to the basics. JIM BEAM

This Jim Beam ad illustrates the cyclical nature of fashion.

could even choose clear gasoline for their cars. Clear products were so ubiquitous that they were spoofed on *Saturday Night Live* in a fake commercial for Crystal Gravy: "You can see your meat!" It was clear that the beginning of the end was in sight for this fad. The comments of one 25-year-old research participant in a study about clear drinks sums up the problem: "When I first started drinking them, I thought they were interesting. But once it became a fad I thought, 'this isn't cool anymore.'"[104]

The first company to identify a trend and act on it has an advantage, whether the firm is Starbucks (gourmet coffee), Nabisco (Snackwells low-fat cookies and crackers), or Taco Bell (value pricing). Nothing is certain, but some guidelines help to predict whether the innovation will endure as a long-term trend or it's just a fad destined to go the way of hula-hoops, Pet Rocks, and Wally Wallwalkers:[105]

● Does it fit with basic lifestyle changes? If a new hairstyle is hard to care for, this innovation will not be consistent with women's increasing time demands. On the other hand, the movement to shorter-term vacations is more likely to last, because this innovation makes trip planning easier for harried consumers who want to get away for a few days at a time.

- What are the benefits? The switch to poultry and fish from beef came about because these meats are healthier, so a real benefit is evident.
- Can it be personalized? Enduring trends tend to accommodate a desire for individuality, whereas styles such as Mohawk haircuts or the grunge look are inflexible and don't allow people to express themselves.
- Is it a trend or a side effect? An increased interest in exercise is part of a basic trend toward health consciousness, although the specific form of exercise that is "in" at any given time will vary (e.g., low-impact aerobics versus in-line skating).
- What other changes have occurred in the market? Sometimes *carryover effects* influence the popularity of related products. The miniskirt fad in the 1960s caused growth in the hosiery market, as sales of pantyhose and tights rose from 10 percent of this product category to more than 80 percent in two years. Now, sales of these items are declining due to today's more casual emphasis in dressing.
- Who has adopted the change? If working mothers, baby boomers, or some other important market segment don't adopt the innovation, it is not likely to become a trend.

■ TRANSFERRING PRODUCT MEANINGS TO OTHER CULTURES

Innovations know no geographic boundaries; in modern times they travel across oceans and deserts with blinding speed. Just as Marco Polo brought noodles from China and colonial settlers introduced Europeans to the "joys" of tobacco, today multinational firms are constantly working to conquer new markets by convincing legions of foreign consumers to desire what they make.

As if understanding the dynamics of one's culture weren't hard enough, these issues get even more complicated when we take on the daunting task of learning about the practices of other cultures. The consequences of ignoring cultural sensitivities can be costly. Think about problems a prominent multinational company like McDonald's encounters as it expands globally:

- During the 1994 soccer World Cup, the fast-food giant made the mistake of reprinting the Saudi Arabian flag, which includes sacred words from the Koran, on disposable packaging used in promotions. Muslims around the world protested this borrowing of sacred imagery and the company had to scramble to correct its mistake.[106]
- In 2002, McDonald's agreed to donate $10 million to Hindu and other groups as partial settlement of litigation involving its mislabeling of French fries and hash browns as being vegetarian (they were cooked in oil containing meat residues).[107]
- Also in 2002, the company abruptly cancelled its plans to introduce a new sandwich called the McAfrika in its Norwegian restaurants. The CEO of McDonald's in Norway acknowledged on national television that introducing this menu item at a time of growing famine in Africa was "coincidental and unfortunate."[108]

In this section, we'll consider some of the issues confronting consumer researchers who are seeking to understand the cultural dynamics of other countries. We'll also consider the consequences of the "Americanization" of global culture. As U.S. (and to some extent, Western European) marketers continue to export Western popular culture to a globe full of increasingly affluent consumers, many are eagerly waiting to replace their traditional products and practices with the likes of McDonald's, Levi's, and MTV. But, as we'll also see, there are plenty of obstacles to success for multinational firms.

Think Globally, Act Locally

As corporations compete in many markets around the world, the debate intensifies regarding the necessity of developing separate marketing plans for each culture versus crafting a single plan that can be implemented everywhere. Let's briefly consider each viewpoint.

Adopt a Standardized Strategy

Starbucks is becoming a household name in Japan (where it is pronounced STAH-buks-zu). Like their American counterparts, local outlets feature comfortable sofas; hip-hop and reggae tunes play in the background. The idea of hanging out in a coffee shop knocking back an oversized gourmet coffee is new to most Japanese, who are accustomed to sipping tea from tiny cups in dimly lit shops. Until Starbucks arrived, locals who did drink coffee associated it with a weak version called "American blend," which was introduced by U.S. soldiers when they arrived after World War II. Starbucks became an instant hit, and now there are well over 300 outlets buzzing with Japanese customers. In addition to the cachet associated with the chain, unlike most Japanese coffee shops (called *kisaten*), Starbucks does not allow smoking. This policy attracts young women, who do not smoke nearly as much as Japanese men.[109]

Starbucks is succeeding by exporting its recipe for success around the world. The company continues to confound local experts by bringing its version of the coffee experience to local cultures that (unlike Japan) have a long history of coffee snobbery. It is opening stores in San Juan and Mexico as part of a push into Latin America, where *cafe con leche* is part of the culture.[110] And talk about a brash move: Now Starbucks is even opening in Austria, which already boasts one coffeehouse for every 530 citizens. These people take their coffee seriously. Again, although some aficionados who are used to ordering their coffee from waiters and drinking it out of china cups turned up their noses at this American intrusion, so far the new Starbucks stores are thriving.[111]

Proponents of a standardized marketing strategy argue that many cultures, especially those of industrialized countries, have become so homogenized that the same approach will work throughout the world. By developing one approach for multiple markets, a company can benefit from economies of scale because it does not have to incur the substantial time and expense of developing a separate strategy for each culture.[112] This viewpoint represents an **etic perspective**, which focuses on commonalities across cultures. An etic approach to a culture is objective and analytical; it reflects impressions of a culture as viewed by outsiders.

Adopt a Localized Strategy

Visitors to the new Walt Disney Studios theme park at Disneyland Paris won't be treated to the voices of American movie stars narrating their guided tours. Instead, European actors like Jeremy Irons, Isabella Rossellini, and Nastassja Kinski will provide commentary—in their native tongues. Disney learned the hard way about the importance of being sensitive to local cultures after it opened its Euro Disney Park in 1992. The company got slammed for creating an entertainment venue that recreated its American locations without catering to local customs (such as serving wine with meals). Visitors to Euro Disney from many countries took offense, even at what seem to be small slights. For example, initially the park only sold a French sausage, which drew complaints from Germans, Italians, and others who believed their own local version to be superior. Euro Disney's CEO explains, "When we first launched there was the belief that it was enough to be Disney. Now we realize that our guests need to be welcomed on the basis of their own culture and travel habits."[113]

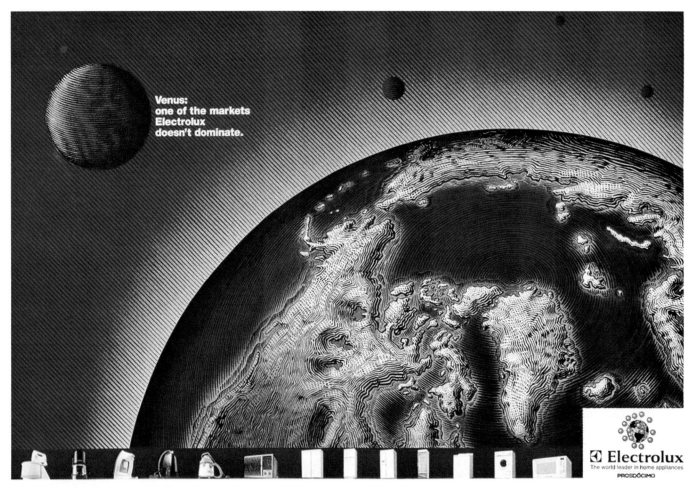

**Venus:
one of the markets
Electrolux
doesn't dominate.**

Electrolux
The world leader in home appliances
PROSDÓCIMO

Globalization has become an integral part of the marketing strategy of many, if not most, major corporations.

Disney's experience supports the view of marketers who endorse an **emic perspective**, which stresses variations across cultures. They feel that each culture is unique, with its own value system, conventions, and regulations. This perspective argues that each country has a *national character*, a distinctive set of behavior and personality characteristics.[114] An effective strategy must be tailored to the sensibilities and needs of each specific culture. An emic approach to a culture is subjective and experiential; it attempts to explain a culture as insiders experience it.

This perspective also reminds us that the downside to crafting a consistent global brand image by ensuring that stores and products look the same in every location can fuel consumers' desires for unique offerings. European fashion houses like Louis Vuitton and Fendi are encountering this craving for uniqueness, as shoppers begin to rebel against the cookie-cutter sameness of luxury products in every market. In the past, these megalabels opened stores around the world carrying almost identical merchandise, but now they are shifting gears as they try to offer more of a mixture of items designed by local artisans. According to the creative director of Prada, "Taste has been standardized by globalization, but there is a trend to rediscover local cultural values, to uncover new stimuli in different cities and in different contexts."[115]

Sometimes this strategy involves modifying a product or the way it is positioned to make it acceptable to local tastes. For example, the Chinese beer Tsingtao is trying to break into the Taiwan market by airing a commercial featuring happy people kneeling on tatami mats while a woman in a kimono sings a traditional

JCDecaux, a French advertising agency, specializes in "street furniture" like these kiosks, newsstands, and public toilets. They represent an emic perspective because each is designed to reflect the local culture.

Japanese tune in Taiwanese dialect. This ad would never be accepted in Tsingtao's home market, where there is strong historical hostility toward Japan. In Taiwan, however, many associate Japanese culture with high status.[116]

In some cases, consumers in one place simply do not like some products that are popular elsewhere. Snapple failed in Japan because consumers were turned off by the drink's cloudy appearance and the pulp floating in the bottles. Similarly, Frito-Lay stopped selling Ruffles potato chips (too salty) and Cheetos (the Japanese didn't appreciate having their fingers turn orange after eating a handful).[117] Cheetos are made in China, but the local version doesn't contain any cheese, which is not a staple of the Chinese diet. Instead, local flavors are available in varieties like Savory American Cream and Japanese Steak.[118]

Adapting a local product to a broader market is a real challenge, but it can be done. For example, an entrepreneur in the Philippines is successfully selling a traditional working-class delicacy called *balut* to the middle class by developing a brand name, standardized outlets, and gourmet sauces to go with it. By the way, this dish is made from duck embryos—Filipino men like to slurp them straight from the egg (feathers, beaks, and all) because they are reputed to enhance sexual stamina. The owner boasts that "Balut is the local Viagra, and we're repackaging it for a new generation."[119] Fries with that?

Cultural Differences Relevant to Marketers

So, which perspective is correct—the emic or the etic? Perhaps it will be helpful to consider some of the ways cultures vary in terms of their product preferences and norms regarding what types of products are appropriate or desirable.

Given the sizeable variations in tastes within the United States alone, it is hardly surprising that people around the world have developed their own unique preferences. Panasonic touted the fact that its rice cooker kept the food from getting too crisp—until the company learned that this is actually a desired attribute in the Middle East. Unlike Americans, Europeans favor dark chocolate over milk chocolate, which they regard as suitable only for children. Sara Lee sells its pound cake with chocolate chips in the United States, raisins in Australia, and coconuts in Hong Kong. Crocodile handbags are popular in Asia and Europe, but not in the United States.[120]

Marketers must be aware of a culture's norms regarding sensitive topics such as taboos and sexuality. Opals signify bad luck to the British, whereas hunting dog or pig emblems are offensive to Muslims. The Japanese are superstitious about the number four. *Shi,* the word for four, is also the word for death. For this reason, Tiffany sells glassware and china in sets of five in Japan.

The language barrier is one obvious problem confronting marketers who wish to break into foreign markets. Travelers abroad commonly encounter signs in tortured English such as a note to guests at a Tokyo hotel saying, "You are invited to take advantage of the chambermaid," a notice at a hotel in Acapulco reassuring people that "The manager has personally passed all the water served here," or a dry cleaner in Majorca who urged passing customers to "drop your pants here for best results." And local product names often raise eyebrows to visiting Americans, who may be surprised to stumble on a Japanese coffee creamer called Creap, a Mexican bread named Bimbo, or even a Scandinavian product that unfreezes car locks called Super Piss.

Chapter 14 noted some gaffes made by U.S. marketers when advertising to ethnic groups in their own country. Imagine how these mistakes are compounded outside of the United States! One technique that is used to avoid this problem is *back-translation,* in which a different interpreter retranslates a translated ad back into its original language to catch errors. Some specific translation obstacles that have been encountered around the world include the following:[121]

- Electrolux vacuum cleaners were marketed in the United States by the Scandinavian manufacturer with the slogan: "Nothing sucks like an Electrolux."
- Colgate introduced a toothpaste in France called Cue, which also happens to be the name of a well-known porn magazine.
- When Parker marketed a ballpoint pen in Mexico, its ads were supposed to say, "It won't leak in your pocket and embarrass you." The translation actually said "It won't leak in your pocket and make you pregnant."
- Fresca (a soft drink) is Mexican slang for lesbian.
- Ford had several problems in Spanish markets. The company discovered that a truck model it called Fiera means "ugly old woman" in Spanish. Its Caliente model, sold in Mexico, is slang for a streetwalker. In Brazil, Pinto is a slang term meaning "small male appendage."
- When Rolls-Royce introduced its Silver Mist model in Germany, it found that the word "mist" translates as excrement. Similarly, Sunbeam's hair curling iron,

called the Mist-Stick, translates as manure wand. To add insult to injury, Vicks is German slang for sexual intercourse, so the company had to change its name to Wicks in this market.

Does Global Marketing Work?

So, after briefly considering some of the many differences one encounters across cultures, what's the verdict? Does global marketing work? Perhaps the more appropriate question is, "*When* does it work?"

Although the argument for a homogenous world culture is appealing in principle, in practice it has met with mixed results. One reason for the failure of global marketing is that consumers in different countries have different conventions and customs, so they simply do not use products the same way. Kellogg, for example, discovered that in Brazil big breakfasts are not traditional—cereal is more commonly eaten as a dry snack.

In fact, significant cultural differences can even show up within the same country: Advertisers in Canada know that when they target consumers in French-speaking Quebec their messages must be much different from those addressed to their fellow countrymen who live in English-speaking regions. Ads in Montreal tend to be a lot racier than those in Toronto, reflecting differences in attitudes toward sexuality between consumers with French versus British roots.[122]

Some large corporations such as Coca-Cola have been successful in crafting a single, international image. Still, even the soft drink giant must make minor modifications to the way it presents itself in each culture. Although Coke commercials are largely standardized, local agencies are permitted to edit them to highlight close-ups of local faces.[123] To maximize the chances of success for these multicultural efforts, marketers must locate consumers in different countries who nonetheless share a common worldview. This is more likely to be the case among people whose frame of reference is relatively more international or cosmopolitan, or who receive much of their information about the world from sources that incorporate a world-wide perspective.

Who is likely to fall into this category? Two consumer segments are particularly good candidates: (1) affluent people who are "global citizens" and who are exposed to ideas from around the world through their travels, business contacts, and media experiences; and (2) young people whose tastes in music and fashion are strongly influenced by MTV and other media that broadcast many of the same images to multiple countries. For example, viewers of MTV Europe in Rome or Zurich can check out the same "buzz clips" as their counterparts in London or Luxembourg.[124]

■ THE DIFFUSION OF CONSUMER CULTURE

Coca-Cola is the drink of choice among young people in Asian countries, and McDonald's is the favorite restaurant.[125] The National Basketball Association sells $500 million of licensed merchandise every year *outside* of the United States.[126] Walk the streets of Lisbon or Buenos Aires, and the sight of Nike hats, GAP T-shirts, and Levi's jeans will accost you at every turn. The allure of consumer culture has spread throughout the world.

However, it's not just about exporting American culture. In a global society, people are quick to borrow from any culture they admire. For example, the cultural scene in Japan influences many Koreans because they believe the Japanese to be sophisticated consumers. Japanese rock bands are more popular in Korea than Korean bands, and shoppers eagerly snap up other exports such as comic books,

Marketing Pitfall

Increasingly, multinational companies are searching for local products that they can extend into global brands. Sometimes, however, they encounter local opposition from those who fear these marketing efforts will dilute the product's national character. That's what is happening to Unilever in Finland. The company wants to turn a cherished local mustard called Turun Sinappi into a global phenomenon by developing new packaging, advertising, and relocating production facilities to Sweden. Organized opposition to this move is being led by members of the "Keep Turun Sinappi Finnish" campaign who insist that the 200-year-old mustard recipe remain exclusively in Finland. More than 200,000 Finns, including 90 percent of the members of the Finnish food, beverages, and consumer products union, signed a petition demanding that Unilever abandon its plans to sell the mustard outside of Finland.[137]

fashion magazines, and game shows. A Korean researcher explains, "Culture is like water. It flows from stronger nations to weaker ones. People tend to idolize countries that are wealthier, freer, and more advanced, and in Asia that country is Japan."[127]

I'd Like to Buy the World a Coke . . .

The West (and especially the United States) is a net exporter of popular culture. Many consumers have learned to equate Western lifestyles in general and the English language in particular with modernization and sophistication, and many American brands are slowly but surely insinuating themselves into local cultures. Indeed, a survey conducted by a marketing research firm in Beijing found that nearly half of all children under 12 think McDonald's is a domestic Chinese brand![128]

Despite the proliferation of American pop culture around the world, there are signs that this invasion is slowing. American TV shows that used to air at prime time on European and Asian channels increasingly occupy fringe time slots as more local programming like the popular German show *The Tunnel* (about escapees from East Germany to West Germany) catch the spotlight. Some local shows "borrow" from American programs; another German hit called *Das Traumschiff* (the "Dream Ship") is a remake of the old American hit *Love Boat*. In fairness, American reality show hits like *Big Brother* and in-your-face game shows like *The Weakest Link* started out as European concepts that U.S. producers imported.[129] One of the biggest reality shows is a Spanish production called *Operación Triunfo* ("Operation Triumph"). Similar to *American Idol*, it's being sold to TV networks in many countries including Russia, Italy, Britain, Greece, Mexico, Brazil, and Portugal.[130]

Political developments are exerting a huge influence on the demand for American products, particularly in regions like the Middle East that oppose U.S. policies. When American warplanes began their bombing campaign in Afghanistan following the events of 9/11, thousands of protestors in Karachi marched through the streets chanting "Death to America" and setting fire to businesses linked to the United States, including KFC restaurants (even though these are locally owned).[131] Coca-Cola estimates that it lost 40 to 50 million cases of soft drink sales in the Gulf, Egypt, and Saudi Arabia in 2002 alone as a result of an anti–U.S. backlash. Procter & Gamble even saw a big dip in sales of its Ariel laundry detergent after it was targeted by a pro-Palestinian boycott—because the brand shared the first name of Ariel Sharon, Israel's prime minister.[132]

Critics in other countries deplore the creeping Americanization of their cultures because of what they view as excessive materialism. City officials in Oaxaca, Mexico successfully fought to bar McDonald's from installing its arches in the town's central plaza.[133] The French have been the most outspoken opponents of American influence on their culture. They have even tried to ban the use of such "Franglish" terms as *le drugstore, le fast food,* and even *le marketing.*[134] Resistance to the diffusion of American culture is best summarized in the words of one French critic who described the Euro Disney theme park as "a horror made of cardboard, plastic, and appalling colors—a construction of hardened chewing gum and idiotic folklore taken straight out of a comic book written for obese Americans."[135]

Opposition to a global fast-food culture also comes from groups like the Slow Food movement that was founded by an Italian journalist to protest the arrival of the first McDonald's restaurant in Rome. This group is promoting what it calls Slow Cities, which stress environmental policies creating public green spaces and finding new ways to dispose of garbage. All members share a commitment to restoring older parts of their cities before agreeing to expand into new areas. They discourage chain stores and fast-food franchises as well as the use or production of any genetically modified agriculture. Today, there are 30 Slow Cities, and 40 more towns have requested membership.[136]

Emerging Consumer Cultures in Transitional Economies

In the early 1980s the Romanian Communist government broadcast the American TV show *Dallas* in order to point out the decadence of Western capitalism. This strategy backfired, and instead the devious (but rich!) J. R. Ewing became a revered icon in parts of Eastern Europe and the Middle East. A popular tourist attraction outside of Bucharest includes a big white log gate that announces (in English) the name, "South Fork Ranch."[138] Western "decadence" appears to be infectious.[139]

More than 60 countries have a Gross National Product of less than $10 billion, and there are at least 135 transnational companies with revenues greater than that. The dominance of these marketing powerhouses has helped to create a **globalized consumption ethic**. Tempting images of luxury cars, glam rock stars on MTV, and modern appliances that make life easier surround us wherever we turn. People the world over begin to share the ideal of a material lifestyle and value well-known brands that symbolize prosperity. Shopping evolves from a wearying, task-oriented struggle to locate even basic necessities to a leisure activity. Possessing these coveted items becomes a mechanism to display one's status (see Chapter 13)—often at great personal sacrifice. In Romania, for example, Kent cigarettes are an underground currency, even though the cost of smoking a pack a day of foreign cigarettes would cost the average Romanian his or her entire yearly salary.

After the downfall of communism, Eastern Europeans emerged from a long winter of deprivation into a springtime of abundance. The picture is not all rosy, however, because attaining consumer goods is not easy for many in **transitional economies**. This description refers to a country (examples include China, Portugal, and Romania) that is struggling with the difficult adaptation from a controlled, centralized economy to a free-market system. In these situations rapid change is required on social, political, and economic dimensions as the populace suddenly is exposed to global communications and external market pressures.[140]

Some of the consequences of the transition to capitalism include a loss of confidence and pride in the local culture, as well as alienation, frustration, and an increase in stress as leisure time is sacrificed to work ever harder to buy consumer goods. The yearning for the trappings of Western material culture is perhaps most evident in parts of Eastern Europe, where citizens who threw off the shackles of communism now have direct access to coveted consumer goods from the United States and Western Europe—if they can afford them. One analyst observed, "as former subjects of the Soviet empire dream it, the American dream has very little to do with liberty and justice for all and a great deal to do with soap operas and the Sears Catalogue."[141]

As the global consumption ethic spreads, rituals and product preferences in different cultures become homogenized. For example, Christmas is now celebrated among some urbanites in Muslim Turkey, though gift-giving even on birthdays is not customary in many parts of the country. In China, Christmas fever is gripping China's newly rising urban middle class as an excuse to shop, eat, and party. People there are snapping up Christmas trees, ornaments, and Christian religious objects (even though the street vendors peddling photos of Jesus and Mary can't always identify who they are). Chinese consumers are embracing Christmas because celebrating the holiday is seen as international and modern, not because it's a traditional Christian celebration. The government encourages this practice because it stimulates consumer spending. To make the holiday even merrier, China exports about $1 billion worth of Christmas products every year and its factories churn out $7.5 billion of the toys people worldwide put under their trees.[142]

Does this homogenization mean that in time consumers who live in Nairobi, New Guinea, or the Netherlands will all be indistinguishable from those in New

Marketing Opportunity

The huge popularity of a humble local product traditionally worn by Brazilian peasants illustrates the diffusion of global consumer culture as consumers hunger for fresh ideas and styles from around the globe. These are simple flip-flops called *Havaianas* (pronounced ah-vai-YAH-nas)—the name is Portuguese for Hawaiians. The lowly shoes, which sell for $2 a pair in Brazil, are associated so strongly with poor people in that country that the expression *pe de chinelo*, or "slipper foot," is a popular slang term for the downtrodden. The main buyers in Brazil continue to be blue-collar workers, but now fashionable men and women in cities from Paris to Sydney are wearing the peasant shoes to trendy clubs and in some cases even to work.

How did these flip-flops make the leap to fashion statement? In an attempt to boost profit margins, a company named Alpargatas introduced new models in colors like lime green and fuchsia that cost twice as much as the original black- or blue-strapped sandal with a cream-colored sole. Then, it launched newer styles, including a masculine surf model. Middle-class Brazilians started to adopt the shoes and even the country's president was seen wearing them. The fashion spread as a few celebrities, including supermodels Naomi Campbell, Kate Moss, and Brazil's own Gisele Bundchen, discovered the flip-flops. Company representatives helped fuel the fire by giving out free sandals to stars at the Cannes Film Festival. The result: Alpargatas' international sales zoomed from virtually zero to over five million sandals sold around the world.[143]

THE GLOBAL LOOKING GLASS

With anti-American sentiment on the rise, international markets have become perilous for U.S.-based multinationals. But that's just business as usual for McDonald's. During the last decade, the Illinois-based chain has been the target of political protests in more than 50 countries. Alas, preventing Ronald McDonald from taking bullets intended for Uncle Sam often means using marketing tricks that would never sit well in Peoria.

FRANCE 1997–2002

Problem:

Backlash against U.S. cultural imperialism. When French farmer Jose Bove vandalized a McDonald's outlet in 1999, his compatriots were thrilled.

McSpin:

Franchise launches ads featuring cowboys who boast that McDonald's France refuses to import American beef "to guarantee maximum hygienic conditions." Ronald McDonald takes a backseat to Asterix, the cartoon defender of French independence.

YUGOSLAVIA 1998

Problem:

Operating under NATO auspices, the U.S. military begins a bombing campaign against Belgrade.

McSpin:

Franchise repositions McDonald's as a symbol of anti-NATO protest. Hands out free burgers at rallies and adds a Serbian nationalist cap to the Golden Arches icon under the slogan "McDonald's is yours."

EGYPT 2001

Problem:

Anti-American boycott sparked by U.S. support for Israel.

McSpin:

Local outlets introduce the McFalafel, rolled out behind an ad jingle sung by Shabaan Abdel Rahim, best known for his chart-topping hit "I Hate Israel."

INDONESIA 2002

Problem:

Anger over U.S. military campaign in Afghanistan triggers protests in the world's most populous Muslim nation.

McSpin:

Outlets install large photos of Indonesian franchise owner making the hajj pilgrimage to Mecca. Staff wears religion-inspired clothing on Fridays, while new TV commercials emphasize local ownership.

SAUDI ARABIA 2002

Problem:

Arab anger at Israel's response to Palestinian uprising triggers boycott of American products.

McSpin:

A Ramadan promotion by the Saudi franchise sends 30 cents from every Big Mac sold to the Red Crescent Society and Nasser Hospital in Gaza for treatment of Palestinian casualties.

Sources: Business 2.0, December, 2002; ***http:// france.attac.org*** (a major French anti-globalization Web site); "McDonald's, Cible Privilégiée de L'anti-Américanisme," *La Monde*, April 27, 2002.

York or Nashville? Probably not, because the meanings of consumer goods often mutate to be consistent with local customs and values. For example, in Turkey some urban women use ovens to dry clothes and dishwashers to wash muddy spinach. Or, a traditional clothing style such as a *bilum* worn in Papua New Guinea may be combined with Western items such as Mickey Mouse shirts or baseball caps.[144] These processes make it unlikely that global homogenization will overwhelm local cultures, but it is likely that there will be multiple consumer cultures, each blending global icons such as Nike's pervasive "swoosh" with indigenous products and meanings.

A process called **creolization** occurs when foreign influences are absorbed and integrated with local meanings. Modern Christianity adapted the pagan Christmas tree into its own rituals. In India handicapped beggars sell bottles of Coke from tricycles, and a popular music hybrid called Indipop mixes traditional styles with rock, rap, and reggae.[145] As we saw in Chapter 14, young Hispanic Americans bounce between hip-hop and *Rock en Espanol*, blend Mexican rice with spaghetti sauce, and spread peanut butter and jelly on tortillas.[146]

The creolization process sometimes results in bizarre permutations of products and services when they are modified to be compatible with local customs. Consider these creolized adaptations, for example:[147]

FINLANDIA
VODKA OF FINLAND

the original Fin

Many advertising messages appeal to people the world over. This Australian ad for a Finnish product would appeal to sophisticated young people from many different cultures.

- In Peru, Indian boys carry rocks painted to look like transistor radios.
- In highland Papua New Guinea, tribesmen put Chivas Regal wrappers on their drums and wear Pentel pens instead of nosebones.
- Bana tribesmen in the remote highlands of Kako, Ethiopia pay to watch *Pluto the Circus Dog* on a Viewmaster.
- When an African Swazi princess marries a Zulu king, she wears a traditional costume of red touraco wing feathers around her forehead and a cape of windowbird feathers and oxtails and the kindis wrapped in a leopard skin. But the ceremony is recorded on a Kodak movie camera while the band plays "The Sound of Music."
- The Japanese use Western words as a shorthand for anything new and exciting, even if they do not understand their meaning. Cars are given names such as Fairlady, Gloria, and Bongo Wagon. Consumers buy *deodoranto* (deodorant) and *appuru pai* (apple pie). Ads urge shoppers to *stoppu rukku* (stop and look), and products are claimed to be *yuniku* (unique).[148] Coca-Cola cans say, "I feel Coke & sound special," and a company called Cream Soda sells products with the slogan, "Too old to die, too young to happy."[149] Other Japanese products with English names include Mouth Pet (breath freshener), Pocari Sweat ("refreshment water"), Armpit (electric razor), Brown Gross Foam (hair-coloring mousse), Virgin Pink Special (skin cream), Cow Brand (beauty soap), and Mymorning Water (canned water).[150]

CHAPTER SUMMARY

- The styles prevalent in a culture at any point in time often reflect underlying political and social conditions. The set of agents responsible for creating stylistic alternatives is termed a *culture production system* (*CPS*). Factors such as the types of people involved in this system and the amount of competition by alternative product forms influence the choices that eventually make their way to the marketplace for consideration by end consumers.

- Culture is often described in terms of high (or elite) forms and low (or popular) forms. Products of popular culture tend to follow a *cultural formula* and contain predictable components. On the other hand, these distinctions are blurring in modern society as imagery from "high art" is increasingly being incorporated into marketing efforts.

- *Reality engineering* occurs as elements of popular culture are appropriated by marketers and converted to vehicles for promotional strategies. These elements include sensory and spatial aspects of everyday existence, whether in the form of products appearing in movies, scents pumped into offices and stores, billboards, theme parks, or video monitors attached to shopping carts.

- *Diffusion of innovations* refers to the process whereby a new product, service, or idea spreads through a population. *Innovators* and *early adopters* are quick to adopt new products, and *laggards* are very slow. A consumer's decision to adopt a new product depends on his or her personal characteristics as well as on characteristics of the innovation itself. Products stand a better chance of being adopted if they demand relatively little change in behavior from users, are easy to understand, and provide a relative advantage compared to existing products.

- The *fashion system* includes everyone involved in the creation and transference of symbolic meanings. Many different products express common *cultural categories* (e.g., gender distinctions). New styles tend to be adopted by many people simultaneously in a process known as *collective selection*. According to meme theory, ideas spread through a population in a geometric progression much as a virus infects many people until it reaches epidemic proportions. Other perspectives on motivations for adopting new styles include psychological, economic, and sociological models of fashion.

- Fashions tend to follow cycles that resemble the product life cycle. The two extremes of fashion adoption, *classics* and *fads*, can be distinguished in terms of the length of this cycle.

- Because a consumer's culture exerts such a big influence on his or her lifestyle choices, marketers must learn as much as possible about differences in cultural norms and preferences when marketing in more than one country. One important issue is the extent to which marketing strategies must be tailored to each culture versus standardized across cultures. Followers of an *etic perspective* believe people in many cultures will appreciate the same universal messages. Believers in an *emic perspective* argue that individual cultures are too unique to permit such standardization; marketers must instead adapt their approaches to be consistent with local values and practices. Attempts at global marketing have met with mixed success; in many cases this approach is more likely to work if the messages appeal to basic values or if the target markets consist of consumers who are more internationally rather than locally oriented.

- The United States is a net exporter of popular culture. Consumers around the world have eagerly adopted American products, especially entertainment vehicles and items that are linked symbolically to a uniquely American lifestyle (e.g., Marlboro cigarettes, Levi's jeans). Despite the continuing "Americanization" of world culture, some consumers are alarmed by this influence, and are instead emphasizing a return to local products and customs. In other cases, they are integrating these products with existing cultural practices in a process known as *creolization*.

KEY TERMS

Advergaming 566
Art product 560
Classic 578
Collective selection 572
Compatibility 570
Complexity 570
Co-optation 556
Craft product 560
Creolization 588
Cultivation hypothesis 564
Cultural categories 571
Cultural formula 561
Cultural gatekeepers 559

Cultural selection 557
Culture production system (CPS) 558
Diffusion of innovations 567
Early adopters 569
Emic perspective 582
Etic perspective 581
Fad 578
Fashion 571
Fashion acceptance cycle 577
Fashion system 570
Globalized consumption ethic 587
Innovation 567
Innovators 568

Knockoff 563
Laggards 567
Late adopters 567
Lead user 569
Meme theory 576
Observability 570
Product placement 564
Reality engineering 563
Relative Advantage 570
Tipping point 576
Transitional economies 587
Trialability 570
Trickle-down theory 575

CONSUMER BEHAVIOR CHALLENGE

1 What are the basic differences between a fad, a fashion, and a classic? Provide examples of each.

2 What is the difference between an art and a craft? How would you characterize advertising within this framework?

3 This chapter mentions some instances in which market research findings influenced artistic decisions, as when a movie ending was reshot to accommodate consumers' preferences. Many people would most likely oppose this practice, claiming that books, movies, records, or other artistic endeavors should not be designed to merely conform to what people want to read, see, or hear. What do you think?

4 Due to higher competition and market saturation, marketers in industrialized countries are increasingly trying to develop Third World markets by encouraging people in underdeveloped countries to desire Western products. Asian consumers alone spend $90 billion a year on cigarettes, and U.S. tobacco manufacturers continue to push relentlessly into these markets. Cigarette advertising, often depicting glamorous Western models and settings, is found just about everywhere, on billboards, buses, storefronts, and clothing, and many major sports and cultural events are sponsored by tobacco companies. Some compa-

nies even hand out cigarettes and gifts in amusement areas, often to preteens. Should this practice be encouraged, even if the products being marketed may be harmful to consumers' health (e.g., cigarettes) or divert needed money away from the purchase of essentials? If you were a trade or health official in a Third World country, what guidelines, if any, might you suggest to regulate the import of luxury goods from advanced economies?

5 Comment on the growing practices described as reality engineering. Do marketers "own" our culture? Should they?

6 Boots with six-inch heels are the latest fashion rage among young Japanese women. Several teens have died after tripping over their shoes and fracturing their skulls. However, followers of the style claim they are willing to risk twisted ankles, broken bones, bruised faces, and other dangers associated with the platform shoes. One teenager said, "I've fallen and twisted my ankle many times, but they are so cute that I won't give them up until they go out of fashion."[151] Many consumers around the world seem to be willing to suffer for the sake of fashion. Others argue that we are merely pawns in the hands of designers, who conspire to force unwieldy fashions down our throats. What do you think? What is and what should be the role of fashion in our society? How important is it for people to be in style? What are the pros and cons of keeping up with the latest fashions? Do you believe that we are at the mercy of designers?

NOTES

1. Khanh T. L. Tran, "Lifting the Velvet Rope: Night Clubs Draw Virtual Throngs with Webcasts," *Wall Street Journal Interactive Edition* (August 30, 1999).
2. Lauren Goldstein, "Urban Wear Goes Suburban," *Fortune* (December 21, 1998): 169–72.
3. Marc Spiegler, "Marketing Street Culture: Bringing Hip-Hop Style to the Mainstream," *American Demographics* (November 1996): 29–34.
4. Joshua Levine, "Badass Sells," *Forbes* (April 21, 1997): 142.
5. Nina Darnton, "Where the Homegirls Are," *Newsweek* (June 17, 1991): 60; "The Idea Chain," *Newsweek* (October 5, 1992): 32.
6. Cyndee Miller, "X Marks the Lucrative Spot, but Some Advertisers Can't Hit Target," *Marketing News* (August 2, 1993): 1.
7. Ad appeared in *Elle* (September 1994).
8. Spiegler, "Marketing Street Culture: Bringing Hip-Hop Style to the Mainstream"; Levine, "Badass Sells."
9. Jeff Jensen, "Hip, Wholesome Image Makes a Marketing Star of Rap's LL Cool J," *Advertising Age* (August 25, 1997): 1.
10. Alice Z. Cuneo, "GAP's 1st Global Ads Confront Dockers on a Khaki Battlefield," *Advertising Age* (April 20, 1998): 3–5.
11. Jancee Dunn, "How Hip-Hop Style Bum-Rushed the Mall," *Rolling Stone* (March 18, 1999): 54–59.
12. Teri Agins, "The Rare Art of 'Gilt by Association': How Armani Got Stars to Be Billboards," *Wall Street Journal Interactive Edition* (September 14, 1999).
13. Eryn Brown, "From Rap to Retail: Wiring the Hip-Hop Nation," *Fortune* (April 17, 2000): 530
14. Martin Fackler, "Hip Hop Invading China," *The Birmingham News* (February 15, 2002): D1.
15. Maureen Tkacik, "'Z' Zips into the Zeitgeist, Subbing for 'S' in Hot Slang," *Wall Street Journal Interactive Edition* (January 4, 2003); Maureen Tkacik, "Slang from the 'Hood Now Sells Toyz in Target," *Wall Street Journal Interactive Edition* (December 30, 2002).
16. Elizabeth M. Blair, "Commercialization of the Rap Music Youth Subculture," *Journal of Popular Culture* 27 (Winter 1993): 21–34; Basil G. Englis, Michael R. Solomon, and Anna Olofsson, "Consumption Imagery in Music Television: A Bi-Cultural Perspective," *Journal of Advertising* 22 (December 1993): 21–34.
17. Spiegler, "Marketing Street Culture: Bringing Hip-Hop Style to the Mainstream."
18. Grant McCracken, "Culture and Consumption: A Theoretical Account of the Structure and Movement of the Cultural Meaning of Consumer Goods," *Journal of Consumer Research* 13 (June 1986): 71–84.
19. Richard A. Peterson, "The Production of Culture: A Prolegomenon," in Richard A. Peterson, ed., *The Production of Culture, Sage Contemporary Social Science Issues* 33 (Beverly Hills, CA: Sage, 1976), 7–22. For a recent study that looked at ways consumers interact with marketers to create cultural meanings, see Lisa Penaloza, "Consuming the American West: Animating Cultural Meaning and Memory at a Stock Show and Rodeo," *Journal of Consumer Research* 28 (December 2001): 369–98.
20. Richard A. Peterson and D. G. Berger, "Entrepreneurship in Organizations: Evidence from the Popular Music Industry," *Administrative Science Quarterly* 16 (1971): 97–107.
21. Elizabeth C. Hirschman, "Resource Ex-change in the Production and Distribution of a Motion Picture," *Empirical Studies of the Arts* 8, no. 1 (1990): 31–51; Michael R. Solomon, "Building Up and Breaking Down: The Impact of Cultural Sorting on Symbolic Consumption," in J. Sheth and E. C. Hirschman, eds., *Research in Consumer Behavior* (Greenwich, CT: JAI Press, 1988), 325–51.
22. See Paul M. Hirsch, "Processing Fads and Fashions: An Organizational Set Analysis of Cultural Industry Systems," *American Journal of Sociology* 77, no. 4 (1972): 639–59; Russell Lynes, *The Tastemakers* (New York: Harper and Brothers, 1954); Michael R. Solomon, "The Missing Link: Surrogate Consumers in the Marketing Chain," *Journal of Marketing* 50 (October 1986): 208–19.
23. Howard S. Becker, "Arts and Crafts," *American Journal of Sociology* 83 (January 1987): 862–89.
24. Herbert J. Gans, "Popular Culture in America: Social Problem in a Mass Society or Social Asset in a Pluralist Society?" in Howard S. Becker, ed., *Social Problems: A Modern Approach* (New York: Wiley, 1966).
25. Karen Breslau, "Paint by Numbers," *Newsweek* (May 13, 2002): 48.
26. Peter S. Green, "Moviegoers Devour Ads," *Advertising Age* (June 26, 1989): 36.
27. John P. Robinson, "The Arts in America," *American Demographics* (September 1987): 42.
28. Michael R. Real, *Mass-Mediated Culture* (Upper Saddle River, NJ: Prentice Hall, 1977).
29. Annetta Miller, "Shopping Bags Imitate Art: Seen the Sacks? Now Visit the Museum Exhibit," *Newsweek* (January 23, 1989): 44.
30. Kim Foltz, "New Species for Study: Consumers in Action," *New York Times* (December 18, 1989): A1.
31. Arthur A. Berger, *Signs in Contemporary Culture: An Introduction to Semiotics* (New York: Longman, 1984).
32. Michiko Kakutani, "Art Is Easier the 2d Time Around," *New York Times* (October 30, 1994): E4.
33. Nigel Andrews, "Filming a Blockbuster Is One Thing; Striking Gold Is Another," *Financial Times* (January 20, 1998).
34. Helene Diamond, "Lights, Camera . . . Research!" *Marketing News* (September 11, 1989): 10.
35. Nigel Andrews, "Filming a Blockbuster is One Thing."
36. "A Brand-New Development Creates a Colorful History," *Wall Street Journal Interactive Edition* (February 18, 1998).
37. Mary Kuntz and Joseph Weber, "The New Hucksterism," *BusinessWeek* (July 1, 1996): 75(2).
38. Michael R. Solomon and Basil G. Englis, "Reality Engineering: Blurring the Boundaries between Marketing and Popular Culture," *Journal of Current Issues and Research in Advertising* 16, no. 2 (Fall 1994): 1–17.
39. Austin Bunn, "Not Fade Away," *New York Times on the Web* (December 2, 2002).
40. Marc Santora, "Circle the Block, Cabby, My Show's On," *New York Times on the Web* (January 16, 2003); Wayne Parry, "Police May Sell Ad Space," *Montgomery Advertiser* (November 20, 2002): A4.
41. T. Bettina Cornwell and Bruce Keillor, "Contemporary Literature and the Embedded Consumer Culture: The Case of Updike's Rabbit," in Roger J. Kruez and Mary Sue MacNealy, eds., *Empirical Approaches to Literature and Aesthetics: Advances in Discourse Processes* 52 (Norwood, NJ: Ablex, 1996), 559–72; Monroe Friedman, "The Changing Language of a Consumer Society: Brand Name Usage in Popular American Novels in the Postwar Era," *Journal of Consumer Research* 11 (March 1985): 927–37; Monroe Friedman, "Commercial Influences in the Lyrics of Popular American Music of the Postwar Era," *Journal of Consumer Affairs* 20 (Winter 1986): 193.
42. Wayne Friedman, "'Tomorrow' Heralds Brave New Ad World," *Advertising Age* (June 24, 2002): 3.
43. Hank Kim and Wayne Friedman, "Brands Get Role in New ABC Show," *Advertising Age* (December 30, 2002): 3.
44. Britt Bill and O'Dwyer Gerad, "The New Billboards: Buggies," *Advertising Age* (August 19, 2002): 11.
45. "Pro Bowler's Skirt Is up for Ad Grabs," *Advertising Age* (September 16, 2002): 16.
46. Robin Givhan, "Designers Caught in a Tangled Web," *Washington Post* (April 5, 1997): C1.
47. Suzanne Vranica, "Sony Ericsson Campaign Uses Actors to Push Camera-Phone in Real Life," *Wall Street Journal Interactive Edition* (July 31, 2002).

48. George Gerbner, Larry Gross, Nancy Signorielli, and Michael Morgan, "Aging with Television: Images on Television Drama and Conceptions of Social Reality," *Journal of Communication* 30 (1980): 37–47.

49. L. J. Shrum, Robert S. Wyer Jr., and Thomas C. O'Guinn, "The Effects of Television Consumption on Social Perceptions: The Use of Priming Procedures to Investigate Psychological Process," *Journal of Consumer Research* 24 (March 1998): 447–68; Stephen Fox and William Philber, "Television Viewing and the Perception of Affluence," *Sociological Quarterly* 19 (1978): 103–12; W. James Potter, "Three Strategies for Elaborating the Cultivation Hypothesis," *Journalism Quarterly* 65 (Winter 1988): 930–39; Gabriel Weimann, "Images of Life in America: The Impact of American T.V. in Israel," *International Journal of Intercultural Relations* 8 (1984): 185–97.

50. "Movie Smoking Exceeds Real Life," *Asbury Park Press* (June 20, 1994): A4.

51. Lynn Elber, "TV Offers Fantasy Depiction of Real-Life Family, Work Life, Study Says," *Montgomery Advertiser* (June 11, 1998): B1

52. Fara Warner, "Why It's Getting Harder to Tell the Shows from the Ads," *Wall Street Journal* (June 15, 1995): B1.

53. Benjamin M. Cole, "Products That Want to Be in Pictures," *Los Angeles Herald Examiner* (March 5, 1985): 36; see also Stacy M. Vollmers and Richard W. Mizerski, "A Review and Investigation into the Effectiveness of Product Placements in Films," in Karen Whitehill King, ed., *Proceedings of the 1994 Conference of the American Academy of Advertising*: 97–102; Solomon and Englis, "Reality Engineering: Blurring the Boundaries Between Marketing and Popular Culture."

54. Wayne Friedman, " 'Minority Report' Stars Lexus, Nokia," *Advertising Age* (June 17, 2002): 41.

55. Denise E. DeLorme and Leonard N. Reid, "Moviegoers' Experiences and Interpretations of Brands in Films Revisited," *Journal of Advertising* 28, no. 2 (1999): 71–90.

56. Cristel Antonia Russell, "Investigating the Effectiveness of Product Placement in Television Shows: The Role of Modality and Plot Connection Congruence on Brand Memory and Attitude," *Journal of Consumer Research* 29 (December 2002): 306–318.

57. Claire Atkinson, "Ad Intrusion Up, Say Consumers," *Advertising Age* (January 6, 2003): 1.

58. Peggy J. Farber, "Schools for Sale," *Advertising Age* (October 25, 1999): 22.

59. Sally Beatty, "In New TV Series, Big-Rig Maker Decides to Team up with Hollywood," *Wall Street Journal Interactive Edition* (October 29, 1999).

60. Jennifer Tanaka and Marc Peyser, "The Apples of Their Eyes," *Newsweek* (November 30, 1998): 58.

61. Nancy Marsden, "Lighting up the Big Screen," *San Francisco Examiner* (August 4, 1998).

62. Joe Flint, "Sponsors Get a Role in CBS Reality Show," *Wall Street Journal Interactive Edition* (January 13, 2000).

63. Stephen J. Gould, Pola B. Gupta, and Sonja Grabner-Kräuter "Product Placements in Movies: A Cross-Cultural Analysis of Austrian, French and American Consumers' Attitudes toward this Emerging, International Promotional Medium," *Journal of Advertising* 29 (Winter 2000): 41–58.

64. Sarah Ellison, "French Cafes Now Serve up Logos du Jour with Au Laits," *Wall Street Journal Interactive Edition* (June 2, 2000).

65. Peter Wonacott, "Chinese TV Is an Eager Medium for (Lots of) Product Placement," *Wall Street Journal Interactive Edition* (January 26, 2000).

66. Gabriel Kahn, "Product Placement Booms in New Bollywood Films," *Wall Street Journal Interactive Edition* (August 30, 2002).

67. Benny Evangelista, "Advertisers Get into the Video Game," *San Francisco Chronicle* (January 18, 1999).

68. Matt Richtel, "Big Mac Is Virtual, but Critics Are Real," *New York Times on the Web* (November 28, 2002).

69. Hassan Fattah and Pamela Paul, "Gaming Gets Serious," *American Demographics* (May 2002): 39–43.

70. Ibid.

71. Tobi Elkin, "Video Games Try Product Placement," *Advertising Age* (May 20, 2002): 157.

72. Lynnette Holloway, "Songs to Start out on Video Games," *New York Times on the Web* (March 10, 2003).

73. Emily Nelson, "Moistened Toilet Paper Wipes out after Launch for Kimberly-Clark," *Wall Street Journal Interactive Edition* (April 15, 2002).

74. Robert Hof, "The Click Here Economy," *BusinessWeek* (June 22, 1998): 122–28.

75. Eric J. Arnould, "Toward a Broadened Theory of Preference Formation and the Diffusion of Innovations: Cases from Zinder Province, Niger Republic," *Journal of Consumer Research* 16

(September 1989): 239–67; Susan B. Kaiser, *The Social Psychology of Clothing* (New York: Macmillan, 1985); Thomas S. Robertson, *Innovative Behavior and Communication* (New York: Holt, Rinehart and Winston, 1971).

76. Jan-Benedict E. M. Steenkamp, Frenkel ter Hofstede, and Michel Wedel, "A Cross-National Investigation into the Individual and National Cultural Antecedents of Consumer Innovativeness," *Journal of Marketing* 63, no. 7 (1999): 55–69.

77. Susan L. Holak, Donald R. Lehmann, and Fareena Sultan, "The Role of Expectations in the Adoption of Innovative Consumer Durables: Some Preliminary Evidence," *Journal of Retailing* 63 (Fall 1987): 243–59.

78. Hubert Gatignon and Thomas S. Robertson, "A Propositional Inventory for New Diffusion Research," *Journal of Consumer Research* 11 (March 1985): 849–67.

79. C. K. Prahalad and Venkatram Ramaswamy, "Co-Opting Customer Competence," *Harvard Business Review* (January–February 2000): 79–87. Eric von Hipple, "Users as Innovators," *Technology Review* 80 (January 1978): 3–11; Jakki Mohr, *Marketing of High-Technology Products and Services* (Upper Saddle River, NJ: Prentice Hall, 2001).

80. Everett M. Rogers, *Diffusion of Innovations*, 3rd ed. (New York: The Free Press, 1983).

81. Umberto Eco, *A Theory of Semiotics* (Bloomington: Indiana University Press, 1979).

82. Fred Davis, "Clothing and Fashion as Communication," in Michael R. Solomon, ed., *The Psychology of Fashion* (Lexington, MA: Lexington Books, 1985): 15–28.

83. Melanie Wallendorf, "The Formation of Aesthetic Criteria through Social Structures and Social Institutions," in Jerry C. Olson, ed., *Advances in Consumer Research* 7 (Ann Arbor, MI: Association for Consumer Research, 1980): 3–6.

84. Grant McCracken, "Culture and Consumption: A Theoretical Account of the Structure and Movement of the Cultural Meaning of Consumer Goods," *Journal of Consumer Research* 13 (June 1986): 71–84.

85. "The Eternal Triangle," *Art in America* (February 1989): 23.

86. Herbert Blumer, *Symbolic Interactionism: Perspective and Method* (Upper Saddle River, NJ: Prentice Hall, 1969); Howard S. Becker, "Art as Collective Action," *American Sociological Review* 39 (December 1973); Richard A. Peterson, "Revitalizing the Culture Concept," *Annual Review of Sociology* 5 (1979): 137–66.

87. For more details, Kaiser, *The Social Psychology of Clothing;* George B. Sproles, "Behavioral Science Theories of Fashion," in Michael R. Solomon, ed., *The Psychology of Fashion* (Lexington, MA: Lexington Books, 1985): 55–70.

88. C. R. Snyder and Howard L. Fromkin, *Uniqueness: The Human Pursuit of Difference* (New York: Plenum Press, 1980).

89. Linda Dyett, "Desperately Seeking Skin," *Psychology Today* (May–June 1996): 14; Alison Lurie, *The Language of Clothes* (New York: Random House, 1981).

90. Harvey Leibenstein, *Beyond Economic Man: A New Foundation for Microeconomics* (Cambridge, MA: Harvard University Press, 1976).

91. Nara Schoenberg, "Goth Culture Moves into Mainstream," *Montgomery Advertiser* (January 19, 2003): 1G.

92. Georg Simmel, "Fashion," *International Quarterly* 10 (1904): 130–55.

93. Tkacik, " 'Z' Zips into the Zeitgeist, Subbing for 'S' in Hot Slang"; Tkacik, "Slang from the 'Hood Now Sells Toyz in Target."

94. Grant D. McCracken, "The Trickle-Down Theory Rehabilitated," in Michael R. Solomon, ed., *The Psychology of Fashion* (Lexington, MA: Lexington Books, 1985): 39–54.

95. Charles W. King, "Fashion Adoption: A Rebuttal to the 'Trickle-Down' Theory," in Stephen A. Greyser, ed., *Toward Scientific Marketing* (Chicago: American Marketing Association, 1963), 108–25.

96. Alf H. Walle, "Grassroots Innovation," *Marketing Insights* (Summer 1990): 44–51.

97. Robert V. Kozinets, "Fandoms' Menace/Pop Flows: Exploring the Metaphor of Entertainment as Recombinant/Memetic Engineering," *Association for Consumer Research* (October 1999). The new science of memetics, which tries to explain how beliefs gain acceptance and predict their progress, was spurred by Richard Dawkins, who in the 1970s proposed culture as a Darwinian struggle among "memes" or mind viruses. See Geoffrey Cowley, "Viruses of the Mind: How Odd Ideas Survive," *Newsweek* (April 14, 1997): 14.

98. Malcolm Gladwell, *The Tipping Point* (New York: Little, Brown and Co., 2000).

99. "Cabbage-Hatched Plot Sucks in 24 Doll Fans," *New York Daily News* (December 1, 1983).

100. "Turtlemania," *The Economist* (April 21, 1990): 32.

101. John Lippman, "Creating the Craze for Pokémon: Licensing Agent Bet on U.S. Kids," *Wall Street Journal Interactive Edition* (August 16, 1999).

102. Anthony Ramirez, "The Pedestrian Sneaker Makes a Comeback," *New York Times* (October 14, 1990): F17.

103. B. E. Aguirre, E. L. Quarantelli, and Jorge L. Mendoza, "The Collective Behavior of Fads: The Characteristics, Effects, and Career of Streaking," *American Sociological Review* (August 1989): 569.

104. Kathleen Deveny, "Anatomy of a Fad: How Clear Products Were Hot and Then Suddenly Were Not," *Wall Street Journal* (March 15, 1994): B1.

105. Martin G. Letscher, "How to Tell Fads from Trends," *American Demographics* (December 1994): 38–45.

106. "Packaging Draws Protest," *Marketing News* (July 4, 1994): 1.

107. "McDonald's to Give $10 Million to Settle Vegetarian Lawsuit," *Wall Street Journal Interactive Edition* (June 4, 2002).

108. Gerard O'Dwyer, "McD's Cancels McAfrika Rollout," *Advertising Age* (September 9, 2002): 14.

109. K. Belson, "As Starbucks Grows, Japan, Too, Is Awash," *New York Times on the Web* (October 21, 2001).

110. "Starbucks Plans 24 Stores in Puerto Rico, Mexico: Will Consumers Buy $5 Coffee in the Land of 50 Cent Cafe?" *Wall Street Journal Interactive Edition* (August 29, 2002).

111. Steven Erlanger, "An American Coffeehouse (or 4) in Vienna," *New York Times on the Web* (June 1, 2002).

112. Theodore Levitt, *The Marketing Imagination* (New York: The Free Press, 1983).

113. Paulo Prada and Bruce Orwall, "Disney's New French Theme Park Serves Wine—and Better Sausage," *Wall Street Journal Interactive Edition* (March 12, 2002).

114. Terry Clark, "International Marketing and National Character: A Review and Proposal for an Integrative Theory," *Journal of Marketing* 54 (October 1990): 66–79.

115. Deborah Ball, "Fashion Houses Implement New Local Marketing Push," *Wall Street Journal Interactive Edition* (June 6, 2002).

116. Jason Dean, "Beer's Taiwan Entry Tests Taste for Chinese Products," *Wall Street Journal Interactive Edition* (July 4, 2002).

117. Norihiko Shirouzu, "Snapple in Japan: How a Splash Dried Up," *Wall Street Journal* (April 15, 1996): B1.

118. Glenn Collins, "Chinese to Get a Taste of Cheese-Less Cheetos," *New York Times* (September 2, 1994): D4.

119. James Hookway, "Philippine Balut Goes Gourmet with an Appeal to Elite Class," *Wall Street Journal Interactive Edition* (May 2, 2002).

120. Julie Skur Hill and Joseph M. Winski, "Goodbye Global Ads: Global Village Is Fantasy Land for Marketers," *Advertising Age* (November 16, 1987): 22.

121. Shelly Reese, "Culture Shock," *Marketing Tools* (May 1998): 44–49; Steve Rivkin, "The Name Game Heats Up," *Marketing News* (April 22, 1996): 8; David A. Ricks, "Products That Crashed into the Language Barrier," *Business and Society Review* (Spring 1983): 46–50; "Speaking in Tongues" 3, no. 1 (Spring 1997): 20–23.

122. Clyde H. Farnsworth, "Yoked in Twin Solitudes: Canada's Two Cultures," *New York Times* (September 18, 1994): E4.

123. Hill and Winski, "Goodbye Global Ads."

124. MTV Europe, personal communication, 1994; see also Teresa J. Domzal and Jerome B. Kernan, "Mirror, Mirror: Some Postmodern Reflections on Global Advertising," *Journal of Advertising* 22 (December 1993): 1–20; Douglas P. Holt, "Consumers' Cultural Differences as Local Systems of Tastes: A Critique of the Personality-Values Approach and an Alternative Framework," *Asia Pacific Advances in Consumer Research* 1 (1994): 1–7.

125. Normandy Madden, "New GenerAsians Survey Gets Personal with Asia-Pacific Kids," *Advertising Age International* (July 13, 1998): 2.

126. "They All Want to Be Like Mike," *Fortune* (July 21, 1997): 51–53.

127. Calvin Sims, "Japan Beckons, and East Asia's Youth Fall in Love," *New York Times* (December 5, 1999): 3.

128. Elisabeth Rosenthal, "Buicks, Starbucks and Fried Chicken, Still China?" *New York Times on the Web* (February 25, 2002).

129. Suzanne Kapner, "U.S. TV Shows Losing Potency around World," *New York Times on the Web* (January 2, 2003).

130. Emma Daly, "In a Spanish Reality TV Show, Even the Losers Win," *New York Times on the Web* (December 4, 2002).

131. B. O'Keefe, "Global Brands," *Fortune* (November 26, 2001): 102–6.

132. Kevin J. Delaney, "U.S. Brands Could Suffer Even Before War Begins," *Wall Street Journal Interactive Edition* (January 28, 2003).

133. Julie Watson, "City Keeps McDonald's from Opening in Plaza," *Montgomery Advertiser* (December 15, 2002): 5AA.

134. John F. Sherry Jr. and Edward G. Camargo, "May Your Life Be Marvelous; French Council Eases Language Ban," *New York Times* (July 31, 1994): 12.

135. Alan Riding, "Only the French Elite Scorn Mickey's Debut," *New York Times* (1992): A1.

136. Matthew Yeomans, "Unplugged," *Wired* (February 2002): 87.

137. Gerard O'Dwyer, "Unilever Angers Finns over Mustard," *Advertising Age* (November 11, 2002): 16.

138. Professor Russell Belk, University of Utah, personal communication (July 25, 1997).

139. Material in this section adapted from Güliz Ger and Russell W. Belk, "I'd Like to Buy the World a Coke: Consumptionscapes of the 'Less Affluent World'," *Journal of Consumer Policy* 19, no. 3 (1996): 271–304; Russell W. Belk, "Romanian Consumer Desires and Feelings of Deservingness," in Lavinia Stan, ed., *Romania in Transition* (Hanover, NH: Dartmouth Press, 1997): 191–208; see also Güliz Ger, "Human Development and Humane Consumption: Well Being Beyond the Good Life," *Journal of Public Policy and Marketing* 16 (1997): 110–25.

140. Professor Güliz Ger, Bilkent University, Turkey, personal communication (July 25, 1997).

141. Erazim Kohák, "Ashes, Ashes . . . Central Europe after Forty Years," *Daedalus* 121 (Spring 1992): 197–215; Belk, "Romanian Consumer Desires and Feelings of Deservingness."

142. David Murphy, "Christmas's Commercial Side Makes Yuletide a Hit in China," *Wall Street Journal Interactive Edition* (December 24, 2002).

143. Miriam Jordan and Teri Agins, "Fashion Flip-Flop: Sandal Leaves the Shower Behind," *Wall Street Journal Interactive Edition* (August 8, 2002).

144. This example courtesy of Professor Russell Belk, University of Utah, personal communication (July 25, 1997).

145. Miriam Jordan, "India Decides to Put Its Own Spin on Popular Rock, Rap and Reggae," *Wall Street Journal Interactive Edition* (January 5, 2000); Rasul Bailay, "Coca-Cola Recruits Paraplegics for 'Cola War' in India," *Wall Street Journal Interactive Edition* (June 10, 1997).

146. Rick Wartzman, "When You Translate 'Got Milk' for Latinos, What Do You Get?" *Wall Street Journal Interactive Edition* (June 3, 1999).

147. Eric J. Arnould and Richard R. Wilk, "Why Do the Natives Wear Adidas: Anthropological Approaches to Consumer Research," *Advances in Consumer Research* 12 (Provo, UT: Association for Consumer Research, 1985): 748–52.

148. Sherry and Camargo, "'May Your Life Be Marvelous'" 174–88.

149. Bill Bryson, "A Taste for Scrambled English," *New York Times* (July 22, 1990): 10; Rose A. Horowitz, "California Beach Culture Rides Wave of Popularity in Japan," *Journal of Commerce* (August 3, 1989): 17; Elaine Lafferty, "American Casual Seizes Japan: Teen-agers Go for N.F.L. Hats, Batman and the California Look," *Time* (November 13, 1989): 106.

150. Lucy Howard and Gregory Cerio, "Goofy Goods," *Newsweek* (August 15, 1994): 8.

151. Calvin Sims, "For Chic's Sake, Japanese Women Parade to the Orthopedist," *New York Times On the Web* (November 26, 1999).

Glossary

ABC model of attitudes a multidimensional perspective stating that attitudes are jointly defined by affect, behavior, and cognition

Absolute threshold the minimum amount of stimulation that can be detected on a given sensory channel

Accommodative purchase decision the process of using bargaining, coercion, compromise, and the wielding of power to achieve agreement among group members who have different preferences or priorities

Acculturation the process of learning the beliefs and behaviors endorsed by another culture

Acculturation agents friends, family, local businesses, and other reference groups that facilitate the learning of cultural norms

Activation models of memory approaches to memory stressing different levels of processing that occur and activate some aspects of memory rather than others, depending on the nature of the processing task

Actual self a person's realistic appraisal of his or her qualities

Adaptation the process that occurs when a sensation becomes so familiar that it no longer commands attention

Advergaming online games merge with interactive advertisements that let companies target specific types of consumers

Affect the way a consumer feels about an attitude object

Age cohort a group of consumers of approximately the same age who have undergone similar experiences

Agentic goals an emphasis on self-assertion and mastery, often associated with traditional male gender roles

AIOs (activities, interests, and opinions) the psychographic variables used by researchers to group consumers

Allegory a story told about an abstract trait or concept that has been personified as a person, animal, or vegetable

Allocentrics people having a group orientation

Androgyny the possession of both masculine and feminine traits

Animism cultural practices whereby inanimate objects are given qualities that make them somehow alive

Anticonsumption the actions taken by consumers that involve the deliberate defacement or mutilation of products

Approach-approach conflict a person must choose between two desirable alternatives

Approach-avoidance conflict a person desires a goal but wishes to avoid it at the same time

Avoidance-avoidance conflict a person faces a choice between two undesirable alternatives

Archetypes a universally shared idea or behavior pattern, central to Carl Jung's conception of personality; archetypes involve themes—such as birth, death, or the devil—that appear frequently in myths, stories, and dreams

Art product a creation viewed primarily as an object of aesthetic contemplation without any functional value

Aspirational reference groups high profile athletes and celebrities used in marketing efforts to promote a product

Atmospherics the use of space and physical features in store design to evoke certain effects in buyers

Attention the assignment of processing activity to selected stimuli

Attention economy a way of operating where the goal is to attract eyeballs, or attention to a Web site

Attitude a lasting, general evaluation of people (including oneself), objects, or issues

Attitude toward the act of buying (A$_{act}$) the perceived consequences of a purchase

Attitude toward the advertisement (A$_{ad}$) a predisposition to respond favorably or unfavorably to a particular advertising stimulus during a particular exposure occasion

Autonomic decision when one family member chooses a product for the whole family

Avatar manifestation of the Hindu deity in superhuman or animal form. In the computing world it has come to mean a cyberspace presence represented by a character that you can move around inside a visual, graphical world

B2C e-commerce businesses selling to consumers through electronic marketing

B2-4B Business to Four Billion—the estimated size of the lower-income market worldwide

Baby boomer a large cohort of people born between the years of 1946 and 1964 who are the source of many important cultural and economic changes

Balance theory a theory that considers relations among elements a person might perceive as belonging together, and people's tendency to change relations among elements in order to make them consistent or "balanced"

Behavior a consumer's actions with regard to an attitude object

Behavioral economics the study of the behavioral determinants of economic decisions

Behavioral influence perspective the view that consumer decisions are learned responses to environmental cues

Behavioral learning theories the perspectives on learning that assume that learning takes place as the result of responses to external events

Binary opposition a defining structural characteristic of many myths in which two opposing ends of some dimension are represented (e.g., good versus evil, nature versus technology)

Bioterrorism terrorist activities aimed at endangering the health of humans and/or the food supply including the release of toxins into air or water and product tampering

Blogosphere the universe of active Weblogs (online diaries)

Body cathexis a person's feelings about aspects of his or her body

Body image a consumer's subjective evaluation of his or her physical self

Boomerang kids grown children who return to their parents' home to live

Brand community a set of consumers who share a set of social relationships based upon usage or interest in a product

Brand equity a brand that has strong positive associations in a consumer's memory and commands a lot of loyalty as a result

Brand personality a set of traits people attribute to a product as if it were a person

Business ethics rules of conduct that guide actions in the marketplace

Business-to-Business (B2B) e-commerce Internet interactions between two or more businesses or organizations

Business-to-business marketers specialists in meeting the needs of organizations such as corporations, government agencies, hospitals, and retailers

Buying center the part of an organization charged with making purchasing decisions

Buzz word of mouth that is viewed as authentic and generated by customers

C2C e-commerce consumer to consumer activity through the Internet

Chunking a process in which information is stored by combining small pieces of information into larger ones

Classic a fashion with an extremely long acceptance cycle

Classical conditioning the learning that occurs when a stimulus eliciting a response is paired with another stimulus that initially does not elicit a response on its own but will cause a similar response over time because of its association with the first stimulus

Closure principle the gestalt principle that describes a person's tendency to supply missing information in order to perceive a holistic image

Co-branding strategies linking products together to create a more desirable connotation in consumer minds

Co-consumers other patrons in a consumer setting

Coercive power influencing a person by social or physical intimidation

Cognition the beliefs a consumer has about an attitude object

Cognitive learning theory approaches that stress the importance of internal mental processes. This perspective views people as problem solvers who actively use information from the world around them to master their environment

Collecting the systematic acquisition of a particular object or set of objects

Collective selection the process by which certain symbolic alternatives tend to be jointly chosen over others by members of a society

Collectivist cultures cultural orientation that encourages people to subordinate their personal goals to those of a stable in-group; values such as self-discipline and group accomplishment are stressed

Communal goals an emphasis on affiliation and the fostering of harmonious relations, often associated with traditional female gender roles

Communications model a framework specifying that a number of elements are necessary for communication to be achieved, including a source, message, medium, receivers, and feedback

Comparative advertising a strategy in which a message compares two or more specifically named or recognizably presented brands and makes a comparison of them in terms of one or more specific attributes

Comparative influence the process whereby a reference group influences decisions about specific brands or activities

Compatibility matching an innovation or product with consumers' lifestyles

Compensatory decision rules a set of rules that allow information about attributes of competing products to be averaged in some way; poor standing on one attribute can potentially be offset by good standing on another

Complexity level of product difficulty to understand or use

Compulsive consumption the process of repetitive, often excessive, shopping used to relieve tension, anxiety, depression, or boredom

Conditioned stimulus a stimulus that produces a learned reaction through association over time

Conformity a change in beliefs or actions as a reaction to real or imagined group pressure

Consensual purchase decision a decision in which the group agrees on the desired purchase and differs only in terms of how it will be achieved

Conspicuous consumption the purchase and prominent display of luxury goods to provide evidence of a consumer's ability to afford them

Consumed consumers those people who are used or exploited, whether willingly or not, for commercial gain in the marketplace

Consumer a person who identifies a need or desire, makes a purchase, and/or disposes of the product

Consumer addiction a physiological and/or psychological dependency on products or services

Consumer behavior the processes involved when individuals or groups select, purchase, use, or dispose of products, services, ideas, or experiences to satisfy needs and desires

Consumer confidence the state of mind of consumers relative to their optimism or pessimism about economic conditions; people tend to make more discretionary purchases when their confidence in the economy is high

Consumer satisfaction/dissatisfaction (CS/D) the overall attitude a person has about a product after it has been purchased

Consumer socialization the process by which people acquire skills that enable them to function in the marketplace

Consumer tribe group of people who share a lifestyle and who can identify with each other because of a shared allegiance to an activity or a product

Consumption communities Web groups where members share views and product recommendations online

Consumption constellations a set of products and activities used by consumers to define, communicate, and perform social roles

Contamination when a place or object takes on sacred qualities due to its association with another sacred person or event

Conventions norms regarding the conduct of everyday life

Coolhunters kids in major markets who roam the streets to report on cutting-edge trends

Co-optation a cultural process by which the original meanings of a product or other symbol associated with a subculture are modified by members of mainstream culture

Core values common general values held by a culture

Corporate paradox the more involved a company appears to be in the dissemination of news about its products, the less credible it becomes

Country-of-origin original country from which a product is produced. Can be an important piece of information in the decision-making process

Craft product a creation valued because of the beauty with which it performs some function; this type of product tends to follow a formula that permits rapid production, and it is easier to understand than an art product

Creolization foreign influences are absorbed and integrated with local meanings

Cultivation hypothesis a perspective emphasizing media's ability to distort consumers' perceptions of reality

Cult products items that command fierce consumer loyalty and devotion

Cultural capital a set of distinctive and socially rare tastes and practices that admits a person into the realm of the upper class

Cultural categories the grouping of ideas and values that reflect the basic ways members of a society characterize the world

Cultural formula a sequence of media events in which certain roles and props tend to occur consistently

Cultural gatekeepers individuals who are responsible for determining the types of messages and symbolism to which members of mass culture are exposed

Cultural selection the process by which some alternatives are selected over others by cultural gatekeepers

Culture the values, ethics, rituals, traditions, material objects, and services produced or valued by the members of a society

Culture jamming the defacement or alteration of advertising materials as a form of political expression

Culture production system (CPS) the set of individuals and organizations responsible for creating and marketing a cultural product

Custom a norm that is derived from a traditional way of doing things

Cybermediary intermediary that helps to filter and organize online market information so that consumers can identify and evaluate alternatives more efficiently

Database marketing tracking consumers' buying habits very closely, and then crafting products and messages tailored precisely to people's wants and needs based on this information

Decay structural changes in the brain produced by learning decrease over time

Decision polarization the process whereby individuals' choices tend to become more extreme (polarized), in either a conservative or risky direction, following group discussion of alternatives

De-ethnicization process whereby a product formerly associated with a specific ethnic group is detached from its roots and marketed to other subcultures

Deindividuation the process whereby individual identities get submerged within a group, reducing inhibitions against socially inappropriate behavior

Demographics the observable measurements of a population's characteristics, such as birthrate, age distribution, and income

Desacralization the process that occurs when a sacred item or symbol is removed from its special place, or is duplicated in mass quantities, and becomes profane as a result

Determinant attributes the attributes actually used to differentiate among choices

Differential threshold the ability of a sensory system to detect changes or differences among stimuli

Diffusion of innovations the process whereby a new product, service, or idea spreads through a population

Discretionary income the money available to a household over and above that required for necessities

Drive the desire to satisfy a biological need in order to reduce physiological arousal

Drive theory concept that focuses on biological needs that produce unpleasant states of arousal

Early adopters people who are receptive to new products and adopt them relatively soon, though they are motivated more by social acceptance and being in style than by the desire to try risky new things

Economics of information perspective in which advertising is an important source of consumer information emphasizing the economic cost of the time spent searching for products

E-fluentials persuasive individuals who influence the purchasing decisions of other consumers, often by sharing their opinions about products in online formats

Ego the system that mediates between the id and the superego

80/20 rule a rule-of-thumb in volume segmentation, which says that about 20 percent of consumers in a product category (the heavy users) account for about 80 percent of sales

Elaborated codes the ways of expressing and interpreting meanings that are more complex and depend on a more sophisticated worldview, which tend to be used by the middle and upper classes

Elaboration likelihood model (ELM) the approach that one of two routes to persuasion (central versus peripheral) will be followed, depending on the personal relevance of a

message; the route taken determines the relative importance of message contents versus other characteristics, such as source attractiveness

Emic perspective an approach to studying for (or marketing to) cultures that stresses the unique aspects of each culture

Encoding the process in which information from short-term memory enters into long-term memory in a recognizable form

Enculturation the process of learning the beliefs and behaviors endorsed by one's own culture

Ethnic pluralism perspective arguing that ethnic groups differ from the mainstream in varying degrees, and that adaptation to a larger society occurs selectively

Ethnic subculture a self-perpetuating group of consumers held together by common cultural ties

Ethnocentrism the belief in the superiority of one's own country's practices and products

Etic perspective an approach to studying (or marketing to) cultures that stresses commonalities across cultures

Evaluative criteria the dimensions used by consumers to compare competing product alternatives

Evoked set those products already in memory plus those prominent in the retail environment that are actively considered during a consumer's choice process

Exchange a transaction in which two or more organizations or people give and receive something of value

Exchange theory the perspective that every interaction involves an exchange of value

Expectancy theory the perspective that behavior is largely "pulled" by expectations of achieving desirable outcomes, or positive incentives, rather than "pushed" from within

Experience the result of acquiring and processing stimulation over time

Experiential perspective an approach stressing the gestalt or totality of the product or service experience, focusing on consumers' affective responses in the marketplace

Expert power authority derived from possessing a specific knowledge or skill

Exposure an initial stage of perception during which some sensations come within range of consumers' sensory receptors

Extended family traditional family structure in which several generations live together

Extended problem solving an elaborate decision-making process, often initiated by a motive that is fairly central to the self-concept and accompanied by perceived risk; the consumer tries to collect as much information as possible, and carefully weighs product alternatives

Extended self the definition of self created by the external objects with which one surrounds oneself

Extinction the process whereby a learned connection between a stimulus and response is eroded so that the response is no longer reinforced

Fad a very short-lived fashion

Family financial officer (FFO) the individual in the family who is in charge of making financial decisions

Family household a housing unit containing at least two people who are related by blood or marriage

Family life-cycle (FLC) a classification scheme that segments consumers in terms of changes in income and family composition and the changes in demands placed on this income

Fantasy a self-induced shift in consciousness, often focusing on some unattainable or improbable goal; sometimes fantasy is a way of compensating for a lack of external stimulation or for dissatisfaction with the actual self

Fashion the process of social diffusion by which a new style is adopted by some group(s) of consumers

Fashion acceptance cycle the diffusion process of a style through three stages: introduction, acceptance, and regression

Fashion system those people and organizations involved in creating symbolic meanings and transferring these meanings to cultural goods

Fear appeals an attempt to change attitudes or behavior through the use of threats or by highlighting negative consequences of noncompliance with the request

Fertility rate a rate determined by the number of births per year per 1,000 women of childbearing age

Figure-ground principle the gestalt principle whereby one part of a stimulus configuration dominates a situation while other aspects recede into the background

Flow state situation in which consumers are truly involved with a product, an ad, or a Web site

Food culture pattern of food and beverage consumption that reflects the values of a social group

Foot-in-the-door technique based on the observation that a consumer is more likely to comply with a request if he or she has first agreed to comply with a smaller request

Frequency marketing a marketing technique that reinforces regular purchasers by giving them prizes with values that increase along with the amount purchased

Functional theory of attitudes a pragmatic approach that focuses on how attitudes facilitate social behavior; attitudes exist because they serve some function for the person

Gemba the one true source of information

Generation X a widely used term to describe "twentysomething" consumers who are (stereotypically) characterized as being confused, alienated, and depressed

Generation Y kids born between 1979 and 1994 (the younger siblings of Gen Xers)

Geodemography techniques that combine consumer demographic information with geographic consumption patterns to permit precise targeting of consumers with specific characteristics

Gerontographics a segmentation approach that divides the mature market into groups based on both level of physical well-being and social conditions such as becoming a grandparent or losing a spouse

Gestalt meaning derived from the totality of a set of stimuli, rather than from any individual stimulus

Gift-giving ritual the events involved in the selection, presentation, acceptance, and interpretation of a gift

Global consumer culture a culture in which people around the world are united through their common devotion to brand name consumer goods, movie stars, celebrities, and leisure activities

Globalized consumption ethic the global sharing of a material lifestyle including the valuing of well-known multinational brands that symbolize prosperity

Goal a consumer's desired end state

Gray market the economic potential created by the increasing numbers of affluent elderly consumers

Green marketing a marketing strategy involving an emphasis on protecting the natural environment

Grid-group theory theory developed by anthropologist Mary Douglas distinguishing between people with high and low group identification and a more or less affirmative relation to the organization of society

Guerrilla marketing promotional strategies that use unconventional locations and intensive word-of-mouth campaigns

Habitual decision-making choices made with little or no conscious effort

Habitus ways in which we classify experiences as a result of our socialization processes

Heavy users a name companies use to identify their customers who consume their products in large volumes

Hedonic consumption the multisensory, fantasy, and emotional aspects of consumers' interactions with products

Heuristics the mental rules-of-thumb that lead to a speedy decision

Hierarchy of effects a fixed sequence of steps that occurs during attitude formation, this sequence varies depending on such factors as the consumer's level of involvement with the attitude object

High-context culture group members tend to be close-knit and are likely to infer meanings that go beyond the spoken word

Homeostasis the state of being in which the body is in physiological balance; goal-oriented behavior attempts to reduce or eliminate an unpleasant motivational state and return to a balanced one

Home shopping parties a gathering where a company representative makes a sales presentation to a group of people who have gathered in the home of a friend or acquaintance

Homogamy the tendency for individuals to marry others similar to themselves

Homophily the degree to which a pair of individuals is similar in terms of education, social status, and beliefs

Hype corporate propaganda planted by companies to create product sensation—dismissed as inauthentic by customers

Hyperreality the becoming real of what is initially simulation or "hype"

Icon a sign that resembles the product in some way

Id the system oriented toward immediate gratification

Ideal of beauty a model, or examplar, of appearance valued by a culture

Ideal self a person's conception of how he or she would like to be

Identity theft occurrence when a criminal uses a person's Social Security number and other personal information to secure credit

Idiocentrics people having an individualist orientation

Impulse buying a process that occurs when the consumer experiences a sudden urge to purchase an item that he or she cannot resist

Index a sign that is connected to a product because they share some property

Individualistic cultures a cultural orientation that encourages people to attach more importance to personal goals than to group goals; values such as personal enjoyment and freedom are stressed

Inertia the process whereby purchase decisions are made out of habit because the consumer lacks the motivation to consider alternatives

Infomediaries people who act as information brokers by representing consumers who want to sell their profiles (including information such as their age, sex, family status, sexual orientation, income level, assets, and current shopping interests) to interested companies

Information power power of knowing something others would like to know

Innovation a product or style that is perceived as new by consumers

Innovators people who are always on the lookout for novel developments and will be the first to try a new offering

Instrumental conditioning also known as operant conditioning, occurs as the individual learns to perform behaviors that produce

positive outcomes and to avoid those that yield negative outcomes

Instrumental values goals endorsed because they are needed to achieve desired end states, or terminal values

Interpretant the meaning derived from a sign or symbol

Interpretation the process whereby meanings are assigned to stimuli

Interpretivism as opposed to the dominant positivist perspective on consumer behavior, instead stresses the importance of symbolic, subjective experience and the idea that meaning is in the mind of the person rather than existing "out there" in the objective world

Invidious distinction the display of wealth or power to inspire envy in others

Involvement the motivation to process product-related information

J.N.D. (just noticeable difference) the minimum difference between two stimuli that can be detected by a perceiver

Kansei engineering a Japanese philosophy that translates customers' feelings into design elements

Kin-network system the rituals intended to maintain ties among family members both immediate and extended

Knockoff a style that has been deliberately copied and modified, often with the intent to sell to a larger or different market

Knowledge structures organized systems of concepts relating to brands, stores, and other concepts

Laddering a technique for uncovering consumers' associations between specific attributes and general values

Laggards consumers who are exceptionally slow to adopt innovations

Late adopters the majority of consumers who are moderately receptive to adopting innovations

Lateral cycling a process in which already-purchased objects are sold to others or exchanged for other items

Latitudes of acceptance or rejection in the social judgment theory of attitudes, the notion that people differ in terms of the information they will find acceptable or unacceptable. They form latitudes of acceptance and rejection around an attitude standard. Ideas that fall within a latitude will be favorable received, but those falling outside of this zone will not.

Lead user an involved, experienced customer (usually a corporate customer) who is very knowledgeable about the field

Learning a relatively permanent change in a behavior caused by experience

Legitimate power the power granted to people by virtue of social agreements

Lifestyle a set of shared values or tastes exhibited by a group of consumers, especially as these are reflected in consumption patterns

Limited problem solving a problem-solving process in which consumers are not motivated to search for information or to rigorously evaluate each alternative; instead they use simple decision rules to arrive at a purchase decision

Long-term memory (LTM) the system that allows us to retain information for a long period of time

Looking-glass self the process of imagining the reaction of others toward oneself

Market beliefs the specific beliefs or decision rules pertaining to marketplace phenomena

Market maven a person who often serves as a source of information about marketplace activities

Market segmentation the process of identifying groups of consumers who are similar to one another in one or more ways, and then devising marketing strategies that appeal to one or more of these groups

Market segmentation strategies targeting a brand only to specific groups rather than to everybody

Masculinism study devoted to the male image and the cultural meanings of masculinity

Masked branding strategy that deliberately hides a product's origin

Match-up hypothesis a celebrity's image and that of the product he or she endorses should be similar to maximize the credibility and effectiveness of the communication

Materialism the importance consumers attach to worldly possessions

Membership reference group ordinary people whose consumption activities provide informational social influence

Meme theory a perspective that uses a medical metaphor to explain how an idea or product enters the consciousness of people over time, much like a virus

Memory a process of acquiring information and storing it over time so that it will be available when needed

Mental accounting principle which states that decisions are influenced by the way a problem is posed

Metaphor the use of an explicit comparison ("A" is "B") between a product and some other person, place, or thing

Modeling imitating the behavior of others

Modified rebuy in the context of the buyclass framework, a task that requires a modest amount of information search and evaluation, often focused on identifying the appropriate vendor

Monomyth a myth with basic characteristics that are found in many cultures

More a custom with strong moral overtones

Motivation an internal state that activates goal-oriented behavior

Motivational research a qualitative research approach, based on psychoanalytic (Freudian) interpretations, with a heavy emphasis on unconscious motives for consumption

Multiattribute attitude models those models that assume that a consumer's attitude (evaluation) of an attitude object depends on the beliefs he or she has about several or many attributes of the object; the use of a multiattribute model implies that an attitude toward a product or brand can be predicted by identifying these specific beliefs and combining them to derive a measure of the consumer's overall attitude

Mystery ads advertisements where the brand is not revealed until the end of the ad

Myth a story containing symbolic elements that expresses the shared emotions and ideals of a culture

Negative reinforcement the process whereby the environment weakens responses to stimuli so that inappropriate behavior is avoided

Negative word-of-mouth the passing on of negative experiences involved with products or services by consumers to other potential customers to influence other's choices

New task in the context of the buyclass framework, a task that requires a great degree of effort and information search

Nodes data that are connected by associative links within knowledge structures

Noncompensatory decision rules choice shortcuts where a product with a low standing on one attribute cannot make up for this position by being better on another attribute

Normative influence the process in which a reference group helps to set and enforce fundamental standards of conduct

Normative social influence the conformity that occurs when a person alters his or her behavior to meet the expectations of a person or group

Norms the informal rules that govern what is right or wrong

Nostalgia a bittersweet emotion; the past is viewed with sadness and longing; many "classic" products appeal to consumers' memories of their younger days

Nuclear family a contemporary living arrangement composed of a married couple and their children

Object in semiotic terms, the product that is the focus of a message

Observability level of product visibility

Observational learning the process in which people learn by watching the actions of others and noting the reinforcements they receive for their behaviors

Opinion leaders those people who are knowledgeable about products and who are frequently able to influence others' attitudes or behaviors with regard to a product category

Organizational buyers people who purchase goods and services on behalf of companies for use in the process of manufacturing, distribution, or resale

Paradigm a widely accepted view or model of phenomena being studied; the perspective that regards people as rational information processors is currently the dominant paradigm, though this approach is now being challenged by a new wave of research that emphasizes the frequently subjective nature of consumer decision making

Parental yielding the process that occurs when a parental decision maker is influenced by a child's product request

Parody display deliberately avoiding status symbols, to seek status by mocking it

Pastiche mixture of images

Perceived age how old a person feels as compared to his or her true chronological age

Perceived risk belief that a product has potentially negative consequences

Perception the process by which stimuli are selected, organized, and interpreted

Perceptual defense the tendency for consumers to avoid processing stimuli that are threatening to them

Perceptual map a research tool used to understand how a brand is positioned in consumers' minds relative to competitors

Perceptual selection process by which people attend to only a small portion of the stimuli to which they are exposed

Perceptual vigilance the tendency for consumers to be more aware of stimuli that relate to their current needs

Permission marketing popular strategy based on the idea that a marketer will be much more successful in persuading consumers who have agreed to let him or her try

Personality a person's unique psychological makeup, which consistently influences the way the person responds to his or her environment

Personality traits identifiable characteristics that define a person

Persuasion an active attempt to change attitudes

Pleasure principle the belief that behavior is guided by the desire to maximize pleasure and avoid pain

Point-of-purchase stimuli (POP) the promotional materials that are deployed in stores or other outlets to influence consumers' decisions at the time products are purchased

Popular culture the music, movies, sports, books, celebrities, and other forms of entertainment consumed by the mass market

Positioning strategy an organization's use of elements in the marketing mix to influence the consumer's interpretation of a product's meaning vis-à-vis competitors

Positive reinforcement the process whereby rewards provided by the environment strengthen responses to stimuli and appropriate behavior is learned

Positivism a research perspective that relies on principles of the "scientific method" and assumes that a single reality exists; events in the world can be objectively measured; and the causes of behavior can be identified, manipulated, and predicted

Principle of cognitive consistency the belief that consumers value harmony among their thoughts, feelings, and behaviors and that they are motivated to maintain uniformity among these elements

Principle of similarity the gestalt principle that describes how consumers tend to group objects that share similar physical characteristics

PRIZM (Potential Rating Index by Zip Market) clustering technique that classifies every zip code in the United States into one of 62 categories, ranging from the most affluent "Blue-Blood Estates" to the least well off "Public Assistance" developed by Claritas, Inc

Problem recognition the process that occurs whenever the consumer sees a significant difference between his or her current state of affairs and some desired or ideal state; this recognition initiates the decision-making process

Product complementarity the view that products in different functional categories have symbolic meanings that are related to one another

Product placement the process of obtaining exposure for a product by arranging for it to be inserted into a movie, television show, or some other medium

Product signal communicates an underlying quality of a product through the use of aspects that are only visible in the ad

Profane consumption the process of consuming objects and events that are ordinary or of the everyday world

Progressive learning model the perspective that people gradually learn a new culture as they increasingly come in contact with it; consumers assimilate into a new culture, mixing practices from their old and new environments to create a hybrid culture

Prospect theory a descriptive model of how people make choices

Psychographics the use of psychological, sociological, and anthropological factors to construct market segments

Psychophysics the science that focuses on how the physical environment is integrated into the consumer's subjective experience

Punishment the learning that occurs when a response is followed by unpleasant events

Purchase momentum initial impulses to buy in order to satisfy our needs increase the likelihood that we will buy even more

Queuing theory the mathematical study of waiting lines

Racial subculture a self-perpetuating group of consumers who are held together by common genetic ties

Rational perspective a view of the consumer as a careful, analytical decision maker who tries to maximize utility in purchase decisions

Reactance a "boomerang effect" that sometimes occurs when consumers are threatened with a loss of freedom of choice; they respond by doing the opposite of the behavior advocated in a persuasive message

Reality engineering the process whereby elements of popular culture are appropriated by marketers and become integrated into marketing strategies

Reality principle principle that the ego seeks ways that will be acceptable to society to gratify the id

Reciprocity norm a culturally learned obligation to return the gesture of a gift with one of equal value

Reference group an actual or imaginary individual or group that has a significant effect on an individual's evaluations, aspirations, or behavior

Referent power the power of prominent people to affect others' consumption behaviors by virtue of product endorsements, distinctive fashion statements, or championing of causes

Refutational argument calling attention to a product's negative attributes as a persuasive strategy where a negative issue is raised and then dismissed. This approach can increase source credibility

Relationship marketing the strategic perspective that stresses the long-term, human side of buyer-seller interactions

Relative advantage the benefits a product can provide over other competing products

Resonance a literary device, frequently used in advertising that uses a play on words (a double meaning) to communicate a product benefit

Response bias a form of contamination in survey research in which some factor, such as the desire to make a good impression on the experimenter, leads respondents to modify their true answers

Restricted codes the ways of expressing and interpreting meanings that focus on the content of objects tend to be used by the working class

Retail theming strategy where stores create imaginative environments that transport shoppers to fantasy worlds or provide other kinds of stimulation

Retrieval the process whereby desired information is recovered from long-term memory

Reward power when a person or group has the means to provide positive reinforcement to a consumer

Risky shift the tendency for individuals to consider riskier alternatives after conferring with a group than if members made their own decisions with no discussion

Rites of passage sacred times marked by a change in social status

Ritual a set of multiple, symbolic behaviors that occur in a fixed sequence and that tend to be repeated periodically

Ritual artifacts items (consumer goods) used in the performance of rituals

Role theory the perspective that much of consumer behavior resembles actions in a play

Sacralization a process that occurs when ordinary objects, events, or people take on sacred meaning to a culture or to specific groups within a culture

Sacred consumption the process of consuming objects and events that are set apart from normal life and treated with some degree of respect or awe

Salience the prominence of a brand in memory

Schema an organized collection of beliefs and feelings represented in a cognitive category

Self-concept the beliefs a person holds about his or her own attributes and how he or she evaluates these qualities

Self-image congruence models the approaches based on the prediction that products will be chosen when their attributes match some aspect of the self

Self-perception theory an alternative (to cognitive dissonance) explanation of dissonance effects; it assumes that people use observations of their own behavior to infer their attitudes toward some object

Semantic meaning symbolic associations in memory

Semiotics a field of study that examines the correspondence between signs and symbols and the meaning or meanings they convey

Sensation the immediate response of sensory receptors (eyes, ears, nose, mouth, fingers) to such basic stimuli as light, color, sound, odors, and textures

Sensory memory the temporary storage of information received from the senses

Service scripts a schema guiding behavior in commercial settings

Sex-typed traits characteristics that are stereotypically associated with one gender or the other

Shaping the learning of a desired behavior over time by rewarding intermediate actions until the final result is obtained

Shopping orientation a consumer's general attitudes and motivations regarding the act of shopping

Short-term memory (STM) the mental system that allows us to retain information for a short period of time

Shrinkage the loss of money or inventory from shoplifting and/or employee theft

Sign the sensory imagery that represents the intended meanings of the object

Silent commerce new trend that enables transactions and information gathering to occur in the background without any direct intervention by consumers or managers

Similie comparing two objects that share a similar property

Single-source data a compilation of information that includes different aspects of consumption and demographic data for a common consumer segment

Skin (graphical interface) an interface (often designed by the user) that visually represents the control panel of a computer program

Sleeper effect the process whereby differences in attitude change between positive and negative sources seem to diminish over time

Social aging theories a perspective to understand how society assigns people to different roles across the life span

Social class the overall rank of people in a society; people who are grouped within the same social class are approximately equal in terms of their income, occupations, and lifestyles

Social comparison theory the perspective that people compare their outcomes with others' as a way to increase the stability of their own self-evaluation, especially when physical evidence is unavailable

Social judgment theory the perspective that people assimilate new information about attitude objects in light of what they already know or feel; the initial attitude acts as a frame of reference, and new information is categorized in terms of this standard

Social marketing the promotion of causes and ideas (social products), such as energy conservation, charities, and population control

Social mobility the movement of individuals from one social class to another

Social power the capacity of one person to alter the actions or outcome of another

Social stratification the process in a social system by which scarce and valuable resources are distributed unequally to status positions that become more or less permanently ranked in terms of the share of valuable resources each receives

Sociometric methods the techniques for measuring group dynamics that involve tracing communication patterns in and among groups

Source attractiveness the dimensions of a communicator that increase his or her persuasiveness; these include expertise and attractiveness

Source credibility a communications source's perceived expertise, objectivity, or trustworthiness

Spreading activation meanings in memory are activated indirectly; as a node is activated, other nodes linked to it are also activated so that meanings spread across the network

Stage of cognitive development the ability to comprehend concepts of increasing complexity as a person matures

Status crystallization the extent to which different indicators of a person's status (income, ethnicity, occupation) are consistent with one another

Status hierarchy a ranking of social desirability in terms of consumers' access to resources such as money, education, and luxury goods

Status symbols products that are purchased and displayed to signal membership in a desirable social class

Stereotype a knowledge structure based on inferences across products

Stimulus discrimination the process that occurs when behaviors caused by two stimuli are different, as when consumers learn to differentiate a brand from its competitors

Stimulus generalization the process that occurs when the behavior caused by a reaction to one stimulus occurs in the presence of other, similar stimuli

Storage the process that occurs when knowledge in long-term memory is integrated with what is already in memory and "warehoused" until needed

Store image a store's "personality," composed of such attributes as location, merchandise suitability, and the knowledge and congeniality of the sales staff

Straight rebuy in the context of the buyclass framework, the type of buying decision that is virtually automatic and requires little deliberation

Subcultures a group whose members share beliefs and common experiences that set them apart from other members of a culture

Subliminal perception the processing of stimuli presented below the level of the consumer's awareness

Superego the system that internalizes society's rules and that works to prevent the id from seeking selfish gratification

Surrogate consumer a professional who is retained to evaluate and/or make purchases on behalf of a consumer

Symbol a sign that is related to a product through either conventional or agreed-upon associations

Symbolic interactionism a sociological approach stressing that relationships with other people play a large part in forming the self; people live in a symbolic environment, and the meaning attached to any situation or object is determined by a person's interpretation of these symbols

Symbolic self-completion theory the perspective that people who have an incomplete self-definition in some context will compensate by acquiring symbols associated with a desired social identity

Syncratic decisions those purchase decisions that are made jointly by both spouses

Synoptic ideal a model of spousal decision making in which the husband and wife take a common view and act as joint decision makers, assigning each other well-defined roles and making mutually beneficial decisions to maximize the couple's joint utility

Taste culture a group of consumers who share aesthetic and intellectual preferences

Terminal values end states desired by members of a culture

Theory of cognitive dissonance theory based on the premise that a state of tension is created when beliefs or behaviors conflict with one another; people are motivated to reduce this inconsistency (or dissonance) and thus eliminate unpleasant tension

Theory of reasoned action an updated version of the Fishbein multiattribute attitude theory that considers factors such as social pressure and A_{act} (the attitude toward the act of buying a product), rather than attitudes toward just the product itself

The Values and Lifestyles (VALS™) System a psychographic segmentation system used to categorize consumers into clusters, or "VALS Types"

Time poverty a feeling of having less time available than is required to meet the demands of everyday living

Tipping point moment of critical mass

Trade dress color combinations that become strongly associated with a corporation

Transitional economies a country that is adapting from a controlled, centralized economy to a free-market system

Triability the ability of the customer to try a product before they purchase it

Tribal marketing linking one's product to the needs of a lifestyle subculture

Trickle-down theory the perspective that fashions spread as the result of status symbols associated with the upper classes "trickling down" to other social classes as these consumers try to emulate those with greater status

Tweens a marketing term used to describe children aged 8–14

Two-factor theory the perspective that two separate psychological processes are operating when a person is repeatedly exposed to an ad: repetition increases familiarity and thus reduces uncertainty about the product but over time boredom increases with each exposure, and at some point the amount of boredom incurred begins to exceed the amount of uncertainty reduced, resulting in wear-out

U-commerce the use of ubiquitous networks that will slowly but surely become a part of us, such as wearable computers or customized advertisements beamed to us on our cell phones

Unconditioned stimulus a stimulus that is naturally capable of causing a response

Underground economy secondary markets (such as flea markets) where transactions are not officially recorded

Uses and gratifications theory views consumers as an active, goal-directed audience that draws on mass media as a resource to satisfy needs

Value a belief that some condition is preferable to its opposite

Value system a culture's ranking of the relative importance of values

Variety seeking the desire to choose new alternatives over more familiar ones

Viral marketing the strategy of getting customers to sell a product on behalf of the company that creates it

Virtual community of consumption a collection of people whose online interactions are based upon shared enthusiasm for and knowledge of a specific consumption activity

Voluntary simplifiers people who believe that once basic material needs are satisfied, additional income does not lead to happiness

Want the particular form of consumption chosen to satisfy a need

Weber's Law the principle that the stronger the initial stimulus, the greater its change must be for it to be noticed

Weblog online personal journal

Word-of-mouth (WOM) product information transmitted by individual consumers on an informal basis

Worldview the ideas shared by members of a culture about principles of order and fairness

Credits

Indexes

Name

Products/Organizations

Subject